VCP-DCV for vSphere

MW01098106

Companion Website and Pearson Test Prep Access Code

Access interactive study tools on this book's companion website, including practice test software, review exercises, Key Term flash card application, a study planner, and more!

To access the companion website, simply follow these steps:

1. Go to **www.pearsonitcertification.com/register**.

2. Enter the **print book ISBN: 9780138169886**.

3. Answer the security question to validate your purchase.

4. Go to your account page.

5. Click on the **Registered Products** tab.

6. Under the book listing, click on the **Access Bonus Content** link.

When you register your book, your Pearson Test Prep practice test access code will automatically be populated with the book listing under the Registered Products tab. You will need this code to access the practice test that comes with this book. You can redeem the code at **PearsonTestPrep.com**. Simply choose Pearson IT Certification as your product group and log into the site with the same credentials you used to register your book. Click the **Activate New Product** button and enter the access code. More detailed instructions on how to redeem your access code for both the online and desktop versions can be found on the companion website.

If you have any issues accessing the companion website or obtaining your Pearson Test Prep practice test access code, you can contact our support team by going to **pearsonitp.echelp.org**.

VCP-DCV for vSphere 8.x Cert Guide

John A. Davis, Steve Baca

Pearson

Hoboken, New Jersey

VCP-DCV for vSphere 8.x Cert Guide

ISBN-13: 978-0-13-816988-6

ISBN-10: 0-13-816988-8

Library of Congress Cataloging-in-Publication Data: 2023914336

1 2023

Trademarks

All terms mentioned in this book that are known to be trademarks or service marks have been appropriately capitalized. Pearson IT Certification cannot attest to the accuracy of this information. Use of a term in this book should not be regarded as affecting the validity of any trademark or service mark.

Warning and Disclaimer

Every effort has been made to make this book as complete and as accurate as possible, but no warranty or fitness is implied. The information provided is on an "as is" basis. The authors and the publisher shall have neither liability nor responsibility to any person or entity with respect to any loss or damages arising from the information contained in this book.

Special Sales

For information about buying this title in bulk quantities, or for special sales opportunities (which may include electronic versions; custom cover designs; and content particular to your business, training goals, marketing focus, or branding interests), please contact our corporate sales department at corpsales@pearsoned.com or (800) 382-3419.

For government sales inquiries, please contact governmentsales@pearsoned.com.

For questions about sales outside the U.S., please contact intlcs@pearson.com.

VICE PRESIDENT, IT PROFESSIONAL
Mark Taub

DIRECTOR, ITP PRODUCT MANAGEMENT
Brett Bartow

EXECUTIVE EDITOR
Nancy Davis

DEVELOPMENT EDITOR
Ellie Bru

MANAGING EDITOR
Sandra Schroeder

SENIOR PROJECT EDITOR
Mandie Frank

COPY EDITOR
Kitty Wilson

INDEXER
Erika Millen

PROOFREADER
Donna E. Mulder

TECHNICAL EDITOR
Joseph Cooper

PUBLISHING COORDINATOR
Cindy Teeters

DESIGNER
Chuti Prasertsith

COMPOSITOR
codeMantra

Pearson's Commitment to Diversity, Equity, and Inclusion

Pearson is dedicated to creating bias-free content that reflects the diversity of all learners. We embrace the many dimensions of diversity, including but not limited to race, ethnicity, gender, socioeconomic status, ability, age, sexual orientation, and religious or political beliefs.

Education is a powerful force for equity and change in our world. It has the potential to deliver opportunities that improve lives and enable economic mobility. As we work with authors to create content for every product and service, we acknowledge our responsibility to demonstrate inclusivity and incorporate diverse scholarship so that everyone can achieve their potential through learning. As the world's leading learning company, we have a duty to help drive change and live up to our purpose to help more people create a better life for themselves and to create a better world.

Our ambition is to purposefully contribute to a world where

- Everyone has an equitable and lifelong opportunity to succeed through learning

- Our educational products and services are inclusive and represent the rich diversity of learners

- Our educational content accurately reflects the histories and experiences of the learners we serve

- Our educational content prompts deeper discussions with learners and motivates them to expand their own learning (and worldview)

While we work hard to present unbiased content, we want to hear from you about any concerns or needs with this Pearson product so that we can investigate and address them.

Please contact us with concerns about any potential bias at https://www.pearson.com/report-bias.html.

Contents at a Glance

Table of Contents

About the Authors

John A. Davis, now an independent contractor and senior integration architect at MEJEER, LLC, became a VMware Certified Instructor (VCI) and VMware Certified Professional (VCP) in 2004. Since then, all of his work has focused on VMware-based technologies. He has experience in teaching official VMware curriculum in five countries and delivering VMware professional services throughout the United States. Recently, his work has involved designing and implementing solutions for hybrid clouds, cloud automation, disaster recovery, and virtual desktop infrastructure (VDI). He has authored several white papers and co-authored *VCP-DCV for vSphere 7.x Cert Guide, VCP6-DCV Cert Guide, and VCAP5-DCA Cert Guide* (VMware Press). He holds several advanced certifications, including VCAP-DCV 2021, VCP-NV 202, and VCP-DTM 2020. He has been a vExpert since 2014. He is the author of the vLoreBlog.com and can be found on Twitter @johnnyadavis.

Steve Baca, VCAP, VCI, VCP, and NCDA, has been in the computer industry for more than 20 years. Originally a computer programmer and a system administrator working on Unix and Windows systems, he migrated over to technical training and wrote a course for Sun Microsystems. After teaching various courses for Sun, he eventually transitioned to VMware about 10 years ago, to do technical training. Currently he is a badged employee for VMware and lives in Omaha, Nebraska. He thoroughly enjoys teaching and writing and believes that the constant evolution of the computer industry requires continuously learning to stay ahead. Steve can be found on Twitter @scbaca1.

Dedication

Dedicated to Madison, Emma, Jaxon, Ethan, Eli, and Robbie, the six wonderful children to whom I am blessed to be known as "Grampy." They fill my days with joy and fun, especially after a hard day of writing or working for their namesake, MEJEER, LLC.
—John Davis

First and foremost, I would like to dedicate this book to my loving wife, Sharyl. Without your support, I would not be able to commit the time necessary to co-author a book. Thank you for believing in me and allowing me to have the time for my many endeavors. I would also like to dedicate this book to my children: Zachary, Brianna, Eileen, Susan, Keenan, and Maura.
—Steve Baca

Acknowledgments

Thanks to my wife and best friend, Delores, who tolerates my late-night writing, supports my recent business venture, and makes me happy every day. Thanks to my parents, Monica and Norman Davis, who provided me with a great education and taught me the importance of hard work. Thanks to God for placing me in an environment with unmeasurable blessings and opportunities.

I would like to thank my co-authors and partners, Steve Baca and Owen Thomas. Thanks to our technical editor, Joe Cooper, for his hard work and dedication. Special thanks to Nancy Davis (executive editor) and Ellie Bru (development editor) for coordinating everything and keeping this project moving.

—John Davis

There are so many people to acknowledge and thank for making this book possible. First, thanks to my wife and family for supporting me while writing this book. I would also like to thank my co-authors, John Davis and Owen Thomas, who deserve much of the credit for this book. Thank you to the production team and editors at Pearson, who do a tremendous amount of work from the initial planning of the book to the final printing.

—Steve Baca

About the Technical Reviewer

Joseph Cooper is a Principal Instructor and a member of America's Tech Lead Team with VMware's Education Department. Joe has spoken at several VMworld conferences, VMUG events, and vForum events, and is a featured instructor in the VMware Learning Zone. Prior to joining VMware, Joe was an instructor at the State University of New York, College at Cortland, where he taught technology courses to sport management and kinesiology students. You can find him on Twitter @joeicooper and on YouTube at https://youtube.com/channel/UCYrPi0AqS8f8QxChAgZa5Sg.

We Want to Hear from You!

As the reader of this book, *you* are our most important critic and commentator. We value your opinion and want to know what we're doing right, what we could do better, what areas you'd like to see us publish in, and any other words of wisdom you're willing to pass our way.

We welcome your comments. You can email or write to let us know what you did or didn't like about this book—as well as what we can do to make our books better.

Please note that we cannot help you with technical problems related to the topic of this book.

When you write, please be sure to include this book's title and author as well as your name and email address. We will carefully review your comments and share them with the author and editors who worked on the book.

Email: community@informit.com

Reader Services

Register your copy of *VCP-DCV for vSphere 8.x Cert Guide* at www.pearsonitcertification.com for convenient access to downloads, updates, and corrections as they become available. To start the registration process, go to www.pearsonitcertification.com/register and log in or create an account.* Enter the product ISBN 9780138169886 and click Submit. When the process is complete, you will find any available bonus content under Registered Products.

*Be sure to check the box that you would like to hear from us to receive exclusive discounts on future editions of this product.

Introduction

This book focuses on one major goal: helping you prepare to pass the VMware vSphere 8.x Professional (2V0-21.23) exam, which is a key requirement for earning the VCP-DCV 2023 certification. This book may be useful for secondary purposes, such as learning how to implement, configure, and manage a vSphere environment or preparing to take other VCP-DCV qualifying exams.

The rest of this introduction provides details on the VCP-DCV certification, the 2V0-21.23 exam, and this book.

VCP-DCV Requirements

The primary objective of the VCP-DCV 2023 certification is to demonstrate that you have mastered the skills to successfully install, configure, and manage VMware vSphere 8 environments. You can find the exam requirements, objectives, and other details on the certification web portal, at http://mylearn.vmware.com/portals/certification/. On the website, navigate to the Data Center Virtualization track and to the VCP-DCV certification. Examine the VCP-DCV 2023 requirements based on your qualifications. For example, if you select that you currently hold no VCP certifications, then the website indicates that your path to certification is to gain experience with vSphere 8.0, attend one of the following required training courses, and pass the Professional vSphere 8.0 (2V0-21.23) exam:

- VMware vSphere: Install, Configure, Manage [V8]
- VMware vSphere: Optimize, Scale, and Secure [V8]
- VMware vSphere: Troubleshooting [V8]
- VMware vSphere: Fast Track [V8]

If you select that you currently hold a VCP-DCV 2020 or newer certification, the website indicates that your path includes a recommendation, but not a requirement, to take a training course.

VMware updates the VCP-DCV certification requirements each year. So, the requirements for the VCP-DCV 2024 certification may differ slightly from VCP-DCV 2023 certification. Likewise, VMware updates the qualifying exams. Each year, as VMware updates the Professional VMware vSphere 8.x exam, the authors of this book will create an appendix to supplement the original book. To prepare for a future version of the exam, download the corresponding online appendix from the book's companion website and use it to supplement the original book.

After you identify your path to certification, you can select the Professional VMware vSphere 8.x (2V0-21.23) exam to closely examine its details and to download the Exam Preparation Guide (also known as the exam blueprint).

Details on the 2V0-21.23 Exam

The 2V0-21.23 exam blueprint provides details on exam delivery, minimum qualifications for candidates, exam objectives, recommended courses, and references to supporting VMware documentation. It also contains 10 sample exam questions. The 2V0-21.23 exam is a proctored exam delivered through Pearson VUE. See Chapter 15, "Final Preparation," for details on registering and taking the exam.

A minimally qualified candidate (MQC) has 6 to 12 months of hands-on experience implementing, managing, and supporting a vSphere environment. The MQC has knowledge of storage, networking, hardware, security, business continuity, and disaster recovery concepts.

The exam characteristics are as follows:

- **Format**: Proctored exam
- **Question type**: Multiple choice
- **Number of questions**: 70
- **Duration**: 135 minutes
- **Passing score**: 300
- **Cost**: $250 (in the United States)

2V0-21.23 Exam Objectives

The 2V0-21.23 exam blueprint lists the exam objectives, which are summarized here:

Section 1: Architectures and Technologies

- Objective 1.1: Identify the pre-requisites and components for a VMware vSphere 8.x implementation
- Objective 1.2: Describe the components and topology of a VMware vCenter architecture

- Objective 1.3: Describe storage concepts

  - 1.3.1: Identify and differentiate storage access protocols for VMware vSphere (NFS, iSCSI, SAN, etc.)

  - 1.3.2: Describe storage datastore types for VMware vSphere

  - 1.3.3: Explain the importance of advanced storage configurations (vStorage APIs for Array Integration (VAAI), vStorage APIs for Storage Awareness (VASA), multipathing, etc.)

  - 1.3.4: Describe storage policies

  - 1.3.5: Describe basic storage concepts in VMware vSAN and VMware Virtual Volumes (vVOLs)

  - 1.3.6: Identify use cases for raw device mapping (RDM), Persistent Memory (PMem), Non-Volatile Memory Express (NVMe), NVMe over Fabrics (NVMe-oF), and RDMA (iSER)

  - 1.3.7: Describe datastore clusters

  - 1.3.8: Describe Storage I/O Control (SIOC)

- Objective 1.4: Describe VMware ESXi cluster concepts

  - 1.4.1: Describe VMware Distributed Resource Scheduler (DRS)

  - 1.4.2: Describe vSphere Enhanced vMotion Compatibility (EVC)

  - 1.4.3: Describe how DRS scores virtual machines

  - 1.4.4: Describe VMware vSphere High Availability (HA)

  - 1.4.5: Identify use cases for fault tolerance

- Objective 1.5: Explain the difference between VMware standard switches and distributed switches

  - 1.5.1: Describe VMkernel networking

  - 1.5.2: Manage networking on multiple hosts with vSphere Distributed Switch (VDS)

  - 1.5.3: Describe networking policies

  - 1.5.4: Manage Network I/O Control (NIOC) on a vSphere Distributed Switch (VDS)

  - 1.5.5: Describe Network I/O Control (NIOC)

- Objective 1.6: Describe VMware vSphere Lifecycle Manager concepts

- Objective 1.7: Describe the basics of VMware vSAN as primary storage

    - 1.7.1: Identify basic vSAN requirements (networking, disk count, and type)

    - 1.7.2: Identify Express Storage Architecture (ESA) concepts for vSAN 8

- Objective 1.8: Describe the role of Virtual Machine Encryption in a data center

    - 1.8.1: Describe vSphere Trust Authority

    - 1.8.2: Describe the role of a Key Management Services (KMS) server in vSphere

- Objective 1.9: Recognize methods of securing virtual machines

    - 1.9.1: Recognize use cases for a virtual Trusted Platform Module (vTPM)

    - 1.9.2: Differentiate between Basic Input or Output System (BIOS) and Unified Extensible Firmware Interface (UEFI) firmware

    - 1.9.3: Recognize use cases for Microsoft virtualization-based security (VBS)

- Objective 1.10: Describe identity federation

    - 1.10.1: Describe the architecture of identity federation

    - 1.10.2: Recognize use cases for identity federation

- Objective 1.11: Describe VMware vSphere Distributed Services Engine

    - 1.11.1: Describe the role of a data processing unit (DPU) in vSphere

- Objective 1.12: Identify use cases for VMware Tools

- Objective 1.13: Describe the high-level components of VMware vSphere with Tanzu

    - 1.13.1: Identify the use case for a Supervisor Cluster and Supervisor Namespace

    - 1.13.2: Identify the use case for vSphere Zones

    - 1.13.3: Identify the use case for a VMware Tanzu Kubernetes Grid (TKG) cluster

Section 2: VMware Products and Solutions

- Objective 2.1: Describe the role of VMware vSphere in the Software-Defined Data Center
- Objective 2.2: Identify use cases for VMware vSphere+
- Objective 2.3: Identify use cases for VMware vCenter Converter
- Objective 2.4: Identify disaster recovery (DR) use cases
  - 2.4.1: Identify VMware vCenter replication options
  - 2.4.2: Identify use cases for VMware Site Recovery Manager (SRM)

Section 3: Planning and Designing (There are no testable objectives for this section.)

Section 4: Installing, Configuring, and Setup

- Objective 4.1: Describe single sign-on (SSO)
  - 4.1.1: Configure a single sign-on (SSO) domain
  - 4.1.2: Join an existing single sign-on (SSO) domain
- Objective 4.2: Configure vSphere distributed switches
  - 4.2.1: Create a distributed switch
  - 4.2.2: Add ESXi hosts to the distributed switch
  - 4.2.3: Examine the distributed switch configuration
- Objective 4.3: Configure Virtual Standard Switch (VSS) advanced virtual networking options
- Objective 4.4: Set up identity sources
  - 4.4.1: Configure identity federation
  - 4.4.2: Configure LDAP integration
- Objective 4.5: Deploy and configure VMware vCenter Server Appliance (VCSA)
- Objective 4.6: Create and configure VMware HA and DRS advanced options (Admission Control, Proactive HA, etc.)

- Objective 4.7: Deploy and configure VMware vCenter High Availability

- Objective 4.8: Set up content library

  - 4.8.1: Create a content library

  - 4.8.2: Add content to the content library

  - 4.8.3: Publish a local content library

- Objective 4.9: Subscribe to content library

  - 4.9.1: Create a subscribed content library

  - 4.9.2: Subscribe to a published content library

  - 4.9.3: Deploy virtual machines (VMs) from a subscribed content library

- Objective 4.10: Manage virtual machine (VM) template versions

  - 4.10.1: Update template in content library

- Objective 4.11: Configure VMware vCenter file-based backup

- Objective 4.12: Configure vSphere Trust Authority

- Objective 4.13: Configure vSphere certificates

  - 4.13.1: Describe Enterprise PKIs role for SSL certificates

- Objective 4.14: Configure vSphere Lifecycle Manager

- Objective 4.15: Configure different network stacks

- Objective 4.16: Configure host profiles

- Objective 4.17: Identify ESXi boot options

  - 4.17.1: Configure Quick Boot

  - 4.17.2: Securely Boot ESXi hosts

- Objective 4.18: Deploy and configure clusters using the vSphere Cluster Quickstart workflow

  - 4.18.1: Use Cluster Quickstart workflow to add hosts

  - 4.18.2: Use Cluster Quickstart workflow to configure a cluster

  - 4.18.3: Use Quickstart to expand clusters

- Objective 4.19: Set up and configure VMware ESXi

  - 4.19.1: Configure Time Configuration

  - 4.19.2: Configure ESXi services

- Objective 5.13: Complete lifecycle activities for VMware vSphere with Tanzu

    - 5.13.1: Update Supervisor cluster

    - 5.13.2: Back up and restore VMware vSphere with Tanzu

Section 6: Troubleshooting and Repairing

- Objective 6.1: Identify use cases for enabling vSphere Cluster Services (vCLS) retreat mode

- Objective 6.2: Differentiate between the main management services in VMware ESXi and vCenter and their corresponding log files

- Objective 6.3: Generate a log bundle

Section 7: Administrative and Operational Tasks

- Objective 7.1: Create and manage virtual machine snapshots

- Objective 7.2: Create virtual machines using different methods (Open Virtualization Format (OVF) templates, content library, etc.)

- Objective 7.3: Manage virtual machines (modifying virtual machine settings, VMware per-VM EVC, latency sensitivity, CPU affinity, etc.)

- Objective 7.4: Manage storage

    - 7.4.1: Configure and modify datastores

    - 7.4.2: Create virtual machine storage policies

    - 7.4.3: Configure storage cluster options

- Objective 7.5: Create DRS affinity and anti-affinity rules for common use cases

- Objective 7.6: Migrate virtual machines

    - 7.6.1: Identify requirements for Storage vMotion, Cold Migration, vMotion, and Cross vCenter Export

- Objective 7.7: Configure role-based access control

- Objective 7.8: Manage host profiles

- Objective 7.9: Utilize VMware vSphere Lifecycle Manager

    - 7.9.1: Describe firmware upgrades for VMware ESXi

    - 7.9.2: Describe VMware ESXi updates

    - 7.9.3: Describe component and driver updates for VMware ESXi

- 7.9.4: Describe hardware compatibility check

- 7.9.5: Describe ESXi cluster image export functionality

- 7.9.6: Create VMware ESXi cluster image

- Objective 7.10: Use predefined alarms in VMware vCenter

- Objective 7.11: Create custom alarms

- Objective 7.12: Deploy an encrypted virtual machine

- 7.12.1: Convert a non-encrypted virtual machine to an encrypted virtual machine

- 7.12.2: Migrate an encrypted virtual machine

- 7.12.3: Configure virtual machine vMotion encryption properties

NOTE   For future exams, download and examine the objectives in the updated exam blueprint. Be sure to use the future Pearson-provided online appendix specific to the updated exam.

NOTE   Section 3 does not apply to the 2V0-21.23 exam, but it may be used for other exams.

Who Should Take This Exam and Read This Book?

The VCP-DCV certification is the most popular certification at VMware; more than 100,000 professionals around the world hold this certification. This book is intended for anyone who wants to prepare for the 2V0-21.23 exam, which is a required exam for VCP-DCV 2023 certification. The audience includes current and prospective IT professionals such as system administrators, infrastructure administrators, and virtualization engineers.

Book Features and Exam Preparation Methods

This book uses several key methodologies to help you discover the exam topics on which you need more review, to help you fully understand and remember those details, and to help you prove to yourself that you have retained your knowledge of those topics. This book does not try to help you pass the exam only by memorization but by truly learning and understanding the topics.

The book includes many features that provide different ways to study so you can be ready for the exam. If you understand a topic when you read it but do not study it any further, you probably will not be ready to pass the exam with confidence. The features included in this book give you tools that help you determine what you know, review what you know, better learn what you don't know, and be well prepared for the exam. These tools include:

- **"Do I Know This Already?" Quizzes**: Each chapter begins with a quiz that helps you determine the amount of time you need to spend studying that chapter.

- **Foundation Topics**: These are the core sections of each chapter. They explain the protocols, concepts, and configuration for the topics in that chapter.

- **Exam Preparation Tasks**: This section of each chapter lists a series of study activities that should be done after reading the "Foundation Topics" section. Each chapter includes the activities that make the most sense for studying the topics in that chapter. The activities include the following:

  - **Key Topics Review**: The Key Topic icon appears next to the most important items in the "Foundation Topics" section of the chapter. The "Key Topics Review" section lists the key topics from the chapter and their page numbers. Although the contents of the entire chapter could be on the exam, you should definitely know the information listed for each key topic. Review these topics carefully.

  - **Memory Tables**: To help you exercise your memory and memorize some important facts, memory tables are provided. The memory tables contain only portions of key tables provided previously in the chapter, enabling you to complete the table or list. Appendix B, "Memory Tables," provides the incomplete tables, and Appendix C, "Memory Tables Answer Key," includes the completed tables (answer keys). These appendixes are also provided on the companion website that is provided with your book.

  - **Define Key Terms**: The VCP-DCV exam requires you to learn and know a lot of related terminology. This section lists some of the most important terms from the chapter and asks you to write a short definition and compare your answer to the glossary.

- **Practice Exams**: The companion website contains an exam engine.

Book Organization

The chapters in this book are organized such that Chapters 1 through 7 provide in-depth material on vSphere concepts, and Chapters 8 through 14 describe procedures for the installation, configuration, and management of vSphere components and features. The authors recommend that you read the entire book from cover to cover at least once. As you read about any topic in Chapters 1 to 7, keep in mind that you can find corresponding "how to" steps in Chapters 8 to 14. As you read about any specific procedure in Chapters 8 to 14, keep in mind that you can find associated details (concepts) in Chapters 1 to 7.

Optionally, you can prepare for the exam by studying for the exam objectives in order, using Table I-1 as a guide. As you prepare for each exam objective, you can focus on the most appropriate chapter and section. You can also refer to related chapters and sections. For example, as you prepare for Objective 1.2 (Describe the components and topology of a VMware vCenter architecture), you should focus on the "vCenter Server Topology" section in Chapter 1, but you may also want to review the "Deploying vCenter Server Components" section in Chapter 8 and the "vSphere Managed Inventory Objects" section in Chapter 5.

When preparing for a specific exam objective, you can use Table I-1 to identify the sections in the book that directly address the objective and the sections that provide related information.

Table I-1   Mapping of Exam Objectives to Book Chapters and Sections

Objective	Description	Chapter/Section	Supporting Chapter/Section
1	**Architectures and Technologies**		
1.1	Identify the prerequisites and components for a VMware vSphere 8.x implementation	1: vSphere Overview, Components, and Requirements ■ Infrastructure Requirements ■ Other Requirements	8: vSphere Installation ■ Installing ESXi Hosts ■ Deploying vCenter Server Components
1.2	Describe the components and topology of a VMware vCenter architecture	1: vSphere Overview, Components, and Requirements ■ vCenter Server Topology	8: vSphere Installation ■ Deploying vCenter Server Components 5: vCenter Server Features and Virtual Machines ■ vSphere Managed Inventory Objects

Objective	Description	Chapter/Section	Supporting Chapter/Section
1	**Architectures and Technologies**		
1.3	Describe storage concepts	2: Storage Infrastructure ■ Storage Models and Datastore Types	
1.3.1	Identify and differentiate storage access protocols for VMware vSphere (NFS, iSCSI, SAN, etc.)	2: Storage Infrastructure ■ Storage Virtualization: Traditional Model	
1.3.2	Describe storage datastore types for VMware vSphere	2: Storage Infrastructure ■ Software-Defined Storage Models ■ Datastore Types	11: Managing Storage ■ Managing Datastores
1.3.3	Explain the importance of advanced storage configurations (vStorage APIs for Array Integration (VAAI), vStorage APIs for Storage Awareness (VASA), multipathing, etc.)	2: Storage Infrastructure ■ VASA ■ VAAI	11: Managing Storage ■ VASA: Registering a Storage Provider ■ VASA: Managing Storage Providers
1.3.4	Describe storage policies	2: Storage Infrastructure ■ Storage Policies	11: Managing Storage ■ Managing Storage Policies
1.3.5	Describe basic storage concepts in VMware vSAN and VMware Virtual Volumes (vVOLs)	2: Storage Infrastructure ■ vSAN Concepts ■ Virtual Volumes (vVols)	2: Storage Infrastructure ■ Storage Virtualization: Traditional Model ■ Software-Defined Storage Models ■ Datastore Types ■ Storage in vSphere with Kubernetes 11: Managing Storage ■ Managing vSAN ■ Managing Datastores ■ Configuring and Managing vVols

Objective	Description	Chapter/Section	Supporting Chapter/Section
1	**Architectures and Technologies**		
1.3.6	Identify use cases for raw device mapping (RDM), Persistent Memory (PMem), Non-Volatile Memory Express (NVMe), NVMe over Fabrics (NVMe-oF), and RDMA (iSER).	2: Storage Infrastructure ■ Raw Device Mappings (RDMs) ■ vVols ■ VMware NVMe	11: Managing Storage ■ Managing RDMs ■ Managing Storage Policies ■ Managing VMware NVMe ■ Managing PMem
1.3.7	Describe datastore clusters	2: Storage Infrastructure ■ Storage DRS (SDRS)	11: Managing Storage ■ Configuring and Managing SDRS
1.3.8	Describe Storage I/O Control (SIOC)	2: Storage Infrastructure ■ NIOC, SIOC, and SDRS	11: Managing Storage ■ Configuring and Managing SIOC
1.4	Describe VMware ESXi cluster concepts	4: Clusters and High Availability ■ Cluster Concepts and Overview ■ Distributed Resources Scheduler (DRS) ■ High Availability (HA)	10: Managing and Monitoring Clusters and Resources ■ Creating and Configuring a vSphere Cluster ■ Creating and Configuring a vSphere DRS Cluster ■ Creating and Configuring a vSphere HA cluster
1.4.1	Describe VMware Distributed Resource Scheduler (DRS)	4: Clusters and High Availability ■ Cluster Concepts and Overview ■ Distributed Resources Scheduler (DRS)	10: Managing and Monitoring Clusters and Resources ■ Creating and Configuring a vSphere DRS Cluster
1.4.2	Describe vSphere Enhanced vMotion Compatibility (EVC)	4: Clusters and High Availability ■ Enhanced vMotion Compatibility (EVC)	10: Managing and Monitoring Clusters and Resources ■ EVC Mode

Objective	Description	Chapter/Section	Supporting Chapter/Section
1	**Architectures and Technologies**		
1.4.3	Describe how DRS scores virtual machines	4: Clusters and High Availability ■ How DRS Scores VMs	10: Managing and Monitoring Clusters and Resources ■ Creating and Configuring a vSphere DRS Cluster
1.4.4	Describe VMware vSphere High Availability (HA)	4: Clusters and High Availability ■ vSphere High Availability (HA)	10: Managing and Monitoring Clusters and Resources ■ Creating and Configuring a vSphere HA cluster
1.4.4.1	Describe Admission Control	4: Clusters and High Availability ■ vSphere HA Admission Control	10: Managing and Monitoring Clusters and Resources ■ Creating and Configuring a vSphere HA cluster
1.4.4.2	Describe vSphere Cluster Services (vCLS)	4: Clusters and High Availability ■ vSphere Cluster Services (vCLS)	
1.4.5	Identify use cases for fault tolerance	4: Clusters and High Availability ■ Fault Tolerance (FT)	10: Managing and Monitoring Clusters and Resources ■ Configuring vSphere Fault Tolerance
1.5	Explain the difference between VMware standard switches and distributed switches	3: Network Infrastructure ■ vSphere Standard Switch (vSS) ■ vSphere Distributed Switch (vDS) ■ vDS Settings and Features	9: Configuring and Managing Virtual Networks ■ Creating and Configuring vSphere Standard Switches ■ Creating and Configuring vSphere Distributed Switches
1.5.1	Describe VMkernel networking	3: Network Infrastructure ■ VMkernel Networking and TCP/IP Stacks	9: Configuring and Managing Virtual Networks ■ Configuring and Managing VMkernel Adapters ■ Configuring TCP/IP Stacks

Objective	Description	Chapter/Section	Supporting Chapter/Section
1	**Architectures and Technologies**		
1.5.2	Manage networking on multiple hosts with vSphere Distributed Switch (VDS)	9: Configuring and Managing Virtual Networks ■ Managing Host Networking with vDS	3: Network Infrastructure ■ vSphere Distributed Switch (vDS)
1.5.3	Describe networking policies	3: Network Infrastructure ■ vSS Networking Policies ■ vDS Networking Policies	9: Configuring and Managing Virtual Networks ■ Networking Policies and Advanced Features
1.5.4	Manage Network I/O Control (NIOC) on a vSphere Distributed Switch (VDS)	9: Configuring and Managing Virtual Networks ■ Configuring Network I/O Control (NIOC)	3: Network Infrastructure ■ Network I/O Control
1.5.5	Describe Network I/O Control (NIOC)	3: Network Infrastructure ■ Network I/O Control	9: Configuring and Managing Virtual Networks ■ Configuring Network I/O Control (NIOC)
1.6	Describe VMware vSphere Lifecycle Manager concepts	13: Managing vSphere and vCenter Server ■ Using vSphere Lifecycle Manager	8: vSphere Installation ■ VMware vSphere Lifecyle Manager Implementation
1.7	Describe the basics of VMware vSAN as primary storage	2: Storage Infrastructure ■ vSAN Concepts	
1.7.1	Identify basic vSAN requirements (networking, disk count, and type)	2: Storage Infrastructure ■ vSAN Requirements	11: Managing Storage ■ Configuring and Managing vSAN
1.7.2	Identify Express Storage Architecture (ESA) concepts for vSAN 8	2: Storage Infrastructure ■ vSAN Concepts	

Objective	Description	Chapter/Section	Supporting Chapter/Section
1	**Architectures and Technologies**		
1.8	Describe the role of Virtual Machine Encryption in a data center	7: vSphere Security ■ Virtual Machine Encryption	
1.8.1	Describe vSphere Trust Authority	7: vSphere Security ■ vSphere Trust Authority (vTA)	12: Managing vSphere Security ■ Configuring and Managing vSphere Trust Authority (vTA)
1.8.1.1	Describe the vSphere Trust Authority architecture	7: vSphere Security ■ vSphere Trust Authority (vTA)	12: Managing vSphere Security ■ Configuring and Managing vSphere Trust Authority (vTA)
1.8.1.2	Recognize use cases for vSphere Trust Authority	7: vSphere Security ■ vSphere Trust Authority (vTA)	
1.8.2	Describe the role of a Key Management Services (KMS) server in vSphere	1: vSphere Overview, Components, and Requirements ■ Infrastructure Requirements	
1.9	Recognize methods of securing virtual machines	7: vSphere Security ■ Virtual Machine Security	
1.9.1	Recognize use cases for a virtual Trusted Platform Module (vTPM)	7: vSphere Security ■ Virtual Trusted Platform Module (vTPM)	
1.9.2	Differentiate between Basic Input or Output System (BIOS) and Unified Extensible Firmware Interface (UEFI) firmware	7: vSphere Security ■ ESXi Secure Boot and TPM	12: Managing vSphere Security ■ Configuring UEFI Secure Boot for ESXi Hosts

Objective	Description	Chapter/Section	Supporting Chapter/Section
1	**Architectures and Technologies**		
1.9.3	Recognize use cases for Microsoft virtualization-based security (VBS)	14: Managing Virtual Machines ■ Virtualization-Based Security	
1.10	Describe identity federation	8: vSphere Installation ■ Configuring Identity Federation	
1.10.1	Describe the architecture of identity federation	8: vSphere Installation ■ Configuring Identity Federation	
1.10.2	Recognize use cases for identity federation	8: vSphere Installation ■ Configuring Identity Federation	
1.11	Describe VMware vSphere Distributed Services Engine	3: Network Infrastructure ■ Network Offloads Compatibility	
1.11.1	Describe the role of a data processing unit (DPU) in vSphere	1: vSphere Overview, Components and Requirements ■ Compute and System Requirements 3: Network Infrastructure ■ Traditional Networking Terminology ■ Network Offloads Compatibility	
1.12	Identify use cases for VMware Tools	5: vCenter Server Features and Virtual Machines ■ VMware Tools	
1.13	Describe the high-level components of VMware vSphere with Tanzu	6: VMware Product Integration ■ vSphere with Tanzu	

Objective	Description	Chapter/Section	Supporting Chapter/Section
1	**Architectures and Technologies**		
1.13.1	Identify the use case for a Supervisor Cluster and Supervisor Namespace	6: VMware Product Integration ■ vSphere with Tanzu ■ vSphere with Tanzu Use Cases	
1.13.2	Identify the use case for vSphere Zones	6: VMware Product Integration ■ vSphere with Tanzu	
1.13.3	Identify the use case for a VMware Tanzu Kubernetes Grid (TKG) cluster	6: VMware Product Integration ■ vSphere with Tanzu	
2	**VMware Products and Solutions**		
2.1	Describe the role of VMware vSphere in the Software-Defined Data Center	1: vSphere Overview, Components, and Requirements ■ VMware SDDC	
2.2	Identify use cases for VMware vSphere+	6: VMware Product Integration ■ vSphere+	
2.3	Identify use cases for VMware vCenter Converter	6: VMware Product Integration ■ vCenter Converter	
2.4	Identify disaster recovery (DR) use cases	6: VMware Product Integration ■ vSphere Replication ■ Site Recovery Manager (SRM)	
2.4.1	Identify VMware vCenter replication options	6: VMware Product Integration ■ vSphere Replication	
2.4.2	Identify use cases for VMware Site Recovery Manager (SRM)	6: VMware Product Integration ■ Site Recovery Manager (SRM)	

Objective	Description	Chapter/Section	Supporting Chapter/Section
3	**Planning and Designing**		
4	**Installing, Configuring, and Setup**		
4.1	Configure single sign-on (SSO)	1: vSphere Overview, Components and Requirements ■ vCenter Server Topology 8: vSphere Installation ■ Configuring Single Sign-On (SSO)	12: Managing vSphere Security ■ Managing SSO
4.1.1	Configure an SSO domain	8: vSphere Installation ■ Deploying vCenter Server Components ■ Configuring Single Sign-On (SSO)	1: vSphere Overview, Components, and Requirements ■ vCenter Server Topology 12: Managing vSphere Security ■ Managing SSO
4.1.2	Join an existing SSO domain	8: vSphere Installation ■ Deploying vCenter Server Components ■ Configuring Single Sign-On (SSO)	1: vSphere Overview, Components, and Requirements ■ vCenter Server Topology 12: Managing vSphere Security ■ Managing SSO
4.2	Configure vSphere distributed switches	9: Configuring and Managing Virtual Networks ■ vSphere Distributed Switches (vDS)	
4.2.1	Create a distributed switch	9: Configuring and Managing Virtual Networks ■ Creating and Configuring vSphere Distributed Switches	
4.2.2	Add ESXi hosts to the distributed switch	9: Configuring and Managing Virtual Networks ■ Adding Hosts to a vDS	

Objective	Description	Chapter/Section	Supporting Chapter/Section
4	**Installing, Configuring, and Setup**		
4.2.3	Examine the distributed switch configuration	9: Configuring and Managing Virtual Networks ■ Creating and Configuring vSphere Distributed Switches	
4.3	Configure Virtual Standard Switch (VSS) advanced virtual networking options	9: Configuring and Managing Virtual Networks ■ Creating and Configuring vSphere Standard Switches ■ Creating and Configuring Standard Port Groups	3: Network Infrastructure ■ vSphere Standard Switch (vSS)
4.4	Set up identity sources	8: vSphere Installation ■ Adding, Editing, and Removing SSO Identity Sources	12: Managing vSphere Security ■ Managing SSO
4.4.1	Configure identity federation	8: vSphere Installation ■ Configuring Identity Federation	12: Managing vSphere Security ■ Managing SSO
4.4.2	Configure LDAP integration	8: vSphere Installation ■ Adding, Editing, and Removing SSO Identity Sources ■ How to Add an LDAP Authentication Source	12: Managing vSphere Security ■ Managing SSO
4.5	Deploy and configure VMware vCenter Server Appliance (VCSA)	8: vSphere Installation ■ vCenter Server Appliance	1: vSphere Overview, Components, and Requirements ■ vCenter Server Topology 13: Managing vSphere and vCenter Server ■ Upgrading to vSphere 7.0 ■ Repointing a vCenter Server to Another Domain

Objective	Description	Chapter/Section	Supporting Chapter/Section
4	**Installing, Configuring, and Setup**		
4.6	Create and configure VMware HA and DRS advanced options (Admission Control, Proactive HA, etc.)	10: Managing and Monitoring Clusters and Resources ■ Creating and Configuring a vSphere DRS Cluster ■ Creating and Configuring a vSphere HA Cluster	4: Clusters and High Availability ■ Distributed Resource Scheduler (DRS) ■ vSphere High Availability (HA)
4.7	Deploy and configure VMware vCenter High Availability	8: vSphere Installation ■ Implementing VCSA HA	1: vSphere Overview, Components, and Requirements ■ vCenter Server Topology ■ vCenter High Availability Requirements 4: Clusters and High Availability ■ vCenter Server High Availability 13: Managing vSphere and vCenter Server ■ Managing the vCenter HA Cluster
4.8	Set up content library	14: Managing Virtual Machines ■ Content Libraries	5: vCenter Server Features and Virtual Machines ■ Content Libraries
4.8.1	Create a content library	14: Managing Virtual Machines ■ Creating a Content Library	
4.8.2	Add content to the content library	14: Managing Virtual Machines ■ Adding Items to a Content Library	
4.8.3	Publish a local content library	14: Managing Virtual Machines ■ Publishing a Content Library	

Objective	Description	Chapter/Section	Supporting Chapter/Section
4	**Installing, Configuring, and Setup**		
4.9	Subscribe to content library	14: Managing Virtual Machines ■ Subscribing to a Content Library	
4.9.1	Create a subscribed content library	14: Managing Virtual Machines ■ Publishing a Content Library	
4.9.2	Subscribe to a published content library	14: Managing Virtual Machines ■ Subscribing to a Content Library	
4.9.3	Deploy virtual machines (VMs) from a subscribed content library	14: Managing Virtual Machines ■ Deploying VMs by Using a Content Library	
4.10	Manage virtual machine (VM) template versions	14: Managing Virtual Machines ■ Managing VM Templates in a Content Library	
4.10.1	Update template in content library	14: Managing Virtual Machines ■ Managing VM Templates in a Content Library	
4.11	Configure VMware vCenter file-based backup	13: Managing vSphere and vCenter Server ■ vCenter Server Backup	
4.12	Configure vSphere Trust Authority	12: Managing vSphere Security ■ Configuring and Managing vSphere Trust Authority (vTA)	7: vSphere Security ■ vSphere Trust Authority (vTA)

Objective	Description	Chapter/Section	Supporting Chapter/Section
4	**Installing, Configuring, and Setup**		
4.13	Configure vSphere certificates	12: Managing vSphere Security ■ Configuring and Managing vSphere Certificates	7: vSphere Security ■ ESXi Host Certificates 13: Managing vSphere and vCenter Server ■ Verifying SSL Certificates for Legacy Hosts
4.13.1	Describe Enterprise PKIs role for SSL certificates	7: vSphere Security ■ vSphere Certificates Overview	12: Managing vSphere Security ■ Configuring and Managing vSphere Certificates
4.14	Configure vSphere Lifecycle Manager	8: vSphere Installation ■ Implementing VMware vSphere Lifecycle Manager	13: Managing vSphere and vCenter Server ■ Using vSphere Lifecycle Manager ■ About VMware Update Manager ■ Update Manager Download Service (UMDS)
4.15	Configure different network stacks	9: Configuring and Managing Virtual Networks ■ Configuring TCP/IP Stacks	3: Network Infrastructure ■ VMkernel Networking and TCP/IP Stacks
4.16	Configure host profiles	8: vSphere Installation ■ Configuring ESXi Using Host Profiles	
4.17	Identify ESXi boot options	8: vSphere Installation ■ ESXi Kernel Options	
4.17.1	Configure Quick Boot	13: Managing vSphere and vCenter Server ■ ESXi Quick Boot	
4.17.2	Securely Boot ESXi hosts	12: Managing vSphere Security ■ Configuring UEFI Secure Boot for ESXi Hosts	7: vSphere Security ■ ESXi Secure Boot and TPM ■ vSphere Trusted Authority (vTA)

Objective	Description	Chapter/Section	Supporting Chapter/Section
4	**Installing, Configuring, and Setup**		
4.18	Deploy and configure clusters using the vSphere Cluster Quickstart workflow	10: Managing and Monitoring Clusters and Resources ■ Creating a Cluster	
4.18.1	Use Cluster Quickstart workflow to add hosts	10: Managing and Monitoring Clusters and Resources ■ Configuring a Cluster with Quickstart	
4.18.2	Use Cluster Quickstart workflow to configure a cluster	10: Managing and Monitoring Clusters and Resources ■ Configuring a Cluster with Quickstart	
4.18.3	Use Quickstart to expand clusters	10: Managing and Monitoring Clusters and Resources ■ Configuring a Cluster with Quickstart	
4.19	Set up and configure VMware ESXi	8: vSphere Installation ■ vSphere Lifecycle ■ Installing ESXi Hosts ■ Initial vSphere Configuration	12: Managing vSphere Security ■ Configuring and Managing ESXi Security
4.19.1	Configure Time Configuration	12: Managing vSphere Security ■ Customizing ESXi Services ■ Configuring ESXi Using Host Profiles 8: vSphere Installation ■ ESXi Configuration Settings	10: Managing and Monitoring Clusters and Resources ■ Configuring a Cluster with Quickstart

Objective	Description	Chapter/Section	Supporting Chapter/Section
4	**Installing, Configuring, and Setup**		
4.19.2	Configure ESXi services	12: Managing vSphere Security ■ Customizing ESXi Services	
4.19.2.1	Configure ESXi Shell	12: Managing vSphere Security ■ SSH and ESXi Shell Security	
4.19.2.2	Configure SSH	12: Managing vSphere Security ■ SSH and ESXi Shell Security	
4.19.3	Configure Product Locker	8: vSphere Installation ■ Configuring ESXi Using Host Profiles	
4.19.4	Configure Lockdown Mode	12: Managing vSphere Security ■ Using Lockdown Mode	7: vSphere Security ■ ESXi Host Access
4.19.5	Configure ESXi firewall	12: Managing vSphere Security ■ Configuring the ESXi Firewall	7: vSphere Security ■ Security Profiles
4.20	Configure VMware vSphere with Tanzu	6: VMware Product Integration ■ vSphere with Tanzu Integration	
4.20.1	Configure a Supervisor Cluster & Supervisor Namespace	6: VMware Product Integration ■ vSphere with Tanzu	
4.20.2	Configure a Tanzu Kubernetes Grid Cluster	6: VMware Product Integration ■ vSphere with Tanzu	

Objective	Description	Chapter/Section	Supporting Chapter/Section
4	**Installing, Configuring, and Setup**		
4.20.3	Configure vSphere Zones	6: VMware Product Integration ■ vSphere with Tanzu	
4.20.4	Configure Namespace permissions	6: VMware Product Integration ■ vSphere with Tanzu	
5	**Performance-tuning, Optimization, Upgrades**		
5.1	Identify resource pools use cases	4: Clusters and High Availability ■ Resource Pools	10: Managing and Monitoring Clusters and Resources ■ Creating a Resource Pool ■ Monitoring and Managing Resource Pool Resources
5.1.1	Explain shares, limits, and reservations (resource management)	4: Clusters and High Availability ■ Shares, Limits, and Reservations	10: Managing and Monitoring Clusters and Resources ■ Shares, Limits, and Reservations ■ Creating a Resource Pool ■ Monitoring and Managing Resource Pool Resources
5.2	Monitor resources of a VMware vCenter Server Appliance (VCSA) and vSphere 8.x environment	10: Managing and Monitoring Clusters and Resources ■ Monitoring and Managing vSphere Resources	4: Clusters and High Availability ■ Cluster Concepts and Overview ■ Distributed Resource Scheduler (DRS)
5.3	Identify and use resource monitoring tools	10: Managing and Monitoring Clusters and Resources ■ Monitoring and Managing vSphere Resources	
5.4	Configure Network I/O Control (NIOC)	9: Configuring and Managing Virtual Networks ■ Configuring Network I/O Control (NIOC)	3: Network Infrastructure ■ Network I/O Control

Objective	Description	Chapter/Section	Supporting Chapter/Section
5	**Performance-tuning, Optimization, Upgrades**		
5.5	Configure Storage I/O Control (SIOC)	11: Managing Storage ■ Configuring and Managing SIOC	2: Storage Infrastructure ■ NIOC, SIOC, and SDRS
5.6	Configure a virtual machine port group to be offloaded to a data processing unit (DPU)	9: Configuring and Managing Virtual Networks ■ vSphere Distributed Switches (vDS)	
5.7	Explain the performance impact of maintaining virtual machine snapshots	5: vCenter Server Features and Virtual Machines ■ Virtual Machine Snapshots	14: Managing Virtual Machines ■ Creating and Managing Virtual Machine Snapshots
5.8	Use Update Planner to identify opportunities to update VMware vCenter	13: Managing vSphere and vCenter Server ■ Using Update Planner	
5.9	Use vSphere Lifecycle Manager to determine the need for upgrades and updates	13: Managing vSphere and vCenter Server ■ Using Lifecycle Manager ■ Upgrading to vSphere 7.0 ■ Using Update Planner	
5.9.1	Update virtual machines	4: Managing Virtual Machines ■ Installing and Upgrading VMware Tools	
5.9.2	Update VMware ESXi	13: Managing vSphere and vCenter Server ■ Using vSphere Lifecycle Manager	
5.10	Use performance charts to monitor performance	10: Managing and Monitoring Clusters and Resources ■ Monitoring and Managing vSphere Resources	

Objective	Description	Chapter/Section	Supporting Chapter/Section
5	**Performance-tuning, Optimization, Upgrades**		
5.11	Perform proactive management with VMware Skyline	10: Managing and Monitoring Clusters and Resources ■ Monitoring and Managing Host Resources and Health	6: VMware Product Integration ■ VMware Skyline
5.12	Use VMware vCenter management interface to update VMware vCenter	13: Managing vSphere and vCenter Server ■ Patching with VAMI	
5.13	Complete lifecycle activities for VMware vSphere with Tanzu	13: Managing vSphere and vCenter Server ■ Using vSphere Lifecycle Manager	
5.13.1	Update Supervisor cluster	13: Managing vSphere and vCenter Server ■ Using vSphere Lifecycle Manager	
5.13.2	Back up and restore VMware vSphere with Tanzu	13: Managing vSphere and vCenter Serve ■ vCenter Server	
6	**Troubleshooting and Repairing**		
6.1	Identify use cases for enabling vSphere Cluster Services (vCLS) retreat mode	4: Clusters and High Availability ■ vSphere Cluster Services (vCLS)	
6.2	Differentiate between the main management services in VMware ESXi and vCenter and their corresponding log files	10: Managing and Monitoring Clusters and Resources ■ ESXi Logs ■ vCenter Server Logs	

Objective	Description	Chapter/Section	Supporting Chapter/Section
6	**Troubleshooting and Repairing**		
6.3	Generate a log bundle	10: Managing and Monitoring Clusters and Resources ■ ESXi Logs ■ vCenter Server Logs ■ Uploading System Logs to VMware 13: Managing vSphere and vCenter Server ■ Monitoring and Managing vCenter Server with the VAMI	
7	**Administrative and Operational Tasks**		
7.1	Create and manage virtual machine snapshots	14: Managing Virtual Machines ■ Creating and Managing Virtual Machine Snapshots	5: vCenter Server Features and Virtual Machines ■ Virtual Machine Snapshots
7.2	Create virtual machines using different methods (Open Virtualization Format (OVF) templates, content library, etc.)	14: Managing Virtual Machines ■ Managing VMs by Using PowerCLI ■ Deploying OVF/OVA Templates ■ Deploying VMs by Using a Content Library	5: vCenter Server Features and Virtual Machines ■ Virtual Machine Cloning 14: Managing Virtual Machines ■ Managing OVF Templates ■ Content Libraries
7.3	Manage virtual machines (modifying virtual machine settings, VMware per-VM EVC, latency sensitivity, CPU affinity, etc.)	14: Managing Virtual Machines ■ Managing EVC Mode and CPU Affinity 10: Managing and Monitoring Clusters and Resources ■ Latency Sensitivity	5: vCenter Server Features and Virtual Machines ■ Virtual Machine Migration

Objective	Description	Chapter/Section	Supporting Chapter/Section
7	**Administrative and Operational Tasks**		
7.4	Manage storage	11: Managing Storage ■ Managing Datastores ■ Managing Storage Policies ■ Managing Multipathing ■ Managing Paths with the vSphere Client	2 : Storage Infrastructure ■ Datastore Types ■ Storage Policies ■ Storage Multipathing and Failover
7.4.1	Configure and modify datastores	11: Managing Storage ■ Managing Datastores	2: Storage Infrastructure ■ Datastore Types
7.4.2	Create virtual machine storage policies	11: Managing Storage ■ Managing Storage Policies	2: Storage Infrastructure ■ Storage Policies
7.4.3	Configure storage cluster options	11: Managing Storage ■ Configuring and Managing Storage DRS ■ Configuring and Managing vSAN	2: Storage Infrastructure ■ SDRS
7.5	Create DRS affinity and anti-affinity rules for common use cases	10: Managing and Monitoring Clusters and Resources ■ Creating Affinity/ Anti-Affinity Rules	4: Clusters and High Availability ■ DRS Rules
7.6	Migrate virtual machines	14: Managing Virtual Machines ■ Migrating Virtual Machines	5: vCenter Server Features and Virtual Machines ■ Virtual Machine Migration ■ vMotion Details ■ Storage vMotion Details
7.6.1	Identify requirements for Storage vMotion, Cold Migration, vMotion, and Cross vCenter Export	14: Managing Virtual Machines ■ Migrating Virtual Machines	5: vCenter Server Features and Virtual Machines ■ Virtual Machine Migration ■ vMotion Details ■ Storage vMotion Details

Objective	Description	Chapter/Section	Supporting Chapter/Section
7	**Administrative and Operational Tasks**		
7.7	Configure role-based access control	12: Managing vSphere Security ■ Configuring and Managing Authentication and Authorization	7: vSphere Security ■ vSphere Permissions 8: vSphere Installation ■ Applying Permissions to ESXi Hosts Using Host Profiles
7.8	Manage host profiles	8: vSphere Installation ■ Configuring ESXi by Using Host Profiles	5: vCenter Server Features and Virtual Machines ■ Host Profiles
7.9	Utilize VMware vSphere Lifecycle Manager	13: Managing vSphere and vCenter Server ■ Using vSphere Lifecycle Manager	8: vSphere Installation ■ Implementing VMware vSphere Lifecycle Manager 14: Managing Virtual Machines ■ Installing and Upgrading VMware Tools
7.9.1	Describe firmware upgrades for VMware ESXi	13: Managing vSphere and vCenter Server ■ Using vSphere Lifecycle Manager	8: vSphere Installation ■ Implementing VMware vSphere Lifecycle Manager
7.9.2	Describe ESXi updates	13: Managing vSphere and vCenter Server ■ Using vSphere Lifecycle Manager	8: vSphere Installation ■ Implementing VMware vSphere Lifecycle Manager
7.9.3	Describe component and driver updates for ESXi	13: Managing vSphere and vCenter Server ■ Using vSphere Lifecycle Manager	8: vSphere Installation ■ Implementing VMware vSphere Lifecycle Manager Implementation
7.9.4	Describe hardware compatibility check	13: Managing vSphere and vCenter Server ■ Using vSphere Lifecycle Manager	8: vSphere Installation ■ Implementing VMware vSphere Lifecycle Manager 5: vCenter Server Features and Virtual Machines ■ VM Hardware/Compatibility 14: Managing Virtual Machines ■ Configuring Virtual Machine Hardware

Objective	Description	Chapter/Section	Supporting Chapter/Section
7	**Administrative and Operational Tasks**		
7.9.5	Describe ESXi cluster image export functionality	13: Managing vSphere and vCenter Server ■ Using vSphere Lifecycle Manager	8: vSphere Installation ■ Implementing VMware vSphere Lifecycle Manager 4: Clusters and High Availability ■ Cluster Concepts and Overview
7.9.6	Create ESXi cluster image	13: Managing vSphere and vCenter Server ■ Using vSphere Lifecycle Manager	
7.10	Use predefined alarms in VMware vCenter	10: Managing and Monitoring Clusters and Resources ■ Alarms	
7.11	Create custom alarms	10: Managing and Monitoring Clusters and Resources ■ Advanced Use Cases for Alarms ■ Creating Alarm Definitions	
7.12	Deploy an encrypted virtual machine	12: Managing vSphere Security ■ Encrypting a Virtual Machine	
7.12.1	Convert a non-encrypted virtual machine to an encrypted virtual machine	12: Managing vSphere Security ■ Encrypting a Virtual Machine	
7.12.2	Migrate an encrypted virtual machine	7: vSphere Security ■ Encrypted vSphere vMotion	
7.12.3	Configure virtual machine vMotion encryption properties	7: vSphere Security ■ Encrypted vSphere vMotion	

Companion Website

Register this book to get access to the Pearson IT Certification test engine and other study materials plus additional bonus content. Check this site regularly for new and updated postings written by the authors that provide further insight into the more troublesome topics on the exam. Be sure to check the box indicating that you would like to hear from us to receive updates and exclusive discounts on future editions of this product or related products.

To access this companion website, follow these steps:

Step 1. Go to **www.pearsonITcertification.com/register** and log in or create a new account.

Step 2. Enter the ISBN **9780138169886**.

Step 3. Answer the challenge question as proof of purchase.

Step 4. Click on the **Access Bonus Content** link in the Registered Products section of your account page to be taken to the page where your downloadable content is available.

NOTE Keep in mind that many of the companion content files—especially image and video files—are very large.

If you are unable to locate the files for this title by following these steps, please visit www.pearsonITcertification.com/contact and select the Site Problems/Comments option. Our customer service representatives will assist you.

How to Access the Pearson Test Prep Practice (PTP) App

You have two options for installing and using the Pearson Test Prep application: a web app and a desktop app. To use the Pearson Test Prep application, start by finding the registration code that comes with the book. You can find the code in these ways:

- You can get your access code by registering the print ISBN (9780138169886) on pearsonitcertification.com/register. Make sure to use the print book ISBN, regardless of whether you purchased an eBook or the print book. After you register the book, your access code will be populated on your account page under the Registered Products tab. Instructions for how to redeem the code are available on the book's companion website by clicking the Access Bonus Content link.

- Premium Edition: If you purchase the Premium Edition eBook and Practice Test directly from the Pearson IT Certification website, the code will be populated on your account page after purchase. Just log in at pearsonitcertification.com, click Account to see details of your account, and click the digital purchases tab.

NOTE   After you register your book, your code can always be found in your account under the Registered Products tab.

Once you have the access code, to find instructions about both the PTP web app and the desktop app, follow these steps:

Step 1.   Open this book's companion website as shown earlier in this Introduction under the heading, "Companion Website."

Step 2.   Click the **Practice Exams** button.

Step 3.   Follow the instructions listed there for both installing the desktop app and using the web app.

Note that if you want to use the web app only at this point, just navigate to pearsontestprep.com, log in using the same credentials used to register your book or purchase the Premium Edition, and register this book's practice tests using the registration code you just found. The process should take only a couple of minutes.

Customizing Your Exams

Once you are in the exam settings screen, you can choose to take exams in one of three modes:

- **Study mode:** Enables you to fully customize your exams and review answers as you are taking the exam. This is typically the mode you use first to assess your knowledge and identify information gaps.

- **Practice Exam mode:** Locks certain customization options, as it is presenting a realistic exam experience. Use this mode when you are preparing to test your exam readiness.

- **Flash Card mode:** Strips out the answers and presents you with only the question stem. This mode is great for late-stage preparation when you really want to challenge yourself to provide answers without the benefit of seeing multiple-choice options. This mode does not provide the detailed score reports that the other two modes do, so you should not use it if you are trying to identify knowledge gaps.

In addition to these three modes, you will be able to select the source of your questions. You can choose to take exams that cover all of the chapters or you can narrow your selection to just a single chapter or the chapters that make up specific parts in the book. All chapters are selected by default. If you want to narrow your focus to individual chapters, simply deselect all the chapters and then select only those on which you wish to focus in the Objectives area.

You can also select the exam banks on which to focus. Each exam bank comes complete with a full exam of questions that cover topics in every chapter. You can have the test engine serve up exams from all test banks or just from one individual bank by selecting the desired banks in the exam bank area. There are several other customizations you can make to your exam from the exam settings screen, such as the time of the exam, the number of questions served up, whether to randomize questions and answers, whether to show the number of correct answers for multiple-answer questions, and whether to serve up only specific types of questions. You can also create custom test banks by selecting only questions that you have marked or questions on which you have added notes.

Updating Your Exams

If you are using the online version of the Pearson Test Prep software, you should always have access to the latest version of the software as well as the exam data. If you are using the Windows desktop version, every time you launch the software while connected to the Internet, it checks if there are any updates to your exam data and automatically downloads any changes that were made since the last time you used the software.

Sometimes, due to many factors, the exam data might not fully download when you activate your exam. If you find that figures or exhibits are missing, you might need to manually update your exams. To update a particular exam you have already activated and downloaded, simply click the Tools tab and click the Update Products button. Again, this is only an issue with the desktop Windows application. If you wish to check for updates to the Pearson Test Prep exam engine software, Windows desktop version, simply click the Tools tab and click the Update Application button. This ensures that you are running the latest version of the software engine.

Credits

Cover: FrameRatio/Shutterstock

Figure 5-1, Figure 5-2, Figure 5-3, Figure 5-4, Figure 8-1, Figure 10-1, Figure 10-2, Figure 10-3, Figure 10-4, Figure 13-1, Figure 13-2: VMware, Inc.

This chapter covers the following topics:

- vSphere Components and Editions

- vCenter Server Topology

- Infrastructure Requirements

- Other Requirements

- VMware Cloud vs. VMware Virtualization

This chapter contains information related to VMware vSphere 8.x Professional (2V0-21.23) exam objectives 1.1, 1.2, 1.8.2, 1.11.1, 2.1, 4.1, 4.1.1, 4.1.2, 4.5, and 4.7.

vSphere Overview, Components, and Requirements

This chapter introduces vSphere 8.0, describes its major components, and identifies its requirements.

"Do I Know This Already?" Quiz

The "Do I Know This Already?" quiz allows you to assess whether you should study this entire chapter or move quickly to the "Exam Preparation Tasks" section. In any case, the authors recommend that you read the entire chapter at least once. Table 1-1 outlines the major headings in this chapter and the corresponding "Do I Know This Already?" quiz questions. You can find the answers in Appendix A, "Answers to the 'Do I Know This Already?' Quizzes and Review Questions."

Table 1-1 "Do I Know This Already?" Foundation Topics Section-to-Question Mapping

Foundations Topics Section	Questions Covered in This Section
vSphere Components and Editions	1, 2
vCenter Server Topology	3, 4
Infrastructure Requirements	5, 6
Other Requirements	7, 8
VMware Cloud vs. VMware Virtualization	9, 10

1. You plan to deploy vSphere 8.0 for three ESXi hosts and want to deploy the minimum vCenter Server edition that supports vMotion. Which vCenter Server edition do you choose?

    a. Essentials

    b. Essentials Plus

    c. Foundation

    d. Standard

2. You plan to deploy vSphere 8.0 and want to minimize virtual machine down-time by proactively detecting hardware failures and placing the host in Quarantine Mode or Maintenance Mode. Which feature do you need?

   a. vSphere High Availability

   b. Proactive HA

   c. Predictive DRS

   d. vCenter HA

3. You are preparing to deploy and manage a vSphere environment. Which vCenter Server component provides Security Assertion Markup Language (SAML) tokens?

   a. vCenter Lookup Service

   b. VMware Directory Service

   c. tcServer

   d. STS

4. You plan to deploy another vCenter Server in your vSphere 8.0 environment and want it to use an existing vSphere Single Sign-On domain. What should you do?

   a. During vCenter Server deployment, join an existing SSO domain.

   b. Prior to vCenter Server deployment, deploy an external PSC.

   c. During vCenter Server deployment, connect to an external PSC.

   d. Configure vCenter HA.

5. You plan to deploy a vCenter Server Appliance 8.0 instance to support 350 ESXi hosts and 4500 virtual machines. Which type of vCenter Server Appliance should you choose?

   a. Small Environment

   b. Medium Environment

   c. Large Environment

   d. X-Large Environment

6. You are interested in booting your ESXi hosts using UEFI. Which of the following is a key consideration?

   a. After installing ESXi 8.0, you can change the boot type between BIOS and UEFI by using the direct console user interface.

   b. ESXi boot from UEFI is deprecated in ESXi 8.0.

    c. After installing ESXi 8.0, you can change the boot type between BIOS and UEFI by using the vSphere Client.

    d. After you install ESXi 8.0, changing the boot type between BIOS and UEFI is not supported.

7. You are planning the backup and recovery for a new vCenter Server Appliance instance, using the file-based backup feature in the vCenter Server Appliance Management Interface. Which protocols are supported? (Choose three.)

    a. NFS

    b. FTP

    c. HTTPS

    d. SCP

    e. TFTP

8. When you are planning for managing a new vSphere 8.0 environment, which of the following are not supported browsers for the vSphere Client? (Choose three.)

    a. Chrome for Windows users

    b. Microsoft Edge for Windows users

    c. Safari for Mac users

    d. Firefox for Mac users

    e. Edge for Mac users

9. You need to include on-premises cloud automation software to improve the delivery of IT services and applications in your vSphere-based SDDC. Which of the following should you choose?

    a. VMware Cloud Assembly

    b. VMware Service Broker

    c. vCloud Director

    d. Aria Automation

10. You want a simple path to the hybrid cloud that leverages a common infrastructure and consistent operational model for on-premises and off-premises data centers. What should you use?

    a. Aria Suite

    b. VMware Cloud Foundation

    c. vCloud Director

    d. Cloud Automation

Foundation Topics

vSphere Components and Editions

VMware vSphere is a suite of products that you can use to virtualize enterprise data centers and build private clouds.

vSphere Components

Table 1-2 describes the installable VMware products that are the core components in a vSphere environment.

Table 1-2 Installable Core vSphere Components

Component	Description
vCenter Server	The major management component in the vSphere environment. Its services include vCenter Server, vSphere Web Client, vSphere Auto Deploy, vSphere ESXi Dump Collector, and the components that were associated with the Platform Services Controller in prior versions: vCenter Single Sign-On, License Service, Lookup Service, and VMware Certificate Authority.
ESXi Server	The physical host (including the hypervisor) on which virtual machines run.

Some optional vSphere features require the deployment of additional components and specific vSphere or vCenter Server editions. Table 1-3 describes two of these optional components, which require the deployment of additional virtual appliances.

Table 1-3 Optional vSphere Components

Optional Component	Description
vSphere Replication	An extension to VMware vCenter Server that provides hypervisor-based virtual machine replication and recovery.
vCenter High Availability	A component that provides protection for vCenter Server Appliance against host, hardware, and application failures. Provides automated active/passive failover with minimal downtime. It can also be used to significantly reduce downtime when you patch vCenter Server Appliance.

Many vSphere features, such as those described in Table 1-4, require specific vSphere configuration, and some require specific licensing, but they do not require the installation or deployment of additional software or virtual appliances.

Table 1-4 Available vSphere Features

Available vSphere Features	Description
vCenter Appliance File-Based Backup and Restore	A feature introduced in vSphere 7.0 that enables you to back up and restore the vCenter Server Appliance instances.
vMotion	A feature that provides live virtual machine migrations with negligible disruption from a source ESXi host to a target ESXi host.
vSphere HA	A feature that provides automated failover protection for VMs against host, hardware, network, and guest OS issues. In the event of host system failure, it performs cold migrations and restarts failed VMs on surviving hosts.
Distributed Resource Scheduler (DRS)	A feature that places and starts VMs on appropriate ESXi hosts and hot-migrates VMs by using vMotion when there is contention for compute resources.
Storage vMotion	A feature that performs live migrations with negligible disruption of VMs from a source datastore to a target datastore.
Fault Tolerance (FT)	A feature that provides automated live failover protection for VMs against host, hardware, network, and guest OS issues.
Distributed Power Management (DPM)	A feature that optimizes power consumption in a vSphere cluster, by moving VM workload to a subset of the cluster's member hosts and placing the other member hosts in Standby Mode.
Proactive HA	A feature that minimizes VM downtime by proactively detecting hardware failures and placing the host in Quarantine Mode or Maintenance Mode.
Content library	A centralized repository that is used to manage and distribute templates, ISO files, scripts, vApps, and other files associated with VMs.
Host profiles	A feature that provides a means to apply a standard configuration to a set of ESXi hosts.

The add-on products in Table 1-5 are commonly used in a vSphere environment and are discussed in this book. These products can be sold separately from vSphere.

Table 1-5 Add-on Products

Product	Description
vSAN	A product that provides a SAN experience in a vSphere environment by leveraging local storage in the ESXi hosts. It tightly integrates with vSphere and is the leading Hyper-Converged Infrastructure (HCI) solution for providing a flash-optimized, secure, and simple-to-use SAN.
NSX	A product that adds software-based virtualized networking and security to a vSphere environment.
Aria Suite (formerly vRealize Suite)	A suite of products that adds operations (Aria Operations Manager), automation (Aria Automation), and orchestration (Aria Orchestrator) to a vSphere environment.

NOTE   Although it is an add-on product, vSAN is covered on the VCP-DCV certification exam and in this book. Other add-on products are briefly described in this book.

The vSphere Host Client is a web-based interface provided by each ESXi host. It is available immediately following the installation of a host. Its primary purpose is to provide a GUI for configuration, management, and troubleshooting purposes when vCenter Server is not available. For example, during the implementation of a new vSphere environment, you could use the vSphere Host Client to create virtual machines for running DNS, Active Directory, and vCenter Server databases prior to deploying vCenter Server. As another example, you could use the vSphere Host Client to power down, troubleshoot, reconfigure, and restart the vCenter Server virtual machine.

The HTML5-based vSphere Client is the preferred web-based GUI for managing vSphere. It is provided by services running in the vCenter Server. The flash-based vSphere Web Client used in previous vSphere versions has been deprecated and is no longer available.

Editions and Licenses

VMware vSphere comes in multiple editions and kits, each having unique feature sets and limitations aimed at addressing unique use cases. With vSphere 8.0, you can choose to use perpetual licenses or subscriptions. When planning for perpetual licenses for a vSphere environment, you should prepare to procure at least three line items: a vCenter Server license, a vSphere license, and support for the environment. The vCenter Server license line item should identify the desired edition and quantity (that is, the number of vCenter Server instances).

Table 1-6 provides a summary of the features that are provided with each edition of vCenter Server 8.0.

Table 1-6   vCenter Server Editions

Feature	Essentials	Essentials Plus	Foundation	Standard
Number of ESXi hosts	3 (2 CPU max)	3 (2 CPU max)	4	2000
vCenter License	Packaged with vSphere license in the Essentials Kit	Packaged with vSphere license in Essentials Plus Kit	Sold separately from vSphere license	Sold separately from vSphere license
Basic vCenter features, like single pane of glass management, Lifecycle Manager, and VMware Converter	Supported	Supported	Supported	Supported

Feature	Essentials	Essentials Plus	Foundation	Standard
Common vCenter features like vMotion, vSphere HA, and vSphere Replication	Not supported	Supported	Supported	Supported
Advanced features like vCenter Server High Availability (VCHA) and vCenter Server Backup and Restore	N/A	N/A	N/A	Supported

You need to obtain vSphere licenses based on the number of CPU sockets and cores per socket in your ESXi server. Each physical socket consumes 1 CPU license, but starting with vSphere 7.0, a socket with more than 32 cores consumes 1 additional CPU license. For example, you can assign 10 vSphere CPU licenses to any of the following combinations of hosts:

- Five hosts with 2 CPUs and 32 cores per CPU

- Five hosts with 1 CPU with 64 cores per CPU

- Two hosts with 2 CPUs and 48 cores per CPU and two hosts with 1 CPU and 20 cores per CPU

The major editions of vSphere 8.0 are Standard and Enterprise Plus. Table 1-7 lists some of the features that are provided with each of these editions.

Table 1-7   Features in vSphere Editions

Feature	Standard	Enterprise Plus
vSphere HA, vSphere Replication, Storage vMotion, Quick Boot, vCenter Backup and Restore, vVols	Supported	Supported
Distributed Switch, Proactive HA, NIOC, SIOC, Storage DRS, DRS, DPM, VM Encryption, Cross-vCenter vMotion, Long Distance vMotion, vTrust Authority, SR-IOV, vSphere Persistent Memory	Not supported	Supported
vSphere Fault Tolerance	Supported up to 2 vCPUs	Supported up to 8 vCPUs

NOTE   Additional licenses are required to use vSAN and Tanzu.

vCenter Server Topology

This section describes the architecture for the vCenter Server.

vSphere 6.x supports multiple vCenter Server topologies and configurations, involving components and technologies such as vCenter Server Appliance, vCenter Server for Windows, embedded database (PostgreSQL), external (SQL Server or Oracle) database, external Platform Services Controller (PSC), embedded PSC, Enhanced Linked Mode, and Embedded Linked Mode. Beginning with vSphere 7.0, the vCenter Server configuration and topology are much simpler.

Beginning with vSphere 7.0, Linux-based vCenter Server Appliances are required, and Windows-based vCenter Servers are not supported. External PSC is not supported. The services provided by PSC in prior vCenter Server versions are directly integrated into vCenter Server Appliance and are no longer described as a part of PSC in most documentation. For example, for vSphere 7.0, the *Platform Services Controller Administration* publication was replaced with the *vSphere Authentication* publication. Table 1-8 describes the main services in vCenter Server Appliance and related services in the ESXi host.

Table 1-8 Services in vCenter Server Appliance

Service	Description
vCenter Single Sign-On	An authentication service that utilizes a secure token exchange mechanism rather than requiring components to authenticate users per component.
Security Token Service (STS)	A component that is part of vCenter Single Sign-On and provides SAML tokens to authenticate users to other vCenter components instead of requiring users to authenticate to each component. A user who authenticates to vCenter Single Sign-On is granted SAML tokens, which are then used for authentication.
Administration server	A component that provides vCenter Single Sign-On administration and configuration from the vSphere Client.
vCenter Lookup Service	A service that contains the topology of the vSphere infrastructure, allowing secure communication between vSphere components.
VMware Directory Service	The directory service for the vCenter Single Sign-On (SSO) domain (vsphere.local).
vCenter Server plug-ins	Applications that add functionality to vCenter. These usually consist of server and client components.
vCenter Server database	A database that contains the status of all virtual machines, ESXi hosts, and users. It is deployed via the vCenter Server deployment wizard.

Service	Description
tcServer	A service that is co-installed with vCenter and is used by web services such as ICIM/Hardware status, Performance charts, WebAccess, Storage Policy Based Services, and vCenter Service status.
License Service	A service that is used to store the available licenses and manage the license assignments for the entire vSphere environment.
vCenter Server Agent	A service that is installed on an ESXi host when that host is added to vCenter's inventory. This service collects, communicates, and runs actions initiated from the vSphere Client.
Host Agent	An administrative agent installed on an ESXi host. Responsible for collecting, communicating, and running actions initiated from the vSphere Host Client.

If you upgrade or migrate a vCenter Server deployment that uses an external PSC, you must converge the PSC into a vCenter Server Appliance instance that you specify. In domains with multiple vCenter Server instances, you must identify the SSO replication partner for each subsequent vCenter Server. If you upgrade or migrate using the GUI-based installer, the wizard prompts you to specify the replication topology. If you upgrade or migrate using the CLI-based installer, you specify the replication topology using the JSON templates. During the upgrade or migration process, the new vCenter Server Appliance 8.0 incorporates the former PSC services, enabling you to decommission the original external PSC.

Single Sign-On (SSO) Domain

Each vCenter Server is associated with a *vCenter Single Sign-On (SSO)* domain, whose default name is vsphere.local. You can change the SSO domain name during deployment. The SSO domain is considered the local domain for authentication to vCenter Server and other VMware products, such as Aria Operations.

During vCenter Server Appliance deployment, you must create an SSO domain or join an existing SSO domain. The domain name is used by the VMware Directory Service (**vmdir**) for all Lightweight Directory Access Protocol (LDAP) internal structuring. You should give your domain a unique name that is not used by Open-LDAP, Microsoft Active Directory, and other directory services.

You can add users and groups to the SSO domain. You can add an Active Directory or LDAP identity source and allow the users and groups in that identity source to authenticate.

Enhanced Linked Mode

You can use Enhanced Linked Mode to link multiple vCenter Server systems. With Enhanced Linked Mode, you can log in to all linked vCenter Server systems simultaneously and manage the inventories of the linked systems. This mode replicates roles, permissions, licenses, and other key data across the linked systems. To join vCenter Server systems in Enhanced Linked Mode, connect them to the same vCenter SSO domain, as illustrated in Figure 1-1. Enhanced Linked Mode requires the vCenter Server Standard licensing level and is not supported with vCenter Server Foundation or vCenter Server Essentials. Up to 15 vCenter Server Appliance instances can be linked together by using Enhanced Linked Mode.

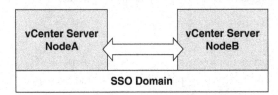

Figure 1-1   Enhanced Linked Mode with Two vCenter Server Appliance Instances

vCenter HA

A *vCenter HA* cluster consists of three vCenter Server instances. The first instance, initially used as the Active node, is cloned twice to a Passive node and to a Witness node. Together, the three nodes provide an active/passive failover solution.

Deploying each of the nodes on a different ESXi instance protects against hardware failure. Adding the three ESXi hosts to a DRS cluster can further protect your environment.

When the vCenter HA configuration is complete, only the Active node has an active management interface (public IP address), as illustrated in Figure 1-2. The three nodes communicate over a private network called a vCenter HA network that is set up as part of the configuration. The Active node continuously replicates data to the Passive node.

All three nodes are necessary for the functioning of this feature. Table 1-9 provides details for each of the nodes.

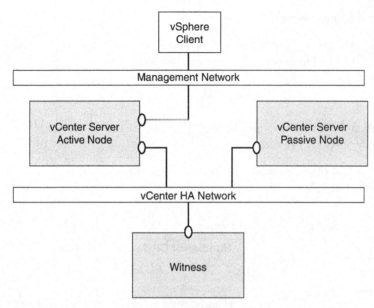

Figure 1-2   vCenter Server HA Nodes

Table 1-9   vCenter HA Node Details

Node Type	Description
Active	Is the active vCenter Server instance.
	Uses a public IP address for the management interface.
	Replicates data to the Passive node using the vCenter HA network.
	Communicates with the Witness node using the vCenter HA network.
Passive	Is cloned from the Active node.
	Uses the vCenter HA network to constantly receive updates from the Active node.
	Automatically takes over the role of the Active node if a failure occurs.
Witness	Is a lightweight clone of the Active node.
	Provides a quorum to protect against a split-brain situation.

Infrastructure Requirements

This section describes some of the main infrastructure requirements that you should address prior to implementing vSphere.

Compute and System Requirements

When planning to implement a vSphere environment, you should prepare sufficient supported compute (CPU and memory) resources, as described in this section.

vCenter Server

vCenter Server Appliance 8.0 can be deployed to an ESXi 6.7 or later host that is managed by a vCenter Server 6.7 or later.

To prepare for deployment of vCenter Server, you should plan to address the compute specifications listed in Table 1-10.

Table 1-10 Compute Specifications for vCenter Server Appliance

Type of Environment	Number of CPUs	Memory
Tiny Environment (up to 10 hosts or 100 virtual machines)	2	14 GB
Small Environment (up to 100 hosts or 1000 virtual machines)	4	21 GB
Medium Environment (up to 400 hosts or 4000 virtual machines)	8	30 GB
Large Environment (up to 1000 hosts or 10,000 virtual machines)	16	39 GB
X-Large Environment (up to 2000 hosts or 35,000 virtual machines)	24	58 GB

NOTE If you want to have an ESXi host with more than 512 LUNs and 2048 paths, you should deploy a vCenter Server Appliance instance for a Large Environment or X-Large Environment component.

ESXi

To install ESXi 8.0, ensure that the hardware system meets the following requirements:

- A supported system platform, as described in the *VMware Compatibility Guide*.
- Two or more CPU cores.
- A supported 64-bit x86 processor, as described in the *VMware Compatibility Guide*.

- The CPU's NX/XD bit enabled in the BIOS.

- 8 GB or more of physical RAM. (VMware recommends 12 GB or more for production environments.)

- To support 64-bit virtual machines, hardware virtualization (Intel VT-x or AMD RVI) enabled on the CPUs.

- One or more supported Ethernet controllers, Gigabit or faster, as described in the *VMware Compatibility Guide*.

- A SCSI disk or a local, non-network RAID LUN with unpartitioned space for the virtual machines.

- For Serial ATA (SATA), a disk connected through supported SAS controllers or supported on-board SATA controllers.

- A boot disk of at least 32 GB of persistent storage such as HDD, SSD, or NVMe. The boot device must not be shared between ESXi hosts.

NOTE SATA disks are considered remote, not local. These disks are not used as scratch partitions by default because they are considered remote. You cannot connect a SATA CD-ROM device to a virtual machine on an ESXi 8.0 host. To use the SATA CD-ROM device, you must use IDE Emulation Mode.

In vSphere 8.0, support for legacy BIOS is limited, and booting ESXi hosts from the Unified Extensible Firmware Interface (UEFI) is recommended. With UEFI, you can boot systems from hard drives, CD-ROM drives, or USB media. vSphere Auto Deploy supports network booting and provisioning of ESXi hosts with UEFI. If your system has supported data processing units (DPUs), you can only use UEFI to install and boot ESXi on the DPUs. You can boot systems from disks larger than 2 TB if the system firmware add-in card firmware supports it, according to vendor documentation.

NOTE Changing the host boot type between legacy BIOS and UEFI is not supported after you install ESXi.

Starting with ESXi 8.0, you can choose to leverage DPUs. In vSphere 8.0, the only supported DPU devices are NVIDIA BlueField and Pensando Distributed Services Card (Pensando DSC).

DPUs are the next step in the evolution of SmartNICs, which are available in PCIe cards that plug into a server. Existing processors such as CPUs and GPUs are not specifically designed to efficiently handle the moving and processing of data. DPUs are designed to process data that x86 CPUs and GPUs can do only inefficiently. A DPU in vSphere 8 makes it possible to offload infrastructure functions from the server's x86 CPU to the DPU. Currently, vSphere supports offloading to DPUs only if NSX is enabled on the ESXi host. NSX traffic and some common virtual switch features can be offloaded to a DPU. Virtual machine traffic and some general network traffic management continues to use the x86 CPU.

NSX and infrastructure services, such as storage and local I/O control, can be offloaded to a DPU. Figure 1-3 shows an instance of ESXi and NSX running directly on a DPU.

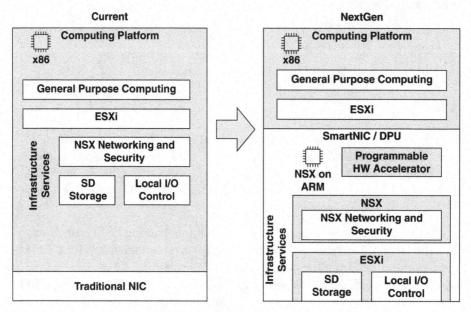

Figure 1-3   An Instance of ESXi and NSX Running Directly on a DPU

Storage Requirements

When preparing to implement a vSphere environment, you should ensure that you have sufficient supported storage resources, as described in this section.

vCenter Server Appliance

As part of preparing for the deployment of vCenter Server 8.0, you should plan to address storage requirements. Table 1-11 lists the storage requirements for a vCenter Server Appliance instance. It allows for Lifecycle Manager, which runs as a service in vCenter Server Appliance.

Table 1-11 Storage Sizes for vCenter Server Appliance

Deployment Size	Default Storage Size	Large Storage Size	X-Large Storage Size
Tiny	579 GB	2019 GB	4279 GB
Small	694 GB	2044 GB	4304 GB
Medium	908 GB	2208 GB	4468 GB
Large	1358 GB	2258 GB	4518 GB
X-Large	2283 GB	2383 GB	4643 GB

ESXi

For best performance of an ESXi 8.0 installation, use a 32 GB or larger persistent storage device for boot devices. Upgrading to ESXi 8.0 requires a 8 GB minimum boot device. When booting from a local disk, SAN, or iSCSI LUN, a 32 GB disk is required to allow for the creation of the boot partition, boot banks, and a VMFS_L ESX=OSData volume. The ESX-OSData volume takes on the role of the legacy/ scratch partition, locker partition for VMware Tools, and coredump destination.

NOTE Upgrading to ESXi 8.0 from versions earlier than 7.x repartitions the boot device and consolidates the original coredump, locker, and scratch partitions into the ESX-OSData volume, which prevents rollback. If you are concerned about upgrading, create a backup of the boot device prior to upgrading; if needed, you can restore from this backup after the upgrade.

The following are additional suggestions for best performance of an ESXi 8.0 installation:

- A local disk of 128 GB or larger for optimal support of ESX-OSData. This disk contains the boot partition, the ESX-OSData volume, and a Virtual Machine File System (VMFS) datastore.

- A device that supports the minimum of 128 terabytes written (TBW).

- A device that delivers at least 100 MBps of sequential write speed.

- To provide resiliency in the event of a device failure, a RAID 1 mirrored device is recommended.

Network Requirements

This section describes some of the key networking requirements for a successful vSphere deployment.

Networking Concepts

In order to prepare for network virtualization in vSphere, you should understand some of the following concepts:

- **Physical network**: This is a network of physical machines that are connected so that they can send data to and receive data from each other.

- **Virtual network**: This is a network of virtual machines running on a physical machine that are connected logically to each other so that they can send data to and receive data from each other.

- **Opaque network**: This is a network created and managed by a separate entity outside vSphere. For example, logical networks that are created and managed by VMware NSX appear in vCenter Server as opaque networks of the type nsx.LogicalSwitch. You can choose an opaque network as the backing for a VM network adapter. To manage an opaque network, use the management tools associated with the opaque network, such as VMware NSX Manager or the VMware NSX API management tools.

- **vSphere standard switch**: This type of virtual switch works much like a physical Ethernet switch. It detects which virtual machines are logically connected to each of its virtual ports and uses that information to forward traffic to the correct virtual machines. A vSphere standard switch can be connected to physical switches by physical Ethernet adapters, also referred to as uplink adapters.

- **VMkernel TCP/IP networking layer**: This layer provides connectivity to hosts and handles the standard infrastructure traffic of vSphere vMotion, IP Storage, Fault Tolerance, and vSAN.

VMware recommends using network segmentation in vSphere environments for separating each type of VMkernel traffic and virtual machine traffic. You can implement network segments by using unique VLANs and IP subnets. Here is a set of commonly used network segments in vSphere:

- Management

- vMotion

- vSphere Replication

- vSphere High Availability Heartbeat

- Fault Tolerance

- IP Storage

- Virtual machine (typically segregated further by application or by other factors, such as test and production)

vCenter Server Network Requirements

Table 1-12 provides details for some of the required network connectivity involving vCenter Server. For each applicable connection, you should ensure that your network and firewall allow the described connectivity.

Table 1-12 Required Ports for vCenter Sever

Protocol/Port	Description	Required For
TCP 22	System port for SSHD	vCenter Server (Must be open for upgrade of the appliance.)
TCP 80	Port for direct HTTP connections; redirects requests to HTTPS port 443	vCenter Server
TCP 88	Required to be open to join Active Directory	vCenter Server
TCP/UDP 389	LDAP port for directory services for the vCenter Server group	vCenter Server to vCenter Server
TCP 443	Default port used by vCenter Server to listen for connections from the vSphere Web Client and SDK clients	vCenter Server to vCenter Server
TCP/UDP 514	vSphere Syslog Collector port for vCenter Server and vSphere Syslog Service port for vCenter Server Appliance	vCenter Server
TCP/UDP 902	Default port that the vCenter Server system uses to send data to managed hosts	vCenter Server
TCP 1514	vSphere Syslog Collector TLS port for vCenter Server	vCenter Server
TCP 2012	Control interface RPC for Single Sign-On	vCenter Server
TCP 2014	RPC port for VMware Certificate Authority (VMCA) APIs	VMCA
TCP/UDP 2020	Authentication framework management	vCenter Server
TCP 5480	vCenter Server Management Interface (formerly known as VAMI)	vCenter Server
TCP/UDP 6500	ESXi Dump Collector port	vCenter Server
TCP 7080, 12721	Secure Token Service (internal ports)	vCenter Server
TCP 7081	vSphere Client (internal ports)	vCenter Server
TCP 7475, 7476	VMware vSphere Authentication Proxy	vCenter Server
TCP 8084	vSphere Lifecycle Manager SOAP port used by vSphere Lifecycle Manager client plug-in	vSphere Lifecycle Manager

Protocol/Port	Description	Required For
TCP 9084	vSphere Lifecycle Manager Web Server Port used by ESXi hosts to access host patch files from vSphere Lifecycle Manager server	vSphere Lifecycle Manager
TCP 9087	vSphere Lifecycle Manager Web SSL port used by vSphere Lifecycle Manager client plug-in for uploading host upgrade files to vSphere Lifecycle Manager server	vSphere Lifecycle Manager
TCP 9443	vSphere Web Client HTTPS	vCenter Server

ESXi Network Requirements

Table 1-13 provides details about some of the required network connectivity involving ESXi. For each applicable connection, you should ensure that your network and firewall allow the described connectivity.

Table 1-13 Required Ports for ESXi

Protocol/Port	Service	Direction	Description
TCP 5988	CIM Server	Inbound	Server for Common Information Model (CIM)
TCP 5989	CIM Secure Server	Inbound	Secure Server for CIM
UDP 8301, 8302	DVSSync	Inbound, outbound	Used for synchronizing states of distributed virtual ports between hosts that have VMware FT record/replay enabled
TCP 902	NFC	Inbound, outbound	ESXi uses Network File Copy (NFC) for operations such as copying and moving data between datastores
UDP 12345, 23451	vSAN Clustering	Inbound, outbound	Used by vSAN nodes for multicast to establish cluster members and distribute vSAN metadata
UDP 68	DHCP	Inbound, outbound	DHCP client for IPv4
UDP 53	DNS	Inbound	DNS client
TCP/UDP 53	DNS	Outbound	DNS client
TCP/UDP 8200, 8100, 8300	Fault Tolerance	Inbound	Traffic between hosts for vSphere Fault Tolerance (FT)
TCP/UDP 80, 8200, 8100, 8300	Fault Tolerance	Outbound	Supports vSphere Fault Tolerance (FT)

Protocol/Port	Service	Direction	Description
TCP 2233	vSAN Transport	Inbound	vSAN reliable datagram transport for vSAN storage I/O
TCP 22	SSH	Inbound	SSH server
TCP 902, 443	vSphere Web Client	Inbound	Allows user connections from vSphere Web Client
TCP/UDP 547	DHCPv6	Outbound	DHCP client for IPv6
UDP 9	WOL	Outbound	Wake-on-LAN
TCP 3260	iSCSI	Outbound	Supports software iSCSI
TCP 8000	vMotion	Outbound	Supports vMotion
UDP 902	vCenter Agent	Outbound	Used by the vCenter Agent

Infrastructure Services

In addition to providing the required compute, storage, and network infrastructure, you should provide supporting infrastructure services, such as Active Directory (AD), Domain Name System (DNS), Network Time Protocol (NTP), and Key Management Services (KMS).

AD

In many vSphere environments, vCenter Single Sign-On (SSO) is integrated with directory services, such as Microsoft Active Directory (AD). SSO can authenticate users from internal users and groups, and it can connect to trusted external directory services such as AD. If you plan to leverage AD for an SSO identity source, you should ensure that the proper network connectivity, service account credentials, and AD services are available and ready for use.

NOTE If the system you use for your vCenter Server installation belongs to a workgroup rather than a domain, vCenter Server cannot discover all domains and systems available on the network when using some features.

DNS

You might want to assign static IP addresses and resolvable fully qualified domain names (FQDNs) to your vSphere components, such as vCenter Server and ESXi hosts. Before installing these components, you should ensure that the proper

IP addresses and FQDN entries are registered in your DNS server. You should configure forward and reverse DNS records.

For example, prior to deploying vCenter Server Appliance, you should assign a static IP address and host name in DNS. The IP must have a valid (internal) domain name system (DNS) registration. During the vCenter Server installation, you must provide the fully qualified domain name (FQDN) or a static IP address. VMware recommends using the FQDN. You should ensure that DNS reverse lookup returns the appropriate FQDN when queried with the IP address of the vCenter appliance. Otherwise, the installation of the Web Server component that supports the vSphere Web client fails.

When you deploy vCenter Server Appliance, the installation of the web server component that supports the vSphere Web Client fails if the installer cannot look up the FQDN for the appliance from its IP address. Reverse lookup is implemented using PTR records. If you plan to use an FQDN for the appliance system name, you must verify that the FQDN is resolvable by a DNS server.

Starting with vSphere 6.5, vCenter Server supports mixed IPv4 and IPv6 environments. If you want to set up vCenter Server Appliance to use an IPv6 address version, use the FQDN or host name of the appliance.

It is important to ensure that each vSphere Web Client instance and each ESXi host instance can successfully resolve the vCenter Server FQDN. It is also important to ensure that the ESXi host management interface has a valid DNS resolution from the vCenter Server and all vSphere Web Client instances. Finally, it is important to ensure that the vCenter Server has a valid DNS resolution from all ESXi hosts and all vSphere Web Clients.

NTP

It is important to provide time synchronization between the nodes. All vCenter Server instances must be time synchronized. ESXi hosts must be time synchronized to support features such as vSphere HA. In most environments, you should plan to use NTP servers for time synchronization. Prior to implementing vSphere, verify that the NTP servers are running and available.

Be prepared to provide the names or IP addresses for the NTP servers when installing vSphere components such as vCenter Server and ESXi. For example, during the deployment of vCenter Server Appliance, you can choose to synchronize time with NTP servers and provide a list of NTP server names or IP addresses, separated by commas. Alternatively, you can choose to allow the appliance to synchronize time with the ESXi host.

NOTE   If a vCenter Server Appliance instance is set for NTP time synchronization, it ignores its **time_tools-sync** Boolean parameter. Otherwise, if the parameter is TRUE, VMware Tools synchronizes the time in the appliance's guest OS with the ESXi host.

KMS

In order to leverage virtual machine encryption or vSAN data-at-rest encryption, you must configure a standard key provider called a Key Management Services (KMS) server. You can also configure a standard key provider along with a virtual Trusted Platform Module (vTPM) to meet the TPM 2.0 requirements for Windows 11 VMs. With vCenter Server 8.0, you can configure a standard key provider, which is called a KMS cluster in vSphere 6.x, to get keys from your KMS. Your KMS should use Key Management Interoperability Protocol (KMIP) 1.1, and your KMS vendor must be compatible with vSphere 8.0, per the *VMware Compatibility Guide*.

Other Requirements

This section describes a few additional requirements for some of the optional components (refer to Table 1-3), available vSphere features (refer to Table 1-4), and add-on products (refer to Table 1-5).

Additional Requirements

The following sections describe some of the requirements for a variety of commonly used vSphere features.

User Interfaces

The vSphere Host Client and vSphere Client utilize HTML5. The flash-based vSphere Web Client is not supported in vSphere 7.0 and later. For Windows and Mac users of vSphere 8.0, VMware supports Microsoft Edge 79 and later, Mozilla Firefox 60 and later, and Google Chrome 75 and later.

vCenter Server File-Based Backup and Restore

With vCenter Server 8.0, if you plan to schedule file-based backups using the vCenter Server Management interface (formerly known as the VAMI), you must prepare an FTP, FTPS, HTTP, HTTPS, SFTP, NFS, or SMB server with sufficient disk space to store the backups.

GUI Installer

You can use the GUI installer to interactively install vCenter Server Appliance. To do so, you must run the GUI deployment from a Windows, Linux, or Mac machine that is in the network on which you want to deploy the instance.

Distributed Power Management (DPM)

DPM requires the ability to wake a host from Standby Mode, which means it needs to be able to send a network command to the host to power on. For this feature, DPM requires iLO, IPMI, or a Wake-on-LAN (WoL) network adapter to be present in each participating host in the cluster. DPM must be supplied with the proper credentials to access the interface and power on the host.

vSphere Replication Requirements

In order to use vSphere Replication 8.6, you must deploy a vSphere Replication Management Service (VRMS) appliance. Optionally, you can add nine additional vSphere Replication Service (VRS) appliances. You should plan for the compute, storage, and network needs of these appliances.

The VRMS appliance requires two vCPUs and 8 GB memory. Optionally, you can configure it for four vCPUs. Each VRS appliance requires two vCPUs and 716 MB memory. The amount of CPU and memory resources consumed by the vSphere Replication agent on each host is negligible.

Each VRMS and VRS appliance contains two virtual disks whose sizes are 16 BG and 17 GB. To thick provision these virtual disks, you must provide 33 GB storage. If you do not reserve the memory, you should provide storage for the VRMS (8 GB) and VRS (716 MB each) swap files.

Each appliance has at least one network interface and requires at least one IP address. Optionally, you can use separate network connections to allow each appliance to separate management and replication traffic.

The main storage requirement for vSphere Replication is to support the target datastore to which the VMs will be replicated. At a minimum in the replication target datastore, you should provide enough storage to replicate each virtual disk, to support each replicated VM's swap file, and to store each VM's multiple point-in-time captures (snapshots).

vCenter High Availability Requirements

The minimum software version for the nodes in a vCenter HA cluster is vCenter Server 6.5. The minimum software versions for the environment (such as a management cluster) where the vCenter HA nodes live are ESXi 6.0 and vCenter Server 6.0. Although not required, VMware recommends that you use a minimum of three ESXi hosts with DRS rules to separate the nodes onto separate hosts. You must use a vCenter Server Appliance Small or larger deployment size (not Tiny) and a vCenter Server Standard (not Foundation) license. A single vCenter Server license is adequate for a single vCenter HA cluster. vCenter HA works with VMFS, NFS, and vSAN datastores.

You must configure the appropriate virtual switch port groups prior to configuring vCenter HA. The vCenter HA network connects the Active, Passive, and Witness nodes, replicates the server state, and monitors heartbeats. The vCenter HA network must be on a different subnet than the management network, must provide less than 10 ms latency between nodes, and must not use a default gateway. The vCenter HA and management network IP addresses must be static.

You can use the Set Up vCenter HA wizard in the vSphere Client to configure vCenter HA. You have the option to perform an automatic configuration or a manual configuration. The automatic configuration requires a self-managed vCenter Server rather than a vCenter Server that resides in a management cluster that is managed by another vCenter Server. The automatic configuration automatically clones the initial (Active node) vCenter Server to create the Witness and Passive nodes. The manual configuration requires you to clone the Active node yourself but gives you more control.

When configuration is complete, the vCenter HA cluster has two networks: the management network on the first virtual NIC and the vCenter HA network on the second virtual NIC.

SDDC Requirements

In a software-defined data center (SDDC) based on vSphere, ESXi provides the hypervisor for running the virtual machines, and vCenter Server provides the virtual infrastructure management.

To build an SDDC, you may plan to implement additional VMware products, such as vSAN, NSX, and Aria Suite. Chapter 2, "Storage Infrastructure," provides details on vSAN, as required in the VCP-DCV exam objectives. Chapter 6, "VMware Product Integration," provides high-level information on the other products, whose details are not explicitly stated in the exam objectives.

vSAN

When preparing to implement vSAN, verify that the ESXi hosts meet the vSAN hardware requirements. All the devices, drivers, and firmware versions in your vSAN configuration must be certified and listed in the vSAN section of the *VMware Compatibility Guide*.

You need to prepare a network for vSAN traffic. This is the network in which you will connect a VMkernel network adapter for each ESXi host. For non-stretched vSAN clusters, the network should provide a maximum round-trip time (RTT) of 1 ms.

NSX

When preparing to implement NSX, ensure that you address the hardware and network latency requirements.

A typical NSX implementation involves deploying NSX Manager and one or more NSX Edge instances. The compute and storage sizes of these objects depend on various factors. You must prepare your environment with the required ESXi version, compute resources, and storage resources based on your NSX design.

You should ensure that the network latency is no higher than 150 ms RTT for NSX Manager connections with vCenter Server and ESXi hosts.

NOTE   Starting with Version 4.0, VMware NSX-T Data Center is known as VMware NSX.

VMware Cloud vs. VMware Virtualization

This section provides brief explanations of virtualization and cloud technologies.

Server Virtualization

VMware vSphere is the industry-leading virtualization and cloud platform. It provides virtualization (abstraction, pooling, and automation) of x86-64 based server hardware and related infrastructure, such as network switches. It provides live workload migrations, high availability, and efficient management at scale in a secured infrastructure.

VMware SDDC

A software-defined data center (SDDC) is a data center that leverages logical infrastructure services that are abstracted from the underlying physical infrastructure. It allows any application to run on a logical platform that is backed by x86-64, any storage, and any network infrastructure. Pioneered by VMware, a SDDC is the ideal architecture for private, public, and hybrid clouds. It extends virtualization concepts to all data center resources and services.

The SDDC includes compute virtualization (vSphere), network virtualization (NSX), and software-defined storage (vSAN and/or vVols) to deliver abstraction, pooling, and automation of the compute, network, and storage infrastructure services. It includes Aria Automation and Aria Operations to deliver policy-based automated management of the data center, services, and applications.

vCloud Suite and Private Clouds

VMware vCloud Suite is an enterprise-ready private cloud software suite that includes vSphere for data center virtualization and VMware Aria Suite for cloud management.

VCF and Hybrid Clouds

A *hybrid cloud* is a combination of a public cloud such as AWS and a private cloud such as an on-premises infrastructure. It is the result of combining any cloud solution with in-house IT infrastructure.

VMware Cloud Foundation (VCF) is the industry's most advanced hybrid cloud platform. It provides a complete set of software-defined services for compute, storage, networking, security, and cloud management to run enterprise apps in private or public environments. It delivers a simple path to the hybrid cloud by leveraging a common infrastructure and consistent operational model for on-premises and off-premises data centers.

VMC on AWS

VMware Cloud (VMC) on AWS is an integrated cloud offering jointly developed by AWS and VMware that provides a highly scalable, secure service that allows organizations to seamlessly migrate and extend their on-premises vSphere-based environments to the AWS cloud. You can use it to deliver a seamless hybrid cloud by extending your on-premises vSphere environment to the AWS cloud.

VMware vCloud Director

VMware vCloud Director is a cloud service-delivery platform used by some cloud providers to operate and manage cloud-based services. Service providers can use vCloud Director to deliver secure, efficient, and elastic cloud resources to thousands of customers.

Cloud Automation

VMware Cloud Assembly and VMware Service Broker are software as a service (SaaS) offerings that address similar use cases to the on-premises cases that VMware Aria Automation addresses.

Exam Preparation Tasks

As mentioned in the section "Book Features and Exam Preparation Methods" in the Introduction, you have some choices for exam preparation: the exercises here, Chapter 15, "Final Preparation," and the exam simulation questions on the companion website.

Review All the Key Topics

Review the most important topics in this chapter, noted with the Key Topic icon in the outer margin of the page. Table 1-14 lists these key topics and the page number on which each is found.

Table 1-14   Key Topics

Key Topic Element	Description	Page Number
Table 1-7	Features in vSphere editions	9
Section	Enhanced Linked Mode	12
List	ESXi system hardware requirements	14
Section	vCenter High Availability Requirements	24
Section	VMware SDDC	26

Complete Tables and Lists from Memory

Print a copy of Appendix B, "Memory Tables" (found on the companion website), or at least the section for this chapter, and complete the tables and lists from memory. Appendix C, "Memory Table Answers" (also on the companion website), includes completed tables and lists to check your work.

Define Key Terms

Define the following key terms from this chapter and check your answers in the glossary:

vSphere HA, Distributed Resource Scheduler (DRS), Proactive HA, vCenter Single Sign-On (SSO), vCenter HA, hybrid cloud, VMware Cloud (VMC)

Answer Review Questions

1. You plan to implement vSphere 8.0 and use vSphere Fault Tolerance to protect virtual machines with two vCPUs. Which is the minimum vSphere edition that you need?

   a. vSphere Essentials Plus

   b. vSphere Foundations

   c. vSphere Standard

   d. vSphere Enterprise Plus

2. You are planning to deploy vSphere 8.0. Where should the VMware Directory Service run?

   a. Nowhere as VMware Directory Service is not used

   b. In an external PSC

   c. Either in an external PSC or in an embedded PSC

   d. In vCenter Server

3. You are planning to deploy ESXi in a vSphere 8.0 environment and want to minimize memory per ESXi host. What is the minimum host memory that VMware recommends for a production environment?

   a. 4 GB

   b. 12 GB

   c. 16 GB

   d. 24 GB

4. You are planning to install vCenter Server 8.0 and want to use the GUI installer. Which of the following are supported locations from which to run the installer? (Choose two.)

   a. The vSphere Host Client on an ESXi host

   b. The vCenter Server Appliance Management Interface

   c. Windows

   d. Mac

5. Which of the following is the industry's most advanced hybrid cloud platform?

   a. VMware Cloud Assembly

   b. VCF

   c. VMC on AWS

   d. Aria Automation

This chapter covers the following topics:

- Storage Models and Datastore Types
- vSAN Concepts
- vSphere Storage Integration
- Storage Multipathing and Failover
- Storage Policies
- Storage DRS (SDRS)

This chapter contains information related to VMware vSphere 8.x Professional (2V0-21.23) exam objectives 1.3, 1.3.1, 1.3.2, 1.3.3, 1.3.4, 1.3.5, 1.3.6, 1.3.7, 1.3.8, 1.7, 1.7.1, 1.7.2, 5.5, 7.4, 7.4.1, 7.4.2, and 7.4.3.

## CHAPTER 2

Storage Infrastructure

This chapter provides details on the storage infrastructure, both physical and virtual, involved in a vSphere 8.0 environment.

"Do I Know This Already?" Quiz

The "Do I Know This Already?" quiz allows you to assess whether you should study this entire chapter or move quickly to the "Exam Preparation Tasks" section. In any case, the authors recommend that you read the entire chapter at least once. Table 2-1 outlines the major headings in this chapter and the corresponding "Do I Know This Already?" quiz questions. You can find the answers in Appendix A, "Answers to the 'Do I Know This Already?' Quizzes and Review Questions."

Table 2-1 "Do I Know This Already?" Foundation Topics Section-to-Question Mapping

Foundation Topics Section	Questions Covered in This Section
Storage Models and Datastore Types	1, 2
vSAN Concepts	3, 4
vSphere Storage Integration	5, 6
Storage Multipathing and Failover	7
Storage Policies	8, 9
Storage DRS (SDRS)	10

1. You need to configure a virtual machine to utilize N-Port ID Virtualization (NPIV). Which of the following is required?

   a. iSCSI

   b. vVOLs

   c. RDM

   d. FCoE

   e. vSAN

2. You are preparing to implement vSphere with Tanzu. Which type of virtual disk must you provide for storing logs, emptyDir volumes, and ConfigMaps?

   a. Ephemeral storage

   b. Container image

   c. Persistent volume

   d. Non-persistent volume

3. You are planning to implement a vSAN stretched cluster. Which of the following statements is true?

   a. You should not enable DRS in automatic mode.

   b. You should disable HA datastore heartbeats.

   c. If PFFT = 1, you may be able to use SMP-FT.

   d. If one of the fault domains is inaccessible, you cannot provision virtual machines.

4. You are planning to implement RAID 6 erasure coding for a virtual disk stored in a vSAN datastore. What percentage of the total capacity will be usable?

   a. 50%

   b. 67%

   c. 75%

   d. 100%

5. You are preparing to leverage VAAI in your vSphere environment. Which of the following primitives will not be available for your virtual machines stored in NFS datastores?

   a. Atomic Test and Set

   b. Full File Clone

   c. Extended Statistics

   d. Reserve Space

6. You are planning to implement vVols. Which of the following are logical I/O proxies?

   a. Data-vVol instances

   b. Storage providers

   c. Storage containers

   d. Protocol endpoints

7. You are explaining how vSphere interacts with storage systems. Which of the following steps may occur when VMware NMP receives an I/O request?

   a. The PSP issues the I/O request on the appropriate physical path.

   b. The SATP issues the I/O request on the appropriate physical path.

   c. The PSP activates the inactive path.

   d. The PSP calls the appropriate SATP.

8. In a vSphere environment where VASA is not implemented, you are planning to leverage storage policies associated with devices in your storage array. Which type of storage policy should you create?

   a. VM storage policy for host-based data services

   b. VM storage policy for vVols

   c. VM storage policy for tag-based placement

   d. vSAN storage policy

9. You are configuring storage policies for use with your vSAN cluster. Which of the following is not an available option?

   a. Number of Replicas per Object

   b. Number of Disk Stripes per Object

   c. Primary Level of Failures to Tolerate

   d. Secondary Level of Failures to Tolerate

10. You are testing Storage DRS (SDRS) in a scenario where the utilized space on one datastore is 82% and the utilized space on another datastore is 79%. You observe that SDRS does not make a migration recommendation. What might be the reason?

    a. The Space Utilization Difference threshold is set too low.

    b. The Space Utilization Difference threshold is set too high.

    c. The Space Utilization Difference threshold is set to 78%.

    d. The Space Utilization Difference threshold is set to 80%.

Foundation Topics

Storage Models and Datastore Types

This section explains how virtual machines access storage and describes the storage models and datastore types available in vSphere.

How Virtual Machines Access Storage

A virtual machine communicates with its virtual disk stored on a datastore by issuing SCSI commands. The SCSI commands are encapsulated into other forms, depending on the protocol that the ESXi host uses to connect to a storage device on which the datastore resides, as illustrated in Figure 2-1.

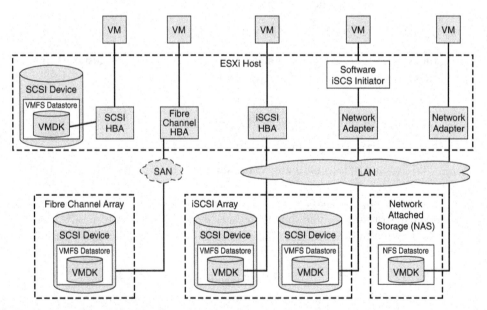

Figure 2-1   Virtual Machine Storage

Storage Virtualization: The Traditional Model

Storage virtualization refers to a logical abstraction of physical storage resources and capacities from virtual machines. ESXi provides host-level storage virtualization. In vSphere environments, a traditional model is built around the storage technologies and ESXi virtualization features discussed in the following sections.

Storage Devices (or LUNs)

In common ESXi vocabulary, the terms *storage device* and *LUN* are used interchangeably. Storage devices, or LUNs, are storage volumes that are presented to a host from a block storage system and are available to ESXi for formatting.

Virtual Disk

Virtual disks are sets of files that reside on a datastore that is deployed on physical storage. From the standpoint of the virtual machine, each virtual disk appears as if it were a SCSI drive connected to a SCSI controller. The physical storage is transparent to the virtual machine guest operating system and applications.

Local Storage

Local storage can be internal hard disks located inside an ESXi host and external storage systems connected to the host directly through protocols such as SAS or SATA. Local storage does not require a storage network to communicate with the host.

Fibre Channel

Fibre Channel (FC) is a storage protocol that a storage area network (SAN) uses to transfer data traffic from ESXi host servers to shared storage. It packages SCSI commands into FC frames. The ESXi host uses Fibre Channel host bus adapters (HBAs) to connect to the FC SAN, as illustrated in Figure 2-1. Unless you use directly connected Fibre Channel storage, you need Fibre Channel switches to route storage traffic. If a host contains FCoE (Fibre Channel over Ethernet) adapters, you can connect to shared Fibre Channel devices by using an Ethernet network.

iSCSI

Internet SCSI (iSCSI) is a SAN transport that can use Ethernet connections between ESXi hosts and storage systems. To connect to the storage systems, your hosts use hardware iSCSI adapters or software iSCSI initiators with standard network adapters.

With hardware iSCSI HBAs, the host connects to the storage through a hardware adapter that offloads the iSCSI and network processing. Hardware iSCSI adapters can be dependent and independent. With software iSCSI adapters, the host uses a software-based iSCSI initiator in the VMkernel and a standard network adapter to connect to storage. Both the iSCSI HBA and the software iSCSI initiator are illustrated in Figure 2-1.

iSER

In addition to traditional iSCSI, ESXi supports the iSCSI Extensions for RDMA (iSER) protocol. When the iSER protocol is enabled, the iSCSI framework on the ESXi host can use the Remote Direct Memory Access (RDMA) transport instead of TCP/IP. You can configure iSER on your ESXi host. The main use case is when you want to use a storage protocol that provides reduced latency, CPU load, and TCP/IP processing compared to iSCSI.

FCoE

If an ESXi host contains FCoE adapters, it can connect to shared Fibre Channel devices by using an Ethernet network.

NAS/NFS

vSphere uses NFS to store virtual machine files on remote file servers accessed over a standard TCP/IP network. ESXi 6.0 and later uses Network File System (NFS) Version 3 or Version 4.1 to communicate with NAS/NFS servers, as illustrated in Figure 2-1. You can use NFS datastores to store and manage virtual machines in the same way that you use the VMFS datastores.

VMFS

The datastores that you deploy on block storage devices use the native vSphere Virtual Machine File System (VMFS) format. VMFS is a special high-performance file system format that is optimized for storing virtual machines.

Raw Device Mappings (RDMs)

A *raw device mapping (RDM)* is a mapping file that contains metadata that resides in a VMFS datastore and acts as a proxy for a physical storage device (LUN), allowing a virtual machine to access the storage device directly. It gives you some of the advantages of direct access to a physical device as well as some of the management advantages of VMFS-based virtual disks. The components involved with an RDM are illustrated in Figure 2-2.

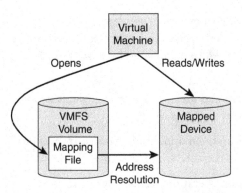

Figure 2-2 RDM Diagram

You can envision an RDM as a symbolic link from a VMFS volume to a storage device. The mapping makes the storage device appear as a file in a VMFS volume. The virtual machine configuration references the RDM, not the storage device. RDMs support two compatibility modes:

- **Virtual compatibility mode**: The RDM acts much like a virtual disk file, enabling extra virtual disk features, such as the use of virtual machine snapshot and the use of disk modes (dependent, independent—persistent, and independent—nonpersistent).

- **Physical compatibility mode**: The RDM offers direct access to the SCSI device, supporting applications that require lower-level control.

Virtual disk files are preferred over RDMs for manageability. You should use RDMs only when necessary. Use cases for RDMs include the following:

- You plan to install in a virtual machine software that requires features inherent to the SAN, such as SAN management, storage-based snapshots, or storage-based replication. The RDM enables the virtual machine to have the required access to the storage device.

- You plan to configure Microsoft Cluster Server (MSCS) clustering in a manner that spans physical hosts, such as virtual-to-virtual clusters and physical-to-virtual clusters. You should configure the data and quorum disks as RDMs rather than as virtual disk files.

Benefits of RDMs include the following:

- **User-friendly persistent names**: Much as with naming a VMFS datastore, you can provide a friendly name to a mapped device rather than use its device name.

- **Dynamic name resolution**: If physical changes (such as adapter hardware changes, path changes, or device relocation) occur, the RDM is updated automatically. The virtual machines do not need to be updated because they reference the RDM.

- **Distributed file locking**: VMFS distributed locking is used to make it safe for two virtual machines on different servers to access the same LUN.

- **File permissions**: Permissions are set on the mapping file to effectively apply permissions to the mapped file, much as they are applied to virtual disks.

- **File system operations**: Most file system operations that are valid for an ordinary file can be applied to the mapping file and redirected to the mapped device.

- **Snapshots**: Virtual machine snapshots can be applied to the mapped volume except when the RDM is used in physical compatibility mode.

- **vMotion**: You can migrate the virtual machine with vMotion, as vCenter Server uses the RDM as a proxy, which enables the use of the same migration mechanism used for virtual disk files.

- **SAN management agents**: RDM enables the use of SAN management agents (SCSI target-based software) inside a virtual machine. This requires hardware-specific SCSI commands as well as physical compatibility mode for the RDM.

- **N-Port ID Virtualization (NPIV)**: You can use NPIV technology, which allows a single Fibre Channel HBA port to register with the fabric by using multiple worldwide port names (WWPNs). This ability makes the HBA port appear as multiple virtual ports, each with its own ID and virtual port name. Virtual machines can claim each of these virtual ports and use them for all RDM traffic. NPIV requires the use of virtual machines with RDMs.

NOTE   To support vMotion involving RDMs, be sure to maintain consistent LUN IDs for RDMs across all participating ESXi hosts.

NOTE   To support vMotion for NPIV-enabled virtual machines, place the RDM files, virtual machine configuration file, and other virtual machines in the same datastore. You cannot perform Storage vMotion when NPIV is enabled.

Software-Defined Storage Models

In addition to abstracting underlying storage capacities from VMs, as traditional storage models do, software-defined storage abstracts storage capabilities. With software-defined storage, a virtual machine becomes a unit of storage provisioning and can be managed through a flexible policy-based mechanism. Software-defined storage involves the vSphere technologies described in the following sections.

vSAN

vSAN is a layer of distributed software that runs natively on each hypervisor in a cluster. It aggregates local or direct-attached capacity, creating a single storage pool shared across all hosts in the vSAN cluster.

vVols

Virtual volumes are encapsulations of virtual machine files, virtual disks, and their derivatives that are stored natively inside a storage system. You do not provision virtual volumes directly. Instead, they are automatically created when you create, clone, or snapshot a virtual machine. Each virtual machine can be associated to one or more virtual volumes.

The *Virtual Volumes (vVols)* functionality changes the storage management paradigm from managing space inside datastores to managing abstract storage objects handled by storage arrays. With vVols, each virtual machine (rather than a datastore) is a unit of storage management. You can apply storage policies per virtual machine rather than per LUN or datastore.

Storage Policy Based Management

Storage Policy Based Management (SPBM) is a framework that provides a single control panel across various data services and storage solutions, including vSAN and vVols. Using storage policies, the framework aligns application demands of virtual machines with capabilities provided by storage entities.

I/O Filters

I/O filters are software components that can be installed on ESXi hosts and can offer additional data services to virtual machines. Depending on the implementation, the services might include replication, encryption, caching, and so on.

Datastore Types

In vSphere, you can use the datastore types described in the following sections.

VMFS Datastore

You can create VMFS datastores on Fibre Channel, iSCSI, FCoE, and local storage devices. ESXi 6.5 and later support VMFS Versions 5 and 6 but not version 3. Table 2-2 compares the features and functionalities of VMFS Versions 5 and 6.

Table 2-2   Comparison of VMFS Version 5 and Version 6

VMFS Features and Functionalities	Version 5	Version 6
Access for ESXi hosts Version 6.5 and later	Yes	Yes
Access for ESXi hosts Version 6.0 and earlier	Yes	No
Datastores per host	1024	1024
512n storage devices	Yes	Yes (default)
512e storage devices	Yes (Not supported on local 512e devices.)	Yes (default)
4Kn storage devices	No	Yes
Automatic space reclamation	No	Yes
Manual space reclamation through the **esxcli** command.	Yes	Yes
Space reclamation from guest OS	Limited	Yes
GPT storage device partitioning	Yes	Yes
MBR storage device partitioning	Yes For a VMFS5 datastore that has been previously upgraded from VMFS3.	No
Storage devices greater than 2 TB for each VMFS extent	Yes	Yes
Support for virtual machines with large-capacity virtual disks, or disks greater than 2 TB	Yes	Yes
Support of small files (1 KB)	Yes	Yes
Default use of ATS-only locking mechanisms on storage devices that support ATS	Yes	Yes
Block size	Standard 1 MB	Standard 1 MB
Default snapshots	VMFSsparse for virtual disks smaller than 2 TB SEsparse for virtual disks larger than 2 TB	SEsparse
Virtual disk emulation type	512n	512n
vMotion	Yes	Yes
Storage vMotion across different datastore types	Yes	Yes
High Availability and Fault Tolerance	Yes	Yes
DRS and Storage DRS	Yes	Yes
RDM	Yes	Yes

When working with VMFS datastores in vSphere 7.0 and later, consider the following:

- **Datastore extents**: A spanned VMFS datastore must use only homogeneous storage devices—either 512n, 512e, or 4Kn. The spanned datastore cannot extend over devices of different formats.

- **Block size**: The block size on a VMFS datastore defines the maximum file size and the amount of space a file occupies. VMFS Version 5 and Version 6 datastores support a 1 MB block size.

- **Storage vMotion**: Storage vMotion supports migration across VMFS, vSAN, and vVols datastores. vCenter Server performs compatibility checks to validate Storage vMotion across different types of datastores.

- **Storage DRS**: VMFS Version 5 and Version 6 can coexist in the same datastore cluster. However, all datastores in the cluster must use homogeneous storage devices. Do not mix devices of different formats within the same datastore cluster.

- **Device Partition Formats**: Any new VMFS Version 5 or Version 6 datastore uses the GUID Partition Table (GPT) to format the storage device, which means you can create datastores larger than 2 TB. If your VMFS Version 5 datastore has been previously upgraded from VMFS Version 3, it continues to use the Master Boot Record (MBR) partition format, which is characteristic for VMFS Version 3. Conversion to GPT happens only after you expand the datastore to a size larger than 2 TB.

NFS

You can create NFS datastores on NAS devices. ESXi 6.0 and later support NFS Versions 3 and 4.1, using two different NFS clients. Table 2-3 compares the capabilities of NFS Versions 3 and 4.1.

Table 2-3 Comparison of NFS Version 3 and Version 4.1 Characteristics

NFS Characteristics	Version 3	Version 4.1
Security mechanisms	AUTH_SYS	AUTH_SYS and Kerberos (krb5 and krb5i)
Encryption algorithms with Kerberos	N/A	AES256-CTS-HMAC-SHA1-96 AES128-CTS-HMAC-SHA1-96
Multipathing	Not supported	Supported through the session trunking

NFS Characteristics	Version 3	Version 4.1
Locking mechanisms	Propriety client-side locking	Server-side locking
Hardware acceleration	Supported	Supported
Thick virtual disks	Supported	Supported
IPv6	Supported	Supported for AUTH_SYS and Kerberos
ISO images presented as CD-ROMs to virtual machines	Supported	Supported
Virtual machine snapshots	Supported	Supported
Virtual machines with virtual disks greater than 2 TB	Supported	Supported

Table 2-4 compares vSphere 8.0 features and related solutions supported by NFS Versions 3 and 4.1.

Table 2-4 Comparison of NFS Version 3 and Version 4.1 Support for vSphere Features and Solutions

NFS Features and Functionalities	Version 3	Version 4.1
vMotion and Storage vMotion	Yes	Yes
High Availability (HA)	Yes	Yes
Fault Tolerance (FT)	Yes	Yes (Supports the new FT mechanism introduced in vSphere 6.0 that supports up to four vCPUs, not the legacy FT mechanism.)
Distributed Resource Scheduler (DRS)	Yes	Yes
Host Profiles	Yes	Yes
Storage DRS	Yes	No
Storage I/O Control	Yes	No
Site Recovery Manager	Yes	Yes, but only with vSphere Replication
Virtual Volumes	Yes	Yes
vSphere Replication	Yes	Yes
vRealize Operations Manager	Yes	Yes

When you upgrade ESXi from a version earlier than 6.5, existing NFS Version 4.1 datastores automatically begin supporting functionalities that were not available in the previous ESXi release, such as vVols and hardware acceleration. ESXi does not support automatic datastore conversions from NFS Version 3 to NFS Version 4.1. You can use Storage vMotion to migrate virtual machines from NFS Version 3 datastores to NFS Version 4.1 datastores. In some cases, storage vendors provide conversion methods from NFS Version 3 to Version 4.1. In some cases, you may be able to unmount an NFS Version 3 datastore from all hosts and remount it as NFS Version 4.1. The datastore should never be mounted using both protocols at the same time.

vVols Datastores

You can create a vVols datastore in an environment with a compliant storage system. A virtual volume, which is created and manipulated out of band by a vSphere APIs for Storage Awareness (VASA) provider, represents a storage container in vSphere. The VASA provider maps virtual disk objects and their derivatives, such as clones, snapshots, and replicas, directly to the virtual volumes on the storage system. ESXi hosts access virtual volumes through an intermediate point in the data path called the protocol endpoint. Protocol endpoints serve as gateways for I/O between ESXi hosts and the storage system, using Fibre Channel, FCoE, iSCSI, or NFS.

vSAN Datastores

You can create a vSAN datastore in a vSAN cluster. vSAN is a hyperconverged storage solution, which combines storage, compute, and virtualization into a single physical server or cluster. The *vSAN Concepts* section describes the concepts, benefits, and terminology associated with vSAN.

Storage in vSphere with Kubernetes

To support the different types of storage objects in Kubernetes, vSphere with Tanzu provides three types of virtual disks: ephemeral storage, container image, and persistent volume.

A vSphere pod requires ephemeral storage to store Kubernetes objects, such as logs, emptyDir volumes, and ConfigMaps. The ephemeral, or transient, storage exists if the vSphere pod exists.

The vSphere pod mounts images used by its containers as image virtual disks, enabling the container to use the software contained in the images. When the vSphere pod lifecycle completes, the image virtual disks are detached from the vSphere pod. You can specify a datastore to use as the container image cache, such that subsequent pods can pull it from the cache rather than from the external container registry.

Some Kubernetes workloads require persistent storage to store the data independently of the pod. Persistent volume objects in vSphere with Tanzu are backed by the First Class Disks on a datastore. A First Class Disk (FCD), which is also called an Improved Virtual Disk, is a named virtual disk that is not associated with a VM. To provide persistent storage, you can use the Workload Management feature in the vSphere Client to associate one or more storage policies with the appropriate namespace.

VMware NVMe

Non-Volatile Memory Express (NVMe) storage is a low-latency, low-CPU-usage, and high-performance alternative to SCSI storage. It is designed for use with faster storage media equipped with non-volatile memory, such as flash devices. NVMe storage can be directly attached to a host using a PCIe interface or indirectly through different fabric transport (NVMe over Fabrics [NVMe-oF]).

In an NVMe storage array, a namespace represents a storage volume. An NVMe namespace is analogous to a storage device (LUN) in other storage arrays. In the vSphere Client, an NVMe namespace appears in the list of storage devices. You can use a device to create a VMFS datastore.

Requirements for NVMe over PCIe

NVMe over PCIe requires the following:

- Local NVMe storage devices
- A compatible ESXi host
- A hardware NVMe over PCIe adapter

Requirements for NVMe over RDMA (RoCE Version 2)

NVMe over RDMA requires the following:

- An NVMe storage array with NVMe over RDMA (RoCE Version 2) transport support
- A compatible ESXi host
- Ethernet switches that support a lossless network
- A network adapter that supports RDMA over Converged Ethernet (RoCE Version 2)

- A software NVMe over RDMA adapter enabled on the ESXi host

- An NVMe controller on the storage array

Requirements for NVMe over Fibre Channel

(e)NVMe over Fibre Channel requires the following:

- A Fibre Channel storage array that supports NVMe

- A compatible ESXi host

- A hardware NVMe adapter (that is, a Fibre Channel HBA that supports NVMe)

- An NVMe controller on the storage array

VMware High-Performance Plug-in (HPP)

VMware provides the High-Performance Plug-in (HPP) to improve the performance of NVMe devices on an ESXi host. HPP replaces NMP for high-speed devices, such as NVMe.

HPP is the default plug-in that claims NVMe-oF targets. In ESXi, the NVMe-oF targets are emulated and presented to users as SCSI targets. The HPP supports only active/active and implicit ALUA targets.

Starting from vSphere 7.0 Update 2, HPP becomes the default plug-in for local NVMe and SCSI devices, but you can replace it with NMP. NMP cannot be used to claim the NVMe-oF targets. HPP should be used for NVMe-oF.

Table 2-5 describes vSphere 7.0 Update 2 and later support for HPP.

Table 2-5   vSphere 7.0 HPP Support

HPP Support	vSphere 7.0 Update 2 and later
Storage devices	Local NVMe PCIe and SCSI
	Shared NVMe-oF (active/active and implicit ALUA targets only)
Multipathing	Yes
Second-level plug-ins	No
SCSI-3 persistent reservations	No
4Kn devices with software emulation	Yes
vSAN	No

Table 2-6 describes the path selection schemes (PSS) HPP uses when selecting physical paths for I/O requests.

Table 2-6   HPP Path Selection Schemes

PSS	Description
FIXED	A designated preferred path is used for I/O requests.
LB-RR (Load Balance—Round Robin)	After transferring a specified number of bytes or I/Os on a current path, the scheme selects the path using the round robin algorithm. You can configure the IOPS and Bytes properties to indicate the criteria for path switching. (This is the default HPP scheme.)
LB-IOPS (Load Balance—IOPS)	After transferring a specified number of I/Os on a current path (1000 by default), the scheme selects an optimal path based on the least number of outstanding bytes.
LB-BYTES (Load Balance—Bytes)	After transferring a specified amount of data on a current path (10 MB by default), the scheme selects an optimal path based on the least number of outstanding I/Os.
LB-Latency (Load Balance—Latency)	The scheme selects an optimal path by considering the latency evaluation time and the sampling I/Os per path.

HPP best practices include the following:

- Use a vSphere version that supports HPP.
- Use HPP for NVMe local and NVMe-oF devices.
- If you use NVMe with Fibre Channel devices, follow your vendor's recommendations.
- If you use NVMe-oF, do not mix transport types to access the same namespace.
- When using NVMe-oF namespaces, make sure that active paths are presented to the host.
- Configure VMs to use VMware Paravirtual controllers.
- Set the latency-sensitive threshold for virtual machines.
- If a single VM drives a significant share of a device's I/O workload, consider spreading the I/O across multiple virtual disks, attached to separate virtual controllers in the VM. Otherwise, you risk the I/O saturating a CPU core.

vSAN Concepts

vSAN virtualizes the local physical storage resources of ESXi hosts by turning them into pools of storage that can be used by virtual machines, based on their quality of service requirements. With vSphere 8.0, *vSAN Express Storage Architecture (ESA)* is available as an alternative architecture for vSAN. The architecture used in previous vSAN versions, vSAN Original Storage Architecture (OSA), is still available in vSphere 8.0.

A two-tiered approach is used in vSAN OSA clusters, where you configure clusters to use hybrid or all-flash disk groups. Hybrid clusters use flash devices for the cache layer and magnetic disks for the storage capacity layer. All-flash clusters use flash devices for both cache and capacity. If a host contributes storage to a vSAN cluster, then it must contribute at least one device for cache and one for capacity in order to form a disk group. Each disk group contains a flash cache device and at least one capacity device. Each host can be configured to use multiple disk groups.

Instead of using disk groups, vSAN ESA clusters use single-tiered storage pools, with all the participating storage devices in a host used for both caching and capacity. In vSAN ESA, all disks are SSDs or NVMe devices, and they all contribute to performance and capacity. vSAN ESA removes the concepts of a disk group and a cache device that existed in the vSAN OSA. Any single device can fail without impacting the availability of data on any of the other devices in the storage pool. This design reduces the size of a failure domain. If a host contributes storage to a vSAN cluster, then it must contribute at least four devices to form a storage pool.

You can enable vSAN on existing host clusters as well as on new clusters. You can expand a datastore by adding to the cluster hosts with capacity devices or by adding local drives to the existing hosts in the cluster. vSAN works best when all ESXi hosts in the cluster are configured similarly, including similar or identical storage configurations. A consistent configuration enables vSAN to balance virtual machine storage components across all devices and hosts in the cluster. Hosts without any local devices can also participate and run their virtual machines on the vSAN datastore.

These are some of the important benefits of vSAN over traditional SAN:

- vSAN does not require a dedicated storage network, as is required on an FC network or a SAN.

- With vSAN, you do not have to pre-allocate and preconfigure storage volumes (LUNs).

- vSAN does not behave like traditional storage volumes based on LUNs or NFS shares. You do not have to apply standard storage protocols, such as FC, and you do not need to format the storage directly.

■ You can deploy, manage, and monitor vSAN by using the vSphere Client rather than other storage management tools.

■ A vSphere administrator, rather than a storage administrator, can manage a vSAN environment.

■ When deploying virtual machines, you can use automatically assigned storage policies with vSAN.

These are some of the important enhancements of vSAN ESA compared to vSAN OSA:

■ vSAN ESA does not require dedicated cache and capacity devices.

■ It makes it possible to increase the write buffer from 600 GB to 1.6 TB.

■ It provides built-in snapshots with minimal VM impact due to long snapshot chains and support with VMware VADP.

■ It provides improved erasure coding with space efficiency.

■ It provides improved compression—up to four times better than with vSAN OSA.

■ It provides HCI mesh support for up to 10 client clusters.

■ It eliminates the complexity of disk groups and their impact related to cache disk failures and compression.

■ It streamlines vSAN File Service failover.

■ It changes cluster-wide settings in vSAN OSA to per-VM settings.

■ It supports any number of disks defined by the hardware, whereas vSAN OSA supports a maximum of 40 disks per host.

vSAN Characteristics

vSAN is like network-distributed RAID for local disks, transforming them into shared storage. vSAN uses copies of VM data, where one copy is local and another copy is on one of the other nodes in the cluster. The number of copies is configurable. Here are some of the features of vSAN:

■ **Shared storage support**: VMware features that require shared storage (that is, HA, vMotion, DRS) are available with vSAN.

■ **On-disk format**: Highly scalable snapshot and clone management are possible on a vSAN cluster.

- **All-flash and hybrid configurations**: vSAN OSA can be used on hosts with all-flash storage or with hybrid storage (that is, a combination of SSDs and traditional HDDs). While in VSAN Express Storage, all disk are SSDs or NVME devices.

- **Fault domains**: Fault domains can be configured to protect against rack or chassis failures, preventing all copies of VM disk data from residing on the same rack or chassis.

- **iSCSI target service**: The vSAN datastore can be visible to and usable by ESXi hosts outside the cluster and by physical bare-metal systems.

- **Stretched cluster**: vSAN supports stretching a cluster across physical geographic locations.

- **Support for Windows Server failover clusters (WSFCs)**: SCSI-3 Persistent Reservations (SCSI3-PR) is supported on virtual disks, which are required for shared disks and WSFCs. Microsoft SQL Server 2012 or later is supported on vSAN. The following limitations apply:

  - Maximum of 6 application nodes in each vSAN cluster

  - Maximum of 64 shared disks per ESXi host

- **vSAN health service**: This service includes health checks for monitoring and troubleshooting purposes.

- **vSAN performance service**: This service includes statistics for monitoring vSAN performance metrics. This can occur at the level of the cluster, ESXi host, disk group, disk, or VM.

- **Integration with vSphere storage features**: Snapshots, linked clones, and vSphere Replication are all supported on vSAN datastores.

- **Virtual machine storage policies**: Policies can be defined for VMs on vSAN. If no policies are defined, a default vSAN policy is applied.

- **Rapid provisioning**: vSAN enables fast storage provisioning for VM creation and deployment from templates.

- **Deduplication and compression**: Block-level deduplication and compression are available space-saving mechanisms on vSAN. In vSAN OSA, compression can be configured at the cluster level and applied to each disk group. In VSAN ESA, compression can be configured on an individual object.

■ **Data at rest encryption**: Data at rest encryption is encryption of data that is not in transit and on which no processes (for example, deduplication or compression) are being carried out. If drives are removed, the data on those drives is encrypted.

■ **SDK support**: vSAN supports an extension (written in Java) of the VMware vSphere Management SDK. It has libraries, code examples, and documentation for assistance in automating and troubleshooting vSAN deployments.

vSAN Terminology

You should get familiar with the following terminology.

■ **Disk group**: In vSAN OSA, a *disk group* is a group of local disks on an ESXi host that contribute to the vSAN datastore. It must include one cache device and from one to seven capacity devices. In a hybrid cluster, a flash disk is the cache device, and magnetic disks are used as capacity devices. In all-flash clusters, flash storage is used for both cache and capacity devices.

■ **Consumed capacity**: This is the amount of physical space used up by virtual machines at any point in time.

■ **Object-based storage**: Data is stored in vSAN by way of objects, which are flexible data containers. Objects are logical volumes with data and metadata spread among nodes in the cluster. Virtual disks are objects, as are snapshots. For object creation and placement, vSAN takes the following into account:

  ■ Virtual disk policy and requirements are verified.

  ■ The number of copies (replicas) is verified; the amount of flash read cache allocated for replicas, number of stripes for replica, and location are determined.

  ■ Policy compliance of virtual disks is ensured.

  ■ Mirrors and witnesses are placed on different hosts or fault domains.

■ **vSAN datastores**: Like other datastores, a vSAN datastore appears in the Storage Inventory view in vSphere. A vSAN cluster provides a single datastore for all the hosts in the cluster, even for hosts that do not contribute storage to vSAN. An ESXi host can mount VMFS and NFS datastores in addition to the vSAN datastore. Storage vMotion can be used to migrate VMs between datastore types.

■ **Objects and components**: vSAN includes the following objects and components:

  ■ **VM home namespace**: The VM home directory where all the VM files are stored

  ■ **VMDK**: Virtual disks for VMs

- **VM swap object**: An object that allows memory to be swapped to disk during periods of contention and that is created at VM power-on

- **Snapshot delta VMDKs**: Change files created when a snapshot is taken of a VM

- **Memory object**: An object created when a VM is snapshotted (and the VM's memory is retained) or suspended

- **Virtual machine compliance status**: Can be Compliant or Noncompliant, depending on whether each of the virtual machine's objects meets the requirements of the assigned storage policy. The status is available on the Virtual Disks page on the Physical Disk Placement tab.

- **Component state**: vSAN has two component states:

  - **Degraded**: vSAN detects a permanent failure of a component.

  - **Absent**: vSAN detects a temporary component failure.

- **Object state**: vSAN has two object states:

  - **Healthy**: At least one RAID 1 mirror is available, or enough segments are available for RAID 5 or 6.

  - **Unhealthy**: No full mirror is available, or not enough segments are available for RAID 5 or 6.

- **Witness**: This is a component consisting of only metadata. It is used as a tiebreaker. Witnesses consume about 2 MB of space for metadata on a vSAN datastore when on-disk format Version 1.0 is used and 4 MB when on-disk format Version 2.0 or later is used.

- **Storage Policy Based Management (SPBM)**: VM storage requirements are defined as a policy, and vSAN ensures that these policies are met when placing objects. If you do not apply a storage policy when creating or deploying VMs, the default vSAN policy is used, with Primary Level of Failures to Tolerate set to 1, a single stripe per object, and a thin provisioned disk.

- **Ruby vSphere Console (RVC)**: This is a command-line interface used for managing and troubleshooting vSAN. RVC provides a cluster-wide view and is included with a vCenter Server deployment.

- **VMware PowerCLI**: vSAN cmdlets are included with PowerCLI to allow administration of vSAN.

- **vSAN Observer**: This is a web-based utility, built on top of RVC, that is used for performance analysis and monitoring. It can display performance statistics on the capacity tier, disk group statistics, CPU load, memory consumption, and vSAN objects in memory and distributed across the cluster.

■ **vSAN Ready Node**: This preconfigured deployment is provided by VMware partners. It is a validated design using certified hardware.

■ **User-defined vSAN cluster**: This vSAN deployment makes use of your selected hardware.

NOTE   In vSAN OSA, the capacity disks contribute to the advertised datastore capacity. The flash cache devices are not included as capacity.

What Is New in vSAN 7.0 and Newer

The following new features are available in vSAN 7.0 and newer.:

■ **vSphere Lifecycle Manager**: vSphere Lifecycle Manager uses a desired-state model to enable simple, consistent lifecycle management for ESXi hosts, including drivers and firmware.

■ **Integrated file services**: The native vSAN File Service enables you to create and present Server Message Block (SMB), NFS Version3, and NFS Version 4.1 file shares, effectively extending vSAN capabilities such as availability, security, storage efficiency, and operations management to files.

■ **Native support for NVMe Hot-Plug**: The Hot-Plug plug-in provides a consistent way of servicing NVMe devices and provides operational efficiency.

■ **I/O redirect based on capacity imbalance with stretched clusters**: This feature improves VM uptime by redirecting all virtual machine I/O from a capacity-strained site to the other site.

■ **Skyline integration with vSphere Health and vSAN Health**: Skyline Health for vSphere and vSAN are available, enabling native, in-product health monitoring and consistent, proactive analysis.

■ **Removal of EZT for shared disk**: vSAN 7.0 eliminates the prerequisite that shared virtual disks using the multi-writer flag must also use the eager zero thick (EZT) format.

■ **Support for vSAN memory as a metric in performance service**: vSAN memory usage is now available in Performance Charts (vSphere Client) and through the API.

- **Visibility of vSphere Replication objects**: vSphere Replication objects are visible in vSAN capacity view.

- **Support for large-capacity drives**: vSAN 7.0 provides support for 32 TB physical capacity drives and up to 1 PB logical capacity when deduplication and compression are enabled.

- **Immediate repair after new witness is deployed**: vSAN immediately invokes a repair object operation after a witness has been added during a replace witness operation.

- **vSphere with Kubernetes integration**: Cloud Native Storage (CNS) is the default storage platform for vSphere with Kubernetes. This integration enables various stateful containerized workloads to be deployed on vSphere with Kubernetes Supervisor and Guest clusters on vSAN, VMFS, and NFS datastores.

- **File-based persistent volumes**: Kubernetes developers can dynamically create shared (read/write/many) persistent volumes for applications. Multiple pods can share data. The native vSAN File Service is the foundation that enables this capability.

- **vVols support for modern applications**: You can deploy modern Kubernetes applications to external storage arrays on vSphere by using the CNS support added for vVols. vSphere now enables unified management for persistent volumes across vSAN, NFS, VMFS, and vVols.

- **vSAN VCG notification service**: You can get notified through email about any changes to vSAN HCL components, such as vSAN ReadyNode, I/O controller, and drives (NVMe, SSD, HDD), and you can get notified through email about any changes.

vSAN Deployment Options

When deploying vSAN, you have several options for the cluster topology, as described in the following sections.

Standard Cluster

A standard vSAN cluster, as illustrated in Figure 2-3, consists of a minimum of 3 hosts and a maximum of 64 hosts, typically residing at the same location and connected on the same Layer 2 network. 10 Gbps network connections are required for all-flash clusters and are recommended for hybrid configurations.

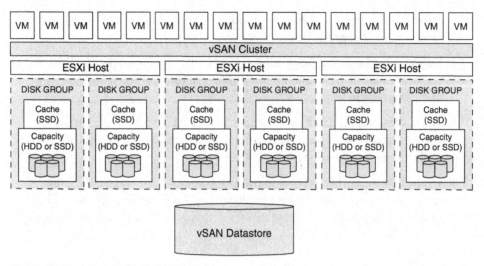

Figure 2-3 A Standard vSAN Cluster

Two-Host vSAN Cluster

The main use case for a two-host vSAN cluster is in a remote office/branch office environment, where workloads require high availability. A two-host vSAN cluster, as illustrated in Figure 2-4, consists of two hosts at the same location, connected to the same network switch or directly connected to one another. You can configure a two-host vSAN cluster that uses a third host as a witness, and the witness can be located separately from the remote office. Usually the witness resides at the main site, along with vCenter Server. For more details on the witness host, see the following section.

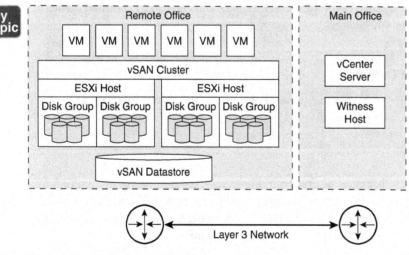

Figure 2-4 A Two-Node vSAN Cluster

Stretched Cluster

You can create a stretched vSAN cluster that spans two geographic sites and continues to function if a failure or scheduled maintenance occurs at one site. Stretched clusters, which are typically deployed in metropolitan or campus environments with short distances between sites, provide an increased level of availability and inter-site load balancing.

You can use stretched clusters for planned maintenance and disaster avoidance scenarios, with both data sites active. If either site fails, vSAN uses the storage on the other site, and vSphere HA can restart virtual machines on the remaining active site.

You should designate one site as the preferred site; it then becomes the only used site in the event that network connectivity is lost between the two sites. A vSAN stretched cluster can tolerate one link failure at a time without data becoming unavailable. During a site failure or loss of network connection, vSAN automatically switches to fully functional sites.

NOTE   A link failure is a loss of network connection between two sites or between one site and the witness host.

Each stretched cluster consists of two data sites and one ***witness host***. The witness host resides at a third site and contains the witness components of virtual machine objects. It contains only metadata and does not participate in storage operations. Figure 2-5 shows an example of a stretched cluster, where the witness node resides at a third site, along with vCenter Server.

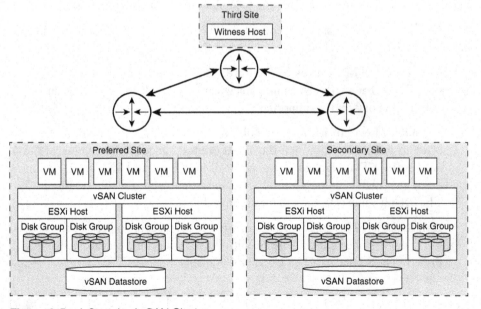

Figure 2-5   A Stretched vSAN Cluster

The witness host acts as a tiebreaker for decisions regarding availability of datastore components. The witness host typically forms a vSAN cluster with the preferred site and forms a cluster with a secondary site if the preferred site becomes isolated. When the preferred site is online again, data is resynchronized.

A witness host has the following characteristics:

- It can use low-bandwidth/high-latency links.

- It cannot run VMs.

- It can support only one vSAN stretched cluster.

- It requires a VMkernel adapter enabled for vSAN traffic with connections to all hosts in the cluster. It can have only one VMkernel adapter dedicated to vSAN but can have another for management.

- It must be a standalone host. It cannot be added to any other cluster or moved in inventory through vCenter Server.

- It can be a physical ESXi host or a VM-based ESXi host.

NOTE   The witness virtual appliance is an ESXi host in a VM, packaged as an OVF or OVA, which is available in different options, depending on the size of the deployment.

Each site in a stretched cluster resides in a separate fault domain. Three default domains are used: the preferred site, the secondary site, and a witness host.

Beginning with vSAN Version 6.6, you can provide an extra level of local fault protection for objects in stretched clusters by using the following policy rules:

- **Primary Level of Failures to Tolerate (PFTT)**: This defines the number of site failures that a virtual machine object can tolerate. For a stretched cluster, only a value of 0 or 1 is supported.

- **Secondary Level of Failures to Tolerate (SFTT)**: This defines the number of additional host failures that the object can tolerate after the number of site failures (PFTT) is reached. For example, if PFTT = 1 and SFTT = 2, and one site is unavailable, then the cluster can tolerate two additional host failures. The default value is 0, and the maximum value is 3.

- **Data Locality**: This enables you to restrict virtual machine objects to a selected site in the stretched cluster. The default value is None, but you can change it to Preferred or Secondary. Data Locality is available only if PFTT = 0.

NOTE   If you set SFTT for a stretched cluster, the Fault Tolerance Method rule applies to the SFTT. The failure tolerance method used for the PFTT is set to RAID 1.

Consider the following guidelines and best practices for stretched clusters:

- DRS must be enabled on a stretched cluster.

- You need to create two host groups, two virtual machines groups, and two VM–Host affinity rules to effectively control the placement of virtual machines between the preferred and secondary sites.

- HA must be enabled on the cluster in such a manner that it respects the VM–Host affinity rules.

- You need to disable HA datastore heartbeats.

- On-disk format Version 2.0 or later is required.

- You need to set Failures to Tolerate to 1.

- Symmetric Multiprocessing Fault Tolerance (SMP-FT) is supported when PFFT is set to 0 and Data Locality is set to Preferred or Secondary. SMP-FT is not supported if PFFT is set to 1.

- Using **esxcli** to add or remove hosts is not supported.

- If one of the three fault domains (preferred site, secondary site, or witness host) is inaccessible, new VMs can still be provisioned, but they are noncompliant until the partitioned site rejoins the cluster. This implicit forced provisioning is performed only when two of the three fault domains are available.

- If an entire site goes offline due to loss of power or network connection, you need to restart the site immediately. Bring all hosts online at approximately the same time to avoid resynchronizing a large amount of data across the sites.

- If a host is permanently unavailable, you need to remove the host from the cluster before performing any reconfiguration tasks.

- To deploy witnesses for multiple clusters, you should not clone a virtual machine that is already configured as a witness. Instead, you can first deploy a VM from OVF, then clone the VM, and then configure each clone as a witness host for a different cluster.

The stretched cluster network must meet the following requirements:

- The management network requires connectivity across all three sites, using a Layer 2 stretched network or a Layer 3 network.

- The vSAN network requires connectivity across all three sites, using a Layer 2 stretched network between the two data sites and a Layer 3 network between the data sites and the witness host.

- The virtual machine network requires connectivity between the data sites but not the witness host. You can use a Layer 2 stretched network or Layer 3 network between the data sites. A VM does not require a new IP address following failover to the other site.

- The vMotion network requires connectivity between the data sites but not the witness host. You can use a Layer 2 stretched or a Layer 3 network between data sites.

vSAN Limitations

Limitations of vSAN include the following:

- No support for hosts participating in multiple vSAN clusters

- No support for vSphere DPM and storage I/O control

- No support for SE sparse disks

- No support for RDM, VMFS, diagnostic partition, and other device access features

vSAN Space Efficiency

You can use space efficiency techniques in vSAN to reduce the amount of space used for storing data. These techniques include the use of any or all of the following:

- **Thin provisioning**: Consuming only the space on disk that is used (and not the total allocated virtual disk space)

- **Deduplication**: Reducing duplicated data blocks by using SHA-1 hashes for data blocks

- **Compression**: Compressing data using LZ4, which is a lightweight compression mechanism

- **Erasure coding**: Creating a stripe of data blocks with a parity block (This is similar to parity with RAID configurations, except it spans ESXi hosts in the cluster instead of disks in the host.)

SCSI UNMAP

SCSI **UNMAP** commands, which are supported in vSAN Version 6.7 Update 1 and later, enable you to reclaim storage space that is mapped to deleted vSAN objects. vSAN supports the SCSI **UNMAP** commands issued in a guest operating system to reclaim storage space. vSAN supports offline unmaps as well as inline unmaps. On Linux, offline unmaps are performed with the **fstrim(8)** command, and inline unmaps are performed when the **mount -o discard** command is used. On Windows, NTFS performs inline unmaps by default.

Deduplication and Compression

All-flash vSAN clusters support deduplication and compression. Deduplication removes redundant data blocks. Compression removes additional redundant data within each data block. Together, these techniques reduce the amount of space required to store data.

In vSAN OSA, deduplication and compression are enabled cluster-wide, but they are applied on a disk group basis. Beginning with vSAN 7 Update 1, you can choose to enable compression only in a cluster, whereas in previous versions, in order to enable compression, you also had to enable deduplication. Compression and deduplication cannot be applied for specific workloads or with vSAN policies. As data moves from the cache tier to the capacity tier, vSAN applies deduplication and then applies compression. When you enable or disable deduplication and compression, vSAN performs a rolling reformat of every disk group on every host; it requires significant disk space and time to complete this operation.

In vSAN ESA, storage compression is enabled by default, but you can use the Storage Policy Based Management (SPBM) framework to disable compression for specific workloads. By adding a policy that uses no compression, you can disable compression for a specific disk or VM. Changing the policy does not change the data state immediately; instead, the change is applied on a subsequent write.

NOTE   Deduplication and compression may not be effective for encrypted VMs.

The amount of storage reduction achieved through deduplication and compression depends on many factors, such as the type of data stored and the number of duplicate blocks. Larger disk groups tend to provide a higher deduplication ratio.

RAID 5 and RAID 6 Erasure Coding

In a vSAN OSA cluster, you can use RAID 5 or RAID 6 erasure coding to protect against data loss while increasing storage efficiency compared with using RAID 1 (mirroring). You can configure RAID 5 on all-flash clusters with four or more fault domains. You can configure RAID 5 or RAID 6 on all-flash clusters with six or more fault domains.

RAID 5 or RAID 6 erasure coding requires less storage space to protect your data than RAID 1 mirroring. For example, if you protect a VM by setting PFTT to 1, RAID 1 requires twice the virtual disk size, and RAID 5 requires 1.33 times the virtual disk size. Table 2-7 compares RAID 1 with RAID 5/6 for a 100 GB virtual disk.

Table 2-7   RAID Configuration Comparison

RAID Configuration	PFTT	Data Size	Required Capacity	Usable Capacity
RAID 1 (mirroring)	1	100 GB	200 GB	50%
RAID 5 or RAID 6 (erasure coding) with four fault domains	1	100 GB	133 GB	75%
RAID 1 (mirroring)	2	100 GB	300 GB	33%
RAID 5 or RAID 6 (erasure coding) with six fault domains	2	100 GB	150 GB	67%
RAID 1 (mirroring)	3	100 GB	400 GB	25%
RAID 5 or RAID 6 (erasure coding) with six fault domains	3	N/A	N/A	N/A

Before configuring RAID 5 or RAID 6 erasure coding in a vSAN OSA cluster, you should consider the following:

- All-flash disk groups are required.

- On-disk format Version 3.0 or later is required.

- A valid license supporting RAID 5/6 is required.

- You can enable deduplication and compression on the vSAN cluster to achieve additional space savings.

- PFTT must be set to less than 3.

- An enhancement in vSAN ESA over vSAN OSA is the ability to deliver RAID 5/6 space efficiency with the performance of RAID 1. Whereas vSAN OSA uses a 3+1 scheme (3 data bits plus 1 parity bit) for RAID 5, vSAN ESA offers a 4+1 scheme and a 2+1 scheme and automatically selects the best scheme, based on the number of hosts in the cluster. In clusters with six or more hosts, vSAN ESA could leverage the 4+1 scheme to use just 125 GB disk space to store 100 GB user data, whereas vSAN OSA with RAID 5 would use 133 GB. In clusters with just three hosts, vSAN ESA could leverage the 2+1 scheme to use just 150 GB disk space to store 100 GB user data, whereas vSAN OSA with RAID 1 would use 200 GB.

vSAN Encryption

You can encrypt data in transit in a vSAN cluster, which means you encrypt data as it moves between hosts. At the same time, you can encrypt data at rest in a vSAN datastore to protect data on storage devices in the event that they are removed from the cluster. Encryption occurs after all other processing, such as deduplication, is performed. All files are encrypted, so all virtual machines and their data are protected. Only administrators with encryption privileges can perform encryption and decryption tasks.

vSAN encryption requires an external key management server (KMS), the vCenter Server system, and ESXi hosts. vCenter Server requests encryption keys from an external KMS. The KMS generates and stores the keys, and vCenter Server obtains the key IDs from the KMS and distributes them to the ESXi hosts. vCenter Server does not store the KMS keys but keeps a list of key IDs.

vSAN uses encryption keys in the following manner:

- vCenter Server requests an AES-256 key encryption key (KEK) from the KMS.

- vCenter Server stores only the ID of the KEK (and not the key itself).

- The host encrypts disk data by using the industry-standard AES-256 XTS mode.

- Each disk has a unique, randomly generated data encryption key (DEK).

- A host key is used to encrypt core dumps, not data. All hosts in the same cluster use the same host key.

- When collecting support bundles, a random key is generated to re-encrypt the core dumps. You can specify a password to encrypt the random key.

NOTE   Each ESXi host uses the KEK to encrypt its DEKs and stores the encrypted DEKs on disk. The host does not store the KEK on disk. If a host reboots, it requests the KEK with the corresponding ID from the KMS. The host can then decrypt its DEKs as needed.

vSAN File Service

You can use *vSAN File Service* to provide vSAN-backed file shares that virtual machines can access as SMB, NFS Version 3, and NFS Version 4.1 file shares. It uses vSAN Distributed File System (vDFS), resilient file server endpoints, and a control plane, as illustrated in Figure 2-6. File shares are integrated into the existing vSAN

SPBM and on a per-share basis. vSAN File Service creates a single vDFS for the cluster and places a file service virtual machine (FSVM) on each host. The FSVMs manage file shares and act as NFS file servers using IP addresses from a static IP address pool.

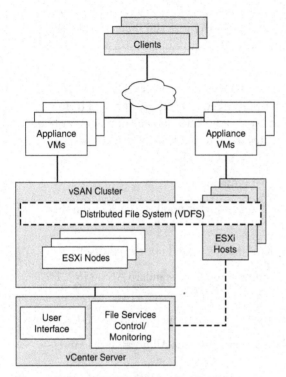

Figure 2-6   vSAN File Service Architecture

vSAN File Service is not supported on a vSAN stretched cluster.

The following are some limits and considerations for vSAN File Service in vSAN Version 8.0:

- File Service VMs are powered off when a vSAN cluster enters Maintenance Mode. (In vSAN prior to Version 7.0 Update 3, File Service VMs are deleted when the vSAN cluster enters Maintenance Mode and are re-created when the cluster exits Maintenance Mode.)

- It supports two-node vSAN clusters and stretched clusters.

- It supports 64 files servers in a 64-host configuration.

- It supports 100 files shares.

- File Service is not supported on vSAN ESA.

vSAN Requirements

Prior to deploying a vSAN cluster, you should address the requirements outlined in the following sections.

vSAN Express Storage Architecture (ESA) Requirements

Consider these vSAN ESA requirements:

- vSAN Ready Nodes

- One 25 Gbps or faster NIC for vSAN

- One 1 Gbps or faster NIC for VMs and for management

- A minimum of 32 GB of RAM for vSAN overhead

- A minimum of four SSDs or NVMe for each host

- Disks of at least 1.6 TB

vSAN Planning and Sizing

When you plan the capacity for a vSAN datastore, you should consider the PFTT and the failure tolerance method, as illustrated previously in Table 2-7. For RAID 1, the required data store capacity can be calculated using the following formula:

Capacity = Expected Consumption Size × (PFTT +1)

For example, say that you plan to use RAID 1 for a 500 GB virtual disk that you expect to be completely filled. In this case, the required capacities are 1000 GB, 1500 GB, and 2000 GB for PFTT set to 1, 2, and 3, respectively.

Keep in mind the following guidelines for vSAN capacity sizing:

- Plan for some extra overhead, as it may be required, depending on the on-disk format version. Version 1.0 adds approximately 1 GB overhead per capacity device. Versions 2.0 and 3.0 add up to 2% overhead per capacity device. Version 3.0 adds 6.2% overhead for deduplication and compression checksums. With vSAN Version 8.0, disk format Version 17 is available.

- Keep at least 30% unused space to avoid vSAN rebalancing.

- Plan for spare capacity to handle potential failure or replacement of capacity devices, disk groups, and hosts.

- Reserve spare capacity to rebuild after a host failure or during maintenance. For example, with PFTT set to 1, at least four hosts should be placed in the cluster because at least three available hosts are required to rebuild components.

- Provide enough spare capacity to make it possible to dynamically change a VM storage policy, which may require vSAN to create a new RAID tree layout for the object and temporarily consume extra space.

- Plan for the space consumed by snapshots, which inherit the storage policy applied to the virtual disk.

- Plan for space consumed by the VM home namespace, which includes the virtual machine's swap file (in vSAN Version 6.7 and later).

When selecting devices to use for vSAN cache hardware (such as PCIe vs. SDD flash devices), in addition to cost, compatibility, performance, and capacity, you should consider write endurance.

When selecting storage controllers for use in a vSAN cluster, in addition to compatibility, you should favor adapters with higher queue depth to facilitate vSAN rebuilding operations. You should configure controllers for passthrough mode rather than RAID 0 mode to simplify configuration and maintenance. You should disable caching on the controller or set it to 100% read.

When sizing hosts, consider using at least 32 GB memory for full vSAN OSA operations based on five disk groups per host and seven capacity devices per disk group.

Fault Domain Planning

If you span your vSAN cluster across multiple racks or blade server chassis, you can configure fault domains to protect against failure of a rack or chassis. A fault domain consists of one or more vSAN cluster member hosts sharing some physical characteristic, such as being in the same rack or chassis. For example, you can configure a fault domain to enable a vSAN cluster to tolerate the failure of an entire physical rack as well as the failure of a single host or another component (such as a capacity device, network link, or network switch) associated with the rack. When a virtual machine is configured with PFTT set to 1, vSAN can tolerate a single failure of any kind and of any component in a fault domain, including the failure of an entire rack.

When you provision a new virtual machine, vSAN ensures that protection objects, such as replicas and witnesses, are placed in different fault domains. If you set a virtual machine's storage policy to PFTT = n, vSAN requires a minimum of $2 \times n + 1$ fault domains in the cluster. A minimum of three fault domains are required to support PFTT = 1.

It is best to configure four or more fault domains in a cluster where PFTT = 1 is used. A cluster with three fault domains has the same restrictions as a three-host cluster, such as the inability to again protect data after a failure and the inability to use the Full Data Migration Mode.

Say that you have a vSAN cluster where you plan to place four hosts per rack. In order to tolerate an entire rack failure, you need to create a fault domain for each rack. To support PFTT = 1, you need to use a minimum of 12 hosts deployed to 3 racks. To support Full Data Migration Mode and the ability to again protect after a failure, deploy a minimum of 16 hosts to 4 racks. If you want Primary Level of Failures to Tolerate set to 2, you need to configure 5 fault domains in the cluster.

When working with fault domains, you should consider the following best practices:

- At a minimum, configure three fault domains in a vSAN cluster. For best results, configure four or more fault domains.

- Each host that is not directly added to a fault domain should reside in its own single-host fault domain.

- You can add any number of hosts to a fault domain. Each fault domain must contain at least one host.

- If you use fault domains, consider creating equal-sized fault domains (with the same number of same-sized hosts).

Hardware Requirements

You should examine the vSAN section of the *VMware Compatibility Guide* to verify that all the storage devices, drivers, and firmware versions are certified for the specific vSAN version you plan to use. For vSAN ESA, each storage pool must have at least four NVMe TLC devices, which are used for both capacity and cache. Table 2-8 lists some of the vSAN OSA storage device requirements.

Table 2-8 vSAN OSA Storage Device Requirements

Component	Requirements
Cache	One SAS or SATA SSD or PCIe flash device is required.
	For a hybrid disk group, the cache device must provide at least 10% of the anticipated storage consumed on the capacity devices in a disk group, excluding replicas.
	The flash devices used for vSAN cache must be dedicated. They cannot be used for vSphere Flash Cache or for VMFS.
Capacity (virtual machine) storage	For a hybrid disk group, at least one SAS or NL-SAS magnetic disk needs to be available.
	For an all-flash disk group, at least one SAS or SATA SSD or at least one PCIe flash device needs to be available.

Component	Requirements
Storage controllers	One SAS or SATA host bus adapter (HBA) or a RAID controller that is in passthrough mode or RAID 0 mode is required.
	If the same storage controller is backing both vSAN and non-vSAN disks, you should apply the following VMware recommendations to avoid issues:
	■ Do not mix the controller mode for vSAN and non-vSAN disks. If the vSAN disks are in RAID mode, the non-vSAN disks should also be in RAID mode.
	■ If VMFS is used on the non-vSAN disks, then use the VMFS datastore only for scratch, logging, and core dumps.
	■ Do not run virtual machines from a disk or RAID group that shares its controller with vSAN disks or RAID groups.
	■ Do not pass through non-vSAN disks to virtual machine guests as RDMs.

The memory requirements for vSAN OSA depend on the number of disk groups and devices that the ESXi hypervisor must manage. According to VMware Knowledge Base (KB) article 2113954, the following formula can be used to calculate vSAN memory consumption in vSAN 7.0.

$$vSANFootprint = HOST\_FOOTPRINT + NumDiskGroups \times DiskGroupFootprint$$

where:

$$DiskGroupFootprint = DISKGROUP\_FIXED\_FOOTPRINT + DISKGROUP\_SCALABLE\_FOOTPRINT + CacheSize \times CACHE\_DISK\_FOOTPRINT + NumCapacityDisks \times CAPACITY\_DISK\_FOOTPRINT$$

For vSAN ESA, each host must have at least 512 GB memory, but the minimum required for your environment depends on the number of devices in the host's storage pool.

The ESXi Installer creates a coredump partition on the boot device, and the default size of this partition is typically adequate. If ESXi host memory is 512 GB or less, you can boot the host from a USB, SD, or SATADOM device. When you boot a vSAN host from a USB device or SD card, the size of the boot device must be at least 4 GB. If ESXi host memory is more than 512 GB, consider the following guidelines:

■ You can boot the host from a SATADOM or disk device with a size of at least 16 GB. When you use a SATADOM device, use a single-level cell (SLC) device.

■ If you are using vSAN Version 6.5 or later, you must resize the coredump partition on ESXi hosts to boot from USB/SD devices.

Cluster Requirements

You should verify that a host cluster contains a minimum of three hosts that contribute capacity to the cluster. A two-host vSAN cluster consists of two data hosts and an external witness host. It is important to ensure that each host that resides in a vSAN cluster does not participate in other clusters.

Software Requirements

For full vSAN OSA capabilities, the participating hosts must be Version 7.0 Update 1, which supports all on-disk formats. For vSAN ESA, ESXi 8.x is required. Following a vSAN upgrade, if you keep the current on-disk format version, you cannot use many of the new features.

Network Requirements

You should ensure that the network infrastructure and configuration support vSAN, as described in Table 2-9.

Table 2-9   vSAN Networking Requirements

Component	Requirement
Host bandwidth	For vSAN OSA hybrid configuration, each host requires 1 Gbps (dedicated).
	For vSAN OSA all-flash configuration or vSAN ESA, each host requires 10 Gbps (dedicated or shared).
Host network	Each vSAN cluster member host cluster (even those that do not contribute capacity) must have a vSAN-enabled VMkernel network adapter connected to a Layer 2 or Layer 3 network.
IP version	vSAN supports IPv4 and IPv6.
Network latency	The maximum round trip time (RTT) between all the member hosts in a standard vSAN clusters is 1 ms.
	The maximum RTT between the two main sites in a stretched vSAN cluster is 5 ms.
	The maximum RTT between each main site and the witness host in a stretched cluster is 200 ms.

License Requirements

You should ensure that you have a valid vSAN license that supports your required features. If you do not need advanced or enterprise features, a standard license is sufficient. An advanced (or enterprise) license is required for advanced features such as RAID 5/6 erasure coding, deduplication, and compression. An enterprise license is required for enterprise features such as encryption and stretched clusters.

After you enable vSAN on a cluster, you must assign the cluster an appropriate vSAN license. Much like vSphere licenses, which are described in Chapter 1, "vSphere Overview, Components, and Requirements," vSAN licenses are subject to per-CPU capacity.

Other vSAN Considerations

The following sections outline some other considerations that are important in planning a vSAN deployment.

vSAN Network Best Practices

Consider the following networking best practices concerning vSAN:

- For hybrid configurations, use dedicated 10 GbE network adapters.

- For all-flash configurations, use dedicated or shared 10 GbE physical network adapters.

- Provision one additional physical NIC as a failover NIC.

- If you use a shared 10 GbE network adapter, place the vSAN traffic on a distributed switch with Network I/O Control (NIOC) configured.

Boot Devices and vSAN

You can boot ESXi from a local VMFS on a disk that is not associated with vSAN.

You can boot a vSAN host from a USB/SD device, but you must use a high-quality 4 GB or larger USB or SD flash drive. If the ESXi host memory is larger than 512 GB, for vSAN 6.5 or later, you must resize the coredump partition on ESXi hosts to boot from USB/SD devices.

You can boot a vSAN host from a SATADOM device, but you must use a 16 GB or larger single-level cell (SLC) device.

Persistent Logging in a vSAN Cluster

When you boot ESXi from a USB or SD device and allocate your local storage to vSAN, you may not have sufficient local space for persistent logging. You should consider using persistent storage other than vSAN for logs, stack traces, and memory dumps. You could use VMFS or NFS, or you could configure the ESXi Dump Collector and vSphere Syslog Collector to send system logs to vCenter Server or to a network server.

vSAN Policies

Storage policies are used in vSAN to define storage requirements for virtual machines. These policies determine how to provision and allocate storage objects within the datastore to guarantee the required level of service. You should assign at least one storage policy to each virtual machine in a vSAN datastore. Otherwise, vSAN assigns a default policy with PFTT set to 1, a single disk stripe per object, and a thin-provisioned virtual disks.

Storage policies, including those specific to vSAN, are covered later in this chapter.

vSphere Storage Integration

In a vSphere 8.0 environment, you have several options for integrating with supported storage solutions, including Virtual Volumes (vVols), vSphere APIs for Storage Awareness (VASA), and vSphere APIs for Array Integration (VAAI).

VASA

Storage vendors or VMware can make use of VASA. Storage providers (VASA providers) are software components that integrate with vSphere to provide information about the physical storage capabilities. Storage providers are utilized by either ESXi hosts or vCenter to gather information about the storage configuration and status and display it to administrators in the vSphere Client. There are several types of storage providers:

- **Persistent storage providers**: These storage providers manage storage arrays and handle abstraction of the physical storage. vVols and vSAN use persistent storage providers.

- **Data storage providers**: This type of provider is used for host-based caching, compression, and encryption.

- **Built-in storage providers**: These storage providers are offered by VMware and usually do not require registration. Examples of these are vSAN and I/O filters included in ESXi installations.

- **Third-party storage providers**: If a third party is offering a storage provider, it must be registered.

The information that storage providers offer may include the following:

- Storage data services and capabilities (which are referenced when defining a storage policy)

- Storage status, including alarms and events

- Storage DRS information

Unless the storage provider is VMware, the vendor must provide the storage provider. There are other requirements related to implementing storage providers as well:

- Contact your storage vendor for information about deploying the storage provider and ensure that it is deployed correctly.

- Ensure that the storage provider is compatible by verifying it with the *VMware Compatibility Guide*.

- Do not install the VASA provider on the same system as vCenter.

- Upgrade storage providers to new versions to make use of new functionalities.

- Unregister and reregister a storage provider when upgrading.

Storage providers must be registered in the vSphere Client to be able to establish a connection between vCenter and the storage provider. VASA is essential when working with vVols, vSAN, vSphere APIs for I/O Filtering (VAIO), and storage VM policies.

NOTE   If vSAN is being used, service providers are registered automatically and cannot be manually registered.

VAAI

VAAI, also known as hardware acceleration or hardware offload APIs, enable ESXi hosts to be able to communicate with storage arrays. They use functions called storage primitives, which allow offloading of storage operations to the storage array itself. The goal is to reduce overhead and increase performance. This allows storage to be responsible for cloning operations and zeroing out disk files. Without VAAI hardware offloading, the VMkernel Data Mover service is used to copy data from the source datastore to the destination datastore, incurring physical network latencies and increasing overhead. The VMkernel always attempts to offload to the storage array by way of VAAI, but if the offload fails, it employs its Data Mover service.

Storage primitives were introduced in vSphere 4.1 and applied to Fibre Channel, iSCSI, and FCoE storage only. vSphere 5.0 added primitives for NAS storage and vSphere thin provisioning. The storage primitives discussed in the following sections are available in vSphere 8.0.

VAAI Block Primitives

The following are the VAAI primitives for block storage:

- **Atomic Test and Set (ATS)**: ATS replaces the use of SCSI reservations on VMFS datastores when updating metadata. With SCSI reservations, only one process can establish a lock on the LUN at a time, leading to contention and SCSI reservation errors. Metadata updates occur whenever a thin-provisioned disk grows, a VM is provisioned, or a vSphere administrator manually grows a virtual disk. With ATS, a lock is placed on a sector of the VMFS datastore when updating metadata. ATS allows larger datastores to be used without running into such contention issues. On storage arrays that do not support VAAI, SCSI reservations are still used.

- **ATS Only flag**: This flag can be set on VMFS datastores that were created as VMFS Version 5 but cannot be enabled on VMFS Version 5 datastores that were upgraded from VMFS Version 3. The ATS Only Flag primitive forces ATS to be used as opposed to SCSI reservations for all metadata updates and operations. To manually enable the ATS Only flag, you use **vmkfstools**, using the following syntax:

```
vmkfstools -configATSOnly 1 [storage path]
```

- **XCOPY (Extended Copy)**: This option allows the VMkernel to offload cloning or Storage vMotion migrations to the storage array, avoiding use of the VMkernel Data Mover service.

- **Write Same (Zero)**: This option is used with eager zeroed thick-provisioned virtual disks to allow the storage device to write the zeros for the disk. This reduces overhead on the ESXi host in terms of CPU time, DMA buffers, and use of the device queue. You use this option whenever you clone a virtual machine with eager zeroed thick-provisioned disks, whenever a thin-provisioned disk expands, or when lazy zeroed thick disks need to be zeroed out (at first write).

VAAI NAS Primitives

The following are the VAAI primitives for NAS:

- **Full File Clone**: This option works the same way as XCOPY but applies to NAS devices as opposed to block storage devices.

- **Fast File Clone/Native Snapshot Support**: This option allows snapshot creation to be offloaded to the storage device for use in linked clones used in VMware Horizon View or in vCloud Director, which leverage reading from replica disks and writing to delta disks.

- **Extended Statistics**: This option allows an ESXi host to get insight into space utilization on a NAS device. For example, when a NAS device is using thin provisioning without the Extended Statistics primitive, the ESXi host lacks visibility into the actual storage usage, leading you to run out of space.

- **Reserve Space**: This option allows thick provisioning of virtual disks on NAS datastores. Prior to this primitive, only thin provisioning could be used on NAS storage devices.

VAAI Thin Provisioning Primitives

If you are using thin provisioning, and VMs are deleted or migrated off a datastore, the array may not be informed that blocks are no longer in use. Multiple primitives, including the following, were added in vSphere 5.0 to add better support for thin provisioning:

- **Thin Provisioning Stun**: Prior to vSphere 5.0, if a thin-provisioned datastore reached 100% space utilization, all VMs on that datastore were paused. After the release of vSphere 5.0, only the VMs requiring extra space are paused, and other VMs are not affected.

- **Thin Provisioning Space Threshold Warning**: When a VM is migrated to a different datastore or is deleted, the SCSI **UNMAP** command is used for the ESXi host to tell the storage array that space can be reclaimed.

Virtual Volumes (vVols)

With vVols, you have a storage operational module that is similar to vSAN, and you can leverage SAN and NAS arrays. As with vSAN, with vVols you can leverage SPBM, which allows you to streamline storage operations. The VASA provider communicates with vCenter Server to report the underlying characteristics of the storage container. You can leverage these characteristics as you create and apply storage policies to virtual machines to optimize the placement and enable the underlying services (such as caching or replication).

The main use case for vVols is to simplify the operational model for virtual machines and their storage. With vVols, the operational model changes from managing space inside datastores to managing abstract storage objects handled by storage arrays.

The major components in vVols are vVols devices, protocol endpoints, storage containers, the VASA provider, and arrays. These components are illustrated in Figure 2-7.

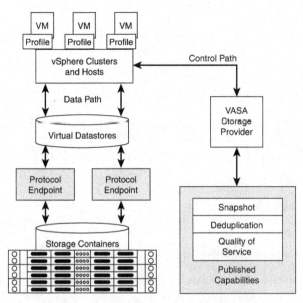

Figure 2-7 vVols Architecture

These are the main characteristics of vVols:

- It has no file system.

- ESXi manages the array through VASA.

- Arrays are logically partitioned into containers, called storage containers.

- vVols objects are encapsulations of VM files, and disks are stored natively on the storage containers.

- Storage containers are pools of raw storage or aggregations of storage capabilities that a storage device can provide to vVols.

- I/O from an ESXi host to a storage array is addressed through an access point called a protocol endpoint (PE).

- PEs are logical I/O proxies, used for communication for vVols and the virtual disk files. These endpoints are used to establish data paths on demand, by binding the ESXi hosts with the PEs.

- Bind requests must be sent from ESXi hosts or vCenter Server before a virtual volume can be used.

- Data services, such as snapshot, replication, and encryption, are offloaded to the array.

- Virtual volumes are managed through the SPBM framework. VM storage policies are required for VMs to use virtual volumes.

There are five types of virtual volumes:

- **Config-vVol**: Metadata
- **Data-vVol**: VMDKs
- **Mem-vVol**: Snapshots
- **Swap-vVol**: Swap files
- **Other-vVol**: Vendor solution specific

Limitations of vVols include the following:

- You cannot use vVols with a standalone ESXi host.
- vVols does not support RDMs.
- A vVols storage container cannot span different physical arrays.
- Host profiles that contain virtual datastores are vCenter Server specific. A profile created by one vCenter Server instance cannot be applied by another vCenter Server instance.

With recent versions of VASA and vSphere, several new features were added, as shown in Table 2-10.

Table 2-10   Recently Added vVOLs Features

VASA Version	vSphere Version	Features
3.5	7.0 Update 1	Enables support for CHAP authentication
		Provides efficient storage vMotion from vVols datastores for thin-provisioned volumes
3.5	7.0 Update 2	Provides a vectored bind for vVols for vMotion workflows
		Enables fast and stable compute with vMotion
		Creates repository folders on a vVols datastore
		Provides vVol stats support
		Provides tools to view near-real-time VASA provider and control path performance
		Provides tools to perform analysis on past data and capture control path metrics from a workflow perspective

VASA Version	vSphere Version	Features
3.5	7.0 Update 3	Provides a vectored snapshot virtual volume, faster snapshots, and shorter stun times
		Provides a faster memory snapshots for VMs on vVols (with up to 500% improvement)
		Provides vectored bind for virtual volumes for the VM power-on workflow
		Provides increased throughput support for backup applications
4.0	7.0 Update 3	Provides the NVMe-oF vVols spec for supporting NVMe protocols for vVols
		Adds a provision for all transport protocols: FC, RDMA, and TCP
		Provides VM power-on improvements
4.0	8.0	Provides VM power-off improvements
		Provides vVols storage improvements and a stable and reliable datastore during flaky connectivity with the VASA provider
		Enables caching of various vVols attributes, such as size and name
		Enables a faster UI datastore browser for large vVols data stores

vSphere 8.0 adds NVMe-oF support for vSphere virtual volumes as part of the VMware-I/O Vendor Program (IOVP) NVMe-FC certification program.

Storage Multipathing and Failover

vSphere provides multipathing and failover, as described in this section.

Multipathing Overview

Multipathing is used for performance and failover. ESXi hosts can balance the storage workload across multiple paths for improved performance. In the event of a path, adapter, or storage processor failure, the ESXi host fails over to an alternate path.

During path failover, virtual machine I/O can be delayed for a maximum of 60 seconds. Active/passive type arrays can experience longer delays than active/active arrays. vSphere supports several types of failover:

- **Fibre Channel failover**: For multipathing, hosts should have at least two HBAs in addition to redundant Fibre Channel switches (the switch fabric) and redundant storage processors. If a host has two HBAs, attached to two Fibre Channel switches, connected to two storage processors, then the datastores attached to the SAN can withstand the loss of any single storage processor, Fibre Channel switch, or HBA.

- **Host-based failover with iSCSI**: As with Fibre Channel failover, with host-based failover with iSCSI, hosts should have at least two hardware iSCSI initiators or two NIC ports used with the software iSCSI initiator. This is in addition to at least two physical switches and at least two storage processors.

- **Array-based failover with iSCSI**: On some storage systems, the storage device abstracts the physical ports from the ESXi hosts, and the ESXi hosts see only a single virtual port. The storage system uses this abstraction for load balancing and path failover. If the physical port where the ESXi host is attached should be disconnected, the ESXi host automatically attempts to reconnect to the virtual port, and the storage device redirects it to an available port.

- **Path failover and virtual machines**: When a path failover occurs, disk I/O could pause for 30 to 60 seconds. During this time, viewing storage in the vSphere client or virtual machines may appear stalled until the I/O fails over to the new path. In some cases, Windows VMs could fail if the failover is taking too long. VMware recommends increasing the disk timeout inside the guest operating system registry to at least 60 seconds to prevent this.

Pluggable Storage Architecture (PSA)

PSA was introduced in vSphere 4 as a way for storage vendors to provide their own multipathing policies, which users can install on ESXi hosts. PSA is based on a modular framework that can make use of third-party multipathing plug-ins (MPPs) or the VMware-provided Native Multipathing Plug-in (NMP), as illustrated in Figure 2-8.

VMware provides generic native multipathing modules, called VMware NMP and VMware HPP. In addition, the PSA offers a collection of VMkernel APIs that third-party developers can use. Software developers can create their own load-balancing and failover modules for a particular storage array. These third-party MPPs can be installed on the ESXi host and run in addition to the VMware native modules or as their replacement. When installed, the third-party MPPs can replace the behavior of the native modules and can take control of the path failover and the load-balancing operations for the specified storage devices.

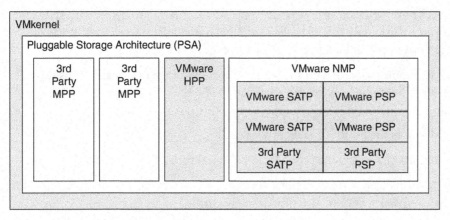

Figure 2-8 Pluggable Storage Architecture

VMware NMP

VMware NMP supports all storage arrays listed on the VMware storage HCL and provides a default path selection algorithm based on the array type. It associates a set of physical paths with a specific storage device (LUN). NMP uses submodules, called Storage Array Type Plug-ins (SATPs) and Path Selection Plug-ins (PSPs).

NMP performs the following operations:

- Manages physical path claiming and unclaiming
- Registers and unregisters logical devices
- Maps physical paths with logical devices
- Supports path failure detection and remediation
- Processes I/O requests to logical devices:
  - Selects an optimal physical path
  - Performs actions necessary to handle path failures and I/O command retries
- Supports management tasks, such as resetting logical devices

Storage Array Type Plug-ins (SATPs)

SATPs are submodules of the VMware NMP and are responsible for array-specific operations. An SATP handles path failover for a device. ESXi offers an SATP for every type of array that VMware supports. ESXi also provides default SATPs that support non-specific active/active, active/passive, ALUA, and local devices.

Each SATP performs the array-specific operations required to detect path state and to activate an inactive path. This allows the NMP module to work with multiple storage arrays without being aware of the storage device specifics.

NMP determines which SATP to use for a specific storage device and maps the SATP with the storage device's physical paths. The SATP implements the following tasks:

- Monitors the health of each physical path

- Reports changes in the state of each physical path

- Performs array-specific actions necessary for storage failover (For example, for active/passive devices, it activates passive paths.)

Table 2-11 provides details on the native SATP modules.

Table 2-11   SATP Module Details

SATP Module	Description
VMW_SATP_LOCAL	SATP for local direct-attached devices. Supports VMW_PSP_MRU and VMW_PSP_FIXED but not VMW_PSP_RR.
VMW_SATP_DEFAULT_AA	Generic SATP for active/active arrays.
VMW_SATP_DEFAULT_AP	Generic SATP for active/passive arrays.
VMW_SATP_ALUA	SATP for ALUA-compliant arrays.

NOTE   You do not need to obtain or download any SATPs. ESXi automatically installs an appropriate SATP for any array you use. Beginning with vSphere 6.5 Update 2, VMW_SATP_LOCAL provides multipathing support for the local devices, except the devices in 4K native format. You are no longer required to use other SATPs to claim multiple paths to the local devices.

Path Selection Plug-ins (PSPs)

VMware PSPs are submodules of NMP. PSPs handle path selection for I/O requests for associated storage devices. NMP assigns a default PSP for each logical device based on the device type. You can override the default PSP.

Each PSP enables and enforces a corresponding path selection policy. Table 2-12 provides details on the native path selection policies.

Table 2-12 VMware Path Selection Policies

PSP Module	Policy	Description
VMW_PSP_MRU	Most Recently Used (VMware)	Initially, MRU selects the first discovered working path.
		If the path fails, MRU selects an alternative path and does not revert to the original path when that path becomes available.
		MRU is default for most active/passive storage devices.
VMW_PSP_FIXED	Fixed (VMware)	FIXED uses the designated preferred path if it is working. If the preferred path fails, FIXED selects an alternative available path but reverts to the preferred path when it becomes available again.
		FIXED is the default policy for most active/active storage devices.
VMW_PSP_RR	Round Robin (VMware)	RR uses an automatic path selection algorithm to rotate through the configured paths. RR sends an I/O set down the first path, sends the next I/O set down the next path, and continues sending the next I/O set down the next path until all paths are used; then the pattern repeats, beginning with the first path. Effectively, this allows all the I/O from a specific host to use the aggregated bandwidth of multiple paths to a specific storage device.
		Both active/active and active/passive arrays use RR. With active/passive arrays, RR uses active paths. With active/active arrays, RR uses available paths.
		The latency mechanism that is activated for the policy by default makes it more adaptive. To achieve better load-balancing results, the mechanism dynamically selects an optimal path by considering the I/O bandwidth and latency for the path.
		RR is the default policy for many arrays.

PSA Summary

To summarize, the PSA performs the following tasks:

- Loads and unloads multipathing plug-ins

- Hides virtual machine specifics from a particular plug-in

- Routes I/O requests for a specific logical device to the MPP managing that device

- Handles I/O queueing to the logical devices

- Implements logical device bandwidth sharing between virtual machines

- Handles I/O queueing to the physical storage HBAs
- Handles physical path discovery and removal
- Provides logical device and physical path I/O statistics

The following process occurs when VMware NMP receives an I/O request for one of its managed storage devices:

Step 1.   The NMP calls the appropriate PSP.

Step 2.   The PSP selects an appropriate physical path.

Step 3.   The NMP issues the I/O request on the selected path.

Step 4.   If the I/O operation is successful, the NMP reports its completion.

Step 5.   If the I/O operation reports an error, the NMP calls the appropriate SATP.

Step 6.   The SATP interprets the errors and, when appropriate, activates the inactive paths.

Step 7.   The PSP selects a new path for the I/O.

When coordinating the VMware native modules and any installed third-party MPPs, the PSA performs the following tasks:

- Loads and unloads MPPs
- Hides virtual machine specifics from MPPs
- Routes I/O requests for a specific logical device to the appropriate MPP
- Handles I/O queuing to the logical devices
- Shares logical device bandwidth between virtual machines
- Handles I/O queuing to the physical storage HBAs

Storage Policies

Storage policies can be used to define which datastores to use when placing virtual machine disks. The following storage policies can be created:

- **VM storage policies for host-based data services**: These policies are rules for services that are offered by the ESXi hosts, such as encryption.
- **VM storage policies for vVols**: These policies allow you to set rules for VMs that apply to vVols datastores. This can include storage devices that are replicated for disaster recovery purposes or have specific performance characteristics.

■ **VM storage policies for tag-based placement**: You can create custom policies for VMs and custom tags for storage devices. This is helpful for storage arrays that do not support VASA and whose storage characteristics are not visible to the vSphere client. For example, you could create a tag named Gold and use it to identify your best-performing storage.

Storage Policy Based Management (SPBM)

You can define a required policy for a VM, such as requiring it to reside on fast storage. You can then use VASA or define storage tags manually. Then a VM can only be placed on a storage device that matches the requirements.

Virtual Disk Types

When creating a virtual disk, you need to determine how you are going to allocate space to that virtual disk. The way space is allocated to a virtual disk is through writing zeros; this process is typically referred to as *zeroing out* the file. For example, if you wanted to create a 20 GB virtual disk and allocate all of the space up front, a VMDK file is created, and 20 GB worth of zeros are written to that file. You can determine when the zeros get written:

■ **Eager zeroed thick**: The disk space for the virtual disk files is allocated and erased (zeroed out) at the time of creation. If the storage device supports VAAI, this operation can be offloaded to the storage array. Otherwise, the VMkernel writes the zeros, and this process could be slow. This method is the slowest for virtual disk creation, but it is the best for guest performance.

■ **Lazy zeroed thick**: The disk space for the virtual disk files is allocated at the time of creation but not zeroed. Each block is zeroed, on demand at runtime, prior to being presented to the guest OS for the first time. This increases the time required for disk format operations and software installations in the guest OS.

■ **Thin provisioned**: The disk space for the virtual disk files is not allocated or zeroed at the time of creation. The space is allocated and zeroed on demand. This method is the fastest for virtual disk creation but the worst for guest performance.

vSAN-Specific Storage Policies

vSAN storage policies define how VM objects are placed and allocated on vSAN to meet performance and redundancy requirements. Table 2-13 describes the vSAN storage policies.

Table 2-13 vSAN Storage Policies

Policy	Description
Primary Level of Failures to Tolerate (PFTT)	This policy defines how many host and device failures a VM object can withstand. For n failures tolerated, data is stored in $n+1$ location. (This includes parity copies with RAID 5 or 6.) If no storage policy is selected at the time of provisioning a VM, this policy is assigned by default. Where fault domains are used, $2n+1$ fault domains, each with hosts adding to the capacity, are required. If an ESXi host isn't in a fault domain, it is considered to be in a single-host fault domain. The default setting for this policy is 1, and the maximum is 3.
Secondary Level of Failures to Tolerate (SFTT)	In stretched clusters, this policy defines how many additional host failures can be tolerated after a site failure's PFTT has been reached. If PFTT = 1, SFTT = 2, and one site is inaccessible, two more host failures can be tolerated. The default setting for this policy is 1, and the maximum is 3.
Data Locality	If PFTT = 0, this option is available. The options for this policy are None, Preferred, and Secondary. This allows objects to be limited to one site or one host in stretched clusters. The default setting for this policy is None.
Failure Tolerance Method	This policy defines whether the data replication mechanism is optimized for performance or capacity. If RAID-1 (Mirroring)—Performance is selected, there will be more space consumed in the object placement but better performance for accessing the space. If RAID-5/6 (Erasure Coding)—Capacity is selected, there will be less disk utilization, but performance will be reduced.
Number of Disk Stripes per Object	This policy determines the number of capacity devices where each VM object replica is striped. Setting this above 1 can improve performance but consumes more resources. The default setting for this policy is 1, and the maximum is 12.
Flash Read Cache Reservation	This policy defines the amount of flash capacity that is reserved for read caching of VM objects. This is defined as a percentage of the size of the VMDK. This is supported only in hybrid vSAN clusters. The default setting for this policy is 0%, and the maximum is 100%.
Force Provisioning	If set to yes, this policy forces provisioning of objects, even when policies cannot be met. The default setting for this policy is no.
Object Space Reservation	This policy defines the percentage of VMDK objects that must be thick provisioned on deployment. The options are as follows: ■ Thin provisioning (default value) ■ 25% reservation ■ 50% reservation ■ 75% reservation ■ Thick provisioning

Policy	Description
Disable Object Checksum	A checksum is used end-to-end in validating the integrity of the data to ensure that data copies are the same as the original. In the event of a mismatch, incorrect data is overwritten. If this policy is set to yes, a checksum is not calculated. The default setting for this policy is no.
IOPS Limit for Object	This policy sets a limit for IOPS of an object. If set to 0, there is no limit.

Storage DRS (SDRS)

You can use vSphere SDRS to manage the storage resources of a datastore cluster. A datastore cluster is a collection of datastores with shared resources and a shared management interface. SDRS provides a number of capabilities for a datastore cluster, as discussed in the following sections.

Initial Placement and Ongoing Balancing

SDRS provides recommendations for initial virtual machine placement and ongoing balancing operations in a datastore cluster. Optionally, SDRS can automatically perform the recommended placements and balancing operations. Initial placements occur when the virtual machine is being created or cloned, when a virtual machine disk is being migrated to another datastore cluster, and when you add a disk to an existing virtual machine. SDRS makes initial placement recommendations (or automatically performs the placement) based on space constraints and SDRS settings (such as space and I/O thresholds).

Space Utilization Load Balancing

You can set a threshold for space usage to avoid filling a datastore to its full capacity. When space usage on a datastore exceeds the threshold, SDRS generates recommendations or automatically performs Storage vMotion migrations to balance space usage across the datastore cluster.

I/O Latency Load Balancing

You can set an I/O latency threshold to avoid bottlenecks. When I/O latency on a datastore exceeds the threshold, SDRS generates recommendations or automatically performs Storage vMotion migrations to balance I/O across the datastore cluster.

SDRS is invoked at the configured frequency (every eight hours by default) or when one or more datastores in a datastore cluster exceeds the user-configurable space utilization thresholds. When Storage DRS is invoked, it checks each datastore's space utilization and I/O latency values against the threshold. For I/O latency, Storage DRS uses the 90th percentile I/O latency measured over the course of a day to compare against the threshold.

SDRS Automation Level

Table 2-14 describes the available SDRS automation levels.

Table 2-14 SDRS Automation Levels

Option	Description
No Automation (manual mode)	Placement and migration recommendations are displayed but do not run until you manually apply the recommendation.
Fully Automated	Placement and migration recommendations run automatically.

SDRS Thresholds and Behavior

You can control the behavior of SDRS by specifying thresholds. You can use the following standard thresholds to set the aggressiveness level for SDRS:

- **Space Utilization**: SDRS generates recommendations or performs migrations when the percentage of space utilization on the datastore is greater than the threshold you set in the vSphere Client.

- **I/O Latency**: SDRS generates recommendations or performs migrations when the 90th percentile I/O latency measured over a day for the datastore is greater than the threshold.

- **Space Utilization Difference**: SDRS can use this threshold to ensure that there is some minimum difference between the space utilization of the source and the destination prior to making a recommendation. For example, if the space used on datastore A is 82% and on datastore B is 79%, the difference is 3. If the threshold is 5, Storage DRS does not make migration recommendations from datastore A to datastore B.

- **I/O Load Balancing Invocation Interval**: After this interval, SDRS runs to balance I/O load.

- **I/O Imbalance Threshold**: Lowering this value makes I/O load balancing less aggressive. Storage DRS computes an I/O fairness metric between 0 and 1, with 1 being the fairest distribution. I/O load balancing runs only if the computed metric is less than 1 – (I/O Imbalance Threshold / 100).

SDRS Recommendations

For datastore clusters, where SDRS automation is set to No Automation (manual mode), SDRS makes as many recommendations as necessary to enforce SDRS rules, balance the space, and balance the I/O resources of the datastore cluster.

Each recommendation includes the virtual machine name, the virtual disk name, the datastore cluster name, the source datastore, the destination datastore, and a reason for the recommendation.

SDRS makes mandatory recommendations when the datastore is out of space, when anti-affinity or affinity rules are being violated, or when the datastore is entering maintenance mode. SDRS makes optional recommendations when a datastore is close to running out of space or when adjustments should be made for space and I/O load balancing.

SDRS considers moving powered-on and powered-off virtual machines for space balancing. Storage DRS considers moving powered-off virtual machines with snapshots for space balancing.

Anti-affinity Rules

To ensure that a set of virtual machines are stored on separate datastores, you can create anti-affinity rules for the virtual machines. Alternatively, you can use an affinity rule to place a group of virtual machines on the same datastore.

By default, all virtual disks belonging to the same virtual machine are placed on the same datastore. If you want to separate the virtual disks of a specific virtual machine on separate datastores, you can do so with an anti-affinity rule.

Datastore Cluster Requirements

Datastore clusters can contain a mix of datastores having different sizes, I/O capacities, and storage array backing. However, the following types of datastores cannot coexist in a datastore cluster:

- NFS and VMFS datastores cannot be combined in the same datastore cluster.

- Replicated datastores cannot be combined with non-replicated datastores in the same SDRS-enabled datastore cluster.

- All hosts attached to the datastores in a datastore cluster must be ESXi 5.0 and later. If datastores in the datastore cluster are connected to ESX/ESXi 4.x and earlier hosts, SDRS does not run.

- Datastores shared across multiple data centers cannot be included in a data-store cluster.

- As a best practice, all datastores in a datastore cluster should have identical hardware acceleration (enabled or disabled) settings.

NIOC, SIOC, and SDRS

In vSphere, you can use Network I/O Control (NIOC), Storage I/O Control (SIOC), and SDRS to manage I/O. These features are often confused by people in the VMware community. Table 2-15 provides a brief description of each feature along with the chapter in this book where you can find more detail.

Table 2-15 Comparing NIOC, SIOC, and SDRS

Feature	Description	Chapter
NIOC	Allows you to allocate network bandwidth to business-critical applications and to resolve situations where several types of traffic compete for common resources.	9
SIOC	Allows you to control the amount of storage I/O that is allocated to virtual machines during periods of I/O congestion by implementing shares and limits.	11
SDRS	Allows you to control and balance the use of storage space and I/O resources across the datastores in a datastore cluster.	11

Exam Preparation Tasks

As mentioned in the section "Book Features and Exam Preparation Methods" in the Introduction, you have some choices for exam preparation: the exercises here, Chapter 15, "Final Preparation," and the exam simulation questions on the companion website.

Review All Key Topics

Review the most important topics in this chapter, noted with the Key Topics icon in the outer margin of the page. Table 2-16 lists these key topics and the page number on which each is found.

Table 2-16   Key Topics

Key Topic Element	Description	Page Number
Paragraph	Raw device mapping	36
Figure 2-4	A two-node vSAN cluster	54
Paragraph	vSAN stretched clusters	55
List	vSAN limitations	58
Paragraph	Native multipathing plug-in	77
Paragraph	SDRS thresholds and behavior	84

Complete Tables and Lists from Memory

Print a copy of Appendix B, "Memory Tables" (found on the companion website), or at least the section for this chapter, and complete the tables and lists from memory. Appendix C, "Memory Tables Answers" (also on the companion website), includes completed tables and lists to check your work.

Define Key Terms

Define the following key terms from this chapter and check your answers in the glossary:

raw device mapping (RDM), virtual volume, Virtual Volumes (vVols), I/O filter, vSAN Express Storage Architecture (ESA),disk group, witness host, vSAN File Service

Review Questions

1. You are deploying datastores in a vSphere environment and want to use the latest VMFS version that supports ESXi 6.5 and later. Which version should you use?

   a. VMFS Version 3

   b. VMFS Version 4

   c. VMFS Version 5

   d. VMFS Version 6

2. You are preparing to manage and troubleshoot a vSAN environment. Which of the following is a command-line interface that provides a cluster-wide view and is included with the vCenter Server deployment?

   a. VMware PowerCLI

   b. vSAN Observer

   c. Ruby vSphere Console

   d. esxcli

3. You want to integrate vSphere with your storage system. Which of the following provides software components that integrate with vSphere to provide information about the physical storage capabilities?

   a. VASA

   b. VAAI

   c. SATP

   d. NMP

4. Which of the following is the default path selection policy for most active/passive storage devices?

   a. VMW_PSP_MRU

   b. VMW_PSP_FIXED

   c. VMW_PSP_RR

   d. VMW_PSP_AP

5. You are deploying virtual machines in a vSphere environment. Which virtual disk configuration provides the best performance for the guest OS?

   a. Thin provisioned

   b. Thick eager zeroed

   c. Thick lazy zeroed

   d. Thin eager zeroed

This chapter covers the following topics:

- Networking Terms and Concepts
- vSphere Standard Switch (vSS)
- vSphere Distributed Switch (vDS)
- vDS Settings and Features
- Other vSphere Networking Features

This chapter contains information related to VMware vSphere 8.x Professional (2V0-21.23) exam objectives 1.5, 1.5.1, 1.5.2, 1.5.3, 1.5.4, 1.5.5, 1.11, 1.11.1, 4.3, 4.15, and 5.4.

## CHAPTER 3

Network Infrastructure

This chapter provides details for the network infrastructure, both physical and virtual, involved in a vSphere 8 environment.

"Do I Know This Already?" Quiz

The "Do I Know This Already?" quiz allows you to assess whether you should study this entire chapter or move quickly to the "Exam Preparation Tasks" section. In any case, the authors recommend that you read the entire chapter at least once. Table 3-1 outlines the major headings in this chapter and the corresponding "Do I Know This Already?" quiz questions. You can find the answers in Appendix A, "Answers to the 'Do I Know This Already?' Quizzes and Review Questions."

Table 3-1   "Do I Know This Already?" Section-to-Question Mapping

Foundation Topics Section	Questions
vSphere Standard Switch (vSS)	1, 2
vSphere Distributed Switch (vDS)	3–5
vDS Settings and Features	6–8
Other vSphere Networking Features	9, 10

1. You are configuring networking policies in your vSphere 8.0 environment. Which of the following policies is not available for a vSS?

   a. Teaming and Failover

   b. Security

   c. Traffic Shaping

   d. Port Blocking

2. You are configuring teaming policies in your vSphere 8.0 environment. Which of the following teaming options is not available for a vSS?

   a. Route Based on Originating Virtual Port

   b. Route Based on Physical NIC Load

   c. Route Based on Source MAC Hash

   d. Use Explicit Failover Order

3. You are configuring virtual networking in your vSphere 8.0 environment. Which of the following policies is available for distributed switches but not for standard switches?

   a. Inbound Traffic Shaping

   b. Outbound Traffic Shaping

   c. IPv6 Support

   d. CDP

4. Using NIOC, you reserved 1.0 Gbps for virtual machine system traffic on a distributed switch with eight 10 Gbps uplinks. If you reserve 512 Mbps for a network resource pool, what is the maximum reservation you can set in another network resource pool?

   a. 0.5 Gbps

   b. 1.0 Gbps

   c. 7.5 Gbps

   d. 79.6 Gbps

5. You want to tag voice over IP data in your vSphere environment. Which step should you take?

   a. Use a vSS

   b. Implement a filtering rule

   c. Implement a rule with Action = Tag

   d. Navigate to Menu > Tags and Custom Attributes

6. You want to leverage LAGs with your vDS. Which of the following is supported?

   a. iSCSI software port binding

   b. Nested ESXi

   c. Multiple LAGs on a single vDS

   d. Multiple LAGs on a single vSS

7. You want to enable a vDS health check for virtual switch teaming. Which of the following is a requirement?

    a. At least two active NICs and two hosts

    b. At least one active NIC from each of two hosts

    c. At least two active NICs from at least one host

    d. At least one active NIC from one host

8. You want to be able to use the vSphere Client to identify the non-Cisco physical switch connected to a virtual switch uplink. Which of the following should you implement?

    a. A vSS with LLDP

    b. A vSS with CDP

    c. A vDS with LLDP

    d. A vDS with CDP

9. You want to use DirectPath I/O in your vSphere 8.0 environment. Which of the following features is supported?

    a. The virtual machine running in a vSphere cluster

    b. Hot adding virtual devices

    c. Snapshots

    d. Fault tolerance

10. You want to create a custom TCP/IP stack for your ESXi 8.0 server. Which one of the following is an available service that you can directly enable for the stack?

    a. vSphere Replication NFC

    b. NFS

    c. vSphere HA heartbeat

    d. iSCSI

Networking Terms and Concepts

Computer networking is built on the TCP/IP protocol suite, which enables all types of computers, from many different vendors, to communicate with one another. This section introduces essential network terminology and concepts for a vSphere environment.

Traditional Networking Terminology

It is important to be familiar with the following commonly used networking terminology:

- **TCP/IP**: Transmission Control Protocol/Internet Protocol (TCP/IP) is a model used in the Internet that allows computers to communicate over long distances. It was developed by the U.S. Department of Defense (DOD) in the 1970s and is defined in RFC documents. It includes components that break data into packets, deliver the packets to the proper destination, and reassemble data from the packets.

- **RFC**: Requests for Comments (RFCs) are the rules of the Internet and are managed by the Internet Engineering Task Force (IETF). Anyone can register to attend an IETF meeting and help draft and define the standards of communication for the Internet.

- **Physical network**: A physical network consists of physical network devices and cabling that allow physical machines, such as ESXi servers, to connect and communicate with other physical machines. A key component of a physical network is the physical Ethernet switch.

- **MAC address**: Each network-connected device has a media access control (MAC) address. You can think of a MAC address as the physical network address of a device. Each server on a network has one or more network interface cards (NICs) that it uses to connect to the network. Each NIC has a unique MAC address. The MAC address is used to identify devices in an Ethernet network.

- **IP address**: In addition to having a MAC address, a device is likely assigned a unique IP address. IP addresses are used to identify devices in an IP network such as the Internet and private subnets.

- **Physical Ethernet switch**: A physical Ethernet switch manages network traffic between devices that are directly connected to its ports. A switch has multiple ports, each of which can be connected to a single device or to another switch. The switch learns the MAC address of each connected device and uses it to build a MAC address table that maps the address to its port number. An Ethernet switch (also called a Layer 2 switch) acts as a traffic cop, directing each received network packet to the proper port, based on the data in the MAC address table. Layer 3 switches use IP routing tables to route traffic between subnets.

- **Opaque network**: An opaque network is a network created and managed by a separate entity outside vSphere, such as a logical segment created by VMware NSX. The opaque network appears as an object in the vSphere Client, but the vCenter Server cannot manage it. You can use the NSX Manager to manage an opaque network.

- **EtherChannel**: An *EtherChannel* is a logical channel formed by bundling together two or more links to aggregate bandwidth and provide redundancy. Other acceptable names for EtherChannel (an IOS term) are port channel (an NX-OS term) and link aggregation group (LAG).

- **LACP**: Link Aggregation Control Protocol (LACP) is a standards-based negotiation protocol used to dynamically build an EtherChannel. It is also known as IEEE 802.1ax (or IEEE 802.3ad). LACP is used to build EtherChannels (LAGs) dynamically. EtherChannels can also be built statically without the use of LACP.

- **IEEE 802.1ax**: This is the IEEE working group that defines port channel, EtherChannel, and link aggregation. Originally, the working IEEE group was 802.3ad, but in 2008 it was replaced by 802.1ax.

- **IEEE 802.3ad**: This is the original IEEE working group for port channel, EtherChannel, and link aggregation. Although it has been replaced with 802.1ax, it is still referred to as IEEE 802.3ad.

- **NIC hardware accelerator**: This is a specialized NIC that is designed for moving data and accelerating the processing by the CPU for networking. One example of a NIC hardware accelerator is a data processing unit (DPU), which is a major evolution of a SmartNIC. As introduced in Chapter 1, "vSphere Overview, Components, and Requirements," vSphere 8.0 can leverage DPUs to offload some infrastructure services. DPUs include flash storage, high-speed ports, hardware accelerators, CPUs, fast path offloading, and virtualized device functions.

Virtual NICs

Much as a physical server may have multiple NICs to connect to physical networks, a virtual machine may have multiple virtual NICs (vNICs) to connect to virtual networks. Much like a physical NIC, each vNIC has a unique MAC address. The vNIC appears as a traditional NIC to a virtual machine's guest OS. The guest OS can assign IP addresses to vNICs.

In addition to requiring network connectivity for virtual machine networking, ESXi requires network connectivity for host management activities and other purposes. To accommodate this need, you should configure one or more VMkernel virtual network adapters on each host. For example, when connecting the vCenter Server or the vSphere Host Client to an ESXi host, you provide the address (IP address or fully qualified host name) of a VMkernel virtual network adapter that is enabled for management traffic. Much as a virtual machine can use multiple virtual network adapters, each ESXi host may use multiple VMkernel network adapters.

Virtual Switch Concepts

A virtual switch is a software construct that acts much like a physical switch to provide networking connectivity for virtual devices within an ESXi host. Each virtual machine may use vNICs to connect to virtual ports on virtual switches. To gain access to the physical network, one or more of the host's physical NICs should be connected to the virtual switch as uplinks. The virtual switch, which resides in the VMkernel, provides traffic management for all vNICs in the host and all the uplink's incoming and outgoing Ethernet frames.

A virtual switch works at Layer 2 of the OSI model. It can send and receive data, provide VLAN tagging, and provide other networking features. A virtual switch maintains a MAC address table that contains only the MAC addresses for the vNICs that are directly attached to the virtual switch. When an Ethernet frame is received by the virtual switch, it passes the frame to the appropriate port, based on its internal MAC address table. The virtual switch updates the physical switch with its internal MAC address table using ARP.

With vSphere 4.0, VMware renamed the original virtual switch vSphere Standard Switch (vSS) and introduced the vSphere Distributed Switch (vDS). A vSS and a vDS behave similarly but are managed and controlled differently. Each vSS is configured and managed by a specific ESXi host. A vDS is configured and managed by the vCenter Server, which pushes the switch's configuration to each participating host. The vDS has many more features than the vSS. All new features are built into the new vDS, while the vSS capabilities are limited.

Each virtual switch has many virtual ports. You can configure port groups (standard port groups) on a vSS. You can configure ports (distributed ports) and port groups (distributed port groups) on a vDS.

VLANs

A *virtual LAN (VLAN)* is a logical partition of a physical network at the data link layer (Layer 2). A VLAN is typically associated with a broadcast domain and is used to isolate the traffic from other networks. A broadcast domain is a collection of network devices that can receive traffic destined to a broadcast address. A physical switch, by default, adheres to this behavior. With VLAN technology, the switch allows a single physical network to be divided into multiple network segments. This is achieved by modifying a unique header of the Ethernet frame and adding a tag to identify the membership within a specific VLAN. A VLAN can be used to subdivide a broadcast domain to limit the number of network devices that can communicate when a broadcast packet is sent.

NOTE   IEEE 802.1Q is the networking standard that supports VLANs on an Ethernet network.

ESXi provides VLAN support by allowing you to assign a VLAN ID to a virtual switch port group. The VMkernel is responsible for all tagging and untagging packets with VLAN IDs as the packets pass through the virtual switch. To properly assign VLANs, you must configure the port group to match the VLAN ID that has been configured at the physical switch. On a single virtual switch, you can configure multiple port groups and assign a unique VLAN ID to each port group. To support the multiple VLANs, the physical NIC that is used as the virtual switch's uplink should connect to a physical switch port that is configured for VLAN trunking.

On a standard port group, the valid VLAN ID range is 1 to 4095, with 4095 being unique. The vSS forwards all packets from all ports to the port group assigned VLAN 4095. One use case is to implement packet sniffing or intrusion detection services in a virtual machine. For sniffing or intrusion detection, you must also enable promiscuous mode for the port group. Another use case is to support VLAN guest tagging.

On a distributed port group, the valid VLAN ID range is 1 to 4094. You cannot assign 4095 to a distributed port group. Instead, you can directly configure VLAN trunking by using a distributed port group. On a distributed port group, you can select the VLAN Trunking option and identify the range of VLANs that are to be trunked. Setting a standard port group for VLAN 4095 is much like setting a distributed port group for VLAN trunking for VLANs 1 to 4094.

For example, say that your organization uses separate VLANs for production traffic (VLAN 101), test/development traffic (VLAN 102), QA traffic (VLAN 103), IP
storage traffic (VLAN 300), vMotion traffic (VLAN 310), and management traffic
(VLAN 500). You want a virtual machine running Wireshark to be able to receive all
virtual machine traffic and management traffic but not IP storage or vMotion traffic.
You can configure the distributed port group to use VLAN trunking range 101 to
103,500. Or, if you wanted to only exclude vMotion and IP storage traffic, you can
define the range 1 to 103,500 to 4094.

vSphere Standard Switch (vSS)

A vSphere Standard Switch (vSS) is also called a host-based switch because it is configured and maintained within a specific ESXi host. The vSS data and management
planes reside within a single host.

Much like a physical Ethernet switch, a vSS maintains and uses a MAC address
table. But with a vSS, the VMkernel directly registers each connected vNIC's MAC
address, along with its virtual port, in the virtual switch's MAC address table. The
vSS does not observe network packets to learn the MAC address. The vSS sends all
packets whose destination address does not match a connected vNIC to the physical
NIC uplinks.

During a default ESXi installation, the host is configured with one virtual switch,
identified as vSwitch0, with a physical NIC uplink, identified as vmnic0. The default
virtual switch contains a virtual machine port group named VM Network and a port
group named Management Network. VM Network is a port group for connecting
virtual machines (a virtual machine port group). Management Network is a port
group that contains a single VMkernel virtual network adapter (vmk0) that is used
for management purposes, such as connecting to vCenter Server. A VMkernel virtual adapter is commonly called a VMkernel port. You can create additional standard
switches. You can add virtual machine port groups and VMkernel virtual network
adapters to existing standard switches. You can assign unique labels and policies to
virtual machine port groups. These policies, which include NIC teaming, security,
and traffic shaping policies, are applied to the virtual machines connected to the port
group.

For example, Figure 3-1 is a diagram representing a standard virtual switch with two
virtual machines connected to a port group named VM Network, two VMkernel
ports (one named Management Network and one named vMotion), and two physical NIC uplinks (vmnic0 and vmnic1).

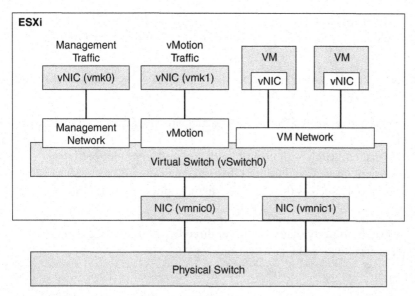

Figure 3-1 A Sample Virtual Switch

Each virtual machine typically has one or more vNICs to allow network communication. To connect a virtual machine to a vSS, you should connect one of its vNICs to a virtual machine port group on the vSS. To allow the virtual machines to communicate with virtual machines on other hosts, connect the port group to one or more physical NIC uplinks in the vSS. The physical NIC should be connected to a physical Ethernet switch. The inbound and outbound Ethernet frames travel through the physical NIC uplink on the vSS. Virtual machines in a port group that do not have a physical NIC uplink can only communicate with other vNICs on the same host and port group.

The vSS provides features such as VLAN tagging, NIC teaming, network security policies, and traffic shaping. The feature set provided by a vSS is smaller than the feature set provided by a vDS or a physical Ethernet switch. The vDS feature set is covered later in this chapter, along with a comparison of vSS and vDS.

A vSS does not have some of the vulnerabilities of a physical switch. For example, it is not susceptible to MAC address flooding attacks because it does not use observed data to populate its MAC address table. The following list contains other common network vulnerabilities and brief explanations about why a vSS is safe from each of them:

- **802.1q tagging attacks**: A vSS does not perform the dynamic trunking required for this type of attack.

- **Double-encapsulation attacks**: A vSS drops any double-encapsulated frames that a virtual machine attempts to send on a port configured for a specific VLAN.

- **Multicast brute-force attacks**: A vSS does not allow frames to leave their correct broadcast domain (VLAN).

- **Spanning tree attacks**: A vSS does not participate in a spanning tree protocol.

A vSS is not a managed switch, so it cannot be configured and monitored using traditional networking models and utilities. Instead, you can manage a vSS by using VMware-provided tools, such as the vSphere Client, vSphere Host Client, vCLI, ESXi shell, or PowerCLI.

The main vSS switch property that you can set directly with the vSphere client is the MTU size, as explained in the next section.

MTU

The standard size for Ethernet packets, or frames, is 1500 bytes. Using larger (jumbo) frames can provide better utilization of a fast network link. To allow jumbo frames on a vSS or vDS, you must set the virtual switch's Maximum Transmission Unit (MTU) setting to a value larger than 1500 bytes, such as 9000 bytes. To use jumbo frames, you must configure the network to support it end to end, including physical NICs and physical switches. To allow a virtual machine to use jumbo frames, you must configure the virtual machine to use the VMXNET3 virtual network adapter. (E1000 and E1000E adapters do not support jumbo frames.) You must also enable jumbo frames inside the guest operating system. To allow VMkernel services such as IP-based storage, vMotion, fault tolerance, and VSAN to use jumbo frames, you must set the MTU setting for the VMkernel network adapter to a value greater than 1500 bytes.

Failure to properly configure MTU to support jumbo frames end to end typically results in poor network performance. With a vDS, you can enable a health check to warn of mismatched configuration between the vDS and the physical network hardware.

vSS Network Policies

You can apply network policies to standard and distributed switches to use and configure specific features. On a vSS, you can apply policies to the switch, and they automatically propagate to each port group. At the port group level, you can override policies applied to the switch and apply unique policies to a port group. On a vDS, you have more flexibility for applying policies, and you can override policies at the port level.

On a vSS, you can set the following network policies:

- Teaming and Failover

- Security

- Traffic Shaping

- VLAN

You can set the policies directly on a vSS. To override a policy at the port group level, just set a different policy on the port group.

A vDS supports additional policies. See the "vDS Network Policies" section, later in this chapter, for details.

NIC Teaming Policies

When you connect two or more physical NICs (pNICs) to the same vSS, you should decide which NIC teaming option to use. The two main purposes of NIC teaming are to improve availability (by eliminating a single point of failure) and to handle large workloads (by spreading traffic across multiple uplinks). The following NIC teaming options are available on vSS and vDS:

- **Route Based on Originating Virtual Port**: This is the default option. Its load balancing is based on the originating port ID of the virtual machine. When a new virtual machine gets connected to the port group, the virtual switch uses the virtual machine's port ID to select one of the pNICs from the active uplinks list to direct outbound traffic. Typically, this results in nearly even virtual machine distribution among the uplinks. If an uplink fails, the switch redirects the traffic from the failed uplink to a surviving uplink.

- **Route Based on IP Hash**: With this load-balancing method, the switch reads the source and destination IP addresses of each outbound packet and uses a hash to determine on which uplink to place the packet. The selection process is resource intensive because the VMkernel examines the header of each Ethernet packet. With this method, a single VM could send packets to different destinations, using different uplinks, which can improve throughput. To support this method, the switch must support IEEE 802.3ad, and you must configure an EtherChannel on the physical switch.

- **Route Based on Source MAC Hash**: This load-balancing method is based on source MAC address. The switch processes each outbound packet header and generates a hash using the least significant bit (LSB) of the MAC address. It uses the hash to decide which active uplink should be used to place the packet.

■ **Use Explicit Failover Order**: When this option is chosen, all outbound traffic uses the first uplink that appears in the active uplinks list. If the first uplink fails, the switch redirects traffic from the failed uplink to the second uplink in the list.

The vDS has additional teaming options that are addressed later in this chapter.

NOTE   For each of these methods, the virtual switch does not consider the virtual machine's active workload in the load-balancing decision making. A vDS offers a load-based NIC teaming option that is addressed later in this chapter.

Table 3-2 lists some advantages and disadvantages for selecting Route Based on IP Hash.

Table 3-2   Advantages and Disadvantages of IP Hash NIC Teaming

Advantages	Disadvantages
A more even distribution of the load compared to Route Based on Originating Virtual Port and Route Based on Source MAC Hash	Highest resource consumption compared to the other load-balancing algorithms
	Requires changes on the physical network
A potentially higher throughput for virtual machines that communicate with multiple IP addresses	Complex to troubleshoot

Network Security Policies

As an administrator, you can define network security policies to protect network traffic against MAC address impersonation and unwanted port scanning. The security policies of the virtual switches are implemented in Layer 2 of the TCP/IP stack. You can use the network security policies to secure traffic against Layer 2 attacks.

It is important to understand how the virtual machine MAC addresses are defined, since they play a part in the security policies. Each vNIC in a virtual machine has an initial MAC address and an effective MAC address. The initial MAC address is assigned when the adapter is created. It can be modified from outside the guest operating system, but it cannot be changed by the guest operating system. The effective MAC address is typically assigned the same value as the initial MAC address when the adapter is created. The effective MAC address can be changed by the guest OS. The effective MAC address is used when filtering incoming packets. When the guest OS changes the effective MAC address, the adapter receives packets destined for the new effective MAC address. When sending a packet, the guest OS typically places its effective MAC address in the source MAC address field of the Ethernet frame.

A guest OS can send frames with an impersonated source MAC address, which facilitates impersonation and malicious attacks. To guard against this risk, you can leverage security policies on vSS port groups and vDS distributed port groups. There are three available options for the network security policies:

- **Promiscuous Mode**: For a vSS port group, the default value is Reject. By default, the vNIC receives only those frames that match the effective MAC address. If this option is set to Accept, the virtual switch sends all frames on the wire to the vNIC, allowing virtual machines to receive packets that are not destined for them. This setting allows the use of tools such as tcpdump and Wireshark inside a guest operating system.

- **MAC Address Changes**: For a vSS port group, the default value is Accept. By default, ESXi accepts the effective MAC address change. If this option is set to Reject, the behavior changes such that ESXi does not honor requests to change the effective MAC address to an address that is different from the initial MAC address. Instead, it disables the virtual switch port until the effective MAC address matches the initial MAC address. The guest OS is unaware that the request was not honored.

- **Forged Transmits**: For a vSS port group, the default value is Accept. By default, ESXi does not compare source and effective MAC addresses and does not drop the packet due to a mismatch. If this option is set to Reject, ESXi compares the source and effective MAC addresses and drops the packet if the addresses do not match.

NOTE   In a vDS, the default value for each of these three security options is Reject.

Traffic Shaping Policy

A virtual machine's network bandwidth can be controlled by enabling traffic shaping. Traffic shaping is defined by average bandwidth, peak bandwidth, and burst size. Network traffic shaping can be configured on standard switches or distributed switches, but by default, traffic shaping is disabled. You can apply a traffic shaping policy to each vSS port group, each vDS distributed port, or each vDS distributed port group. On a standard switch, traffic shaping can be configured only for outbound traffic. On a vDS, it can be configured for both outbound and inbound traffic. When you enable traffic shaping for a standard switch or port group, you can configure the following options:

- **Average Bandwidth**: This is the allowed average load for a port. It is the allowed number of kilobits per second for traffic through a port, averaged over time.

- **Peak Bandwidth**: This is the allowed maximum number of kilobits per second of traffic through a port when it is sending or receiving a burst of traffic. This number tops the bandwidth that a port uses when it is using its burst bonus that is configured using the Burst Size parameter. The Peak Bandwidth setting cannot be smaller than the Average Bandwidth setting.

- **Burst Size**: This is the maximum number of kilobytes to allow in a burst. If this parameter is set, a port might gain a burst bonus when it does not use all its allocated bandwidth. You can define an average bandwidth allotment for the virtual machines connected to a port group. If the virtual machines have not used the allotted bandwidth, the system may grant a burst bonus, allowing the virtual machines to send some data, limited by the burst size, at a faster rate (up to the peak bandwidth).

VLAN Policies

You can apply a VLAN policy to a vSS, such that all port groups on the vSS are associated with a single VLAN. Optionally, you can override the VLAN setting per port group, such that all the virtual machines in the port group are associated with the same VLAN. A major use case for multiple virtual machine port groups is to provide a simple means to place different sets of virtual machines onto separate VLANs. In this case, you should apply a unique VLAN policy to each virtual machine port group.

VLANs are described in the "VLANs" section of this chapter.

vSphere Distributed Switch (vDS)

A *vSphere Distributed Switch (vDS)* acts as a single virtual switch for all associated hosts in a data center. It provides centralized provisioning, monitoring, and management of virtual networks for associated hosts and virtual machines. You create and configure distributed switches on a vCenter Server system. The vCenter Server propagates the switch configuration to each connected ESXi host in the form of a host proxy switch. The ESXi host provides the data plane for the I/O traffic. The data plane implements the packet switching, filtering, tagging, and other features for the Ethernet packet. The management plane is provided by vCenter Server. Figure 3-2 shows the architecture of a vDS, including its management plane and data plane.

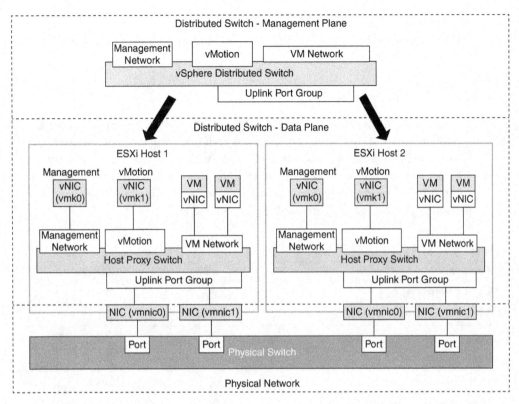

Figure 3-2 vDS Architecture

Distributed Port Groups

The ports in a vDS, which are called *distributed ports*, are where the VMkernel virtual network adapters and virtual machine vNICs connect. A set of distributed ports is a called a *distributed port group*. A vDS provides distributed port groups to simplify the configuration and management of distributed ports. You can apply unique network labels to each distributed port group. You can configure NIC teaming, VLAN, security, traffic shaping, and other policies to a distributed port group, which applies the policies to the underlying distributed ports. When you connect a vNIC to a vDS, you can choose the distributed port group rather than a specific distributed port.

Uplink Port Groups

An uplink port group is similar to a distributed port group, except that it is used to manage the physical connections for hosts. An uplink port group, which is defined during the creation of a distributed switch, contains one or more uplinks. An uplink (dvuplink) is where you map the hosts' physical NICs that connect the vDS to the physical network. When you change settings that involve uplink port groups (such as NIC teaming settings), the settings are automatically applied to each host and the appropriate NICs.

vSS and vDS Comparison

You can define a custom name for each vDS, distributed port group, and uplink port group by using the vSphere Client. At the switch level, you can make several more settings and take more actions with a vDS than with a vSS, such as creating private VLANs and configuring port mirroring sessions. vDS offers many advantages over vSS but requires Enterprise Plus licensing. Table 3-3 provides a side-by-side comparison of the features that are available in vSS and vDS.

Table 3-3 Comparison of vSS and vDS Features

Feature	vSS	vDS
Layer 2 switch	X	X
VLAN segmentation (802.1q tagging)	X	X
IPv6 support	X	X
NIC teaming	X	X
Outbound traffic shaping	X	X
Cisco Discovery Protocol (CDP)	X	X
Inbound traffic shaping		X
VM network port block		X
Private VLANs		X
Load-based NIC teaming		X
Data center–level management		X
Network vMotion		X
Per-port policy settings		X
Port state monitoring		X
NetFlow		X
Port mirroring		X

vDS Network Policies

On a vDS, you have more flexibility in terms of applying policies than you do with a vSS. You can apply policies to a distributed port group, and those policies then automatically propagate to each distributed port. At the distributed port level, you can override policies applied to the distributed port group and apply unique policies to a distributed port. Likewise, you can apply policies to uplink port groups and override the policies at the uplink port level.

At the distributed port group level, you can control which network policies can be overridden at the distributed port group level. For example, if you configure the distributed port group to allow VLAN policy override at the port level, you can set a VLAN ID directly on a distributed port. Otherwise, you cannot.

As with a vSS, you can apply the following network policies for vDS:

- Teaming and Failover
- Security
- Traffic Shaping
- VLAN

As mentioned earlier, you can apply these policies at the distributed port group and distributed port levels.

With a vDS, you can apply the following additional policies, which are addressed in upcoming sections in this chapter:

- Monitoring
- Traffic Filtering and Marking
- Resources Allocation
- Port Blocking

Compared to a vSS, a vDS provides additional teaming and failover options, which are addressed in the "Load-Based NIC Teaming" and "LACP Support" sections in this chapter. Compared to a vSS, a vDS provides additional traffic shaping options, which are addressed in the "Inbound Traffic Shaping" section in this chapter.

Inbound Traffic Shaping

Distributed virtual switches can do both inbound and outbound traffic shaping, whereas standard virtual switches handle just outbound traffic shaping. Specifically, you can configure the average bandwidth, peak bandwidth, and burst size on a distributed port group and apply it to ingress or egress traffic (inbound or outbound to the distributed port).

Port-Blocking Policies

When needed, you can block traffic to specific distributed ports. For example, if a virtual machine is broadcasting a lot of traffic due to a broken or hacked application and starts consuming a large portion of the network bandwidth, you may want to temporarily block traffic to its distributed port. This is particularly useful if you are a network administrator who has permission to modify the vDS but do not have permission to modify the virtual machine.

As with other policies, to allow individual port blocking, you first need to allow port blocking policy override on the distributed port group. Optionally, you can block all ports in a port group.

Load-Based NIC Teaming

In addition to the NIC teaming options (Originating Virtual Port ID, Source MAC Hash, IP Hash, and Explicit Failover Order) provided by standard switches, a vDS offers load-based teaming. Load-based NIC teaming (or Route Based on Physical NIC Load) checks the current load on the uplinks and takes steps to migrate traffic from overloaded uplinks to less active uplinks. With load-based teaming, each vNIC is initially assigned to an uplink, based on the originating virtual port ID. If an uplink's load exceeds 75% of its capacity over a 30-second interval, then the port ID of the virtual machine with the highest I/O is moved to a different uplink.

Load-based teaming offers lower overhead than IP-based load balancing, and it does not require the physical switches to support 802.3ad (EtherChannel/link aggregation).

Resource Allocation Policy

When you apply a resource allocation policy to a distributed port group, you can assign a *network resource pool* to the port group. Network resource pools leverage Network I/O Control (NIOC) to allocate resources for network traffic, as explained in the following sections.

Network I/O Control (NIOC)

NIOC was introduced in vSphere 4.1, when VMware added support for physical NICs with speeds greater than 1 Gbps. It became common for servers to have fewer NICs with multiple types of network traffic sharing the bandwidth. VMware uses NIOC as an additional layer of packet scheduling in the hypervisor to prioritize network traffic.

When you enable NIOC in a vDS in vSphere 8, each virtual port has a network port queue where the network scheduler gets the packet and transmits it based on the shares, reservations, and limit settings for each network port. The vDS recognizes the following network traffic types: management, Fault Tolerance, NFS, vSAN, vMotion, vSphere Replication, vSphere Data Protection Backup, NVMe over TCP, and virtual machine traffic. With default settings, NIOC does not directly limit or guarantee network bandwidth to any system traffic type. In other words, the reservation for each traffic type is 0, and the limit is set to unlimited. By default, NIOC provides a higher relative priority to virtual machine traffic, and this priority is applied during periods of network contention. In other words, there are twice as many default virtual machine traffic shares (100) as there are shares for the other types of system traffic (50).

You can change the limit for any system traffic type to reflect the maximum bandwidth (in Mbps or Gbps) that the traffic type can consume on a single physical NIC.

You can change the reservation for any system traffic type to establish a specific bandwidth (in Mbps) that the traffic type is guaranteed on a single physical NIC. This bandwidth cannot exceed 75% of the bandwidth of the lowest-capacity NIC that is servicing the traffic type. If you reserve resources for virtual machine traffic, you can use network resource pools to delegate the reserved resources.

Network Resource Pools

A network resource pool is a mechanism that enables you to apply a part of the bandwidth that is reserved for virtual machine system traffic to a set of distributed port groups. By default, no network resource pools exist.

For example, if you reserve 2 Gbps for virtual machine system traffic on a distributed switch with four uplinks, the total aggregated bandwidth available for virtual machine reservation on the switch is 8 Gbps. Each network resource pool can reserve a portion of the 8 Gbps capacity. If you create a network pool named PG-A and set it to reserve 3 Gbps, then you have 5 Gbps that you can use for other network pools, as illustrated in Figure 3-3.

The bandwidth quota that is dedicated to a network resource pool is shared among the distributed port groups associated with the pool and is applied to the virtual machines connected to the associated distributed ports.

With NIOC Version 3, you can set shares, reservations, and limits on virtual machine vNICs, much as you can for a virtual machine's CPU and memory. To fulfill the network reservations (guarantees), NIOC uses a traffic placement engine. For virtual machines that have network reservation configured, the distributed switch attempts to place the virtual network adapter traffic on a physical adapter that can supply the required bandwidth and is in the scope of the active teaming policy. The total bandwidth reservation for virtual machines in a network resource pool cannot exceed the reservation of the pool.

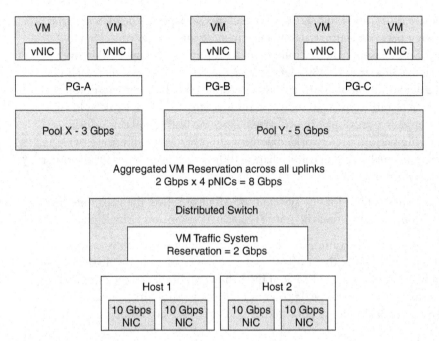

Figure 3-3   Network Resource Pools Example

The actual limit and reservation applied to a virtual network adapter may be impacted by a distributed port group's traffic shaping policy. For example, if a vNIC's limit is set to 300 Mbps, and the average bandwidth and peak bandwidth applied by traffic shaping are 200 Mbps, then the effective limit becomes 200 Mbps.

To meet the network guarantees (reservation) for a virtual machine, vSphere implements admission control at the host and cluster levels, based on bandwidth reservation and teaming policy. A distributed switch applies bandwidth admission control by using NIOC to verify the following:

- A physical adapter is available that can supply the guaranteed bandwidth to the VM network adapters.

- The virtual network adapter's reservation is less than the free quota in the network resource pool.

With NIOC Version 3, a vSphere DRS cluster places the virtual machine on a host that can fulfill the reserved bandwidth for the virtual machine, according to the active teaming policy. In the following situations, vSphere DRS migrates a virtual machine to another host to satisfy the virtual machine's bandwidth reservation:

- The reservation is changed to a value that the initial host can no longer satisfy.

- A physical adapter that carries traffic from the virtual machine is offline.

In the event of a host failure or isolation, vSphere HA powers on a virtual machine on another host in the cluster, according to the bandwidth reservation and teaming policy. To use network admission control in a vSphere DRS or vSphere HA cluster, you should perform the following tasks:

- Allocate bandwidth for the virtual machine system traffic.

- Configure the bandwidth requirements of virtual machines connected to the distributed switch.

NetFlow and Monitoring Policy

Cisco introduced the *NetFlow* feature in the mid-1990s, and eventually it became an open source feature controlled by the IETF. VMware added NetFlow Version 5 to the vSphere 5.0 release. NetFlow is a switch feature that collects IP network traffic as it enters or exits an interface. NetFlow data provides an overview of traffic flows, based on the network source and destination. The main purpose is to collect IP network traffic that is flowing through a vDS. The current supported version for the vDS is NetFlow Version 10, which is identified as IPFIX.

NetFlow allows administrators to forward network flows to a centralized NetFlow collector. These flows can include virtual machine-to-virtual machine flows, virtual machine-to-physical device flows, and physical device-to-virtual machine flows. The collector can be a physical device on the network or a virtual machine. The collector gathers the flows to enable network analysis and troubleshooting. You can set a sampling rate to collect network flows. For example, if you set the sampling rate to 4, NetFlow samples one packet and then drops (skips) the next four packets. If the sampling rate is zero, NetFlow samples every packet (that is, skips zero packets).

By default, NetFlow is turned off on a vDS. If you enable it, you can set Collector IP Address, Collector Port, and other settings. To collect data from only the virtual machines on the same host, you can enable Process Internal Flows Only.

After configuring NetFlow on a vDS, you can configure monitoring policies on vDS port groups and ports.

Traffic Filtering and Marking Policy

With a vDS, you can implement a traffic filtering and marking policy to protect the virtual network from unwanted traffic and security attacks. The traffic filtering in a vDS uses simple filtering rules, much like the filtering in many physical switches. As an example, you could create a simple Permit rule that allows the specified traffic while blocking everything else. Or you could create a Deny rule that blocks the specified traffic while allowing everything else.

A marking policy allows you to mark traffic with a priority tag that is used during times of contention on a physical switch. In essence, it allows you to apply a tag to the Ethernet header or IP header as the Ethernet frame enters and exits your virtual switch. You can mark the traffic with a Class of Service (CoS) tag in a Layer 2 Ethernet header. Or you could mark the traffic with a Differentiated Service Code Point (DSCP) tag in a Layer 3 IP header. Higher tagged packets move to the front of the queue on a physical Ethernet switch during times of contention, and lower or untagged packets are sent using best-effort service.

With a vDS, you can apply filters on data traveling between the vNIC and the distributed port and between the uplink port and the physical NIC. These are the major steps in the process:

Step 1.   Enable traffic filtering and marking on the distributed port group or uplink port group.

Step 2.   Mark traffic on the distributed port group or uplink port group.

Step 3.   Configure filters on the distributed port group or uplink port group.

Step 4.   Define traffic rules for the distributed port group or uplink port group.

When marking traffic, you can create a rule in which you configure qualifiers to identify the data to be tagged and set Action to Tag. You can use system traffic qualifiers (such as NFS), MAC traffic qualifiers (to match by MAC address and VLAN ID), and IP traffic qualifiers (to match by IP version and IP address).

For example, to mark voice over IP (VoIP) traffic whose source IP is 192.168.2.0, you can create a rule that specifies the following parameters:

- **Action**: Tag
- **DSCP Value**: 26
- **Traffic Direction**: Egress
- **Traffic Qualifiers**: IP Qualifier
- **Protocol**: UDP
- **Destination Port**: 5060
- **Source Address:** IP address matches 192.168.2.0 with prefix length 24

vDS Settings and Features

The following sections provide details on other vDS settings and features.

Private VLANs

Private VLANs (PVLANs) are an extension of the VLAN standard that is not double encapsulated but that allows a VLAN to effectively be subdivided into other VLANs. This is useful for a hosting provider that has run out of VLANs or in any environment where 4094 VLANs are not enough.

A VLAN that is to be subdivided becomes known as the primary private VLAN. This primary PVLAN is then carved up into one or multiple secondary PVLANs that exist only within the primary. When a virtual machine or VMkernel port sends a packet, that packet is tagged at the distributed port group level on the vDS. Because this is not double encapsulation, packets travel with only one VLAN tag at a time. However, physical switches could be confused by seeing MAC addresses tagged with more than one VLAN tag, unless the physical switches are PVLAN aware and have their PVLAN tables configured appropriately. If the physical network is configured correctly, it identifies that the secondary PVLAN exists as part of the primary.

There are three different types of secondary PVLANs:

- **Promiscuous**: Nodes in a promiscuous secondary PVLAN can communicate with other nodes in the same PVLAN and all nodes in any secondary (community or isolated) PVLANs in the same primary PVLAN.

- **Community**: Nodes in a community secondary PVLAN can communicate with other nodes in the same PVLAN and nodes in a promiscuous secondary PVLAN in the same primary PVLAN. Nodes in a community secondary PVLAN cannot communicate with nodes in other community or isolated secondary PVLANs.

- **Isolated**: Nodes in an isolated secondary PVLAN can communicate with nodes in a promiscuous secondary PVLAN in the same primary PVLAN. Nodes in an isolated secondary PVLAN cannot communicate with other nodes in the same PVLAN or with nodes in other community or isolated secondary PVLANs.

Data Center–Level Management

The vSphere Client provides a single pane of glass for provisioning, configuring, and managing a vDS, which can be used by up to 2500 ESXi servers. At the data center level, you can perform many network management tasks, such as the following.

- Create a vDS

- Attach hosts to the vDS

- Create distributed port groups

- Assign policies to port groups

- Migrate virtual machines and VMkernel virtual network adapters to the vDS

- Monitor alerts, tasks, and events

- Monitor port state

- Manage network resources

Network Offloads Compatibility

One of the major new features in vSphere 8 is vSphere Distributed Services Engine (vDSE), which is a result of VMware's Monterey project, introduced at VMworld 2020. With vDSE, infrastructure services are distributed across the different compute resources available on the ESXi host, and networking functions are offloaded to the DPU. vDSE accelerates infrastructure functions on the DPU by introducing a vDS on the DPU and VMware NSX Networking and Observability, which allows you to proactively monitor, identify, and mitigate network infrastructure bottlenecks. vDSE can offload networking operations from the host CPUs to DPUs, leveraging a feature called Network Offloads Compatibility. When a vDS is backed by the DPU, the traffic forwarding logic is offloaded from host CPUs to the DPU. Network Offloads Compatibility must be selected and configured during vDS creation. It cannot be configured after you add hosts to a vDS. After enabling Network Offloads Compatibility, you can only add ESXi hosts that are backed by DPU to the vDS.

In vSphere 8.0, the following features are supported by a DPU-backed vDS:

- Creation and deletion of the vSphere distributed switch

- Configuration management

- vSphere distributed switch health checks

- Link Aggregation Control Protocol (LACP)

- Port mirroring

- Private LANs

- Link Layer Discovery Protocol

In vSphere 8.0, the following features are not supported by a DPU-backed vDS:

- Network I/O control

- Traffic-shaping policies

- DV filter

- Network resource pools

A DPU is supported only on a vSphere Lifecycle Manager cluster. A DPU requires a minimum version combination of vSphere 8.0, NSX 4.0.1.1, and Edge Version 20.

A vDS is required to use vDSE. A DPU-backed vDS with ESXi supports the following modes:

- **Non-offloading mode before NSX is enabled**: If NSX is not enabled, the DPU is used as a traditional NIC, and no offloading is supported.

- **Offloading mode after NSX is enabled**: If NSX 4.0.1.1 is enabled, certain networking and NSX features are offloaded to the DPU.

With NSX 4.0.1.1, the following NSX capabilities are supported and will be handled by the DPU:

- Networking:

  - Geneve overlay and VLAN-based segments

  - Distributed IPv4 and IPv6 routing

  - NIC teaming across the SmartNIC/DPU ports

- Visibility and operations (NSX tools):

  - NSX Traceflow

  - IPFIX

  - Packet Capture

  - Port mirroring

  - Statistics

One use case for vDSE is to offload to the DPU the encapsulation and decapsulation of Geneve packets for NSX networking and processing of NSX security.

Port State Monitoring

In the vSphere Client, you can view details for each vDS port, such as the connected virtual machine, the runtime MAC address, and the link state (link up, link down, blocked, or information unavailable).

Port State with vMotion

A virtual machine connected to a vDS maintains its virtual switch connection when migrating to a different ESXi host. From a virtual networking perspective, the virtual machine has not moved. It remains connected to the same distributed port, with no disruption to the policies and statistics that are tied to that distributed port.

When you perform a migration of a virtual machine connected to a vSS, the virtual machine is attached to a different port on a different virtual switch. The policies and statistics associated with the original port are not carried with the virtual machine. The virtual machine is subject to the policies associated with the destination port group and virtual switch.

Port Mirroring

Port mirroring allows administrators to duplicate everything that is happening on one distributed port to then be visible on another distributed port. With port mirroring, you can do granular per-port network analysis by gathering the entire traffic stream coming into and going out a monitored port. To get started, you create a port mirroring session in which you identify the session type, session properties, traffic source, and destination.

For the session type, you can specify one of the following options:

- **Distributed Port Monitoring**: Mirrors packets from a set of distributed ports to other distributed port groups.

- **Remote Mirroring Source**: Mirrors packets from a set of distributed ports to specific uplinks.

- **Remote Mirroring Destination**: Mirrors packets from a set of VLANs to distributed ports.

- **Encapsulated Remote Mirroring (L3) Source**: Mirrors packets from a set of distributed ports to the IP address of a remote agent.

The session properties are dependent on the session type and include the following settings:

- **Name**: Uniquely identifies the session.

- **Status**: Enables or disables the session.

- **Description**: Describes the session.

- **Sampling Rate**: Sets the rate at which packets are sampled.

- **Normal I/O on Destination Ports**: Available only for distributed port and uplink destinations. You can disable this option to allow mirrored traffic out on destination ports but disallow mirrored traffic in on destination ports.

- **Mirrored Packet Length**: Limits the size of mirrored frames.

- **Traffic Source**: Identifies the source of the traffic.

Typically, the mirrored data is sent to a network sniffer or an intrusion detection system.

Port Binding and Allocation

Virtual network adapters (for virtual machines and the VMkernel) must connect to virtual switch ports to communicate on a network. Port binding determines how virtual machines are bound, or attached, to virtual switch ports. To control port assignment, you can choose to use static binding or ephemeral binding:

- **Static binding**: With static binding (which is the default), when a vNIC attaches to a port in a distributed port group, the connection is static, which means the virtual machine remains attached to the port, regardless of the power state of the virtual machine. This binding is performed and controlled by vCenter Server.

- **Ephemeral binding**: Ephemeral means there is no binding of the vNIC to a specific virtual switch port. With this setting, virtual switch ports are created and deleted on demand by the host. At any moment, the number of ports for an ephemeral distributed port group is equivalent to the number of running vNICs connected to the port group.

NOTE   Having an available ephemeral port group is useful in cases where vCenter Server is down and you need to assign a virtual machine to a port group. For example, if a vCenter Server Appliance (VCSA) device is connected to a distributed port group with static binding, you may fail to reconnect the VCSA device to the network after restoring the VCSA device because vCenter is required to assign the port. In this case, you should be successful in connecting the restored VCSA device to the ephemeral distributed port group because the ESXi host will assign the port.

You can control the number of ports and the port allocation in a distributed port group. The port allocation can be elastic or fixed:

- **Elastic**: By default, ports in the port group are created and removed on demand. For example, if the port group is configured for eight ports and elastic port allocation, you can connect nine vNICs to the port group because when you connect the eighth vNIC to the port group, eight more ports are automatically added.

- **Fixed**: The number of ports in the port group is static. Ports are not automatically created or removed. For example, if the port group is configured for eight ports and fixed port allocation, you cannot connect nine vNICs to the port group. When you attempt to connect the ninth vNIC to the port group, you get the error "no free port is available."

In vSphere 8.0, the default settings for a distributed port group are static binding, elastic port allocation, and eight ports.

In the past, the ephemeral setting seemed like the easiest way to go because it required the least administrative effort to address an ever-growing environment. That changed in vSphere 5.1, when static port binding became "elastic" by default.

LACP Support

In vSphere 8.0, a vDS supports LACP. This means you can connect ESXi hosts to physical switches by using dynamic link aggregation. You can create multiple link aggregation groups (LAGs) on a distributed switch to aggregate the bandwidth of physical NICs on ESXi hosts that are connected to LACP port channels. This enables you to increase the network bandwidth, redundancy, and load balancing to the port groups. You need to configure each LAG with two or more ports and connect physical NICs to the ports. Within a LAG, the ports are teamed, such that the network traffic is load balanced between the ports using an LACP hashing algorithm.

For each LAG on a vDS, a LAG object is created on each associated host proxy switch. The same number of ports that you assign to the LAG on the vDS are assigned to the corresponding LAG on the proxy switch on each host, as illustrated in Figure 3-4.

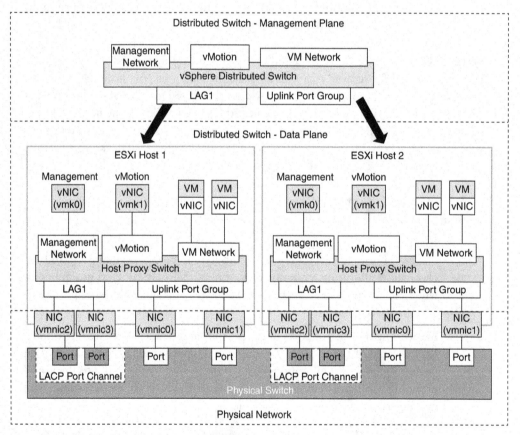

Figure 3-4 LACP Configuration with a vDS

On a host proxy switch, a physical NIC can connect to just one LAG port. On a distributed switch, a LAG port can connect to multiple physical NICs from different hosts. The physical NICs that are connected to the LAG ports must connect to links that participate in an LACP port channel on the physical switch.

A vDS supports up to 64 LAGs. With ESXi 8.0, a host supports up to 32 LAGs. The LAG configuration for a vDS may be limited by the physical network configuration.

The following limitations apply for LACP support in a vDS:

- LACP support is not compatible with software iSCSI port binding. (iSCSI multipathing is supported if iSCSI port binding is not used.)

- LACP support settings do not exist in host profiles.

- LACP is not supported with nested ESXi.

- LACP support does not work with the ESXi dump collector.

- LACP control packets (LACPDU) are not mirrored by vDS port mirroring.

- The vDS teaming and failover health check (see the following section) does not support LAG ports. (LAG port connectivity is checked by LACP.)

- Enhanced LACP support works only when a single LAG handles traffic per distributed port group.

vDS Health Check

By default, vDS health checks are disabled, but you can enable them to check for several specific network inconsistencies. A health check identifies problems but does not attempt to fix the problems. You can use vDS health checks to regularly examine certain settings on distributed and physical switches to identify common errors in the networking configuration. The default interval between health checks is 1 minute. Health checks generate MAC addresses to use during testing. Depending on the selected options, the number of generated MAC addresses can be significant. If you disable health checking, the MAC addresses age out of your environment. For this reason, you may want to enable health checks temporarily.

Table 3-4 provides a summary of the vDS health checks available.

Table 3-4   vDS Health Checks

Health Check	Required vDS Configuration
Checks whether the VLAN trunk ranges on the distributed switch match the trunk port configuration on the connected physical switch ports.	At least two active physical NICs
Checks for matching MTU settings on the distributed switch, the physical network adapter, and the physical switch ports.	At least two active physical NICs
Checks whether the virtual switch teaming policy matches the physical switch port-channel settings.	At least two active physical NICs and two hosts

The potential values for VLAN Health Status, MTU Health Status, and Teaming and Failover Health Status include Normal, Warning, and Unknown. If the VLAN trunk ranges configured on a distributed switch match the trunk ranges on a physical switch, VLAN Health Status is set to Normal. If the MTU settings configured on the distributed switch match the MTU settings on the physical switch, MTU Health Status is set to Normal. If the physical switch ports participate in an EtherChannel and the distributed port group teaming policy is IP hash, Teaming and Failover Health Status is set to Normal. Also, if the distributed port group teaming policy is set to Port Based, MAC Hash, or Explicit Failover, and physical switch ports do not participate in an EtherChannel, Teaming and Failover Health Status is set to Normal.

Other vSphere Networking Features

The following sections provide details on other networking features supported in vSphere 8.0 that are not covered earlier in this chapter.

Multicast Filtering Mode

vDS 6.0.0 and later support basic multicast filtering mode and multicast snooping mode.

Basic Multicast Filtering

In basic multicast filtering mode, a virtual switch (vSS or vDS) forwards multicast traffic for virtual machines according to the destination MAC address of the multicast group, which is based on the MAC address generated from the last 23 bits of the IPv4 address of the group. When a guest operating system joins a multicast group, it pushes the group multicast MAC address to the network through the virtual switch. The virtual switch records the port to destination multicast MAC address mapping in a local forwarding table. The switch does not interpret IGMP messages. Instead, it sends messages directly to the local multicast router, which interprets the messages and takes the appropriate action.

The basic mode has the following restrictions:

- A virtual machine may receive packets from the wrong groups because the switch forwards packets based on the multicast group's destination MAC address, which can potentially be mapped to up to 32 IP multicast groups.

- Due to a limitation of the forwarding model, a virtual machine that is subscribed for traffic from more than 32 multicast MAC addresses may receive packets from the wrong groups.

- The switch does not filter packets based on source address, as defined in IGMP Version 3.

Multicast Snooping

vDS 6.0.0 and later support multicast snooping, which forwards multicast traffic based on the Internet Group Management Protocol (IGMP) and Multicast Listener Discovery (MLD) messages from virtual machines. Multicast snooping supports IGMP Version 1, IGMP Version 2, and IGMP Version 3 for IPv4 multicast group addresses and MLD Version 1 and MLD Version 2 for IPv6 multicast group addresses. The switch dynamically detects when a virtual machine sends a packet containing IGMP or MLD membership information through a switch port and creates a record about the destination IP address of the group. The switch automatically removes the entry for a group from the lookup records whenever a virtual machine does not renew its membership on time.

When using vDS multicast snooping mode, a virtual machine can receive multicast traffic on a single switch port from up to 256 groups and 10 sources.

Discovery Protocol

Switch discovery protocols help vSphere administrators identify the physical switch ports to which a vSS or vDS is connected. Cisco Discovery Protocol (CDP) support was introduced with ESX 3.x. CDP is available for standard switches and distributed switches that are connected to Cisco physical switches. Link Layer Discovery Protocol (LLDP) is supported in vSphere 5.0 and later for vDS (5.0.0 and later) but not for vSS.

CDP enables you to determine which Cisco switch port is connected to a vSS or a vDS. When CDP is enabled for a vDS, you can view the properties of the Cisco switch, such as device ID, software version, and timeout. You can set CDP Type to any of the following values:

- **Listen**: ESXi collects and displays details about the associated Cisco switch port but does not share information about the vDS with the Cisco switch.

- **Advertise**: ESXi shares information about the vDS with the Cisco switch but does not collect or display details about the associated Cisco switch port.

- **Both**: ESXi collects and displays information about the associated Cisco switch port and shares information about the vDS with the Cisco switch.

LLDP enables you to determine which physical switch port is connected to a vDS. When LLDP is enabled for a vDS, you can view the properties of the physical switch, such as chassis ID, system name and description, and device capabilities. You can set the CDP Type to Listen, Advertise, or Both, as previously explained for CDP.

In the vSphere client, to view the physical switch information, you can select a host, navigate to Configure > Networking > Physical Adapters, select an adapter, and choose either the CDP or LLDP tab in the details pane.

TCP Segmentation Offload

TCP Segmentation Offload (TSO, which is referred to as large segment offload or large send offload [LSO] in VMXNET3's latest attributes) allows the segmentation of traffic to be offloaded from the virtual machine and from the VMkernel to the physical NIC. The network adapter separates large frames (up to 64 KB) into MTU-sized frames. One of the jobs of the TCP layer is to segment the data stream to the size of the Ethernet frame. If the frame size is 1500 bytes and an application is transmitting 8 Kbps, it is the job of the TCP layer to segment it down to 1500-byte packets. This occurs in the guest operating system. However, if a physical NIC supports TSO, the adapter can do the work instead, resulting in less overhead and better performance. To use TSO, it must be enabled along the data path, including the physical NIC, vNIC, VMkernel, and guest OS. By default, it is enabled in the VMkernel, the VMXNET2 vNIC, and the VMXNET 3 vNIC.

DirectPath I/O

DirectPath I/O allows a virtual machine to access physical PCI functions on platforms that have an I/O memory management unit (IOMMU). You can enable DirectPath I/O passthrough for a physical NIC on an ESXi host to enable efficient resource usage and to improve performance. After enabling DirectPath I/O on the physical NIC on a host, you can assign it to a virtual machine, allowing the guest OS to use the NIC directly and bypassing the virtual switches.

NOTE   Do not enable DirectPath I/O passthrough for the USB controller for an ESXi host that is configured to boot from a USB device or an SD card attached to a USB channel.

The following features are not available for DirectPath-enabled virtual machines:

- Hot addition and removal of virtual devices
- Suspend and resume
- Record and replay
- Fault tolerance
- High availability
- DRS (The virtual machine can be part of a cluster but cannot migrate across hosts.)
- Snapshots

Single Root I/O Virtualization (SR-IOV)

Single Root I/O Virtualization (SR-IOV) is a feature that allows a single Peripheral Component Interconnect Express (PCIe) device to appear as multiple devices to the hypervisor (ESXi) or to a virtual machine's guest operating system. SR-IOV is useful for supporting an application in a guest OS that is sensitive to network latency.

SR-IOV-enabled devices provide virtual functions (VFs) to the hypervisor or guest operating system. VFs are lightweight PCIe functions that support data exchange with limited support for configuration changes. The virtual machine can take advantage of SR-IOV by exchanging Ethernet frames directly with the physical network adapter, bypassing the VMkernel. This improves network performance by reducing latency and improves CPU efficiency. The downside of this approach is that the environment must meet certain requirements, and several features are not supported.

Although a virtual switch (vSS or vDS) does not handle the network traffic of an SR-IOV-enabled virtual machine, you can control the assigned VFs by using switch configuration policies at the port group level or port level. For example, the VF driver (guest OS) cannot modify the MAC address if it is not allowed in the security policy for the port group or port.

To use SR-IOV in vSphere 8.0, your environment must meet the requirements described in Table 3-5.

Table 3-5 SR-IOV Requirements

Component	Requirements
Physical host	Must use an Intel or AMD processor.
	Must support IOMMU and SR-IOV.
	IOMMU and SR-IOV must be enabled in the BIOS.
Physical network adapter	Must be supported by the server vendor for use with the host system and SR-IOV for the specific ESXi release.
	SR-IOV must be enabled in the firmware.
	Must use MSI-X interrupts.
Physical function (PF) driver in ESXi	Must be certified by VMware.
	Must be installed on the ESXi host, which may require custom installation.
Guest OS	Must be supported by the NIC vendor for the specific ESXi release.
Virtual function (VF) driver in guest OS	Must be compatible with the NIC and supported on the guest OS release.
	Must be Microsoft WLK or WHCK certified for Windows virtual machines.
	Must be installed on the operating system and may require custom installation.

The following features are not available for SR-IOV-enabled virtual machines, and attempts to configure these features may result in unexpected behavior:

- vSphere vMotion
- Storage vMotion
- vShield
- NetFlow
- VXLAN Virtual Wire
- vSphere High Availability
- vSphere Fault Tolerance
- vSphere DRS
- vSphere DPM
- Virtual machine suspend and resume
- Virtual machine snapshots
- MAC-based VLAN for passthrough virtual functions
- Hot addition and removal of virtual devices, memory, and vCPU
- Participation in a cluster environment
- Network statistics for a virtual machine NIC using SR-IOV passthrough

Each NIC must have SR-IOV-supported drivers and may require SR-IOV to be enabled on the firmware.

An SR-IOV NIC can operate in one of three modes in ESXi:

- **Non SR-IOV Mode**: The NIC is not used to provide VFs to virtual machines.
- **SR-IOV Only Mode**: The NIC provides VFs to virtual machines but does not back other virtual machine traffic. In the vSphere Client, the NIC appears in a separate list (External SR-IOV Adapters) in the switch topology page.
- **Mixed Mode**: The NIC services virtual machines with and without SR-IOV.

DirectPath I/O and SR-IOV offer similar performance benefits and trade-offs, but you use them to accomplish different goals. You can use SR-IOV in workloads with extremely high packet rates or very low latency requirements, where you want multiple virtual machines to share the same physical NIC (with the same physical function). With DirectPath I/O, you can map only one physical NIC to one virtual machine.

VMkernel Networking and TCP/IP Stacks

The VMkernel networking layer provides connectivity for the hypervisor and handles system services traffic, such as management, vMotion, IP-based storage, provisioning, Fault Tolerance logging, vSphere Replication, vSphere Replication NFC, and vSAN. You can create multiple VMkernel virtual network adapters to support these services. For each VMkernel adapter, you can select which system service it supports. Each VMkernel adapter requires IP configuration and virtual switch configuration. You can choose to configure multiple system services to share networks, or you can configure a separate network for each system service. In addition to using separate virtual and physical network infrastructure to support each system service, you can use separate VMkernel TCP/IP stacks.

The VMkernel provides multiple TCP/IP stacks that you can use to isolate the system services traffic. You can use the preexisting stacks (default, vMotion, and Provisioning) and create custom stacks, as described here:

- **Default TCP/IP stack**: This stack provides networking support for management traffic and for all VMkernel traffic types. You can choose to use just this stack and ignore the other available stacks.

- **vMotion TCP/IP stack**: This stack supports the traffic for vMotion. You can use this stack to improve the isolation for the vMotion traffic. After you create a VMkernel adapter on this stack, you can no longer use the default stack for vMotion. (vMotion is automatically disabled on VMkernel adapters on the default stack.)

- **Provisioning TCP/IP stack**: This stack supports the traffic for virtual machine cold migration, cloning, and snapshot migration. It also supports the Network File Copy (NFC) traffic used for cloning virtual disks with long-distance vMotion. You can use this stack to isolate provisioning traffic and place it on a separate gateway. After you create a VMkernel adapter on this stack, you can no longer use the default stack for provisioning. (Provisioning is automatically disabled on VMkernel adapters on the default stack.)

- **Custom TCP/IP stack**: You can create custom stacks to isolate the networking of custom applications.

When you create a VMkernel virtual network adapter, you should configure the settings described in Table 3-6.

Table 3-6 VMkernel Adapter Settings

Setting	Description
IP Settings	Provide IPv4 or IPv6 configuration details, such as IPv4 address, mask, and gateway.
MTU	Set this option as described in the "MTU" section in this chapter.
TCP/IP Stack	Select a standard or custom stack, as described in this section.
Available Services	Select which of the following system services to enable for the adapter: ■ Management ■ Motion ■ IP-based storage ■ Provisioning ■ Fault Tolerance logging ■ vSphere Replication ■ vSphere Replication NFC ■ vSAN

Exam Preparation Tasks

As mentioned in the section "Book Features and Exam Preparation Methods" in the Introduction, you have some choices for exam preparation: the exercises here, Chapter 15, "Final Preparation," and the exam simulation questions on the companion website.

Review All Key Topics

Review the most important topics in this chapter, noted with the Key Topic icon in the outer margin of the page. Table 3-7 lists these key topics and the page number on which each is found.

Table 3-7   Key Topics for Chapter 3

Key Topic Element	Description	Page Number
List	vSS networking policies	101
Section	vSS and vDS comparison	106
Section	Resource allocation policy	108
Section	Port mirroring	116
List	LACP with vDS limitations	119
List	SR-IOV limitations	124

Complete Tables and Lists from Memory

Print a copy of Appendix B, "Memory Tables" (found on the companion website), or at least the section for this chapter, and complete the tables and lists from memory. Appendix C, "Memory Table Answers" (also on the companion website), includes completed tables and lists to check your work.

Define Key Terms

Define the following key terms from this chapter and check your answers in the glossary:

EtherChannel, virtual LAN (VLAN), vSphere Distributed Switch (vDS), network resource pool, NetFlow, private VLAN (PVLAN), port mirroring, Single Root I/O Virtualization (SR-IOV)

Review Questions

1. You are configuring traffic shaping policies for your vSS. Which one of the following is not an available setting?

   a. Peak Bandwidth

   b. Minimum Bandwidth

   c. Average Bandwidth

   d. Burst Size

2. You want to implement network security policies at the lowest available level. Which approach should you choose?

   a. Use standard switches and apply policies on the individual ports.

   b. Use standard switches and choose override on the port groups.

   c. Use distributed switches and apply policies on the individual ports.

   d. Use distributed switches and apply policies on the distributed port groups.

3. You created a distributed port group with default settings. Which of the following statements is true?

   a. The port group is set for fixed allocation and 8 ports.

   b. The port group is set for elastic allocation and 8 ports.

   c. The port group is set for fixed allocation and 16 ports.

   d. The port group is set for elastic allocation and 16 ports.

4. You want to address an application's sensitivity to network latency by implementing a technology that presents a physical device with multiple virtual functions. Which one of the following should you implement?

   a. DirectPath I/O

   b. TSO

   c. LACP

   d. SR-IOV

5. You want to control the use of NetFlow within your distributed switch. Which type of network policy should you implement?

   a. Traffic shaping

   b. Monitoring

   c. Resource allocation

   d. Filtering and marking

This chapter covers the following topics:

- Cluster Concepts and Overview
- Distributed Resource Scheduler (DRS)
- vSphere High Availability (HA)
- Other Resource Management and Availability Features

This chapter contains information related to VMware vSphere 8.x Professional (2V0-21.23) exam objectives 1.4, 1.4.1, 1.4.2, 1.4.3, 1.4.4, 1.4.4.1, 1.4.4.2, 1.4.5, 4.6, 4.7, 5.1, 5.1.1, 5.2, 6.1, 7.5, and 7.9.5.

## CHAPTER 4

Clusters and High Availability

This chapter provides details on clusters and high availability in vSphere 8.0.

"Do I Know This Already?" Quiz

The "Do I Know This Already?" quiz allows you to assess whether you should study this entire chapter or move quickly to the "Exam Preparation Tasks" section. In any case, the authors recommend that you read the entire chapter at least once. Table 4-1 outlines the major headings in this chapter and the corresponding "Do I Know This Already?" quiz questions. You can find the answers in Appendix A, "Answers to the 'Do I Know This Already?' Quizzes and Review Questions."

Table 4-1 "Do I Know This Already?" Foundation Topics Section-to-Question Mapping

Foundation Topics Section	Questions
Cluster Concepts and Overview	1
Distributed Resource Scheduler (DRS)	2–4
vSphere High Availability (HA)	5–7
Other Resource Management and Availability Features	8–10

1. You want to implement EVC to ensure that vMotion is enabled across a specific set of ESXi hosts. Which of the following are requirements? (Choose two.)

    a. Hosts must be connected to a DRS cluster.

    b. Hosts must be connected to a vCenter Server.

    c. CPUs must be configured with a custom compatibility mask.

    d. You must select either Enable EVC for AMD Hosts or Enable EVC for Intel Hosts.

2. In vSphere 8.0, you want to configure the DRS migration threshold such that it is at the minimum level at which virtual machine happiness is considered. Which of the following values should you choose?

   a. Level 1

   b. Level 2

   c. Level 3

   d. Level 4

   e. Level 5

3. Which of the following is not a good use for resource pools in DRS?

   a. To delegate control and management

   b. To impact the use of network resources

   c. To impact the use of CPU resources

   d. To impact the use of memory resources

4. You want to use shares to give high-priority resource access to a set of virtual machines in a resource pool, without concern for the relative number of objects in the pool compared to other pools. Which feature is helpful?

   a. Limits

   b. Standard shares

   c. Scalable shares

   d. DRS advanced settings

5. You are configuring vSphere HA in a cluster. You want to configure the cluster to use a specific host as a target for failovers. Which setting should you use?

   a. Host Failures Cluster Tolerates

   b. Define Host Failover Capacity By set to Cluster Resource Percentage

   c. Define Host Failover Capacity By set to Slot Policy (Powered-on VMs)

   d. Define Host Failover Capacity By set to Dedicated Failover Hosts

   e. Define Host Failover Capacity By set to Disabled

6. You are enabling VM Monitoring in a vSphere HA cluster. You want to set the monitoring level such that its failure interval is 60 seconds. Which of the following options should you choose?

   a. High

   b. Medium

    c. Low

    d. Normal

7. You are configuring Virtual Machine Component Protection (VMCP) in a vSphere HA cluster. Which of the following statements is true?

    a. For PDL and APD failures, you can control the restart policy for virtual machines by setting it to Conservative or Aggressive.

    b. For PDL failures, you can control the restart policy for virtual machines by setting it to Conservative or Aggressive.

    c. For APD failures, you can control the restart policy for virtual machines by setting it to Conservative or Aggressive.

    d. For PDL and APD failures, you cannot control the restart policy for virtual machines.

8. You want to configure your environment to use predictive metrics when making placement and balancing decisions. What feature is required?

    a. Predictive DRS

    b. Aria Automation

    c. Proactive HA

    d. Slot Policy

9. You are configuring vSphere Fault Tolerance (FT) in a vSphere 8.0 environment. What is the maximum number of virtual CPUs you can use with an FT-protected virtual machine?

    a. One

    b. Two

    c. Four

    d. Eight

10. You are concerned about service availability for your vCenter Server. Which of the following statements is true?

    a. If a vCenter service fails, VMware Service Lifecycle Manager restarts it.

    b. If a vCenter service fails, VMware Lifecycle Manager restarts it.

    c. If a vCenter service fails, vCenter Server HA restarts it.

    d. VMware Service Lifecycle Manager is a part of the PSC.

Foundation Topics

Cluster Concepts and Overview

A vSphere cluster is a set of ESXi hosts that are intended to work together as a unit. When you add a host to a cluster, the host's resources become part of the cluster's resources. vCenter Server manages the resources of all hosts in a cluster as one unit. In addition to creating a cluster, assigning a name, and adding ESXi objects, you can enable and configure features on a cluster, such as vSphere Distributed Resource Scheduler (DRS), VMware Enhanced vMotion Compatibility (EVC), Distributed Power Management (DPM), vSphere High Availability (HA), and vSAN.

In the vSphere Client, you can manage and monitor the resources in a cluster as a single object. You can easily monitor and manage the hosts and virtual machines in the DRS cluster.

If you enable VMware EVC on a cluster, you can ensure that migrations with vMotion do not fail due to CPU compatibility errors. If you enable vSphere DRS on a cluster, you can allow automatic resource balancing using the pooled host resources in the cluster. If you enable vSphere HA on a cluster, you can allow rapid virtual machine recovery from host hardware failures, using the cluster's available host resource capacity. If you enable DPM on a cluster, you can provide automated power management in the cluster. If you enable vSAN on a cluster, you use a logical SAN that is built on a pool of drives attached locally to the ESXi hosts in the cluster.

You can use the Quickstart workflow in the vSphere Client to create and configure a cluster. The Quickstart page provides three cards: Cluster Basics, Add Hosts, and Configure Cluster. For an existing cluster, you can use Cluster Basics to change the cluster name and enable cluster services, such as DRS and vSphere HA. You can use the Add Hosts card to add hosts to the cluster. You can use the Configure Cluster card to configure networking and other settings on the hosts in the cluster.

In addition, in vSphere 7.0 and later, you can configure a few general settings for a cluster. For example, when you create a cluster, even if you do not enable DRS, vSphere, HA, or vSAN, you can choose to manage all hosts in the cluster with a single image. With this option, all hosts in a cluster inherit the same image, which reduces variability between hosts, improves your ability to ensure hardware compatibility, and simplifies upgrades. This feature requires hosts to already be ESXi 7.0 or above. It replaces baselines. Once it is enabled, baselines cannot be used in this cluster.

NOTE   Do not confuse a vSphere cluster with a datastore cluster. In vSphere, datastore clusters and vSphere (host) clusters are separate objects. Although you can directly enable a vSphere cluster for vSAN, DRS, and vSphere HA, you cannot directly enable it for datastore clustering. You create datastore clusters separately. See Chapter 2, "Storage Infrastructure," for details on datastore clusters.

vSphere Cluster Services (vCLS)

vCLS, which is implemented by default in all vSphere clusters, ensures that cluster services remain available even if vCenter Server becomes unavailable. When you deploy a new cluster in vCenter Server 7.0 Update 3 or upgrade a vCenter Server to Version 7.0 Update 3, vCLS virtual appliances are automatically deployed to the cluster. In clusters with three or more hosts, three vCLS appliances are automatically deployed with anti-affinity rules to separate the appliances. In smaller clusters, the number of vCLS VMs matches the number of hosts.

In vSphere 8.0, each vCLS VM is configured with one vCPU, 128 MB memory, and no vNIC. The datastore for each vCLS VM is automatically selected based on the rank of the datastores connected to the cluster's hosts, with preference given to shared datastores. You can control the datastore choice by using the vSphere Client to select the cluster, navigating to Configure > vSphere Cluster Service > Datastores, and clicking the Add button. vCLS VMs are always powered on and should be treated as system VMs, where only administrators perform selective operations on the vCLS VMs. vCenter Server manages the health of vCLS VMs. You should not back up or take snapshots of these VMs. You can use the Summary tab for a cluster to examine the vCLS health, which is either Healthy, Degraded, or Unhealthy.

If you want to place a datastore hosting a vCLS VM into Maintenance Mode, you must either manually migrate the vCLS VM with Storage vMotion to a new location or put the cluster in Retreat Mode. In Retreat Mode, the health of vCLS is degraded, DRS stops functioning, and vSphere HA does not perform optimal placement when responding to host failure events. To put a cluster in Retreat Mode, you need to obtain its cluster domain ID from the URL of the browser after selecting the cluster in the vSphere Client. Then you apply the cluster domain ID, which is in the form *domain-*c(*number*), to create a new vCenter Server advanced setting with the entry **config.vcls. clusters.***domain-***c(***number***).enabled** that is set to False.

Enhanced vMotion Compatibility (EVC)

EVC is a cluster setting that can improve CPU compatibility between hosts for supporting vMotion. vMotion migrations are live migrations that require compatible instruction sets for source and target processors used by the virtual machine. The source and target processors must come from the same vendor class (AMD or Intel) to be vMotion compatible. The clock speed, cache size, and number of cores can differ between source and target processors. When you start a vMotion migration or a migration of a suspended virtual machine, the wizard checks the destination host for compatibility; it displays an error message if problems exist. By using EVC, you can allow vMotion between some processors that would normally be incompatible.

The CPU instruction set that is available to a virtual machine guest OS is determined when the virtual machine is powered on. This CPU feature set is based on the following items:

- The host CPU family and model
- Settings in the BIOS that might disable CPU features
- The ESX/ESXi version running on the host
- The virtual machine's compatibility setting
- The virtual machine's guest operating system

EVC ensures that all hosts in a cluster present the same CPU feature set to virtual machines, even if the actual CPUs on the hosts differ. If you enable the EVC cluster setting, you can configure the EVC Mode with a baseline CPU feature set. EVC ensures that hosts in a cluster use the baseline feature set when presenting an instruction set to a guest OS. EVC uses AMD-V Extended Migration technology for AMD hosts and Intel FlexMigration technology for Intel hosts to mask processor features; this allows hosts to present the feature set of an earlier processor generation. You should configure EVC Mode to accommodate the host with the smallest feature set in the cluster.

The EVC requirements for hosts include the following:

- ESXi 6.7 or later is required.
- Hosts must be attached to a vCenter Server.
- CPUs must be from a single vendor (either Intel or AMD).
- If the AMD-V, Intel-VT, AMD NX, or Intel XD features are available in the BIOS, they need to be enabled.
- Check the *VMware Compatibility Guide* to ensure that CPUs are supported for EVC Mode.

NOTE You can apply a custom CPU compatibility mask to hide host CPU features from a virtual machine, but VMware does not recommend doing so.

You can configure the EVC settings by using the Quickstart > Configure Cluster workflow in the vSphere Client. You can also configure EVC directly in the cluster settings. The options for VMware EVC are Disable EVC, Enable EVC for AMD

Hosts, and Enable EVC for Intel Hosts. You can also configure per-VM EVC, as described in Chapter 5, "vCenter Server Features and Virtual Machines."

If you choose Enable EVC for Intel Hosts, you can set the EVC Mode setting to one of the options described in Table 4-2.

Table 4-2 EVC Modes for Intel

Level	EVC Mode	Description
L0	Intel Merom	Smallest Intel feature set for EVC mode.
L1	Intel Penryn	Includes the Intel Merom feature set and exposes additional CPU features, including SSE4.1.
L2	Intel Nehalem	Includes the Intel Penryn feature set and exposes additional CPU features, including SSE4.2 and POPCOUNT.
L3	Intel Westmere	Includes the Intel Nehalem feature set and exposes additional CPU features, including AES and PCLMULQDQ.
L4	Intel Sandy Bridge	Includes the Intel Westmere feature set and exposes additional CPU features, including AVX and XSAVE.
L5	Intel Ivy Bridge	Includes the Intel Sandy Bridge feature set and exposes additional CPU features, including RDRAND, ENFSTRG, FSGSBASE, SMEP, and F16C.
L6	Intel Haswell	Includes the Intel Ivy Bridge feature set and exposes additional CPU features, including ABMX2, AVX2, MOVBE, FMA, PERMD, RORX/MULX, INVPCID, and VMFUNC.
L7	Intel Broadwell	Includes the Intel Haswell feature set and exposes additional CPU features, including Transactional Synchronization Extensions, Supervisor Mode Access Prevention, Multi-Precision Add-Carry Instruction Extensions, PREFETCHW, and RDSEED.
L8	Intel Skylake	Includes the Intel Broadwell feature set and exposes additional CPU features, including Advanced Vector Extensions 512, Persistent Memory Support Instructions, Protection Key Rights, Save Processor Extended States with Compaction, and Save Processor Extended States Supervisor.
L9	Intel Cascade Lake	Includes the Intel Skylake feature set and exposes additional CPU features, including VNNI and XGETBV with ECX = 1.
L10	Intel Ice Lake	Includes the Intel Cascade Lake feature set and exposes additional CPU features, including HA extensions, Vectorized AES, User Mode Instruction Prevention, Read Processor ID, Fast Short REP MOV, WBNOINVD, Galois Field New Instructions, and AVX512 Integer Fused Multiply Add, Vectorized Bit Manipulation, and Bit Algorithms Instructions.
L11	Intel Sapphire Rapids	Includes the Intel Ice Lake feature set and exposes additional CPU features, including Control-Flow Enforcement Technology, Advanced Matrix Extensions, Supervisor Protection Keys, AVX-VNNI, AVX512 FP16, AVX512 BF16, CLDEMOTE, SERIALIZE, WBNOINVD, and MOVDIRI instructions.

If you choose Enable EVC for AMD Hosts, you can set the EVC Mode setting to one of the options described in Table 4-3.

Table 4-3 EVC Modes for AMD

Level	EVC Mode	Description
A0	AMD Opteron Generation 1	Smallest AMD feature set for EVC mode.
A1	AMD Opteron Generation 2	Includes the AMD Generation 1 feature set and exposes additional CPU features, including CPMXCHG16B and RDTSCP.
A3	AMD Opteron Generation 3	Includes the AMD Generation 2 feature set and exposes additional CPU features, including SSE4A, MisAlignSSE, POPCOUNT, and ABM (LZCNT).
A2, B0	AMD Opteron Generation 3 (without 3DNow!)	Includes the AMD Generation 3 feature set without 3DNow support.
B1	AMD Opteron Generation 4	Includes the AMD Generation 3 no3DNow feature set and exposes additional CPU features, including SSSE3, SSE4.1, AES, AVX, XSAVE, XOP, and FMA4.
B2	AMD Opteron Piledriver	Includes the AMD Generation 4 feature set and exposes additional CPU features, including FMA, TBM, BMI1, and F16C.
B3	AMD Opteron Steamroller	Includes the AMD Piledriver feature set and exposes additional CPU features, including XSAVEOPT RDFSBASE, RDGSBASE, WRFSBASE, WRGSBAS, and FSGSBASE.
B4	AMD Zen	Includes the AMD Steamroller feature set and exposes additional CPU features, including RDRAND, SMEP, AVX2, BMI2, MOVBE, ADX, RDSEED, SMAP, CLFLUSHOPT, XSAVES, XSAVEC, SHA, and CLZERO.
B5	AMD Zen 2	Includes the AMD Zen feature set and exposes additional CPU features, including CLWB, UMIP, RDPID, XGETBV with ECX = 1, WBNOINVD, and GMET.
B6	AMD Zen 3	Includes the AMD Zen 2 feature set and exposes additional CPU features, including always serializing LFENCE, INVPCID, PSFD, SSBD, PCID, PKU, VAES, VPCLMULQDQ, and shadow stacks.
B7	AMD Zen 4	Includes the AMD Zen 3 feature set and exposes additional CPU features, including Fast Short CMPSB and STOSB, Automatic IBRS, AVX512BF16, AVX512BITALG, AVX512BW, AVX512CD, AVX512DQ, AVX512F, AVX512IFMA, AVX512VBMI, AVX512VBMI2, AVX512VL, AVX512VNNI, AVX512VPOPCNTDQ, GFNI, IBRS, and Upper Address Ignore.

Starting with vSphere 7.0 Update 1, EVC provides a feature for Virtual Shared Graphics Acceleration (vSGA), allowing multiple virtual machines to share GPUs and leverage the 3D graphics acceleration capabilities.

vSAN Services

You can enable DRS, vSphere HA, and vSAN at the cluster level. The following sections provide details on DRS and vSphere HA. For details on vSAN, see Chapter 2.

Distributed Resource Scheduler (DRS)

DRS distributes compute workload in a cluster by strategically placing virtual machines during power-on operations and live migrating (vMotion) VMs when necessary. DRS provides many features and settings that enable you to control its behavior.

You can set DRS Automation Mode for a cluster to one of the following:

- **Manual**: DRS does not automatically place or migrate virtual machines. It only makes recommendations.

- **Partially Automated**: DRS automatically places virtual machines as they power on. It makes recommendations for virtual machine migrations.

- **Fully Automated**: DRS automatically places and migrates virtual machines.

You can override Automation Mode at the virtual machine level.

Recent DRS Enhancements

VMware added many improvements to DRS beginning with vSphere 6.5. For example, in vSphere 7.0, DRS runs once every minute rather than every 5 minutes, as in older DRS versions. The newer DRS versions tend to recommend smaller (in terms of memory) virtual machines for migration to facilitate faster vMotion migrations, whereas older versions tend to recommend large virtual machines to minimize the number of migrations. Older DRS versions use an imbalance metric that is derived from the standard deviation of load across the hosts in the cluster. Newer DRS versions focus on virtual machine happiness. Newer DRS versions are much lighter and faster than the older versions.

Newer DRS versions recognize that vMotion is an expensive operation and account for it in their recommendations. In a cluster where virtual machines are frequently powered on and the workload is volatile, it is not necessary to continuously migrate virtual machines. DRS calculates the gain duration for live migrating a virtual machine and considers the gain duration when making recommendations.

In vSphere 8.0, when PMEM is present, DRS performance can be improved by leveraging memory statistics to optimize VM placement.

The following sections provide details on other recent DRS enhancements.

Network-Aware DRS

In vSphere 6.5, DRS considers the utilization of host network adapters during initial placement and load balancing, but it does not balance the network load. Instead, its goal is to ensure that the target host has sufficient available network resources. It works by eliminating hosts with saturated networks from the list of possible migration hosts. The threshold used by DRS for network saturation is 80% by default. When DRS cannot migrate VMs due to network saturation, the result may be an imbalanced cluster.

Beginning with vSphere 7.0, DRS uses a new cost modeling algorithm that is flexible and balances network bandwidth along with CPU and memory usage.

Virtual Machine Distribution

Starting with vSphere 6.5, you can enable an option to distribute a more even number of virtual machines across hosts. The main use case for this is to improve availability. The primary goals of DRS—to ensure that all VMs are getting the resources they need and that the load is balanced in the cluster—remain unchanged. But with this new option enabled, DRS also tries to ensure that the number of virtual machines per host is balanced in the cluster.

Memory Metric for Load Balancing

Historically, vSphere has used the Active Memory metric for load-balancing decisions. In vSphere 6.5 and 6.7, you have the option to set DRS to balance the load based on the Consumed Memory metric. vSphere 7.0 and later do not support the option to change this behavior.

Virtual Machine Initial Placement

Starting with vSphere 6.5, DRS began to use a new initial placement algorithm that is faster, lighter, and more effective than the previous algorithm. In earlier versions, DRS takes a snapshot of the cluster state when making virtual machine placement recommendations. With the new algorithm, DRS does not snapshot the cluster state, which allows for more accurate recommendations and faster virtual machine power on. In vSphere 6.5, the new placement feature is not supported for the following configurations:

- Clusters where DPM, Proactive HA, or HA Admission Control is enabled

- Clusters with DRS configured in Manual Mode

- Virtual machines with the Manual DRS Override setting enabled

- Virtual machines that are FT enabled

- Virtual machines that are part of a vApp

In vSphere 6.7 and later, the new placement is available for all configurations.

Enhancements to the Evacuation Workflow

Prior to vSphere 6.5, when evacuating a host entering Maintenance Mode, DRS waited to migrate templates and power off virtual machines until after the completion of vMotion migrations, leaving those objects unavailable for use for a long time. Starting with vSphere 6.5, DRS prioritizes the migration of virtual machine templates and powered-off virtual machines over powered-on virtual machines, making those objects available for use without the need to wait on vMotion migrations.

Prior to vSphere 6.5, the evacuation of powered-off virtual machines was inefficient. In versions since vSphere 6.5, these evacuations occur in parallel, making use of up to 100 re-register threads per vCenter Server. This means that you may see only a small difference when evacuating up to 100 virtual machines.

In versions since vSphere 6.7, DRS is more efficient at evacuating powered-on virtual machines from a host that is entering Maintenance Mode. Instead of simultaneously initiating vMotion for all the powered-on VMs on the host, as in previous versions, DRS initiates vMotion migrations in batches of eight at a time. Each vMotion batch is issued after the previous batch completes. The vMotion batching makes the entire workflow more controlled and predictable.

DRS Support for NVM

In versions since vSphere 6.7, DRS supports virtual machines running on next-generation persistent memory devices, known as non-volatile memory (NVM) devices. NVM is exposed as a datastore that is local to the host. Virtual machines can use the datastore as an NVM device exposed to the guest (Virtual Persistent Memory [vPMem]) or as a location for a virtual machine disk (Virtual Persistent Memory Disk [vPMemDisk]). DRS is aware of the NVM devices used by virtual machines and guarantees that the destination ESXi host has enough free persistent memory to accommodate placements and migrations.

How DRS Scores VMs

Historically, DRS balanced the workload in a cluster based on host compute resource usage. In versions since vSphere 7.0, DRS balances the workload based on virtual machine happiness. A virtual machine's DRS score is a measure of its happiness, which, in turn, is a measure of the resources available for consumption by the virtual machine. The higher the DRS score for a VM, the better its resource availability. DRS moves virtual machines to improve their DRS scores. DRS also calculates a DRS score for a cluster, which is a weighted sum of the DRS scores of all the virtual machines in the cluster.

In versions since Sphere 7.0, DRS calculates the core for each virtual machine on each ESXi host in the cluster every minute. Simply put, DRS logic computes an ideal throughput (demand) and an actual throughput (goodness) for each resource (CPU, memory, and network) for each virtual machine. The virtual machine's efficiency for a particular resource is a ratio of the goodness over the demand. A virtual machine's DRS score (total efficiency) is the product of its CPU, memory, and network efficiencies.

When calculating the efficiency, DRS applies resource costs. For CPU resources, DRS includes costs for CPU cache, CPU ready, and CPU tax. For memory resources, DRS includes costs for memory burstiness, memory reclamation, and memory tax. For network resources, DRS includes a network utilization cost.

DRS compares a virtual machine's DRS score for the host on which it currently runs. DRS determines whether another host can provide a better DRS score for the virtual machine. If so, DRS calculates the cost for migrating the virtual machine to the host and factors that score into its load-balancing decision.

DRS Rules

You can configure rules to control the behavior of DRS.

A VM–host affinity rule specifies whether the members of a selected virtual machine DRS group can run on the members of a specific host DRS group. Unlike a virtual machine–to–virtual machine (VM–VM) affinity rule, which specifies affinity (or anti-affinity) between individual virtual machines, a VM–host affinity rule specifies an affinity relationship between a group of virtual machines and a group of hosts. There are *required* rules (designated by "must") and *preferential* rules (designated by "should").

A VM–host affinity rule includes the following components:

- One virtual machine DRS group

- One host DRS group

- A designation of whether the rule is a requirement ("must") or a preference ("should") and whether it is affinity ("run on") or anti-affinity ("not run on")

A VM–VM affinity rule specifies whether selected individual virtual machines should run on the same host or whether they should be kept on separate hosts. This type of rule is used to create affinity or anti-affinity between individual virtual machines. When an affinity rule is created, DRS tries to keep the specified virtual machines together on the same host. You might want to do this, for example, for performance reasons.

With an anti-affinity rule, DRS tries to keep the specified virtual machines apart. You can use such a rule if you want to guarantee that certain virtual machines are always on different physical hosts. In that case, if a problem occurs with one host, not all virtual machines are at risk. You can create VM–VM affinity rules to specify whether selected individual virtual machines should run on the same host or be kept on separate hosts.

VM–VM affinity rule conflicts can occur when you use multiple VM–VM affinity and VM–VM anti-affinity rules. If two VM–VM affinity rules are in conflict, you cannot enable both of them. For example, if one rule keeps two virtual machines together and another rule keeps the same two virtual machines apart, you cannot enable both rules. Select one of the rules to apply and disable or remove the conflicting rule. When two VM–VM affinity rules conflict, the older one takes precedence, and the newer rule is disabled. DRS tries to satisfy only enabled rules and ignores disabled rules. DRS gives higher precedence to preventing violations of anti-affinity rules than violations of affinity rules.

NOTE A VM–VM rule does not allow the "should" qualifier. You should consider these as "must" rules.

DRS Migration Sensitivity

Prior to vSphere 7.0, DRS used a migration threshold to determine when virtual machines should be migrated to balance the cluster workload. In vSphere 7.0 and newer, DRS is designed to be more virtual machine centric and workload centric rather than cluster centric. You can set the DRS Migration Sensitivity parameter to one of the following values:

- **Level 1**: DRS only makes recommendations to fix rule violations or to facilitate a host entering Maintenance Mode.

- **Level 2**: DRS expands on Level 1 by making recommendations in situations that are at or close to resource contention. It does not make recommendations just to improve virtual machine happiness or cluster load distribution.

- **Level 3**: DRS expands on Level 2 by making recommendations to improve VM happiness and cluster load distribution. This is the default level.

- **Level 4**: DRS expands on Level 3 by making recommendations for occasional bursts in the workload and reacts to sudden load changes.

- **Level 5**: DRS expands on Level 4 by making recommendations dynamic and greatly varying workloads. DRS reacts to the workload changes every time.

Resource Pools

Resource pools are container objects in the vSphere inventory that are used to compartmentalize the CPU and memory resources of a host, a cluster, or a parent resource pool. Virtual machines run in and draw resources from resource pools. You can create multiple resource pools as direct children of a standalone host or a DRS cluster. You cannot create child resource pools on a host that has been added to a cluster or on a cluster that is not enabled for DRS.

You can use resource pools to organize VMs. You can delegate control over each resource pool to specific individuals and groups. You can monitor resources and set alarms on resource pools. If you need a container just for organization and permission purposes, consider using a folder. If you also need resource management, then consider using a resource pool. You can assign resource settings such as shares, reservations, and limits to resource pools.

Use Cases

You can use resource pools to compartmentalize a cluster's resources and then use the resource pools to delegate control to individuals or organizations. Table 4-4 provides some use cases for resource pools.

Table 4-4 Resource Pool Use Cases

Use Case	Details
Flexible hierarchical organization	Add, remove, modify, and reorganize resource pools, as needed.
Resource isolation	Use resource pools to allocate resources to separate departments, in such a manner that changes in a pool do not unfairly impact other departments.
Access control and delegation	Use permissions to delegate activities, such as virtual machine creation and management, to other administrators.
Separation of resources from hardware	In a DRS cluster, perform resource management independently of the actual hosts.
Managing multitier applications	Manage the resources for a group of virtual machines (in a specific resource pool), which is easier than managing resources per virtual machine.

Shares, Limits, and Reservations

You can configure CPU and memory shares, reservations, and limits on resource pools, as described in Table 4-5.

Table 4-5 Shares, Limits, and Reservations

Option	Description
Shares	Shares specify the relative importance of a virtual machine or a resource pool. If a virtual machine has twice as many shares of a resource as another virtual machine, it is entitled to consume twice as much of that resource when these two virtual machines are competing for resources. Shares can be thought of as priority under contention.
	Shares are typically set to High, Normal, or Low, and these values specify share values with a 4:2:1 ratio. You can also select Custom and assign a specific number of shares (to express a proportional weight).
	A resource pool uses its shares to compete for the parent's resources and is allocated a portion based on the ratio of the pool's shares compared with its siblings. Siblings share the parent's resources according to their relative share values, bounded by the reservation and limit.
	For example, consider a scenario where a cluster has two child resource pools with normal CPU shares, another child resource pool with high CPU shares, and no other child objects. During periods of contention, each of the pools with normal shares would get access to 25% of the cluster's CPU resources, and the pool with high shares would get access to 50%.
Reservations	A reservation specifies the guaranteed minimum allocation for a virtual machine or a resource pool. A CPU reservation is expressed in megahertz, and a memory reservation is expressed in megabytes. You can power on a virtual machine only if there are enough unreserved resources to satisfy the reservation of the virtual machine. If the virtual machine starts, then it is guaranteed that amount, even when the physical server is heavily loaded.
	For example, if you configure the CPU reservation for each virtual machine as 1 GHz, you can start eight VMs in a resource pool where the CPU reservation is set for 8 GHz and expandable reservations are disabled. But you cannot start additional virtual machines in the pool.
	You can use reservations to guarantee a specific amount of resources for a resource pool. The default value for a resource pool's CPU or memory reservation is 0. If you change this value, it is subtracted from the unreserved resources of the parent. The resources are considered reserved, regardless of whether virtual machines are associated with the resource pool.

Option	Description
Expandable reservations	You can enable expandable reservations to effectively allow a child resource pool to borrow from its parent. Expandable reservations, which are enabled by default, are considered during admission control. When powering on a virtual machine, if the resource pool does not have sufficient unreserved resources, the resource pool can use resources from its parent or ancestors. For example, say that in a resource pool where 8 GHz is reserved and expandable reservations are disabled, you try to start nine virtual machines each with 1 GHz, but the last virtual machine does not start. If you enable expandable reservations in the resource pool, and its parent pool (or cluster) has sufficient unreserved CPU resources, you can start the ninth virtual machine.
Limits	A limit specifies an upper bound for CPU or memory resources that can be allocated to a virtual machine or a resource pool. You can set a limit on the amount of CPU and memory allocated to a resource pool. The default is unlimited. For example, if you power on multiple CPU-intensive virtual machines in a resource pool, where the CPU limit is 10 GHz, then, collectively, the virtual machines cannot use more than 10 GHz CPU resources, regardless of the pool's reservation settings, the pool's share settings, or the amount of available resources in the parent.

Table 4-6 provides the CPU and memory share values for virtual machines when using the High, Normal, and Low settings. For resource pools, the share values are equivalent to those of a virtual machine with four vCPUs and 16 GB memory.

Table 4-6   Virtual Machine Shares

Setting	CPU Share Value	Memory Share Value
High	2000 per vCPU	20 per MB
Normal	1000 per vCPU	10 per MB
Low	500 per vCPU	5 per MB

For example, the share values for a resource pool configured with normal CPU shares and high memory shares are 4000 (that is, 4×1000) CPU shares and 327,680 (that is, $16 \times 1024 \times 20$) memory shares.

NOTE   The relative priority represented by each share changes with the addition and removal of virtual machines in a resource pool or cluster. It also changes as you increase or decrease the shares on a specific virtual machine or resource pool.

Enhanced Resource Pool Reservation

In versions since vSphere 6.7, DRS uses a two-pass algorithm to allocate resource reservations to children. The old allocation model does not reserve more resources than the current demand, even when the resource pool is configured with a higher reservation. When a spike in virtual machine demand occurs after resource allocation is complete, DRS does not make the remaining pool reservation available to the virtual machine until the next allocation operation occurs. As a result, a virtual machine's performance may be temporarily impacted. In the new allocation model, each allocation operation uses two passes. In the first pass, the resource pool reservation is allocated based on virtual machine demand. In the second pass, excess pool reservation is allocated proportionally, limited by the virtual machine's configured size, which reduces the performance impact due to virtual machine spikes.

Scalable Shares

In versions since vSphere 7.0, DRS provides scalable shares. The main use case for scalable shares is a scenario in which you want to use shares to give high-priority resource access to a set of virtual machines in a resource pool, without concern for the relative number of objects in the pool compared to other pools. With standard shares, each pool in a cluster competes for resource allocation with its siblings, based on the share ratio. With scalable shares, the allocation for each pool factors in the number of objects in the pool.

For example, consider a scenario in which a cluster with 100 GHz CPU capacity has a high-priority resource pool with CPU Shares set to High and a low-priority resource pool with CPU Shares set to Normal, as shown in Figure 4-1. This means that the share ratio between the pools is 2:1, so the high-priority pool is effectively allocated twice the CPU resources as the low-priority pool whenever CPU contention exists in the cluster. The high-priority pool is allocated 66.7 GHz, and the low-priority pool is effectively allocated 33.3 GHz. In this cluster, 40 virtual machines of equal size are running, with 32 in the high-priority pool and 8 in the low-priority pool. The virtual machines are all demanding CPU resources, causing CPU contention in the cluster. In the high-priority pool, each virtual machine is allocated 2.1 GHz. In the low-priority pool, each virtual machine is allocated 4.2 GHz.

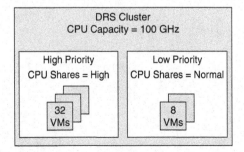

Figure 4-1   Scalable Shares Example

If you want to change the resource allocation such that each virtual machine in the high-priority pool is effectively allocated more resources than the virtual machines in the low-priority pool, you can use scalable shares. If you enable scalable shares in the cluster, DRS effectively allocates resources to the pools based on the Shares settings and the number of virtual machines in the pool. In this example, the CPU shares for the pools provide a 2:1 ratio. Factoring this with the number of virtual machines in each pool, the allocation ratio between the high-priority pool and the low-priority pool is 2 times 32 to 1 times 8, or simply 8:1. The high-priority pool is allocated 88.9 GHz, and the low-priority pool is allocated 11.1 GHz. Each virtual machine in the high-priority pool is allocated 2.8 GHz. Each virtual machine in the low-priority pool is allocated 1.4 GHz.

vSphere High Availability (HA)

vSphere HA is a cluster service that provides high availability for the virtual machines running in the cluster. You can enable vSphere High Availability (HA) on a vSphere cluster to provide rapid recovery from outages and cost-effective high availability for applications running in virtual machines. vSphere HA provides application availability in the following ways:

- It protects against server failure by restarting the virtual machines on other hosts in the cluster when a host failure is detected, as illustrated in Figure 4-2.

- It protects against application failure by continuously monitoring a virtual machine and resetting it if a failure is detected.

- It protects against datastore accessibility failures by restarting affected virtual machines on other hosts that still have access to their datastores.

- It protects virtual machines against network isolation by restarting them if their host becomes isolated on the management or vSAN network. This protection is provided even if the network has become partitioned.

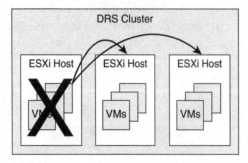

Figure 4-2 vSphere HA Host Failover

Benefits of vSphere HA over traditional failover solutions include the following:

- Minimal configuration

- Reduced hardware cost

- Increased application availability

- DRS and vMotion integration

vSphere HA can detect the following types of host issues:

- **Failure**: A host stops functioning.

- **Isolation**: A host cannot communicate with any other hosts in the cluster.

- **Partition**: A host loses network connectivity with the primary host.

When you enable vSphere HA on a cluster, the cluster elects one of the hosts to act as the primary host. The primary host communicates with vCenter Server to report cluster health. It monitors the state of all protected virtual machines and secondary hosts. It uses network and datastore heartbeating to detect failed hosts, isolation, and network partitions. vSphere HA takes appropriate actions to respond to host failures, host isolation, and network partitions. For host failures, the typical reaction is to restart the failed virtual machines on surviving hosts in the cluster. If a network partition occurs, a primary host is elected in each partition. If a specific host is isolated, vSphere HA takes the predefined host isolation action, which may be to shut down or power down the host's virtual machines. If the primary host fails, the surviving hosts elect a new primary host. You can configure vSphere to monitor and respond to virtual machine failures, such as guest OS failures, by monitoring heartbeats from VMware Tools.

NOTE Although vCenter Server is required to implement vSphere HA, the health of an HA cluster is not dependent on vCenter Server. If vCenter Server fails, vSphere HA still functions. If vCenter Server is offline when a host fails, vSphere HA can fail over the affected virtual machines.

vSphere HA Requirements

When planning a vSphere HA cluster, you need to address the following requirements:

- The cluster must have at least two hosts, licensed for vSphere HA.

- Hosts must use static IP addresses or guarantee that IP addresses assigned by DHCP persist across host reboots.

- Each host must have at least one—and preferably two—management networks in common.

- To ensure that virtual machines can run any host in the cluster, the hosts must access the same networks and datastores.

- To use VM Monitoring, you need to install VMware Tools in each virtual machine.

- IPv4 or IPv6 can be used.

NOTE   The Virtual Machine Startup and Shutdown (automatic startup) feature is disabled and unsupported for all virtual machines residing in a vSphere HA cluster.

vSphere HA Response to Failures

You can configure how a vSphere HA cluster should respond to different types of failures, as described in Table 4-7.

Table 4-7   vSphere HA Response to Failure Settings

Option	Description
Host Failure Response > Failure Response	If Enabled, the cluster responds to host failures by restarting virtual machines. If Disabled, host monitoring is turned off, and the cluster does not respond to host failures.
Host Failure Response > Default VM Restart Priority	You can indicate the order in which virtual machines are restarted when the host fails (higher-priority machines first).
Host Failure Response > VM Restart Priority Condition	The restart priority condition must be met before HA restarts the next priority group.
Response for Host Isolation	You can indicate the action that you want to occur if a host becomes isolated. You can choose Disabled, Shutdown and Restart VMs, or Power Off and Restart VMs.
VM Monitoring	You can indicate the sensitivity (Low, High, or Custom) with which vSphere HA responds to lost VMware Tools heartbeats.
Application Monitoring	You can indicate the sensitivity (Low, High, or Custom) with which vSphere HA responds to lost application heartbeats.

NOTE   If multiple hosts fail, the virtual machines on the failed host migrate first in order of priority, and then the virtual machines from the next host migrate.

Heartbeats

The primary host and secondary hosts exchange network heartbeats every second. When the primary host stops receiving these heartbeats from a secondary host, it checks for ping responses or the presence of datastore heartbeats from the secondary host. If the primary host does not receive a response after checking for a secondary host's network heartbeat, ping, or datastore heartbeats, it declares that the secondary host has failed. If the primary host detects datastore heartbeats for a secondary host but no network heartbeats or ping responses, it assumes that the secondary host is isolated or in a network partition.

If any host is running but no longer observes network heartbeats, it attempts to ping the set of cluster isolation addresses. If those pings also fail, the host declares itself to be isolated from the network.

vSphere HA Admission Control

vSphere uses admission control when you power on a virtual machine. It checks the amount of unreserved compute resources and determines whether it can guarantee that any reservation configured for the virtual machine is configured. If so, it allows the virtual machine to power on. Otherwise, it generates an "Insufficient Resources" warning.

vSphere HA Admission Control is a setting that you can use to specify whether virtual machines can be started if they violate availability constraints. The cluster reserves resources so that failover can occur for all running virtual machines on the specified number of hosts. When you configure vSphere HA admission control, you can set the options described in Table 4-8.

Table 4-8   vSphere HA Admission Control Options

Option	Description
Host Failures Cluster Tolerates	Specifies the maximum number of host failures for which the cluster guarantees failover
Define Host Failover Capacity By set to Cluster Resource Percentage	Specifies the percentage of the cluster's compute resources to reserve as spare capacity to support failovers
Define Host Failover Capacity By set to Slot Policy (for powered-on VMs)	Specifies a slot size policy that covers all powered-on VMs
Define Host Failover Capacity By set to Dedicated Failover Hosts	Specifies the designated hosts to use for failover actions
Define Host Failover Capacity By set to Disabled	Disables admission control
Performance Degradation VMs Tolerate	Specifies the percentage of performance degradation the VMs in a cluster are allowed to tolerate during a failure

If you disable vSphere HA admission control, then you enable the cluster to allow virtual machines to power on regardless of whether they violate availability constraints. In the event of a host failover, you may discover that vSphere HA cannot start some virtual machines.

In vSphere 8.0, the default admission control setting is Cluster Resource Percentage, which reserves a percentage of the total available CPU and memory resources in the cluster. For simplicity, the percentage is calculated automatically by defining the number of host failures to tolerate (FTT). The percentage is dynamically changed as hosts are added to the cluster or removed from it. Another new enhancement is the Performance Degradation VMs Tolerate setting, which controls the amount of performance reduction that is tolerated after a failure. A value of 0% indicates that no performance degradation is tolerated.

With the Slot Policy option, vSphere HA admission control ensures that a specified number of hosts can fail, leaving sufficient resources in the cluster to accommodate the failover of the impacted virtual machines. Using the Slot Policy option, when you perform certain operations, such as powering on a virtual machine, vSphere HA applies admission control in the following manner:

Step 1.   HA calculates the slot size, which is a logical representation of memory and CPU resources. By default, it is sized to satisfy the requirements for any powered-on virtual machine in the cluster. For example, it may be sized to accommodate the virtual machine with the greatest CPU reservation and the virtual machine with the greatest memory reservation.

Step 2.   HA determines how many slots each host in the cluster can hold.

Step 3.   HA determines the current failover capacity of the cluster, which is the number of hosts that can fail while still leaving enough slots to satisfy all the powered-on virtual machines.

Step 4.   HA determines whether the current failover capacity is less than the configured failover capacity (provided by the user).

Step 5.   If the current failover capacity is less than the configured failover capacity, admission control disallows the operation.

If a cluster has a few virtual machines that have much larger reservations than the others, they will distort slot size calculation. To remediate this, you can specify an upper bound for the CPU or memory component of the slot size by using advanced options. You can also set a specific slot size (CPU size and memory size). The next section describes the advanced options that affect the slot size.

vSphere HA Advanced Options

You can set vSphere HA advanced options by using the vSphere Client or in the fdm.cfg file on the hosts. Table 4-9 provides some of the advanced vSphere HA options.

Table 4-9 Advanced vSphere HA Options

Option	Description
das.isolationaddress$X$	Provides the addresses to use to test for host isolation when no heartbeats are received from other hosts in the cluster. If this option is not specified (which is the default setting), the management network default gateway is used to test for isolation. To specify multiple addresses, you can set das.isolationaddress$X$, where X is a number between 0 and 9.
das.usedefaultisolationaddress	Specifies whether to use the default gateway IP address for isolation tests.
das.isolationshutdowntimeout	For scenarios where the host's isolation response is to shut down, specifies the period of time that the virtual machine is permitted to shut down before the system powers it off.
das.slotmeminmb	Defines the maximum bound on the memory slot size.
das.slotcpuinmhz	Defines the maximum bound on the CPU slot size.
das.vmmemoryminmb	Defines the default memory resource value assigned to a virtual machine whose memory reservation is not specified or is zero. This is used for the Host Failures Cluster Tolerates admission control policy.
das.vmcpuminmhz	Defines the default CPU resource value assigned to a virtual machine whose CPU reservation is not specified or is zero. This is used for the Host Failures Cluster Tolerates admission control policy. If no value is specified, the default of 32 MHz is used.
das.heartbeatdsperhost	Specifies the number of heartbeat datastores required per host. The default is 2. The acceptable values are 2 to 5.
das.config.fdm. isolationPolicyDelaySec	Specifies the number of seconds the system delays before executing the isolation policy after determining that a host is isolated. The minimum is 30. A lower value results in a 30-second delay.
das.respectvmvmantiaffinityrules	Determines whether vSphere HA should enforce VM–VM anti-affinity rules even when DRS is not enabled.

Virtual Machine Settings

To use the Host Isolation Response Shutdown and Restart VMs setting, you must install VMware Tools on the virtual machine. If a guest OS fails to shut down in 300 seconds (or a value specified by das.isolationshutdowntimeout), the virtual machine is powered off.

You can override the cluster's settings for Restart Priority and Isolation Response for each virtual machine. For example, you might want to prioritize virtual machines providing infrastructure services such as DNS or DHCP.

At the cluster level, you can create dependencies between groups of virtual machines. You can create VM groups, host groups, and dependency rules between the groups. In the rules, you can specify that one VM group cannot be restarted if another specific VM group is started.

VM Component Protection (VMCP)

Virtual Machine Component Protection (VMCP) is a vSphere HA feature that can detect datastore accessibility issues and provide remediation for affected virtual machines. When a failure occurs such that a host can no longer access the storage path for a specific datastore, vSphere HA can respond by taking actions such as creating event alarms or restarting a virtual machine on other hosts. The main requirements are that vSphere HA is enabled in the cluster and that ESX 6.0 or later is used on all hosts in the cluster.

The failures VMCP detects are permanent device loss (PDL) and all paths down (APD). PDL is an unrecoverable loss of accessibility to the storage device that cannot be fixed without powering down the virtual machines. APD is a transient accessibility loss or other issue that is recoverable.

For PDL and APD failures, you can set VMCP to either issue event alerts or to power off and restart virtual machines. For APD failures only, you can additionally control the restart policy for virtual machines by setting it to Conservative or Aggressive. With the Conservative setting, the virtual machine is powered off only if HA determines that it can be restarted on another host. With the Aggressive setting, HA powers off the virtual machine regardless of the state of other hosts.

Virtual Machine and Application Monitoring

VM Monitoring restarts specific virtual machines if their VMware Tools heartbeats are not received within a specified time. Likewise, Application Monitoring can restart a virtual machine if the heartbeats from a specific application in the virtual machine are not received. If you enable these features, you can configure the monitoring settings to control the failure interval and reset period. Table 4-10 lists these settings.

Table 4-10 VM Monitoring Settings

Setting	Failure Interval	Reset Period
High	30 seconds	1 hour
Medium	60 seconds	24 hours
Low	120 seconds	7 days

The Maximum per-VM Resets setting can be used to configure the maximum number of times vSphere HA attempts to restart a specific failing virtual machine within the reset period.

vSphere HA Best Practices

You should provide network path redundancy between cluster nodes. To do so, you can use NIC teaming for the virtual switch. You can also create a second management network connection, using a separate virtual switch.

When performing disruptive network maintenance operations on the network used by clustered ESXi hosts, you should suspend the Host Monitoring feature to ensure that vSphere HA does not falsely detect network isolation or host failures. You can reenable host monitoring after completing the work.

To keep vSphere HA agent traffic on the specified network, you should ensure that the VMkernel virtual network adapters used for HA heartbeats (enabled for management traffic) do not share the same subnet as VMkernel adapters used for vMotion and other purposes.

You use the das.isolationaddress.X advanced option to add an isolation address for each management network.

Proactive HA

Proactive High Availability (Proactive HA) integrates with select hardware partners to detect degraded components and evacuate VMs from affected vSphere hosts before an incident causes a service interruption. Hardware partners offer a vCenter Server plug-in to provide the health status of the system memory, local storage, power supplies, cooling fans, and network adapters. As hardware components become degraded, Proactive HA determines which hosts are at risk and places them into either Quarantine Mode or Maintenance Mode. When a host enters Maintenance Mode, DRS evacuates its virtual machines to healthy hosts, and the host is not used to run virtual machines. When a host enters Quarantine Mode, DRS leaves the current virtual machines running on the host but avoids placing or migrating virtual machines to the host. If you prefer that Proactive HA simply make evacuation recommendations rather than automatic migrations, you can set Automation Level to Manual.

The vendor-provided health providers read sensor data in the server and provide the health state to vCenter Server. The health states are Healthy, Moderate Degradation, Severe Degradation, and Unknown.

Other Resource Management and Availability Features

This section describes other vSphere features related to resource management and availability.

Predictive DRS

Predictive DRS is a feature in vSphere 6.5 and later that leverages the predictive analytics of VMware Aria Operations, formerly known as vRealize Operations (vROps), and vSphere DRS. Together, these two products can provide workload balancing prior to the occurrence of resource utilization spikes and resource contention. Every night, Aria Operations calculates dynamic thresholds, which are used to create forecasted metrics for the future utilization of virtual machines. Aria Operations passes the predictive metrics to vSphere DRS to determine the best placement and balance of virtual machines before resource utilization spikes occur. Predictive DRS helps prevent resource contention on hosts that run virtual machines with predictable utilization patterns.

The following prerequisites are needed to run Predictive DRS:

- vCenter Server 6.5 or later is required.
- Predictive DRS must be configured and enabled in both vCenter Server and Aria Operations.
- The vCenter Server and Aria Operations clocks must be synchronized.

Distributed Power Management (DPM)

The vSphere Distributed Power Management (DPM) feature enables a DRS cluster to reduce its power consumption by powering hosts on and off, as needed, based on cluster resource utilization. DPM monitors the cumulative virtual machine demand for memory and CPU resources in the cluster and compares this to the available resources in the cluster. If sufficient excess capacity is found, vSphere DPM directs the host to enter Standby Mode. When DRS detects that a host is entering Standby Mode, it evacuates the virtual machines. Once the host is evacuated, DPM powers it off, and the host is in Standby Mode. When DPM determines that capacity is inadequate to meet the resource demand, DPM brings a host out of Standby Mode by powering it on. Once the host exits Standby Mode, DRS migrates virtual machines to it.

To power on a host, DPM can use one of three power management protocols: Intelligent Platform Management Interface (IPMI), Hewlett-Packard Integrated Lights-Out (iLO), or Wake-on-LAN (WoL). If a host supports multiple protocols, they are used in the following order: IPMI, iLO, WOL. If a host does not support one of these protocols, DPM cannot automatically bring a host out of Standby Mode.

DPM is very configurable. As with DRS, you can set DPM's automation to be manual or automatic.

NOTE Do not disconnect a host that is in Standby Mode or remove it from a DRS cluster without first powering it on. Otherwise, vCenter Server is not able to power the host back on.

To configure IPMI or iLO settings for a host, you can edit the host's Power Management settings. You should provide credentials for the Baseboard Management Controller (BMC) account, the IP address of the appropriate NIC, and the MAC address of the NIC.

Using WOL with DPM requires that the following prerequisites be met:

- ESXi 3.5 or later is required.

- vMotion must be configured.

- The vMotion NIC must support WOL.

- The physical switch port must be set to automatically negotiate the link speed.

Before enabling DPM, use the vSphere Client to request the host to enter Standby Mode. After the host powers down, right-click the host and attempt to power on. If this is successful, you can allow the host to participate in DPM. Otherwise, you should disable power management for the host.

You can enable DPM in a DRS cluster's settings. You can set Automation Level to Off, Manual, or Automatic. When this option is set to Off, DPM is disabled. When it is set to Manual, DPM makes recommendations only. When it is set to Automatic, DPM automatically performs host power operations as needed.

Much as with DRS, with DPM you can control the aggressiveness of DPM (that is, the DPM threshold) with a slider bar in the vSphere Client. The DRS threshold and the DPM threshold are independent of one another. You can override automation settings per host. For example, for a 16-host cluster, you might want to set DPM Automation to Automatic on only 8 of the hosts.

Fault Tolerance (FT)

If you have virtual machines that require continuous availability as opposed to high availability, you can consider protecting the virtual machines with *vSphere Fault*

Tolerance (FT). vSphere FT provides continuous availability for a virtual machine (the primary VM) by ensuring that the state of a secondary VM is identical at any point in the instruction execution of the virtual machine.

If the host running the primary VM fails, an immediate and transparent failover occurs. The secondary VM becomes the primary VM host without losing network connection or in-progress transactions. With transparent failover, there is no data loss, and network connections are maintained. The failover is fully automated and occurs even if vCenter Server is unavailable. Following the failover, FT spawns a new secondary VM and reestablishes redundancy and protection, assuming that a host with sufficient resources is available in the cluster. Likewise, if the host running the secondary VM fails, a new secondary VM is deployed. vSphere Fault Tolerance can accommodate symmetric multiprocessor (SMP) virtual machines with up to eight vCPUs.

Use cases for FT include the following:

- Applications that require continuous availability, especially those with long-lasting client connections that need to be maintained during hardware failure

- Custom applications that have no other way of being clustered

- Cases in which other clustering solutions are available but are too complicated or expensive to configure and maintain

Before implementing FT, consider the following requirements:

- CPUs must be vMotion compatible.

- CPUs must support hardware MMU virtualization.

- A low-latency 10 Gbps network is required for FT Logging.

- Virtual machine files other than VMDK files must be stored on shared storage.

- A vSphere Standard License is required for FT protection of virtual machines with up to two virtual CPUs.

- A vSphere Enterprise Plus License is required for FT protection of virtual machines with up to eight virtual CPUs.

- Hardware Virtualization (HV) must be enabled in the host BIOS.

- Hosts must be certified for FT.

- The virtual memory reservation should be set to match the memory size.

- vSphere HA must be enabled on the cluster.

- SSL certificate checking must be enabled in the vCenter Server settings.

- The hosts must use ESXi 6.x or later.

You should also consider the following VMware recommendations concerning vSphere FT:

- VMware recommends a minimum of two physical NICs.

- VMware recommends that the host BIOS power management settings be set to Maximum Performance or OS-Managed Performance.

- You should have at least three hosts in the cluster to accommodate a new secondary VM following a failover.

The following vSphere features are not supported for FT-protected virtual machines:

- Snapshots (An exception is that disk-only snapshots created for vStorage APIs for Data Protection [VADP] backups are supported for FT but not for legacy FT.)

- Storage vMotion

- Linked clones

- Virtual Volumes datastores

- Storage-based policy management (However, vSAN storage policies are supported.)

- I/O filters

- Disk encryption

- Trusted Platform Module (TPM)

- Virtual Based Security (VBS)–enabled VMs

- Universal Point in Time snapshots (a next-generation vSAN feature)

- Physical raw device mappings (RDMs) (However, virtual RDMs are supported for legacy FT.)

- Virtual CD-ROMs for floppy drives backed by physical devices

- USB devices, sound devices, serial ports, and parallel ports

    - N-Port ID Virtualization (NPIV)

- Network adapter passthrough

- Hot plugging devices (Note that the hot plug feature is automatically disabled when you enable FT on a virtual machine.)

- Changing the network where a virtual NIC is connected

- Virtual Machine Communication Interface (VMCI)

- Virtual disk files larger than 2 TB

- Video devices with 3D enabled

You should apply the following best practices for FT:

- Use similar CPU frequencies in the hosts.

- Use active/standby NIC teaming settings.

- Ensure that the FT Logging network is secure (that is, FT data is not encrypted).

- Enable jumbo frames and 10 Gbps for the FT network. Optionally, configure multiple NICs for FT Logging.

- Place ISO files on shared storage.

- If vSAN is used for primary or secondary VMs, do not also connect those virtual machines to other storage types. Also, place the primary and secondary VMs in separate vSAN fault domains.

- Keep vSAN and FT Logging on separate networks.

In vSphere 6.5, FT is supported with DRS only when EVC is enabled. You can assign a DRS automation to the primary VM and let the secondary VM assume the same setting. If you enable FT for a virtual machine in a cluster where EVC is disabled, the virtual machine DRS automation level is automatically disabled. In versions since vSphere 6.7, EVC is not required for FT to support DRS.

To enable FT, you first create a VMkernel virtual network adapter on each host and connect to the FT Logging network. You should enable vMotion on a separate VMkernel adapter and network.

When you enable FT protection for a virtual machine, the following events occur:

- If the primary VM is powered on, validation tests occur. If validation is passed, then the entire state of the primary VM is copied and used to create the secondary VM on a separate host. The secondary VM is powered on. The virtual machine's FT status is Protected.

- If the primary VM is powered off, the secondary VM is created and registered to a host in the cluster but not powered on. The virtual machine FT Status setting is Not Protected, VM not Running. When you power on the primary VM, the validation checks occur, and the secondary VM is powered on. Then FT Status changes to Protected.

Legacy FT VMs can exist only on ESXi hosts running on vSphere versions earlier than 6.5. If you require legacy FT, you should configure a separate vSphere 6.0 cluster.

vCenter Server High Availability

vCenter Server High Availability (vCenter HA) is described in Chapter 1, "vSphere Overview, Components, and Requirements." vCenter HA implementation is covered in Chapter 8, "vSphere Installation." vCenter HA management is covered in Chapter 13, "Managing vSphere and vCenter Server."

VMware Service Lifecyle Manager

If a vCenter service fails, *VMware Service Lifecycle Manager* (vmon) restarts it. VMware Service Lifecycle Manager is a service that runs in a vCenter server that monitors the health of services and takes preconfigured remediation action when it detects a failure. If multiple attempts to restart a service fail, the service is considered failed.

NOTE Do not confuse VMware Service Lifecyle Manager with VMware vSphere Lifecycle Manager, which provides simple, centralized lifecycle management for ESXi hosts through the use of images and baselines.

Exam Preparation Tasks

As mentioned in the section "Book Features and Exam Preparation Methods" in the Introduction, you have some choices for exam preparation: the exercises here, Chapter 15, "Final Preparation," and the exam simulation questions on the companion website.

Review All Key Topics

Review the most important topics in this chapter, noted with the Key Topic icon in the outer margin of the page. Table 4-11 lists these key topics and the page number on which each is found.

Table 4-11   Key Topics for Chapter 4

Key Topic Element	Description	Page Number
Section	Network-aware DRS	140
Section	How DRS scores VMs	142
List	DRS migration sensitivity	143
Section	Scalable shares	147
List	vSphere HA requirements	149
Table 4-7	vSphere HA response to failure settings	150
List	vSphere FT requirements	158

Complete Tables and Lists from Memory

Print a copy of Appendix B, "Memory Tables" (found on the companion website), or at least the section for this chapter, and complete the tables and lists from memory. Appendix C, "Memory Table Answers" (also on the companion website), includes completed tables and lists to check your work.

Define Key Terms

Define the following key terms from this chapter and check your answers in the glossary:

Virtual Machine Component Protection (VMCP), Proactive High Availability (Proactive HA), Predictive DRS, vSphere Fault Tolerance (FT), VMware Service Lifecycle Manager

Review Questions

1. You are configuring EVC. Which of the following is not a requirement?

    a. A vSphere cluster

    b. A DRS cluster

    c. CPUs in the same family

    d. CPUs with the same base instruction set

2. In vSphere 8.0, you want to configure the DRS migration threshold such that it is at the maximum level at which resource contention is considered but virtual machine happiness is not. Which of the following values should you choose?

    a. Level 1

    b. Level 2

    c. Level 3

    d. Level 4

    e. Level 5

3. In a vSphere cluster, which of the following statements is true if the primary host detects datastore heartbeats for a secondary host but no network heartbeats or ping responses?

    a. The primary host declares that the secondary host is isolated.

    b. The primary host assumes that the secondary host is isolated or in a network partition.

    c. The primary host takes the host isolation response action.

    d. The primary host restarts the virtual machines on the failed secondary host.

4. You want to configure vSphere HA. Which of the following is a requirement?

    a. IPv4 must be used for all host management interfaces.

    b. vMotion must be enabled on each host.

    c. The Virtual Machine Startup and Shutdown (automatic startup) feature must be enabled on each virtual machine.

    d. Host IP addresses must persist across reboots.

5. You are configuring vSphere Distributed Power Management (DPM) in your vSphere 8.0 environment. Which of the following is not a requirement for using Wake-on-LAN (WoL) in DPM?

    a. The management NIC must support WOL.

    b. vMotion is configured.

    c. The vMotion NIC must support WOL.

    d. The physical switch port must be set to auto negotiate the link speed.

This chapter covers the following topics:

- vCenter Server and vSphere

- Virtual Machine File Structure

- Virtual Machine Snapshots

- Virtual Machine Settings

- Virtual Machine Migration

- Virtual Machine Cloning

This chapter contains information related to VMware vSphere 8.x Professional (2V0-21.23) exam objectives 1.2, 1.12, 4.8, 5.7, 7.1, 7.2, 7.3, 7.6, 7.6.1, 7.8, and 7.9.4.

vCenter Server Features and Virtual Machines

This chapter provides details on vCenter Server features that have not been covered in previous chapters. It covers virtual machine features such as file structure, migrations, and cloning. Chapters 13, "Managing vSphere and vCenter Server," and 14, "Managing Virtual Machines," provide details on managing vCenter Server, vSphere, and virtual machines.

"Do I Know This Already?" Quiz

The "Do I Know This Already?" quiz allows you to assess whether you should study this entire chapter or move quickly to the "Exam Preparation Tasks" section. In any case, the authors recommend that you read the entire chapter at least once. Table 5-1 outlines the major headings in this chapter and the corresponding "Do I Know This Already?" quiz questions. You can find the answers in Appendix A, "Answers to the 'Do I Know This Already?' Quizzes and Review Questions."

Table 5-1 "Do I Know This Already?" Foundation Topics Section-to-Question Mapping

Foundation Topics Section	Questions
vCenter Server and vSphere	1, 2
Virtual Machine File Structure	3
Virtual Machine Snapshots	4
Virtual Machine Settings	5, 6
Virtual Machine Migration	7–9
Virtual Machine Cloning	10

1. You just installed a new vCenter Server. Using the vSphere Client, which of the following objects can be the first object that you create in the inventory?

    a. A cluster

    b. A host

    c. A virtual machine

    d. A data center

    e. A datastore

    f. A virtual machine folder

2. You want to create a content library for your vCenter Server. Which type of content library cannot be modified directly?

    a. A library backed by vSAN

    b. A local library

    c. A published library

    d. A subscribed library

3. You are providing support for a virtual machine named Server01 in a vSphere 8.0 environment. Which of the following is the virtual disk data file?

    a. Server01.vmdk

    b. Server01-flat.vmdk

    c. Server01.vmx

    d. Server01-data.vmdk

4. You have taken multiple snapshots for a virtual machine. In the vSphere Client Snapshot Manager, where is the You Are Here icon located?

    a. Under the parent snapshot

    b. Under the child snapshot

    c. Under the latest snapshot

    d. Under the associate delta file

5. You are configuring a virtual machine in vSphere 8.0. Which of the following devices cannot be configured or removed?

    a. SIO controller

    b. SCSI controller

    c. Parallel port

    d. PCI device

6. You are using the vSphere Client to edit a virtual machine in vSphere 8.0. Which of the following is not available on the VM Options tab?

   a. General Options

   b. Encryption Options

   c. Snapshot Options

   d. vApp Options

7. From the vSphere Client, you want to migrate virtual machines to another vCenter Server without needing to enter credentials for the target vCenter Server. Which of the following is required? (Choose two.)

   a. Advanced Cross vCenter vMotion

   b. Separate single sign-on domains

   c. Enhanced Linked Mode

   d. Time synchronization

   e. vSphere Standard License

8. You want to perform multiple simultaneous virtual machine migrations for a four-node DRS cluster with a 10 GigE vMotion network and multiple datastores. Which of the following operations are allowed without any queuing?

   a. Nine simultaneous vMotion migrations

   b. Nine simultaneous vMotion migrations without Shared Storage

   c. One Storage vMotion operation and four vMotion operations

   d. Four simultaneous vMotion and five provisioning operations involving the same host

9. You are optimizing your vSphere environment. Which of the following is not helpful for improving vMotion performance?

   a. Using NIOC to increase shares for vMotion traffic

   b. Using traffic shaping to limit the bandwidth that is available to vMotion traffic

   c. Using multiple-NIC vMotion

   d. Using jumbo frames

10. You want to use instant clones in vSphere. Which of the following statements is true?

    a. You can use the vSphere Host Client to perform an instant clone.

    b. You can use the vSphere Client to perform an instant clone.

    c. A sample major use case for instant clones is a large-scale deployment in a VMware Horizon VDI.

    d. The source virtual machine must be powered down.

Foundation Topics

vCenter Server and vSphere

Previous chapters provide details about the vSphere topology, storage infrastructure, network infrastructure, and vSphere clusters. This section provides details about other features, such as the vSphere inventory, host profiles, and content libraries.

vSphere Managed Inventory Objects

This section describes the vSphere inventory and object types, which should be planned prior to implementing vSphere. It provides information on creating and configuring inventory objects during vSphere implementation.

The *vSphere inventory* is a collection of managed virtual and physical objects. Depending on the object type, you can configure objects and perform operations such as setting permissions, monitoring tasks, monitoring events, and setting alarms. You can organize many of the objects by placing them into folders, which makes managing them easier.

All inventory objects except for hosts can be renamed to represent their purposes. For example, they can be named after company departments, locations, or functions.

NOTE Many systems that rely on vCenter Server, such as VMware Horizon, also refer to vCenter objects according to their names. Take care when renaming vCenter inventory objects such as data centers, folders, and datastores if you have deployed any external systems that rely on vCenter Server.

NOTE Inventory object names cannot exceed 214 bytes (UTF-8 encoded).

Data Centers

In the vSphere inventory, a *data center* is a container object that is an aggregation of all the different types of objects used to work in a virtual infrastructure. Other than an optional folder to contain data centers, you cannot create any object in the inventory until you create a data center.

Data centers are often used to contain all the objects in a physical data center. For example, if you use a single vCenter Server to manage vSphere assets in San Francisco and Chicago, you might want to use corresponding virtual data centers to organize each city's assets. You could create data center objects named San Francisco and Chicago and place each ESXi host, virtual machine, and other object in the appropriate data center.

Within each data center, there are four separate hierarchies:

- Virtual machines (and templates)
- Hosts (and clusters)
- Networks
- Datastores

A data center is a namespace for networks and datastores. The names for these objects must be unique within a data center. You cannot use identical datastore names within the same data center, but you can use identical datastore names within two different data centers. Virtual machines, templates, and clusters do not need to have unique names within the data center but must have unique names within their folder.

Folders

In the vSphere inventory, folders are container objects that allow you to group objects of a single type. A folder can contain data centers, clusters, datastores, networks, virtual machines, templates, or hosts. For example, one folder can contain hosts and a folder containing hosts, but it cannot contain hosts and a folder containing virtual machines.

You can create data center folders directly under the root vCenter Server and use them to organize your data centers. Within each data center is one hierarchy of folders for virtual machines and templates, one for hosts and clusters, one for datastores, and one for networks.

When creating or modifying a folder, the only available setting is the folder name. You can use folders when assigning permissions and configuring alarms.

Clusters

A *cluster* is a set of ESXi hosts that are intended to work together as a unit. When you add a host to a cluster, the host's resources become part of the cluster's resources. vCenter Server manages the resources of all hosts in a cluster as one unit. In addition to creating a cluster, assigning a name, and adding ESXi objects, you can enable and configure features on a cluster, such as VMware EVC, vSphere DRS, and vSphere HA.

If you enable VMware EVC on a cluster, you can ensure that migrations with vMotion do not fail due to CPU compatibility errors. If you enable vSphere DRS on a cluster, you can allow automatic resource balancing by using the pooled host resources in the cluster. If you enable vSphere HA on a cluster, you can allow rapid virtual machine recovery from host hardware failures by using the cluster's available host resource capacity.

Cluster features are covered in detail in Chapter 4, "Clusters and High Availability."

Resource Pools

In the vSphere inventory, *resource pools* are container objects that are used to compartmentalize the CPU and memory resources of a host or cluster. Virtual machines run in resource pools, using resources provided by the resource pools. You can create multiple resource pools as direct children of a standalone host or cluster.

You can use resource pools to organize VMs. You can delegate control over each resource pool to specific individuals and groups. You can monitor resources and set alarms on resource pools. If you need a container just for organization and permission purposes, consider using a folder. If you also need resource management, then consider using a resource pool.

If DRS is enabled, you can use the vSphere Client to create resource pools in the cluster and assign resource settings, such as reservations and limits. Otherwise, you can create resource pools directly on specific ESXi hosts.

You can configure resource settings for resource pools, such as reservations, limits, and shares. See Chapter 4 for more details on resource pools.

Hosts

In the vSphere inventory, hosts are objects that represent your ESXi servers. After installing an ESXi host, you can choose to add it to the vSphere inventory, in which case you need to provide credentials for a user who is assigned the administrator role directly on the host.

The vpxa agent in the ESXi server maintains communication with vCenter Server. It is an interface between the vCenter Server and the ESXi hostd service, which drives the main operations on the host, such as powering on a virtual machine.

For maintenance and troubleshooting activities, you can disconnect a host from the vCenter Server; when you do this, you do not remove it from vCenter Server, but you suspend related vCenter Server monitoring activities. You can connect hosts that are disconnected. If you choose to remove a host from inventory, the host and all its associated virtual machines are removed.

If the SSL certificate used by vCenter Server is replaced or changed, the vCenter Server is unable to decrypt the host passwords. You need to reconnect the certificate and resupply the host credentials.

To remove a host from the vSphere inventory, you must first enter Maintenance Mode.

Networks

In the vSphere inventory, a network is an object that is used to connect a set of virtual network adapters. Each ESXi host may have multiple VMkernel virtual network adapters. Each virtual machine may have multiple virtual network adapters. Each virtual network adapter may be connected to a port group (on a standard virtual switch) or a distributed port group (on a vSphere distributed switch). All virtual machines that connect to the same port group belong to the same network in the virtual environment, even if they are on different physical servers. You can manage networks by monitoring, setting permissions, and setting alarms on port groups and distributed port groups.

Chapter 3, "Network Infrastructure," provides details on networks.

Datastores

In the vSphere inventory, datastores are objects that represent physical storage resources in the data center. A datastore is the storage location for virtual machine files. The physical storage resources can come from local SCSI disks of the ESXi host, Fibre Channel SAN disk arrays, iSCSI SAN disk arrays, or network attached storage (NAS) arrays. VMFS datastores can be backed by local SCSI, Fibre Channel, or iSCSI. NFS datastores can be backed by NAS. vSAN datastores can be built in VSAN clusters.

Chapter 2, "Storage Infrastructure," provides details on datastores.

Virtual Machines

In the vSphere inventory, virtual machines are represented in a manner that reflects the current inventory view. For example, in the Hosts and Clusters view, each virtual machine is a descendant of the ESXi host on which it runs. In the Networks view, each virtual machine is a descendant of the network to which it connects.

Templates

In the vSphere inventory, *templates* are objects that are effectively non-executable virtual machines. A template is a primary copy of a virtual machine that can be used to create and provision new virtual machines. A template can have a guest operating system and application software installed. Templates are often customized during deployment to ensure that each new virtual machine has a unique name and network settings.

For more details on templates, see the "Virtual Machine Cloning" section, later in this chapter.

vApps

A *vApp* is a container object in vSphere that provides a format for packaging and managing applications. Typically, a vApp is a set of virtual machines that runs a single application and allows you to manage the application as a single unit. You can specify a unique boot order for the virtual machines in a vApp, which allows you to gracefully start an application that spans multiple virtual machines. You can apply resource management settings to a vApp in a similar manner as you would to a resource pool.

Host Profiles

A *host profile* is a feature that enables you to encapsulate the configuration of one host and apply it to other hosts. A host profile is especially helpful in an environment where an administrator manages multiple hosts and clusters with vCenter Server. The following are characteristics of host profiles:

- Host profiles are automated and centrally managed.
- Host profiles are used for host configuration and configuration compliance.
- Host profiles can improve efficiency by reducing the need for repetitive manual tasks.
- A host profile captures the configuration of a reference host and stores the configuration as a managed object.
- Host profiles provide parameters for configuring networking, storage, security, and other host-level settings.
- A host profile can be applied to individual hosts, a cluster, or a set of hosts and clusters.
- A host profile makes it easy to ensure that all hosts in a cluster have a consistent configuration.

You can use the following workflow to leverage a host profile to apply a consistent host configuration in your vSphere environment:

Step 1.   Set up and configure a reference host.

Step 2.   Create a host profile from the reference host.

Step 3.   Attach hosts or clusters to the host profile.

Step 4.   Check the compliance of the hosts with the host profile. If all hosts are compliant with the reference host, you do not need to take additional steps.

Step 5.   If the hosts are not fully compliant, remediate the hosts by applying the host profile.

> **NOTE**   If you want a host profile to use directory services for authentication, the reference host must be configured to use a directory service.

In previous releases, vSphere requires that the reference host be available for certain tasks, such as editing, importing, and exporting the host profile. In versions since vSphere 6.0, a dedicated reference host is not required for these tasks.

Auto Deploy uses host profiles to configure ESXi.

Content Libraries

A *content library* is a repository that can be used to share files such as virtual machine templates, vApps, and image files among a set of vCenter Servers. Content libraries, which were introduced in vSphere 6.0, address the fact that multiple vCenter Servers do not directly share associated files such as Open Virtualization Format (OVF) and image (ISO) files. A great use case is a company that has multiple sites, each managed by a dedicated vCenter Server, where the OVF files and ISO files that are used at one site are not directly available for use at other sites. In such a case, you can create a content library at one site and publish it to serve the other sites. At the other sites, you can create subscribed libraries that automatically synchronize with the published library. For example, you can create a local content library using the main office vCenter Server, publish it, and subscribe to it from branch office vCenter Servers.

A subscribed content library can be configured to download metadata only whenever it receives notification of a change. In such a case, the subscribing library reflects the most recent changes, but it is not burdened with supplying the storage space for every published file. Instead, the administrator can choose whether to download the data for the entire library or per item.

Three types of content libraries can be used: local, published, and subscribed. A local content library is the simplest form. You can allow, modify, and delete content in a content library. A published library is a local library where content is published for subscription. A subscribed library is a library whose content you cannot change or publish. It receives its content from a published library.

Each content library is built on a single storage entity, which may be a VMFS datastore, an NFS datastore, a CIFS share, a local disk, or a vSAN datastore. In vSphere 8.0, the following maximum limitations apply:

- 1000 libraries per vCenter Server

- 1000 items per library

- 16 concurrent synchronization operations per published library

- 9 virtual disk files per OVA/OVF template

After one library is set to subscribe to another library, synchronization occurs. Automatic synchronization occurs every 24 hours by default and can be modified using an API. The content library service, which is named vmware-vdcs, is installed as part of the vCenter Server installation and uses the same database as vCenter Server.

Simple versioning is used to keep libraries synchronized. Version numbers are assigned to the libraries and to each item in the library. These numbers are incremented whenever content is added or modified. A library does not store previous versions or provide rollback.

The following sequence occurs between a subscribed library and a published library:

Step 1.   The library service on the subscriber connects to the library services on the publisher by using the VMware Content Subscription Protocol (VCSP) and checks for updates.

Step 2.   The subscriber pulls the lib.json file from the publisher, and the lib. json file for each library is examined to determine if discrepancies exist between the publisher and the subscriber.

Step 3.   The library service uses VCSP to determine what data has changed and sends a request to the transfer service to copy the required files.

Step 4.   The subscriber updates the versioning information in the database.

In versions since vSphere 6.5, you can mount an ISO file directly from the content library, apply a guest OS customization specification during VM deployment, and update existing templates. The content library's performance is then improved. The Optimized HTTP Sync option stores content in a compressed format, which reduces the synchronization time. The content library leverages new features in vCenter Server 6.5, including vCenter HA and backup/restoration.

In previous versions of vSphere, content libraries supported only OVF templates. As a result, virtual machine templates and vApp templates were converted to OVF files when you uploaded them to a content library. Starting with vSphere 6.7 Update 1, content libraries support virtual machine templates. Therefore, templates in the content library can be either the OVF template type or the VM template type. vApp templates are still converted to OVF files when you upload them to a content library. The distribution of VM templates requires that the respective vCenter Server instances be in Enhanced Linked Mode or Hybrid Linked Mode and that the respective hosts be connected through a network.

To allow a user to manage a content library and its items, you can assign the Content Library administrator role, which is a sample role, to that user as a global permission. Users who are assigned the administrator role at a vCenter Server level cannot see the libraries unless they have a read-only global permission.

Starting with vSphere 7.0 Update 3, you can protect the OVF items by applying default OVF security policy to a content library.

In vSphere 7.0 and later, with Content Libraries you can manage VM templates in an efficient and flexible manner. You can edit the contents of the VM templates by checking them out, making the necessary changes, and checking them in.

You can track history of changes over time by using the vertical timeline view. The vertical timeline view provides you with detailed information about the different VM template versions, the updates that privileged users have made, and when the last change was made. By using the vertical timeline, you can revert VM templates back to their previous state or delete the previous version of a VM template.

In addition, you can deploy a virtual machine from the latest version of the VM template without any disruption while it is checked out for update. You can update the virtual machine and check it back in into the same VM template.

Virtual Machine File Structure

A virtual machine consists of several files that are stored in a datastore. The key files are the configuration file, virtual disk file, NVRAM setting file, and log file. Table 5-2 provides details for virtual machine files. You can configure virtual machine settings through the vSphere Client, **esxcli**, or the vSphere Web Services SDK.

NOTE Do not directly change, move, or delete virtual machine files without guidance from a VMware Technical Support representative.

Table 5-2 Virtual Machine Files

File	Description
vmname.vmx	Virtual machine configuration file
vmname.vmxf	Additional virtual machine configuration file
vmname.vmdk	Virtual disk characteristics (metadata) file
vmname-flat.vmdk	Virtual disk data file (commonly called a flat file)
vmname.nvram or nvram	Virtual machine BIOS or UEFI configuration file
vmname.vmsd	Virtual machine snapshot file
vmname.vmsn	Virtual machine snapshot data file
vmname.vswp	Virtual machine swap file
vmname.vmss	Virtual machine suspend file
vmware.log	Current virtual machine log file
vmware-#.log	Old virtual machine log file, where # is a number starting with 1

Additional files can be created when you perform specific operations, such as when you create snapshots. If you convert a virtual machine to a template, the .vmtx file replaces the virtual machine configuration file (the .vmx file).

By default, when you create a virtual machine, the system creates a folder in the datastore and assigns a folder name that is similar to the virtual machine name. In cases where the default folder name is already in use, the system appends a number to the new folder to make it unique.

Configuration File

A virtual machine's configuration file is a text file that contains all of the virtual machine's settings, including a description of the virtual hardware. For example, a portion of the contents of a VMX file for a CentOS virtual machine named server1 could include the following text:

```
displayName = "server1"
guestOS = "centos-64"
nvram = "server1.nvram"
scsi0:0.fileName = "server1.vmdk"
```

If this virtual machine is sized with two virtual CPUs and 1024 GB memory, the contents of the VMX file may also include the following text:

```
numvcpus = "2"
memSize = "1024"
```

Virtual Disk Files

The name of the VMDK file that contains metadata for a virtual disk is included in the VMX file as shown in the previous example (`scsi0:0.fileName = "server1.vmdk"`). The VMDK metadata file is a text file that contains details about the virtual disk, such as the numbers of cylinders, heads, and sectors, as shown in the following sample content:

```
ddb.geometry.cylinders = "1305"
ddb.geometry.heads = "255"
ddb.geometry.sectors = "63"
```

The VMDK metadata file also contains the names of other files associated with the virtual disk, such as data (extent) files, as shown in the following sample content:

```
# Extent description
RW 20971520 VMFS "server1-flat.vmdk"
```

Snapshot Files

When you take a snapshot of a virtual machine, the system creates a few files. For example, if you take a snapshot of a powered-off virtual machine named server1 that has only one virtual disk and no previous snapshots, the following files may be created:

- **server1-000001-sesparse.vmdk**: A delta data disk that stores changes made since the creation of the snapshot
- **server1-000001.vmdk**: A VMDK metadata file for the delta disk
- **server1-Snapshot1.vmsn**: Snapshot data

The following section provides more details on virtual machine snapshots.

Virtual Machine Snapshots

A *virtual machine snapshot* captures the state of a virtual machine and the data in the virtual machine at a specific point in time. Snapshots are useful when you want to return the state of a virtual machine to a point that was previously captured. For example, you can create a snapshot of a virtual machine just prior to installing and testing software in the virtual machine. This enables you to revert the virtual machine to its original state when you finish testing.

You can take multiple snapshots of a virtual machine. If you take multiple snapshots without reverting the virtual machine, the snapshots are created in a linear fashion, as shown in Figure 5-1. The vSphere Client represents the snapshot hierarchy of a virtual machine as a tree, where the root node is the virtual machine and the branch nodes are the snapshots. If you revert the virtual machine to a snapshot, the state of your virtual machine is associated with that snapshot, as shown in Figure 5-2. If you create another snapshot, you add branches to the snapshot tree, as shown in Figure 5-3.

Figure 5-1   Linear Snapshots

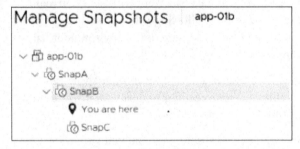

Figure 5-2   Post-Reversion Snapshot Tree

Figure 5-3   New Branch in a Snapshot Tree

Each branch in a snapshot tree can have up to 32 snapshots.

In the vSphere Client, you can perform several snapshot operations, including taking a snapshot, reverting to a snapshot, and deleting a snapshot. When taking a snapshot, you can choose whether to snap the memory and whether to quiesce the guest OS. In cases where no snapshot exists but delta files exist, you can choose to consolidate the disks.

Snapshot Use Cases

The following are some common use cases for snapshots:

- **Change rollbacks**: Prior to upgrading or making a configuration change to an application, you can take a virtual machine snapshot to provide a rollback option.

- **Guest OS upgrade rollbacks**: Prior to upgrading the guest OS, you can take a virtual machine snapshot to provide a rollback option.

- **Training and development labs**: You can take snapshots of a set of virtual machines used in a lab environment prior to allowing user access. When the user finishes experimenting, you can revert the state of the environment back to the original state for the next user.

- **Backups**: A backup utility may first trigger a virtual machine snapshot and then copy the virtual machine files without needing to deal with open files. Following the backup, the utility deletes the snapshot.

- **Troubleshooting and triage**: Taking a snapshot of a troubled virtual machine enables you to later choose to return the virtual machine to its exact state when it experienced the issue.

- **Linked clones**: Automation and virtual desktop software, such as vRealize Automation and Horizon, may leverage virtual machine snapshots to allow you to use fast provisioning (linked clone) methods by which new virtual machines share a base virtual disk. For example, to use a linked clone in a vRealize Automation blueprint, you need to identify a virtual machine snapshot.

What a Snapshot Preserves

A snapshot preserves the following information:

- **Virtual machine settings**: The virtual machine directory, which includes the disks added or changed after you take the snapshot

- **Disk state**: The state of each virtual disk of the VM

- **Memory state**: (Optional) The contents of the virtual machine's memory, captured only if the VM is powered on and the checkbox Snapshot the Virtual Machine's Memory is selected (which it is by default).

- **Power state**: Whether the virtual machine is powered on, powered off, or suspended when you take the snapshot (If you revert to a snapshot that includes the memory state, the virtual machine is returned to its preserved power state.)

Parent Snapshots

The first virtual machine snapshot that you create is the base snapshot. Taking a snapshot creates a delta disk file for each disk attached to the virtual machine and, optionally, a memory file. The delta disk files and memory file are stored with the base VMDK file. The parent (current) snapshot is always the snapshot that appears immediately above the You Are Here icon in the Snapshot Manager. If you revert to a snapshot, that snapshot becomes the parent of the You Are Here current state. When you have multiple snapshots, each child snapshot has a parent snapshot.

NOTE   The parent snapshot is not always the snapshot that you took most recently.

Snapshot Behavior

Taking a snapshot preserves the disk state by creating a series of delta disks for each attached virtual disk or virtual raw device mapping (RDM). Taking a snapshot creates a snapshot object in the Snapshot Manager that represents the virtual machine state and settings. Each snapshot creates a delta disk for each virtual disk. When you take a snapshot, the system prevents the virtual machine from writing to the current data (VMDK) file and instead directs all writes to the delta disk. The delta disk represents the difference between the current state of the virtual disk and the state that existed at the time that you took the parent snapshot. Delta disk files can expand quickly and can become as large as the configured size of the virtual disk if the guest operating system writes to every block of the virtual disk.

When you take a snapshot, you capture the state of the virtual machine, the virtual disks, and (optionally) the virtual memory in a set of files, such as the delta, database, and memory files. By default, the delta disks are stored with the corresponding virtual disk files, and the memory and database files are stored in the virtual machine directory.

Flat File

A virtual disk involves a metadata file and a data file, each with the .vmdk extension. The metadata VMDK file contains information about the virtual disk, such as geometry and child–parent relationship information. The data VMDK file is called the flat file, and its name contains the word flat. Only the names of the metadata files appear in the vSphere Client datastore browser. In normal circumstances, the virtual machine's guest OS and applications write to the flat file.

Delta Disk Files

When you create a snapshot, you create a delta disk for each virtual disk. SEsparse is the default format for all delta disks on the VMFS6 datastores. The delta (child) disk represents the difference between the current state of the virtual disk and the state that existed at the time that you took the parent snapshot. A delta disk has two VMDK files: One is a small metadata file, and the other is a data file. Delta disk data files are also called redo logs.

Database File

The database file is a file with the .vmsd extension that contains snapshot details required by the Snapshot Manager. It contains details on the relationships between snapshots and child disks.

Memory File

The memory file is a file with the .vmsn extension that includes the active state of the virtual machine's memory. Capturing the memory state of the virtual machine lets you revert to a powered-on state. Memory snapshots take longer to create than nonmemory snapshots. The size of the memory impacts the amount of time required to create the snapshot.

Limitations

The use of snapshots can impact a virtual machine's performance and can be limited in some scenarios, as summarized in the following list:

- Snapshots are not supported for RDM physical mode disks or for iSCSI initiators in a guest OS.

- Snapshots of powered-on or suspended virtual machines with independent disks are not supported.

- A quiesced snapshot requires a supported guest operating system and active VMware Tools services.

- Snapshots are not supported with PCI vSphere DirectPath I/O devices.

- Snapshots are not supported for virtual machines configured for bus sharing.

- Although taking snapshots may be a useful step for a backup utility, a snapshot is not a backup by itself. A snapshot does not provide a redundant copy of data. If the base flat file is lost or corrupted, you cannot restore the virtual machine by reverting to a snapshot.

- Snapshots can negatively affect the performance of a virtual machine. The performance degradation is impacted by factors such as the age of the snapshot, the depth of the snapshot tree, and the amount of data in the delta files.

- Snapshot operations can take much longer to finish when they involve virtual disks larger than 2 TB.

- Deleting a large snapshot that is part of the current path (as indicated by You Are Here in the Snapshot Manager) can negatively impact the performance and the health of the virtual machine. To minimize risk, you can shut down the virtual machine prior to deleting the snapshot.

Virtual Machine Settings

This section provides information on virtual machine settings in vSphere 8.0.

VM Hardware/Compatibility

You can configure a virtual machine's compatibility setting to control which ESXi host versions can be used to run the virtual machine. In the vSphere Client, you can set the Compatible With option for a virtual machine to a compatible ESXi version, such as ESXi 8.0 and later or ESXi 6.7 Update 2 and later. The compatibility setting determines which ESXi host versions the virtual machine can run on and the hardware features available to the virtual machine. At the host, cluster, or data center level, you can set the Default VM Compatibility setting. (See Chapter 14 for details.)

Virtual hardware devices perform the same function for the virtual machines as physical hardware devices do for traditional servers. Each virtual machine has CPU, memory, and disk resources. All modern operating systems provide support for virtual memory, allowing software to use more memory than is present in the server hardware. Similarly, ESXi can provide to its virtual machines VM memory totaling more than the capacity of the host's physical memory.

You can add virtual hardware devices to a virtual machine by editing the virtual machine's settings in the vSphere Client. Not all devices are configurable. For example, the PCI and SIO virtual hardware devices are part of the virtual motherboard but cannot be configured or removed. You can enable the Memory Hotplug or CPU Hotplug settings in order to add memory or CPU resources to a running virtual machine. Memory Hotplug is supported on all 64-bit operating systems, but some guest operating systems may not be able to make use of the added memory without restarting. The ESXi license and other factors for the host where the virtual machine runs may impact the available devices for the virtual machine. For a list of hardware devices and their functions, see Table 5-3.

Table 5-3   Virtual Machine Hardware Devices

Device	Description
CPU	At least one vCPU but not more than the number of logical CPUs in the host.
	You can set advanced CPU features, such as the CPU identification mask and hyperthreaded core sharing.
Chipset	The virtual motherboard consists of VMware-proprietary virtual devices, based on the following chips:
	■ Intel 440BX AGPset 82443BX host bridge/controller
	■ Intel 82371AB (PIIX4) PCI ISA IDE Xcelerator
	■ National Semiconductor PC87338 ACPI 1.0 and PC98/99 Compliant SuperI/O
	■ Intel 82093AA I/O advanced programmable interrupt controller
DVD/CD-ROM drive	One by default.
	You can configure the virtual DVD/CD-ROM device to connect to client devices, host devices, or datastore ISO files.
	You can add and remove virtual DVD/CD-ROM devices.
Hard disk	A virtual disk is backed by a set of files, as discussed earlier in this chapter.
IDE 0, IDE 1	Two virtual Integrated Drive Electronics (IDE) interfaces are present by default.
Keyboard	The virtual keyboard is mapped to the user keyboard when you connect to the virtual machine console.
Memory	The size of the virtual memory becomes the size of memory that the guest OS perceives to be physical memory.
Network adapter	You can configure the number of virtual network adapters (NICs) and the adapter type used by each virtual machine.
Parallel port	You can add, remove, and configure virtual parallel ports.
PCI controller	One PCI controller, which is located on the virtual motherboard, is presented to the virtual machine. It cannot be removed or modified.

Device	Description
PCI device	If you configured devices to be reserved for PCI passthrough on the host, you can add up to 16 PCI vSphere DirectPath devices to a virtual machine.
Pointing device	The virtual pointing device is mapped to the user's pointing device when you connect to the virtual machine console.
Serial port	You can configure a virtual machine with up to 32 virtual serial ports. You can add, remove, or configure virtual serial ports.
SATA controller	Provides access to virtual disks and DVD/CD-ROM devices. The SATA virtual controller appears to the guest OS as an AHCI SATA controller.
SCSI controller	Provides access to virtual disks. The SCSI virtual controller appears to the guest OS as different types of controllers, including LSI Logic Parallel, LSI Logic SAS, and VMware Paravirtual.
SIO controller	Provides serial and parallel ports and floppy devices and performs system management activities. One SIO controller is available to the virtual machine, but it cannot be configured or removed.
USB controller	The virtual USB controller is the software virtualization of the USB host controller function in the virtual machine.
USB device	You can add multiple virtual USB devices to a virtual machine that you map to USB devices connected to an ESXi host or a client computer.
VMCI	The Virtual Machine Communication Interface (VMCI) device provides a high-speed communication channel between a virtual machine and the hypervisor. You cannot add or remove VMCI devices.
NVMe controller	NVM Express (NVMe) is a logical device interface specification for accessing non-volatile storage media attached through a PCI Express (PCIe) bus in real and virtual hardware.
NVDIMM controller	Provides access to the non-volatile memory resources of the host.
NVDIMM device	You can add up to 64 virtual non-volatile dual in-line memory module (NVDIMM) devices to a virtual machine.
TPM device	You can add a virtual Trusted Platform Module (TPM) 2.0 device to a virtual machine to allow the guest OS to store sensitive information, perform cryptographic tasks, or attest the integrity of the guest platform.

Virtual Disk Provisioning

You can configure the provisioning type for a virtual disk to thin provisioned, lazy zeroed thick provisioned, or eager zeroed thick provisioned, as described in the section "Virtual Disk Types" in Chapter 2:

- With thin provisioning, storage blocks are not allocated during disk creation, which allows for fast provisioning but requires allocation and zeroing at runtime.

- With thick eager zeroed, storage blocks are allocated and zeroed during provisioning, which allows for fast runtime.

- With thick lazy zeroed provisioning, storage blocks are pre-allocated but not pre-zeroed.

Your choice for the provisioning type depends on each virtual machine's use case. For example, if you want to minimize the virtual machine startup time and minimize its risk, you may choose thick provision lazy zeroed.

VMware Tools

VMware Tools is a set of software modules and services, including services that can communicate with the VMkernel. This communication allows integration with vSphere for activities such as customizing the guest OS, running scripts in the guest OS, and synchronizing time. If you use guest operating systems without VMware Tools, many VMware features are not available. VMware Tools enhances the performance of the guest OS by enabling the latest drivers for virtual devices, enabling memory functions (such as ballooning), and more. It includes drivers such as SVGA, Paravirtual SCSI, VMXNet NIC, mouse, audio, guest introspection, and memory control drivers. Prior to upgrading the hardware for a virtual machine, you should upgrade VMware Tools.

VMware Tools includes the VMware user process named **vmtoolsd**, which enables copy and paste and mouse control and automatically sets the screen resolution for some non-Windows guests. It enhances the performance of the virtual machine's guest operating system and improves management of the virtual machine. It includes device drivers and other software that is essential for the VM. VMware Tools gives you more control over the virtual machine interface.

Virtual Machine Options

To edit a virtual machine setting, you can navigate to and manipulate settings on the VM Options tab. Many of these options have dependencies with the ESXi hosts, data centers, clusters, or resource pools on which the virtual machine resides. Table 5-4 describes the available virtual machine options.

Table 5-4 Virtual Machine Options Tab Options

Category	Description
General Options	Settings include virtual machine name, configuration file location, and the working directory location.
Encryption Options	Settings allow you to enable or disable virtual machine encryption or vMotion encryption.
Power Management	Settings allow you to choose how to respond when the guest OS is placed on standby. The choices are to suspend the virtual machine or put the guest OS into standby mode.
VMware Tools	Settings allow you to choose how to respond to specific power operations. For example, you can choose whether to power off the virtual machine or shut down the guest when the red power-off button is clicked.
Virtualization Based Security (VBS)	For virtual machines running the modern Windows OS versions, you can enable VBS to add an extra level of protection.
Boot Options	Settings include firmware, boot delay, and failed boot recovery parameters.
Advanced Options	Settings include logging, debugging, swap file location, and configuration parameters.
Fibre Channel NPIV	Settings allow the virtual machine to use N-Port ID Virtualization (NPIV), including whether to generate new worldwide names (WWNs).
vApp Options	Settings allow you to control vApp functionality for the virtual machine, such as enable/disable and IP allocation policy. vApp settings that are made directly to a virtual machine override settings made on the vApp.

Virtual Machine Advanced Settings

As indicated in Table 5-4, you can use the vSphere Client to edit the advanced settings for a virtual machine on its VM Options tab. You can set a virtual machine's advanced settings to enable or disable logging. You can enable or disable hardware acceleration. You can set debugging and statistics to Run Normally, Record Debugging Information, Record Statistics, or Record Statistics and Debugging. For applications that are highly sensitive to latency, you can set Latency Sensitivity to High.

Under Advanced Settings, you can select Configuration Parameters, where you can directly manipulate the virtual machine's low-level settings, as illustrated in Figure 5-4.

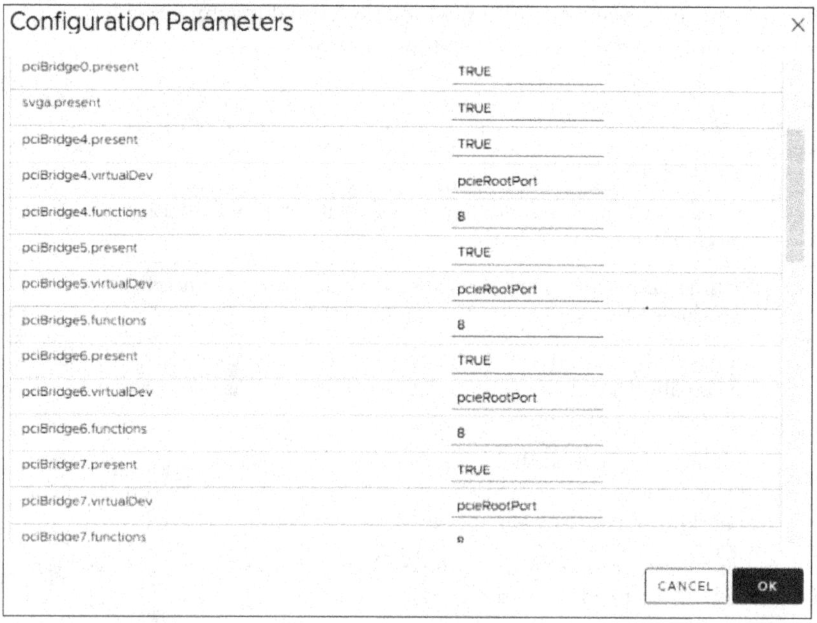

Configuration Parameters   ×

pciBridge0.present	TRUE
svga.present	TRUE
pciBridge4.present	TRUE
pciBridge4.virtualDev	pcieRootPort
pciBridge4.functions	8
pciBridge5.present	TRUE
pciBridge5.virtualDev	pcieRootPort
pciBridge5.functions	8
pciBridge6.present	TRUE
pciBridge6.virtualDev	pcieRootPort
pciBridge6.functions	8
pciBridge7.present	TRUE
pciBridge7.virtualDev	pcieRootPort
pciBridge7.functions	8

CANCEL   OK

Figure 5-4 Sample Virtual Machine Configuration Parameters

Virtual Machine Migration

This section provides information such as concepts, prerequisites, and data flow details for each migration type. Chapter 14 provides information on performing migrations.

Migrating Virtual Machines

You can migrate virtual machines from one compute resource or storage location to another while the virtual machine is stopped (cold) or running (hot). For example, if you want to balance the workload, you can migrate some virtual machines from busy ESXi hosts or datastores (or both) to other hosts and datastores. As another example, if you want to perform maintenance (such as an upgrade), you can migrate all virtual machines from an ESXi host or datastore, perform the maintenance, and optionally migrate virtual machines back to the original location.

Moving a virtual machine between the inventory folder or resource pools in the same data center is not considered a migration. Cloning and copying virtual machines are also not forms of migration.

Each migration type involves a unique set of requirements, such as minimum privileges required to perform the operation.

NOTE To migrate virtual machines with disks larger than 2 TB, the source and destination ESXi hosts must be Version 6.0 and later.

Cold Migrations

Moving a powered-off or suspended virtual machine to a new host, new datastore, or both is considered a cold migration. The required privilege is Resource.Migrate Powered Off Virtual Machine.

Hot Migrations

Moving a powered-on virtual machine to a new host, new datastore, or both is considered a hot migration. During the migration, vCenter Server must take steps to ensure that active connections and services of the virtual machine are not interrupted.

Cross-Host Migrations

Moving a virtual machine, whether hot or cold, to a new host is considered a cross-host migration. In vSphere Client wizards that involve cross-host migrations, you can choose a destination host. Alternatively, when available and properly configured, you can choose a DRS cluster, resource pool, or vApp as the destination.

The cross-host migration wizards include a Compatibility panel to identify any compatibility issues or warnings. If the panel displays the message "Compatibility Checks Succeeded," you can proceed with no concern. If the panel displays an error, the migration is disabled for the associated hosts. If it displays a warning message, the migration is not disabled, and you can proceed, bearing in mind the warning. For hot migrations, the compatibility check accommodates vMotion CPU compatibility checking.

For a virtual machine using an NVDIMM device and PMem storage, the destination host or cluster must have available PMem resources to pass the compatibility check. For a cold migration involving a virtual machine that does not have an NVDIMM device but uses PMem storage, you can choose a target host or cluster without available PMem resources. The hard disks use the storage policy and datastore selected for the virtual machine's configuration files.

Cross-Datastore Migrations

Moving a virtual machine, whether hot or cold, to a new datastore is considered a cross-datastore migration.

Cross-vCenter Server Migrations

Moving a virtual machine, whether hot or cold, to a new vCenter Server is considered a cross-vCenter Server migration. To perform a standard, cross-vCenter Server migration with Enhanced Linked Mode, you must meet the following requirements:

- The associated vCenter Servers and ESXi hosts must be Version 6.0 or later.

- The cross-vCenter Server and long-distance vMotion features require an Enterprise Plus license.

- The vCenter Server instances must be time-synchronized with each other for correct vCenter Single Sign-On token verification.

- For migration of compute resources only, both vCenter Server instances must be connected to the shared virtual machine storage.

- Both vCenter Server instances must be in the same vCenter Single Sign-On domain.

With Advanced Cross vCenter vMotion (XVM), you can migrate virtual machines between vCenter Server, without Enhanced Linked Mode, by providing the credentials of the other vCenter Server when prompted by the wizard. To perform a cross-vCenter migration using Advanced Cross vCenter vMotion, you must meet the following requirements:

- The vCenter Sever where you initiate the migration must be Version 7.0 Update 1c or later.

- For powered-on virtual machines, you must have a vSphere Enterprise Plus license.

- For powered-off virtual machines, a vSphere Standard license will suffice.

Virtual Machine Migration Limitations

vCenter Server limits the number of simultaneous virtual machine migration and provisioning operations that occur per host, network, and datastore. Each of the network, datastore, and host limits must be satisfied for the operation to proceed. vCenter Server uses a costing method by which each migration and provisioning operation is assigned a cost per resource. Operations whose costs cause resources to exceed their limits are queued until other operations complete.

Limits depend on the resource type, ESXi version, migration type, and other factors, such as network type. ESXi Versions 6.0 to 8.0 have consistent limits:

- **Network limits**: Network limits apply only to vMotion migrations. Each vMotion migration has a network resource cost of 1. The network limit depends on the network bandwidth for the VMkernel adapter enabled for vMotion migration. For 1 GigE the limit is 4, and for 10 GigE it is 8.

■ **Datastore limits**: Datastore limits apply to vMotion and Storage vMotion migrations. Each vMotion migration has a resource cost of 1 against the shared datastore. Each Storage vMotion migration has a resource cost of 16 against both the source and destination datastores. The datastore limit per datastore is 128.

■ **Host limits**: Host limits apply to vMotion, Storage vMotion, and cold migrations. They also apply to virtual machine provisioning operations, including new deployments, and cloning. Provisioning and vMotion operations have a host cost of 1. Storage vMotion operations have a host cost of 4. The host limit per host is 8.

For costing purposes, a hot migration that is both a cross-host and cross-datastore migration (vMotion migration without shared storage) is considered to be a combination of a vMotion and Storage vMotion migration and applies the associated network, host, and datastore costs. vMotion migration without shared storage is equivalent to Storage vMotion migration with a network cost of 1.

Consider the following examples for a four-node DRS cluster with a 10 GigE vMotion network:

■ If you perform nine simultaneous vMotion migrations, the ninth migration is queued due to the network limit, even if different hosts are involved.

■ If you perform nine simultaneous hot cross-host and cross-datastore migrations involving the same datastore, the ninth migration is queued due to the datastore limit, even if the migrations are split as to whether the datastore is the source or the target.

■ You can simultaneously perform one Storage vMotion and four vMotion operations involving a specific host.

TCP/IP Stacks

You can use the vMotion TCP/IP stack to isolate vMotion traffic and assign it to a dedicated default gateway, routing table, and DNS configuration. To use the vMotion TCP/IP stack, select vMotion from the TCP/IP Stack drop-down menu when configuring the associated VMkernel virtual network adapter. When you assign a VMkernel virtual network adapter to the vMotion stack, you cannot use the adapter for purposes other than vMotion. Likewise, you can use the provisioning TCP/IP stack to isolate traffic for cold migration, cloning, and snapshots. To use the provisioning TCP/IP stack, select Provisioning from the TCP/IP Stack drop-down menu when configuring the associated VMkernel virtual network adapter. When you assign a VMkernel virtual network adapter to the provisioning stack, you cannot use the adapter for purposes other than provisioning.

vMotion Details

This section provides details on the vMotion feature in vSphere.

vMotion Overview

A hot cross-host migration is called a ***vMotion*** migration. A hot migration across hosts and datastores is often called a vMotion migration without shared storage. A hot cross-vCenter Server migration is often called a cross-vCenter Server vMotion migration. Although the term *vMotion migration* may be used to describe any hot cross-host migration, this section provides details on just the traditional vMotion migration, in which shared storage is used and cross-datastore migration does not occur.

During a vMotion migration, the entire state of the virtual machine is moved to the new host. The state includes the current memory content and all the information that defines and identifies the virtual machine. The memory content includes the components of the operating system, applications, and transaction data that are in the memory. The state includes all the data that maps to the virtual machine hardware elements, such as BIOS, devices, CPU, MAC addresses for the Ethernet cards, chipset states, and registers. The associated virtual disk remains in the original location on storage that is shared between the source and destination hosts. After the virtual machine state is migrated to the destination host, the virtual machine continues execution on the destination host.

vMotion Requirements

As explained in the section "Enhanced vMotion Compatibility (EVC)" in Chapter 4, vMotion requires that the destination host's processors be compatible with the source host's processors to support live migration. Specifically, the destination processors must come from the same family and provide the same instruction set as the source processors. You can enable EVC in the cluster to broaden the vMotion compatibility.

Starting with vSphere 6.7, you can enable EVC at the virtual machine level to facilitate the migration of the virtual machine beyond the cluster and across vCenter Server systems and data centers. You can change the per-VM EVC mode only when the virtual machine is powered off. The per-VM EVC overrides but cannot exceed the cluster EVC setting.

Before using vMotion, you must address its host configuration requirements. Each host must meet the licensing, shared storage, and networking requirements for vMotion.

For standard vMotion migration, you must configure the source and destination hosts with shared storage to enable the migrated virtual machines to remain in the same datastore throughout the migration. Shared storage may be implemented with Fibre Channel, iSCSI, or NAS storage. The datastore may be VMFS or NFS. You can also leverage a vSAN datastore to meet the shared storage requirement for vMotion migrations between cluster members.

NOTE Hot migrations that are cross-host and cross-datastore migrations do not required shared storage, and they are often called vMotion migrations without shared storage.

For vMotion migration, you must configure each host with a VMkernel virtual network interface connected to a virtual switch with an uplink that uses at least one physical network interface card (NIC). VMware recommends that the network connection be made to a secured network. The vMotion network must provide at least 250 Mbps of dedicated bandwidth per concurrent vMotion session. For long-distance migrations, the maximum supported network round-trip time for vMotion migrations is 150 milliseconds. For faster vMotion migrations, consider using 10 Gbps NICs instead of 1 Gbps NICs. As of vSphere 8.0, you can notify applications running inside the guest OS whenever a vMotion event starts and finishes. This notification allows latency-sensitive applications to prepare and even delay a vSphere vMotion operation.

To improve vMotion migration times even further, consider implementing multi-NIC vMotion. With multi-NIC vMotion, multiple paths are used simultaneously to carry the vMotion workload. To configure multi-NIC vMotion, you can enable vMotion traffic for two VMkernel virtual network adapters that are configured to use separate paths. For example, you can follow these steps to enable multi-NIC vMotion, as illustrated in Figure 5-5:

Step 1.   On a virtual switch, attach two uplink adapters connected to the vMotion network.

Step 2.   Connect two VMkernel adapters enabled for vMotion.

Step 3.   For the first VMkernel adapter, set the first uplink path to Active and the second uplink path to Standby.

Step 4.   For the second VMkernel adapter, set the first uplink path to Standby and the second uplink path to Active.

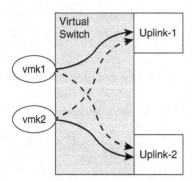

Figure 5-5 Multi-NIC vMotion

For more vMotion performance improvements, you can use Network I/O Control (NIOC) to guarantee network bandwidth to vMotion traffic. You can also use jumbo frames. To avoid network saturation, you can use traffic shaping to limit the average and peak bandwidth available to vMotion traffic.

By default, you cannot use vMotion to migrate a virtual machine that is attached to a standard switch with no physical uplinks. To change this behavior, you can set the vCenter Server advanced setting config.migrate.test.CompatibleNetworks.VMOn-VirtualIntranet to False.

> **NOTE**   During a vMotion migration without shared storage, the virtual disk data is transferred over the vMotion network.

In vSphere 8.0, if you enable network offloads to a data processing unit (DPU) device, you can use vMotion when both hosts have DPU devices, but you must prepare the vCenter Server system and VMware NSX as follows:

- Enable network offload compatibility on the vSphere Distributed Switch (vDS).

- Connect hosts to the vDS according to the DPU model.

- Deploy NSX and configure an NSX transport node for the vDS.

- Enable Universal Pass Through (UPT) support on the virtual machine that is to be migrated.

vMotion Migration and Data Flow Details

During a vMotion migration, the state of the running virtual machines is copied to the destination host over the designated vMotion network, the virtual machine is stopped on the source ESXi host, and the VM is resumed on the target ESXi host. The process involves the following phases:

- **Compatibility check**: Intended to ensure that requirements are met and that the destination host can run the virtual machine.

- **Pre-copy**: Briefly stuns the source memory and starts memory trackers. Copies memory page from source to target. Tracks which source pages are modified after the pre-copy so these pages (dirty pages) can be re-sent later.

- **Iterations of pre-copy**: If dirty pages exist, repeats the pre-copy of just the dirty pages and scans for new dirtied pages. Continues iteration until no dirty pages exist or until vMotion determines that the final page copy can be completed in less than 500 ms.

- **Switchover**: Quiesces and suspends the virtual machine execution on the source host, transfers checkpoint data, and starts the execution of the virtual machine using the checkpoint data on the target host.

The stun time (that is, the time at which the virtual machine is not running anywhere) is typically between 100 ms and 200 ms. Stun time is much higher than this when vGPUs are involved.

Encrypted vMotion

When migrating encrypted virtual machines, vSphere vMotion always uses encryption. For non-encrypted virtual machines, you can select one of the following vMotion encryption options:

- **Disabled**: Do not use encryption.

- **Opportunistic**: Use encryption if the source and destination hosts support it.

- **Required**: If the source or destination host does not support encrypted vMotion, do not allow the migration.

NOTE   Only ESXi Versions 6.5 and later use encrypted vSphere vMotion. To use vMotion to migrate encrypted virtual machines across vCenter Server instances, you must use the vSphere API.

Storage vMotion Details

This section provides details on the Storage vMotion feature in vSphere.

Storage vMotion Overview

Storage vMotion migration is a hot cross-datastore migration. Storage vMotion enables you to migrate a virtual machine and its disk files from one datastore to another while the virtual machine is running. Use cases for Storage vMotion include preparing for datastore maintenance (such as upgrading the underlying storage array), optimizing performance (redistribution of storage load), and transforming the virtual disk provisioning type. When you use Storage vMotion on a virtual machine, you can migrate all the virtual machine files to a single location, migrate individual virtual disks, or separate virtual disks from other virtual machine files.

NOTE Migration with Storage vMotion changes virtual machine files on the destination datastore to match the inventory name of the virtual machine. The migration renames all virtual disk, configuration, snapshot, and NVRAM files. If the new names exceed the maximum filename length, the migration fails.

Storage vMotion Requirements and Limitations

The following are the major requirements and limitations for Storage vMotion in vSphere 8.0:

- Virtual disks in nonpersistent mode are not supported for Storage vMotion. For virtual compatibility mode RDMs, you can migrate just the mapping file or include the migration of the data to a virtual disk file. For physical compatibility mode RDMs, you can only migrate the mapping file.

- Storage vMotion migration is not supported during VMware Tools installation.

- You cannot use Storage vMotion to migrate virtual disks larger than 2 TB from a VMFS Version 5 datastore to a VMFS Version 3 datastore.

- The source host on which the virtual machine is running must have a license that includes Storage vMotion.

- ESXi 4.0 and later hosts do not require vMotion configuration to perform Storage vMotion migrations.

- The host on which the virtual machine is running must have access to both the source and target datastores.

Storage vMotion Data Flow Details

The following major steps are automatically performed by Storage vMotion in vSphere 8.0:

Step 1.   The virtual machine's home directory is copied to the destination datastore.

Step 2. A hidden (shadow) virtual machine starts using the copied files. The underlying processes (worlds) are visible to the **esxtop** utility. The virtual machine continues to run in preexisting worlds.

Step 3. An initial copy of the source virtual disk is made to the destination datastore, and change block tracking (CBT) is leveraged to track blocks that are changed after they are copied.

Step 4. Step 3 is repeated until the number of changed blocks is small enough to support a fast switchover.

Step 5. The system invokes a fast suspend and resume operation that transfers the running virtual machine to the idling hidden virtual machine. The virtual machine now runs in the new worlds. The preexisting worlds that were associated with the virtual machine are removed.

Virtual Machine Cloning

vSphere provides many cloning options, as described in this section.

Clones

When you clone a virtual machine, vCenter Server creates a virtual machine that is a copy of the original virtual machine. The virtual disk files, configuration file, and other files are copied from the original virtual machine to the new virtual machine. The new virtual machine is commonly referred to as a *clone*. The new virtual machine files are named and stored based on parameters you provide during the deployment. You can choose to make some configuration changes and customizations during the cloning process. The contents of some of the files, such as the configuration file, are modified. At the end of the operation, you can manage both the original virtual machine and the new virtual machine as inventory objects in vCenter Server.

Cold Clones

A cold clone occurs when the source virtual machine is powered down prior to starting the clone operation. In this case, vCenter Server does not have to worry about interrupting the execution of the source virtual machine.

Hot Clones

A hot clone occurs when the source virtual machine is running during a clone operation. In this case, the vCenter Server must avoid disrupting the execution of the source virtual machine. To do so, it takes a virtual machine snapshot prior to copying data and removes the snapshot at the end of the operation.

Linked Clones

A linked clone is a virtual machine that is cloned in such a manner that it shares its virtual disk files with the original virtual machine (parent). The shared files are static. Much like a virtual machine that has a snapshot, a linked clone writes its virtual disk changes to separate data files. Compared to a full clone, a linked clone operation is faster and conserves disk space. You cannot use the vSphere Client to directly create linked clones. You can use PowerCLI (via the **-LinkedClone** parameter with the **New-VM** command) or other VMware products to create linked clones. For example, in VMware Horizon you can create desktop pools based on linked clones, and in vCloud Director you can use fast provisioning.

Rapid Provisioning with Templates

As stated previously, templates are objects in the vSphere inventory that are effectively non-executable virtual machines.

You can convert a virtual machine to a template and vice versa. But the main use case for templates is for rapid deployment of new similar virtual machines from a single template. In such a case, you are effectively cloning the template again and again, allowing the template to remain unchanged and ready for future use. To update a template, such as to install the most recent guest OS updates, you can temporarily convert the template to a virtual machine, apply the updates, and convert back to a template.

When you deploy a virtual machine from a template, vCenter Server creates a virtual machine that is a copy of the original template. The virtual disk files, configuration file, and other files are copied from the template to the new virtual machine. The new virtual machine files are named and stored based on parameters you provide during the deployment. You can choose to make some configuration changes and customizations during the cloning process. The contents of some of the files, such as the configuration file, are modified. At the end of the operation, you can manage both the original template and the new virtual machine as inventory objects in vCenter Server.

Deploying a virtual machine from a template is a lot like cloning a virtual machine. In either case, you create a new virtual machine by copying a source object. For template deployments, the source object is a template. For virtual machine cloning, the source object is a virtual machine.

Instant Clones

Starting with vSphere 6.7, you can use the instant clone technology to hot clone a running virtual machine in a manner that is like a combination of vMotion and linked clone technology. The result of an instant clone operation is a new virtual machine (destination virtual machine) that is identical to the source virtual machine. The processor state, virtual device state, memory state, and disk state of the destination virtual machine match those of the source virtual machine. To avoid network conflicts, you can customize the MAC addresses of the virtual NICs, but the guest customization feature is not supported for instant clones. You cannot use the vSphere Client to perform an instant clone operation.

A common use case for instant clones is just-in-time deployment in a VMware Horizon virtual desktop infrastructure (VDI). Instant clones enable you to perform large-scale deployments by creating virtual machines from a controlled point in time. For example, VMware Horizon uses Instant Clone to improve the provisioning process for virtual desktops. Compared to View Composer, which uses linked clones, instant clones eliminate some steps (such as reconfiguration and checkpoints) and replace other steps to greatly reduce the provisioning time. Other use cases are large deployments of identical virtual servers in the cloud and situations where you want to reduce boot storms and provisioning times.

During an instant clone (vmFork) operation, the system quiesces and stuns the source virtual machine, creates and transfers a checkpoint, customizes the destination MAC address and UUID, and forks the memory and disk. The destination virtual machine shares the parent virtual machine's disk and memory for reads. For writes, the destination machine uses copy on write (COW) to direct disk and memory changes to delta files and private memory space.

The requirements for instant clones may depend on the software applications that use the API to perform the cloning operations. For example, VMware Horizon 7.1 requires static port binding, ESXi 6.0 Update 1 or later, and a distributed virtual switch.

Instant cloned virtual machines are fully independent vCenter Server inventory objects. You can manage instant clone destination virtual machines as you would regular virtual machines, without any restrictions.

Exam Preparation Tasks

As mentioned in the section "Book Features and Exam Preparation Methods" in the Introduction, you have some choices for exam preparation: the exercises here, Chapter 15, "Final Preparation," and the exam simulation questions on the companion website.

Review All Key Topics

Review the most important topics in this chapter, noted with the Key Topic icon in the outer margin of the page. Table 5-5 lists these key topics and the page number on which each is found.

Table 5-5 Key Topics for Chapter 5

Key Topic Element	Description	Page Number
Procedure	Host profile workflow	176
List	Content library limitations	177
List	Files in a virtual machine snapshot	180
List	Use cases for snapshots	182
List	Requirements for cross-vCenter Server migrations	192
Section	Virtual machine migration limitations	192
Section	vMotion requirements	194
Section	Instant clones	200

Complete Tables and Lists from Memory

Print a copy of Appendix B, "Memory Tables" (found on the companion website), or at least the section for this chapter, and complete the tables and lists from memory. Appendix C, "Memory Table Answers" (also on the companion website), includes completed tables and lists to check your work.

Define Key Terms

Define the following key terms from this chapter and check your answers in the glossary:

vSphere inventory, data center, cluster, resource pool, template, vApp, host profile, content library, virtual machine snapshot, VMware Tools, vMotion, Storage vMotion

Review Questions

1. Which of the following is not a valid use case for virtual machine snapshots?

   a. Rolling back guest OS changes

   b. Recovering from the accidental deletion of a flat file

   c. Troubleshooting

   d. Linking a clone in a vRA blueprint

2. You are troubleshooting a virtual machine by using the vSphere Client. Which of the following is not a valid debugging and statistics advanced setting?

   a. Record Trivial

   b. Record Debugging

   c. Run Normal

   d. Record Statistics

3. Which of the following is the proper order of phases that occur during a vMotion operation?

   a. Compatibility check, pre-copy, switchover

   b. Pre-copy, compatibility check, switchover

   c. Pre-copy, switchover, compatibility check

   d. Compatibility check, switchover, pre-copy

4. You want to hot migrate a virtual machine from one ESXi host and VMFS datastore on one storage array to another ESXi host and VMFS datastore on a separate storage array. Which of the following statements is true?

   a. This operation is not supported in vSphere 8.0.

   b. The virtual disk data is transferred over the management network.

   c. The virtual disk data is transferred over the vMotion network.

   d. You must perform the operation in two separate steps: in vMotion and in Storage vMotion.

5. You are supporting thousands of virtual machines in a vSphere environment. Which of the following features is associated with vmFork?

   a. Instant clone

   b. Linked clone

   c. Snapshot

   d. Cross-vCenter vMotion

This chapter covers the following topics:

- vSphere Add-ons
- Aria Suite
- Desktop and Application Virtualization
- Replication and Disaster Recovery
- Private, Public, and Hybrid Clouds
- Networking and Security

This chapter contains information related to VMware vSphere 8.x Professional (2V0-21.23) exam objectives 1.13, 1.13.1, 1.13.2, 1.13.3, 2.2, 2.3, 2.4, 2.4.1, 2.4.2, 4.20, 4.20.1, 4.20.2, 4.20.3, 40.20.4, and 5.11.

## CHAPTER 6

VMware Product Integration

This chapter provides information on vSphere 8.0 integration with other VMware products, including Aria Suite, Site Recovery Manager, Horizon, and NSX.

"Do I Know This Already?" Quiz

The "Do I Know This Already?" quiz allows you to assess whether you should study this entire chapter or move quickly to the "Exam Preparation Tasks" section. In any case, the authors recommend that you read the entire chapter at least once. Table 6-1 outlines the major headings in this chapter and the corresponding "Do I Know This Already?" quiz questions. You can find the answers in Appendix A, "Answers to the 'Do I Know This Already?' Quizzes and Review Questions."

Table 6-1 "Do I Know This Already?" Foundation Topics Section-to-Question Mapping

Foundation Topics Section	Questions
vSphere Add-ons	1
Aria Suite	2, 3
Desktop and Application Virtualization	4–6
Replication and Disaster Recovery	7
Private, Public, and Hybrid Clouds	8, 9
Networking and Security	10

1. You want to streamline the development of modern applications by using a familiar single stack for containers and virtual machines. Which of the following products should you use?

    a. VMware Horizon

    b. VMware App Volumes

    c. VMware AppStack

    d. vSphere with Tanzu

2. You want to provide continuous performance optimization and intelligent remediation in your vSphere software-defined data center. Which of the following products should you use?

    a. VMware Aria for Logs

    b. VMware Aria Operations

    c. VMware Aria Automation

    d. VMware Aria Operations for Networks

3. You want to decrease time and effort spent on root cause analysis in your data center. Which of the following products should you use?

    a. VMware Aria for Logs

    b. VMware Aria Operations

    c. VMware Aria Automation

    d. VMware Aria Operations for Networks

4. You want to deliver VDI using stateless virtual desktops and just-in-time delivery of user profile data and applications. Which products should you choose? (Choose two.)

    a. VMware Horizon

    b. Dynamic Environment Manager

    c. vSphere Replication

    d. HCX

    e. App Volumes

5. You want to use App Volumes in your Horizon VDI environment. Which other environments can benefit from App Volumes? (Choose two.)

    a. VCF

    b. VMware on AWS

    c. Citrix XenApp

    d. RDSH

6. You want to provide replication for your vSphere virtual machines to a remote site. Which of the following includes the required software?

    a. vSphere Essentials

    b. Aria Suite

    c. vSphere Foundations

    d. vSphere Standard

7. Which of the following are use cases for VMware Site Recovery Manager? (Choose two.)

   a. Replicate data

   b. Planned migrations

   c. Disaster recovery

   d. VDI

   e. Data center automation

8. You want to use a platform that provides Cloud Builder and SDDC Manager. Which product should you choose?

   a. HCX

   b. Aria Automation

   c. VCF

   d. Aria Operations for Networks

9. You want to implement a workload mobility platform that simplifies application migration, workload rebalancing, and business continuity across hybrid clouds. Which product should you implement?

   a. HCX

   b. Aria Automation

   c. VCF

   d. Aria Operations for Networks

10. You want to adopt zero-trust security and automated network deployment. Which of the following products should you use?

    a. VMware NSX

    b. HCX

    c. VCF

    d. AppDefense

Foundation Topics

vSphere Add-ons

This section addresses the following products that are part of vSphere or directly related to vSphere but that are not covered in detail in other chapters of this book:

- **vSphere with Tanzu**: A vSphere edition that natively provides support for containers in the hypervisor

- **vSphere+**: A product that transforms an on-premise vSphere environment to a SaaS (software as a service)-based infrastructure.

- **vCenter Converter**: A product that facilitates the conversion of physical and other servers into virtual machines running in vSphere

- **vSphere Replication**: A virtual machine replication feature that is included with specific vSphere editions

- **VMware Skyline**: A proactive support offering for many VMware products, including vSphere

vSphere with Tanzu

You can enable vSphere with Tanzu on vSphere clusters to turn the clusters into a platform for running Kubernetes workloads with a Kubernetes control plane in the hypervisor layer. You can deploy vSphere pods for running Kubernetes containers natively or create upstream Kubernetes clusters through the VMware Tanzu Kubernetes Grid. vSphere 8 documentation typically uses the term *supervisor* to refer to a vSphere cluster enabled for vSphere with Tanzu, whereas vSphere 7 documentation uses the term *supervisor cluster*.

A DevOps engineer can run Kubernetes workloads within a vSphere namespace, use Tanzu Kubernetes Grid to deploy and manage multiple upstream Kubernetes clusters, deploy Kubernetes containers directly in vSphere pods on the supervisor, and deploy standard VMs. A vSphere pod, which is the equivalent of a Kubernetes pod, is a VM with a small footprint running one or more Linux containers. Its compute size, storage size, and resource reservations are precisely configured for its workload. vSphere pods are only supported with supervisors that are configured with NSX as the networking stack. Figure 6-1 is a logical diagram of these components.

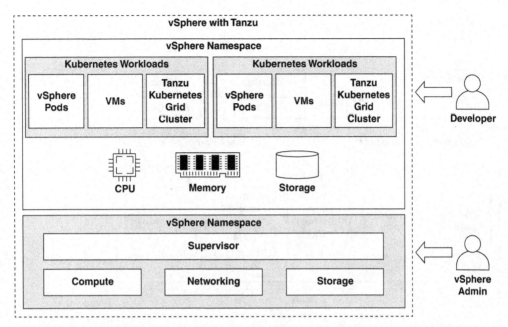

Figure 6-1 vSphere with Tanzu

A vSphere namespace is a domain and resource boundary where vSphere pods, VMs, and Tanzu Kubernetes Grid clusters can run. A vSphere administrator can create vSphere namespaces on the supervisor. Initially, a namespace has unlimited resources within the supervisor. However, it is possible to set limits on the namespace's compute and storage resource, which is backed by vSphere resource pools and Kubernetes storage quotas. You can provide DevOps engineers and other user groups with access to vSphere namespaces by applying permissions to user groups available via vCenter Single Sign-on identity sources or via an OpenID Connect (OIDC) provider registered with the supervisor. Figure 6-2 shows the architecture of a single-cluster supervisor.

You can provide high availability for Kubernetes workloads against cluster-level failures by using vSphere zones. You can use the vSphere Client to create vSphere zones and map them to vSphere clusters. You can deploy a supervisor on three vSphere zones for high availability. Alternatively, you can deploy a supervisor on a single vSphere cluster, which creates a vSphere zone automatically. You can also deploy a supervisor to a cluster that is already mapped to a zone.

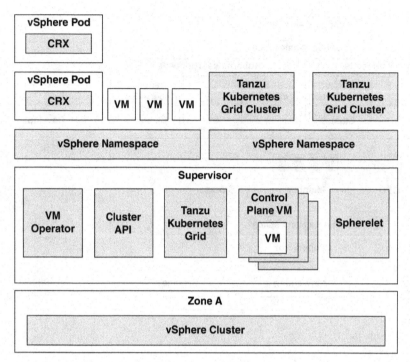

Figure 6-2   Single-Cluster Supervisor

In a three-zone supervisor, a namespace resource pool is created on each vSphere cluster that is mapped to a zone. The namespace spreads across all three vSphere clusters in each zone. Tanzu Kubernetes Grid can be used to make Kubernetes available as a utility, much like an electrical grid. Operators and developers can use this grid to create and manage clusters using a declarative manner that is familiar to Kubernetes users. Tanzu Kubernetes Grid deploys clusters using a configuration of Kubernetes open source software that is supported by VMware. You can provision and operate upstream Tanzu Kubernetes Grid clusters on supervisors by using Tanzu Kubernetes Grid.

A three-zone supervisor has the following components:

- **Supervisor control plane VM**: The zones are load balanced, and each has its own IP address.

- **Tanzu Kubernetes Grid and Cluster API**: Modules running on the supervisor enable provisioning and management of Tanzu Kubernetes Grid clusters.

- **Virtual Machine Service**: A module deploys standalone VMs and VMs that make up Tanzu Kubernetes Grid clusters.

Figure 6-3 shows the architecture of a three-zone supervisor.

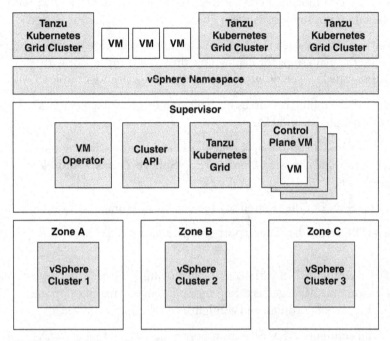

Figure 6-3   A Three-Zone Supervisor

vSphere with Tanzu Use Cases

The following are key use cases for vSphere with Tanzu:

- Streamlining application development for hybrid and public clouds

- Modernizing applications using existing infrastructure

- Accelerating innovation using a single infrastructure stack

- Boosting application performance and resiliency

vSphere with Tanzu Integration

The steps to implement vSphere with Tanzu are dependent on your choice for the networking stack, in addition to other considerations. You can choose between the following options for the networking stack when deploying a supervisor:

- NSX

- vSphere Distributed Switch (vDS)and the HAProxy load balancer

- vDS networking with the NSX Advanced Load Balancer

In vSphere 8.0 with Tanzu, NSX for the networking stack supports vSphere pods, Tanzu Kubernetes clusters, Embedded Harbor Registry, and load balancing. vDS for the networking stack does not support vSphere Pods or Embedded Harbor Registry.

Each choice for the networking stack involves a unique implementation workflow. For example, here are the main steps for deploying a three-node supervisor with NSX as the networking stack:

Step 1. Configure the compute resources by deploying three vSphere clusters and configuring DRS and HA.

Step 2. Use the vSphere Client to map a zone to each cluster by selecting the vCenter Server and choosing **Configure** > **vSphere Zones** > **Add New vSphere Zone**.

Step 3. Configure vSAN or other shared storage and create storage policies.

Step 4. Create a vDS, create distributed port groups, and add the hosts to the vDS.

Step 5. Deploy and configure NSX Manager by deploying NSX Manager nodes, adding a Compute Manager, creating transport zones, creating IP pools, creating uplinks and profiles, and configuring NSX on the cluster.

Step 6. Deploy and configure NSX Edge transport nodes by creating an NSX Edge cluster, creating an NSX Tier-0 uplink segment, and creating an NSX Tier-0 gateway.

Step 7. Deploy and configure the supervisor.

These are the high-level steps for deploying and configuring a supervisor:

Step 1. In the vSphere Client, use **Home** > **Workload Management** > **Get Started** to provide a name, vSphere cluster, storage, load balancer, network mode, and other settings for the supervisor.

Step 2. Assign a license to the supervisor by selecting **Workload Management** > **Supervisors** > **Configure** > **Licensing**.

Step 3. Select **Workload Management** > **Namespaces** > **Create Namespace** to create the namespace and assign its compute resource limits, storage limits, permissions, and security policy.

Step 4. Select **Workload Management** > **Supervisors** > **Configure** to generate the CSR and then select **Workload Platform Management** > **Actions** > **Replace Certificate**.

Step 5. Integrate the Tanzu Kubernetes Grid on the supervisor with Tanzu Mission Control by setting the registration URL at **Workload Management** > **Configure** > **TKG Service Tanzu Mission Control**.

Step 6. Set the default container network interface (CNI) by selecting **Workload Management** > **Configure** > **TKG Service**.

Step 7. Change the control plane size and the management network settings of the supervisor by selecting **Workload Management** > **Supervisors** > **Configure** and setting the **Network** and **Control Plane Size** options.

To view the state and settings of a vSphere namespace using the vSphere Client, expand the vSphere cluster in the inventory pane, select the Namespaces resource pool, and examine the Status, Permissions, Storage, Capacity and Usage, and Tanzu Kubernetes cards. To change permissions, storage, or resource limit settings, select the appropriate option in the appropriate card, such as Manage Permissions, Edit Storage, or Edit Limits.

You can create a Tanzu Kubernetes Grid workload cluster by using these high-level steps:

Step 1. Install the Tanzu CLI in a bootstrap machine (Windows, Linux, or Mac).

Step 2. Install Kubernetes CLI and other tools in the bootstrap machine.

Step 3. Connect the Tanzu CLI to the supervisor.

Step 4. Create a configuration file with a Kubernetes-style object specification for the cluster object

Step 5. Create the cluster with the **tanzu cluster create** command.

vSphere+

VMware vSphere+ brings together on-premises and cloud components to form a hybrid solution. It is a cloud-connected subscription-based offering that connects the existing vCenter Server and ESXi hosts you have running on premises today with VMware Cloud. Workloads continue to run on premises, but the management platform runs in the cloud. vSphere+ is designed to transform existing on-premises deployments into SaaS-enabled infrastructure, providing centralized management and high-value cloud services through the VMware Cloud console. The on-premises vCenter Server is connected to a Cloud console through a VMware cloud gateway.

The Cloud console centralizes many tasks that would normally need to be performed separately from multiple vCenter instances. It provides administrative services, such as vCenter lifecycle management, global inventory, event view, security health check, VM provisioning, and configuration management services.

With vSphere+, you get developer services, such as Tanzu Kubernetes Grid service, VM service, network service, storage service, Tanzu integrated service, and Tanzu Mission Control Essentials.

vSphere+ Use Cases

The following are key use cases for vSphere+:

- Activating hybrid cloud services for business-critical applications running on premises, including disaster recovery and ransomware protection

- Transforming on-premises infrastructure into SaaS-enabled infrastructure

- Providing a unified infrastructure management experience for a distributed environment via the VMware Cloud console

- Transforming on-premises infrastructure into an enterprise-ready Kubernetes platform

vSphere+ Integration

The transition from on-premises vSphere to vSphere+ involves an in-place upgrade and a license conversion. The upgrade involves connecting the on-premises vCenter Server to VMware Cloud via one or more cloud gateways. It may require upgrading vCenter Server to the latest release. After that, you convert your vSphere licenses to subscriptions.

vCenter Converter

VMware *vCenter Converter* (also called Converter Standalone) is a free solution that automates the process of converting existing Windows and Linux machines into virtual machines running in a vSphere environment. The source machines can be physical servers or virtual machines in non-ESXi environments. You can use Converter to convert virtual machines running in VMware Workstation, VMware Fusion, Hyper-V, and Amazon EC2 Windows to virtual machines running in vSphere.

With Converter, you can hot clone Windows servers without disrupting users of the source Windows Server. With hot cloning, you can minimize downtime when converting existing Windows and Linux servers to virtual machines running in vSphere.

Converter offers a centralized management console that allows users to queue and monitor multiple simultaneous remote and local conversions.

vCenter Converter Use Cases

The following are common use cases for vCenter Converter:

- Creating virtual machine templates based on existing servers

- Converting from physical to virtual servers

- Migrating VMs from non-vSphere environments

vCenter Converter Integration

Converter is a standalone product that you can install on a Windows system. You can install it locally on a Windows desktop or on a server instance. To enable remote creation and management of tasks, you can install Converter's server and worker components on a Windows server in your data center and install the client component on multiple desktops. The server component installs an agent component on each Windows source machine prior to hot cloning.

In the Converter user interface, you can specify a vCenter Server as the destination for a conversion operation. You must provide credentials with sufficient privileges to create the virtual machine in the vSphere environment.

VMware vSphere Replication

VMware vSphere Replication is included in multiple editions of vSphere. See the section "Replication and Disaster Recovery," later in this chapter, for details.

VMware SkyLine

VMware *Skyline* is a proactive support technology, developed by VMware Global Services, that is available to customers with an active Production Support or Premier Services agreement. Skyline helps you avoid problems before they occur and reduces the amount of time spent on support requests.

The Skyline architecture includes Skyline Collector, a standalone on-premises virtual appliance for secure, automatic data collection. It also includes Skyline Advisor, a self-service web portal for accessing your VMware inventory, proactive findings, recommendations, and risks. You can segment data by factors such as region and lines of business. You can use VMware Cloud Services console to control user access and permissions. With a Premier Services agreement, you can access executive summary reports and view more powerful recommendations.

You can use Skyline Advisor to access Skyline Log Assist, which automatically (with your permission) uploads support log bundles to VMware Technical Support and eliminates manual procedures for log gathering and uploading. If you approve a request in Skyline Advisor, the requested logs are automatically uploaded to VMware Support. Likewise, you can choose to proactively push log files to VMware Support by using Log Assist within Skyline Advisor.

VMware SkyLine Use Cases

Skyline is commonly used to avoid issues and streamline resolution in a vSphere environment.

VMware SkyLine Integration

See Chapter 10, "Managing and Monitoring Clusters and Resources," for instructions on configuring vCenter Server integration with Skyline Health.

Aria Suite

This section covers the Aria Suite, formerly known as vRealize Suite, which is a set of products that provides a layer for operations, automation, and analysis for software-defined data centers and hybrid clouds.

Aria Operations

Aria Operations Manager (formerly known as vRealize Operations) provides operations management for private, hybrid, and multi-cloud environments in a single pane of glass. It offers full-stack visibility from physical, virtual, and cloud infrastructure to virtual machines, containers, and applications. It provides continuous performance optimization, efficient capacity planning, cost management, and integrated compliance. It offers self-driving operations and intelligent remediation. It is available as an on-premises offering and as a SaaS offering.

Aria Operations provides intelligent alerts, trending, and forecasting functionality. It uses current, historical, and predicted data for capacity analysis. For example, it calculates and provides a Days Remaining metric for many managed objects, such as vSphere clusters and datastores. This metric represents the number of days until the resource is predicted to have insufficient capacity. It applies customizable policies for everything it does. For example, you can use policies to adjust headroom buffers and provisioning lead times that impact capacity analysis.

Aria Operations provides many native dashboards for management and troubleshooting. In addition, it offers many management packs to extend its operations beyond just vSphere. For example, you can install VMware-provided and third-party management packs that support operations for vSAN, NSX, third-party network gear, third-party storage system, and third-party software applications. Each management pack has its own unique requirements, which typically include installing the pack and connecting it to a management endpoint for the managed entity.

Aria Operations Use Cases

The following are common use cases for Aria Operations:

- Continuous performance optimization

- Integrated compliance

- Next-generation operations platform

- Capacity and cost management and planning
- Intelligent remediation

Aria Operations Integration

In the Aria Operations user interface, you can use the Solutions page to add a vCenter Server adapter instance (cloud account). You configure the instance by providing the address and user credentials for connecting to vCenter Server. At a minimum, the user account must have Read privileges assigned at the data center or vCenter Server level. To collect virtual machine guest OS metrics, the credential must have Performance > Modify Intervals permission enabled in the target. Additional requirements exist to allow Aria Operations to perform automated actions in vSphere.

Aria for Logs

Aria for Logs (formerly known as vRealize Log Insight) is a software product that provides intelligent log management for infrastructure and applications for any environment. It is a highly scalable log management solution that provides intuitive dashboards, analytics, and third-party extensibility. It collects and automatically identifies structure in all types of machine-generated log data, such as application logs, network traces, configuration files, messages, performance data, and system state dumps. It builds a high-performance index for performing analytics. It monitors and manages machine data at scale.

Aria for Logs is especially useful in a large environment with multiple vCenter Server instances and complex infrastructure. You can configure Aria for Logs to collect and analyze data from the vCenter Servers, ESXi hosts, guest operating systems, network infrastructure, storage infrastructure, and more. It provides a single pane of glass you can use to analyze data from the entire stack when troubleshooting.

Aria for Logs Use Cases

Aria for Logs is commonly used to decrease time and effort spent on root cause analysis and to aid in centralized log management and analysis.

Aria for Logs Integration

To collect alarms, events, and tasks data from a vSphere environment, you must connect Aria for Logs to one or more vCenter Server systems. Aria for Logs can collect events, tasks, alerts, and other structured data directly from the vCenter Server. It can also collect unstructured data from ESXi hosts and the vCenter Server via syslog.

When connecting the vCenter Server to Aria for Logs, you must provide a service account with appropriate privileges. To collect structured data from the vCenter Server, the service account must have the System.View privilege. To collect syslog data from ESXi hosts, the account must have the following privileges:

- Host.Configuration.Change settings
- Host.Configuration.Network configuration
- Host.Configuration.Advanced Settings
- Host.Configuration.Security Profile and Firewall

See the "Aria for Logs" section in Chapter 10 for instructions on configuring vRLI to integrate with vCenter Server.

Aria Automation

Aria Automation (formerly known as vRealize Automation) is an automation platform for private and multi-cloud environments. It delivers self-service automation, DevOps for infrastructure, and network automation that help you increase your business's agility, productivity, and efficiency. With Aria Automation, your internal IT teams, DevOps engineers, developers, and others get the infrastructure, applications, and resources they need as a service with a public cloud–like experience. Customers benefit from increased speed, flexibility, reliability, and scalability, and you maintain security and control.

Aria Automation includes Cloud Assembly, Service Broker, and Code Stream:

- You can use Cloud Assembly to iteratively develop and deploy blueprints for your vSphere environment and other clouds.
- You can use Service Broker to create, manage, and use self-service catalog items.
- You can use Code Stream to create pipelines that automate your entire DevOps lifecycle, including automation of software testing and release.

With Cloud Assembly, you can build blueprints that automatically provision virtual machines based on existing virtual machines and templates in your vSphere environment. In a blueprint, you define the provisioning method, such as full clone or linked clone. You can configure the blueprint to provision multiple virtual machines, applications, and networks. For example, you can develop a blueprint to deploy a multitier application involving multiple virtual machines, networks, and software components. You can publish the blueprints and use Service Broker to make them available as a service in the self-service catalog. You can configure Aria Automation to allow consumers to provision the multitier application and its networks on demand and to destroy it when it is no longer needed.

Aria Automation Use Cases

The following are common use cases for Aria Automation:

- **Self-service private and hybrid clouds**: Aria Automation provides a self-service catalog for delivering IaaS in an on-premises vSphere environment, private clouds built on VMware Cloud Foundation, and VMware Cloud Foundation on AWS.

- **Multi-cloud automation with governance**: An organization that uses Aria Automation can extend self-service automation to multiple public clouds, including Amazon Web Services, Microsoft Azure, and Google Cloud Platform.

- **DevOps**: Aria Automation provides automation for continuous integration/continuous development (CI/CD) pipelines.

- **Kubernetes automation**: Aria Automation can be used to automate Kubernetes cluster and namespace provisioning management and support.

Aria Automation Integration

To begin using Aria Automation, you need to deploy an Aria Automation instance to a management vSphere cluster. The deployment typically involves three Aria Automation virtual appliances and three VMware Identity Manager (vIDM) appliances. To facilitate the deployment of these appliances, you can deploy and use the Aria Lifecycle Manager (LCM) appliance.

To provide vSphere automation using Aria Automation, you need to add at least one vCenter cloud account. The vCenter Server that you use for a cloud account manages the user workload vSphere clusters. The cloud account provides the credentials that Aria Automation uses to connect to vCenter Server. Some of the required, key privileges are datastore space allocation, folder manipulation, network assignment, virtual machine configuration, content library management, virtual machines interaction, and snapshot management.

Aria Orchestrator

Aria Orchestrator (formerly known as vRealize Orchestrator) is a modern workflow automation platform that simplifies complex infrastructure processes. It is a key component of Aria Automation for providing custom workflows within on-demand services and providing anything as a service (XaaS). It can be used independently to run prebuilt workflows and to create custom workflows. It automates management and operational tasks of VMware and third-party systems, such as ticketing systems, change management systems, and IT asset management systems.

In a vSphere environment, you may frequently perform some operational tasks. For example, say that you frequently receive requests to support the update procedure for a complex application involving multiple virtual machines. For each update, you are required to take the following actions:

Step 1.   Shut down the virtual machines, one by one, in a specific order, ensuring that each shutdown operation completes prior to beginning the next shutdown.

Step 2.   Create a snapshot of each virtual machine.

Step 3.   Power on the virtual machines, one by one, in a specific order, ensuring that the guest OS and application services for each one are running prior to beginning the next power on.

Step 4.   Inform the application team that the application is ready for update.

Step 5.   Following a successful update, delete the snapshots.

With Aria Orchestrator, you can build workflows to automate all or portions of such an operation. For example, Aria Orchestrator provides out-of-the-box workflows for virtual machine power and snapshot operations. You can build a custom workflow that leverages the existing workflows as nested workflows. In the custom workflow, you can add data input, conditional paths, looping, and monitoring.

Aria Orchestrator Use Cases

Aria Orchestrator is typically used to orchestrate common vSphere operations tasks, orchestrate common data center infrastructure and application tasks, and provide XaaS for an Aria Orchestrator environment.

Aria Orchestrator Integration

You can configure Aria Orchestrator to use Aria Automation authentication or vSphere authentication. To use vSphere authentication, in the Aria Orchestrator Control Center, set Configure Authentication Provider > Authentication Mode to vSphere and configure it to use the credentials of the local administrator account of the vCenter Single Sign-On (SSO) domain (administrator@vsphere.local by default). With Aria Orchestrator, you must use vCenter Server 6.0 or later. To add a vCenter Server instance, you run the provided Add a vCenter Server Instance workflow.

Aria Operations for Networks

Aria Operations for Networks (formerly known as vRealize Network Insight) helps you build an optimized, highly available, and secure network infrastructure for hybrid clouds and multi-clouds. It accelerates micro-segmentation planning and implementation. It provides auditing for changes to the security posture and helps you ensure compliance. It facilitates troubleshooting across network infrastructure (virtual and physical) and security infrastructure.

Aria Operations for Networks provides network visibility and analytics to accelerate micro-segmentation security, minimize risk during application migration, optimize network performance, and manage NSX, SD-WAN VeloCloud, and Kubernetes deployments.

Aria Operations for Networks Use Cases

The following are common use cases for Aria Operations for Networks.

- **Plan application security and migration**: Aria Operations for Networks accelerates microsegmentation deployment for private clouds and public clouds.

- **Optimize and troubleshoot virtual and physical networks**: Aria Operations for Networks enables you to reduce the mean time to resolution for application connectivity issues, eliminate network bottlenecks, and audit network and security changes.

- **Manage and scale NSX**: Aria Operations for Networks covers multiple NSX Manager instances and increases your availability by proactively detecting configuration issues.

Aria Operations for Networks Integration

You can add VMware managers, such as vCenter Server, VMware NSX Manager, and VMware NSX-T Manager, to Aria Operations for Networks for data collection. To add a vCenter Server to Aria Operations for Networks as a data source, you need to have the following privileges applied and propagated at the root level:

- System.Anonymous

- System.Read

- System.View

- Global.Settings

To support IPFIX, you also need the Modify and Port Configuration Operation privilege on the distributed switches and Modify and Policy Operation on the distributed port groups.

To identify VM-to-VM paths, you must install VMware Tools in the virtual machines.

Desktop and Application Virtualization

This section addresses VMware products for desktop and application virtualization.

VMware Horizon

VMware Horizon is a platform for securely delivering virtual desktops and applications in private clouds and hybrid clouds. It enables provisioning and management of desktop pools that have thousands of virtual desktops each. It streamlines the management of images, applications, profiles, and policies for desktops and their users. It integrates with VMware Workspace ONE Access, which establishes and verifies end-user identity with multifactor authentication and serves as the basis for conditional access and network microsegmentation policies for Horizon virtual desktops and applications.

Horizon includes instant clones and works with VMware Dynamic Environment Manager and VMware App Volumes to dynamically provide just-in-time (JIT) delivery of user profile data and applications to stateless desktops.

Horizon provisions large pools of virtual desktops from a small set of base virtual desktops by integrating with vCenter Server. Horizon makes the provisioning requests, which are carried out by vCenter Server in the appropriate vSphere clusters. vSphere provides the environment, including the compute, storage, and network resources for running the virtual desktops. With vSphere DRS and vSphere HA, it provides load balancing and high availability.

VMware Horizon Use Cases

The following are common use cases for VMware Horizon:

- Remote users
- Kiosk and task users
- Call centers
- Bring-your-own-device (BYOD) deployments
- Graphics-intensive applications

VMware Horizon Integration

To get started with Horizon, in the vSphere environment, you need to prepare vSphere clusters to be used as resources for virtual desktop provisioning. You must add vCenter Server instances by using the Horizon console. When adding a vCenter Server instance, you need to provide the vCenter Server address and appropriate user credentials. You can use the administrator account in the SSO domain (administrator@vsphere.local by default) or, preferably, an account that is assigned the minimum privileges. The minimum privileges include virtual machine provisioning, configuring, and interaction, plus other privileges such as folder management and datastore allocation. The use of instant clones requires additional privileges.

App Volumes

VMware *App Volumes* is a set of application and user management solutions for VMware Horizon, Citrix Virtual Apps and Desktops, and Remote Desktop Services Host (RDSH) virtual environments. It streamlines your ability to deliver, update, assign, and manage applications and users across virtual desktop infrastructure (VDI) and published application environments. With App Volumes, you install an application once, using a provisioning computer, collect the application components in application packages, and centrally control the mapping of application packages to desktops.

Application packages and companion writable volumes are stored in virtual disk files and attached to virtual machines to deliver applications. Updates to applications involve updating or replacing application packages or their mappings to desktops.

In RDSH environments, applications are installed on servers and delivered via Remote Desktop. Using App Volumes with RDSH simplifies the installation and management of the application on the server. Instead of attaching an application package to desktops, you attach the application package to RDSH servers and allow RDSH to deliver the application to users.

App Volumes Use Cases

The following are common use cases for App Volumes:

- Application virtualization in VMware Horizon VDI environments
- Application virtualization in Citrix XenDesktop and XenApp environments
- Virtualization for RDSH-delivered applications

App Volumes Integration

To integrate App Volumes with vSphere, the main step is to use the App Volumes management console to register a vCenter Server as a machine manager. This requires a specific set of privileges in vCenter Server, such as privileges to use the datastores, to view and stop sessions, and to configure virtual disks for virtual machines.

Replication and Disaster Recovery

This section addresses VMware products for replication and disaster recovery.

vSphere Replication

vSphere Replication is an extension to VMware vCenter Server that provides hypervisor-based virtual machine replication and recovery. It provides virtual machine replication between the following source and destination combinations:

- Data center to data center
- Cluster to cluster within a data center
- Multiple source sites to a shared target site

vSphere Replication provides many benefits over storage-based replication:

- Lower cost per virtual machine
- Flexibility in storage vendor selection at the source and target sites
- Lower overall cost per replication

vSphere Replication is compatible with most vSphere features, including vMotion, Storage vMotion, vSphere HA, DRS, Storage DRS, vSAN, and DPM. It is not compatible with vSphere Fault Tolerance.

vSphere Replication Use Cases

vSphere Replication is commonly used for disaster recovery, virtual machine recovery, and data center migrations.

vSphere Replication Integration

vSphere Replication does not require separate licensing. Instead, it is included as a feature of the following vSphere license editions, with no limit on the number of replicated virtual machines:

- vSphere Essentials Plus
- vSphere Standard
- vSphere Enterprise
- vSphere Enterprise Plus

A minimum vSphere Replication deployment involves a single virtual appliance per site that provides vSphere Replication Management Service (VRMS) and vSphere Replication Service (VRS). It requires that specific network ports—including TCP 80, 443, and 902—be open for ESXi hosts. Likewise, it requires TCP ports 80, 443, 10443, and 7444 to be open for the vCenter Server.

vSphere Replication provides hypervisor-based replication, in which a vSphere Replication agent in the hypervisor collects and transmits changed blocks to the target VRS appliance. The method is similar to the Change Block Tracking (CBT) feature in ESXi, but it is a mechanism that is unique to vSphere Replication and prevents compatibility issues with technologies leveraging CBT.

It is possible to connect up to nine virtual appliances running just VRS for each vCenter Server instance. A single VRMS appliance and nine VRS appliances can work in unison to provide replication for a single vCenter Server environment for up to 4000 replicated virtual machines when using vSphere 8 and vSphere Replication 8.6.

Prior to installing vSphere Replication, you need to set the vCenter Server advanced setting VirtualCenter.FQDN to the fully qualified domain name of the vCenter Server. To install vSphere Replication, you use the standard vSphere OVF deployment wizard in the vSphere Client. Then you use the vCenter Server Appliance Management Interface (VAMI) to register the appliance with vCenter Single Sign-On. Successful registration produces a Site Recovery option on the vSphere Client home page. To replicate between sites, you deploy vSphere Replication to both sites and configure a vSphere Replication connection between the sites, using the Site Recovery page in the vSphere Client.

Configuring vSphere Replication involves the following steps:

Step 1. In the vSphere Client, navigate to **Home > Site Recovery > Open Site Recovery**.

Step 2. Select a vSphere connected pair and click **View Details**.

Step 3. Click the **Replications** tab.

Step 4. Select **Outgoing** or **Incoming** and click the **Create New Replication** icon.

Step 5. Complete the wizard to configure the replication settings, such as those for the target, seed, recovery point objective (RPO), point in time instances, and quiescing options.

To recover a virtual machine, you follow these steps:

Step 1. In the vSphere Client, navigate to **Home > Site Recovery > Open Site Recovery**.

Step 2.   Select a vSphere connected pair and click **View Details**.

Step 3.   Click the **Replications** tab.

Step 4.   Select a replication instance in the **Incoming** section.

Step 5.   Click the **Recover** icon.

Step 6.   Choose **Synchronize Recent Changes** to perform a final synchroniza-tion or **Use Latest Available Data** to continue without performing a final synchronization.

Step 7.   Optionally, select **Power on the Virtual Machine After Recovery**.

Step 8.   Complete the wizard by selecting the target folder, compute resource, and other options.

You can leverage alarms in vCenter Server to get alerts about issues in vSphere Replication, such as issues with the connection, a VRS instance, or a specific replication. For example, you configure an alarm to be triggered whenever a configured replication exceeds the configured RPO.

vSphere Replication 8.6 offers the following additional options when replicating a virtual machine:

- Recovery point objective (RPO)
- Guest file system quiescing
- Data compression
- Data encryption
- Multiple points in time (MPIT)
- Replication seeds

Site Recovery Manager (SRM)

VMware *Site Recovery Manager (SRM)* is a business continuity solution that you can use to orchestrate planned migrations, test recoveries, and disaster recoveries. For data replication, SRM integrates with vSphere Replication and supported storage-based replication products. In SRM you can build recovery plans that include recovery steps, virtual machine priority groups, dependencies, IP address changes, and resource mappings. You can run a single plan in one of three modes:

- **Planned Migration Mode**: In Planned Migration Mode, SRM automatically shuts down the source virtual machines prior to migration, performs a final data synchronization, and stops if errors occur.

- **Disaster Recovery Mode**: In Disaster Recovery Mode, SRM attempts to shut down and synchronize the source virtual machines but continues with recovery.

- **Test Mode**: In Test Mode, SRM leaves the source machines running while it brings up another instance of each virtual machine, using snapshots at the recovery site in an isolated network. During a test recovery, the source machines continue to be replicated and protected. After a test recovery, you should run a cleanup to shut down and remove the target site snapshots.

SRM is tightly integrated with vSphere Replication in vSphere 8.0. To use SRM, you begin by navigating to Home > Site Recovery in the vSphere Client.

SRM Use Cases

SRM is commonly used for disaster recovery, disaster recovery testing, and data center migrations.

SRM Integration

Prior to installing SRM, you should implement a supported replication technology, such as EMC RecoverPoint or vSphere Replication. You need to deploy SRM to both the source and target sites. You can install a Windows-based version of SRM in a supported Windows server, or you can deploy the SRM virtual appliance. In most cases, you should deploy the SRM appliance, which includes an embedded vPostgreSQL database that supports a full-scale SRM environment.

At each site, you need to deploy an SRM server and register it with a vCenter Server. SRM requires a separate vCenter Server at the source site and at the target site.

SRM uses Transport Layer Security (TLS) and solution user authentication for secured connections with vCenter Server. It assigns a private key and a certificate to the solution user and registers it with the vCenter Single Sign-On service. When you pair SRM instances across vCenter Servers that do not use Enhanced Linked Mode, Site Recovery Manager creates an additional solution user at the remote site.

Private, Public, and Hybrid Clouds

This section addresses VMware products for private, public, and hybrid clouds.

VMware Cloud Foundation (VCF)

VCF is a hybrid cloud platform built on a full-stack hyperconverged infrastructure (HCI) technology. It provides a single easy-to-deploy architecture that enables consistent, secure infrastructure and operations across private and public clouds.

VCF provides the following features:

- Automated bring-up of the software stack, including vSphere, vCenter Server, vSAN, NSX-T, and Aria Suite

- Simplified provisioning in workload domains built on vSphere, vSAN, and NSX-T

- Application-focused management, leveraging vSphere with Tanzu to support virtual machines and containers in the same platform

- With Automated Lifecycle Management (LCM), simplified updates for all components in the stack

- Multi-instance management, which allows multiple VCF instances to be managed together

Each version of VCF includes a set of specific VMware products and specific versions. For example, these are the main components in a private cloud powered by VCF 4.5:

- Cloud Builder 4.5

- SDDC Manager 4.5

- vCenter Server 7.0U3h

- ESXi 7.0U3g

- vSAN 7.0U3g

- NSX-T 3.2.1.2

- Aria Suite 8.8.2

Cloud Builder is the VCF component that automates the deployment of the entire software-defined stack. SDDC Manager is the VCF component that automates the entire system lifecycle and simplifies day-to-day management and operations.

The standard model for VCF uses separate virtual infrastructure domains for running management and user workloads. VCF also supports a consolidated model, in which the management and user workloads run in the same virtual infrastructure domain.

VCF Use Cases

VCF is commonly used for private clouds, hybrid clouds, modern applications, and VDI.

VCF Integration

To get started with VCF, you should prepare ESXi hosts for the implementation of the management domain, address network and environment prerequisites, fill in the deployment parameter workbook, deploy the VMware Cloud Builder appliance, and use Cloud Builder to deploy the management domain, including vCenter Server.

VMware Hybrid Cloud Extension (HCX)

VMware HCX is a workload mobility platform that simplifies application migration, workload rebalancing, and business continuity across on-premises data centers, private clouds, and hybrid clouds. HCX enables you to migrate thousands of virtual machines, migrate from non-vSphere platforms, upgrade vSphere versions, balance workload between on-premises and cloud, and implement replication to protect against disaster.

VMware HCX enables you to schedule and migrate thousands of vSphere virtual machines within and across data centers without requiring a reboot. HCX offers many services with each VMware HCX license (Advanced or Enterprise), as listed in Table 6-2.

Table 6-2 VMware HCX Services

Service	License	Description
Interconnect	Advanced	Creates secured connections between HCX instances, supporting migration, replication, disaster recovery, and management operations.
WAN Optimization	Advanced	Optimizes the performance of the connection provided by HCX Interconnect through a combination of deduplication, compression, and line conditioning techniques.
Network Extension	Advanced	Extends (that is, provides Layer 2 adjacency for) the virtual machine networks between source and remote HCX-enabled environments.
Bulk Migration	Advanced	Migrates a set of virtual machines using VMware vSphere Replication in parallel between HCX-enabled sites.
vMotion Migration	Advanced	Migrates a single virtual machine between HCX-enabled sites with no service interruption, using vMotion.
Disaster Recovery	Advanced	Protects virtual machines from disaster by using replication and recovery.
Mobility Groups	Enterprise	Allows you to group virtual machines by application, network, or other aspects for migration and monitoring.

Service	License	Description
OS Assisted Migration	Enterprise	Leverages HCX Sentinel software in the guest OS to migrate Windows and Linux virtual machines to a vSphere-enabled data center. Uses a gateway appliance at the source and a receiver appliance at the destination.
Replication Assisted vMotion (RAV)	Enterprise	Migrates a set of virtual machines in parallel, using VMware vSphere Replication and vMotion between HCX-enabled sites with no service interruption.
Site Recovery Manager (SRM) Integration	Enterprise	Integrates HCX functionality with the VMware SRM for protection and orchestrated recovery operations.
Traffic Engineering: Application Path Resiliency and TCP Flow Conditioning	Enterprise	Optimizes network traffic for HCX Interconnect and Network Extension services. The Application Path Resiliency service creates multiple tunnel flows for both Interconnect and Network Extension traffic. The TCP Flow Conditioning service adjusts and optimizes the segment size to reduce fragmentation and reduce the overall packet rate.
Mobility Optimized Networking (MON)	Enterprise	Integrates HCX Network Extension with NSX Dynamic Routing to enable optimal networking between migrated virtual machines and other virtual machines. Works with new or existing network extensions to NSX-T 3.0 Data Center.

HCX Use Cases

HCX is commonly used for cloud adoption and migration, workload rebalancing, and business continuity.

HCX Integration

To integrate HCX into an on-premises vSphere environment, you need to implement HCX components that connect the environment to another environment, such as a hosted private cloud or hybrid cloud. The following are the key components, which provide the services described in Table 6-2:

- HCX Connector and HCX Cloud Installation
- HCX-IX Interconnect Appliance

- HCX WAN Optimization Appliance
- HCX Network Extension Virtual Appliance

VMware HCX is used in VMware on AWS, Azure VMware Solution, and other hybrid cloud solutions.

VMware Cloud (VMC) on AWS

VMware Cloud (VMC) on Amazon Web Services (AWS) is an integrated cloud offering jointly developed by AWS and VMware. VMC on AWS enables you to migrate virtual machines between your on-premises vSphere environment, and a vSphere environment running in AWS. With VMC on AWS, you can deploy a software-defined data center (SDDC) on demand that you configure and manage using your vSphere Client and the VMware Cloud Services console.

VMC on AWS provides workloads with access to many AWS services, including database, AI/ML, and security services. It provides simplicity for hybrid cloud operations by enabling you to use the same VCF technologies (vSphere, vSAN, NSX, vCenter Server) across the on-premises environment and the AWS cloud. It does not require custom, on-premises hardware. To migrate virtual machines to or from an on-premises vSphere environment to VMC on AWS, you can perform a live migration via vMotion or use VMware HCX.

Azure VMware Solution

Azure VMware Solution combines VMware's SDDC software with the Microsoft Azure global cloud service ecosystem to provide a hosted private cloud. Azure VMware Solution is managed to meet performance, availability, security, and compliance requirements. Currently, you cannot use on-premises vCenter Server to manage the hosted private cloud. Instead, you use vCenter Server and NSX Manager in a hosted private cloud.

You can set up VMware HCX for an Azure VMware Solution private cloud. HCX enables migration of VMware workloads to the cloud and other connected sites. If you meet standard cross-vCenter vMotion requirements, you can migrate on-premises virtual machines to the hosted private cloud. To configure HCX, you deploy an HCX virtual appliance in your on-premises vSphere environment and connect it to HCX in your hosted private cloud.

You can use Azure Migrate to migrate on-premises vSphere virtual machines to Azure.

Networking and Security

This section addresses VMware products for networking and security.

NSX

VMware NSX Data Center (NSX) is a network virtualization and security platform that enables a software-defined approach to networking that extends across data centers, clouds, and application frameworks. NSX enables you to provision and manage networks independently of the underlying hardware, much as you do with virtual machines. You can reproduce a complex network in seconds and create multiple networks with diverse requirements.

NSX provides a new operational model for software-defined networking and extends it to the virtual cloud network. It provides a complete set of logical networking, security capabilities, and services, such as logical switching, routing, firewalling, load balancing, virtual private networking, quality of service (QoS), and monitoring.

NOTE   Starting with Version 4.0.0.1 (which is equivalent to Version 4.0 for on-premises NSX), VMware NSX-T Data Center is now known as VMware NSX.

VMware NSX-T Data Center (NSX-T) was originally developed for non-vSphere environments, but now it now supports vSphere. Although VMware previously offered separate NSX-V (end-of-life) and NSX-T products, starting with Version 4.0, VMware NSX-T Data Center is known as VMware NSX.

The NSX platform provides the following components:

- NSX managers
- NSX edge nodes
- NSX distributed routers
- NSX service routers
- NSX segments (logical switches)

NSX provides a data plane, a control plane, and a management plane.

NSX Use Cases

The following are common use cases for NSX:

- Adoption of zero-trust security

- Multi-cloud networking

- Automated network deployment

- Networking and security for cloud-native applications (containers)

NSX Integration

To prepare for an NSX installation, you need to meet the requirements for deploying its components, such as the NSX managers and edge nodes. Typically, a three-node NSX Manager cluster is deployed to a management vSphere cluster, and the NSX edges are deployed in a shared edge and compute cluster.

After deploying the required virtual appliances from OVF, you log in to NSX Manager and add a vCenter Server as a compute manager. When adding the vCenter Server compute manager, you should use the administrator account of the Single Sign-On domain (administrator@vsphere.local by default) or use a custom account configured with the appropriate privileges. Next, you deploy NSX edges to vSphere clusters managed by the vCenter Server and create the transport zones and transport nodes.

Starting with vSphere 7.0 and NSX-T 3.0, you can run NSX directly on a vDS (Version 7.0 or later). This provides simpler integration in vCenter Server as well as some other benefits. When creating transport nodes on ESXi hosts, you use vDS as the host switch type.

Exam Preparation Tasks

As mentioned in the section "Book Features and Exam Preparation Methods" in the Introduction, you have some choices for exam preparation: the exercises here, Chapter 15, "Final Preparation," and the exam simulation questions on the companion website.

Review All Key Topics

Review the most important topics in this chapter, noted with the Key Topic icon in the outer margin of the page. Table 6-3 lists these key topics and the page number on which each is found.

Table 6-3   Key Topics for Chapter 6

Key Topic Element	Description	Page Number
List	Use cases for vSphere with Tanzu	211
List	Use cases for Aria Operations	216
List	Use cases for Aria Automation	219
List	Use cases for Aria Orchestrator	220
List	Use cases for Horizon	222
List	Use cases for App Volumes	223
List	Use cases for NSX	233

Complete Tables and Lists from Memory

Print a copy of Appendix B, "Memory Tables" (found on the companion website), or at least the section for this chapter, and complete the tables and lists from memory. Appendix C, "Memory Table Answers" (also on the companion website), includes completed tables and lists to check your work.

Define Key Terms

Define the following key terms from this chapter and check your answers in the glossary:

vCenter Converter, Skyline, Aria for Logs, Aria Automation, VMware Horizon, App Volumes, vSphere Replication, Site Recovery Manager (SRM)

Review Questions

1. You want to build custom workflows to support XaaS. Which product should you use?

   a. Aria for Logs

   b. Aria Orchestrator

   c. Aria Operations

   d. App Volumes

2. You need to provide virtual desktops and applications to remote users and call centers. Which product should you implement?

   a. VCF

   b. Aria Suite

   c. AppDefense

   d. Horizon

3. You want to configure vSphere Replication using the vSphere Client. Which of the following is the correct navigation path?

   a. Home > vCenter Server > vSphere Replication

   b. Home > Site Recovery > Open Site Recovery

   c. Home > Host and Clusters > Replications

   d. Home > Administration > Replication

4. Which of the following products provides connection, WAN optimization, and bulk migrations?

   a. Aria Suite

   b. vSphere Replication

   c. SRM

   d. HCX

5. For your virtual infrastructure, you want to adopt zero-trust security, implement multi-cloud networking, and use automated network deployment. Which product should you consider?

   a. VMware Horizon

   b. VMware SRM

   c. VMware Aria

   d. VMware NSX

This chapter covers the following topics:

- vSphere Certificates
- vSphere Permissions
- ESXi and vCenter Server Security
- vSphere Network Security
- Virtual Machine Security
- Available Add-on Security

This chapter contains information related to VMware vSphere 8.x Professional (2V0-21.23) exam objectives 1.8, 1.8.1, 1.8.1.1, 1.8.1.2, 1.9, 1.9.1, 1.9.2, 4.12, 4.13, 4.13.1, 4.17.2, 4.19.4, 4.19.5, 7.7, 7.12.2, and 7.12.3.

vSphere Security

This chapter covers topics related to hardening a vSphere environment.

"Do I Know This Already?" Quiz

The "Do I Know This Already?" quiz allows you to assess whether you should study this entire chapter or move quickly to the "Exam Preparation Tasks" section. In any case, the authors recommend that you read the entire chapter at least once. Table 7-1 outlines the major headings in this chapter and the corresponding "Do I Know This Already?" quiz questions. You can find the answers in Appendix A, "Answers to the 'Do I Know This Already?' Quizzes and Review Questions."

Table 7-1 "Do I Know This Already?" Foundation Topics Section-to-Question Mapping

Foundations Topics Section	Questions Covered in This Section
vSphere Certificates	1, 2
vSphere Permissions	3, 4
ESXi and vCenter Server Security	5, 6
vSphere Network Security	7
Virtual Machine Security	8, 9
Available Add-on Security	10

1. You are preparing to import certificates for your vSphere 8.0 environment. Which of the following is not a requirement?

   a. x509 Version 3

   b. PKCS8 and PKCS1 PEM format

   c. Digital signature and key encipherment keys

   d. 1024 to 16,384-bit keys

2. You are making plans for ESXi host certificates. Which of the following is not a valid certificate mode?

   a. VMware Endpoint Certificate Store Mode

   b. VMware Certificate Authority Mode

   c. Custom Certificate Authority Mode

   d. Thumbprint Mode

3. You are preparing to apply permissions in vCenter Server. Which of the following is a system role?

   a. Read-only

   b. Virtual machine user

   c. Datastore consumer

   d. Content library administrator

4. You are configuring permissions in vCenter Server. Which privilege is required for a user to use Storage vMotion to migrate a virtual machine?

   a. Resource.Migrate Powered On Virtual Machine

   b. Resource.Migrate Powered Off Virtual Machine

   c. Resource.Assign Virtual Machine to Resource Pool on the Cluster

   d. Resource.Assign Virtual Machine to Resource Pool on the VM Folder

5. You are hardening your ESXi hosts. Which of the following is true concerning normal Lockdown Mode?

   a. All users with administrator privileges on the host can access the DCUI.

   b. All users in the Exception Users list can access the DCUI.

   c. No one can access the DCUI.

   d. Users identified in the host's DCUI.Access advanced option can access the DCUI.

6. You are creating user accounts in the vCenter SSO domain. With default settings, which of the following is a valid password?

   a. VMware1!

   b. VMworld!

   c. VMwareR0cks

   d. VMwarerocks!!

7. You are configuring IPsec on your ESXi hosts. Which of the following commands can you use to list the available security associations on an ESXi host?

   a. **esxcli network ipsec sa list**

   b. **esxcli network ip ipsec sa list**

   c. **esxcli network ip ipsec list**

   d. **esxcli network ip sa list**

8. You want to migrate virtual machines across vCenter instances. Which of the following statements is true concerning vMotion migration across vCenter Server instances?

   a. You cannot use vMotion across vCenter Servers.

   b. The source and target vCenter Servers must share the same KMS cluster.

   c. vMotion migration of encrypted virtual machines is not supported.

   d. Encrypted vMotion migration of non-encrypted virtual machines is not supported.

9. You are hardening virtual machines in your vSphere 8 environment. Which of the following options can be set to TRUE to disable an unexposed feature?

   a. tools.guestlib.enableHostInfo

   b. tools.setInfo.sizeLimit

   c. vmx.log.keepOld

   d. isolation.tools.ghi.launchmenu.change

10. You want to use microsegmentation to protect the applications and data in your vSphere environment. What should you implement?

   a. VMware AppDefense

   b. VMware NSX

   c. VMware vRealize Automation

   d. VMware vRealize Log Insight

Foundation Topics

vSphere Certificates

This section describes the use of certificates in a vSphere environment.

vSphere Certificates Overview

In vSphere, security is provided by using certificates to encrypt communications, authenticate services, and sign tokens. By default, vSphere can provision vCenter Server components and ESXi hosts with VMware Certificate Authority (VMCA) certificates. You can, however, have vSphere use custom certificates, which are stored in the *VMware Endpoint Certificate Store (VECS)*.

VMCA is vSphere's internal certificate authority, which provides all the necessary vCenter Server and ESXi certificates. It is automatically installed on each vCenter Server and immediately secures the environment without any required modification.

vCenter Server supports custom certificates that are generated and signed from your own enterprise public key infrastructure (PKI). vCenter Server also supports custom certificates that are generated and signed by trusted third-party certificate authorities (CAs), such as VeriSign or GoDaddy. You can replace the existing VMCA-signed solution user and STS certificates with custom certificates. If you do so, you bypass VMCA and become responsible for all certificate provisioning and monitoring. You can replace the VMCA root certificate with a certificate that is signed by an enterprise CA or a third-party CA, in which case VMCA signs the custom root certificate each time it provisions certificates, making VMCA an intermediate CA (see Figure 7-1). VMware does not recommend either of these approaches. If you use the VMCA as an intermediate CA or use custom certificates, you might encounter significant complexity, potentially resulting in a negative impact to your security and increased operational risk.

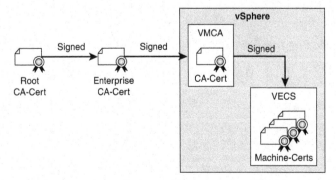

Figure 7-1 VMCA as an Intermediate CA

vSphere provides core identity services, as described in Table 7-2.

Table 7-2 Core Identity Services in vSphere

Service	Description
VMware Directory Service (vmdir)	Serves as an identity source that handles SAML certificate management for authentication with vCenter Single Sign-On.
VMware Certificate Authority (VMCA)	Issues certificates for VMware solution users, machine certificates for machines on which services are running, and ESXi host certificates. VMCA can be used as is, or it can be used as an intermediary certificate authority.
VMware Authentication Framework Daemon (VMAFD)	Includes VMware Endpoint Certificate Store (VECS) and several internal authentication services.

VECS is a local (client-side) repository for certificates, private keys, and other certificate information that can be stored in a keystore. You can choose not to use VMCA as your certificate authority and certificate signer, but you must use VECS to store all vCenter certificates and keys. ESXi certificates are stored locally on each host and not in VECS. The stores included in VECS are described in Table 8-9 in Chapter 8, "vSphere Installation."

VMware recommends that you use either VMCA default certificates or a hybrid mode. If you use VMCA in a hybrid approach, you replace the vCenter Server SSL certificates and allow VMCA to manage certificates for solution users and ESXi hosts. Optionally, for high-security deployments, you can replace the ESXi host SSL certificates. Table 7-3 summarizes VMware's recommended modes for managing certificates.

Table 7-3 Recommended Modes for Managing Certificates

Mode	Description	Advantages
VMCA Default Certificates	VMCA provides all the certificates for vCenter Server and ESXi hosts.	This is the lowest-overhead option. VMCA manages the certificate lifecycle for vCenter Server and ESXi hosts.
VMCA Default Certificates with External SSL Certificates (hybrid mode)	You replace the vCenter Server SSL certificates and allow VMCA to manage certificates for solution users and ESXi hosts. Optionally, for high-security deployments, you can replace the ESXi host SSL certificates as well.	VMCA manages internal certificates, but you get the benefit of using your corporate-approved trusted SSL certificates.

Certificate Requirements

The following requirements apply to all imported certificates:

- The key size is 2048 bits to 16,384 bits.

- VMware supports PKCS8 and PKCS1 (RSA key) PEM formats. When you add keys to VECS, they are converted to PKCS8.

- x509 Version 3 is required.

- SubjectAltName must contain DNS Name=*machine_FQDN*.

- CRT format is required.

- The digital signature and key encipherment keys are available.

- Enhanced Key Usage can either be empty or contain Server Authentication.

VMCA does not support the following certificates:

- Certificates with wildcards

- The algorithms md2WithRSAEncryption 1.2.840.113549.1.1.2, md5WithR-SAEncryption 1.2.840.113549.1.1.4, and sha1WithRSAEncryption 1.2.840.113549.1.1.5

- The algorithm RSASSA-PSS with OID 1.2.840.113549.1.1.10

If you do not generate certificate signing requests (CSRs) using Certificate Manager, you need to ensure that a CSR includes the fields listed in Table 7-4.

Table 7-4 Required Fields for a CSR

String	X.500 Attribute Type
CN	commonName
L	localityName
ST	stateOrProvinceName
O	organizationName
OU	organizationalUnitName
C	countryName
STREET	streetAddress
DC	domainComponent
UID	userid

If you use VMCA as an intermediate CA, you can use the vSphere Certificate Manager to create a CSR or you can create a CSR manually. When you create a CSR manually, in addition to the previously stated requirements, you should consider the requirements in Table 7-5, which are based on the specific certificate types.

NOTE Do not use CRL distribution points, authority information access, or certificate template information in any custom certificates.

Table 7-5 Requirements for Certificates When VMCA Is an Intermediate CA

Certificate Type	Additional Requirements
Root certificate	Set CA extension to true and include CertSign. For example, use the following in the CSR: basicConstraints = critical, CA:true keyUsage = critical, digitalSignature,keyCertSign
Machine SSL certificate	No additional requirements
Solution user certificate	Use a different Name value for each solution user, which may appear as CN under Subject, depending on the tool

VMCA provisions an environment with certificates, including machine SSL certificates for secure connections, solution user certificates for service authentication with vCenter Single Sign-On, and ESXi host certificates (see Table 7-6).

Table 7-6 Certificates in vSphere

Certificate	Provisioned	Details
ESXi certificate	VMCA (default)	Stored locally on an ESXi host in the /etc/vmware/ssl directory when the host is first added to vCenter Server and when it reconnects.
Machine SSL certificate	VMCA (default)	Stored in VECS. Used to create SSL sockets for SSL client connections, for server verification, and for secure communication such as HTTPS and LDAPS. Used by the reverse proxy service, the vCenter Server service (**vpxd**), and the VMware Directory service (**vmdir**). Uses X.509 Version 3 certificates to encrypt session information.

Certificate	Provisioned	Details
Solution user certificate	VMCA (default)	Stored in VECS.
		Used by solution users to authenticate to vCenter Single Sign-On through SAML token exchange.
vCenter Single Sign-On SSL signing certificate	During installation	Used throughout vSphere for authentication, where a SAML token represents the user's identity and contains group membership information.
		You can manage this certificate from the command line. Changing this certificate in the file system leads to unpredictable behavior.
VMware Directory Service (**vmdir**) SSL certificate	During installation	Starting with vSphere 6.5, the machine SSL certificate is used as the **vmdir** certificate.
vSphere Virtual Machine Encryption Certificates	Depends	Used for virtual machine encryption, which relies on an external Key Management Services (KMS) server.
		Depending on how the solution authenticates to the KMS server, it might generate certificates and store them in VECS.

A solution user presents a certificate to vCenter Single Sign-On when it first authenticates, after a reboot, and after a timeout has elapsed. The timeout (Holder-of-Key Timeout) can be set from the vSphere Client and defaults to 2,592,000 seconds (30 days).

VECS includes the following solution user certificate stores:

- **Machine**: Used by the license server and the logging service.

- **vpxd**: Used by the vCenter service (vpxd) to authenticate to vCenter Single Sign-On.

- **vpxd-extension**: Used by the Auto Deploy service, inventory service, and other services that are not part of other solution users.

- **vsphere-webclient**: Used by the vSphere Client and some additional services, such as the performance chart service.

- **wcp**: Used by vSphere with Kubernetes.

NOTE Do not confuse the machine solution user certificate with the machine SSL certificate. The machine solution user certificate is used for SAML token exchange. The machine SSL certificate is used for secure SSL connections for a machine.

ESXi Host Certificates

In vSphere 6.0 and later, vCenter Server supports several certificate modes for ESXi hosts, as described in Table 7-7.

Table 7-7 Certificate Modes for ESXi Hosts

Mode	Description
VMware Certificate Authority Mode (default)	Use this mode when VMCA provisions an ESXi host as either the top-level CA or an intermediate CA. In this mode, you can refresh and renew certificates from the vSphere Client.
Custom Certificate Authority Mode (CA)	Use this mode with custom certificates signed by a third-party or an enterprise CA. In this mode, you cannot refresh and renew certificates from the vSphere Client.
Thumbprint Mode	Use this legacy (vSphere 5.5) mode only for troubleshooting. In this mode, vCenter Server checks the certificate format, not the certificate's validity. For example, expired certificates are accepted. Some vCenter 6.x and later services might not work correctly in this mode.

NOTE If you apply custom certificates to hosts but do not change the certificate mode to Custom Certificate Authority, VMCA might replace custom certificates when you select Renew in the vSphere Client.

You can use the vSphere Client to view expiration data for certificates, whether they are signed by VMCA or a third party. The vCenter Server raises yellow alarms for hosts where certificates expire shortly (that is, in less than 8 months) and red alarms where certificates are in the Expiration Imminent state (that is, expire in less than 2 months).

ESXi hosts that boot from installation media have autogenerated certificates. When a host is added to the vCenter Server system, it is provisioned with a certificate that is signed by VMCA as the root CA.

vSphere Permissions

This section describes the permissions model in vSphere.

Authentication and Authorization

vCenter Single Sign-On (SSO) is responsible for authenticating vCenter Server users. The user accounts may be defined directly in the SSO domain or in a supported identity source. vCenter Server uses permissions and roles to provide authorization, and this controls what an authenticated user can do. It allows you to assign a permission to an object in the vCenter Server inventory by specifying which privileges a specific user or group has on that object.

The default SSO domain name is vsphere.local, but you can change it during domain creation. Initially, only the SSO domain administrator is authorized to log in to vCenter Server. By default, the SSO domain administrator is administrator@vsphere.local. You can create additional users in the SSO domain. You can add supported identity sources to SSO, including Active Directory over LDAP, a native Active Directory (Integrated Windows Authentication, which is deprecated) domain, or an OpenLDAP directory service.

Starting in vSphere 7.0, vCenter Server supports federated authentication, where you configure a connection to an external identity provider to replace vCenter Server as the identity provider. Currently, vCenter Server supports only Active Directory Federation Services (AD FS) as an external identity provider.

The permissions model for vCenter Server systems relies on assigning permissions to objects in the object hierarchy. A permission involves the assignment of a user (or group) and a role to an inventory object.

When you add a new identity source to SSO, all users can be authenticated, but they effectively have the no access role to the vCenter Server inventory.

Inventory Hierarchy and Objects

You can assign permissions to objects at different levels of the inventory hierarchy, such as ESXi hosts, clusters, virtual machines, folders, resource pools, datastores, and networks. You can also assign permissions to a global root object to apply the permissions to all objects in all solutions. You can apply permissions to container objects and can optionally allow the permissions to propagate to descendant objects. Most objects inherit permissions from their parents via a single path, but virtual machines inherit permissions from virtual machine folders, hosts, resource pools, and so on, as you can see in Figure 7-2. If an object inherits permissions from two parent objects, then its inherited permissions are determined by the union of the permissions. Figure 7-2 shows the vSphere inventory hierarchy in vSphere 8.0.

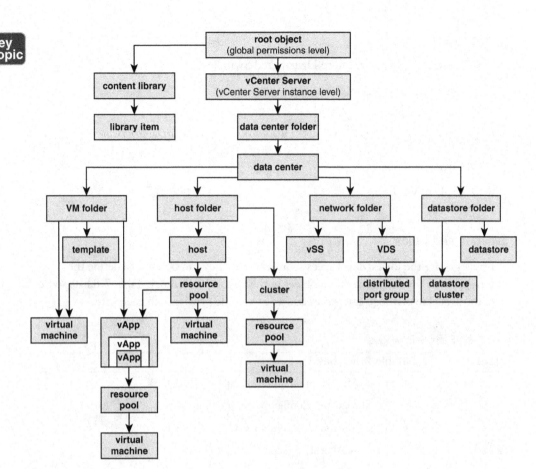

Figure 7-2 vSphere 8.0 Inventory Hierarchy

An object might have multiple permissions but only one permission for each user or group. In other words, you cannot assign to an object two permissions that specify the same group. If multiple permissions are applied to a specific object using multiple groups and if a specific user belongs to more than one of these groups, then the effective permission for that user on that object is the union of the privileges in applicable roles.

Privileged users can define permissions on managed objects, including the following:

- Clusters
- Data centers
- Datastores
- Datastore clusters
- Folders

- Hosts

- Networks (except vSphere Distributed Switches)

- Distributed port groups

- Resource pools

- Templates

- Virtual machines

- vSphere vApps

Privileges and Roles

Privileges are the lowest-level access controls, and they can be used to define the actions that a user can take on an object in the vSphere inventory. Table 7-8 lists some of the available privilege categories and a few sample privileges in each category.

Table 7-8 Sample Privileges

Category	Sample Privileges
Virtual machine configuration	■ Virtual Machine.Configuration.Add Existing Disk ■ Virtual Machine.Configuration.Add New Disk ■ Virtual Machine.Configuration.Change CPU Count
Datastore	■ Datastore.Allocate Space ■ Datastore.Browse Datastore ■ Datastore.Remove File
Virtual machine snapshot	■ Virtual Machine.Snapshot Management.Create Snapshot ■ Virtual Machine.Snapshot Management.Rename Snapshot ■ Virtual Machine.Snapshot Management.Revert to Snapshot

A role is composed of a set of privileges. Out of the box, the vCenter Server provides many roles. You cannot modify the vCenter Server system roles. The main system roles are described in Table 7-9. You can modify the sample roles, but VMware recommends that you not modify these roles directly but instead clone the roles and modify the clones to suit your case.

NOTE Changes to roles take effect immediately, even for users who are currently logged in to vCenter Server. One exception is with searches, where a change is not realized until the next time the user logs in to vCenter Server.

Table 7-9 The Main System Roles in vCenter Server 8.0

System Role	Description
Read-only	Allows the user to view the state of an object and details about the object. For example, users with this role can view virtual machine attributes but cannot open the VM console.
Administrator	Includes all privileges of the read-only role and allows the user to view and perform all actions on the object. If you have the administrator role in an object, you can assign privileges to individual users and groups. If you have the administrator role in vCenter Server, you can assign privileges to users and groups in the default SSO identity source. By default, the administrator@vsphere.local user has the administrator role in both vCenter Single Sign-On and vCenter Server.
No access	Prevents users from viewing or interacting with the object. New users and groups are effectively assigned this role by default.

There are a number of sample roles in vCenter Server 8.0:

- Resource pool administrator (sample)
- Virtual machine user (sample)
- VMware consolidated backup user (sample)
- Datastore consumer (sample)
- Network administrator (sample)
- Virtual machine power user (sample)
- Content library administrator (sample)
- Content library registry administrator (sample)

To become familiar with the privileges in a role, you can edit the role and explore the privileges that are included in the role. For example, if you edit the virtual machine console user role, you see that it only includes some privileges in the Virtual Machine > Interaction category and no other privileges. Specifically, it includes only these privileges:

- Acknowledge alarm
- Answer question
- Configure CD media
- Configure floppy media
- Connect devices

- Console interaction
- Install VMware tools
- Power off
- Power on
- Reset
- Suspend

NOTE   If you create a role, it does not inherit privileges from any of the system roles.

Permissions

The permissions model for vCenter Server systems relies on assigning permissions to objects in the object hierarchy. A permission is the assignment of a user (or group) and a role to an inventory object. A permission is set on an object in the vCenter object inventory. Each permission associates the object with a group (or user) and a role, as illustrated in Figure 7-3. For example, you can select a virtual machine object, add one permission that gives the read-only role to Group 1, and add a second permission that gives the administrator role to User 2.

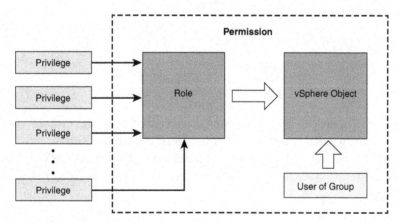

Figure 7-3   vSphere Permissions Diagram

Global Permissions

Most entities that appear in the vCenter Server inventory are managed objects whose access can be controlled using permissions. You cannot modify permissions on entities that derive permissions from the root vCenter Server system, such as the following:

- Custom fields
- Licenses
- Roles
- Statistics intervals
- Sessions

The global root object is used to assign permissions across solutions. The vCenter Server is an example of a solution, and it is attached as a child to the global root object in the hierarchy. The content library and tag category objects are also attached as children to the global root object. Global permissions are permissions that are applied to the global root object and span solutions. For example, a global permission can be applied to both vCenter Server and Aria Orchestrator. Each solution has its own root object in the hierarchy, whose parent is the global root object. You can give a group of users read permissions to all objects in both object hierarchies.

Best Practices for Roles and Permissions

VMware recommends the following best practices when configuring roles and permissions in a vCenter Server environment:

- Where possible, assign roles to groups rather than to individual users.
- Grant permissions to users (or groups) only on the objects where they are required. Use the minimum permissions to meet the required functionality.
- If you assign a restrictive role to a group, check to ensure that the group does not contain the administrator user or other users who require administrative privileges.
- Use folders to group objects. For example, to grant modify permission on one set of hosts and view permission on another set of hosts, place each set of hosts in a folder.
- Use caution when adding a permission to the root vCenter Server objects. Users with privileges at the root level have access to global data on vCenter Server, such as roles, custom attributes, and vCenter Server settings.
- Consider enabling propagation when you assign permissions to an object. Propagation ensures that new objects in the object hierarchy inherit permissions.

For example, you can assign a permission to a virtual machine folder and enable propagation to ensure that the permission applies to all VMs in the folder.

- Use the no access role to mask or hide specific areas of the hierarchy. The no access role restricts access for the users or groups with that role.

> **NOTE** Changes to licenses propagate to all linked vCenter Server systems in the same vCenter Single Sign-On domain.

Required Privileges for Common Tasks

Many tasks require permissions on multiple objects in the inventory. Consider the following:

- To perform any operation that consumes storage space, such as taking a snapshot, you must have the Datastore.Allocate Space privilege on the target datastore in addition to having the directly required privileges on the major object.

- Moving an object in the inventory hierarchy requires appropriate privileges on the object itself, the source parent object (such as a folder or cluster), and the destination parent object.

- Deploying a virtual machine directly to a host or cluster requires the Resource. Assign Virtual Machine to Resource Pool privilege because each host or cluster has its own implicit resource pool.

Table 7-10 shows the required privileges for a few common tasks.

Table 7-10 Required Permissions for Common Tasks

Task	Required Privileges
Create a virtual machine	On the destination folder or in the data center: ■ Virtual Machine.Inventory.Create New ■ Virtual Machine.Configuration.Add New Disk ■ Virtual Machine.Configuration.Add Existing Disk ■ Virtual Machine.Configuration.Raw Device On the destination host or cluster or in the resource pool: ■ Resource.Assign Virtual Machine to Resource Pool On the destination datastore or in the datastore folder: ■ Datastore.Allocate Space On the network: ■ Network.Assign Network

Task	Required Privileges
Deploy a virtual machine from a template	On the destination folder or in the data center: ■ Virtual Machine.Inventory.Create from Existing ■ Virtual Machine.Configuration.Add New Disk On a template or in a template folder: ■ Virtual Machine.Provisioning.Deploy Template On the destination host or cluster or in the resource pool: ■ Resource.Assign Virtual Machine to Resource Pool On the destination datastore or in a datastore folder: ■ Datastore.Allocate Space On the network that the virtual machine will be assigned to: ■ Network.Assign Network
Take a virtual machine snapshot	On the virtual machine or in a virtual machine folder: ■ Virtual Machine.Snapshot Management.Create Snapshot On the destination datastore or in a datastore folder: ■ Datastore.Allocate Space
Move a virtual machine into a resource pool	On the virtual machine or in a virtual machine folder: ■ Resource.Assign Virtual Machine to Resource PoolVirtual Machine.Inventory.Move In the destination resource pool: ■ Resource.Assign Virtual Machine to Resource Pool
Install a guest operating system on a virtual machine	On the virtual machine or in a virtual machine folder: ■ Virtual Machine.Interaction.Answer Question ■ Virtual Machine.Interaction.Console Interaction ■ Virtual Machine.Interaction.Device Connection ■ Virtual Machine.Interaction.Power Off ■ Virtual Machine.Interaction.Power On ■ Virtual Machine.Interaction.Reset ■ Virtual Machine.Interaction.Configure CD Media ■ Virtual Machine.Interaction.Configure Floppy Media ■ Virtual Machine.Interaction.Tools Install

Task	Required Privileges
	On a datastore containing the installation media ISO image: ■ Datastore.Browse Datastore On the datastore to which you upload the installation media ISO image: ■ Datastore.Browse DatastoreDatastore.Low Level File Operations
Migrate a virtual machine with vMotion	On the virtual machine or in a virtual machine folder: ■ Resource.Migrate Powered On Virtual Machine ■ Resource.Assign Virtual Machine to Resource Pool On the destination host or cluster or in a resource pool: ■ Resource.Assign Virtual Machine to Resource Pool
Cold migrate (relocate) a virtual machine	On the virtual machine or in a virtual machine folder: ■ Resource.Migrate Powered Off Virtual Machine ■ Resource.Assign Virtual Machine to Resource Pool On the destination host or cluster or in a resource pool: ■ Resource.Assign Virtual Machine to Resource Pool On the destination datastore: ■ Datastore.Allocate Space
Migrate a virtual machine with Storage vMotion	On the virtual machine or in a virtual machine folder: ■ Resource.Migrate Powered On Virtual Machine On the destination datastore: ■ Datastore.Allocate Space
Move a host into a cluster	On the host: ■ Host.Inventory.Add Host to Cluster On the destination cluster: ■ Host.Inventory.Add Host to Cluster ■ Host.Inventory.Modify. Cluster

How Permissions Are Applied by vCenter Server

As you assign each permission, you can choose whether to allow the permission to propagate to child objects. This setting is made for each permission and cannot be universally applied. The default setting is to allow propagation to child objects. The propagation is applied to the vSphere inventory hierarchy as shown in Figure 7-2.

If conflicting permissions are applied to an object and to its ancestors, the permissions that are assigned at a lower-level object in the inventory hierarchy override permissions assigned at a higher-level object. If multiple permissions are assigned to the same object in different groups that contain a specific user, then that user's effective permission is the union of the associated privileges. Permissions assigned to a user override permissions assigned to groups containing the user when the permissions are applied to the same object. For example, consider the following scenario, which is illustrated in Figure 7-4:

- One cluster exists in the inventory, and it contains host-01 and host-02.

- The user account User-A is a member of groups Group-01 and Group-02.

- The user account User-B is a member of group Group-01.

- The user account User-C is a member of group Group-02.

- The user account User-D is a member of groups Group-01 and Group-03.

- The user account User-E is a member of groups Group-02 and Group-04.

Propagate to Child Objects is enabled for each of the following permissions:

- A permission assigns Group-01 the administrator role on the cluster.

- A permission assigns Group-02 the administrator role on host-01.

- A permission assigns Group-02 the read-only role on host-02.

- A permission assigns User-D the read-only role on the cluster.

- A permission assigns Group-03 the no access role on host-02.

- A permission assigns Group-04 the read-only role on host-01.

- A permission assigns Group-04 the no access role on host-02.

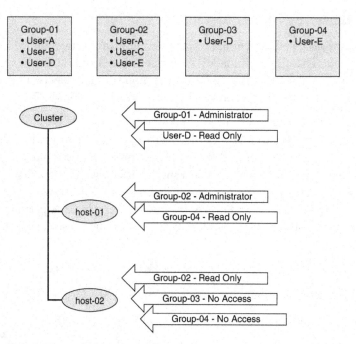

Figure 7-4 vSphere Permission Example

In this scenario, the following effective permissions apply:

- User-A:

  - Can perform all tasks on the cluster object

  - Can perform all tasks on the host-01 object

  - Can only view the host-02 object

- User-B:

  - Can perform all tasks on the cluster object

  - Can perform all tasks on the host-01 object

  - Can perform all tasks on the host-02 object

- User-C:

  - Cannot view or perform any task on the cluster object

  - Can perform all tasks on the host-01 object

  - Can only view the host-02 object

- User-D

    - Can only view the cluster object

    - Can only view the host-01 object

    - Cannot view or perform any task on the host-02 object

- User-E

    - Cannot view or perform any task on the cluster object

    - Can perform all tasks on the host-01 object

    - Can only view the host-02 object

ESXi and vCenter Server Security

ESXi has many built-in security features, such as CPU isolation, memory isolation, and device isolation. An ESXi host is protected with a firewall that is intended to permit only required network traffic. Starting with vSphere 6.0, ESXi hosts participate in the certificate infrastructure and, by default, are provisioned with certificates that are signed by VMCA.

Optionally, you can further harden ESXi by configuring features such as Lockdown Mode, certificate replacement, and smart card authentication for enhanced security. You should consider limiting direct access to ESXi hosts, using security profiles, using host profiles, and managing certificates. In addition, you can take other security measures, such as using multiple networks to segregate ESXi network functions and implementing UEFI Secure Boot for ESXi hosts.

Built-in Security Features

The following are some of vSphere's built-in security features:

- ESXi Shell and SSH are disabled by default.

- By default, ESXi runs only services that are essential to managing its functions.

- By default, all ports that are not required for management access to the host are closed.

- By default, weak ciphers are disabled, and communications from clients are secured by SSL. Default certificates created on ESXi use PKCS#1 SHA-256 with RSA encryption as the signature algorithm.

- A Tomcat web service is used internally by ESXi to support access by web clients. ESXi is not vulnerable to the Tomcat security issues reported in other use cases because the service has been modified to run only functions that a web client requires for administration and monitoring.

- VMware monitors all security alerts that can affect ESXi security and issues security patches when needed.

- Secure services such as SSH and SFTP are available and should be used instead of insecure counterparts, such as Telnet and FTP.

- ESXi provides the option of using UEFI Secure Boot.

- When a TPM 2.0 chip is available in the hardware and configured in the system UEFI BIOS, ESXi works with Secure Boot to enhance security and trust assurance rooted in hardware.

Security Profiles

You can customize many of the essential security settings for a host through the Security Profile panel in the vSphere Client. You can use security profiles to customize services and configure the ESXi firewall. Table 7-11 describes the services that are available for viewing and managing through the vSphere Client for a default vSphere installation, along with the default state for each of them. You can use the vSphere Client to start, stop, and restart individual services.

Table 7-11   ESXi Security Profile Services

Service	Default State	Description
Direct Console User Interface (DCUI)	Running	Allows you to interact with an ESXi host from the local console host by using text-based menus
ESXi Shell	Stopped	Is available from the DCUI or from SSH
SSH	Stopped	Allows remote connections through Secure Shell
Load-Based Teaming Daemon	Running	Enables load-based teaming
attestd	Stopped	Enables the vSphere Trust Authority Attestation Service
kmxd	Stopped	Enables the vSphere Trust Authority Key Provider Service
Active Directory Service	Stopped	Is started on hosts after you configure ESXi for Active Directory
NTP Daemon	Stopped	Enables the Network Time Protocol daemon
PC/SC Smart Card Daemon	Stopped	Is started on hosts after you enable the host for smart card authentication

Service	Default State	Description
CIM Server	Running	Can be used by Common Information Model (CIM) applications
SNMP Server	Stopped	Enables the SNMP daemon
Syslog Server	Stopped	Enables the syslog daemon
VMware vCenter Agent (**vpxa**)	Running	Connects the host to vCenter Server
X.Org Server	Stopped	Is internally used for virtual machine 3D graphics

Table 7-12 lists the firewall ports that are installed by default in ESXi 7.0. On a specific host, the list of actual services and firewall ports can be impacted by the currently installed VMware Installation Bundles (VIBs).

Table 7-12 Incoming and Outgoing Firewall Ports

Firewall Service	Incoming Port(s)	Outgoing Port(s)
CIM Server	5988 (TCP)	—
CIM Secure Server	5989 (TCP)	—
CIM SLP	427 (TCP,UDP)	427 (TCP,UDP)
DHCPv6	546 (TCP,UDP)	547 (TCP,UDP)
DVSSync	8301, 8302 (UDP)	8301, 8302 (UDP)
HBR	—	44046, 31031 (TCP)
NFC	902 (TCP)	902 (TCP)
WOL	—	9 (UDP)
vSAN Clustering	12345, 23451 (UDP)	12345, 23451 (UDP)
DCHP Client	68 (UDP)	68 (UDP)
DNS Client	53 (UDP)	53 (TCP,UDP)
Fault Tolerance	8100, 8200, 8300 (TCP,UDP)	80, 8100, 8200, 8300 (TCP,UDP)
NSX Distributed Logical Router Service	6999 (UDP)	6999 (UDP)
Software iSCSI Client	—	3260 (TCP)
rabbitmqproxy	—	5671 (TCP)
vSAN Transport	2233 (TCP)	2233 (TCP)
SNMP Server	161 (UDP)	—
SSH Server	22 (TCP)	—

Firewall Service	Incoming Port(s)	Outgoing Port(s)
vMotion	8000 (TCP)	8000 (TCP)
VMware vCenter Agent	—	902 (UDP)
vSphere Web Access	80 (TCP)	—
vsanvp	8080 (TCP)	8080 (TCP)
RFB Protocol	5900–5964 (TCP)	—
vSphere Lifecycle Manager	80, 9000 (TCP)	80, 9000 (TCP)
I/O Filter	9080 (TCP)	—

NOTE The RFB protocol (TCP 5900–5964) and OpenWSMAN daemon (TCP 8889) are firewall ports for services that are not visible in the vSphere Client by default.

ESXi Password Hardening

One step in hardening an ESXi host is to harden the password required to use its predefined local administrator account, which is called root. By default, the ESXi host enforces passwords for its local user accounts, which may be used to access the host via the Direct Console User Interface (DCUI), the ESXi Shell, Secure Shell (SSH), or the vSphere Client. You can modify the ESXi password requirements by setting the Security.PasswordQualityControl advanced option for the host. For example, you can set Security.PasswordQualityControl to configure the ESXi host to accept passphrases, which it does not accept by default.

Joining an ESXi Host to a Directory Service

You can join an ESXi host to a directory service, such as Active Directory, and configure permissions to allow the associated users to connect directly to the ESXi host using DCUI, ESXi Shell, SSH, or the vSphere Host Client. The main reason for doing this is to reduce the number of local ESXi user accounts that you must create and manage. Another reason is to provide users with the means to directly access ESXi with an existing user account whose password is already hardened.

vSphere Authentication Proxy

You can add ESXi hosts to an Active Directory domain by using the vSphere Authentication Proxy instead of adding the hosts explicitly to the Active Directory domain. To do this, you can add the host's IP address to the vSphere Authentication

Proxy access control list. By default, the vSphere Authentication Proxy autho-
rizes the host based on its IP address. You can enable client authentication to have
vSphere Authentication Proxy check the host's certificate. If you are using Auto
Deploy, you can configure a reference host to point to the Authentication Proxy, set
up a rule that applies the reference host's profile to other hosts provisioned by Auto
Deploy, let Auto Deploy store the host's IP address in the access control list, and join
the host to the AD domain.

ESXi Host Access

You can implement Lockdown Mode to force operations to be performed through
vCenter Server. You can choose to use Strict Lockdown Mode, which disables the
DCUI service, or Normal Lockdown Mode, which allows DCUI access for some
users. In Normal Lockdown Mode, user accounts that are in the Exception Users
list and have administrator privileges on the host can access the DCUI. A common
use case for this is to provide access to service accounts, such as backup agents. Also,
in Normal Lockdown Mode, users identified in the host's DCUI.Access advanced
option can access the DCUI. If the ESXi shell or SSH is enabled and the host is
placed in Lockdown Mode, accounts in the Exception Users list who have administrator privileges can use these services. For all other users, ESXi Shell or SSH access
is disabled. The main use case for this is to provide user access in the event of catastrophic failure. Starting with vSphere 6.0, ESXi or SSH sessions for users who do
not have administrator privileges are terminated.

Control MOB Access

The vCenter Server Managed Object Browser (MOB) provides a means to explore
the vCenter Server object model. Its primary use is for debugging. It provides the
ability to make some configuration changes, so it may be considered a vulnerability
for malicious attacks. The MOB is disabled by default. You should enable it only for
debugging or for tasks that require it, such as extracting an old certificate from a system. To enable the MOB, you can use the vSphere Client to set the host's advanced
system setting Config.HostAgent.plugins.solo.enableMob. You should not use the
vim-cmd tool in the ESXi shell for this purpose.

ESXi Secure Boot and TPM

Unified Extensible Firmware Interface (UEFI) is firmware that effectively replaces
BIOS and offers better features, such as more primary partitions, firmware-based
network functions, faster boot time, Secure Boot, and support for larger disks.

UEFI Secure Boot is a mechanism which ensures that only trusted code is loaded by
the UEFI firmware prior to OS handoff. When Secure Boot is enabled, the UEFI

firmware validates the digitally signed kernel of an OS against a digital certificate stored in the UEFI firmware. Starting with vSphere 6.5, ESXi supports Secure Boot if it is enabled in the hardware. ESXi Version 6.5 and later supports UEFI Secure Boot at each level of the boot stack.

ESXi is composed of digitally signed packages called vSphere Installation Bundles (VIBs). These packages are never broken open. At boot time, the ESXi file system maps to the content of those packages. By leveraging the same digital certificate in the host UEFI firmware that is used to validate the signed ESXi kernel, the kernel validates each VIB by using the Secure Boot verifier against the firmware-based certificate, ensuring a cryptographically "clean" boot.

When Secure Boot is enabled, ESXi prevents the installation of unsigned code on ESXi. To install unsigned code such as beta drivers, you must disable Secure Boot. When Secure Boot is enabled, the Secure Boot verifier runs, detects the unsigned VIB, and crashes the system, which produces the purple screen of death (PSOD) event, which identifies the VIB that must be removed. To remediate, you need to boot the ESXi host with Secure Boot disabled, remove the VIB, and reboot with Secure Boot enabled.

ESXi can use *Trusted Platform Module (TPM)* chips, which are secure cryptoprocessors that enhance host security by providing a trust assurance rooted in hardware as opposed to software. TPM is an industry standard for secure cryptoprocessors. TPM chips are found in most of today's computers, including laptops, desktops, and servers. vSphere 8.0 supports TPM Version 2.0.

A TPM 2.0 chip attests to an ESXi host's identity. Host attestation is the process of authenticating and attesting to the state of the host's software at a given point in time. UEFI Secure Boot, which ensures that only signed software is loaded at boot time, is a requirement for successful attestation. The term *attestation* in this use case means the ESXi host has provided evidence that the host booted up with Secure Boot enabled, which ensures that only signed code is being used.

TPM chips can store artifacts (passwords, certificates, or encryption keys) used to authenticate an ESXi host. At each power on, the ESXi host loads the UEFI firmware and validates the boot loader against the digital certificate stored in the firmware. The boot loader contains a component called vmkboot, which validates the signature of the ESXi kernel. vmkboot uses the TPM 2.0 API to write measured values, represented as SHA-512 hashes of modules and settings, to the TPM device, including whether Secure Boot was enabled. Once the boot loader has been successfully validated, it loads the VMkernel, including the init process, which runs the Secure Boot verifier code, which validates all of the VIBs. If all of the VIBs pass the certificate check, other processes and virtual machines are permitted to start.

vSphere Trust Authority (vTA)

In an environment where TPM attestation is used, you can implement the vSphere Trust Authority (vTA), which uses its own management cluster to serve as a hardware root of trust. Ideally, the vTA trusted hosts cluster is small and separate from all other clusters and has very few administrators. In vSphere 6.7, you can leverage TPM and vCenter Server to identify hosts that failed attestation, but you cannot automatically prevent secured/encrypted workloads from migrating to those hosts. Also, you cannot encrypt vCenter Server. Starting with vSphere 7.0, with vTA, you can enable the trusted hosts cluster to handle the attestation of other hosts and to take over the distribution of the encryption keys from the Key Management Services (KMS) servers. This removes vCenter Server from the critical path for key distribution and enables you to encrypt vCenter Server. A trusted infrastructure consists of at least one vSphere Trust Authority cluster, at least one trusted cluster, and at least one external KMIP-compliant KMS server, as illustrated in Figure 7-5, which is a diagram from the *VMware vSphere 7.0 Security Guide*.

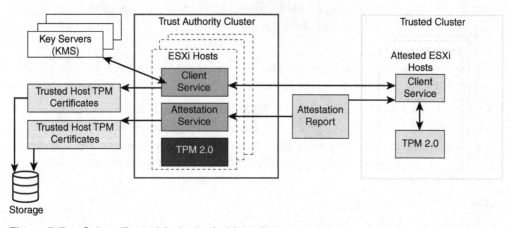

Figure 7-5 vSphere Trusted Authority Architecture

vCenter Server Security

You should follow VMware guidelines, summarized in this section, to ensure the security of a vCenter Server environment.

User Access

The user accounts defined in the local operating system (localos) of the Linux-based vCenter Server Appliance have no permissions defined in the vCenter Server environment. The localos user accounts—such as root, sshd, and vdtc—are not members of any SSO domain (vsphere.local) group to which permissions are applied. No one should attempt to use these accounts to log in to the vSphere Client. You should not use these accounts when configuring permissions or group memberships. Do not allow users to log in directly to the localos of the vCenter Server appliance. Log in locally only when required.

By default, the only accessible user account in the SSO domain is administrator, which has full control of the environment. If you use the default SSO domain name, the user account is admnistrator@vsphere.local. Ideally, you should integrate vSphere with a supported enterprise directory service, such as Active Directory, to allow users seamless access without requiring additional user accounts. Alternatively, you can create other user accounts in the SSO domain for your users. You should ensure that each user can access the environment with a unique account that is assigned the minimally required privileges.

> **NOTE** Do not confuse the administrator (root) of the localos with the SSO administrator (administrator@vsphere.local by default). By default, no localos user account has administrator privileges in vCenter Server.

For users who require the administrator role, you should assign the role to the appropriate user accounts or group accounts to avoid using the SSO administrator account.

The vCenter Server connects to each ESXi host with the vpxuser account defined on the host. By default, vCenter Server changes the vpxuser password automatically every 30 days on each connected ESXi host. To change this behavior, you can change the value of the vCenter Server advanced setting VimPasswordExpirationInDays.

vCenter SSO Password Policy

The password for the SSO administrator account and other SSO domain user accounts is controlled by the SSO password policy. By default, this password must meet the following requirements:

- At least eight characters
- At least one uppercase character
- At least one lowercase character
- At least one numeric character
- At least one special character

In addition, the password cannot be more than 20 characters long, and it cannot contain non-ASCII characters. SSO administrators can change the default password policy.

Restricting Administrative Privileges

You should use permissions to assign the administrator role to just the specific users and group that truly require it. You should create and use custom roles with only the required privileges when creating permissions. In other words, you should apply the principle of least privileges when configuring permissions in vCenter Server.

By default, a user with the administrator role can interact with files and applications in a virtual machine's guest operating system. If administrators do not require this interaction, consider applying a role without the guest operations privilege.

Restricting vCenter Server Access

You should minimize the number of users who can log directly in to the vCenter Server localos, as they could intentionally or unintentionally cause harm by altering settings and modifying processes. Allow only users with legitimate purposes to log in to the system and ensure that the login events are audited.

You should secure the network where vCenter Server is connected by applying the information in the "vSphere Network Security" section, later in this chapter.

Controlling Datastore Browser Access

Assign the Datastore.Browser datastore privilege only to users and user groups who truly require it.

vCenter Server and Client Certificates

You should ensure that vSphere Client users and other client applications heed certificate verification warnings to prevent man-in-the-middle (MITM) attacks.

You should remove any expired or revoked certificates from the vCenter Server to avoid MITM attacks.

Time Synchronization

You should ensure that all systems, such as vCenter Server, ESXi, and supporting services, use the same relative time source. The time source must be in sync with an acceptable time standard, such as Coordinated Universal Time (UTC). Time synchronization is critical for many vSphere features, such as vSphere HA. It is also critical for securing vSphere.

Time synchronization is essential for certificate validation. Time synchronization simplifies troubleshooting and auditing. Incorrect time settings make it difficult to analyze and correlate log files related to detecting attacks and conducting security audits.

vSphere Network Security

You can use firewalls, segmentation, VLANs, and other measures to secure the networks used by your virtual machines and the vSphere environment. It is important to put vCenter Server on the management network only. In addition, you should avoid putting the vCenter Server system on other networks, such as your production network or storage network, or on any other network that has access to the Internet. vCenter Server does not need access to the network where vMotion operates.

Firewalls

You can use traditional physical firewalls, virtual machine–based firewalls, and hypervisor-based firewalls (such as NSX Distributed Firewall) to protect traffic to and from the vCenter Server, ESXi hosts, virtual machines, and other vSphere components. Ideally, you could use firewalls to allow only the required traffic between specific vSphere components, virtual machines, and network segments.

Segmentation and Isolation

You should keep different virtual machine zones within a host on different network segments to reduce the risk of data leakage and threats. Such threats include Address Resolution Protocol (ARP) spoofing, in which an attacker manipulates the ARP table to remap MAC and IP addresses and gains access to network traffic to and from a host. Attackers use ARP spoofing to generate MITM attacks, perform denial of service (DoS) attacks, and hijack systems. You can implement segmentation by using one of two approaches:

- **Use separate physical network adapters for virtual machine zones**: This may be the most secure method.

- **Set up virtual local-area networks (VLANs) for virtual machine zones**: This may be the most cost-effective method.

You should isolate the vSphere management network, which provides access to the management interface on each component. In most cases, you should place the vSphere management port group in a dedicated VLAN and ensure that the network segment is not routed except to other management-related networks. Likewise, you should isolate IP-based storage traffic and vMotion traffic.

Internet Protocol Security

You can configure Internet Protocol Security (IPsec) on ESXi hosts to enable authentication and encryption of incoming and outgoing packets. You can configure security associations to control *how* the system encrypts the traffic. For each association, you configure a name, a source, a destination, and encryption parameters. You can configure security policies to determine *when* the system should encrypt traffic. Security policies include information such as source, destination, protocol, direction, mode, and a security association.

To list the available security associations, you can use this command in ESXi:

```
esxcli network ip ipsec sa list
```

To add a security association, you can use the **esxcli network ip ipsec sa add** command with one or more of the options listed in Table 7-13.

Table 7-13 IPsec Options

Option	Description
--sa-source=*source address*	Required. Specify the source address.
--sa-destination=*destination address*	Required. Specify the destination address.
--sa-mode=*mode*	Required. Specify the mode: either transport or tunnel.
--sa-spi=*security parameter index*	Required. Specify the security parameter index, in hexadecimal.
--encryption-algorithm=*encryption algorithm*	Required. Specify the algorithm as one of the following parameters: ■ **3des-cbc0** ■ **aes128-cbc** ■ **null** (no encryption)
--integrity-algorithm=*authentication algorithm*	Required. Specify the authentication algorithm: either **hmac-sha1** or **hmac-sha2-256**.
--integrity-key=*authentication key*	Required. Specify the authentication key. You can enter keys as ASCII text or in hexadecimal.
--sa-name=*name*	Required. Provide a name for the security association.

General Networking Security Recommendations

The following are additional general networking security recommendations:

■ If spanning tree is enabled, ensure that physical switch ports are configured with PortFast.

■ Ensure that NetFlow traffic for a vSphere Distributed Switch (vDS) is sent only to authorized collector IP addresses.

■ Ensure that only authorized administrators have access to virtual networking components by using the role-based access controls.

■ Ensure that port groups are not configured to the value of the native VLAN.

- Ensure that port groups are not configured to VLAN values reserved by upstream physical switches.

- Ensure that port groups are not configured to VLAN 4095 except in the case of Virtual Guest Tagging (VGT).

- On distributed virtual switches, restrict port-level configuration overrides. The port-level override option is disabled by default.

- Ensure that vDS port mirror traffic is sent only to authorized collector ports or VLANs.

Network Security Policies

You should connect virtual machines to standard virtual switch port groups or distributed virtual switch port groups that are configured with an appropriate security policy. The network security policy provides three options, which may each be set to Reject or Accept, as described in Table 7-14.

Table 7-14 Network Security Policies

Option	Setting	Description
Promiscuous Mode	Accept	The virtual switch forwards all frames to the virtual network adapter.
	Reject	The virtual switch forwards only the frames that are addressed to the virtual network adapter.
MAC Address Changes	Accept	If the guest operating system changes the effective MAC address of the virtual adapter to a value that differs from the MAC address assigned to the adapter in the VMX file, the virtual switch allows the inbound frame to pass.
	Reject	If the guest operating system changes the effective MAC address of the virtual adapter to a value that differs from the MAC address assigned to the adapter in the VMX file, the virtual switch drops all inbound frames to the adapter. If the guest OS changes the MAC address back to its original value, the virtual switch stops dropping the frames and allows inbound traffic to the adapter.
Forged Transmits	Accept	The virtual switch does not filter outbound frames. It permits all outbound frames, regardless of the source MAC address.
	Reject	The virtual switch drops any outbound frame from a virtual machine virtual adapter that uses a source MAC address that differs from the MAC address assigned to the virtual adapter in the VMX file.

On a distributed virtual switch, you can override the security policy per virtual port.

Virtual Machine Security

To harden a virtual machine, you can follow best practices, configure UEFI, implement security policies, protect against denial of service attacks, and implement encryption, as described in this section.

Virtual Machine Hardening Best Practices

To harden virtual machines, you should apply the following best practices:

- **General protection**: In most respects, you should treat virtual machine as you would a physical server when it comes to applying security measures. For example, be sure to install guest operating systems patches, protect with antivirus software, and disable unused serial ports.

- **Templates**: Carefully harden the first virtual machine deployment of each guest O/S and verify hardening completeness. Convert the virtual machine into a template and use the template to deploy virtual machines, as needed.

- **Virtual machine console**: Minimize the use of this console. Use it only when required. Use remote tools such as SSH and Remote Desktop to access virtual machines. Consider limiting the number of console connections to just one.

- **Virtual machine resource usage**: Prevent virtual machines from taking over resources on the ESXi host to minimize the risk of denial of service to other virtual machines. Configure each virtual machine with enough virtual hardware but not more virtual hardware resources than needed. For example, configure each virtual machine with enough virtual memory to handle its workload and meet application vendor recommendations, but do not provide much more memory than you expect it will need. Consider setting reservations or shares to ensure that critical virtual machines have access to enough CPU and memory.

- **Unnecessary services**: Disable or uninstall any function for the guest operating system that is not required in order to reduce the number of components that can be attacked and to reduce its resource demand. For example, turn off screen savers, disable unneeded guest operating system services, and disconnect the CD/DVD drive.

- **Unnecessary hardware devices**: To minimize potential attack channels, disable any hardware devices that are not required, such as floppy drives, serial ports, parallel ports, USB controllers, and CD-ROM drives.

Configuring UEFI Boot

Starting with vSphere 6.5, if the operating system supports UEFI Secure Boot, you can configure your VM to use UEFI boot. Prerequisites are UEFI firmware virtual hardware Version 13 or later, VMware Tools Version 10.1 or later, and an operating system that supports UEFI Secure Boot. For Linux virtual machines, the VMware host guest file system is not supported in Secure Boot Mode and should be removed from VMware Tools before you enable Secure Boot. If you turn on Secure Boot for a virtual machine, you can load only signed drivers into that virtual machine.

In a guest operating system that supports UEFI Secure Boot, each piece of boot software is signed, including the bootloader, the operating system kernel, and operating system drivers. The default configuration includes several code-signing certificates, including a Microsoft certificate for booting Windows, a Microsoft certificate for third-party code, and a VMware certificate for booting ESXi inside a virtual machine. The virtual machine default configuration includes one certificate: the Microsoft Key Exchange Key (KEK) certificate.

If you turn on Secure Boot for a virtual machine, you can only load signed drivers in the guest OS.

Disabling Unexposed Features

Some virtual machine settings are useful for other platforms (such as VMware Workstation and VMware Fusion) but can be disabled in a vSphere environment. To reduce potential risk, consider setting the following advanced virtual machine options to TRUE:

- isolation.tools.unity.push.update.disable

- isolation.tools.ghi.launchmenu.change

- isolation.tools.memSchedFakeSampleStats.disable

- isolation.tools.getCreds.disable

- isolation.tools.ghi.autologon.disable

- isolation.bios.bbs.disable

- isolation.tools.hgfsServerSet.disable

Other Common Settings

You should consider the following options that are commonly used to address specific potential security threats:

- **Disk shrinking**: Because disk shrinking, which involves reclaiming unused disk space from a virtual machine, can take considerable time to complete and its invocation can result in a temporary denial of service, you should disable disk shrinking by using the following lines in the VMX file:

```
isolation.tools.diskWiper.disable = "TRUE"

isolation.tools.diskShrink.disable = "TRUE"
```

- **Copying and pasting**: Copy and paste operations are disabled by default in new virtual machines. In most cases, you should retain this default to ensure that one user of the virtual machine console cannot paste data that was originally copied from a previous user. Ensure that the following lines remain in the VMX files:

```
isolation.tools.copy.disable = "TRUE"

isolation.tools.paste.disable = "TRUE"
```

- **Connecting devices**: By default, the ability to connect and disconnect devices is disabled. One reason is to prevent one user from accessing a sensitive CD-ROM device that was left in the drive. Another reason is to prevent users from disconnecting the network adapter, which could lead to denial of service. Ensure that the following lines remain in the VMX file:

```
isolation.device.connectable.disable = "TRUE"

isolation.device.edit.disable = "TRUE"
```

- **Logging**: Uncontrolled virtual machine logging could lead to denial of service if the associated datastore runs out of disk space. VMware recommends keeping 10 log files. To set this on a virtual machine, set the following in the VMX file:

```
vmx.log.keepOld = "10"
```

Alternatively, to limit the number of log files for virtual machines on an ESXi host, add the previous line to the host's /etc/vmware/config file. A more aggressive measure is to disable virtual machine logging with the following statement in the VMX file:

```
logging = "FALSE"
```

- **VMX file size**: By default, the size of each VMX file is 1 MB because uncontrolled file sizes can lead to denial of service if the datastore runs out of disk space. Occasionally, *setinfo* messages that define virtual machine characteristics or identifiers are sent as name/value pairs from the virtual machine to the VMX file. If needed, you can increase the size of the VMX file limit by using the following statement in the VMX file and replacing the numeric value with a larger value:

```
tools.setInfo.sizeLimit = "1048576"
```

If tools.setInfo.sizeLimit is not set in the virtual machine's advanced options, the default size applies. In most cases, you can keep the default setting as a security measure.

■ **Performance counters**: VMware Tools provides performance counters on CPU and memory from the ESXi host into the virtual machine for use by PerfMon. This feature is disabled by default because an adversary could potentially make use of this information to attack the host. Ensure that the following line remains in the VMX files, as it blocks some (but not all) performance metrics:

```
tools.guestlib.enableHostInfo = "FALSE"
```

Virtual Machine Risk Profiles

VMware's *vSphere 6.0 Hardening Guide* provides guidelines for addressing vulnerabilities based on risk profiles. When you can apply this hardening guide to your environment, the first step is to apply the appropriate risk profile, based on the sensitivity of your environment and data. The hardening guide offers three risk profiles:

■ **Risk Profile 1**: Intended to be implemented in just the most secure environments, such as top-secret government environments.

■ **Risk Profile 2**: Intended to be implemented in sensitive environments to protect sensitive data such as data that must adhere to strict compliance rules.

■ **Risk Profile 3**: Intended to be implemented in all production environments.

Starting with vSphere 6.7, the *vSphere Hardening Guide* is replaced with the *vSphere Security Configuration Guide*. The risk profiles are removed, primarily because the only remaining Risk Profile 1 setting is ESXi.enable-strict-lockdown-mode. Instead of identifying risk profiles, the new guide simply describes the current guidelines for configuring the vCenter, ESXi, hardware, virtual machines, and guest OS.

Protecting Virtual Machines Against Denial-of-Service Attacks

As mentioned earlier, the size limit of the virtual machine configuration file (VMX file) is 1 MB by default, but you can change it by using the tools.setInfo.sizeLimit parameter to avoid filling the datastore and causing denial of service.

Virtual Machine Communication Interface (VMCI) is a high-speed communication mechanism for virtual machine-to-ESXi host communication. In some VMware products, including ESXi 4.x, VMCI also provides high-speed communication between virtual machines on the same ESXi host. In ESXi 5.1, the guest-to-guest VMCI is removed. In a VMX file, the vmci0.unrestricted parameter is used to control VMCI isolation for virtual machines running on ESX/ESXi 4.x and ESXi 5.0, but it has no effect on virtual machines running on ESXi 5.1 and later. Any DoS concerns related to VMCI in previous vSphere versions do not apply to vSphere 8.0.

Non-administrative users in the guest operating system can shrink virtual disks to reclaim the disk's unused space. However, if you shrink a virtual disk repeatedly, the disk can become unavailable, leading to denial of service. To prevent this, you could disable the ability to shrink virtual disks by following these steps:

Step 1.   Shut down the virtual machine.

Step 2.   Modify the advanced settings in the virtual machine options.

Step 3.   Set isolation.tools.diskWiper.disable and isolation.tools.diskShrink.disable to TRUE.

Controlling VM Device Connections

As mentioned earlier in this chapter, the ability to connect and disconnect devices is disabled by default for new virtual machines. In most cases, you should not change this behavior. You should verify that the following settings exist in your VMX files, especially if the virtual machines were deployed from a non-hardened template or were originally built on older ESXi hosts:

```
isolation.device.connectable.disable = "TRUE"
isolation.device.edit.disable = "TRUE"
```

If these parameters are set to FALSE, then in a guest operating system, any user or process, with or without root or administrator privileges, could use VMware Tools to change device connectivity and settings. The user or process could then connect or disconnect devices, such as network adapters and CD-ROM drives, and modify device settings. This functionality could allow the user or process to connect a CD-ROM with sensitive data or disconnect a network adapter, which could lead to denial of service for other users.

Virtual Machine Encryption

Starting with vSphere 6.5, you can protect your virtual machines, virtual disks, and other virtual machine files by using virtual machine encryption. In vSphere 6.5 and 6.7, you must set up a trusted connection between vCenter Server and a KMS server. The KMS server generates and stores keys. It passes the keys to vCenter Server for distribution. Starting in vSphere 7.0, you can remove the need for vCenter to request keys from the KMS server by configuring vTA and making encryption keys conditional to cluster attestation.

You can use the vSphere Client or the vSphere API to add key provider instances to a vCenter Server system. vCenter Server uses Key Management Interoperability Protocol (KMIP) to allow flexibility in choosing a KMS server. If you use multiple key provider instances, all instances must be from the same vendor and must replicate keys. If you use different KMS server vendors in different environments, you can add a key provider for each KMS server and specify a default key provider. The first key provider that you add becomes the default key provider, but you can change it.

Only vCenter Servers (not the ESXi hosts) have the credentials for logging in to the KMS server. vCenter Server obtains keys from the KMS server and pushes them to the hosts. Two types of keys are used for virtual machine encryption:

- **Data encryption keys (DEKs)**: DEKs are internal keys that are generated by the ESXi host and used to encrypt virtual machines and disks. DEKs are XTS-AES-256 keys.

- **Key encryption key (KEKs)**: KEKs are the keys that vCenter Server requests from the KMS server. KEKs are AES-256 keys. vCenter Server stores only the ID of each KEK and not the key itself. These keys are used to encrypt the DEKs as they are written to an encrypted virtual machine's VMX file.

You can encrypt an existing virtual machine or virtual disk by changing its storage policy. Encryption works with any guest OS because encryption occurs at the hypervisor level. Encryption keys and configuration are not contained in the virtual machine's guest OS. Encryption works with any supported storage type, including VMware vSAN.

You can encrypt virtual disks only for encrypted virtual machines. You cannot encrypt the virtual disk of an unencrypted VM. You can encrypt virtual machine files (NVRAM, VSWP, and VMSN files), virtual disk files, and coredump files. Log files, virtual machine configuration files, and virtual disk descriptor files are not encrypted. For each virtual machine, you can use the vSphere Client to encrypt and decrypt virtual disks independently.

Coredumps are always encrypted on ESXi hosts where Encryption Mode is enabled. Coredumps on the vCenter Server system are not encrypted. To perform cryptographic operations, you must be assigned the cryptographic operations privilege.

ESXi uses KEKs to encrypt the internal keys and stores the encrypted internal keys on disk. ESXi does not store the KEK on disk. If a host reboots, vCenter Server requests the KEK with the corresponding ID from the KMS server and makes it available to ESXi, which decrypts the internal keys as needed. In addition to VMDK files, most virtual machine files that contain guest data are encrypted, such as the NVRAM, VSWP, and VMSN files. The key that vCenter Server retrieves from the KMS server unlocks an encrypted bundle in the VMX file that contains internal keys and other secrets.

VM encryption uses vSphere APIs for I/O Filtering (VAIO), which is typically called IOFilter. IOFilter is an ESXi framework that allows for the interception of virtual machine I/O in the virtual SCSI (vSCSI) emulation layer, which is just below the virtual machine and above the file system. It enables VMware and third-party developers to develop services using virtual machine I/O, such as encryption, caching, and replication. It is implemented entirely in user space, which cleanly isolates it from the core architecture and core functionality of the hypervisor. In the event of any failure, only the virtual machine in question is impacted. Multiple filters can be enabled for a particular virtual machine or a virtual disk, which are typically chained in a manner such that I/O is processed serially by each of these filters before the I/O is passed down to VMFS or completed within one of the filters.

The default administrator system role includes all cryptographic operations privileges. A new default role, the no cryptography administrator role, supports all administrator privileges except for the cryptographic operations privileges. You can create a custom role that contains granular cryptographic operations privileges such as by setting Cryptographic Operations to Encrypt (which allows a user to encrypt a virtual machine or virtual disk) or setting Cryptographic Operations to Add Disk (which allows a user to add a disk to an encrypted virtual machine).

The vSphere Client can be used to encrypt and decrypt virtual machines. To re-encrypt a virtual machine, you must use the API. You can use the API to perform a deep re-encryption (replacing the DEK and KEK) or a shallow re-encryption (replacing just the KEK) of a virtual machine. A deep re-encryption requires that the virtual machine be powered off and free from snapshots. A shallow re-encryption is permitted on a virtual machine with one snapshot (not multiple snapshots). The **crypto-util** command-line utility can be used to decrypt coredumps, check for file encryption, and perform management tasks on the ESXi host.

The specific steps and keys used during an encryption operation depend on the provider type. For the Standard key provider:

- The ESXi host generates internal XTS-AES-256 keys to use as data encryption keys (DEKs), which it uses to encrypt virtual machines and virtual disks.

- vCenter Server requests AES-256 keys from the KMS server to use as the key encryption key (KEK). vCenter Server stores only the KEK ID, not the key itself.

- ESXi uses the KEK to encrypt the internal keys. It stores the encrypted internal key on disk but does not store the KEK on disk. If the host reboots, vCenter Server requests the KEK using the corresponding ID from the KMS server and provides it to the host.

For the vSphere Trust Authority trusted key provider:

- The trusted cluster's vCenter Server determines if the default trusted key provider is accessible to the ESXi host and adds the trusted key provider to the virtual machine ConfigSpec.

- Whenever an ESXi host creates a virtual machine, if an attestation token is not already available to the host, it requests one from the Attestation Service.

- The Key Provider Service validates the attestation token and creates a KEK. It encrypts (wraps) the KEK using its primary key. It returns the KEK ciphertext and KEK plaintext to the trusted host.

- The ESXi host generates a data encryption key (DEK), which it uses to encrypt virtual machines and virtual disks.

- The hosts uses the KEK to encrypt (wrap) the DEK. It stores the key ciphertext from the key provider alongside the encrypted data.

Encrypted vSphere vMotion

Encrypted vSphere vMotion provides confidentiality, integrity, and authenticity of the data that is transferred with vSphere vMotion. Starting with vSphere 6.5, vSphere vMotion uses encryption when migrating encrypted virtual machines. You cannot turn off encrypted vSphere vMotion for encrypted virtual machines. For virtual machines that are not encrypted, you can set Encrypted vMotion to one of the following states:

- **Disabled**: Do not use encrypted vSphere vMotion.

- **Opportunistic**: Use encrypted vSphere vMotion if the source and target hosts support it. (This is the default.)

- **Required**: If the source or destination host does not support encrypted vSphere vMotion, do not allow migration with vSphere vMotion.

The following rules concerning encrypted vMotion across vCenter Server instances apply:

- Encrypted vMotion of unencrypted and encrypted virtual machines is supported.

- The source and destination vCenter Server instances must share the KMS cluster that was used to encrypt the virtual machine.

- The name of the shared KMS cluster must be the same on each vCenter Server instance.

- You must have the Cryptographic Operations.Migrate privilege on the virtual machine.

- You must have the Cryptographic Operations.EncryptNew privilege on the destination vCenter Server.

- If the destination ESXi host is not in Safe Mode, then you also need the Cryptographic Operations.RegisterHost privilege on the destination vCenter Server.

- You cannot change the virtual machine storage policy or perform a key change.

NOTE   Only ESXi Versions 6.5 and later use encrypted vSphere vMotion.

When using vTA, the following requirements apply:

- The destination host must be configured with vTA and must be attested.

- Encryption cannot change on migration.

- You can migrate a standard encrypted virtual machine onto a trusted host.

- You cannot migrate a vTA encrypted virtual machine onto a non-trusted host.

Virtual Trusted Platform Module (vTPM)

A *virtual Trusted Platform Module (vTPM)* is a software-based representation of a physical TPM 2.0 chip. A vTPM uses software to perform the same functions that a TPM chip performs in hardware. A vTPM uses the NVRAM file, which is encrypted using virtual machine encryption, as its secure storage. A hardware TPM chip includes a preloaded key called the endorsement key (EK), which includes a private key and a public key. For vTPM, the EK is provided either by VMCA or by a third-party CA. An important use case for vTPM is to support Windows security features in Windows 10 and above and Windows Server 2016 and above. For example, one specific use case is to use vTPM to meet the Windows 11 requirement for TPM 2.0.

You can add a vTPM to either a new virtual machine or an existing virtual machine, which enables the guest operating system to create and store keys that are private. The keys are not exposed to the guest operating system itself, even if the guest operating system is compromised. The keys can be used only by the guest operating system for encryption or signing. With an attached vTPM, a third party can remotely attest to (validate) the identity of the firmware and the guest operating system.

When you configure a vTPM, VM encryption automatically encrypts the virtual machine files but not the disks. The backup of a VM with a vTPM must include all virtual machine data, including the NVRAM file. In order to successfully restore the VM, the backup must include the NVRAM file, and you must ensure that the encryption keys are available.

To use a vTPM, the following requirements must be met:

- Virtual machine hardware Version 14 using Extensible Firmware Interface (EFI) firmware

- vCenter Server 6.7 or later

- Virtual machine encryption (for home files) and KMS server

- Windows Server 2016 (64 bit) or Windows 10 (64 bit)

You can add a vTPM as you create a virtual machine by selecting Customize Hardware > Add New Device > Trusted Platform Module. Likewise, you can add a vTPM to an existing (powered-down) virtual machine. In the vSphere Client, you can identify which virtual machines are enabled with vTPM by using Show/Hide Column for a selected object, such as a host or cluster.

Beginning with vSphere 8, you can leverage the TPM Provision Policy feature when cloning a virtual machine that includes a vTPM. The policy lets you choose if you want to clone or replace the vTPM. Cloning the vTPM results in copying its workload-related keys. When you choose Replace, the vTPM is replaced, and you avoid the risk of the cloned virtual machine having access to any stored secrets from the source virtual machine.

Virtual Intel Software Guard Extension (vSGX)

Intel Software Guard Extension (SGX) is a processor-specific technology that application developers can use to protect code and data from disclosure or modification. It allows user-level code to define enclaves, which are private regions of memory. It prevents code running outside an enclave from accessing content in the enclave.

If Intel SGX technology is available on your hardware, your virtual machines can use virtual Intel SGX (vSGX). To enable vSGX for a virtual machine, the following requirements must be met:

- Virtual machine hardware Version 17 and EFI firmware

- vCenter Server 7.0 and ESXi 7.0 or later

- Linux, Windows Server 2016 (64 bit) or later, or Windows 10 (64 bit) guest OS

- Intel Coffee Lake CPU or later

When vSGX is enabled on a virtual machine, the following features are not supported for that machine:

- vMotion/DRS migration

- Virtual machine suspend and resume

- Memory snapshots (Virtual machine snapshots are supported without snapshotting the memory.)

- Fault tolerance

Available Add-on Security

You can further secure your environment by procuring and implementing additional features that are not provided natively in vSphere, including the VMware products vRealize Aria Operations and NSX.

Compliance Using VMware Aria Operations

You can implement VMware Aria Operations, formerly known as vRealize Operations Manager to provide a single-pane-of-glass monitoring solution for your virtual infrastructure, applications, storage, and network devices. Aria Operations provides an open and extensible platform supported by third-party management packs. It monitors performance and availability metrics, performs predictive analysis of the data, and enables proactive remediation of emerging issues. In addition, you can use Aria Operations to monitor objects in your vSphere environment—such as vCenter Servers, hosts, virtual machines, distributed port groups, and datastores—to ensure compliance with the appropriate standards. You can use Aria Operations to define and analyze compliance standards.

You can customize Aria Operations policies in accordance with the *vSphere Security Configuration Guide* to enable vSphere alerts for ESXi hosts, vCenter Server, and virtual machines that are in violation of the guide. In addition, hardening guides for regulatory standards are delivered as management packs (PAK files) that you can upload, license, and install. For example, you can install management packs for the following regulatory standards:

- Health Insurance Portability and Accountability Act (HIPAA)

- Payment Card Industry Data Security Standard (PCI DSS)

- CIS security standards

- Defense Information Systems Agency (DISA) security standards

- Federal Information Security Management Act (FISMA) security standards

- International Organization for Standardization (ISO) security standards

Aria Operations collects compliance data from vSphere objects, generates compliance alerts, and creates reports based on the compliance results.

VMware NSX

You can implement VMware NSX to add a distributed logical firewall, microsegmentation, and additional security measures to your vSphere environment.

NSX provides Distributed Firewall (DFW), which runs in the VMkernel as a VIB package on all NSX-prepared ESXi hosts. DFW offers near-line-rate performance, virtualization, identity awareness, automated policy creation, advanced service insertion, and other network security features. DFW enhances your physical security by removing unnecessary hairpinning from the physical firewalls and reduces the amount of traffic on the network. It enables *micro-segmentation*, which effectively enables you to place a firewall on each VM network connection.

Micro-segmentation decreases the level of risk and increases the security posture of a vSphere environment. Micro-segmentation involves the following capabilities:

- Distributed stateful firewalling

- Topology-agnostic segmentation

- Centralized policy control

- Granular control

- Network-based isolation

With NSX, isolation can be achieved by leveraging VXLAN technology and virtual networks (that is, logical switches). Isolation can also be achieved by using traditional networking methods, such as implementing ACLs, firewall rules, and routing policies. For example, in a brownfield environment, you could choose to keep existing VLAN segmentation to isolate VMkernel traffic and VM zones while using NSX DFW to implement application segmentation.

With NSX, you can implement virtual machine–to–virtual machine protection, which is commonly referred to as east–west protection, in more than one manner. For example, you could implement multiple Layer 2 segments with Layer 3 isolation (see Figure 7-6), or you could implement a single Layer 2 segment and use DFW rules for isolation (see Figure 7-7).

NSX provides other security features, such as Service Composer, which you can use to configure security groups and security policies. A security policy is a collection of firewall rules, endpoint services, and network introspection services. Security groups may be populated statically or dynamically based on containers (such as folders and clusters), security tags, Active Directory groups, and regular expressions. You can map a security policy to a security group.

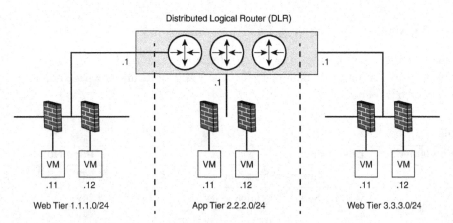

Figure 7-6 Example with Multiple Layer 2 Segments

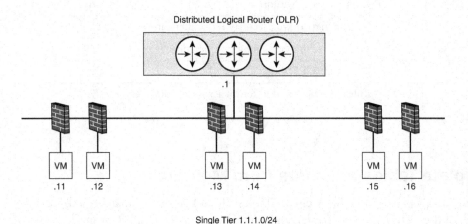

Figure 7-7 Example with a Single Layer 2 Segment

NSX includes other security features, such as SpoofGuard, the Edge firewall, and a virtual private network (VPN).

Exam Preparation Tasks

As mentioned in the section "Book Features and Exam Preparation Methods" in the Introduction, you have some choices for exam preparation: the exercises here, Chapter 15, "Final Preparation," and the exam simulation questions on the companion website.

Review All the Key Topics

Review the most important topics in this chapter, noted with the Key Topics icon in the outer margin of the page. Table 7-15 lists these key topics and the page number on which each is found.

Table 7-15 Key Topics for Chapter 7

Key Topic Element	Description	Page Number
Figure 7-2	vSphere inventory hierarchy	247
List	vCenter Server 7.0 sample roles	249
Paragraph	How permissions are applied by vCenter Server	255
List	Built-in security features	257
Paragraph	vSphere Trust Authority (vTA)	263
List	General networking security recommendations	267
List	Virtual machine hardening best practices	269
Paragraph	Configure UEFI boot	270
List	Rules for encrypted vMotion across vCenter Server instances	276

Complete Tables and Lists from Memory

Print a copy of Appendix B, "Memory Tables" (found on the companion website), or at least the section for this chapter, and complete the tables and lists from memory. Appendix C, "Memory Tables Answers" (also on the companion website), includes completed tables and lists to check your work.

Define Key Terms

Define the following key terms from this chapter and check your answers in the glossary:

VMware Endpoint Certificate Store (VECS), VMware Directory Service (**vmdir**), VMware Certificate Authority (VMCA), Trusted Platform Module (TPM), virtual Trusted Platform Module (vTPM), Intel Software Guard Extension (SGX), microsegmentation

Review Questions

1. You are preparing to implement certificates in your vSphere environment. Which of the following does VCMA support in custom certificates when it is used as a subordinate CA?

   a. CRL distribution points

   b. Authority information access

   c. CRT format

   d. Certificate template information

2. On which of the following can you set permissions in vCenter Server?

   a. Licenses

   b. Datastores

   c. Roles

   d. Sessions

3. You are examining the default security profile in your vSphere environment. Which of the following services is stopped by default?

   a. DCUI

   b. Load-Based Teaming Daemon

   c. CIM Server

   d. SNMP Server

4. You are hardening a vCenter Server and see that it contains some expired certificates. What is the main purpose of removing expired and revoked certificates from vCenter Server?

   a. To avoid DoS attacks

   b. To avoid MITM attacks

   c. To avoid automatic virtual machine shutdown due to expired certificates

   d. To avoid ARP spoofing

5. You want to enable UEFI boot for your virtual machines. Which of the following is a requirement?

    a. Virtual hardware Version 11 or later

    b. VMware Tools Version 11 or later

    c. Virtual hardware Version 12 or later

    d. VMware Tools Version 10.1 or later

This chapter covers the following topics:

- Installing ESXi Hosts
- Deploying vCenter Server Components
- Configuring Single Sign-On (SSO)
- Initial vSphere Configuration

This chapter contains information related to VMware vSphere 8.x Professional (2V0-21.23) exam objectives 1.1, 1.2, 1.6, 1.10, 1.10.1, 1.10.2, 4.1, 4.1.1, 4.1.2, 4.4, 4.4.1, 4.4.2, 4.5, 4.7, 4.14, 4.16, 4.17, 4.19, 4.19.1, 4.19.3, 7.7, 7.8, 7.9, 7.9.1, 7.9.2, 7.9.3, 7.9.4, and 7.9.5.

vSphere Installation

This chapter discusses the procedures involved in installing and configuring a vSphere 8.0 environment.

"Do I Know This Already?" Quiz

The "Do I Know This Already?" quiz allows you to assess whether you should study this entire chapter or move quickly to the "Exam Preparation Tasks" section. In any case, the authors recommend that you read the entire chapter at least once. Table 8-1 outlines the major headings in this chapter and the corresponding "Do I Know This Already?" quiz questions. You can find the answers in Appendix A, "Answers to the 'Do I Know This Already?' Quizzes and Review Questions."

Table 8-1 "Do I Know This Already?" Foundation Topics Section-to-Question Mapping

Foundations Topics Section	Questions Covered in This Section
Installing ESXi Hosts	1, 2
Deploying vCenter Server Components	3, 4
Configuring Single Sign-On (SSO)	5–7
Initial vSphere Configuration	8–10

1. You are preparing to deploy vSphere 8.0. Which of the following is a prerequisite for installing ESXi interactively?

   a. Download the ESXi installer ISO.

   b. Download the ESXi installer OVF.

   c. Download the GUI installer for Windows or Mac.

   d. Download the ESXi MSI.

2. You are preparing to do a scripted installation of ESXi 8.0. Where is the default installation script located?

   a. /etc/vmware/weasel/ks.py

   b. /etc/vmware/weasel/ks.cfg

   c. /etc/vmware//ks.cfg

   d. /etc/vmware/ks.py

3. You are preparing to install vCenter Server 8.0 using a deployment command. To perform a pre-deployment check, which command should you use?

   a. **vcsa-deploy-precheck** *path-to-JSON-file*

   b. **vcsa-deploy install --precheck** *path-to-JSON-file*

   c. **vcsa-deploy install --verify-only** *path-to-JSON-file*

   d. **vcsa-deploy precheck** *path-to-JSON-file*

4. You are installing vSphere 8.0 and want to document the location of certificates. Where are the ESXi certificates stored?

   a. Locally on the ESXi hosts

   b. In VECS

   c. In the vCenter Server database

   d. In VMCA

5. You are adding an OpenLDAP authentication source for your recently deployed vCenter Server. Which of the following is not a requirement?

   a. All users must have the object of class **inetOrgPerson**.

   b. All groups must have the object of class **groupOfUniqueNames**.

   c. All groups must have the group membership attribute **uniqueMember**.

   d. All users must be members of the OpenLDAP group.

6. You are deploying a new vSphere environment and need to control which users can manage certificates. For which vCenter Server group should you manipulate Single Sign-On domain group membership?

   a. DCAdmins

   b. SolutionUsers

   c. CAAdmins

   d. SystemConfiguration_Administrators

7. You are adding an Active Directory (Integrated Windows Authentication) identity source and want to ensure that future machine name changes do not cause issues. Which of the following allows you to do this?

   a. Select Use Service Principal Name (SPN) and provide a UPN.

   b. Select Use Machine Account and provide a UPN.

   c. Select Use Service Principal Name (SPN) and provide a base DN for users.

   d. Select Use Machine Account and provide a base DN for users.

8. You are deploying vCenter Server in a secured network that has no Internet access. What do you need to install in order to download updates?

   a. Update Manager Download Service

   b. Update Manager Proxy Service

   c. Lifecycle Manager Download Service

   d. Lifecycle Manager Proxy Service

9. You are implementing vCenter HA. How will you connect the nodes to the vCenter HA network?

   a. Connect NIC 1 on the Active and Passive nodes and NIC 0 to the vCenter HA network. Do not connect the Witness node to the vCenter HA network.

   b. Connect NIC 1 on the Active and Passive nodes and NIC 0 on the Witness node to the vCenter HA network.

   c. Connect NIC 0 on the Active, Passive, and Witness nodes to the vCenter HA network.

   d. Connect NIC 1 on the Active, Passive, and Witness nodes to the vCenter HA network.

10. You are installing new ESXi hosts and want to configure boot options. Which of the following **kernelopt** options has been deprecated in ESXi 7.0?

    a. **autoCreateDumpFile**

    b. **autoPartitionCreateUSBCoreDumpPartition**

    c. **skipPartitioningSsds**

    d. **autoPartitionOnlyOnceAndSkipSsd**

Foundation Topics

Installing ESXi Hosts

To begin a vSphere deployment, you should install and configure at least one ESXi host by using the information in this section. Optionally, you can apply the information here to install and configure additional ESXi hosts. In many cases, administrators choose to deploy the first ESXi host and then deploy vCenter Server and use vCenter Server along with other tools, such as host profiles, to facilitate the deployment and configuration of the remaining ESXi hosts.

You have several choices for installing ESXi, such as using the interactive wizard, using scripts, and using Auto Deploy. These choices are covered in this section. Using host profiles to configure ESXi hosts after installation is discussed later in this chapter.

Installing ESXi Interactively

You can use the following procedure—which is very useful in small environments with fewer than five ESXi hosts—to install ESXi interactively:

Step 1.   Verify that all the target machine hardware is supported and meets minimum requirements.

Step 2.   Gather and record the information that will be required during the installation (see Table 8-2).

Step 3.   Verify that the server hardware clock is set to **UTC**. This setting is in the system BIOS or UEFI. If you plan to install ESXi on NVIDIA or Pensando DPUs, you must use UEFI.

Step 4.   Download the ESXi installer ISO and boot the hardware system from it.

Step 5.   If the system has supported DPUs, select the DPU on which you want to install ESXi.

Step 6.   On the Select a Disk page, select the drive on which to install ESXi and press **Enter**. If you select a disk containing VMFS or vSAN data, respond to the choices provided by the installer. If you select an SD or USB device, you should respond to the prompt to select a persistent disk with at least 32 MB free space for the ESXi-OSData partition.

Step 7.   Select the keyboard type and language for the host.

Step 8.   Enter a password to be used by the root account.

Step 9.   When prompted to do so, remove the bootable media and press **Enter** to reboot the host.

Table 8-2 Information Required for ESXi Installation

Information	Required or Optional	Details
Keyboard layout	Required	Default: US English
VLAN ID	Optional	Range: 0–4094
		Default: None
IP address	Optional	Default: DHCP
Subnet mask	Optional	Default: Based on the configured IP address
Gateway	Optional	Default: Based on the configured IP address and subnet mask
Primary DNS	Optional	Default: Based on the configured IP address and subnet mask
Secondary DNS	Optional	Default: None
Host name	Required for static IP settings	Default: None
Install location	Required	At least 5 GB if you install on a single disk
		Default: None
Migrate existing ESXi settings; preserve VMFS datastore	Required if you are installing ESXi on a drive with an existing ESXi installation	Default: None
Root password	Required	Must contain at least 8 to 40 characters and meet other requirements
		Default: None

The default behavior is to configure the ESXi management network using DHCP. You can override the default behavior and use static IP settings for the management network after the installation is completed. If your host is not yet assigned an IP address or if you want to change the IP address, you can use the following procedure to select the appropriate network adapter, configure the VLAN, and set the IP configuration for the host's management network interface:

Step 1. Log on to the Direct Console User Interface (DCUI), which appears on the host's monitor.

Step 2. If needed, use the DCUI to change the network adapter used for management:

   a. Select **Configure Management Network** and press **Enter**.

   b. Select **Network Adapters** and press **Enter**.

   c. Select a network adapter and press **Enter**.

Step 3.   If needed, use the DCUI to change the VLAN used for management:

a. Select **Configure Management Network** and press **Enter**.

b. Select **VLAN** and press **Enter**.

c. Enter the appropriate VLAN ID for the network connection.

Step 4.   If needed, use the DCUI to change the IP configuration used for management:

a. Select **Configure Management Network** and press **Enter**.

b. Select **IPv4 Configuration** and press **Enter**.

c. Select **Set Static IPv4 Address and Network Configuration**.

d. Enter the IP address, subnet mask, and default gateway and press **Enter**.

NOTE   It is important for the IP address of the management network to remain consistent. If you do not select a static IP address, make sure that you create a DHCP reservation for the MAC address of your first physical NIC, which ESXi calls VMNIC0.

You can use the DCUI to configure DNS by following this procedure:

Step 1.   Select **Configure Management Network** and press **Enter**.

Step 2.   Select **DNS Configuration** and press **Enter**.

Step 3.   Select **Use the Following DNS server Addresses and Hostname**.

Step 4.   Enter the primary server, an alternative server (optional), and the host name.

When ESXi is installed and the management network is configured, you can manage the host and make other configuration changes by using the vSphere Host Client.

Scripted ESXi Installation

Installation scripts provide an efficient way to deploy multiple hosts and/or to deploy hosts remotely.

You can use an installation script that includes the settings for installing ESXi. The script can be applied to all of the hosts that need to have the same configuration. Only supported commands can be used in the installation script. This can be modified for settings that need to be unique for each host. The installation script can be in any of the following locations:

- FTP server
- HTTP/HTTPS server

- NFS server

- USB flash drive

- CD-ROM drive

To start the installation script, you can enter boot options at the ESXi installer boot command line. At boot time, you can press Shift+O in the boot loader (see Figure 8-1) to specify boot options and access the kickstart file. If you are installing using PXE boot, options can be passed through the **kernelopts** line of the boot. cfg file. The location of the installation script is defined by setting the **ks=**_filepath_ option, where _filepath_ is the location of the kickstart file. If **ks=**_filepath_ is not included in the script, the text installer runs.

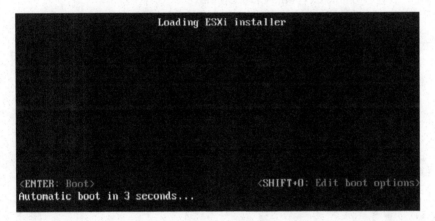

Figure 8-1 ESXi Installer

Follow these steps to start the installation script:

Step 1.   Start the host.

Step 2.   When the Loading ESXi Installer window appears (see Figure 8-1), press **Shift+O** to define the options.

Step 3.   At the **runweasel** command prompt, enter **ks=** along with the path to the installation script and the command-line options. For example, you could enter the following options to boot the host from a script named ks-script-01 residing on the server 192.168.1010.10 and set the host's IP address to 192.168.100.101:

```
ks=http://192.168.100.10/kickstart/ks-script-01.cfg
nameserver=192.168.1.100 ip=192.168.100.101 netmask=
255.255.255.0 gateway=192.168.100.101
```

To successfully perform a scripted installation, you may need to enter boot options to access the script file. Table 8-3 shows some of these options.

Table 8-3 Boot Options for ESXi Scripted Installation

Boot Option	Description
BOOTIF=*hwtype-MAC address*	Is similar to the **netdevice** option except in the PXELINUX format.
gateway=*ip address*	Serves as a gateway for downloading the installation script.
ip=*ip address*	Indicates the IP address used for downloading the installation script.
ks=*cdrom:/path*	Performs a scripted installation with the script at *path*, which resides on the CD in the CD-ROM drive.
ks=*file://path*	Performs a scripted installation with the script at *path*.
ks=*protocol://serverpath*	Performs a scripted installation with a script located on the network at the given URL. *protocol* can be **http**, **https**, **ftp**, or **nfs** (for example, **ks=nfs://host/porturl-path**).
ks=*usb*	Performs a scripted installation, accessing the script from an attached USB drive.
ks=*usb://path*	Performs a scripted installation with the script file at the specified path, which resides on a USB drive.
ksdevice=*device* or **netdevice=***device*	Tries to use a network adapter device when looking for an installation script and installation media. For *device*, specify a MAC address, such as 00:50:56:C0:00:01, or a vmnic## name.
nameserver=*ip address*	Specifies the domain name server to be used for downloading the installation script and installation media.
netmask=*subnet mask*	Specifies the subnet mask used for downloading the installation script.
vlanid=*vlanid*	Specifies the VLAN used for downloading the installation script.

There is a default installation script included with the ESXi installer, and it can be used to install ESXi onto the first disk that is detected. The default ks.cfg installation script is in the initial RAM disk at /etc/vmware/weasel/ks.cfg. The location of the default ks.cfg file can be defined with the **ks=file://etc/vmware/weasel/ks.cfg** boot option. When using the ks.cfg script for the installation, the default root password is myp@ssw0rd. The installation script on the installation media can't be modified. After the ESXi host has been installed, the vSphere Host Client or the vSphere Web Client logged in to the vCenter Server that manages the ESXi host can be used to change any of the default settings.

Example 8-1 shows the contents of the default script provided with ESXi 8.0, which includes an option to support DPUs.

Example 8-1 Default Installation Script

```
#
# Sample scripted installation file
#

# Accept the VMware End User License Agreement
vmaccepteula

# Set the root password for the DCUI and Tech Support Mode
rootpw myp@ssw0rd

# Install on the first local disk available on machine
install --firstdisk --overwritevmfs
 In case your system has DPUs, you also specify a PCI slot:
install --firstdisk --overwritevmfs --dpuPciSlots=<PCIeSlotID>

# Set the network to DHCP on the first network adapter
network --bootproto=dhcp --device=vmnic0

# A sample post-install script
%post --interpreter=python --ignorefailure=true
import time
stampFile = open('/finished.stamp', mode='w')
stampFile.write( time.asctime() )
```

You can see that this default script sets the root password to myp@ssw0rd, installs on the first disk, overwrites any existing VMFS datastore, and sets the network interface to use DHCP. When creating your own script, you can specify many options, a few of which are shown in Table 8-4.

Table 8-4 Sample Options for the ESXi Installation Script

Command	Options	Description
clearpart (optional)	--ignoredrives=	Removes partitions on all drives except those specified.
	--overwritevmfs	Allows overwriting of VMFS partitions on the specified drives.
dryrun	N/A	Parses and checks the installation script but does not perform the installation.

Command	Options	Description
install	**--disk=**	Specifies the disk to partition. Acceptable values can use various forms, as in these examples:
		Path:
		--disk=/vmfs/devices/disks/mpx.vmhba1:C0:T0:L0
		MPX name:
		--disk=mpx.vmhba1:C0:T0:L0
		VML name:
		--disk=vml.000000034211234
		vmkLUN UID:
		--disk=vmkLUN_UID
	--ignoressd	Excludes solid-state disks from eligibility for partitioning.
	--overwritevsan	Used to install ESXi on a disk—either SSD or HDD (magnetic)—that is already in a vSAN disk group.
network	**--bootproto=**	Specifies whether the IP address should be set statically or via DHCP.
	--ip=	Sets an IP address for the machine to be installed, in the form *xxx.xxx.xxx.xxx*. Required with the **bootproto=static** option and ignored otherwise.
	--nameserver	Designates the primary name server as an IP address. Used with the **bootproto=static** option. You can omit this option if you do not intend to use DNS.

Using Auto Deploy

vSphere Auto Deploy makes it possible to install ESXi on hundreds of physical hosts. Experienced administrators can use Auto Deploy to efficiently manage large environments. Hosts use network booting to boot from a central Auto Deploy server. Hosts can be configured with a host profile created from a reference host, if desired. This host profile could be created to prompt for input. After the hosts boot and are configured, they are then managed by vCenter Server, like other ESXi hosts. Auto Deploy can also be configured for stateless caching or stateful installations.

With *stateless caching*, which is the default, Auto Deploy does not store ESXi configuration or state data within the host. Instead, Auto Deploy uses image profiles and host profiles to maintain the host configuration. During subsequent boots, the host must connect to the Auto Deploy server to retrieve its configuration. If a network boot fails, the ESXi host can use a local cache to boot from the last-known ESXi image.

With stateful installations, Auto Deploy is used to boot the host, but the installation and configuration are written to a local disk. On subsequent boots, the host boots from the local disk where this host configuration is stored.

Auto Deploy can be configured and managed using a graphical user interface (GUI) in vSphere 6.5 and later. The PowerCLI method is also available, but the GUI provides an easier-to-use option. For the Auto Deploy GUI to be visible in the vSphere Web Client, both the Image Builder and Auto Deploy services must be running when you're logging in to vCenter Server. The Image Builder feature in the GUI enables you to download ESXi images from the VMware public repository or to upload ZIP files containing ESXi images or drivers. You can customize the images by adding or removing components and optionally export images to ISO or ZIP files for use elsewhere. You can compare two images to see how their contents differ.

You can use the Deployed Hosts tab to view hosts that are provisioned with Auto Deploy and to perform tests and remediations.

The architecture for Auto Deploy includes many components, as described in Table 8-5 and illustrated in Figure 8-2.

Table 8-5 Auto Deploy Components

Component	Description/Purpose
Auto Deploy server	Uses a rules engine, a set of images, a set of host profiles, and required infrastructure to manage ESXi deployments.
Rules engine	Assigns image profiles and host profiles to each host.
Host profile	Defines host-specific configurations, such as networking, NTP, and host permissions. You can use host customization in conjunction with host profiles to provide details that are unique to each host, such as IP address.
Auto Deploy PowerCLI	Serves as a command-line engine for driving Auto Deploy.
Image Builder PowerCLI	Serves as a command-line engine for building images.
vCenter Server	Manages the vSphere inventory and provides host profiles.
DHCP server	Provides IP configuration to the host and redirects the host to the PXE server.
PXE server	Boots the host and directs it to the TFTP server.
TFTP server	Provides the appropriate boot image.
Software depot	Holds a collection of VIBs either online (accessible via HTTP) or offline (accessible via a USB drive or CD/DVD).
Image profile	Holds a collection of VIBs used to install the ESXi server and saved as ZIP files or ISO images. You can obtain image profiles from VMware and VMware partners, and you can create custom image profiles by using ESXi Image Builder.

Component	Description/Purpose
vSphere Installation Bundle (VIB)	Packages a collection of files (such as drivers) into an archive similar to a ZIP file. Each VIB is released with an acceptance level that cannot be changed. The host acceptance level assigned to each host determines which VIBs can be installed to the host. These are the acceptance levels, from highest to lowest: ■ VMwareCertified ■ VMwareAccepted ■ Partner Supported ■ CommunitySupported

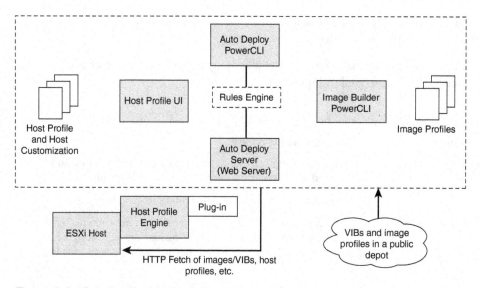

Figure 8-2   Auto Deploy Architecture

By default, Auto Deploy provisions hosts with certificates that are signed by the VMware Certificate Authority (VMCA), but you can change this to make the Auto Deploy server a subordinate certificate authority of your third-party certificate authority. With ESXi 8.0, Auto Deploy provides a third option that allows you to generate a certificate outside vSphere. For this option, you could generate custom certificates with a script or provider such as Verisign, assign certificates to stateless hosts based on the boot NIC's MAC address or BIOS UUID, update the VMware Endpoint Certificate Store (VECS) using PowerCLI, and add the CA public certificate to the TRUSTED_ROOTS store in VECS.

You control the behavior of the vSphere Auto Deploy server by using rules. The rules engine checks the rule set for matching host patterns to decide which items (image profile, host profile, vCenter Server location, or script object) to use to provision each host. Rules can assign image profiles and host profiles to a set of hosts. A rule can identify target hosts by boot MAC address, Basic Input/Output System (BIOS), universally unique identifier (UUID), System Management BIOS (SMBIOS) information, vendor, model, or fixed DHCP IP address. You can create rules by using the vSphere Web Client or vSphere Auto Deploy cmdlets with PowerCLI. For example, to create a new deployment rule named Rule-01 that places all hosts in a folder named Auto-deployed Hosts, you can use the following PowerCLI command:

```
New-DeployRule -Name Rule-01 -Item "Auto-deployed Hosts" -allhosts
```

To modify the rule so that it applies only to a set of hosts in a specific IP range, you can use the Set-DeployRule cmdlet:

```
Set-DeployRule -DeployRule Rule-01 -Pattern
"ipv4=192.168.100.101-192.168.100.112"
```

Table 8-6 describes some of the common Auto Deploy PowerCLI cmdlets.

Table 8-6 Common Auto Deploy PowerCLI cmdlets

cmdlet	Description
Get-DeployCommand	Returns a list of Auto Deploy cmdlets.
New-DeployRule	Creates a new rule with the specified items and patterns.
Set-DeployRule	Updates an existing rule with the specified items and patterns. You cannot update a rule that is part of a rule set.
Get-DeployRule	Retrieves the rules with the specified names.
Copy-DeployRule	Clones and updates an existing rule.
Add-DeployRule	Adds one or more rules to the working rule set and, by default, also to the active rule set. Use the **NoActivate** parameter to add a rule to the working rule set only.
Remove-DeployRule	Removes one or more rules from the working rule set and from the active rule set. Run this command with the **-Delete** parameter to completely delete the rule.
Set-DeployRuleSet	Explicitly sets the list of rules in the working rule set.
Get-DeployRuleSet	Retrieves the current working rule set or the current active rule set.
Switch-ActiveDeployRuleSet	Activates a rule set so that any new requests are evaluated through the rule set.
Get-VMHostMatchingRules	Retrieves rules that match a pattern. For example, you can retrieve all rules that apply to a host or hosts. Use this cmdlet primarily for debugging.

cmdlet	Description
Test-DeployRulesetCompliance	Checks whether the items associated with a specified host are in compliance with the active rule set.
Repair-DeployRulesetCompliance	Given the output of **Test-DeployRulesetCompliance**, this cmdlet updates the image profile, host profile, and location for each host in the vCenter Server inventory. The cmdlet might apply image profiles, apply host profiles, or move hosts to the prespecified folders or clusters on the vCenter Server system.
Apply-EsxImageProfile	Associates the specified image profile with the specified host.
Get-VMHostImageProfile	Retrieves the image profile in use by a specified host. This cmdlet differs from the **Get-EsxImageProfile** cmdlet in the Image Builder PowerCLI.
Repair-DeployImageCache	Deploys a new image cache. Use this cmdlet only if the Auto Deploy image cache is accidentally deleted.
Get-VMHostAttributes	Retrieves the attributes for a host that are used when the Auto Deploy server evaluates the rules.
Get-DeployMachineIdentity	Returns a string value that Auto Deploy uses to logically link an ESXi Host in vCenter to a physical machine.
Set-DeployMachineIdentity	Logically links a host object in the vCenter Server database to a physical machine. Use this cmdlet to add hosts without specifying rules.
Get-DeployOption	Retrieves the Auto Deploy global configuration options. This cmdlet currently supports the **vlan-id** option, which specifies the default VLAN ID for the ESXi Management Network of a host provisioned with Auto Deploy. Auto Deploy uses the value only if the host boots without a host profile.
Set-DeployOption	Sets the value of a global configuration option. Currently supports the **vlan-id** option for setting the default VLAN ID for the ESXi Management Network.

The first time a host boots using Auto Deploy, the following sequence of events occurs:

1. The host starts a PXE boot sequence. The DHCP server assigns an IP address and redirects the host to the TFTP server.

2. The host downloads and executes the iPXE file (configured by the DHCP server) and applies the associated configuration file.

3. The host makes an HTTP boot request to the vSphere Auto Deploy server. The HTTP request includes hardware and network information.

4. The vSphere Auto Deploy server queries the rules engine and streams data (the ESXi image) from the image profile and the host profile.

5. The host boots using the image profile. If the vSphere Auto Deploy server provided a host profile, the host profile is applied to the host.

6. vSphere Auto Deploy adds the host to the proper inventory location and cluster in the vCenter Server system.

7. If the host is part of a DRS cluster, virtual machines from other hosts might be migrated to the host.

NOTE   If a host profile requires a user to specify certain information, such as a static IP address, the host is placed in Maintenance Mode when the host is added to the vCenter Server system. You must reapply the host profile and update the host customization to have the host exit Maintenance Mode.

Deploying vCenter Server Components

VMware vCenter 7.0 and later is only available as a prebuilt Linux-based virtual appliance. It is no longer available to be installed on Windows systems. This section provides information on deploying vCenter Server components.

vCenter Server Database

As of vCenter 7.0, only one database can be used: an included version of the VMware-specific distribution of PostgreSQL.

NOTE   The vCenter installation program allows migration from a Windows-based vCenter Server to the vCenter Server Appliance, including migration from Oracle or Microsoft SQL to the embedded PostgreSQL database.

Platform Services Controller (PSC)

In vSphere 6.x, the Platform Services Controller (PSC) component could be deployed externally to vCenter Server. Beginning with vSphere 7.0, the services that the PSC provided in vSphere 6.x, such as SSO, VMCA, and License Service, are consolidated into vCenter Server. These services cannot be deployed as separate virtual appliances. Because the services are now part of vCenter, they are no longer listed as part of the PSC. For example, in vSphere 7.0, the *vSphere Authentication* publication replaces the *Platform Services Controller Administration* publication.

vCenter Server Appliance

As of vSphere 7.0, the vCenter Server is only available as a prebuilt virtual appliance that consists of the following:

- Photon OS 3.0
- vSphere Authentication Services
- PostgreSQL
- The VMware vSphere Lifecycle Manager extension for the vSphere Client
- VMware vCenter Lifecycle Manager

The vCenter Server 8.0 deployment wizard helps you determine the resource allocation for the virtual appliance, based on the size of your environment. To prepare for a vCenter Server 8.0 deployment, you should download the vCenter Server Appliance installer ISO file and mount it to a virtual machine or physical machine from which you want to perform the deployment. To use the vCenter Server Appliance GUI (or CLI) installer, you can use a machine that is running a supported version of a Windows, Linux, or Mac operating system, as shown in Table 8-7.

Table 8-7 Requirements for GUI/CLI Installers

Operating System	Supported Versions	Minimum Hardware Configuration
Windows	■ Windows 10,11 ■ Windows 2016 x64 bit ■ Windows 2019 x64 bit ■ Windows 2022 x64 bit	4 GB RAM, 2 CPUs having 4 cores with 2.3 GHz, 32 GB hard disk, 1 NIC
Linux	■ SUSE 15 ■ Ubuntu 18.04, 20.04, and 21.10	4 GB RAM, 1 CPU having 2 cores with 2.3 GHz, 16 GB hard disk, 1 NIC With the CLI installer, 64-bit OS
macOS	■ macOS 10.15 and 11.12 ■ macOS Catalina, Big Sur, and Monterey	8 GB RAM, 1 CPU having 4 cores with 2.4 GHz, 150 GB hard disk, 1 NIC

You can use the GUI or CLI installers to do the following:

- Deploy or upgrade vCenter Server Appliance.
- Converge prior vCenter installations with external PSCs to the current vCenter Server version.

- Migrate a Windows-based vCenter Server to the Linux-based vCenter Server Appliance.

- Restore a vCenter Server Appliance from a file-based backup.

Deploying VCSA Using the GUI Installer

You can use the GUI installer to deploy a vCenter Server Appliance. To perform a GUI-based deployment, you download the vCenter Server Appliance installer on a network client machine, run the deployment wizard from the client machine, and provide the required information.

Using the GUI installer involves two stages. In the first stage, you navigate through the installation wizard, choose the deployment type, provide the appliance settings, and deploy the OVA. Alternatively, you can use the vSphere Web Client or the vSphere Host Client to deploy the OVA.

In the second stage of using the GUI installer, you use a wizard to configure the appliance time synchronization, configure vCenter Single Sign-On (SSO), and start the services in the newly deployed appliance. Alternatively, you can use a web browser to access the appliance's vCenter Server Appliance Management Interface (VAMI) at https://*FQDN*:5480. If you use the alternative approach in the first stage, then you must use it in the second stage. To use the GUI installer to deploy the VCSA, you can follow these steps:

Step 1. In the vCenter Server Appliance installer, navigate to the appropriate subdirectory in the **vcsa-ui-installer** directory and run the installer executable file:

- For Windows, use the **win32** subdirectory and the **installer.exe** file.
- For Linux, use the **lin64** subdirectory and the **installer** file.
- For macOS, use the **mac** subdirectory and the **Installer.app** file.

Step 2. On the Home page, click **Install**.

Step 3. On the next page, click **Next**.

Step 4. Read and accept the license agreement and click **Next**.

Step 5. Connect to the target server where you want to deploy the appliance and make one of two choices:

- Provide the FQDN (or IP address) and credentials for the target ESXi host and provide the appropriate certificate.

■ Provide the FQDN (or IP address) and credentials for the target vCenter Server (that is managing the hosts on which this new vCenter Server will be deployed), provide the appropriate certificate, and specify the appropriate location in the vSphere inventory.

Step 6. On the next page, set the appliance's name and root user password, following these rules:

■ The appliance name must not contain a percent sign (%), backslash (\), or forward slash (/) and must be no more than 80 characters in length.

■ The password must contain only lowercase ASCII characters without spaces, must have at least eight characters, and must contain a number, uppercase and lowercase letters, and a special character, such as an exclamation point (!), hash symbol (#), at sign (@), or parentheses (()).

Step 7. Select the deployment size: Tiny, Small, Medium, Large, or X-Large (refer to Chapter 1, "vSphere Overview, Components, and Requirements").

Step 8. Select the storage size for the appliance (as explained in Chapter 1).

Step 9. Select an available datastore and select the disk provisioning type. Optionally, with vSphere 8.0, you can choose to create a new vSAN cluster or vSAN Express Storage Architecture (vSAN ESA) cluster and choose the appropriate disks to claim.

Step 10. On the Configure Network Settings page, fill in the network settings, such as virtual switch port group, IP configuration, and communication ports.

Step 11. On the Ready to Complete page, click **Finish**.

Step 12. Wait for the OVA to deploy and then click **Continue** to proceed with Stage 2.

Step 13. On the Introduction page, click **Next**.

Step 14. Choose a time configuration option:

■ Synchronize Time with the ESXi Host
■ Synchronize Time with NTP Servers

Step 15. Optionally, enable SSH connections into the appliance.

Step 16. Create a new SSO domain or join an existing domain:

■ **Create a new SSO domain**: Enter the domain (such as vsphere.local), set the SSO administrator account (which is administrator@vsphere.local by default) password, provide an SSO site name, and confirm the password.

- **Join an existing SSO domain**: Enter the PSC FQDN containing the SSO server, provide the HTTPS port that PSC will use, provide the target SSO domain name (such as vsphere.local), and enter the SSO administrator account password.

Step 17. Optionally, choose the option to join the VMware Customer Experience Improvement Program (CEIP).

Step 18. On the Ready to Complete page, click **Finish** and then click **OK**.

Deploying VCSA Using the CLI

You can use the CLI installer to perform a silent VCSA deployment. The CLI deployment process includes downloading the installer, preparing a JSON configuration file with the deployment information, and running the deployment command. The VCSA installer contains JSON templates for all deployment types. This enables you to deploy an appliance with minimum effort by copying the appropriate JSON template, changing a few values, and using it with the CLI installer. The steps are as follows:

Step 1. In the vCenter Server Appliance installer, navigate to one of the following directories:

- In Windows, **/vcsa-cli-installer/win32**
- In Linux, **/vcsa-cli-installer/lin64**
- In macOS, **/vcsa-cli-installer/mac**

Step 2. Copy the templates from the **install** subfolder to your desktop.

Step 3. Use a text editor to modify the JSON template for your use case. Modify the default parameter values with your appropriate values and add additional parameters, as necessary. For example, to use an IPv4 DHCP assignment, in the **network** subsection of the template, change the value of the **mode** parameter to **dhcp** and remove the default configuration parameters that are used for a static assignment, as shown here:

```
"network": {
"ip_family": "ipv4",
 "mode": "dhcp"
},
```

Step 4. Save the file in UTF-8 format.

Table 8-8 shows some of the available JSON templates for vCenter Server 8.0.

Table 8-8   JSON Templates

Template	Description
embedded_vCSA_on_ESXi.json	Contains the minimum configuration parameters required for the deployment of a vCenter Server appliance on an ESXi host
vCSA_with_cluster_on_ESXi.json	Contains the minimum configuration parameters required for the deployment of a vCenter Server appliance with a single node vSAN and a vLCM managed cluster on an ESXi host
embedded_vCSA_on_VC.json	Contains the minimum configuration parameters required for the deployment of a vCenter Server appliance on a vCenter Server instance
embedded_vCSA_replication_on_ESXi.json	Contains the minimum configuration parameters required for the deployment of a vCenter Server appliance as a replication partner to another embedded vCenter Server on an ESXi host
embedded_vCSA_replication_on_VC.json	Contains the minimum configuration parameters required for the deployment of a vCenter Server appliance replication partner to another vCenter Server appliance on a vCenter Server instance

NOTE   When using the CLI installer, you must strictly use only ASCII characters for the command-line and JSON configuration file values, including usernames and passwords.

Prior to running the deployment command, you can run a pre-deployment check by using this command:

```
vcsa-deploy install --verify-only path-to-JSON-file
```

When you are ready, you can run the deployment command:

```
vcsa-deploy install --accept-eula --acknowledge-ceip optional_
arguments path-to-JSON-file
```

vCenter Server Post-Installation

After installing vCenter Server, you should be able to access the vSphere Client at https://*vcenter_server_ip_address_or_fqdn*/ui and the vSphere Web Client at https://*vcenter_server_ip_address_or_fqdn*/vsphere-client.

The *VMware Enhanced Authentication Plug-in* provides integrated Windows authentication and Windows-based smart card functionality. In the vSphere 6.5 release, the VMware Enhanced Authentication Plug-in replaced the Client Integration Plug-in.

To install the VMware Enhance Authentication Plug-in, you can use the following procedure:

Step 1.   In a web browser, open the vSphere Web Client.

Step 2.   At the bottom of the vSphere Web Client login page, click **Download Enhanced Authentication Plug-in**.

Step 3.   Save the plug-in to your computer and run the executable.

Step 4.   Follow the wizard for both the VMware Enhanced Authentication Plug-in and the VMware Plug-in Service, which are run in succession.

Step 5.   When the installations are complete, refresh the browser.

Step 6.   In the External Protocol Request dialog box, click **Launch Application**.

If you install the plug-in from an Internet Explorer browser, you must first disable Protected Mode and enable pop-up windows on your web browser.

Configuring and Managing VMware Certificate Authority (VMCA)

VMware Certificate Authority (VMCA), which runs in the vCenter Server Appliance, is responsible for issuing certificates for VMware solution users, certificates for machines running required services, and certificates for ESXi hosts. *VMware Endpoint Certificate Service (VECS)* is a local repository for certificates and private keys. VECS is a mandatory component that is used when VMCA is not signing certificates. VECS includes a set of keystores, including machine SSL certificates, trusted roots, certificate revocation lists (CRLs), and solution users (including machine, vpxd, vpx-extension, and vSphere-webclient). VECS does not store ESXi certificates. ESXi certificates are stored locally on the ESXi hosts in the /etc/vmware/ssl directory. Table 8-9 describes the stores included in VECS.

Table 8-9   VECS Stores

Store	Description
Machine SSL store (MACHINE_SSL_CERT)	Used by the reverse proxy service on each ESXi host and by the **vmdir** service.
Trusted root store (TRUSTED_ROOTS)	Contains all trusted root certificates.

Store	Description
Solution user stores: ■ Machine ■ vpxd ■ vpxd-extension ■ vsphere-webclient ■ wcp	VECS includes one store for each solution user: ■ License Server (machine) ■ vCenter service daemon (vpxd) ■ vCenter Extensions (vpxd-extension) ■ vSphere Client (vsphere-webclient) ■ vSphere with Tanzu (wcp)
vSphere Certificate Manager utility backup store (BACKUP_STORE)	Used by VMCA to support certificate reversion.
Other stores	Other stores might be added by solutions. For example, the Virtual Volumes solution adds an SMS store.

As described in Chapter 7, "vSphere Security," you can bypass VMCA by using custom certificates or configure VMCA to operate as a subordinate CA, but neither of these options is recommended. Instead, VMware recommends that you use the VMCA in the default manner or the hybrid manner, where you replace the vCenter Server SSL certificates, and allow VMCA to manage certificates for solution users and ESXi hosts.

NOTE

The VMCA in vSphere 8.0 does not support the use of CRLs, and it does not enforce certificate revocation. If you suspect that a certificate was compromised, you should remove it and consider replacing all certificates.

When you use VMCA in the default manner, so that it acts as the CA for vSphere, no real configuration is required other than to configure web browsers to trust VMCA. VMCA can handle all certificate management in a vSphere environment where the administrator has historically elected not to replace certificates. During an upgrade to vSphere 6.0, all self-signed certificates are replaced with certificates signed by VMCA.

Using VMCA in a subordinate CA manner requires you to replace the VMCA root certificate with a certificate signed by a third-party CA, making the VMCA certificate an intermediate certificate of the CA. To use VMCA in the subordinate CA manner, follow this procedure:

Step 1.   Launch the vSphere Certificate Manager utility.

Step 2.   Select **Option 2**, which is to replace the VMCA root certificate with a custom signing certificate and replace all certificates.

Step 3.   When prompted to do so, provide the password for the SSO domain administrator account.

Step 4.   Select **Option 1** to generate a certificate signing request (CSR) and key. When prompted to do so, specify the directory where you want to save the CSR and key.

Step 5.   Provide the CSR (root_signing_cert.csr) to your CA to generate the sub ordinate signing certificate.

Step 6.   Use a text editor to copy content from intermediate CA certificates and the root CA certificate into a single file (root_signing_chain.cer).

Step 7.   In Certificate Manager, return to **Option 2** and follow the prompts to replace the certificates on the local machine.

Step 8.   Import the root signing certificate (root_signing_chain.cer) and root signing key (root_signing_cert.key).

Step 9.   When prompted to do so, provide a value for each item, such as country, name, and organization.

When you complete these steps, the VMCA root certificate is replaced with a custom signing certificate.

NOTE   For more details on this procedure, see https://kb.vmware.com/s/article/2112016.

Configuring Single Sign-On (SSO)

In addition to deploying one or more VCSAs and creating a vCenter Single Sign-On (SSO) domain in a new vSphere environment, you need to configure SSO. Configuring SSO includes adding and editing SSO identity sources, configuring SSO users, and configuring SSO policies.

SSO and Identity Sources Overview

To access vCenter Server, users must log in using SSO domain user accounts or user accounts from identity sources registered in SSO. The acceptable identity sources are Active Directory (with integrated Windows authentication), Active Directory as a Lightweight Directory Access Protocol (LDAP) server, and OpenLDAP. Local operating system user accounts, such as root, are not used to access vCenter Server.

The SSO domain is available immediately as an identity source. This domain was called vsphere.local in vSphere 5.5, but in vSphere 6.x and higher, you can assign the SSO domain name during installation.

The Active Directory over LDAP identity source is preferred over the Active Directory (Integrated Windows Authentication) option. A future update to Microsoft Windows will require strong authentication and encryption for Active Directory, which will impact how vCenter Server authenticates to Active Directory. To continue using Active Directory as the identity source for vCenter Server, you should plan to enable Secure LDAP (LDAPS).

Adding, Editing, and Removing SSO Identity Sources

You can use the *vSphere Client* to add SSO identity sources by following these steps:

Step 1.   Log in with the vSphere Client to the vCenter Server using administrator@vsphere.local or another member of the SSO administrators group.

Step 2.   Navigate to **Home > Administration > Single Sign On > Configuration**.

Step 3.   Click **Identity Sources** and then click **Add Identity Source**.

Step 4.   Select one of the following available identity sources and enter the appropriate settings:

- Active Directory (Integrated Windows Authentication)
- Active Directory over LDAP
- OpenLDAP
- Local operating system of the SSO server

Step 5.   Click **Add**.

To remove an SSO identity source, follow these steps:

Step 1.   In the vSphere Web Client, navigate to **Administrator > Single Sign-On > Configuration > Identity Sources** and select the identity source.

Step 2.   Click the **Delete Identity Source** icon.

Step 3.   When prompted to do so, click **Yes** to confirm.

You can configure a default domain for SSO. The default SSO domain allows users to authenticate without identifying a domain name. Users from other identity sources must identify the domain name during authentication. To configure a default domain using the vSphere Client, follow these steps:

Step 1.   Navigate to **Home > Administration > Single Sign On > Configuration**.

Step 2.   Click **Identity Sources** and then click **Add Identity Source**.

Step 3.   Select an identity source and click **Set as Default**.

Adding an Active Directory Identity Source

To permit Active Directory authentication in vSphere, you need to add one or more Active Directory domains as identity sources in SSO. In scenarios where the SSO server is a member of an Active Directory domain, that domain may be added as an Active Directory integrated Windows authentication (which is deprecated) identity source. You can add other Active Directory domains to SSO as Active Directory LDAP server identity sources.

Before you can add an integrated Active Directory identity source, you need to ensure that the server where SSO is installed is in the domain. You add the vCenter Server Appliance to the domain by using the following procedure:

Step 1.   Log on to the vSphere Web Client using the SSO domain administrator account (such as administrator@vsphere.local).

Step 2.   From the left pane, select **Administration > Single Sign On > Configuration**.

Step 3.   Select the **Identity Provider** tab.

Step 4.   Select **Active Directory** as the type and click **Join AD**.

Step 5.   Enter Active Directory details such as the domain, organizational unit, username, and password.

Step 6.   Click **OK**.

Step 7.   Right-click the node and select **Reboot**.

After the appliance reboots, you can add an Active Directory (Integrated Windows Authentication) identity source.

When adding an Active Directory (Integrated Windows Authentication) identity source, you need to provide information for the following parameters:

- **Domain Name**: Enter the FDQN of the domain.

- **Use Machine Account**: Select this option to use the local machine account as the Server Principal Name (SPN). Do not use this option if you plan to rename the machine.

- **Use Service Principal Name (SPN)**: Select this option instead of Use Machine Account if you prefer to specify a unique SPN instead of using the machine name as the SPN. If you choose this option, you must also provide the SPN, UPN, and password, as follows:

  - **Service Principal Name (SPN)**: If you selected the Use Service Principal Name option, you need to provide a unique name that includes the domain name, such as STS/domain.com.

- **User Principal Name (UPN)**: If you selected the User Service Principal Name option, you need to provide a username that can authenticate the Active Directory domain.

- **Password**: If you selected the Use Service Principal Name option, you need to provide a password that is associated with the UPN.

> **NOTE**   The user account must have read access to the organizational units that contain users and groups. If a user's account does not have sufficient permission or is locked or disabled, then authentications and searches in the Active Directory domain fail.

When adding an Active Directory over LDAP identity source, you need to provide information for the following parameters:

- **Name**: Specify the logical name for the identity source.

- **Base DN for Users**: Specify the base distinguished name for users.

- **Base DN for Groups**: Specify the base distinguished name for groups.

- **Domain Name**: Specify the FDQN of the domain.

- **Domain Alias**: Specify the domain's NetBIOS name.

- **Username**: Specify a username in the domain that has at least read access to the specified user and group base DNs.

- **Password**: Specify the password that is associated with the username.

- **Connect To**: Specify which domain controller to connect to.

- **Primary Server URL**: Specify the primary domain controller's URL, in the form ldap://*hostname:port* or ldaps://*hostname:port*.

- **Secondary Server URL**: Specify the secondary domain controller's URL, in the form ldap://*hostname:port* or ldaps://*hostname:port*.

- **SSL Certificate**: When using LDAPS in the URL parameters, specify the certificate.

You can add additional user accounts from other identity sources to the SSO administrators group. To add additional user accounts from other identity sources to the administrators group in the SSO domain, you can follow these steps:

Step 1.   Log in to the vSphere Web Client with the SSO domain administrator account.

Step 2.   Navigate to **Home > Administration > Single Sign-On > Users and Groups**.

Step 3. Navigate to **Group** > **Administrators** > **Group Members** and select the **Add Member** icon.

Step 4. Select the additional identity source from the **Domain** drop-down menu.

Step 5. Select the account you would like to add.

Step 6. Click **OK**.

Adding an LDAP Authentication Source

To use OpenLDAP for authentication, one or more LDAP authentication sources have to be added in vCenter. In order to use OpenLDAP for authentication, the following requirements must be met:

- The OpenLDAP schema must be RFC 4519 compliant.

- All users must have the object class **inetOrgPerson**.

- All groups must have the object class **groupOfUniqueNames**.

- All groups must have the group membership attribute **uniqueMember**.

- All users and group objects must have **entryUUID** configured.

When configuring OpenLDAP, you need to provide information for the following parameters:

- **Name**: Specify the logical name for the identity source.

- **Base DN for Users**: Specify the base distinguished name for users.

- **Base DN for Groups**: Specify the base distinguished name for groups.

- **Domain Name**: Specify the FDQN of the domain.

- **Domain Alias**: Specify the domain name in capital letters if no alias is defined.

- **Username**: Specify a username in the domain that has at least read access to the specified user and group base DNs.

- **Password**: Specify the password that is associated with the username.

- **Primary Server URL**: Specify the primary server's URL, in the form ldap://*hostname:port* or ldaps://*hostname:port*.

- **Secondary Server URL**: Specify the secondary server's URL, in the form ldap://*hostname:port* or ldaps://*hostname:port*.

- **SSL certificate**: When using LDAPS in the URL parameters, specify the certificate.

Enabling and Disabling Single Sign-On (SSO) Users

To manage SSO users, you can use the vSphere Client. For example, to add an SSO user, follow these steps:

Step 1. Log on to the vCenter Server by using administrator@vsphere.local or another user in the SSO administrators group.

Step 2. Navigate to **Home > Administration > Single Sign-On > Users and Groups**.

Step 3. Select the **Users** tab and click **Add User**.

Step 4. Provide the username and password. Optionally provide values for the other fields.

Step 5. Click **OK**.

In a similar manner, you can create an SSO group by selecting the Users tab in step 3 and providing details in step 4. You can also use the Groups tab to select a group and use the Add Member icon (in the details section) to add users to the group. When adding a user to a group, use the Domain drop-down to select the SSO domain or another identity source and select a user account from the provided list.

To disable or enable an SSO user account, select the user account in Users and Groups, click the ellipsis icon, and click Disable or Enable.

The SSO domain—which is called vsphere.local by default—provides several predefined groups. You can add users from Active Directory domains or other identity sources to these predefined groups. Some SSO privileges are determined solely based on membership in these groups. For example, a user who is a member of the CAAdmins group can manage VMCA, and a user who is a member of the LicenseService.Administrators group can manage licenses.

The SSO domain contains many predefined groups, including the following:

- **Users**: This group contains all users in the SSO domain.

- **DCAdmins**: Members of this group can perform domain controller administrator actions on VMware Directory Service.

- **SolutionUsers**: Each solution user authenticates individually to vCenter Single Sign-On with a certificate. By default, VMCA provisions solution users with certificates. Do not explicitly add members to this group.

- **CAAdmins**: Members have administrator privileges for VMCA. Adding members to these groups is not usually recommended, but a user must be a member of this group to perform most certificate management operations, such as using the **certool** command.

- **SystemConfiguration.BashShellAdministrators**: Members can enable and disable access to the BASH shell.

- **SystemConfiguration.Administrators**: Members can view and manage the system configuration and perform tasks such as restarting services.

- **LicenseSevice.Administrators**: Members have full write access to all licensing-related data and can add, remove, assign, and un-assign serial keys for all product assets registered in licensing service.

- **Administrators**: Members can perform SSO administration tasks for VMware Directory Service (**vmdir**).

Configuring SSO Policies

SSO provides policies that enforce security rules in the environment. You can configure SSO password policies, SSO lockout policies, and SSO token policies. To configure these policies, you can use the vSphere Client to select Administration > Single Sign-On > Configuration and then select Password Policy, Lockout Policy, or Token Policy and click Edit. For each set of policies, you need to set the appropriate password policy parameters, as described in Table 8-10.

Table 8-10 SSO Policies and Parameters

SSO Policy Parameter	Policy Setting	Details
Password Policy	Description	Password policy description.
	Maximum lifetime	The maximum number of days a password can exist before the user must change it.
	Restrict reuse	The number of the user's previous passwords that cannot be selected.
	Maximum length	The maximum number of characters that are allowed in the password.
	Minimum length	The minimum number of characters that are allowed in the password, which must be no fewer than the combined minimum of alphabetic, numeric, and special character requirements.
	Character requirements	The minimum number of different character types that are required in the password. The types include special, alphabetic, uppercase, lowercase, and numeric.
	Identical adjacent characters	The number of identical adjacent characters that are supported in a password. The value must be greater than 0.

SSO Policy Parameter	Policy Setting	Details
Lockout Policy	Description	Description of the lockout policy.
	Max number of failed login attempts	The maximum number of failed login attempts that are allowed before the account is locked.
	Time interval between failures	The time period in which failed login attempts must occur to trigger a lockout.
	Unlock time	The amount of time the account stays locked. The value 0 specifies that an administrator must explicitly unlock the account.
Token Policy	Clock tolerance	The time difference, in milliseconds, that SSO tolerates between a client clock and a domain controller clock. If the time difference is greater than the specified value, SSO declares the token to be invalid.
	Maximum token renewal count	The maximum number of times a token may be renewed before a new security token is required.
	Maximum token delegation count	The maximum number of times a single holder-of-key token can be delegated.
	Maximum bearer token lifetime	The lifetime value of a bearer token before the token must be reissued.
	Maximum holder-of-key token lifetime	The lifetime value of a holder-of-key token before the token is marked invalid.

Configuring Identity Federation

Starting with vSphere 7.0, vCenter Server supports federated authentication, where vSphere Client user login attempts are redirected to the external identity provider. Corporate credentials (including multifactor authentication) can then be used to log in. After authentication, the identity provider redirects the user back to the vSphere Client via a cryptographic token used for authorization.

Identity Federation utilizes OAuth2 and OIDC protocols for information exchange. Identity Federation replaces traditional Active Directory, integrated Windows authentication, and LDAP/LDAPS authentication for vCenter. vSphere Single Sign-On is not replaced, however, to allow additional administration or emergency access.

The following requirements apply to Active Directory Federation Services:

- AD Federation Services for Windows Server 2016 R2 or higher must be deployed.

- AD Federation Services must be connected to Active Directory.

- An application group for vCenter is created in AD Federation Services for configuration (see https://kb.vmware.com/s/article/78029).

- The AD Federation Services server certificate must be signed by a certificate authority. If self-signed certificates are used, the root CA certificate has to be imported to the vCenter JRE truststore.

The following requirements apply to vSphere to support Identity Federation:

- vSphere 7.0 or later is required.

- Communication is possible between the vCenter Server and AD Federation Services endpoint, authorization, token, logout, JWKS, and other advertised endpoints.

- The VcIdentityProviders.Manage privilege is required in vCenter to create, update, or delete a vCenter Server identity provider for Federation Services authentication. If a user should be limited to viewing the identity provider configuration and not changing it, you need to use the VcIdentityProviders. Read privilege.

Follow these steps to enable Identity Federation:

Step 1. Add your AD FS server certificate (or a CA or intermediate certificate that signed the AD FS server certificate) to the trusted root certificates store.

Step 2. In the vSphere Client, navigate to **Home > Administration > Configuration > Single Sign On**. Select the **Identity Provider** tab.

Step 3. Click the **i** next to Change Identity Provider.

Step 4. Copy the URIs in the pop-up (as they will be needed to configure the AD Federation Services server) and then close the pop-up.

Step 5. Create an OpenID Connect configuration in AD Federation Services and configure it for the vCenter Server. A shared secret and identifying information must be established between the identity provider and vCenter. An OpenID Connect configuration known as an application group is created in AD Federation Services; it contains a server application and a web API. These components define the information that vCenter uses to trust and communicate with the AD Federation Services server. To create the AD Federation Services application group, the two redirect URIs from step 4 are used. It is important to copy or record the following information:

  - Client identifier
  - Shared secret
  - OpenID address of the AD Federation Services server

Step 6. On the **Identity Provider** tab, click **Change Identity Provider**, select **Microsoft ADFS**, and click **Next**.

Step 7. Enter the following information:

- Client identifier
- Shared secret
- OpenID address of the AD Federation Services server

Click **Next**.

Step 8. Enter the user and group information for Active Directory over LDAP to search for users and groups and click **Next**.

Step 9. Review the configuration information and click **Finish**.

Step 10. Go to **Home > Administration > Single Sign On > Users and Groups**.

Step 11. On the **Groups** tab, click **Administrators (group)** and click **Add Members**.

Step 12. From the drop-down, select **Microsoft ADFS**, and in the text box under the drop-down menu, enter **vcenter** and wait for the drop-down to show a selection. Then select **vCenter Admins** and add it to the group.

Step 13. Click **Save**.

Step 14. Log in to vCenter with an AD user's credentials to verify functionality.

Initial vSphere Configuration

This section covers some of the vSphere settings, components, and features that are typically configured in conjunction with a new vSphere deployment.

Implementing vSphere Client

The vSphere Client, which is the primary vSphere GUI, is HTML5 based and uses the Clarity style user interface. The vSphere Client is a service that is installed automatically when you install vCenter Server.

Implementing VMware vSphere Lifecycle Manager

Starting with vSphere 7.0, *vSphere Lifecycle Manager (vLCM)* replaces VMware Update Manager from prior versions. vLCM adds to the functionality of Update Manager to include features and capabilities for ESXi lifecycle management at the cluster level. vLCM operates as a service that runs on the vCenter Server. This service is available via the vSphere Client immediately after the vCenter Server deployment;

no special steps are required to install vLCM unless you need to install the optional module VMware vSphere Update Manager Download Service (UMDS).

In scenarios where vCenter Server is installed in a secured network with no Internet access, you can install UMDS and use it to download updates. You can use UMDS to export the updates to a portable media drive that you then present to vLCM. Or, if network connectivity exists between the vCenter Server and UMDS, you can automate the export process by leveraging the web server on the UMDS machine.

NOTE   See Chapter 13, "Managing vSphere and vCenter Server," for more details on vSphere Lifecycle Manager.

Configuring the vCenter Server Inventory

This section describes the procedures you use to create an inventory hierarchy that includes data centers, folders, clusters, and resource pools.

To create a data center, you can follow these steps:

Step 1.   Log on to the vSphere Client as a user with the data center. Create data center privilege.

Step 2.   Right-click the vCenter Server in the inventory and select **New Datacenter**.

Step 3.   Provide a name for the data center and click **OK**.

To create a folder, you can follow these steps:

Step 1.   In the vSphere Client, right-click the appropriate parent object (a data center or another folder).

Step 2.   Select **New Folder**. If the parent object is a folder, the new folder type is automatically set to match the parent; otherwise, specify the folder type as **Host and Cluster** folder, **Storage** folder, or **VM and Template** folder.

Step 3.   Provide a name for the folder and click **OK**.

To add an ESXi host, you must address the following prerequisites:

- Ensure that the appropriate data center and (optionally) folder objects are created in the vCenter Server inventory.

- Obtain the root account credentials for the host.

- Verify that the host and vCenter Server can communicate via port 902 or a custom port.

- Verify that any NFS mounts on the host are active.

- For a host with more than 512 LUNs and 2048 paths, verify that the vCenter Server instance is set to support a Large or X-Large environment.

To add an ESXi host, you can follow these steps:

Step 1. Log on to the vSphere Client as a user with the Host.Inventory.Add standalone host privilege.

Step 2. Right-click the data center or folder in the inventory and select **Add Host**.

Step 3. Provide the host's FQDN (or IP address) and credentials.

Step 4. Provide licensing information (using a new or existing license).

Step 5. Optionally, set the Lockdown Mode, remote access, and virtual machine folder information and continue navigating to the final wizard page.

Step 6. Click **OK**.

To implement vCenter HA, you can use the following procedure to configure vCenter HA:

Step 1. In the vSphere Client, select the vCenter Server in the inventory pane.

Step 2. Select **Configure > Select vCenter HA > Set Up vCenter HA**.

Step 3. If your vCenter Server is managed by another vCenter Server in a different SSO domain, complete the following steps:

    a. Click **Management vCenter Server Credentials**. Provide the FQDN and Single Sign-On credentials and click **Next**.

    b. If you see a certificate warning displayed, review the SHA1 thumbprint and click **Yes** to continue.

Step 4. In the Resource Settings section, select the vCenter HA network for the active node from the drop-down menu.

Step 5. Click the checkbox if you want to automatically create clones for Passive and Witness nodes.

Step 6. For the Passive node, follow these steps:

    a. Click **Edit** and provide details for the Passive node virtual machine, such as the name, compute resources, and datastore.

    b. Select the Management (NIC 0) and vCenter HA (NIC 1) networks.

    c. Complete the settings and click **Finish**.

Step 7. For the Witness node, follow these steps:

    a. Click **Edit** and provide details for the passive node virtual machine, such as the name, compute resources, and datastore.

      b. Select the vCenter HA (NIC 1) network.

      c. Complete the settings and click **Finish**.

Step 8. Click **Next**.

Step 9. In the IP Settings section, provide the IP address details.

Step 10. Click **Finish**.

Using Host Profiles

NOTE This section provides details on using host profiles to configure ESXi hosts.

Starting with vSphere 8, you can use vSphere configuration profiles to manage host configuration at the cluster level, using a declarative model. You can only enable vSphere configuration profiles on clusters managed with a single image. Enabling vSphere configuration profiles is a permanent change that prevents you from using host profiles for the hosts in the cluster.

Configuring ESXi Using Host Profiles

During the implementation of vSphere, you can use host profiles to efficiently deploy a standard configuration to a set of ESXi hosts. To do so, you can configure a single ESXi host, create a host profile from that host, and apply the profile to other recently deployed hosts. This process reduces the time required to configure ESXi hosts and minimizes the risk of misconfigured hosts. The host profile contains all the networking, storage, security, and other host-level settings. The host from which the profile is created is known as the reference host. You can attach a host profile to individual hosts, a cluster, or all the hosts and clusters managed by a vCenter Server.

Applying a Host Profile

After attaching a host profile, you can check compliance of the associated hosts and remediate as necessary.

You can use this procedure to create a host profile from a reference host:

Step 1. Navigate to the host profiles main view and click **Extract Host Profile**.

Step 2. Select the host that acts as the reference host and click **Next**.

Step 3. Enter a name and description for the new profile and click **Next**.

Step 4. Review the summary information for the new profile and click **Finish**.

You can use this procedure to attach a profile to an ESXi host or cluster:

Step 1.   From the host profiles main view, select the host profile to be applied to the host or cluster.

Step 2.   Click **Attach/Detach Hosts and Clusters**, select the host or cluster from the expanded list, and click **Attach**.

Step 3.   Optionally, click **Attach All** to attach all listed hosts and clusters to the profile.

Step 4.   Optionally, enable **Skip Host Customization**; if you do, you do not need to customize hosts during this process.

Step 6.   Click **Next**.

Step 7.   Optionally, update or change the user input parameters for the host profiles policies by customizing the host.

Step 8.   Click **Finish** to finish attaching the host or cluster to the profile.

You can use this procedure to remediate an ESXi host:

Step 1.   Navigate to the host profiles main view.

Step 2.   Right-click a host profile and select **Remediate**.

Step 3.   Select the host or hosts you want to remediate with the host profile.

Step 4.   Optionally, enter the host customizations to specify host properties or browse to import a host customization file.

Step 5.   Click **Pre-check Remediation** to check whether the selected hosts are ready for remediation.

Step 6.   Select the checkbox to reboot the host if a reboot is required in order to complete the remediation process. To manually reboot the host after the process, do not select the checkbox.

Step 7.   Review the tasks that are necessary to remediate the host profile and click **Finish**.

Editing Host Profiles

To edit a host profile, you can use this procedure:

Step 1.   Navigate to the host profiles main view.

Step 2.   Select the host profile that you want to edit and click the **Configure** tab.

Step 3.   Click **Edit Host Profile**.

Step 4.   Optionally, click the **Name and Description** tab to change the profile name and description.

Step 5. In the Edit Host Profile page, expand each category to view or edit a specific policy or setting.

Step 6. Select **All** to view all host profile configurations or select **Favorites** to view only those configurations.

Step 7. Optionally, in the search field, filter the configuration names and values you want to view. For example, enter **SNMP**, and all configurations that relate to SNMP are displayed.

Step 8. Optionally, customize the hosts. Make any changes to the available configuration values for this profile and click **Save**.

Applying Permissions to ESXi Hosts by Using Host Profiles

You can use host profiles to apply ESXi host permissions to be used when users access a host directly. To configure the host profile with the appropriate permissions, you can use the vSphere Client (not the vSphere Web Client) and follow this procedure:

Step 1. Select **View > Management > Host Profiles**.

Step 2. Select an existing profile and click **Edit Profile**.

Step 3. In the profile tree, locate and expand **Security Configuration**.

Step 4. Right-click on the **Permission Rules** folder and click **Add Profile**.

Step 5. Expand **Permissions Rules** and select **Permission**.

Step 6. On the Configuration Details tab, click the **Configure Permission** drop-down menu and select **Require a Permission Rule**.

Step 7. Enter the name of a user or group, in the format *domain\name*, where *domain* is the domain name, and *name* is the username or group name.

Step 8. If a group name is used, select the **Name Refers to a Group of Users** checkbox.

Step 9. Enter the assigned role name, which is case sensitive. This can be the name of a built-in role on the host or a custom role that you have created on the host. For system roles, use the non-localized role name, such as **Admin** for the administrator role or **ReadOnly** for the read-only role.

Step 10. Optionally, select **Propagate Permission**.

Step 11. Click **OK**.

After configuring the host profile, you can use it to apply the permissions to new or existing ESXi hosts.

VMware Tools

Ideally, you should install VMware Tools in all your virtual machines. When deploying a new vSphere environment, you should install VMware Tools in any virtual machines deployed as part of the virtual infrastructure and management. For example, if you use virtual machines to run Active Directory domain controllers, DNS servers, or DHCP servers, consider installing VMware Tools.

VMware Tools is a suite of utilities that you install in the operating system of a virtual machine. VMware Tools enhances the performance and management of the virtual machine. You can use the following procedure to install VMware Tools in a virtual machine using the VMware Host Client:

Step 1.   Click **Virtual Machines** in the VMware Host Client inventory.

Step 2.   Select a powered-on virtual machine from the list. (The virtual machine must be powered on to install VMware Tools.)

Step 3.   Open a console to the virtual machine and log in with administrator or root privileges.

Step 4.   Click **Actions**, select **Guest OS** from the drop-down menu, and select **Install VMware Tools**.

Step 5.   Use the guest OS to complete the installation.

This procedure is useful for installing VMware Tools in a DNS, Active Directory domain controller, database server, or other virtual machine that you may deploy prior to deploying vCenter Server.

ESXi Configuration Settings

This section describes how to configure some common ESXi host setting using the vSphere Host Client.

To use the vSphere Host Client, open a supported web browser connected to your ESXi server by using its fully qualified name or IP address and the root account. To view the host's settings, click on Manage in the left pane and then select System, Hardware, Licensing, Packages, Services, or Security and Users.

To change the host time or date, choose System > Time and Date. Use the interface to set a specific date and time. Click Edit NTP Setting to specify the NTP servers and NTP Service Status. Optionally, click on Edit PTP Settings to provide PTP Client and PTP Service Status settings.

To manage the host's license, choose Licensing and then use the Add License and Remove Licenses buttons. To manage services, choose Services and then select a specific service and an action, such as Start or Stop. Optionally, you can choose

Policy and then select whether the service should start and stop manually, automatically with the host, or automatically with the firewall port.

To configure authentication, certificates, user roles, Lockdown Mode, acceptance level, and roles, choose Security and Users. From there, to create a user, select Users > Add Users. To configure Lockdown Mode, select Lockdown Mode and then select Edit Settings or Add User Exception. To manage roles, choose Roles and then click Add Role or select a specific role and click Edit Role.

Advanced ESXi Host Options

This section describes how to configure some advanced options for ESXi hosts.

ESXi Advanced System Settings

You can use the vSphere Host Client or the vSphere Client to set advanced attributes on ESXi hosts. You should change the advanced options only when you get specific instructions to do so from VMware technical support or a knowledge base article.

To change a host's advanced settings using the vSphere Host Client, you can navigate to Manage > System > Advanced Settings. To change a host's advanced settings using the vSphere Client, you can select the host and navigate to Configure > System > Advanced System Settings.

For example, to set the host's product locker directory to shared storage, you can locate and edit the UserVars.ProductLockerLocation setting. The default value is /locker/packages/vmtoolsRepo/. You can change this to a path on shared storage. This setting controls where the host finds ISO images for installing VMware Tools. The main reason for setting it to shared storage is to save space on the host's local disk.

ESXi Kernel Options

Starting with ESXi 7.0, disk partitioning in boot devices has changed from previous ESXi versions. The changes include the following:

- The system boot partition is now larger.
- The boot banks are now larger.
- The coredump, tools, and scratch partitions have been consolidated into a single VMFS-L-based ESX-OSData volume.
- Coredumps default to a file in the ESX-OSData volume.

You need to issue boot options at the time of boot, either by defining the kernel options in the ESXi boot.cfg file or by manually entering the boot options after pressing Shift+O in the ESXi boot loader. Table 8-11 lists the kernel options.

Table 8-11   ESXi 7.0 Kernel Options

Kernel Option	Description
autoPartition=TRUE/FALSE (default FALSE)	This option, if set to TRUE, defines automatic partitioning of the unused local storage devices at boot time. The boot disk gets partitioned with boot bands, ESXi-OSData, and, if the disk is larger than 128 GB, a VMFS partition. Any new empty device discovered will be auto-partitioned as well. Auto-partitioning can be set for only the first unused device with the setting autoP artitionOnlyOnceAndSkipSsd=TRUE. On hosts with USB boot and VMFS-L, ESX-OSData does not exist on other local disks.
	If a storage device has both a scratch partition and a coredump partition, the scratch partition is converted to ESX-OSData; otherwise, the first unused disk identified is partitioned with ESX-OSData as well.
skipPartitioningSsds=TRUE/ FALSE (default FALSE)	If this option is set to TRUE, local SSDs are excluded from automatic partitioning.
autoPartitionOnlyOnceAndSkipSs d=TRUE/FALSE (default FALSE)	If this option is set to TRUE, SSD/NVMe devices are excluded, and the ESXi host automatically partitions the first unused local disk if there is no VMFS-L ESX-OSData volume.
allowCoreDumpOnUSB=TRUE/ FALSE (default FALSE)	If this option is set to TRUE, ESXi can write kernel crash coredumps to the VMFS-L Locker volume on a USB boot device.
dumpSize (default:0 (automatically sized))	This option sets the size of the coredump file (in megabytes) created on the system VMFS-L volume. This is limited to one-half of the space available on the VMFS-L volume.
autoCreateDumpFile=TRUE/ FALSE (default TRUE)	This option, when set to TRUE, automatically creates a coredump file. This is attempted in the following order: ■ VMFS-L ESX-OSData ■ USB VMFS-L ■ Local VMFS

NOTE   The following kernel boot options have been deprecated and are no longer supported in ESXi 7.0 and later:

■ **--no-auto-partition**

■ **autoPartitionCreateUSBCoreDumpPartition**

■ **autoPartitionDiskDumpPartitionSize**

Exam Preparation Tasks

As mentioned in the section "Book Features and Exam Preparation Methods" in the Introduction, you have some choices for exam preparation: the exercises here, Chapter 15, "Final Preparation," and the exam simulation questions on the companion website.

Review All the Key Topics

Review the most important topics in this chapter, noted with the Key Topic icon in the outer margin of the page. Table 8-12 lists these key topics and the page number on which each is found.

Table 8-12 Key Topics for Chapter 8

Key Topic Element	Description	Page Number
Section	Installing ESXi interactively	290
List	First-time boot sequence using Auto Deploy	300
List	Deploying VCSA using the GUI installer	303
Procedure	Using VMCA in a subordinate CA manner	308
Procedure	Adding an Active Directory over LDAP identity source	312
Section	Enabling Identity Federation	316
Procedure	Implementing vCenter HA	320

Complete Tables and Lists from Memory

Print a copy of Appendix B, "Memory Tables" (found on the companion website), or at least the section for this chapter, and complete the tables and lists from memory. Appendix C, "Memory Table Answers" (also on the companion website), includes completed tables and lists to check your work.

Define Key Terms

Define the following key terms from this chapter and check your answers in the glossary:

stateless caching, VMware Enhanced Authentication Plug-in, VMware Certificate Authority (VMCA), VMware Endpoint Certificate Service (VECS), vSphere Client, VMware Lifecycle Manager (vLCM)

Review Questions

1. You are using the GUI installer for vCenter Server 8.0. Which of the following statements is true?

   a. In the first stage, you choose the deployment type. In the second stage, you navigate through the installation wizard.

   b. In the first stage, you provide the appliance settings. In the second stage, you navigate through the installation wizard.

   c. In the first stage, you choose the deployment type. In the second stage, you deploy the OVA.

   d. In the first stage, you provide the appliance settings. In the second stage, you configure SSO.

2. You are adding an Active Directory over LDAP identity source. Which setting must you provide?

   a. UPN

   b. SPN

   c. Use machine account

   d. Base DN for users

3. You are implementing a new vSphere environment and want to install services for updating the ESXi hosts. What should you do?

   a. Deploy a VMware Update Manager appliance.

   b. Deploy a vSphere Lifecycle Manager appliance.

   c. Deploy vCenter Server with Update Manager embedded.

   d. Nothing; the software service is included in vCenter Server.

4. You are implementing Auto Deploy and want to control its behavior with rules. Which of the following is not a means by which a rule can identify target hosts?

   a. MAC address

   b. Model

   c. Serial number

   d. BIOS UUID

5. You are using host profiles to deploy a standard configuration to ESXi hosts. Which of the following provides the proper order of operation?

   a. Click Attach Host Profile, click Pre-check Remediation, click Remediate.

   b. Click Attach Host Profile, click Remediate, click Pre-check Remediation, click Finish.

   c. Click Pre-check Remediation, click Remediation, click Remediate.

   d. Click Pre-check Remediation, click Remediate, click Attach Host Profile, click Finish.

This chapter covers the following topics:

- vSphere Standard Switches (vSS)
- vSphere Distributed Switches (vDS)
- VMkernel Networking
- Configuring and Managing Networking Features
- Managing Host Networking with vDS

This chapter contains information related to VMware vSphere 8.x Professional (2V0-21.23) exam objectives 1.5.1, 1.5.1, 1.5.2, 1.5.3, 1.5.4, 1.5.5, 4.2, 4.2.1, 4.2.2, 4.2.3, 4.3, 4.15, 5.4, and 5.6.

## CHAPTER 9

Configuring and Managing Virtual Networks

This chapter describes how to configure and manage virtual network infrastructure in a vSphere 8 environment.

"Do I Know This Already?" Quiz

The "Do I Know This Already?" quiz allows you to assess whether you should study this entire chapter or move quickly to the "Exam Preparation Tasks" section. In any case, the authors recommend that you read the entire chapter at least once. Table 9-1 outlines the major headings in this chapter and the corresponding "Do I Know This Already?" quiz questions. You can find the answers in Appendix A, "Answers to the 'Do I Know This Already?' Quizzes and Review Questions."

Table 9-1 "Do I Know This Already?" Foundation Topics Section-to-Question Mapping

Foundation Topics Section	Questions
vSphere Standard Switches (vSS)	1, 2
vSphere Distributed Switches (vDS)	3, 4
VMkernel Networking	5
Configuring and Managing Networking Features	6–8
Managing Host Networking with vDS	9, 10

1. You want to connect physical adapters to an existing vSphere Standard Switch. Which of the following steps should you take?

   a. Select Manage Physical Adapters and click the Add Adapters button.

   b. Select VMkernel Adapters.

   c. Create a port group and then add the adapter to it.

   d. Create an uplink port group and then add the adapter to it.

2. You are assigning a VLAN ID to a standard port group. What is the acceptable range?

   a. 1–4094

   b. 0–4095

   c. 0–4094

   d. 1–1095

3. You are modifying an existing vDS. Which of the following options is not available on the General settings page?

   a. Name

   b. Number of Uplinks

   c. Network I/O Control

   d. VLAN ID

4. You are modifying an existing vDS. Which of the following options is not available on the Advanced settings page?

   a. Traffic Filtering and Marking

   b. MTU

   c. Multicast Filtering Mode

   d. Discovery Protocol

5. You are adding a VMkernel adapter to a vDS. Which one of the following is not an available setting?

   a. SR-IOV

   b. MTU

   c. TCP/IP Stack

   d. Available Services

6. You enabled NIOC for a distributed switch, and you want to change shares for the system traffic. Which of the following is not an available system traffic type?

   a. Fault Tolerance

   b. vSAN

   c. vSphere HA Heartbeat

   d. NFS

7. You are configuring port mirroring for a distributed switch. Which of the following is not an available session type?

   a. Distributed port monitoring

   b. Port group

   c. Remote mirroring destination

   d. Encapsulated remote mirroring (L3) source

8. You want to implement LAGs to support your vSphere 8.0 networking. Which of the following steps should you take to prepare?

   a. Ensure that all the NICs in a LAG are configured with the same speed and duplexing.

   b. Ensure that the number of ports in a single port channel is equivalent to the number of participating ESXi hosts.

   c. Ensure that the number of ports in a single port channel on the switch is equivalent to or greater than the number of participating NICs from a specific ESXi host.

   d. Ensure that the number of participating NICs on each host is greater than the number of ports in the port channel.

9. You want to enable vDS health checks in your vSphere 8.0 environment. Which of the following is a valid choice for a health check service that you can enable or disable in the vSphere Client?

   a. MTU and Failover

   b. VLAN and MTU

   c. VLAN and Teaming

   d. MTU and Teaming

10. You are configuring rules to mark network packets. Which of the following is not a valid option for qualifying packets?

    a. Destination IP address

    b. Source IP address

    c. Source and destination MAC addresses

    d. VM guest OS type

Foundation Topics

vSphere Standard Switches (vSS)

This section addresses the creation and configuration of vSS and standard port groups.

Creating and Configuring vSphere Standard Switches

You can use the following procedure to create a vSS that provides network connectivity for hosts and virtual machines:

Step 1. In the vSphere Client, select an ESXi host in the inventory pane and navigate to **Configure > Networking > Virtual Switches**.

Step 2. Click **Add Networking**.

Step 3. Select a connection type (**VMkernel Network Adapter, Physical Network Adapter**, or **Virtual Machine Port Group for a Standard Switch**) for which you want to use the new standard switch and click **Next**.

Step 4. Select **New Standard Switch**, optionally change the MTU setting (from the default 1500), and click **Next**.

Step 5. Carry out the appropriate steps for the selection you made in step 3:

- On the Create a Standard Switch page, to add physical network adapters to the standard switch, take the following steps. Otherwise, click **Next**.
  - **a.** In the Assigned Adapters window, click the **Add Adapter** (green plus sign) button.
  - **b.** From the list of available network adapters, select one or more adapters.
  - **c.** Click **OK** and then click **Next**.
- If you created a new standard switch with a VMkernel adapter, use the Port Properties page to configure the adapter:
  - **a.** Provide a network label that indicates its purpose, such as vMotion or NFS.
  - **b.** Optionally, set a VLAN ID.
  - **c.** Select **IPv4, IPv6,** or **IPv4 and IPv6**.
  - **d.** Set MTU to a custom size for the VMkernel adapter or choose to get the MTU from a switch.

        e. Select a TCP/IP stack for the VMkernel adapter. (You cannot change it later.)

        f. If you use the default TCP/IP stack, select from the available services (**vMotion, Provisioning, Fault Tolerance Logging, Management, vSphere Replication, vSphere Replication NFC**, or **vSAN**).

        g. Click **Next**.

        h. Configure the IP settings and click **Next**.

    ■ If you created a new standard switch with a virtual machine port group, use the Connection Settings page to configure the port group:

        a. Provide a network label for the port group.

        b. Optionally, assign a VLAN ID.

        c. Click **Next**.

Step 6.   On the Ready to Complete page, click **Finish**.

NOTE If you create a standard switch without physical network adapters, all traffic on that switch is confined to that switch. You can create a standard switch without physical network adapters if you want a group of virtual machines to be able to communicate with each other but with nothing else.

You can make vSS configuration settings, including settings that control switch-wide defaults for ports. Such settings can be overridden by port group settings. To modify the settings of a vSS, select the host in the vSphere Client inventory pane and click Edit. You can then adjust the following settings:

■ **Number of vSS ports**: The number of ports on a standard switch is dynamically scaled up and down. You cannot explicitly set the number of ports in a vSS. A vSS can expand up to the maximum number of ports supported on the host, which is based on the maximum number of virtual machines the host can handle.

■ **Maximum transmission unit (MTU)**: You can enable jumbo frames on a vSS by increasing the MTU setting from the standard 1500 bytes. You can set the MTU between 1280 bytes and 9000 bytes.

■ **Physical network adapter**: Virtual machines connected to a vSS can only reach the physical networks through uplink physical network adapters. If you can connect two or more adapters to a vSS, they are transparently teamed.

To change or add physical adapters that are assigned to a vSS, you can use the following procedure:

Step 1. In the vSphere Client, select the ESXi host in the inventory pane and navigate to **Configure > Networking > Virtual Switches**.

Step 2. Navigate to the appropriate standard switch and select **Manage Physical Adapters**.

Step 3. In the Manage Physical Adapters window, click the **Add Adapter** (green plus sign) button.

Step 4. In the Add Physical Adapters to Switch window, select one or more adapters to assign to the vSS and click **OK**.

Step 5. In the Manage Physical Adapters window, use the up and down buttons to set each assigned vSS adapter to **Active**, **Standby**, or **Unused**. Click **OK**.

To view the MAC address and other characteristics of a host's physical NICs, you can select the host and navigate to Configure > Networking > Physical Adapters. To change the speed and duplexing of an adapter, select the adapter, click Edit, and make the change.

When configuring networks for the virtual machines in your vSphere environment, consider whether you want to migrate the virtual machines among a set of hosts. If you do, be sure that the hosts are in the same broadcast domain (that is, the same Layer 2 subnet). ESXi does not support migration of virtual machines between hosts in different broadcast domains as a virtual machine may lose access to required resources in the destination network. Even if your network provides high availability or includes intelligent switches that can resolve the virtual machine's needs across different networks, you may experience significant lag times as the Address Resolution Protocol (ARP) table updates.

Creating and Configuring Standard Port Groups

You can use the following procedure to add a virtual machine port group to a standard virtual switch:

Step 1. In the vSphere Client, right-click a host in the inventory pane and select **Add Networking**.

Step 2. For Select Connection Type, select **Virtual Machine Port Group for a Standard Switch** and click **Next**.

Step 3. For **Select Target Device**, choose whether to create a new standard switch or use an existing switch:

- If the new port group is for an existing standard switch, click **Browse**, select the standard switch, click **OK**, and click **Next**.

- If you are creating a new standard switch, you can assign physical network adapters to the standard switch or you can choose to create the standard switch with no assigned physical network adapters:

   a. Click **Add Adapters**.

   b. Select an adapter from the Network Adapters list.

   c. Use the Failover Order Group drop-down menu to assign the adapter to **Active Adapters**, **Standby Adapters**, or **Unused Adapters** and click **OK**.

   d. Use the up and down arrows in the Assigned Adapters list to change the position of the adapter, if needed.

   e. Click **Next**.

Step 4. On the Connection Settings page, set a network label for the port group and, optionally, set a VLAN ID. Click **Next**.

Step 5. On the Ready to Complete page, click **Finish**.

On a standard switch port group, the VLAN ID reflects the VLAN tagging mode in the port group, as shown in Table 9-2.

Table 9-2 VLAN ID Details

VLAN ID	VLAN Tagging Mode	Description
0	External switch tagging (EST)	The virtual switch does not pass traffic associated with a VLAN.
1 to 4094	Virtual switch tagging (VST)	The virtual switch tags traffic with the entered tag.
4095	Virtual guest tagging (VGT)	Virtual machines handle VLANs. The virtual switch passes traffic from any VLAN.

You can edit an existing standard switch port group by using the following procedure:

Step 1. In the vSphere Client, select a host in the inventory pane and navigate to **Configure > Networking > Virtual Switches**.

Step 2. Select the appropriate standard switch and navigate to the switch's topology diagram.

Step 3. In the topology diagram, click on the name of the port group and click the **Edit Settings** icon.

Step 4. On the Properties page, optionally change the port group's network label and VLAN ID.

Step 5.   On the Security page, optionally override the switch settings concerning MAC address impersonation and using promiscuous mode.

Step 6.   On the Traffic Shaping page, optionally override the switch settings for throttling network traffic based on average and peak bandwidth.

Step 7.   On the Teaming and Failover page, optionally override the teaming and failover settings inherited from the standard switch. Optionally configure traffic distribution across the physical adapters and the failover order.

Step 8.   Click **OK.**

To remove a port group from a standard switch, navigate to the switch's topology, select the port group, and click the Remove Selected Port Group icon.

vSphere Distributed Switches (vDS)

This section addresses the creation and configuration of vSphere Distributed Switches (vDS) and distributed port groups.

Creating and Configuring vSphere Distributed Switches

You can use the vSphere Client to create a vDS:

Step 1.   In the vSphere Client, right-click a data center in the inventory pane and select **Distributed Switch > New Distributed Switch.**

Step 2.   On the Name and Location page, enter a name for the new distributed switch or accept the generated name and click **Next.**

Step 3.   On the Select Version page, select a distributed switch version (**8.0.0**, **7.0.3, 7.0.2, 7.0.0, 6.6.0,** or **6.5.0**) and click **Next.** Features released with vSphere versions later than the version selected are not supported for the distributed switch.

Step 4.   On the Configure Settings page, provide the following vDS settings:

- For Version 8.0.0 and above, select the type of network offloads compatibility to control if network and security functions are offloaded to a DPU. You can choose **None, Pensando,** or **NVIDIA BlueField.** When you choose an option other than None, NIOC is disabled.

- Select the number of uplinks. The number of uplink ports determines how many physical NICs are connected per ESXi host.

- Enable or disable Network I/O Control. If it is enabled, it prioritizes network traffic.

- Optionally, select the **Create a Default Port Group** checkbox to create a new distributed port group with default settings for this switch. Enter a port group name or accept the generated name.

- If your system has custom port group requirements, create distributed port groups that meet those requirements after you add the distributed switch.

Click **Next**.

Step 5.   On the Ready to Complete page, review the settings you selected and click **Finish**.

In step 4, if you are deploying vDS 8.0 or higher, you can set Network Offloads Compatibility to Pensando or NVIDIA BlueField. With this setting, the network and security functions will be offloaded to the DPU device. DPU is a smart network card (SmartNIC) that has compute capability embedded in it. You can offload the networking functionality from the ESXi host to DPU for better performance. You can configure network offloads compatibility during the creation of the distributed switch, but you cannot modify the setting that associates hosts to the distributed switch.

If you plan on using NSX-T, set the vDS version to 7.0.0 or later and use NSX-T 3.0 or later.

Upgrading a vDS

You can upgrade a vDS from Version 6.x to a later version, but you cannot revert a vDS to an earlier version. As a rollback plan, you should export the distributed switch configuration prior to upgrading. In the export wizard, choose the option to include the distributed port groups. If an issue emerges, you can re-create the vDS by importing the switch configuration file and choosing the Preserve Original Distributed Switch and Port Group Identifiers option.

It is possible to both export and import vDS configurations:

- **Exporting a vDS configuration**: To export a vDS configuration, select it in the inventory pane, select Settings > Export Configuration, and use the wizard. In the wizard, select whether you want to include the configuration of the distributed port groups in the export. Optionally, you can provide a description for the export. The file is saved to your local system.

- **Importing a vDS configuration**: To import a vDS configuration, right-click a data center in the inventory pane, select Distributed Switch > Import Distributed Switch, and use the wizard. In the wizard, to assign the keys from the configuration file to the switch and its port groups, select the Preserve Original Distributed Switch and Port Group Identifiers checkbox.

Upgrading a distributed switch causes the hosts and virtual machines attached to the switch to experience brief downtime. VMware recommends performing the upgrade during a maintenance window and changing the DRS mode to manual (and ignoring DRS recommendations) during the upgrade.

You can use the following procedure to upgrade a vDS:

Step 1.   In the vSphere Client, navigate to **Networking**, right-click the distributed switch in the inventory pane, and select **Upgrade > Upgrade Distributed Switch**.

Step 2.   Select the vSphere Distributed Switch version (**8.0.0**, **7.0.3**, **7.0.2**, **7.0.0**, **6.6.0**, or **6.5.0**) that you want to upgrade the switch to and click **Next**.

Step 3.   Complete the wizard and click **Finish**.

> **NOTE**   If some ESXi hosts are incompatible with the selected target version, you should upgrade (or remove) the incompatible hosts or select another distributed switch version.

Modifying a vSphere Distributed Switch

To use the vSphere Client to configure general properties on an existing vDS, you can use the following procedure:

Step 1.   Select **Home > Networking**.

Step 2.   Select the vDS in the navigation pane and navigate to **Configure > Settings > Properties**.

Step 3.   Click **Edit**.

Step 4.   Click **General**.

Step 5.   Change the general setting of the distributed switch, including name, number of uplinks, whether Network I/O Control is enabled or disabled, and description.

Configuring NetFlow on a vDS

To configure NetFlow on a vDS, you can use the following procedure:

Step 1.   In the vSphere Client home page, select the distributed switch in the inventory pane.

Step 2.   Select **Actions > Settings > Edit NetFlow**.

Step 3. Provide the collector IP address and collector port of the NetFlow collector.

Step 4. Set an observation domain ID that identifies information related to the switch.

Step 5. Optionally, set the switch IP address and provide an IP address if you want to see the information from the distributed switch in the NetFlow collector under a single network device (IP address) instead of under a separate device for each host.

Step 6. Optionally, set the Active Flow Export Timeout and Idle Flow Export Timeout options to time values, in seconds, to wait before sending information after the flow is initiated.

Step 7. Optionally, to change the portion of data that the switch collects, configure the sampling rate.

Step 8. Optionally, to collect data on network activity between virtual machines on the same host, enable **Process Internal Flows Only**.

Step 9. Click **OK**.

Configuring Advanced vDS Settings

To configure advanced properties for an existing vDS, you can use the following procedure:

Step 1. In the vSphere Client, select the distributed switch in the inventory pane and navigate to **Configure** > **Settings** > **Properties**.

Step 3. Click **Edit**.

Step 4. Click **Advanced**.

Step 5. Set the MTU (in bytes), multicast filtering mode (basic or IGMP/MLD snooping), discovery protocol, and administrator contact.

Creating and Configuring Distributed Port Groups

You can use the following procedure to add a distributed port group to a vDS to create a network for connecting virtual machines and VMkernel adapters:

Step 1. In the vSphere Client, right-click a distributed switch in the inventory pane and select **Distributed Port Group** > **New Distributed Port Group**.

Step 2. In the wizard, provide a name for the new distributed port group or accept the generated name and click **Next**.

Step 3. On the **Configure Settings** page, optionally change any of the following properties:

- **Port Binding**: Choose **Static** or **Ephemeral**.
- **Port Allocation**: Choose **Elastic** or **Fixed**.
- **Number of Ports**: Increase or decrease the value from the default (which is 8).
- **Network Resource Pool**: Select an available pool.
- **VLAN**: Set VLAN Type to **None**, **VLAN**, **VLAN Trunking**, or **Private VLAN** and provide the corresponding settings.
- **Advanced**: Select the **Customize Default Policy Configuration** checkbox.

Click **Next**.

Step 4. If you selected the **Customize Default Policy Configuration** checkbox in step 4, you can use the following pages to customize policies:

- On the Security page, provide your choices for accepting or rejecting Promiscuous Mode, MAC Address Changes, and Forged Transmits and click **Next**.
- On the Traffic Shaping page, enable ingress traffic shaping or egress traffic shaping, or both. If you enable traffic shaping, you can set the average bandwidth, peak bandwidth, and burst size. Click **Next**.
- On the Teaming and Failover page, optionally set the Load Balancing, Network Failure Detection, Notify Switches, Failback, and Failover Order options. Click **Next**.

Step 5. On the Monitoring page, enable or disable NetFlow and click **Next**.

Step 6. On the Miscellaneous Settings page, click **Next**.

Step 7. On the Ready to Complete page, review the settings and click **Finish**.

VMkernel Networking

This section describes the procedures for configuring VMkernel networking.

Configuring and Managing VMkernel Adapters

To create a VMkernel virtual network adapter on a standard switch, you can use the Add Networking wizard, as described earlier in this chapter, in the "Creating and Configuring vSphere Standard Switches" section. To open the wizard, you can right-click a host in the inventory pane and select Add Networking. In the wizard, you can choose whether to add the adapter to a new standard switch or to an existing standard switch.

To add a VMkernel adapter to a distributed port group, you can use the following procedure:

Step 1. In the vSphere Client, right-click a distributed port group in the inventory pane and select **Add VMkernel Adapters**.

Step 2. On the Select Hosts page, click **Attached Hosts** (green plus sign), select the appropriate hosts, and click **Next**.

Step 3. Configure the VMkernel adapter IP, MTU, Stack and Available Services settings, as previously described.

Step 4. Complete the wizard and click **Finish**.

To view information about the VMkernel adapters in a host, select the host in the inventory pane and select Configure > Networking > VMkernel Adapters. To view details, select a specific adapter and examine the All, Properties, IP Settings, and Policies tabs. To modify a VMkernel adapter, select the adapter and click Edit.

Configuring TCP/IP Stacks

To view and edit the configuration of existing TCP/IP stacks on a host, you can use the following procedure:

Step 1. In the vSphere Client, select the host in the inventory pane and navigate to **Configure** > **Networking** > **TCP/IP Configuration**.

Step 2. Select any of the stacks in the table, such as **Default, vMotion, Provisioning**, or a custom stack.

Step 3. Examine the details pane, which may include DNs, routing, IPv4/IPv6 routing tables, a control algorithm, and the maximum number of allowed connections.

Step 4. Click **Edit** and use the following pages to modify the selected stack.

Step 5. On the DNS Configuration page, choose one of the following methods:

- **Obtain Settings Automatically from a VMkernel Network Adapter**: Select an existing VMkernel adapter.
- **Enter Settings Manually**: Provide the host name, domain name, preferred DNS server, alternate DNS server, and search domains.

Step 6. On the Routing page, edit the VMkernel gateway settings.

Step 7. On the Name page, edit the name of the stack.

Step 8.   On the Advanced page, edit the maximum number of connections and the congestion control algorithm.

Step 9.   Click **OK**.

To create a custom TCP/IP stack, you can use the following command in the ESXi shell:

```
esxcli network ip netstack add -N="stack_name"
```

After creating a custom stack, you can use the previously described procedure to configure the stack. When creating a VMkernel virtual network adapter, you can select any existing custom stack or predefined stack (default, vMotion, or provisioning).

Configuring and Managing Networking Features

This section describes the procedures for implementing networking features supported by vSphere.

Configuring Network I/O Control (NIOC)

To guarantee minimum bandwidth for system traffic and for virtual machines, you can enable and configure NIOC. You can enable NIOC on a distributed switch by using the following procedure:

Step 1.   In the vSphere Client, select the distributed switch in the inventory pane and navigate to **Actions** > **Settings** > **Edit Settings**.

Step 2.   From the Network I/O Control drop-down menu, select **Enable**.

Step 3.   Click **OK**.

By default, NIOC applies shares to each network traffic type as follows:

- **Management traffic**: 50 shares
- **Fault Tolerance (FT) traffic**: 50 shares
- **NFS traffic**: 50 shares
- **vSAN traffic**: 50 shares
- **vMotion traffic**: 50 shares
- **vSphere Replication (VR) traffic**: 50 shares
- **vSphere Data Protection backup traffic**: 50 shares
- **Virtual machine traffic**: 100 shares

To configure resource allocation for system traffic, you can use the following procedure:

Step 1. In the vSphere Client, select the distributed switch in the inventory pane.

Step 2. On the Configure tab, expand **Resource Allocation**.

Step 3. Click **System Traffic**.

Step 4. Select the appropriate traffic type and click **Edit**.

Step 5. Set the desired values for Shares, Reservation, and Limit.

Step 6. In the Reservation text box, enter a value for the minimum bandwidth that must be available for the traffic type.

Step 7. In the Limit text box, set the maximum bandwidth that system traffic of the selected type can use.

Step 8. Click **OK** to apply the allocation settings.

Creating a Network Resource Pool

If you enabled NIOC on a distributed switch and reserved bandwidth for the virtual machine feature, then you can create a set of network resource pools and allocate the reserved bandwidth among the pools. The total reservation from the virtual network adapters of the powered-on associated VMs must not exceed the quota of the pool. You can create a network pool by using the following procedure:

Step 1. In the vSphere Client, select the distributed switch in the inventory pane.

Step 2. On the Configure tab, expand **Resource Allocation**.

Step 3. Click **Network Resource Pools**.

Step 4. Click the **Add** button.

Step 5. Provide a name and a description for the pool.

Step 6. Set the reservation quota (in Mbps).

Step 7. Click **OK**.

NOTE The maximum quota that you can assign to the pool is equal to the aggregated reservation for virtual machine system traffic minus the quotas of the other network resource pools.

After creating a network resource pool, you can assign a distributed port group to the resource pool by using the following procedure:

Step 1.   In the vSphere Client, right-click a distributed port group in the inventory pane and select **Edit Settings**.

Step 2.   In the settings, click **General**.

Step 3.   In the Network Resource Pool drop-down menu, select the network resource pool and click **OK**.

Finally, you can set the network shares, reservation, and limit settings for individual virtual machines that are connected to the distributed port group in a network resource pool by using the following procedure:

Step 1.   In the vSphere Client, select a virtual machine in the inventory pane and navigate to **Actions > Edit Settings**.

Step 2.   Expand the **Network Adapter** section of the VM network adapter.

Step 3.   Either add and configure a new network adapter or select an existing network adapter.

Step 4.   Configure the network adapter's Shares, Reservation, and Limit settings.

Step 5.   Click **OK**.

Using Private VLANs

To use private VLANs (PVLANs), you must first define the PVLANs on a vDS. You can use the following procedure to do so:

Step 1.   In the vSphere Client, select a distributed switch in the inventory pane and navigate to **Configure > Settings > Private VLAN**.

Step 2.   Click **Edit**.

Step 3.   To add a primary VLAN, above Primary VLAN ID click the **plus sign** (+) button.

Step 4.   To add a secondary VLAN, in the right pane click the **plus sign** (+) button.

Step 5.   For Secondary VLAN type, select either **Isolated** or **Community**.

Step 6.   Click **OK**.

After creating the PVLANs, you can use them when assigning the VLAN network policies for distributed port groups and distributed ports, just as you do with standard VLANs.

Using DirectPath I/O

To allow virtual machines to access a physical NIC using DirectPath I/O, you must first enable DirectPath I/O for the NIC. You can do so with this procedure:

Step 1.   In the vSphere Client, select the ESXi host in the inventory.

Step 2.   On the Configure tab, expand **Hardware** and click **PCI Devices**.

Step 3.   Click **Edit**.

Step 4.   Select the NIC that has a green icon, indicating that it is active and ready. (An orange icon indicates that the device state has changed, and you must reboot the host prior to using the NIC.)

Step 5.   Click **OK**.

Now you are ready to use the following procedure to configure a virtual machine for DirectPath access to the passthrough NIC:

Step 1.   In the vSphere Client, locate the virtual machine in the inventory pane.

Step 2.   Power off the virtual machine.

Step 3.   Select **Actions > Edit Settings**.

Step 4.   Select the **Virtual Hardware** tab.

Step 5.   Select **Memory** and set Limit to **Unlimited**.

Step 6.   Click **Add New Device** and select **Other Devices > PCI Device**.

Step 7.   From the New PCI Device drop-down menu, select the appropriate passthrough device and click **OK**.

Step 8.   Power on the virtual machine.

Single Root I/O Virtualization (SR-IOV)

To enable a virtual machine to use the capabilities of SR-IOV, you must enable the SR-IOV virtual functions on the host and connect a virtual machine. To enable SR-IOV on a host, you can use the following procedure:

Step 1.   In the vSphere Client, select the host in the inventory pane.

Step 2.   Select the **Configure** tab and select **Networking > Physical Adapters**. Examine the SR-IOV property to see which NICs supports SR-IOV.

Step 3.   Select the NIC and click **Edit Adapter Settings**.

Step 4.   Under SR-IOV, set Status to **Enabled**.

Step 5.   In the Number of Virtual Functions text box, type the number of virtual functions that you want to configure for the adapter.

Step 6.   Click **OK**.

Step 7.   Restart the host.

You can use the following vCLI command to examine a host's virtual functions:

```
esxcli network sriovnic
```

To associate a virtual machine with one or more virtual functions as SR-IOV passthrough network adapters, you should first verify the following:

- Virtual functions exist on the host.
- Passthrough networking devices for the virtual functions are active in the host's PCI Devices list.
- The virtual machine compatibility is ESXi 5.5 and later.
- The guest OS is Red Hat Enterprise Linux 6 or later or Windows.

You can use the following procedure to implement SR-IOV for a virtual machine:

Step 1.   In the vSphere Client, select the virtual machine in the inventory pane.

Step 2.   Power off the virtual machine.

Step 3.   Select **Actions > Edit Settings**.

Step 4.   Select the **Virtual Hardware** tab.

Step 5.   From the Add New Device drop-down menu, select **Network Adapter**.

Step 6.   Expand the **New Network** section and connect the virtual machine to a port group. (The virtual NIC does not use this port group for data traffic. The port group is used to identify the networking properties, such as VLAN tagging, to apply on the data traffic.)

Step 7.   Select **Adapter Type > SR-IOV Passthrough**.

Step 8.   From the Physical Function drop-down menu, select the physical NIC.

Step 9.   To allow changes in the MTU of packets from the guest operating system, use the Guest OS MTU Change drop-down menu.

Step 10.   Expand the **Memory** section, select **Reserve All Guest Memory (All Locked)**, and click **OK**.

Step 11.   Power on the virtual machine.

The host selects a free virtual function from the physical adapter and maps it to the SR-IOV passthrough adapter. The host validates all properties of the virtual machine adapter and the underlying virtual function against the settings of the port group to which the virtual machine belongs.

NOTE   The step to reserve all the guest memory is required to allow the I/O memory management unit (IOMMU) and the passthrough device to access the memory using direct memory access (DMA).

Optionally, you can use the virtual switch, port group, or port to set the MTU size, security policy for VF traffic, and VLAN tagging mode.

You can enable SR-IOV with host profiles. In a host profile, expand General System Settings > Kernel Module. Select the appropriate physical function driver and provide the number of virtual functions that you want to provide for each physical function. The details depend on your hardware.

Configuring and Managing Port Mirroring

To configure port mirroring, you can use the following procedure:

Step 1.   In the vSphere Client, select a vDS in the inventory pane and navigate to **Configure > Settings > Port Mirroring**.

Step 3.   Click **New**.

Step 4.   Select one of the following options for Session Type:

- **Distributed Port Monitoring**
- **Remote Mirroring Source**
- **Remote Mirroring Destination**
- **Encapsulated Remote Mirroring (L3) Source**

Click **Next**.

Step 5.   Provide the following applicable session properties:

- **Name, Status, Description, and Sampling Rate**
- **Normal I/O on Destination Ports**
- **Mirrored Packet Length**

Click **Next**.

Step 6.   Identify the traffic source by using the following options:

- **Add Existing Ports from a List**: Click **Select Distributed Ports**, select each port, and click **OK**.

- **Add Existing Ports by Port Number**: Click **Add Distributed Ports**, enter the port number, and click **OK**.

- **Set Traffic Direction**: Select **Ingress**, **Egress**, or **Ingress/Egress**.

- **Specify the Source VLAN**: If you selected a remote mirrored destination, click **Add** and provide a VLAN ID.

Click **Next**.

Step 7.   Select the destination by using the following information:

- **Select a destination distributed port:** Click either **Select Distributed Ports** or **Add Distributed Ports** to add by port number.

- **Select an uplink**: Select an uplink and click **Add**.

- **Select ports or uplinks**: Select distributed ports and uplinks.

- **Specify IP address**: Click **Add** and provide an IP address.

Click **Next**.

You can use a similar procedure to edit port mirroring sessions; however, in step 2, you should select a session and click **Edit**. To remove a session, click **Remove**.

Configuring and Managing Link Aggregation Groups (LAGs)

This section provides information on configuring ESXi hosts to connect to physical switches using dynamic link aggregation. It involves creating link aggregation groups (LAGs) on distributed switches using host NICs that are connected to LACP port channels on physical switches.

To get started, you must create an LACP port channel on a physical switch for each LAG on each participating ESXi host. The steps are hardware dependent and are not covered here. Before you create the port channel, you should consider the following requirements:

- The number of ports in each port channel must match the number of physical NICs that will be aggregated on the host (a minimum of two).

- The same hashing algorithm must be used for the port channel and the associated LAG on the vDS.

- All the NICs in a LAG must be configured with the same speed and duplexing.

Before creating the LAG on a vDS in vSphere 8.0, you should address the following requirements:

- An LACP port channel must be available on a physical switch and configured to support the host, including the appropriate number of ports, speed, duplexing, and hashing (load balancing) algorithm.

- The vDS must be Version 6.5 or later.

- Enhanced LACP must be supported on the distributed switch, so use the vSphere Client to select the vDS in the inventory pane, navigate to Summary > Features, and verify that Link Aggregation Control Protocol is set to Enhanced Support.

Enhanced LACP for vDS supports the following load-balancing modes (hashing algorithms):

- Destination IP address
- Destination IP address and TCP/UDP port
- Destination IP address and VLAN
- Destination IP address, TCP/UDP port, and VLAN
- Destination MAC address
- Destination TCP/UDP port
- Source IP address
- Source IP address and TCP/UDP port
- Source IP address and VLAN
- Source IP address, TCP/UDP port, and VLAN
- Source MAC address
- Source TCP/UDP port
- Source and destination IP address
- Source and destination IP address and TCP/UDP port
- Source and destination IP address and VLAN
- Source and destination IP address, TCP/UDP port, and VLAN
- Source and destination MAC address

- Source and destination TCP/UDP port

- Source port ID

- VLAN

To change the LACP feature state from Basic Support to Enhanced Support, you can use the following procedure:

Step 1. In the vSphere Client, select the vDS in the inventory pane and navigate to **Summary > Features**.

Step 2. Verify that Link Aggregation Control Protocol is set to **Basic Support**.

Step 3. Select **Actions > Upgrade**.

Step 4. Select **Enhance LACP Support**.

Step 5. Navigate through the wizard to verify the port group accessibility and LACP configuration prerequisites.

Step 6. If the prerequisite verifications passed, complete the wizard and click **Finish**.

Step 7. Verify that Link Aggregation Control Protocol is set to **Enhanced Support**.

Step 8. Navigate to the **Configure** tab and verify that **LACP** appears in the Settings section.

You can use the following procedure to create a LAG:

Step 1. In the vSphere Client, select the distributed switch in the inventory pane, navigate to **Configure > Settings**, and select **LACP**.

Step 2. Click the **New Link Aggregation Group** icon.

Step 3. Provide the following information:

a. A name for the LAG

b. The number of ports to include in the LAG (which must match the number of ports in the LACP port channel)

c. The LACP negotiating mode (If the corresponding LACP-enabled physical switch ports are set to **Active**, then set the LAG's mode to **Passive** and vice versa.)

d. The load-balancing mode (which must match the load-balancing mode in the LACP port channel)

Step 4.   If you want to override the VLAN and NetFlow policies for each individual uplink port, set the VLAN and NetFlow policies for the LAG.

Step 5.   Click **OK**.

The LAG is now available for use. It appears as unused in the teaming and failover settings of the distributed port groups. To use the LAG as the uplink for a distributed port group, you can use the following procedure:

Step 1.   In the vSphere Client, select the distributed switch in the inventory pane.

Step 2.   Use the following steps to set the LAG as **Standby** for the appropriate distributed port groups:

   a. Select **Actions** > **Distributed Port Group** > **Manage Distributed Port Groups**.

   b. Select **Teaming and Failover** and click **Next**.

   c. Select the port groups where you want to use the LAG.

   d. In Failover Order, select the LAG and use the arrow keys to move it to the **Standby Uplinks** list.

   e. Complete the wizard and click **Finish**.

Step 3.   Use the following steps to assign the host's physical NICs to the LAG:

   a. Select **Actions** > **Add and Manage Hosts** > **Manage Host Networking**.

   b. Select the host and click **Next**.

   c. On the Select Network Adapter Tasks page, select **Manage Physical Adapters** and click **Next**.

   d. On the Manage Physical Adapters page, select a NIC and click **Assign an Uplink**.

   e. Select a LAG port and click **OK**.

   f. Repeat steps d and e for each NIC you want to include in the LAG.

   g. Complete the wizard and click **Finish**.

Step 4.   Use the following steps to activate the LAG for the appropriate distributed port groups:

   a. Select **Actions** > **Distributed Port Group** > **Manage Distributed Port Groups**.

   b. Select **Teaming and Failover** and click **Next**.

   c. Select the port groups where you previously set the LAG for standby.

    d. In Failover Order, select the LAG and use the arrow keys to move it to the **Active Uplinks** list.

    e. Move each standalone uplink to the **Unused** list.

    f. Complete the wizard and click **Finish**.

Managing Host Networking with vDS

This section describes the steps for managing host networking using vDS.

Adding Hosts to a vDS

To prepare for adding ESXi hosts to a vDS, you should do the following:

Step 1.   Create distributed port groups for virtual machines.

Step 2.   Create distributed port groups for VMkernel networking, such as management, vMotion, and Fault Tolerance.

Step 3.   Configure uplinks on the distributed switch for physical NICs that you want to connect to the switch.

Step 4.   Configure the vDS to support the hosts' VMs. For example, set the vDS's MTU and discovery protocols.

You can use the Add and Manage Hosts wizard to add multiple hosts at a time. To do so, follow these steps:

Step 1.   In the vSphere Client, select the distributed switch in the inventory pane and navigate to **Actions > Add and Manage Hosts**.

Step 2.   On the Select Task page, select **Add Hosts** and click **Next**.

Step 3.   On the Select Hosts page, click **New Hosts**.

Step 4.   Select the appropriate hosts in your data center, click **OK**, and then click **Next**.

Step 5.   On the next page, select the tasks for configuring network adapters to the distributed switch and click **Next**.

Step 6.   On the Manage Physical Network Adapters page, do the following:

    a. From the On Other Switches/Unclaimed list, select an unclaimed physical NIC or select a NIC to migrate from another virtual switch.

    b. Click **Assign Uplink**.

    c. Select an uplink and click **OK**.

Step 7.   Click **Next**.

Step 8.   On the next page, do the following:

    a. Select a VMkernel adapter and click **Assign Port Group**.

    b. Select a distributed port group and click **OK**.

Step 9.   Click **Next**.

Step 10.   Optionally, on the Migrate VM Networking page, select the checkbox **Migrate Virtual Machine Networking** to configure virtual machine networking and then complete the following steps:

    a. To connect all network adapters of a virtual machine to a distributed port group, select the virtual machine or select an individual network adapter to connect only that adapter.

    b. Click **Assign Port Group**.

    c. Select a distributed port group from the list, click **OK**, and then click **Next**.

Step 11.   Click **Finish**.

> **NOTE**   In the vSphere inventory, the hosts that you add must reside in the same data center as the vDS.

Managing Host Physical Network Adapters on a vDS

You can configure the physical NICs for multiple hosts connected to a single vDS at the same time. For consistent network configuration, you can use the following procedure to assign the same physical NIC from each host to the same vDS uplink:

Step 1.   In the vSphere Client, select the distributed switch in the inventory pane and navigate to **Actions > Add and Manage Hosts**.

Step 2.   In the wizard, select **Manage Host Networking** and click **Next**.

Step 3.   On the Select Hosts page, click **Attached Hosts** (green plus sign) and select the appropriate hosts. Click **Next**.

Step 4.   When you see all the ESXi hosts you selected on the Select Hosts page, click **Next**.

Step 5.   On the Manage Physical Adapters page, select a physical NIC from the On Other Switches/Unclaimed list to assign an uplink to the adapter.

Step 6.   Click **Assign Uplink**.

Step 7.   Select an uplink or select **Auto-assign** and click **OK**.

Step 8.   Click **Next**.

Step 9.   Continue through the wizard. Optionally, you can use the wizard to migrate VMkernel adapters and virtual machines.

Step 10.   Click **Finish**.

Migrating VMkernel Network Adapters to a vDS

You can use the following procedure to migrate VMkernel network adapters to a vDS:

Step 1.   In the vSphere Client, select the distributed switch in the inventory pane and navigate to **Actions > Add and Manage Hosts**.

Step 2.   In the wizard, select **Manage Host Networking** and click **Next**.

Step 3.   On the Select Hosts page, click the **Attached Hosts** button (green plus sign) and select the appropriate hosts. Click **Next**.

Step 4.   Click **Next**.

Step 5.   Continue through the wizard. Optionally, you can use the wizard to make changes and migrate virtual machines.

Step 6.   On the Manage VMkernel Adapters page, select a VMkernel adapter from each host, click **Assign Port Group**, click **OK**, and click **Next**.

Step 7.   Click **Finish**.

> **NOTE**   If you migrate or create VMkernel adapters for iSCSI, verify that the teaming and failover policy of the target distributed port group meets the requirements for iSCSI:
>
> - Verify that only one uplink is active, the standby list is empty, and the rest of the uplinks are unused.
> - Verify that only one physical NIC per host is assigned to the active uplink.

Removing Hosts from a vDS

Prior to removing an ESXi host for a vDS, you should migrate all the host's virtual machines, VMkernel adapters, and physical NICs from the vDS. To remove hosts from a vDS, follow these steps:

Step 1.   In the vSphere Client, select the vDS in the inventory pane and navigate to **Actions > Add and Manage Hosts**.

Step 2.   Select **Remove Hosts** and click **Next**.

Step 3.   Select the hosts you want to remove and click **Next**.

Step 4.   Click **Finish**.

Migrating Virtual Machines to a vDS

If you want to relocate a virtual machine to a vDS, you can edit each virtual machine and change the network to which to the vNICs are connected. To migrate a set of virtual machines from multiple networks to the distributed port groups of a specific vDS, you can use the following procedure:

Step 1.   In the vSphere Client, select the distributed switch in the inventory pane and navigate to **Actions > Add and Manage Hosts**.

Step 2.   In the wizard, select **Manage Host Networking** and click **Next**.

Step 3.   On the Select Hosts page, click the **Attached Hosts** button (green plus sign) and select the appropriate hosts. Click **Next**.

Step 4.   Click the **Next** button to navigate through the wizard until you reach the Migrate VM Networking page.

Step 5.   Check the **Migrate Virtual Machine Networking** box and examine the list of virtual machines that appears.

Step 6.   Select a virtual machine, click **Assign Port Group**, and select the distributed port group where the virtual machine should connect.

Step 7.   Repeat steps 5 and 6 for each virtual machine that you want to migrate and then click **Next**.

Step 8.   On the Ready to Complete page, click **Finish**.

To migrate a set of virtual machines from one network (distributed port group or standard port group) to another, you can use the following procedure:

Step 1.   In the vSphere Client, select the network in the inventory pane and navigate to **Actions > Migrate VMs to Another Network**.

Step 2.   In the wizard, select **Destination Network**, click **OK**, and click **Next**.

Step 3.   On the next page, select the virtual machines that you want to migrate and click **Next**.

Step 4.   On the Ready to Complete page, click **Finish**.

Monitoring the State of Ports in a Distributed Port Group

You can use the following procedure to examine the ports in a distributed port group:

Step 1.   In the vSphere Client, select a distributed port group in the inventory pane.

Step 2.   Click the **Ports** tab and examine the list of ports that exist in the port group.

Step 3.   To sort the rows by the data in a specific column (such as Port ID), click on the header for the appropriate column.

Step 4.   To filter the list using data in the column, click on the **Filter** icon in the column and enter a value. For example, to search for a port for a virtual machine with MAC address ending with 83, click on **Runtime MAC Address** and enter **83**.

Step 5.   To examine details for a port, click on the port and examine the details pane beneath the list of ports. Click the **Network Connection**, **Policies**, and **Traffic Filtering and Marking** tabs to see related details. Click on **Statistics** to view statistics on the amount of data and number of packets flowing into and out of the port.

Using the vDS Health Check

You can choose whether and when to use the vDS Health Check feature. For example, you could choose to enable it only temporarily, as you plan and make vDS configuration changes. By default it is disabled. You can use the following procedure to enable or disable Health Check for a vDS:

Step 1.   In the vSphere Client, select the vDS in the inventory pane and navigate to **Configure > Setting > Health Check**.

Step 2.   Click the **Edit** button.

Step 3.   For each for the following available health checks, choose **Enabled** or **Disabled** and set the interval, in minutes:

- VLAN and MTU
- Teaming and Failover

Step 4.   Click **OK**.

You can view a vDS health check by using this procedure:

Step 1. In the vSphere Client, select the vDS in the inventory pane and navigate to **Monitor > Health**.

Step 2. On the Host Member Health Status page, examine the overall, VLAN, MTU, and teaming and failover health statuses of the hosts connected to the switch.

Step 3. For more detail, select any host in the list and examine the details pane. In the details pane, select the **VLAN**, **MTU**, or **Teaming and Failover** tabs to get details on specific health checks.

Networking Policies and Advanced Features

To view the policies applied to a distributed port group, select the port group in the inventory pane, select Configure > Policies, and examine the applied security, ingress traffic shaping, egress traffic shaping, VLAN, and teaming and failover policies. To change the policies applied to a distributed port group, you can use the following procedure:

Step 1. In the vSphere Client, select the distributed port group in the inventory pane, navigate to **Configure > Policies**, and click the **Edit** button.

Step 2. On the left side, select any of the following policies and use the associated page to make changes:

- **Security**: On the Security page, provide your choices for accepting or rejecting promiscuous mode, MAC address changes, and forged transmits.

- **Traffic Shaping**: On the Traffic Shaping page, you can enable **Ingress Traffic Shaping** or **Egress Traffic Shaping** or both. If you enable traffic shaping, you can set the **Average Bandwidth**, **Peak Bandwidth**, and **Burst Size** options.

- **Teaming and Failover**: On the Teaming and Failover page, you can set the **Load Balancing**, **Network Failure Detection**, **Notify Switches**, **Failback**, and **Failover Order** options.

- **Monitoring**: On the Monitoring page, you can enable or disable NetFlow.

Step 3. Select any of the following categories and use the associated page to modify switch settings:

- **General**: On the General page, modify settings such as **Name**, **Port Binding**, **Port Allocation**, **Number of Ports**, **Network Resource Pool**, and **Description**.

- **Advanced**: On the Advanced page, choose **Allowed** or **Disabled** for each policy to indicate whether the policy can be overridden at the port level.

- **Miscellaneous**: On the Miscellaneous page, you can set Block All Ports to **Yes** or **No**.

Step 4.   Click **OK**.

To configure a traffic filtering and marking policy for a vDS, for example, you can use the following procedure:

Step 1.   In the vSphere Client, select a distributed port group or uplink port group in the inventory pane and navigate to **Configure > Settings > Traffic Filtering and Marking**.

Step 2.   Click **Enable and Reorder**.

Step 3.   Click **Enable All Traffic Rules**.

Step 4.   Click **OK**.

Step 5.   To create a rule to mark traffic, use the following steps:

   a. Click **Add**.

   b. Select **Action > Tag** and configure the tag either for **CoS** or **DSCP**.

   c. Set the traffic direction and specify the traffic qualifiers (system, MAC, or IP).

   d. Optionally, click the **Enable Qualifier** checkbox and provide information for qualifying the packets to mark. You can use the following tabs to qualify data:

      - **IP**: Identify packets by source and destination addresses and ports.

      - **MAC**: Identify packets by source and destination addresses and by VLAN.

      - **System Traffic**: Identity data by system traffic type (such as management or vMotion).

   e. Click **OK**.

Step 6.   To create a rule to filter traffic, repeat step 5 but configure the action to either allow traffic to pass or to block the traffic.

Exam Preparation Tasks

As mentioned in the section "Book Features and Exam Preparation Methods" in the Introduction, you have some choices for exam preparation: the exercises here, Chapter 15, "Final Preparation," and the exam simulation questions on the companion website.

Review All the Key Topics

Review the most important topics in this chapter, noted with the Key Topic icon in the outer margin of the page. Table 9-3 lists these key topics and the page number on which each is found.

Table 9-3   Key Topics for Chapter 9

Key Topic Element	Description	Page Number
Procedure	Creating a vSphere Standard Switch	334
Procedure	Creating and configuring distributed port groups	341
Procedure	Configuring TCP/IP stacks	343
Section	Configuring Network I/O Control	344
Procedure	Configuring and managing port mirroring	349
Section	Adding hosts to a vDS	354

Complete Tables and Lists from Memory

Print a copy of Appendix B, "Memory Tables" (found on the companion website), or at least the section for this chapter, and complete the tables and lists from memory. Appendix C, "Memory Table Answers" (also on the companion website), includes completed tables and lists to check your work.

Define Key Terms

No new terms are defined in this chapter.

Review Questions

1. You want to use VLAN guest tagging with your vSphere Standard Switch. What setting should you make on the standard port group?

   a. Set VLAN ID to 0.

   b. Set VLAN ID to 4095.

   c. Set VLAN Type to Trunking.

   d. Set VLAN Type to Guest Tagging.

2. You are preparing to upgrade a vDS to Version 8.0.0. What step should you take prior to upgrading?

   a. Copy the vDS.

   b. Back up vCenter Server.

   c. Export the vDS configuration, including the distributed port group configuration.

   d. Export the vDS configuration, excluding the distributed port group configuration.

3. You enabled NIOC, reserved virtual machine system traffic, and created a network resource pool. Which of the following steps do you need to take to allow a virtual machine to use the network resource pool?

   a. Edit the virtual machine and set the network resources allocation policy.

   b. Add the virtual machine to the resource pool.

   c. Assign the network resource pool to the distributed port group where the virtual machines are connected.

   d. In the inventory pane, drag and drop the virtual machine onto the network resource pool.

4. You are creating a VMkernel virtual adapter for vMotion traffic. Which of the following is not a valid option?

   a. In a standard switch, assign the adapter to the vMotion stack.

   b. In a distributed switch, assign the adapter to the vMotion stack.

   c. In a standard switch, assign the adapter to the default stack.

   d. In a distributed switch, assign the adapter to the provisioning stack.

5. You want to enable NetFlow in a distributed port group. Which of the following steps should you take?

   a. Change the distributed port group's monitoring policy.

   b. Change the distributed port group's security policy.

   c. In the distributed port group's Advanced settings, set NetFlow to Enable.

   d. Enable port mirroring on the distributed port group.

This chapter covers the following topics:

- Creating and Configuring a vSphere Cluster

- Creating and Configuring a vSphere DRS Cluster

- Creating and Configuring a vSphere HA Cluster

- Monitoring and Managing vSphere Resources

- Events, Alarms, and Automated Actions

- Logging in vSphere

This chapter contains information related to VMware vSphere 8.x Professional (2V0-21.23) exam objectives 1.4, 1.4.1, 1.4.2, 1.4.3, 1.4.4, 1.4.4.1, 1.4.5, 4.6, 4.18, 4.18.1, 4.18.2, 4.18.3, 4.19.1, 5.1, 5.1.1, 5.2, 5.3, 5.10, 5.11, 6.2, 6.3, 7.3, 7.5, 7.10, and 7.11.

Managing and Monitoring Clusters and Resources

This chapter discusses managing and monitoring vSphere clusters and resources.

"Do I Know This Already?" Quiz

The "Do I Know This Already?" quiz allows you to assess whether you should study this entire chapter or move quickly to the "Exam Preparation Tasks" section. In any case, the authors recommend that you read the entire chapter at least once. Table 10-1 outlines the major headings in this chapter and the corresponding "Do I Know This Already?" quiz questions. You can find the answers in Appendix A, "Answers to the 'Do I Know This Already?' Quizzes and Review Questions."

Table 10-1 "Do I Know This Already?" Foundation Topics Section-to-Question Mapping

Foundation Topics Section	Questions
Creating and Configuring a vSphere Cluster	1
Creating and Configuring a vSphere DRS Cluster	2, 3
Creating and Configuring a vSphere HA Cluster	4, 5
Monitoring and Managing vSphere Resources	6–8
Events, Alarms, and Automated Actions	9
Logging in vSphere	10

1. In a cluster that you initially created using Quickstart and for which you chose the option Configure Network Settings Later, you now want to add a host. Which of the following is a true statement?

   a. You cannot use Quickstart to add more hosts to the cluster.

   b. You can use Quickstart to add hosts to the cluster and configure the host networking.

   c. You can use Quickstart to add hosts to the cluster but must manually configure the host networking.

   d. You can edit the cluster and change the Configure Networking Settings Later option.

2. You are creating a resource pool in a DRS cluster. Which of the following statements are true? (Choose three.)

   a. When you create a child resource pool, the system applies admission control.

   b. If you choose Scale Descendant's Shares, child pools use scalable shares.

   c. The default CPU reservation is 0.

   d. The default memory limit is 0.

   e. The default reservation type is Fixed (Non-Expandable).

3. You are configuring a vSphere HA cluster. Which of the following is not a valid setting for Define Host Failover Capacity?

   a. Standby

   b. Cluster Resource Percentage

   c. Slot Policy (for powered-on VMs)

   d. Dedicated Failover Hosts

4. You want to configure VMCP in a vSphere cluster. Which of the following settings is valid?

   a. In the vSphere HA settings, select Failures and Responses > Datastore with PDL and choose Power Off and Restart VMs–Conservative Restart Policy.

   b. In the vSphere HA settings, select Failures and Responses > Datastore with PDL and choose Power Off and Restart VMs.

   c. In the vSphere DRS settings, select Failures and Responses > Datastore with APD and choose Power Off and Restart VMs–Conservative Restart Policy.

   d. In the vSphere DRS settings, select Failures and Responses > Datastore with APD and choose Power Off and Restart VMs–Aggressive Restart Policy.

5. You are configuring a vSphere HA cluster and want to configure proactive HA. Which of the following is not a requirement?

   a. Host.Config.Quarantine and Host.Config.Maintenance privileges

   b. A vendor-supplied vSphere Client plug-in

   c. A VMware-supplied plug-in

   d. vSphere DRS

6. You are experiencing poor performance for an application in a virtual machine. You learn from guest OS software and the vSphere client performance charts that the guest OS is paging. Which of the following is likely to fix the problem?

    a. Increase the memory in the ESXi host.

    b. Increase the memory size of the virtual machine.

    c. Migrate the virtual machine to a host that has plenty of free memory.

    d. Reserve all of the virtual machine's memory.

7. You are configuring virtual disks for the virtual machines in your vSphere environment. Which provisioning type is the best choice when you care more about optimizing the space usage than about performance or availability risk?

    a. Thin

    b. Thick eager zeroed

    c. Thick lazy zeroed

    d. Sparse

8. You are using ESXTOP to analyze vSphere performance. Which of the following statistics is the best indicator of some resource contention?

    a. %USED

    b. %DRPTX

    c. OVHD

    d. READ/s

9. You are configuring alarms in your vSphere environment. Which of the following is not a valid event type?

    a. Error

    b. Warning

    c. Information

    d. Audit

10. You are examining vSphere logs. Which of the following logs contains data about the agent that manages and configures the ESXi host?

    a. /var/log/vmkernel.log

    b. /var/log/vpxa.log

    c. /var/log/hostd.log

    d. /var/log/vmksummary.log

Creating and Configuring a vSphere Cluster

By using the vSphere Client, you can create a vSphere cluster and use its Quickstart feature to configure the cluster, or you can manually create the cluster. You can configure DRS, vSphere HA, and EVC on the cluster, as described in this chapter. You can also configure vSAN on the cluster, as described in Chapter 11, "Managing Storage."

Creating a Cluster

To create a vSphere cluster that you plan to configure using Quickstart, you should ensure that the hosts have the same ESXi version and patch level. If you are adding hosts to the vCenter Server inventory, you need the credentials for the root user account for the hosts. You must have the Host.Inventory.Create Cluster privilege. To create a cluster that you manage with a single image, verify that you have a supported ESXi 7.0 or later image available in the vSphere Lifecycle Manager depot. You can use the following procedure to create the cluster:

Step 1.   In the vSphere Client, right-click a data center in the inventory pane and select **New Cluster**.

Step 2.   Enter a name for the cluster.

Step 3.   Optionally, for each of the following services, slide the switch to the right to enable the service:

- vSphere DRS
- vSphere HA
- vSAN

If you enable DRS, you can optionally change its automation setting. (The default is Fully Automated using Threshold Level 3.)

Step 4.   Optionally, to create a cluster that you manage with a single image, select **Manage All Hosts in the Cluster with a Single Image** and then do the following:

- Select an ESXi version (image) from the drop-down menu.
- Optionally, select options from the Vendor Addon and Vendor Addon Version drop-down menus.

Step 5.   Click **OK**.

Configuring a Cluster with Quickstart

To modify an existing cluster, you can select the cluster in the inventory pane and click Configure > Configuration > Quickstart. On the Quickstart page are three cards: Cluster Basics, Add Hosts, and Configure Cluster. To change the name and the enabled cluster services, click Cluster Basics > Edit.

To add a host to a cluster, you can use the following procedure.

Step 1. In the vSphere Client, select a cluster in the inventory pane and navigate to **Configure > Configuration > Quickstart > Add Hosts**.

Step 2. In the wizard, click **New Hosts > Add Host** and provide the name (or IP address) and credentials for each host that you want to add that is not already in the vCenter Server inventory.

Step 3. Optionally, select the **Use the Same Credentials for All Hosts** option.

Step 4. Click **Existing Hosts > Add** and select each host that you want to add that is already in the vCenter Server inventory. Click **Next**.

Step 5. On the Host Summary page, click **Next**.

Step 6. When managing a cluster with a single image, you can select a host whose image you should be used for the cluster on the Import Image page. Click **Next**.

Step 7. On the Ready to Complete page, click **Finish**.

Step 8. Monitor the progress under Recent Tasks, where you can see any errors.

Step 9. When the task is complete, you can view the number of hosts and the health on the **Add Hosts** card. Optionally, select **Re-validate**.

Step 10. Use the inventory pane to verify that the hosts are attached to the cluster and are in Maintenance Mode.

To configure cluster settings and host networking in a cluster, you can use the following procedure:

Step 1. In the vSphere Client, select a cluster in the inventory pane and navigate to **Configure > Configuration > Quickstart**.

Step 2. Optionally, if you want to configure the cluster manually, click **Skip Quickstart**, which is irreversible. Otherwise, continue with the following steps to use Quickstart to configure the cluster.

Step 3. Click **Configure Cluster > Configure**.

Step 4.   On the Distributed Switches page, you can either select the irreversible option **Configure Networking Settings Later** or use the following steps to configure the cluster networking:

    a. Specify the number of distributed switches to create (up to three).

    b. Enter a unique name for each distributed switch. Alternatively, click **Use Existing** and select an existing compatible distributed switch and distributed port group.

    c. To set up the vMotion network, select a distributed switch and assign a new port group to it.

    d. In the Physical Adapters section, for each physical network adapter, assign a distributed switch name from the drop-down menu. Ensure that each new distributed switch is assigned to at least one physical adapter. For any existing distributed switch, to avoid an error, select the physical adapter that is currently mapped to the switch.

    e. Click **Next**.

    f. If you enabled the vSphere DRS feature during cluster creation, in the vMotion Traffic page that appears, provide the VLAN ID, protocol type, and IP configuration.

Step 5.   Click **Next**.

Step 6.   In the Advanced Options page, configure the following options:

    a. If you enabled vSphere HA during cluster creation, use the options in the High Availability section to enable or disable host failure monitoring, virtual machine monitoring, and admission control. For admission control, you can specify the number of hosts for failover capacity.

    b. If you enabled vSphere DRS during cluster creation, use the options in the Distributed Resource Scheduler section to set the automation level and migration threshold.

    c. In the Host Options section, set the Lockdown Mode and enter an NTP server address.

    d. Optionally, in the Enhanced vMotion Capability section, use the options to enable EVC and select a mode.

Step 7.   Click **Next**.

Step 8.   On the Ready to Complete page that appears, review the settings and click **Finish**.

You can extend a cluster by adding more hosts. If you initially selected the Skip Quickstart option, then you should add hosts manually. If you previously used

Quickstart but selected Configure Networking Settings Later, you can add hosts by using Quickstart but must manually configure the host networking. To extend a cluster, you can use the following procedure:

Step 1. In the vSphere Client, right-click a configured cluster in the inventory pane and select **Add Hosts**.

Step 2. In the wizard, select hosts from the vCenter Server inventory and add new hosts (by providing names and credentials) to include in the cluster.

Step 3. On the Ready to Complete page, click **Finish**.

Step 4. On the Configure Hosts card of the Extend Cluster Guide page that appears, select **Configure**. If you previously used Quickstart to configure the host networking, the vMotion Traffic page appears. Provide the VLAN ID, protocol type, and IP configuration. A pop-up window appears, informing you that the configuration for the hosts that exist in the cluster is applied to the newly added hosts.

Step 5. Click **Continue**.

After successful validation, the Configure button in the Configure Hosts card becomes inactive, and the Re-validate button is available.

If you enable DRS, the default Automation Level setting is Fully Automated, and the default Threshold setting is 3. If you enable HA, the default values are Host Monitoring and Admission Control Are Enabled and VM Monitoring Is Disabled. You can override the default values later in the workflow.

If you select an image for managing all the hosts in the cluster, you can later edit the image specification on the Updates tab. If you do not choose an image to manage hosts, you must manage the cluster by using baselines and baseline groups. You can switch from using baselines to using images later.

Starting with vSphere 7.0, you can use vSphere Lifecycle Manager to upgrade and update the hosts in a cluster. A vSphere Lifecycle Manager image is a combination of vSphere software, driver software, and firmware for specific host hardware. You can assign an image to a cluster used to control the software set to be installed on the hosts, including the ESXi version, additional VMware-provided software, and vendor software, such as firmware and drivers.

The image that you define during cluster creation is not immediately applied to the hosts. If you do not set up an image for a cluster, the cluster uses baselines and baseline groups. For more information about using images and baselines to manage hosts in clusters, see the *Managing Host and Cluster Lifecycle* documentation.

EVC Mode

As previously described, you can configure EVC by using Quickstart > Configure Cluster. You can also configure EVC directly in the cluster settings. You can set VMware EVC to Disable EVC, Enable EVC for AMD Hosts, or Enable EVC for Intel Hosts.

If you choose Enable EVC for AMD Hosts, you can set the mode to one of the options listed in Table 4-3 in Chapter 4, "Clusters and High Availability."

If you choose Enable EVC for Intel Hosts, you can set the mode to one of the options listed in Table 4-2 in Chapter 4.

To view the EVC modes for all of a cluster's virtual machines in the vSphere Client, you can select a cluster, navigate to its VMs tab, and select Show/Hide Columns > EVC Mode.

Creating and Configuring a vSphere DRS Cluster

This section describes how to create and configure a vSphere DRS cluster.

Creating a vSphere DRS Cluster

To create a vSphere DRS cluster, follow the procedure in the section "Creating a Cluster," earlier in this chapter, and ensure that you choose to enable the DRS service. Use the information in the rest of this section to configure the DRS cluster.

Creating a Resource Pool

You can use the following procedure to create a child resource pool in a DRS cluster:

Step 1.   In the vSphere Client, navigate to **Hosts and Clusters**, right-click a DRS cluster in the inventory, and select **New Resource Pool**.

Step 2.   Provide a name for the resource pool.

Step 3.   Optionally, select the **Scale Descendant's Shares** checkbox to enable scalable shares. (Enabling this option causes any child resource pools to use scalable shares, which scale dynamically when virtual machines are added and removed.)

Step 4.   Optionally, set CPU and Memory Shares to **Low**, **Normal**, **High**, or **Custom**. If you select Custom, enter a numeric value.

Step 5.   Optionally, set CPU and Memory Reservation to a numeric value (the default is 0) and a unit of measure (**MB**, **GB**, **MHz**, or **GHz**).

Step 6. Optionally, set CPU and Memory Limit to a numeric value (the default is Unlimited) and a unit of measure (**MB**, **GB**, **MHz**, or **GHz**).

Step 7. Optionally, deselect the **CPU** and **Memory Expandable** checkboxes (which are selected by default).

Step 8. Click **OK**.

> **NOTE** When you create a child resource pool, the vSphere Client prompts you for resource pool attribute information. The system uses admission control to ensure that you do not allocate resources that are not available. If you choose Scale Descendant's Shares, each descendant pool will also use scalable shares. You cannot change this behavior for each child pool.

Configuring Advanced DRS Options

This section describes how to configure some advanced options for vSphere DRS.

Creating Affinity/Anti-Affinity Rules

Table 10-2 provides some common use cases for VM-to-VM (or VM–VM) affinity and anti-affinity rules.

Table 10-2 Use Cases for VM–VM Rules

Use Case	Rule Details
To improve application and communication performance for a multinode application.	Use VM–VM affinity rules to ensure that sets of virtual machines that engage in significant data exchange reside on the same host, such that the data transfer occurs within the host system hardware and does not traverse the physical network infrastructure.
To improve application availability for a multinode application	Use VM–VM anti-affinity rules to ensure that sets of peer virtual machines reside on separate hosts, such that the failure of a single host does not result in the failure of all the peer application nodes.

You can use the following procedure to create a VM–VM affinity or anti-affinity rule:

Step 1. Browse to the cluster in the vSphere Client.

Step 2. Navigate to **Configure > VM/Host Rules** and click **Add**.

Step 3. In the Create VM/Host Rule dialog box, type a name for the rule.

Step 4. From the Type drop-down menu, select either **Keep Virtual Machines Together** (affinity) or **Separate Virtual Machines** (anti-affinity).

Step 5.   Click **Add**.

Step 6.   Select at least two virtual machines to which the rule will apply and click **OK**.

Step 7.   Click **OK**.

Configuring Predictive DRS

To configure predictive DRS, you can use the following procedure:

Step 1.   In the vRealize Operations (vROps) GUI, select the appropriate vCenter Server adapter instance and choose **Advanced Settings**.

Step 2.   Set Provide Data to vSphere Predictive DRS to **True**.

Step 3.   In the vSphere Client, select the cluster in the inventory pane and navigate to **Cluster > Services > vSphere DRS > Edit**.

Step 4.   Check the **Predictive DRS** checkbox.

Creating and Configuring a vSphere HA Cluster

This section describes how to create and configure a vSphere HA cluster.

Creating a vSphere HA Cluster

To create a vSphere HA cluster, follow the procedure in the section "Creating a Cluster," earlier in this chapter, and ensure that you choose to enable the vSphere HA service. Use the information in the rest of this section to configure the vSphere HA cluster.

Configuring Advanced vSphere HA Options

You can use the following procedure to add vSphere HA advanced options, as described in Table 4-9:

Step 1.   In the vSphere Client, select a vSphere HA cluster in the inventory pane and navigate to **Configure > vSphere Availability > Edit > Advanced Options**.

Step 2.   Click **Add**.

Step 3.   Enter the name of the advanced option and the value.

Step 4.   Click **OK**.

Configuring vSphere HA Admission Control

To configure admission control for a vSphere HA cluster, you can use the following procedure:

Step 1. In the vSphere Client, select the vSphere HA cluster in the inventory pane and navigate to **Configure > vSphere Availability > Edit**.

Step 2. Click **Admission Control** and set Host Failures Cluster Tolerates to the maximum number of host failures you want the cluster to support.

Step 3. Select one of the following options for Define Host Failover Capacity By, as described in Table 4-8 in Chapter 4:

- **Cluster Resource Percentage**
- **Slot Policy** (for powered-on VMs)
- **Dedicated Failover Hosts**
- **Disabled** (which disables admission control)

Step 4. Optionally, set Performance Degradation VMs Tolerate to a percentage.

Step 5. Click **OK**.

Configuring VMCP

To configure Virtual Machine Component Protection (VMCP) in a vSphere HA cluster, you can use the following procedure:

Step 1. In the vSphere Client, select the cluster in the inventory pane and navigate to **Configure > vSphere Availability > Edit**.

Step 2. Select **Failures and Responses > Datastore with PDL** and choose one of the following:

- **Issue Events**
- **Power Off and Restart VMs**

Step 3. Select **Failures and Responses > Datastore with APD** and choose one of the following:

- **Issue Events**
- **Power Off and Restart VMs–Conservative Restart Policy**
- **Power Off and Restart VMs–Aggressive Restart Policy**

Configuring Virtual Machine and Application Monitoring

You can use the following procedure to turn on and configure virtual machine and application monitoring in a vSphere HA cluster:

Step 1. In the vSphere Client, select the vSphere HA cluster in the inventory pane and navigate to **Configure > vSphere Availability > Edit**.

Step 2. Select **Failures and Responses > VM Monitoring.**

Step 3. Select **VM Monitoring** to turn on VMware Tools heartbeats.

Step 4. Select **Application Monitoring** to turn on application heartbeats.

Step 5. To set the heartbeat monitoring sensitivity, move the slider between Low and High or select **Custom** and provide a custom value.

Step 6. Click **OK.**

Configuring Proactive HA

To get started with implementing Proactive HA, you need to install a supported vendor-supplied vSphere Client plug-in and register the proactive HA provider. When you turn on proactive HA in a cluster, you can select from the list of providers for installed plug-ins that are monitoring every host in the cluster. You can use the following procedure to configure proactive HA in a cluster:

Step 1. Ensure that the following prerequisites are met:

- vSphere HA and DRS are enabled.
- To allow remediation actions, ensure that you have the Host.Config. Quarantine and Host.Config.Maintenance privileges.

Step 2. In the vSphere Client, select the cluster in the inventory pane and navigate to **Configure > vSphere Availability > Edit**.

Step 3. Select **Turn on Proactive HA.**

Step 4. Click **Proactive HA Failures and Responses.**

Step 5. Set Automation Level to **Manual** or **Automated.**

Step 6. Set Remediation to one of the following:

- **Quarantine Mode for All Failures**
- **Quarantine Mode for Moderate and Maintenance Mode for Severe Failure (Mixed)**
- **Maintenance Mode for All Failures**

Configuring vSphere Fault Tolerance

Before enabling vSphere Fault Tolerance (FT) for a virtual machine, you must prepare the hosts and cluster by doing the following:

Step 1.   Configure vSphere HA on the cluster.

Step 2.   On each participating host, configure a vMotion port group, a VMkernel adapter enabled for vMotion, a Fault Tolerance logging network, and a VMkernel adapter enabled for FT Logging.

To turn on FT for a virtual machine, you can use the following procedure:

Step 1.   In the vSphere Client, right-click the virtual machine in the inventory pane and select **Fault Tolerance > Turn On Fault Tolerance**.

Step 2.   Click **Yes**.

Step 3.   Select a datastore on which to place the secondary VM configuration files and click **Next**.

Step 4.   Select a host on which to place the secondary VM and click **Next**.

Step 5.   Review your selections and then click **Finish**.

Before FT is turned on for a virtual machine, FT performs several validation steps related to the FT requirements listed in Chapter 4. The virtual machine datastores and memory are replicated as FT is turned on. This may take several minutes, during which the virtual machine status does not appear as protected. When the replication completes and the state of the secondary VM is synchronized with that of the primary VM, the status changes to Protected.

To test FT failover for a virtual machine, right-click the virtual machine and select Fault Tolerance > Test Failover. Likewise, you can select Fault Tolerance > Test Restart Secondary to restart the Secondary VM.

Monitoring and Managing vSphere Resources

You can use the vSphere *client performance charts* to view compute, storage, and network resource usage for virtual machines, hosts, and clusters. For a more granular look from the host perspective, you can use the *ESXTOP* utility. You can use vCenter Server alarms to bring attention to conditions and events that may call for human intervention, such as low resource availability on a cluster, host, or datastore. To bring multi-vCenter Server monitoring, predictive analysis, and intelligent operations to an environment, you can consider integrating vRealize Operations (vROps).

Metrics

Performance metrics are organized into logical groups based on the object or object device, as shown in Table 10-3.

Table 10-3   Metrics

Metric Group	Description
Cluster Services	Performance metrics on vSphere host clusters.
CPU	CPU utilization metrics for hosts, virtual machines, resource pools, or compute resources.
Datastore	Datastore utilization metrics.
Disk	Disk utilization metrics for hosts, virtual machines, or datastores.
Memory	Memory utilization metrics for hosts, virtual machines, resource pools, or compute resources.
Network	Network utilization metrics for physical NICs, virtual NICs, and other network devices.
Power	Energy and power utilization metrics for hosts.
Storage Adapter	Data traffic metrics for host bus adapters (HBAs).
Storage Path	Data traffic metrics for paths.
System	Overall system availability metrics, such as the system heartbeat and uptime. These counters are available directly from hosts and from vCenter Server.
Virtual Disk	Disk utilization and disk performance metrics for virtual machines.
Virtual Flash	Virtual flash metrics.
Virtual Machine Operations	Virtual machine power and provisioning operations metrics in a cluster or data center.
vSphere Replication	Virtual machine replication metrics.

Disk metrics include I/O performance, such as latency and read/write speeds, and utilization metrics for storage as a finite resource.

The value obtained for memory utilization is one of the following:

- For virtual machines, *memory* refers to the guest physical memory, which is the virtual memory the hypervisor presents to the guest as physical memory.

- For hosts, *memory* refers to the machine memory, which is the physical memory in the host system.

vSphere Client Performance Charts

The vSphere client performance charts enable you to view performance metrics in different types of charts, depending on the selected object and metric type, as described in Table 10-4.

Table 10-4 Performance Chart Types

Chart Type	Description	Example
Line chart	Displays metrics for a single inventory object, where data for each metric is represented by a separate line.	A network chart for a host can include one line chart showing the number of packets received and another line chart showing the number of packets transmitted.
Bar chart	Displays metrics for objects, where each bar represents metrics for an object.	A bar chart can display metrics for datastores, where each datastore is represented as a bar. Each bar displays metrics based on the file type, such as virtual disk or snapshot.
Pie chart	Displays metrics for a single object, where each slice represents a category or child object.	A datastore pie chart can display the amount of storage space occupied by each virtual machine or by each file type.
Stacked chart	Displays metrics for child objects.	A host's stacked CPU usage chart displays metrics for the 10 virtual machines on the host that are consuming the most CPU. The Other amount displays the total CPU usage of the remaining virtual machines.

Overview and advanced performance charts are available for data center, cluster, host, resource pool, vApp, and virtual machine objects. Overview performance charts are also available for datastores and datastore clusters. Performance charts are not available for network objects. Charts are organized into views, which you can use to see related data together on one screen. You can specify the time range or data collection interval. Advanced charts contain more information than overview charts. You can print, configure, and export advanced charts (in PNG, JPEG, or CSV formats).

Overview Performance Charts

You can use the vSphere Client to examine the overview performance charts for data centers, clusters, datastores (and datastore clusters), hosts, resource pools, vApps, and virtual machines.

To view a performance chart, you can use the following procedure:

Step 1.   In the vSphere Client, select an appropriate object in the inventory pane and navigate to **Monitor > Performance**.

Step 2.   Select a view.

Step 3.   Select a predefined or custom time range.

Table 10-5 lists the available performance chart views by object type.

Table 10-5   Views by Object Type

Object Type	View List Items
Data center	**Clusters**: Thumbnail CPU and memory charts for each cluster and stacked charts for total data center CPU and memory. **Storage**: Space utilization charts for each datastore by file type.
Datastore and datastore cluster	**Space**: Space utilization charts by datastore, by file type, and by virtual machine. **Performance**: Disk performance (latency, throughput, and queuing) charts for the datastore (or datastore cluster, when Storage DRS is enabled) by virtual machine, by virtual disk, and by file type.
Cluster	**Home**: CPU and memory charts for the cluster. **Resource pools and virtual machines**: Thumbnail charts for resource pools and virtual machines and stacked charts for total cluster CPU and memory usage. **Hosts**: Thumbnail charts for each host and stacked charts for total cluster CPU, memory, disk usage, and network usage.
Host	**Home**: CPU, memory, disk, and network charts for the host. **Virtual machines**: Thumbnail charts for virtual machines, and stacked charts for total CPU usage and total host memory usage.
Resource Pool	**Home**: CPU and memory charts for the resource pool. **Resource pools and virtual machines**: Thumbnail charts for resource pools and virtual machines and stacked charts for total resource CPU and memory usage.
vApps	**Home**: CPU and memory charts for the resource pool. **Resource pools and virtual machines**: Thumbnail charts for resource pools and virtual machines and stacked charts for total vApp CPU and memory usage.
Virtual Machine	**Storage**: Space utilization charts for the virtual machine by file type and by datastore. **Fault tolerance**: CPU and memory charts that display metrics for the fault-tolerant primary and secondary virtual machines. **Home**: CPU, memory, network, and host thumbnail charts and disk performance charts for the virtual machine.

NOTE   When Storage I/O Control is disabled, the values for the Storage I/O Normalized Latency metrics are zeros.

Advanced Performance Charts

For more granularity, you can use advanced performance charts or create your own custom charts. Advanced performance charts are especially useful when overview performance charts do not provide sufficient data for troubleshooting a specific issue. Advanced performance charts include the following features:

- **Customizable**: You can change and save chart settings.

- **More information**: You can include data counters that are not supported in other performance charts. You can hover over a data point to see details at that point.

- **Exportable**: You can save an image to a file or spreadsheet. You can export the data to a spreadsheet.

Figure 10-1 shows an example of an advanced performance chart that includes memory metrics for a virtual machine.

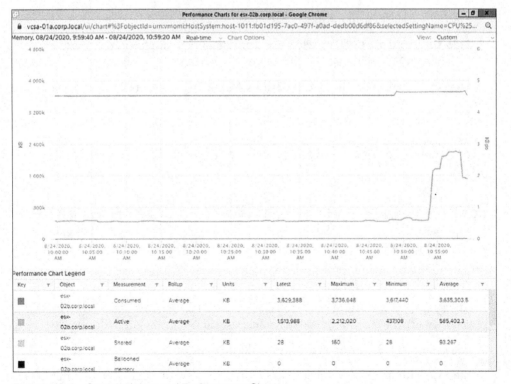

Figure 10-1   Sample Advanced Performance Chart

You can use the following procedure to access an advanced performance chart:

Step 1.   In the vSphere Client, select an appropriate object in the inventory pane and navigate to **Monitor > Performance**.

Step 2.   Click **Advanced**.

Step 3.   Optionally, select an appropriate view from View drop-down list.

Step 4.   Optionally, click the **Popup Chart** icon to open the chart in a separate window.

Step 5.   Click **Chart Options**.

Step 6.   Under Chart Metrics, select an appropriate metric group.

Step 7.   Select a time span. If you choose **Custom Interval**, then select one of the following:

  ■ **Last**: Specify the number of hours, days, weeks, or months.

  ■ **From**: Specify beginning and ending times.

Step 8.   Under Target Objects, select the appropriate inventory objects. (Optionally, use the **All** or **None** buttons.)

Step 9.   Select an appropriate chart type.

Step 10.   Under Counters, select the data counters to display in the chart. (Optionally, use the **All** or **None** buttons.)

Step 11.   Optionally, click **Save Options As** and save your settings as a custom chart.

NOTE   Pop-up charts are useful for maximizing the available real estate for a chart and for comparing two separate charts side by side.

NOTE   For the stacked graph type, you can use only one measurement unit. In addition, per-virtual-machine stacked graphs are available only for hosts. You can click on a counter's description name to display details, such as whether the selected metric can be stacked for each virtual machine.

After you create a custom chart, the chart is added to the View drop-down list. You can then use the chart in the same manner as you would any prebuilt view.

You can use the following procedure to delete a custom chart:

Step 1.   In the vSphere Client, select an appropriate object in the inventory pane and navigate to **Monitor > Performance**.

Step 2.   Select **Advanced > Chart Options**.

Step 3.   Select the chart and click **Delete Options**.

You can use the following procedure to save data from an advanced performance chart to a file either in a graphic format or in a comma-separated values (CSV) format:

Step 1.   In the vSphere Client, select an object in the inventory pane and navigate to **Monitor > Performance**.

Step 2.   Click **Advanced**.

Step 3.   Optionally, select a view or change chart options until you are satisfied with the chart.

Step 4.   Click the **Export** icon.

Step 5.   Select one of the following options:

- **To PNG**: Exports a bitmap image to PNG format.
- **To JPEG**: Exports a bitmap image to JPEG format.
- **To CSV**: Exports text data to CSV format.
- **To SVG**: Exports a vector image to SVG format.

Step 6.   Provide a filename and location.

Step 7.   Click **Save**.

Troubleshooting and Optimizing Performance

Table 10-6 provides the likely causes and potential solutions for some sample symptoms, based on vSphere performance metrics.

Table 10-6   CPU Performance Analysis

Symptoms	Likely Causes	Potential Solutions
Host: CPU usage is consistently high. **Virtual machine**: CPU usage is above 90%. CPU ready is above 20%. Application performance is poor.	■ The host has insufficient CPU resources to meet the demand. ■ Too many virtual CPUs are running on the host. ■ Storage or network operations are placing the CPU in a wait state. ■ The guest OS generates too much load for the CPU.	■ Add the host to a DRS cluster. ■ Increase the number of hosts in the DRS cluster. ■ Migrate one or more virtual machines to other hosts. ■ Upgrade the physical CPUs of the host.

Symptoms	Likely Causes	Potential Solutions
		■ Upgrade ESXi to the latest version.
		■ Enable CPU-saving features such as TCP segmentation offload, large memory pages, and jumbo frames.
		■ Increase the amount of memory allocated to the virtual machines, which may improve cached I/O and reduce CPU utilization.
		■ Reduce the number of virtual CPUs assigned to virtual machines.
		■ Ensure that VMware Tools is installed.
		■ Compare the CPU usage of troubled virtual machines with that of other virtual machines on the host or in the resource pool. (Hint: Use a stacked graph.)
		■ Increase the CPU limit, shares, or reservation on the troubled virtual machine.
Host: Memory usage is consistently 94% or higher. Free memory is 6% or less. **Virtual machine**: Swapping is occurring. (Memory usage may be high or low.)	■ The host has insufficient memory resources to meet the demand.	■ Ensure that VMware Tools is installed and that the balloon driver is enabled for all virtual machines.
		■ Reduce the memory size on oversized virtual machines.
		■ Reduce the memory reservation of virtual machines where it is set higher than needed.
		■ Add the host to a DRS cluster.
		■ Increase the number of hosts in the DRS cluster.
		■ Migrate one or more virtual machines to other hosts.
		■ Add physical memory to the host.

Symptoms	Likely Causes	Potential Solutions
Virtual machine: Memory usage is high. **Guest OS**: Memory usage is high. Paging is occurring.	■ The guest OS is not provided sufficient memory by the virtual machine.	■ Increase the memory size of the virtual machine.
Virtual machine: CPU ready is low. **Guest OS**: CPU utilization is high.	■ The guest OS is not provided sufficient CPU resources by the virtual machine.	■ Increase the number of CPUs for the virtual machine. ■ Migrate the virtual machine to a host with faster CPUs.
Datastore: Space utilization is high.	■ Snapshot files are consuming a lot of datastore space. ■ Some virtual machines are provisioned with more storage space than required. ■ The datastore has insufficient storage space to meet the demand.	■ Delete or consolidate virtual machine snapshots. ■ Convert some virtual disks to be thin provisioned. ■ Migrate one or more virtual machines (or virtual disks) to other datastores. ■ Add the datastore to a Storage DRS datastore cluster. ■ Add datastores with available space to the datastore cluster. ■ Add more storage space to the datastore.
Disk: Device latency is greater than 15 ms.	■ Problems are occurring with the storage array.	■ Migrate the virtual machines to datastores backed by other storage arrays.
Disk: VMkernel latency is greater than 4 ms. Queue latency is greater than zero.	■ The maximum throughput of a storage device is not sufficient to meet the demand of the current workload.	■ Migrate the virtual machines to datastores backed by storage devices (LUNs) with more spindles. ■ Balance virtual machines and their disk I/O across the available physical resources. ■ Use Storage DRS I/O balancing. Add more disks (spindles) to the storage device backing the datastore. ■ Configure the queue depth and cache settings on the RAID controllers. Adjust the Disk. SchedNumReqOutstanding parameter.

Symptoms	Likely Causes	Potential Solutions
		■ Configure multipathing.
		■ Increase the memory size of the virtual machine to eliminate any guest OS paging. Increase the guest OS caching of disk I/O.
		■ Ensure that no virtual machine swapping or ballooning is occurring.
		■ Defragment guest file systems.
		■ Use eager zeroed thick provisioned virtual disks.
Network: The number of packets dropped is greater than zero. Latency is high. The transfer rate is low.	■ The maximum throughput of a physical network adapter is not sufficient to meet the demand of the current workload.	■ Install VMware Tools on each virtual machine and configure the guest OS to use the best-performing network adapter driver (such as vmxnet3).
	■ Virtual machine network resource shares are too few.	■ Migrate virtual machines to other hosts or to other physical network adapters.
	■ Network packet size is too large, which results in high network latency. Use the VMware AppSpeed performance monitoring application or a third-party application to check network latency.	■ Verify that all NICs are running in full duplex mode.
		■ Implement TCP Segmentation Offload (TSO) and jumbo frames.
		■ Assign additional physical adapters as uplinks for the associated port groups.
	■ Network packet size is too small, which increases the demand for the CPU resources needed for processing each packet. Host CPU, or possibly virtual machine CPU, resources are not enough to handle the load.	■ Replace physical network adapters with high-bandwidth adapters.
		■ Place sets of virtual machines that communicate with each other regularly on the same ESXi host.

Symptoms	Likely Causes	Potential Solutions
Performance charts are empty.	■ Some metrics are not available for pre-ESXi 5.0 hosts. ■ Data is deleted when you move objects to vCenter Server or remove them. ■ Performance chart data for inventory objects that were moved to a new site by VMware vCenter Site Recovery Manager is deleted from the old site and not copied to the new site. ■ Performance charts data is deleted when you use VMware vMotion across vCenter Server instances. ■ Real-time statistics are not available for disconnected hosts or powered-off virtual machines. ■ Non-real-time statistics are rolled up at specific intervals. For example, 1-day statistics might not be available for 30 minutes after the current time, depending on when the sample period began. ■ The 1-day statistics are rolled up to create one data point every 30 minutes. If a delay occurs in the roll-up operation, the 1-week statistics might not be available for 1 hour after the current time. It takes 30 minutes for the 1-week collection interval, plus 30 minutes for the 1-day collection interval.	■ Upgrade hosts to a later version of ESXi. ■ Allow time for data collection on objects that were recently added, migrated, or recovered to the vCenter Server. ■ Power on all hosts and allow time for real-time statistics to collect. ■ Allow time for the required roll-ups for non-real-time statistics.

Symptoms	Likely Causes	Potential Solutions
	The 1-week statistics are rolled up to create one data point every 2 hours. If a delay occurs in the roll-up operations, the 1-month statistics might not be available for 3 hours. It takes 2 hours for the 1-month collection interval, plus 1 hour for the 1-week collection interval.	
	The 1-month statistics are rolled up to create one data point every day. If a delay occurs in the roll-up operations, the statistics might not be available for 1 day and 3 hours. It takes 1 day for the past year collection interval, plus 3 hours for the past month collection interval. During this time, the charts are empty.	

Monitoring and Managing Cluster Resources

On a Summary tab for a vSphere DRS cluster, you can see the Capacity, Used, and Free metrics for CPU, Memory, and Storage resources, as shown in Figure 10-2.

To examine the CPU and memory usage more closely, you can navigate to Monitor > vSphere DRS and select CPU Utilization or Memory Utilization. Each of these pages shows a bar graph, where each bar represents the total resource (CPU or memory) usage of a specific host and each bar is split into sections representing the resource usage of individual virtual machines. Likewise, you can select Monitor > vSphere DRS > Network Utilization to examine the network utilization of each host in the cluster.

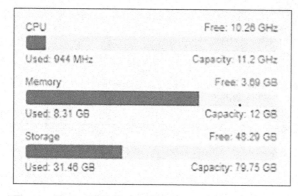

CPU   Free: 10.26 GHz

Used: 944 MHz   Capacity: 11.2 GHz

Memory   Free: 3.69 GB

Used: 8.31 GB   Capacity: 12 GB

Storage   Free: 48.29 GB

Used: 31.46 GB   Capacity: 79.75 GB

Figure 10-2 DRS Cluster Resource Usage

The Summary tab shows the vSphere DRS score, the number of DRS recommendations, and the number of DRS faults, as shown in Figure 10-3.

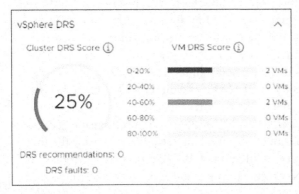

Figure 10-3 Sample DRS Score

If DRS is in manual mode, you can click on the number of DRS recommendations on the Summary tab, which is a link that takes you to the DRS Recommendations page. On the DRS Recommendations page, you can view the current recommendations, select those that you want to apply, and click the Apply Recommendations button. Each recommendation includes a description, such as which virtual machine to migrate to which host, and a reason, such as balance average memory loads.

Optionally, you can click the Run DRS Now button to make DRS perform its analysis and potentially generate new recommendations.

Monitoring and Managing Resource Pool Resources

To view resource pool configuration details, you can select a DRS cluster in the inventory pane and navigate to Hosts > Resource Pools. On that page, you can see all the resource pools that are direct children of the cluster. For each pool, you see the CPU and memory resource settings, including Reservation, Limit, Shares Setting (such as Low or Custom), Shares Value (numeric share value), and Allocation Type (Expandable or Non-Expandable). You can click on the name of a resource pool, which is a link to the pool's Summary page, which shows the current capacity, usage, and free compute resources for the resource pool. The summary page also shows the number of virtual machines, powered-on virtual machines, child resource pools, and vApps in the pool.

For more detail, you can navigate to Monitor > Utilization or to Monitor > Resource Allocation and select CPU, Memory, or Storage. For both CPU and memory resources, the Utilization page shows the resource configuration and the consumed, active, and worst-case allocation. The Utilization page also shows a breakdown of guest memory, including the Active Guest Memory, Swapped, Compressed, and Ballooned metrics.

You can use overview and advanced performance charts with resource pools. When you see undesired behavior, you can edit the settings for an existing resource pool to change the pool's CPU and memory shares, reservations, and limits. For example, consider a scenario where you configure two resource pools in a cluster with 100 GHz CPU capacity. In a pool with 40 virtual machines, you set CPU Shares to High. In another pool, which has 8 virtual machines, you set CPU Shares to Normal. You see in the performance charts that the virtual machines in the pool with the 40 virtual machines have greater CPU Ready values than the virtual machines in the other pool. You realize that although you used higher CPU shares for the first pool, the virtual machines are experiencing more CPU contention than are virtual machines in the second pool. To correct this, you could take one of the following actions:

- Increase the CPU shares on the first pool by using a custom value.

- Change the CPU shares on the second pool to Low.

- Set an appropriate CPU reservation on the first pool.

- Set an appropriate CPU limit on the second pool.

- Change the configuration to use scalable shares.

Monitoring and Managing Host Resources and Health

You can use the vSphere Client to monitor the state of host hardware components, such as CPUs, memory, fans, temperature, voltage, power, network, battery, storage, cable (interconnect), software components, watchdog, and PCI devices. To view the host hardware health status with the vSphere Client, you can use the following procedure:

Step 1. In the vSphere Client, select the host in the inventory pane and navigate to **Monitor > Hardware Health**.

Step 2. Select the type of information to view:

- **Sensors**
- **Storage Sensors**
- **Alerts and Warnings**
- **System Event Log**

The host health monitoring tool presents data gathered using Systems Management Architecture for Server Hardware (SMASH) profiles. The information displayed depends on the sensors available on the server hardware.

NOTE   You can also set alarms to trigger when the host health status changes.

If you participate in the Customer Experience Improvement Program (CEIP), you can configure Skyline Health to perform online health checks. If CEIP is not enabled, the Internet connectivity check is unavailable. A Skyline deployment includes a Cloud Services Organization and a Skyline Collector. The Skyline Organization is a logical container associated with your VMware Cloud Services account that gives you access to the Skyline Advisor in the Cloud Services Console. The Skyline Collector is a virtual appliance that you deploy within your environment to collect data and send it to csa.vmware.com.

You can use the following procedure to configure Skyline Health:

Step 1.   In the vSphere client, select a vCenter Server or a host in the inventory pane and navigate to **Monitor > Skyline Health**.

Step 2.   Expand the **Online Health Connectivity** category and select one of the following options:

- **CEIP**: Verifies whether CEIP is enabled for the vCenter Server.
- **Online Health Connectivity (Internet Check)**: Verifies vCenter Server to vmware.com connectivity via HTTPS/443.
- **Advisor**: Provides additional features, such as automatic support log bundle transfer with Log Assist. (Advisor is included in Production and Premier Support contracts.)
- **Audit CEIP Collected Data**: Allows you to view data collected and sent for CEIP.
- **Number of Online Health Checks Performed Successfully**: Indicates, as it says, how many checks have been performed successfully.

Step 3.   Expand the following categories and examine the related health warnings:

- **Compute Health Checks**
- **Network Health Checks**
- **Security Health Check**
- **Storage Health Checks**
- **General Health Checks**

Step 4.   Click **Retest** to run the health checks immediately.

Step 5.   Optionally, if issues are discovered, click the **Ask VMware** button to request a knowledge base article that describes how to resolve the issue.

> **NOTE** If you have access to Skyline Advisor, you can log in to Cloud Services at https://skyline.vmware.com/advisor by using your My VMware account and use the dashboard to view findings and recommendations discovered by Skyline.

Monitoring and Managing Virtual Machine Resources

Table 10-7 lists and describes some of the key metrics for monitoring virtual machines.

Table 10-7 Virtual Machine Metrics

Metric	Unit	Description
CPU Usage	%	Indicates the CPU workload for the virtual machine.
CPU Ready Time	ms	Indicates the amount of time a virtual CPU is ready to work (that is, has a workload and is ready to be scheduled) but is waiting to be scheduled on hardware. High CPU Ready Time is a sign of CPU contention.
Memory Consumed	KB	Indicates the amount of physical memory currently backing the virtual machine.
Memory Active	KB	Indicates the amount of consumed memory that is actively being read or written by the guest OS.
Memory Swap In Rate	Kbps	Indicates the amount of memory read from the virtual machine's swap file over time.
Disk Usage	Kbps	Indicates the disk throughput.
Virtual Disk Read Latency	ms	Indicates the average amount of time for a read operation to complete.
Network Usage	Kbps	Indicates the amount of data transmitted and received over time.
Network Transmit Packets Dropped	number	Indicates the number of packets transmitted to the network that were dropped.

Shares, Limits, and Reservations

You can set the CPU and memory shares, reservation, and limit on a virtual machine by using the following procedure:

Step 1. In the vSphere Client, right-click your virtual machine in the inventory and select **Edit Settings**.

Step 2. Edit the **Shares**, **Reservation**, and **Limit** values under CPU Resources.

Step 3. Set the **Shares**, **Reservation**, and **Limit** values under Memory Resources.

Step 4. Click **OK**.

The relative priority represented by each share changes whenever additional sibling virtual machines are powered on or powered off. Likewise, each share's relative priority changes whenever the shares on siblings are increased or decreased. This affects all virtual machines in the same resource pool.

For example, consider the following scenario:

- All virtual machines have the same number of vCPUs.

- Two virtual machines are run in a resource pool with CPU Limit set to 8 GHz.

- The virtual machines are CPU bound (that is, they are demanding more CPU resources than they are receiving).

- The virtual machines' CPU shares are set to Normal.

- You should expect each virtual machine's performance chart to show CPU Utilization as 4 GHz.

- When you power on a third CPU-bound sibling virtual machine with CPU Shares value set to High, you should expect to see that the new virtual machine uses 4 GHz and the first two machines drop to 2 GHz each.

To understand the impact of shares, consider another scenario, where a set of sibling virtual machines are frequently CPU bound and are using all the resources in their parent resource pool. During these periods of CPU contention in the resource pool, you see significantly high CPU Ready Time values on each of the virtual machines. You are only concerned about improving the performance of one specific virtual machine, so you increase its CPU Shares value. The CPU's Ready Time setting for that machine should decrease during periods of CPU contention, and the CPU Ready Time settings of its siblings should rise.

To guarantee that a specific amount of resources are always available to a running virtual machine, even when the physical server is heavily loaded, you can set its CPU or memory reservation. The vCenter Server or ESXi host allows you to power on a virtual machine only if there are enough unreserved resources to satisfy the virtual machine's reservation. Likewise, your attempts to increase the reservation on a running virtual machine (or a resource pool) succeed only if there are enough unreserved resources to satisfy the request. In the previous scenario, if you want to ensure that a virtual machine always has access to at least 1 GHz, regardless of the number or resource settings of siblings, you should set its CPU reservation to 1 GHz.

NOTE   The default CPU and memory reservation for a virtual machine is zero, meaning that its guest OS is not guaranteed any specific amount of either resource. Instead, with default settings, shares would be applied during periods of compute resource contention.

You can set limits for CPU, memory, and storage I/O for a virtual machine to establish an upper bound (maximum) amount of resources that can be allocated to the virtual machine. The host never allocates more than the limit, even when there are unused resources on the system. By default, the limits are set to Unlimited, which means the virtual machine's configured memory becomes its effective limit. Using limits has both benefits and drawbacks:

- **Benefits**: If you are concerned that the performance of a virtual machine may deteriorate as you add virtual machines to the cluster, you could set limits on the virtual machine to simulate having fewer available resources and measure its performance.

- **Drawbacks**: You might be wasting idle resources because the system prevents virtual machines from exceeding the limits that you set, even when the system is underutilized and idle resources are available.

NOTE   If you want to reduce the risk that a virtual machine may consume excessive resources and impact the performance of other virtual machines, you can consider setting low shares on the virtual machine. Low shares decrease the virtual machine's access to the resource during periods of resource contention but also do not prevent the virtual machine from using idle resources.

Admission Control

When you power on a virtual machine, the system checks the amount of available unreserved CPU and memory resources. The system determines whether it can guarantee the reservation for the virtual machine. This process is called *admission control*. If enough unreserved CPU and memory are available (or if there is no reservation), the virtual machine is powered on. Otherwise, an "Insufficient Resources" warning appears.

NOTE   Each virtual machine, including VMs with no user-specified memory reservation, may have some reservation for its memory overhead. The memory overhead reservation is considered by admission control.

NOTE   When the vSphere Distributed Power Management (DPM) feature is enabled and some hosts are in Standby Mode, their unreserved resources are considered available for admission control. If a virtual machine cannot be powered on without these resources, vSphere DPM makes a recommendation to power on one or more standby hosts.

VMware Tools and Microsoft Windows Perfmon

When VMware Tools is installed, VMware provides performance counters that enable you to view data within a Windows guest OS by using the Microsoft Windows Performance Monitor (Perfmon) utility. VMware provides virtual machine–specific performance counter libraries for the Windows Perfmon utility, which enables administrators to accurately examine virtual machine usage data and guest OS usage data within a single pane of glass.

For a Windows virtual machine where VMware Tools is installed, you can use the following procedure to examine VMware-specific statistics in the Windows Perfmon utility:

Step 1.   Log on to Windows and click **Start** > **Run**.

Step 2.   Enter **Perfmon** and press **Enter**.

Step 3.   In the Performance dialog box, click **Add**.

Step 4.   In the Add Counters dialog box, select **Use Local Computer Counters**.

Step 5.   Select a performance object whose name begins with **VM** (that is, a virtual machine performance object).

Step 6.   Select the counters that you want to display for that object.

Step 7.   If the performance object has multiple instances, select the instances you want to display.

Step 8.   Click **Add**.

Step 9.   Examine the data for the selected performance object.

Step 10.   Click **Close**.

Latency Sensitivity

If you have a latency-sensitive application, such as voice over IP (VoIP) or a media player application, you can edit the virtual machine's settings and set VM Options > Advanced > Latency Sensitivity to High. With this setting, you should ensure that all the virtual machine's configured CPU and memory are reserved. With this setting, the system effectively gives exclusive physical CPU access to each virtual CPU. If the virtual machine is in a DRS cluster, DRS automatically creates a VM–host soft affinity rule.

The Impact of Virtual Machine Configurations

The specific settings you configure for a virtual machine can impact its performance, as summarized in Table 10-8.

Table 10-8   The Impact of Virtual Machine Configurations

Configuration	Impact
Compute oversize/ undersize	An oversized compute size for a virtual machine may result in wasted resources. With an undersized compute size, the virtual machine may experience poor performance.
Virtual disk oversize/ undersize	An oversized virtual disk may result in wasted resources. With an undersized virtual disk, the virtual machine may experience denial of service.
VMDK provisioning types	If a virtual disk is thin provisioned, then you may be maximizing the use of your storage space while decreasing the virtual machine's performance and increasing its risk of denial of service.
Resource reservations	If a resource is reserved, you may be improving and guaranteeing the guest OS performance while reducing the density of virtual machines on the resource.
Independent disks	If a virtual disk is set to Independent Mode, then you are prevented from taking snapshots of it. If it is set to Independent–Nonpersistent, all changes are discarded when you power off or reset the virtual machine.
Guest OS type	The choice for the guest OS type during virtual machine creation directly impacts the type of virtual devices that are used in the virtual machine.
VMware Tools version	The VMware Tools version impacts the set of device drivers it provides to the guest OS.
Permissions	The permissions set on a virtual machine impacts who can use (power on, open a console), who can modify (change virtual hardware settings), and who can manage (set permissions, migrate) the virtual machine.

Other Virtual Machine Resource Management Features

You can configure virtual machines to support SRIOV, VGPU, RDMA, and Direct-Path I/O passthrough, as discussed in Chapter 14, "Managing Virtual Machines."

ESXTOP

ESXTOP is a utility that provides a detailed real-time look at resource usage from the ESXi shell. You can run ESXTOP in Interactive, Batch, or Replay Mode. You must have root user privileges. RESXTOP is a similar tool that can be installed and run from a Linux server and connected to ESXi hosts.

By default, when you issue the command **esxtop**, the utility opens in Interactive Mode to show the CPU panel, where statistics for each virtual machine and other groups are displayed in separate rows. To see just virtual machine statistics, you can press Shift+V. Each column provides CPU statistics, such as %USED, %WAIT, %RDY, %CSTP, and %SWPWT. To see statistics for the multiple worlds (processes) that comprise a virtual machine, you can press the E key and enter the virtual machine's ID. Figure 10-4 shows an example of an ESXTOP CPU panel, displaying virtual machine statistics with one virtual machine (GID 33791) expanded.

```
1:24:45pm up  1:31, 562 worlds, 3 VMs, 4 vCPUs; CPU load average: 0.12, 0.14, 0.19
PCPU USED(%):   11   11 AVG:   11
PCPU UTIL(%):   11   11 AVG:   11

     GID NAME               NWLD   %USED    %RUN   %SYS  %WAIT %VMWAIT    %RDY   %IDLE  %OVRLP   %CSTP  %MLMTD  %SWPWT
   24851 kms-01b              10   12.86   12.92   0.06 984.53    0.31    2.84  185.43    0.07    0.00    0.00    0.00
   33791 vmx                   1    0.08    0.01   0.07  99.97       -    0.01    0.00    0.00    0.00    0.00    0.00
   33791 NetWorld-VM-135       1    0.00    0.00   0.00  99.98       -    0.00    0.00    0.00    0.00    0.00    0.00
   33791 vmast.135915          1    0.09    0.10   0.00  99.35       -    0.54    0.00    0.00    0.00    0.00    0.00
   33791 vmx-vthread-135       1    0.00    0.00   0.00  99.99       -    0.00    0.00    0.00    0.00    0.00    0.00
   33791 vmx-filtPoll:wi       1    0.00    0.00   0.00  99.98       -    0.00    0.00    0.00    0.00    0.00    0.00
   33791 vmx-mks:win10         1    0.01    0.01   0.00  99.98       -    0.00    0.00    0.00    0.00    0.00    0.00
   33791 vmx-svga:win10        1    0.00    0.00   0.00  99.99       -    0.00    0.00    0.00    0.00    0.00    0.00
   33791 vmx-vcpu-0:win1       1    1.55    1.55   0.00  96.95    0.17    1.50   96.78    0.02    0.00    0.00    0.00
   33791 LSI-135915:0          1    0.00    0.00   0.00  99.99       -    0.00    0.00    0.00    0.00    0.00    0.00
   33780 app-01b               9    1.04    1.00   0.03 897.71    0.80    1.19   97.11    0.00    0.00    0.00    0.00
```

Figure 10-4 Sample ESXTOP CPU Panel

You can change the view from the CPU panel to other panels by using keystrokes. For example, you can press the M key for the memory panel, the V key for the virtual machine storage panel, or the N key for the network panel. Table 10-9 describes some of the important statistics available for each panel.

Table 10-9 Important ESXTOP Panels and Metrics

Panel	Statistic	Description
CPU	%USED	Percentage of physical CPU core cycles used by the virtual machine.
CPU	%RUN	Percentage of total time scheduled for the virtual machine without accounting for hyperthreading, system time, co-stopping, and waiting: %RUN = 100% − %RDY − %CSTP − %WAIT
CPU	%RDY	Percentage of time the virtual machine was ready to run but was not provided CPU resources on which to execute. Indicator of CPU contention on the host.
CPU	%WAIT	Percentage of time the virtual machine spent in the blocked or busy wait state, including idle time. %WAIT includes %SWPWT.

Panel	Statistic	Description
CPU	%CSTP	Percentage of time a virtual machine spends in a ready, co-descheduled state. A high value indicates that the virtual machine's multiple CPUs are in contention.
CPU	%SWPWT	Percentage of time a virtual machine spends waiting for the host to swap memory.
Memory	MEMSZ	Amount of physical memory allocated to a virtual machine: MEMSZ = GRANT + MCTLSZ + SWCUR + "Never Touched"
Memory	GRANT	Amount of guest physical memory mapped to a virtual machine.
Memory	CNSM	Amount of the memory consumed by the virtual machine: CNSM = GRANT – Shared Memory
Memory	SWCUR	Amount of memory swapped by the virtual machine.
Memory	SWR/s	Rate at which the host swaps in memory from disk for the virtual machine.
Memory	OVHD	Amount of memory used for virtual machine overhead, which is memory charged to the virtual machine that is not used by the guest OS.
Virtual Machine Storage	READS/s	Number of read commands issued per second.
Virtual Machine Storage	WRITES/s	Number of write commands issued per second.
Virtual Machine Storage	MBREAD/s	Megabytes read per second.
Virtual Machine Storage	LAT/rd	Average latency (in milliseconds) per read.
Network	PKRRX/s	Number of packets received per second.
Network	MbTX/s	Megabits transmitted per second.
Network	%DRPTX	Percentage of transmit packets dropped. Indicates that the physical network adapter cannot meet the demand, perhaps due to the load from other virtual machines.
Network	%DRPRX	Percentage of receive packets dropped. Indicates that insufficient CPU resources are available for network processing.

NOTE   The Network panel contains a row for each NIC in a virtual machine rather than a row for each virtual machine. The E and Shift+V keystrokes are not applicable to the Network panel.

You can use the **-b** argument to run ESXTOP in Batch Mode, where you can collect statistics in a CSV file. You can later manipulate this file with other tools, such as Microsoft Perfmon or Excel. For example, you can use the following command to collect statistics in a file named mydata.csv:

```
esxtop -b > mydata.csv
```

You can use ESXTOP in Replay Mode, where it uses pre-collected data rather than real-time data. To collect the data, you should run **vm-support** in Snapshot Mode, specifying the data collection interval and duration (in seconds), as shown in the following example:

```
vm-support -S -d 3600 -I 5
```

After collecting the data, you must unpack and decompress the resulting tar file. Then you can run ESXTOP in Replay Mode, providing the path to the data file, as shown here:

```
esxtop -R vm-support_dir_path
```

VIMTOP

VIMTOP is a tool you can run in vCenter Server Appliance to see resource usage for the services that are running. It is like ESXTOP but displays services, such as vCenter Server, Certificate Manager, vPostgres, and ESXi Agent Manager, rather than virtual machines and ESXi worlds (processes). You can use VIMTOP to identify which service is using the most compute, disk, or network resources whenever vCenter Server is running poorly.

vCenter Server Management

In vCenter Server Management (formerly known as the VAMI), you select Monitor to view the resource usage of the vCenter Server. To see compute usage graphs, select Monitor > CPU and Memory. To see the usage of each storage partition, select Monitor > Disks. To use a graph where you can select and view specific network metrics, select Monitor > Network.

You can navigate to Monitor > Database to view database utilization of alarms, events, tasks, and statistics. You can also view the overall space utilization of the database and database log.

Events, Alarms, and Automated Actions

vSphere has a configurable events and alarms subsystem that tracks events throughout vSphere and stores the data in log files and in the vCenter Server database. It enables you to specify the conditions under which alarms are triggered. Alarms can change state from normal (green) to warning (yellow) to alert (red), depending on changing conditions. Triggered alarms can automatically launch alarm actions.

Events

Events are simply recorded incidents, such as user actions or system actions, involving a host or any object managed by vCenter Server. The following are a few examples:

- A license key expires.
- A virtual machine is migrated.
- A virtual machine is powered on.
- A host connection is lost.

Event data includes details such as who generated the event, when it occurred, and what type of event it was. Table 10-10 describes the types of events.

Table 10-10   Event Types

Event Type	Description
Audit	Provides data concerning events that are tracked, including action details such as who did it, when it occurred, and the IP address of the user. This data is crucial for the security framework.
Information	Indicates that the operation completed successfully.
Warning	Indicates a potential risk to the system that needs to be addressed. This event does not terminate the process or operation.
Alert	Indicates that a fatal problem has occurred in the system and terminates the process or operation.

Viewing Events in the vSphere Client

You can use the following procedure to view events in the vSphere Client:

Step 1.   In the vSphere Client, select an object in the inventory pane and navigate to **Monitor > Events**.

Step 2.   Select an event to see its details.

Step 3.   Use the column headings to sort the events, show columns, hide columns, and filter the events.

Viewing the System Event Log

To view system events that are recorded in the vCenter Server database, you can use the following procedure:

Step 1.   Log on to the vSphere Client as a user with the Global.Diagnostics privilege.

Step 2.   Select the vCenter Server in the inventory pane.

Step 3.   Navigate to **Monitor > Hardware Health**.

Step 4.   Click **System Event Log**.

Step 5.   Optionally, click **Export**.

Streaming Events to a Remote Syslog Server

You can enable remote streaming, such that the vCenter Server streams newly generated events to a remote syslog server. In the syslog server, the events have the following format:

```
<syslog-prefix> : Event [eventId] [partInfo] [createdTime]
[eventType] [severity] [user] [target] [chainId] [desc]
```

Messages that are longer than 1024 characters are split into multiple syslog messages.

As an alternative to streaming events, you can forward events. When you forward events, the events are sent to a remote server rather than recorded.

You can use the following procedure to forward vCenter Server logs to a remote syslog server:

Step 1.   Log on to VAMI as root.

Step 2.   Select **Syslog**.

Step 3.   In the Forwarding Configuration section, click **Configure**.

Step 4.   In the Create Forwarding Configuration pane, enter the server address of the destination host. The maximum number of supported destination hosts is three.

Step 5.   Select a protocol (**TLS**, **TCP**, **RELP**, or **UDP**) to use.

Step 6.   Provide a port number.

Step 7.   Optionally, add more destination servers.

Step 8.   Click **Save**.

Step 9.   Optionally, click **Send Test Message**.

You can configure events to be written to the vCenter Server streaming facility. Event streaming is disabled by default. You can use the following procedure to stream events to a remote syslog server:

Step 1.   In the vSphere Client, select the vCenter Server in the inventory pane and navigate to **Configure** > **Settings** > **Advanced Settings**.

Step 2.   Click **Edit**.

Step 3.   Enable the **vpxd.event.syslog** option.

Alarms

An alarm is a notification that is activated in response to an event, a set of conditions, or the state of an inventory object. Table 10-11 describes the elements that are used in an alarm definition.

Table 10-11   Alarm Definition Elements

Element	Description
Name	A name (label) that is used to identify the alarm
Description	Text that is useful for understanding the purpose of the alarm
Targets	The type of object that is monitored by the alarm
Alarm Rules	A set of rules that defines the alarm's triggers, severity, and actions
Last Modified	The date of the most recent change to the alarm definition

vSphere 8.0 provides many preconfigured alarms for hosts, virtual machines, datastores, licenses, host flash capacity, vSAN, Fault Tolerance, host system, VASA providers, storage policies compliance, vSphere HA, Storage DRS, virtual switches, datastore clusters, and more. These alarms are triggered by specific events or conditions. They are intended to alert you when something is becoming unhealthy or unavailable or when the workload or performance of something is abnormal. You can use the vSphere Client to edit, disable, enable, and delete alarms.

You can create custom alarms. For example, you might want to monitor the memory usage of all virtual machines in a specific vSphere cluster. In the vSphere Client, you can select the cluster in the inventory, create an alarm for the cluster, set the alarm's Targets value to virtual machine, and configure rules with triggers based on memory usage.

NOTE   You can enable, disable, and modify alarms only from the object at which the alarm is defined. For example, if you define a virtual machine memory alarm on a cluster, you cannot change the alarm at the individual virtual machine level.

Viewing and Acknowledging Triggered Alarms

To view triggered alarms, you can use the following procedure:

Step 1.   In the vSphere Client, select an object in the inventory pane and navigate to **Monitor > Issues and Alarms**.

Step 2.   Click **Triggered Alarms**.

Step 3.   Optionally, select an alarm and click **Acknowledge**.

You can acknowledge an alarm to let other users know that you are taking ownership of the issue and to prevent the alarm from sending more email messages. The alarm, however, is still visible in the system.

NOTE   After you acknowledge an alarm in the vSphere Client, its alarm actions are discontinued. Alarms are not cleared or reset when acknowledged.

To clear an alarm (that is, reset its state to normal), you need the Alarm.Set Alarm Status privilege. You can select a triggered alarm and choose Reset to Green.

Creating Alarm Definitions

To create or configure an alarm, you must use a user account with the Alarms.Create Alarm or Alarms.Modify Alarm privilege. To create an alarm, you can use the following procedure:

Step 1.   In the vSphere client, select an object in the inventory pane and navigate to **Configure > More > Alarm Definitions**.

Step 2.   Click **Add**.

Step 3.   Provide the name, description, target type, and target for the alarm.

Step 4.   Click **Next**.

Step 5.   Create an alarm rule by specifying the following:

- **Conditions**: Set this option to **Trigger, Arguments, Operator**, or **Threshold**.
- **Severity**: Set this option to **Warning** or **Critical**.
- **Actions**: Set this option to **Send Email Notifications, Send SNMP Traps**, or **Run Script**.

Step 6.   Optionally, click **Add Another Rule, Duplicate Rule**, or **Remove Rule**.

Step 7.   Click **Next**.

Step 8.   Specify alarm reset rules by enabling the **Reset the Alarm to Green** option and providing details, such as arguments, operators, and actions.

Step 9.   Click **Next**.

Step 10.   Click **Enable This Alarm**.

To edit an alarm, select an inventory object, navigate to Configure > Alarm Definitions, select the alarm, and choose Edit. Apply steps 3 through 10 from the preceding procedure.

Alarm Actions

Alarm actions are operations that are automatically triggered by alarms. Table 10-12 provides details on available alarm actions.

Table 10-12   Alarm Actions

Action	Details
Send Email Notification	Indicates the recipient email address.
	Requires that you first configure the mail settings for your vCenter Server. You must set the primary receiver URL to the DNS name or IP address of your SNMP receiver. You should set the receiver port to an appropriate value between 1 and 65535 and set the community string to an appropriate community identifier.
Send SNMP Traps	Requires that you first configure the SNMP Receivers settings for your vCenter Server. You must set Mail.Server to the DNS name or IP address of your SMTP gateway. You must set Mail.Sender to the email address of the sender.
Run Scripts	Provides the full pathname of the command or script, formatted into a single string. The execution occurs on the vCenter Server Appliance.
Advanced Actions	Only applicable to alarms that target virtual machines and hosts. Examples of host actions include Enter Maintenance Mode and Exit Maintenance Mode. Examples of virtual machine actions include Migrate VM and Reboot Guest on VM.

Advanced Use Cases for Alarms

You can create custom alerts with notifications for many purposes, such as the following:

- Something has failed or disconnected (such as host connection failure or VASA provider disconnection).

- Something is not performing well (such as excessive CPU ready time, memory swapping, disk latency, or packets dropped).

- Health is poor (such as vSAN health, key management server health, or vCenter HA cluster health).

Logging in vSphere

It is important that you understand logging in vSphere components and related products and that you be prepared to implement logging.

ESXi Logs

Table 10-13 provides details on most of the ESXi log files, including the location and purpose of each of them. You should become familiar with each of them and learn which logs are useful for various troubleshooting scenarios. For example, when troubleshooting virtual machine issues, the only directly useful logs are vmkernel, vmkwarning, hostd, and the specific virtual machine's log files. When troubleshooting issues related to the connection between an ESXi host and the vCenter Server, the vpxa log is most useful.

Table 10-13 ESXi Log Files

Component	Location	Description
VMkernel	/var/log/vmkernel.log	Data related to virtual machines and ESXi
VMkernel warnings	/var/log/vmkwarning.log	Data related to virtual machines
VMkernel summary	/var/log/vmksummary.log	Data related to uptime and availability statistics for ESXi
ESXi host agent	/var/log/hostd.log	Data related to the agent that manages and configures the ESXi host and its virtual machines
vCenter agent	/var/log/vpxa.log	Data related to the agent that communicates with vCenter Server
ESXi Shell	/var/log/shell.log	Data related to each command typed into the ESXi shell as well as shell events
Authentication	/var/log/auth.log	Data related to event authentication for the local system
System messages	/var/log/syslog.log	General log messages that can be used for troubleshooting

Component	Location	Description
Virtual machines	vmware.log, located in the same folder as the virtual machine configuration file	Data related to virtual machine power events, system failure information, tool status and activity, time sync, virtual hardware changes, vMotion migrations, machine clones, and more
Trusted infrastructure agent	/var/run/log/kmxa.log	Data related to the client service on the ESXi trusted host
Key provider service	/var/run/log/kmxd.log	Data related to the vSphere Trust Authority key provider service
Attestation service	/var/run/log/attestd.log	Data related to the vSphere Trust Authority attestation service
ESX token service	/var/run/log/esxtokend.log	Data related to the vSphere Trust Authority ESXi token service
ESX API forwarder	/var/run/log/esxapiadapter. log	Data related to the vSphere Trust Authority API forwarder
Quick Boot	/var/log/loadESX.log	Data related to restarting an ESXi host through Quick Boot

You can use the ESXi host client to examine the logs on a specific ESXi host by navigating to Monitor > Logs and selecting a specific log file. You can scroll through the log and search for specific text. You can select a log, click Actions, and choose Open in New Window or Generate a Support Bundle.

Likewise, you can use the ESXi Direct Console User Interface (DCUI) to view system logs. In the DCUI, after you click View System Logs and select the log you want, you can use the Enter key (or Spacebar) to scroll through the log messages and press the forward slash (/) key to begin a search.

If you have the Global.Diagnostics privilege, you can also use the vSphere Client to export a host's system logs by following these steps:

Step 1.   In the vSphere Client, right-click an ESXi host in the inventory pane.

Step 2.   Click **Export System Logs**.

Step 3.   Select the appropriate objects.

Step 4.   Optionally, click **Gather Performance Data**.

Step 5.   Optionally, provide a password for encrypted coredumps.

Step 6.   Click **Export Logs**.

Step 7.   Monitor the status of the Downloading Log Bundles task in the Recent Tasks pane.

When you finish this process, the file is located in the default location. On a Windows desktop, the location is the Downloads folder, and the filename begins with VMware-vCenter-support.

NOTE In step 3, you can select or deselect entire categories, such as System, Virtual Machines, and Storage. You can also select or deselect specific objects within each category, such as logs and coredumps.

You can collect ESXi log files by using the **/usr/bin/vm-support** command, which generates a file named using the following format:

```
esx-date-unique-xnumber.tgz
```

vCenter Server Logs

The main logs in a vCenter Server appliance are located in /var/log/vmware. The most important logs are in the vpxd subdirectory. Some other sibling subdirectories include vsan-health, vsphere-ui, and vpostgres. The following logs are associated vCenter Server authentication services:

- **VMware Directory Service**: /var/log/vmware/vmdird/
- **VMware Single Sign-On**: /var/log/vmware/sso/
- **VMWare Certificate Authority (VMCA)**: /var/log/vmware/vmcad/
- **VMware Endpoint Certificate Store (VECS)**: /var/log/vmware/vmafdd/
- **VMware Lookup Service**: /var/log/vmware/sso/lookupServer.log

Uploading System Logs to VMware

To export system logs from the vCenter Server and all its hosts, you can use the procedure outlined in the section "ESXi Logs" but begin by selecting the vCenter Server instead of a specific host. In the wizard, you can select which hosts to include, and you can optionally select Include vCenter Server and vSphere UI Client Logs.

You can export a vCenter Server instance's support bundle by using the URL shown on the DCUI home screen (https://*FQDN*:443/appliance/support-bundle).

Alternatively, you can run the **vc-support.sh** script in the vCenter Server appliance Bash Shell to collect the support bundle.

You can directly upload a log package to an open VMware service request by using the following procedure:

Step 1.   In the vSphere Client, navigate to **Administration > Support**.

Step 2.   Click **Upload File to Service Request**.

Step 3.   Provide a service request ID.

Step 4.   Click **Choose File**, select the appropriate log bundle, and click **OK**.

Log Levels

The default log level setting is Info; this is where errors, warnings, and informational level are logged. You can change the log level to lower levels, such as Verbose, which is useful for troubleshooting and debugging but is not recommended for normal use in production environments. You can use the vSphere Client to change the logging level by selecting the vCenter Server, selecting Configure > Settings > General > Edit, and setting the logging settings to the appropriate levels, as described in Table 10-14.

Table 10-14   vCenter Server Logging Options

Logging Option	Description
None (Disable Logging)	No vCenter Server logging occurs.
Error (Errors Only)	The vCenter Server collects only error entries in its log files.
Warning (Warning and Errors)	The vCenter Server collects warning and error entries in its log files.
Info (Normal Logging)	The vCenter Server collects information, warning, and error entries in its log files.
Verbose (Verbose)	The vCenter Server collects verbose, information, warning, and error entries in its log files.
Trivia (Extended Verbose)	The vCenter Server collects trivia, verbose, information, warning, and error entries in its log files.

Although setting the logging level to Verbose or Trivia may be beneficial for troubleshooting, doing so for long durations may cause noticeable vCenter Server performance degradation. VMware recommends that you use these levels in rare cases, such as while actively troubleshooting, and that you reset the logging level immediately afterward. Changes to the logging level are saved in the vCenter Server configuration file /etc/vmware-vpx/vpxd.cfg. You can make additional changes to logging behavior by editing the advanced settings of a vCenter Server. For example, you can use the vSphere Client to edit the following settings, which impact log size, retention, rotation, and compression:

- config.log.level
- config.log.maxFileNum

- config.log.maxFileSize
- config.log.compressOnRoll

NOTE By default, vCenter Server vpxd log files are rolled up and compressed into .gz files. You can turn off compression for vpxd log files by adding the log.compressOnRoll key with the value false to the vCenter Server advanced settings.

Configuring Syslog on ESXi Hosts

You can use the following procedure to configure the syslog service for a host:

Step 1. In the vSphere Client, select a host in the inventory pane and navigate to **Configure** > **System** > **Advanced System Settings**.

Step 2. Click **Edit**.

Step 3. Filter for **syslog**.

Step 4. To set up logging globally for the following options, select the appropriate option and enter the appropriate value:

- **Syslog.global.defaultRotate**: Maximum number of logs to keep when rotating logs.

- **Syslog.global.defaultSize**: Size of log (in KB) before triggering a log rotation.

- **Syslog.global.LogDir**: Directory in a VMFS or NFS datastore to store logs specified in the format [*datastore*] */path*. For example, to store logs in the /vmfs/volumes/VMFS-01/systemlogs folder, specify [VMFS-01] /systemlogs.

- **Syslog.global.logDirUnique**: A subdirectory for the host at the specified path, which is useful when multiple hosts use the same shared datastore for logging.

- **Syslog.global.LogHost**: Remote syslog host and port to which messages are forwarded. For example, to forward to a server named syslogsvr-1 using port 1514, specify ssl://syslogsvr-1:1514.

Step 5. Optionally, select specific log names and change the number of rotations and log size for just the specific log.

Step 6. Click **OK**.

You can control how log files are maintained for virtual machines. A new log file is created each time you power on or resume a virtual machine or whenever the file size exceeds the vmx.log.rotateSize value, unless the value is 0 (default). VMware recommends saving 10 log files, each one limited to no less than 2 MB. If you need logs for a longer time span, you can set vmx.log.keepOld to 20.

You can use the following procedure to change the number of log files for a single virtual machine:

Step 1. In the vSphere Client, right-click a host or a virtual machine in the inventory pane and click **Edit Settings**.

Step 2. Select **VM Options > Advanced**.

Step 3. Click **Edit Configuration**.

Step 4. Add or edit the **vmx.log.keepOld** parameter, set to the appropriate number.

Step 5. Click **OK**.

NOTE To set the vmx.log.keepOld value for all virtual machines on a specific host, edit the /etc/vmware/config file and add or edit a line like the following:

```
vmx.log.keepOld = "10"
```

You can modify the /etc/vmware/logfilters file on a host to change its logging behavior. In this file, you can add entries specifying the following options:

- Add **numLogs** to specify the maximum number of log entries before the specified log messages are filtered and ignored. Use 0 to filter and ignore all the specified log messages.

- Add **Ident** to specify one or more system components to apply the filter.

- Add **logRegexp** to specify a case-sensitive phrase to filter the log messages by their content.

- Add the following line to the /etc/vmsyslog.conf file: **enable_logfilters = true**.

- Run the command **esxcli system syslog reload**.

vRealize Log Insight (vRLI)

To collect and analyze vSphere data using vRLI, after you deploy vRLI, follow these steps:

Step 1. In the vRLI web interface, navigate to the **Administration** tab.

Step 2. Click **Integration > vSphere**.

Step 3. Provide the host name and credentials required to connect to a vCenter Server.

Step 4. Click **Test Connection**.

Step 5. If you use an untrusted SSL certificate, click **Accept** in the dialog.

Step 6. Click **Save**.

Step 7. Use the vRLI web interface to configure the data collection from vCenter.

Exam Preparation Tasks

As mentioned in the section "Book Features and Exam Preparation Methods" in the Introduction, you have some choices for exam preparation: the exercises here, Chapter 15, "Final Preparation," and the exam simulation questions on the companion website.

Review All the Key Topics

Review the most important topics in this chapter, noted with the Key Topic icon in the outer margin of the page. Table 10-15 lists these key topics and the page number on which each is found.

Table 10-15 Key Topics for Chapter 10

Key Topic Element	Description	Page Number
List	Add a host using Quickstart	369
Table 10-2	Use cases for VM–VM rules	373
List	Configuring vSphere HA admission control	375
Section	Configuring proactive HA	376
Section	Performance graph overview	379
List	Configuring Skyline Health	391
Section	The impact of virtual machine configuration	396

Complete Tables and Lists from Memory

Print a copy of Appendix B, "Memory Table" (found on the companion website), or at least the section for this chapter, and complete the tables and lists from memory. Appendix C, "Memory Table Answers" (also on the companion website), includes completed tables and lists to check your work.

Define Key Terms

Define the following key terms from this chapter and check your answers in the glossary:

client performance charts, ESXTOP, CPU Ready Time, VIMTOP

Review Questions

1. You are creating a resource pool in a vSphere DRS cluster. Which of the following is a default setting?

   a. Memory Limit is disabled.

   b. CPU Shares is 0.

   c. Memory Reservation is 0.

   d. CPU Reservation is normal.

2. You want to configure predictive DRS in your vSphere cluster. Which of the following is a requirement?

   a. Set DRS to Fully Automated.

   b. In the cluster, set Provide Data to vSphere Predictive DRS to True.

   c. In Aria Operations, set Provide Data to vSphere Predictive DRS to True.

   d. In Aria Automation, set Provide Data to vSphere Predictive DRS to True.

3. You are configuring a vSphere HA cluster and do not want it to automatically reserve resources for failure. What setting should you use?

   a. Set Cluster Resource Percentage to 0.

   b. Set Cluster Resource Percentage to 100.

   c. Set Define Host Failover Capacity to Dedicated Host Failures.

   d. Set Define Host Failover Capacity to Disabled.

4. You want to use a command-line tool that shows real-time CPU statistics for the services running in the vCenter Server. Which should you choose?

   a. VIMTOP

   b. ESXTOP

   c. Performance charts

   d. vCenter Server Management Interface

5. You are examining vSphere logs. Which of the following logs is in the same folder as the virtual machine configuration file?

   a. vpxa.log

   b. vmksummary.log

   c. auth.log

   d. vmware.log

This chapter covers the following topics:

- Configuring and Managing vSAN
- Managing Datastores
- Storage DRS and SIOC
- iSCSI, iSER, NVMe, and PMem
- Multipathing, Storage Policies, and vVols

This chapter contains information related to VMware vSphere 8.x Professional (2V0-21.23) exam objectives 1.3.1, 1.3.2, 1.3.3, 1.3.4, 1.3.5, 1.3.6, 1.3.7, 1.3.8, 1.7.1, 5.5, 7.4, 7.4.1, 7.4.2, and 7.4.3.

## CHAPTER 11

Managing Storage

This chapter provides information on configuring and managing storage in a vSphere environment.

"Do I Know This Already?" Quiz

The "Do I Know This Already?" quiz allows you to assess whether you should study this entire chapter or move quickly to the "Exam Preparation Tasks" section. In any case, the authors recommend that you read the entire chapter at least once. Table 11-1 outlines the major headings in this chapter and the corresponding "Do I Know This Already?" quiz questions. You can find the answers in Appendix A, "Answers to the 'Do I Know This Already?' Quizzes and Review Questions."

Table 11-1 "Do I Know This Already?" Foundation Topics Section-to-Question Mapping

Foundation Topics Section	Questions
Configuring and Managing vSAN	1, 2
Managing Datastores	3, 4
Storage DRS and SIOC	5, 6
iSCSI, iSER, NVMe, and PMem	7, 8
Multipathing, Storage Policies, and vVols	9, 10

1. You are configuring a hybrid vSAN OSA cluster in a vSphere environment. By default, what percentage of the flash space is used as a write buffer?

   a. 100%

   b. 70%

   c. 30%

   d. 0%

2. You are configuring vSAN in a vSphere environment. Which of the following is supported when using Quickstart to configure a vSAN cluster?

    a. Hosts with no local storage

    b. Hosts with an existing vSAN configuration

    c. Hosts with dissimilar network configurations

    d. Hosts with local storage

3. You want to increase the size of a VMFS 6 datastore. Which of the following statements is true?

    a. The only means to increase the size of a datastore is to add an extent.

    b. If Expandable = NO, you cannot add an extent to the datastore.

    c. If the datastore is 100% full, you cannot increase its capacity.

    d. If Expandable = YES, you can increase the datastore size using available space on the storage device that is backing the datastore.

4. You are configuring NFS datastores for your vSphere 8.0 environment. Which of the following statements is true?

    a. You can use multiple IP addresses with any NFS datastore.

    b. You can use multiple IP addresses with NFS Version 4.1 but not with NFS Version 3.

    c. You can use multiple IP addresses with NFS Version 3 but not with NFS Version 4.1.

    d. You cannot use multiple IP addresses with any version of NFS.

5. In a vSphere 8 environment, you are configuring SIOC and want to change the threshold it uses to begin prioritizing I/O based on shares. Which of the following options is the acceptable range?

    a. 1 to 100 ms

    b. 5 to 100 ms

    c. 30 to 100 ms

    d. 10 to 50 ms

6. You want to perform maintenance on a datastore that is a member of a datastore cluster. Which of the following actions should you take?

    a. Right-click the host and choose Enter Maintenance Mode.

    b. Right-click the datastore and choose Enter Maintenance Mode.

    c. Right-click the host and choose Enter SDRS Maintenance Mode.

    d. Right-click the datastore and choose Enter SDRS Maintenance Mode.

7. You need to configure an ESXi 8.0 host to access shared NVMe devices using RDMA over Converged Ethernet (RoCE) Version 2. Which steps should you take? (Choose three.)

   a. Configure a VMkernel network adapter.

   b. Add a software adapter to the host's network adapters.

   o. Navigate to Storage Adapters > RDMA Adapters and verify the VMkernel adapter bindings.

   d. Navigate to Networking > RDMA Adapters and verify the VMkernel adapter bindings.

   e. Add a software adapter to the host's storage adapters.

8. In a vSphere 8.0 environment, you want to allow a virtual machine to use NVDIMMs as standard memory. What should you configure?

   a. vPMemDisk

   b. vPMem

   c. NVMe-oF

   d. RDMA

9. You want to set the path selection policy for a storage device managed by NMP such that it uses a preferred path. Which of the following policies should you choose?

   a. FIXED

   b. LB_RR

   c. VMW_PSP_FIXED

   d. VMW_PSP_RR

10. You are preparing to configure vVols in a vSphere 8.0 environment. Which of the following components should you configure in the storage system? (Choose two.)

    a. Protocol endpoints

    b. Storage containers

    c. LUNs

    d. Virtual volumes

Foundation Topics

Configuring and Managing vSAN

This section provides information on configuring and managing vSAN clusters and vSAN datastores.

Preparing for vSAN

Before creating and configuring vSAN clusters, you should be aware of the following vSAN characteristics:

- At a minimum, a standard vSAN cluster must include three hosts with capacity devices. It can include hosts with or without capacity devices. To use a vSAN datastore, an ESXi host must be a member of the vSAN cluster.

- Multiple vSAN clusters can be configured in a single vCenter Server instance. For best results, use uniformly configured hosts in all the vSAN clusters.

- For vSAN Original Storage Architecture (OSA), if a host contributes capacity, it must have at least one flash cache device and one capacity device. For vSAN Express Storage Architecture (ESA), if a host contributes capacity, then it must contribute at least four devices forming a storage pool.

- Only local (or directly attached) devices can participate in vSAN. vSAN does not share devices with other vSphere features.

- For vSAN OSA, in hybrid clusters, magnetic disks are used for capacity, and flash devices serve as a read cache and a write buffer. In a hybrid cluster, 70% of the flash space is used for the read cache, and 30% is used for the write buffer.

- For vSAN OSA, in all-flash clusters, one designated flash device is used as a write cache, and additional flash devices are used for capacity. No read cache is used. All read requests come directly from the flash pool capacity.

- To use the full set of vSAN OSA capabilities, the ESXi hosts that participate in vSAN clusters must be Version 7.0 Update 1 or later.

- To use vSAN 8.0 ESA, ESXi 8.0 or later is required.

It is important to ensure that you meet all the vSAN hardware, cluster, software, and network requirements described in Chapter 2, "Storage Infrastructure."

Creating a vSAN Cluster with Quickstart

Quickstart, which is described in Chapter 10, "Managing and Monitoring Clusters and Resources," allows you to quickly create, configure, and expand a vSAN cluster, using recommended default settings for networking, storage, and services. It uses the vSAN health service to help you validate and correct configuration issues, using a checklist consisting of green messages, yellow warnings, and red failures.

To use Quickstart to configure a vSAN cluster, the hosts must use ESXi 6.0 Update 2 or later. The hosts must have a similar network configuration to allow Quickstart to configure network settings based on cluster requirements. You can use Quickstart to configure vSAN on an existing cluster by using the following procedure:

Step 1. In the vSphere Client, select the cluster in the Hosts and Clusters inventory and click **Configure** > **Configuration** > **Quickstart**.

Step 2. On the Cluster Basics card, click **Edit**, select the vSAN service, and optionally select other services, such as DRS and vSphere HA. Optionally, select **Enable vSAN ESA**. Then click **Finish**.

Step 3. Click **Add Hosts** > **Add** and use the wizard to add hosts to the cluster.

Step 4. On the Cluster Configuration card, click **Configure** and use the wizard to configure the following:

   a. On the Configure the Distributed Switches page, enter networking settings, including distributed switches, port groups, and physical adapters.

   b. On the vMotion Traffic page, enter vMotion IP address information.

   c. On the Storage Traffic page, enter storage IP address information.

   d. On the Advanced Options page, provide vSAN cluster settings. Optionally, provide settings for DRS, HA, and EVC.

   e. On the Claim Disks page, select disks on each host to claim for vSAN. For OSA, choose one cache device and at least one capacity device. For ESA, choose at least four capacity devices.

   f. Optionally, on the Create Fault Domains page, define fault domains for hosts that can fail together.

   g. On the Ready to Complete page, verify the cluster settings and click **Finish**.

Manually Enabling vSAN

You can use the following procedure to manually enable vSAN:

Step 1.   Prepare a VMkernel network adapter on each participating host:

   a. In the vSphere Client, select a host in the inventory pane and navigate to **Networking > VMkernel Adapters**.

   b. Click the **Add Networking** icon.

   c. Use the wizard to configure the adapter's network settings and to enable vSAN.

Step 2.   In the inventory pane, right-click a data center and select **New Cluster**.

Step 3.   Provide a name for the cluster.

Step 4.   Optionally, configure other cluster settings, such as DRS, vSphere HA, and EVC.

Step 5.   Add hosts to the cluster.

Step 6.   Navigate to **Configure > vSAN > Services**.

Step 7.   Select **I need local vSAN Datastore**, click **Configure**, and select one of the following configuration types:

   ■ **Standard vSAN Cluster**

   ■ **Two Host Cluster**

   ■ **Stretched Cluster**

Step 8.   Click **Configure** and, optionally, select **vSAN ESA**.

Step 9.   In the Services page, optionally configure the following:

   ■ (For vSAN OSA only) **Space Efficiency**: Choose **None**, **Compression Only**, or **Deduplication and Compression**.

   ■ **Encryption**: Optionally, enable **Data at-rest encryption** and specify a key provider. Optionally, enable **Data in-transit encryption** and specify a rekey interval.

   ■ **Disk Format Options**: Optionally, enable **Allow Reduced Redundancy** and **RDMA support**.

   Click **Next**.

Step 9.   On the Claim Disks page, select the disks for use by the cluster and click **Next**.

Step 10. Follow the wizard to complete the configuration of the cluster, based on the fault tolerance mode:

- **For a two-host vSAN cluster**: Choose a witness host for the cluster and claim disks for the witness host.
- **For a stretched cluster**: Define fault domains for the cluster, choose a witness host, and claim disks for the witness host.
- **If you selected fault domains**: Define the fault domains for the cluster.

Step 11. On the Ready to Complete page, click **Finish**.

NOTE Deduplication is not available in vSAN ESA.

Editing vSAN Settings

You can modify the settings of an existing vSAN cluster by using the following procedure:

Step 1. In the vSphere Client, select the cluster in the inventory pane and navigate to **Configure > vSAN > Services**.

Step 2. Click **Edit**.

Step 3. Optionally modify the following settings:

- (For vSAN OSA only) **Deduplication and Compression** or **Compression Only**
- **vSAN Encryption**
- **vSAN Performance Service**
- **iSCSI Target**
- **Advanced Settings > Object Repair Timer**
- **Advanced Settings > Site Read Locality for stretched clusters**
- **Thin Swap Provisioning**
- **Large Cluster Support for Up to 64 Hosts**
- **Automatic Rebalance**

Step 4. Click **Apply**.

Licensing vSAN

You need a vSAN license to use vSAN beyond the evaluation period. The license capacity is based on the total number of CPUs in the hosts participating in the cluster. The vSAN license is recalculated whenever ESXi hosts are added to or removed from the vSAN cluster. Some advanced features, such as all-flash configuration and stretched clusters, require special licenses.

The Global.Licenses privilege is required on the vCenter Server. You can use the following procedure to assign a vSAN license to a cluster:

Step 1. In the vSphere Client, select the vSAN cluster in the inventory pane.

Step 2. On the **Configure** tab, right-click the vSAN cluster and choose **Assign License.**

Step 3. Select an existing license and click **OK.**

Viewing a vSAN Datastore

When you enable vSAN on a cluster, a vSAN datastore is created. You can use the following procedure to review the capacity and other details of a vSAN datastore:

Step 1. In the vSphere Client, navigate to **Home > Storage.**

Step 2. Select the vSAN datastore.

Step 3. On the Configure tab, review the following:

- Capacity (total capacity, provisioned space, and free space)
- Datastore capabilities
- Policies

Configuring vSAN and vSphere HA

You can enable vSphere HA and vSAN on the same cluster, but this configuration requires ESXi Version 5.5 Update 1 or later and requires a minimum of three ESXi hosts. The following networking differences apply when using vSAN and vSphere HA together:

- The vSphere HA traffic flows over the vSAN network rather than the management network.
- vSphere HA uses the management network only when vSAN is disabled.

Before you enable vSAN on an existing vSphere HA cluster, you must first disable vSphere HA. After vSAN is enabled, you can re-enable vSphere HA.

Table 11-2 describes the vSphere HA networking differences between clusters where vSAN is enabled and is not enabled.

Table 11-2 Network Differences in vSAN and non-vSAN Clusters

Factor	vSAN Is Enabled	vSAN Is Not Enabled
Network used by vSphere HA	vSAN network	Management network
Heartbeat datastores	Any datastore, other than a vSAN datastore, that is mounted to multiple hosts in the cluster	Any datastore that is mounted to multiple hosts in the cluster
Host isolation criteria	Isolation addresses not pingable and vSAN storage network inaccessible	Isolation addresses not pingable and management network inaccessible

When configuring the vSphere HA admission control policy, you must account for a vSAN rule set's Primary Level of Failures to Tolerate setting. This setting must not be lower than the capacity reserved by the vSphere HA admission control setting. If vSphere HA reserves less capacity, failover activity might be unpredictable. For example, for an eight-host cluster, if you set the vSphere HA admission control to more than 25% of the cluster resources, then you should not set the vSAN rule's Primary Level of Failures to Tolerate setting higher than two hosts.

Setting the HA Capacity Reservation Setting

Capacity can be reserved for failover in the vSphere HA admission control policies. Such a reservation must be coordinated with the vSAN policy Primary Level of Failures to Tolerate. The HA reserved capacity cannot be higher than the vSAN Primary Level of Failures to Tolerate setting.

For example, if you set vSAN Primary Level of Failures to Tolerate to 1, the HA admission control policy must reserve resources equal to those of one host. If you set the vSAN Primary Level of Failures to Tolerate to 2, the HA admission control policy must reserve resources equal to those of two ESXi hosts.

Disabling vSAN

You can use the following procedure to disable vSAN for a host cluster, which causes all virtual machines located on the vSAN datastore to become inaccessible:

Step 1.   In the vSphere Client, select the cluster in the inventory pane.

Step 2.   Verify that the host in the cluster is in Maintenance Mode.

Step 3.   Select **Configure > vSAN > Services**.

Step 4.   Click **Turn Off vSAN**.

Step 5.   In the dialog box that appears, confirm your selection.

NOTE   If you intend to use virtual machines while vSAN is disabled, you should first migrate the virtual machines to another datastore.

Shutting Down and Restarting vSAN

In vSAN 7.0 Update 3 and later, to shut down an entire vSAN cluster prior to performing some maintenance activities, you can use the Shutdown Cluster Wizard. In the vSphere Client, right-click the vSAN cluster and choose Shutdown Cluster. In the wizard, verify that the prechecks are successful, provide a reason for the shutdown, and complete the wizard.

After you perform maintenance activities, you can restart a vSAN cluster. To restart a vSAN cluster, right-click the vSAN cluster, choose Restart Cluster, and monitor the progress.

NOTE   If you have a vSphere with Tanzu environment, you must follow the specified order when shutting down or starting up the components.

Deploying vSAN with vCenter Server

You can simultaneously deploy a VCSA and create a vSAN cluster by using the vCenter Server installer and following these steps:

Step 1.   Create a single-host vSAN cluster.

Step 2.   Place the vCenter Server on the host in the cluster.

Step 3.   Choose **Install** on a new vSAN cluster containing the target host.

This process deploys a one-host vSAN cluster. After the deployment, you can use the vSphere Client to configure the vSAN cluster and add additional nodes to the cluster.

Expanding a vSAN Cluster

You can expand a vSAN cluster by adding to the cluster ESXi hosts with storage. Keep in mind that ESXi hosts without local storage can also be added to a vSAN cluster. You can use the following procedure to expand a vSAN cluster by adding hosts:

Step 1.   In the vSphere Client, right-click a cluster in the inventory pane and select **Add Hosts**.

Step 2.   Using the wizard, add hosts by using one of the following options:

- **New Hosts**: Provide the host name and credentials.
- **Existing Hosts**: Select a host in the inventory that is not yet in the cluster.

Step 3.   Complete the wizard and click **Finish** on the final page.

You can also use the following procedure to move multiple existing ESXi hosts into a vSAN cluster by using host profiles:

Step 1.   In the vSphere Client, navigate to **Host Profiles**.

Step 2.   Click the **Extract Profile from a Host** icon.

Step 3.   Select a host in the vSAN cluster that you want to use as the reference host and click **Next**.

Step 4.   Provide a name for the new profile and click **Next**.

Step 5.   On the next wizard page, click **Finish**.

Step 6.   In the Host Profiles list, select the new host profile and attach multiple hosts to the profile.

Step 7.   Click the **Attach/Detach Hosts and Clusters to a Host Profile** icon.

Step 8.   Detach the reference vSAN host from the host profile.

Step 9.   In the Host Profiles list, select the new host profile and click the **Check Host Profile Compliance** icon.

Step 10.   Select **Monitor > Compliance**.

Step 11.   Right-click the host and select **All vCenter Actions > Host Profiles > Remediate**.

Step 12.   When prompted, provide appropriate input parameters for each host and click **Next**.

Step 13.   Review the remediation tasks and click **Finish**.

The hosts and their resources are now part of the vSAN cluster.

You can use the following procedure to add hosts to a vSAN cluster by using Quickstart:

Step 1.   Verify that no network configuration that was previously performed through the Quickstart workflow has been modified from outside the Quickstart workflow.

Step 2.   In the vSphere Client, select the vSAN cluster in the inventory and click **Configure > Configuration > Quickstart**.

Step 3.   Click **Add Hosts > Launch**.

Step 4.   Use the wizard to provide information for new hosts or to select existing hosts from the inventory.

Step 5.   Complete the wizard and click **Finish** on the last page.

Step 6.   Click **Cluster Configuration** > **Launch**.

Step 7.   Provide networking settings for the new hosts.

Step 8.   On the Claim Disks page, select disks on each new host.

Step 9.   On the Create Fault Domains page, move the new hosts into their corresponding fault domains.

Step 10.   Complete the wizard and click **Finish**.

NOTE   When adding a host to a vSAN cluster by using Quickstart, the vCenter Server must not be running on the host.

Working with Maintenance Mode

Before shutting down, rebooting, or disconnecting a host that is a member of a vSAN cluster, you must put the ESXi host in Maintenance Mode. Consider the following guidelines for using Maintenance Mode for vSAN cluster member hosts:

- When entering host Maintenance Mode, you must select a data evacuation mode, such as Ensure Accessibility or Full Data Migration.

- When a vSAN cluster member host enters Maintenance Mode, the cluster capacity is automatically reduced.

- Each impacted virtual machine may have compute resources, storage resources, or both on the host entering Maintenance Mode.

- Ensure that Accessibility Mode, which is faster than Full Data Migration Mode, migrates only the components from the host that are essential for running the virtual machines. It does not re-protect your data. When in this mode, if you encounter a failure, the availability of your virtual machine is affected, and you might experience unexpected data loss.

- When you select Full Data Migration Mode, your data is automatically re-protected against a failure (if the resources are available and Primary Level of Failures to Tolerate is set to 1 or more). In this mode, your virtual machines can tolerate failures, even during planned maintenance.

- When working with a three-host cluster, you cannot place a server in Maintenance Mode with Full Data Migration Mode.

Prior to placing a vSAN cluster member host in Maintenance Mode, you must do the following:

- If using Full Data Migration Mode, ensure that the cluster has enough hosts and available capacity to meet the requirements of the Primary Level of Failures to Tolerate policy.

- Verify that remaining hosts have enough flash capacity to meet any flash read cache reservations. To analyze this, you can run the following VMware Ruby vSphere Console (RVC) command:

  ```
  vsan.whatif_host_failures
  ```

- Verify that the remaining hosts have devices with sufficient capacity to handle stripe width policy requirements, if selected.

- Make sure that you have enough free capacity on the remaining hosts to handle the data that must be migrated from the host entering Maintenance Mode.

You can use the Confirm Maintenance Mode dialog box to determine how much data will be moved, the number of objects that will become noncompliant or inaccessible, and whether sufficient capacity is available to perform the operation. You can use the Data Migration Pre-check button to determine the impact of data migration options when placing a host into Maintenance Mode or removing it from the cluster.

To place a vSAN cluster member host in Maintenance Mode, you can use the following procedure:

Step 1. In the vSphere Client, select the cluster in the inventory pane.

Step 2. Optionally, use the following steps to run Data Migration Pre-check:

  a. Click **Data Migration Pre-check**.

  b. Select a host and a data migration option and click **Pre-check**.

  c. View the test results and decide whether to proceed.

Step 3. Right-click the host and select **Maintenance Mode > Enter Maintenance Mode**.

Step 4. Select one of the following data evacuation modes:

  - **Ensure Accessibility**: If hosts are powered off or removed from a vSAN cluster, vSAN makes sure the virtual machines on the ESXi host that is removed can still run those virtual machines. This moves some of the virtual machine data off the vSAN cluster, but replica data remains. If you have a three-host cluster, this is the only evacuation mode available.

- **Full Data Migration**: As its name implies, this mode moves all the VM data to other ESXi hosts in the cluster. This option makes sense if you are removing the host from the cluster permanently. If a virtual machine has data on the host and that data is not migrated off, the host cannot enter this mode.
- **No Data Migration**: If this option is selected, vSAN does not move any data from this ESXi host.

Click OK.

Managing vSAN Fault Domains

Fault domains provide additional protection against outage in the event of a rack or blade chassis failure. A *vSAN fault domain* contains at least one vSAN host, depending on the physical location of the host. With fault domains, vSAN can withstand rack, blade chassis, host, disk, or network failure within one fault domain, as the replica and witness data are stored in a different fault domain.

You can use the following procedure to create a new fault domain in a vSAN cluster:

Step 1. In the vSphere Client, examine each host in a vSAN cluster.

Step 2. Verify that each host is running ESXi 6.0 or later (to support fault domains) and is online.

Step 3. Select the vSAN cluster in the inventory pane and click **Configure > vSAN > Fault Domains**.

Step 4. Click the **Add** (plus sign) icon.

Step 5. In the wizard, provide a name for the fault domain.

Step 6. Select one or more hosts to add to the fault domain.

Step 7. Click **Create**.

You can use the vSphere Client to add hosts to an existing fault domain by selecting Configure > vSAN > Fault Domains and dragging the host to the appropriate fault domain. Likewise, you can drag a host out of a fault domain to remove the host from the fault domain and create a single-host fault domain.

Extending a vSAN Datastore Across Two Sites

A vSAN stretched cluster extends across two physical data center locations to provide availability in the event of site failure as well as provide load balancing between sites. With a stretched vSAN cluster, both sites are active, and if either site fails, vSAN uses storage on the site that is still up. One site must be designated as the preferred site, which makes the other site the secondary, or nonpreferred, site.

You can use the following procedure to leverage Quickstart to create a stretched cluster across two sites:

Step 1. Ensure that the following prerequisites are met:

- You have a minimum of three hosts (preferred site, secondary site, witness).
- ESXi 6.0 Update 2 or later is used on each host.
- The hosts in the cluster do not have any existing vSAN or networking configuration.

Step 2. Click **Configure > Configuration > Quickstart**.

Step 3. Click **Cluster Configuration > Edit**.

Step 4. In the wizard, provide a cluster name, enable vSAN, and optionally enable other features, such as DRS or vSphere HA. Optionally, enable vSAN ESA.

Step 5. Click **Finish**.

Step 6. Click **Add Hosts > Add**.

Step 7. In the wizard, provide information for new hosts or select existing hosts from the inventory. Click **Finish**.

Step 8. Click **Cluster Configuration > Configure**.

Step 9. In the wizard, configure the following:

- Configure settings for distributed switch port groups, physical adapters, and the IP configuration associated with vMotion and storage.
- Set vSAN Deployment Type to **Stretched Cluster**.
- On the Claim Disks page, select disks on each host to be used by vSAN. For vSAN ESA, optionally select **I Want vSAN to Manage the Disks**.
- On the Create Fault Domains page, define fault domains for the hosts in the preferred site and the secondary site.
- On the Select Witness Host page, select a host to use as a witness host. This host cannot be part of the cluster and can have only one VMkernel adapter configured for vSAN data traffic.
- On the Claim Disks for Witness Host page, select disks on the witness host for cache and capacity.
- On the Ready to Complete page, verify the cluster settings and click **Finish**.

When creating a vSAN stretched cluster, DRS must be enabled on the cluster. There are also several DRS requirements for stretched vSAN clusters:

- Two host groups must be created: one for the preferred site and another for the secondary site.

- Two VM groups must be created: one for the preferred site VMs and one for the VMs on the secondary site.

- Two VM–host affinity rules must be created for the VMs on the preferred site and VMs on the secondary site.

- VM–host affinity rules must be used to define the initial placement of virtual machines on ESXi hosts in the cluster.

In addition to the DRS requirements, there are also HA requirements for stretched vSAN clusters:

- HA must be enabled.

- HA rules should allow the VM–host affinity rules in the event of a failover.

- HA datastore heartbeats should be disabled.

vSAN has numerous requirements for implementing stretched clusters:

- Stretched clusters must use on-disk format Version 2.0 or higher. If your vSAN cluster is not using on-disk format Version 2.0, it must be upgraded before you configure the stretched vSAN cluster.

- Failures to Tolerate must be set to 1.

- Symmetric Multiprocessing Fault Tolerance (SMP-FT) VMs are supported only when Primary Level of Failures to Tolerate (PFTT) is set to 0 and Data Locality is either Preferred or Secondary. SMP-FT VMs with PFTT set to 1 or higher are not supported.

- If hosts are disconnected or fail in a not responding state, the witness cannot be added or removed.

- Adding ESXi hosts via **esxcli** commands on stretched clusters is not supported.

Managing Devices in a vSAN Cluster

You can use the following procedure to create a disk group on a vSAN OSA cluster member host:

Step 1.   In the vSphere Client, select the cluster in the inventory pane and navigate to **Configure > vSAN > Disk Management**.

Step 2.   Select the host and click **Create Disk Group**.

Step 3. Select the flash device to be used for the cache.

Step 4. Select the type of capacity disks to use (**HDD** for hybrid or **Flash** for all-flash).

Step 5. Select the devices you want to use for capacity.

Step 6. Click **Create** or **OK**.

You can use the following procedure to claim storage devices for a vSAN cluster:

Step 1. In the vSphere Client, select the cluster in the inventory pane and navigate to **Configure > vSAN > Disk Management > Claim Unused Disks**.

Step 2. Select a flash device to be used for the cache and click **Claim** for the cache tier.

Step 3. Select one or more devices (**HDD** for hybrid or **Flash** for all-flash) to be used as capacity and click **Claim** for the capacity tier.

Step 4. Click **Create** or **OK**.

You can use a similar process to claim disks to be used for vSAN ESA storage pools, but you do not need to specify whether a disk is used for capacity or cache.

For vSAN OSA, to verify that the proper role (cache or capacity) has been assigned to each device in an all-flash disk group, examine the Disk Role column at the bottom of the Disk Management page. If the vSAN cluster is set to claim disks in manual mode, you can use the following procedure to add additional local devices to an existing disk group:

Step 1. In the vSphere cluster, select the vSAN cluster in the inventory pane and navigate to **Configure > vSAN > Disk Management**.

Step 2. Select the disk group and click **Add Disks**.

Step 3. Select the device and click **Add**.

The additional devices must be the same type (flash or HDD) as existing devices in the disk group.

NOTE If you add a used device that contains residual data or partition information, you must first clean the device. For example, you can run the RVC command **host_wipe_vsan_disks**.

You can use the following procedure to remove specific devices from a disk group or remove an entire disk group:

Step 1.   In the vSphere cluster, select the vSAN cluster in the inventory pane.

Step 2.   Click **Configure** > **vSAN** > **Disk Management**.

Step 3.   To remove a disk group, select the disk group, click **Remove**, and select a data evacuation mode.

Step 4.   To remove a device, select the disk group, select the device, click **Remove**, and select a data evacuation mode.

Step 5.   Click **Yes** or **Remove**.

NOTE   You should typically remove specific devices from a disk group or remove an entire disk group only when you are upgrading a device, replacing a failed device, or removing a cache device. Deleting a disk group permanently deletes the data stored on the devices. Removing one flash cache device or all capacity devices from a disk group removes the entire disk group.

If ESXi does not automatically identify your devices as being flash devices, you can use the following procedure to manually mark them as local flash devices. For example, flash devices that are enabled for RAID 0 Mode rather than Passthrough Mode may not be recognized as flash. Marking these devices as local flash makes them available for use as vSAN cache devices. Before starting the following procedure, you should verify that the device is local and not in use:

Step 1.   In the vSphere cluster, select the vSAN cluster in the inventory pane and navigate to **Configure** > **vSAN** > **Disk Management**.

Step 2.   Select a host to view the list of available devices.

Step 3.   In the **Show** drop-down menu, select **Not in Use**.

Step 4.   Select one or more devices from the list and click **Mark as Flash Disk**.

Step 5.   Click **Yes**.

Likewise, you can use this procedure in other scenarios where you want to change how a device is identified. In step 4, you can choose Mark as HDD Disk, Mark as Local Disk, or Mark as Remote.

Increasing Space Efficiency in a vSAN Cluster

To increase space efficiency in a vSAN cluster, you can use SCSI Unmap, deduplication, compression, RAID5 erasure coding, and RAID 6 erasure encoding.

Unmap capability is disabled by default. To enable SCSI Unmap on a vSAN cluster, use the RVC command **vsan.unmap_support --enable**.

NOTE Unmap capability is disabled by default. When you enable Unmap on a vSAN cluster, you must power off and then power on all VMs. VMs must use virtual hardware Version 13 or above to perform Unmap operations.

For vSAN OSA, deduplication and compression are enabled as a cluster-wide setting but are applied per disk group. When deduplication and compression are enabled, vSAN OSA performs a rolling reformat of every disk group on every host. Depending on the data stored on the vSAN datastore, this process might take a long time. Do not perform such operations frequently. If you plan to disable deduplication and compression, you must first verify that enough physical capacity is available to place your data. After enabling deduplication and compression in vSAN OSA, you should consider the following:

- For efficiency, consider adding a disk group to cluster capacity instead of incrementally adding disks to an existing disk group.

- When you add a disk group manually, add all the capacity disks at the same time.

- You cannot remove a single disk from a disk group. You must remove the entire disk group in order to make modifications.

- A single disk failure causes an entire disk group to fail.

To enable deduplication and compression for an existing vSAN OSA cluster, should verify that the cluster is all-flash. Then, you can edit the vSAN cluster as previously described and select either Deduplication and Compression or Compression Only. You can optionally select Allow Reduced Redundancy.

When you enable deduplication and compression, vSAN updates the on-disk format of each disk group of the cluster by evacuating data from the disk group, removing the disk group, and re-creating it with a new format. This operation does not require virtual machine migration or DRS. If you choose the Allow Reduced Redundancy option, the virtual machines may continue to keep running even if the cluster does not have enough resources for the disk group to be fully evacuated. In this case, your virtual machines might be at risk of experiencing data loss during the operation.

> **NOTE**   Compression is enabled by default in vSAN ESA, but you can create and leverage a storage policy to change this behavior. Such a change would apply to just new writes. Old blocks are left uncompressed even after compression is turned on for an object and vice versa.

Using Encryption in a vSAN Cluster

When planning to implement vSAN encryption, you should consider the following:

- Encryption services are implemented differently in vSAN OSA than in vSAN ESA.

- In vSAN ESA, data encryption and other services reside at the top of the storage stack. In vSAN ESA, as a VM issues a write operation, vSAN encrypts the data once, after compression occurs, meaning that all vSAN traffic transmitted across hosts is also encrypted. This eliminates the need to encrypt the data on other hosts holding the object and the need decrypt and re-encrypt (which are required with vSAN OSA).

- In vSAN 8.0, for both ESA and OSA, data-at-rest encryption is a cluster-based service. Encryption in ESA must be configured during the initial cluster configuration, and once configured, it cannot be disabled at a later time. Encryption in OSA can be enabled or disabled as needed, but encrypting a cluster requires a rolling disk group evacuation.

- You can separately encrypt data in transit in a vSAN cluster and data at rest in a vSAN datastore. Data-in-transit encryption includes all data and metadata transferred between the member hosts using AES-256 encryption. Although in-flight data encryption may already be occurring with ESA, it does not use a unique hash for each data packet. To ensure the highest level of security, enable data-in-transit encryption on a per-cluster basis.

- To enable data-in-transit encryption, use the vSphere Client to navigate to the cluster's Configure > Services page and enable the Data-in-Transit Encryption option.

- To enable data-at-rest encryption for a vSAN datastore, you must implement a key management server (KMS) cluster server that is Key Management Interoperability Protocol (KMIP) 1.1 compliant and is in the vSphere compatibility matrices.

- You should not deploy the KMS server on the same vSAN datastore that it will help encrypt.

- Encryption is CPU intensive. Enable AES-NI in your BIOS.

- In a stretched vSAN cluster, the witness host only stores metadata and does not participate in data-at-rest encryption.

- You should establish a policy regarding the data-at-rest encryption of coredumps because they contain sensitive information such as keys for hosts. In the policy, consider the following:

  - You can use a password when you collect a vm-support bundle.

  - The password re-encrypts coredumps that use internal keys based on the password.

  - You can later use the password to decrypt the coredumps in the bundle.

  - You are responsible for keeping track of the password. It is not saved anywhere in vSphere.

To use data-at-rest encryption in a vSAN datastore, you must either provide a native key provider or provide a standard key provider and establish trust. You can use the following procedure to add a standard key provider to vCenter Server:

Step 1.   Ensure that the user has the Cryptographer.ManageKeyServers privilege.

Step 2.   In the vSphere Client, select the vCenter Server in the inventory pane and navigate to **Configure > Key Providers**.

Step 3.   Click **Add Standard Key Provider** and specify the following KMS information in the wizard:

  - For a KMS cluster, select **Create New Cluster**.
  - Specify the cluster name, alias, and address (FQDN or IP address).
  - Specify the port, proxy, and proxy port.

Step 4.   Click **Add**.

NOTE   Connecting to a KMS through a proxy server that requires a username or password is not supported. Connecting to a KMS by using only an IPv6 address is not supported.

You can use the following procedure to establish a trusted connection for a standard key provider:

Step 1.   In the vSphere Client, select the vCenter Server in the inventory pane and navigate to **Configure > Key Management Servers**.

Step 2.   Select the KMS instance and click **Establish Trust with KMS**.

Step 3.   Select one of the following options, as appropriate for the selected KMS instance:

- **Root CA Certificate**
- **Certificate**
- **New Certificate Signing Request**
- **Upload Certificate and Private Key**

When multiple KMS clusters are used, you can use the following procedure to identify a default KMS cluster:

Step 1.   In the vSphere Client, select the vCenter Server in the inventory pane and navigate to **Configure > Key Management Servers**.

Step 2.   Select the KMS cluster and click **Set KMS Cluster as Default**.

Step 3.   Click **Yes**.

Step 4.   Verify that the word **default** appears next to the cluster name.

You can make vCenter Server trust the KMS by using the following procedure:

Step 1.   In the vSphere Client, select the vCenter Server in the inventory pane and navigate to **Configure > Key Management Servers**.

Step 2.   Select the KMS instance and do one of the following:

- Select **All Actions > Refresh KMS Certificate > Trust**.
- Select **All Actions > Upload KMS Certificate > Upload File**.

In vSphere 7.0 Update 2 and later, you can use the built-in vSphere Native Key Provider to enable vSAN data-at-rest encryption. To configure a vSphere Native Key Provider using the vSphere Client, select the vCenter Server, select Configure > Security > Key Providers, select Add Native Key Provider, provide a name, and complete the wizard. You should configure the vCenter Server file-based backup and restore and store the backups securely as they contain the key derivation key.

If you want to enable encryption on a vSAN cluster, you need the following privileges:

- Host.Inventory.EditCluster
- Cryptographer.ManageEncryptionPolicy
- Cryptographer.ManageKMS
- Cryptographer.ManageKeys

You can use the following procedure to enable encryption on a vSAN cluster:

Step 1.   In the vSphere Client, select the cluster in the inventory pane and navigate to **vSAN > Services**.

Step 2.   Click the **Edit** button.

Step 3.   In the vSAN Services dialog, enable **Encryption** and select a KMS cluster.

Step 4.   Optionally, select the **Erase Disks Before Use** checkbox, based on the following:

- If this is a new cluster with no virtual machines, you can deselect the checkbox.
- If it is an existing cluster with unwanted data, select the checkbox, which increases the processing time for each disk.

Step 5.   Click **Apply**.

To generate new encryption keys, you can use the following procedure:

Step 1.   Log on to the vSphere Client as a user with **Host.Inventory.EditCluster** and **Cryptographer.ManageKeys** privileges.

Step 2.   In the vSphere Client, select the cluster in the inventory pane and navigate to **Configure > vSAN > Services**.

Step 3.   Click **Generate New Encryption Keys**.

Step 4.   To generate a new Key Encryption Key (KEK), click **Apply**. Each host's Key Encryption Key (DEK) is re-encrypted with the new KEK.

Step 5.   Optionally, select **Also Re-encrypt All Data on the Storage Using New Keys**.

Step 6.   Optionally, select the **Allow Reduced Redundancy** checkbox, although note that doing so might put your data at risk during the disk reformatting operation.

If a host member of a vSAN cluster that uses encryption has an error, the resulting coredump is encrypted. Coredumps that are included in the vm-support package are also encrypted.

Using vSAN Policies

Virtual machine performance and availability requirements can be defined for vSAN, if required. Once virtual machines are created, their storage policy is enforced on the vSAN datastore. Underlying components of virtual disks are spread across the vSAN datastore to meet the requirements defined in the storage policy. Storage providers provide information about the physical storage to vSAN to assist with placement and monitoring.

Creating a vSAN Storage Policy

The following procedure can be used to create a vSAN storage policy:

Step 1.   In the vSphere Client, go to **Policies and Profiles > VM Storage Policies**.

Step 2.   Click on the **Create a New VM Storage Policy** icon.

Step 3.   On the Name and Description page, select an appropriate vCenter Server, enter a name and description for the policy, and click **Next**.

Step 4.   On the Policy Structure page, select **Enable Rules for "vSAN" Storage** and click **Next**.

Step 5.   On the vSAN page, set the policy:

  a. On the Availability tab, set Site Disaster Tolerance and Failures to **Tolerate**.

  b. On the Storage Rule tab, define the encryption, space efficiency, and storage tier rules.

  c. On the Advanced Policy Rules tab, set Disk Stripes per Object and IOPS Limit.

  d. On the Tags tab, click **Add Tag Rule** and configure its options.

  Click **Next**.

Step 6.   On the Storage Compatibility page, review the list of compatible datastores and click **Next**.

Step 7.   On the Review and Finish page, review all the settings and click **Finish**.

Changing the vSAN Default Storage Policy

vSAN datastore default policies can be changed, if desired, using the following procedure:

Step 1.   In the vSphere Client storage inventory view, right-click the vSAN datastores and select **Configure**.

Step 2.   Select **General**, click **Edit** to the default storage policy, and select a storage policy to be defined as the new default.

Step 3.   Click **OK**.

Viewing vSAN Storage Providers

vSAN 6.7 and above register one storage provider for all vSAN clusters managed by vCenter. To access the storage providers, use the URL https://VCfqdn:VCport/vsanHealth/vsanvp/version.xml.

To view the vSAN storage providers, in the vSphere client, select a vCenter Server and navigate to Configure > Storage Providers.

Each ESXi host has a vSAN storage provider, but only one is active. Storage providers on other ESXi hosts are in standby. If an ESXi host with an active storage provider fails, a storage provider from another host activates.

Using vSAN File Service

You can use the following procedure to configure (enable) the *vSAN file service* on a vSAN cluster, which enables you to create file shares:

Step 1. Address the following prerequisites:

- Identify a set of available IPv4 addresses—preferably one per host (for best performance)—that are from the same subnet and are part of the forward and reverse lookup zones in the DNS server.
- If using a distributed vSphere Switch, create a dedicated distributed port group.
- Ensure that vDS 6.6.0 or higher is in use.
- Promiscuous Mode and forged transmits are enabled during file services configuration. If an NSX-based network is used, you must provide similar settings.

Step 2. In the vSphere Client, select the vSAN cluster and select **Configure > vSAN > Services**.

Step 3. In the File Service row, click **Enable**.

Step 4. In the wizard, select a network and select one of the following options:

- **Automatic**: Automatically searches for and downloads the OVF
- **Manual**: Allows you to manually select an OVF and associated files (CERT, VMDK, and so on)

Select **Enable**.

vSAN files services are now enabled, and a File Services Virtual Machine (FSVM) is placed on each host.

To configure vSAN File Services, select the vSAN cluster and navigate to Configure SAN Services. Choose Configure Domain and use its wizard to configure domain name, networking, and directory services.

To create a share, you can use the following procedure:

Step 1.   In the vSphere Client, select the vSAN cluster in the inventory pane and navigate to **Configure > vSAN > File Service Shares**.

Step 2.   Click **Add**.

Step 3.   In the wizard, enter the following general information:

- **Protocol**: Select either SMB or NFS. If you select SMB, you can optionally choose the **Protocol Encryption** option. With SMB, you can hide files and folders by using the **Access Based Enumeration** option. If you select NFS, you can choose **NFS3**, **NFS4**, or **NFS3 and NFS 4**. If you choose NFS, you can choose **AUTH_SYS** or **Kerberos** security.

- **Name**: Specify a name.

- **Storage Policy**: Select the vSAN default storage policy.

- **Storage Space Quotas**: Set the share warning threshold and the share hard quota.

- **Labels**: Specify up to five labels (key/value pairs) per share, a label key (up to 250 characters), and a label value (fewer than 1000 characters).

Click **Next**.

Step 4.   On the Net Access Control page, select one of the following options:

- **No Access**: Use this option to prevent access to the file share.

- **Allow Access from Any IP**: Use this option to allow access from any IP address.

- **Customize Net Access**: Use this option to control whether specific IP addresses can access, read, or modify the file share. You can configure Root Squash based on IP address.

Click **Next**.

Step 5.   On the Review page, click **Finish**.

NOTE   In releases prior to vSAN 7.0 Update 3, when a host enters Maintenance Mode, its FSVM is deleted after the Protocol Stack container moves to another VM. When the host exits Maintenance Mode, a new VM is provisioned.

Managing Datastores

This section provides information on managing datastores in a vSphere 8.0 environment.

Managing VMFS Datastores

You can set up Virtual Machine File System (VMFS) datastores on any SCSI-based storage device that is discovered by a host, such as a Fibre Channel device, an iSCSI device, or a local device. To view a host's SCSI devices, you can use the following procedure:

Step 1.   In the vSphere Client, select an ESXi host in the inventory pane and navigate to **Configure > Storage > Storage Adapters**.

Step 2.   Select a storage adapter.

Step 3.   Optionally, click the **Rescan Adapter** or **Rescan Storage** button.

Step 4.   In the details pane, select the **Devices** tab and examine the details for each discovered SCSI device, including type, capacity, and assigned datastores.

Step 5.   Optionally, to manipulate a specific device, select the device and click the **Refresh**, **Attach**, or **Detach** button.

To create a VMFS 6 datastore on a SCSI device, you can use the following procedure:

Step 1.   In the vSphere Client, right-click a host in the inventory pane and select **Storage > New Datastore**.

Step 2.   For datastore type, select **VMFS** and click **Next**.

Step 3.   Provide a name for the datastore, select an available SCSI device, and click **Next**.

Step 4.   Select **VMFS 6** and click **Next**.

Step 5.   Keep the default Partition Configuration setting **Use All Available Partitions**. Alternatively, set the datastore size, block size, space reclamation granularity, and space reclamation priority.

Step 6.   Click **Next**.

Step 7.   On the Ready to Complete page, click **Finish**.

You can increase the size of a VMFS datastore by adding an extent or by expanding the datastore within its own extent. A VMFS datastore can span multiple devices. Adding an extent to a VMFS datastore means adding a storage device (LUN) to the datastore. A spanned VMFS datastore can use any extent at any time. It is not required to fill up a specific extent before using the next one.

A datastore is expandable when the backing storage device has free space immediately after the datastore extent. You can use the following procedure to increase the size of a datastore:

Step 1.   In the vSphere Client, right-click the datastore in the inventory pane and select **Increase Datastore Capacity**.

Step 2.   Select a device from the list of storage devices, based on the following.

- To expand the datastore, select a storage device whose Expandable column contains YES.

- To add an extent to the datastore, select a storage device whose Expandable column contains NO.

Step 3.   Review the available configurations in the partition layout.

Step 4.   In the menu, select one of the following available configuration options, depending on your previous selections:

- **Use Free Space to Expand the Datastore**: Select this option to expand the existing datastore and disk partition to use the adjacent disk space.

- **Use Free Space**: Select this option to deploy an extent in the remaining free space.

- **Use All Available Partitions**: Select this option to reformat a disk and deploy an extent using the entire disk. (This option is available only for non-blank disks.)

Step 5.   Set the capacity. (The minimum extent size is 1.3 GB.) Click **Next**.

Step 6.   Click **Finish**.

NOTE   If a shared datastore becomes 100% full and has powered-on virtual machines, you can increase the datastore capacity—but only from the host where the powered-on virtual machines are registered.

Each VMFS datastore is assigned a universally unique ID (UUID). A storage device operation, such as a LUN snapshot, LUN replication, or LUN ID change, might produce a copy of the original datastore such that both the original and a copy device contain a VMFS datastore with identical signatures (UUID). When ESXi detects a VMFS datastore copy, it allows you to mount it with the original UUID or mount it with a new UUID. The process of changing the UUID is called *resignaturing*.

To allow a host to use the original datastore and the copy, you can choose to resignature the copy. If the host will only access the copy, you could choose to mount the copy without resignaturing.

Consider the following points related to resignaturing:

- When resignaturing a datastore, ESXi assigns a new UUID to the copy, mounts the copy as a datastore that is distinct from the original, and updates all corresponding UUID references in the virtual machine configuration files.

- Datastore resignaturing is irreversible.

- After resignaturing, the storage device is no longer treated as a replica.

- A spanned datastore can be resignatured only if all its extents are online.

- The resignaturing process is fault tolerant, so if the process is interrupted, you can resume it later.

- You can mount the new VMFS datastore without risk of its UUID conflicting with UUIDs of any other datastore from the hierarchy of device snapshots.

To mount a VMFS datastore copy on an ESXi host, you can use the following procedure:

Step 1. In the vSphere Client, select the host in the inventory page and navigate to **Configure** > **Storage Adapters**.

Step 2. Rescan storage.

Step 3. Unmount the original VMFS datastore, which has the same UUID as the VMFS copy.

Step 4. Right-click the host and select **Storage** > **New Datastore**.

Step 5. Select **VMFS** as the datastore type.

Step 6. Enter the datastore name and placement (if necessary).

Step 7. In the list of storage devices, select the device that contains the VMFS copy.

Step 8. Choose to mount the datastore and select one of the following options:

   a. Mount Options > **Assign a New Signature**
   b. Mount Options > **Keep Existing Signature**

Step 9. Click **Finish**.

Beginning with vSphere 7.0, you can use clustered virtual machine disks (VMDKs) on a VMFS 6 datastore to support Windows Server Failover Clustering (WSFC). When creating the VMFS 6 datastore, you can use the vSphere Client to choose a device whose Clustered VMDK Support attribute is set to Yes. To enable support for clustered VMDKs, you should therefore set Clustered VMDK Support to Yes. Ensure that the datastore is being used only by ESXi 7.0 or later hosts that are managed by the same vCenter Server 7.0 or later. After the datastore is created, select it in the vSphere Client and set Datastore Capabilities > Clustered VMDK to Enable. After enabling this setting, you can place the clustered virtual disks on the datastore. To disable the setting, you need to first power off the virtual machines that have clustered virtual disks.

Table 11-3 provides details on other administrative operations that you can perform on VMFS datastores.

Table 11-3 VMFS Datastore Operations

Operation	Steps	Notes
Change datastore name	1. Right-click the datastore and select **Rename.** 2. Provide a name (42-character limit).	If the host is managed by vCenter Server, you must rename the datastore from vCenter Server, not from the vSphere Host Client. You can successfully rename a datastore that has running virtual machines.
Unmount datastore	1. Ensure that **Storage DRS** and **Storage I/O Control** are not enabled for the datastore. 2. Right-click the datastore and select **Unmount Datastore**. 3. Select the hosts.	When you unmount a datastore, it remains intact but can no longer be seen from the specified hosts. Do not perform other configuration operations on the datastore during the unmount operation. Ensure that the datastore is not used by vSphere HA heartbeating (which could trigger a host failure event and cause virtual machines to restart).
Mount datastore	1. Right-click the datastore and select **Mount Datastore** (if the datastore is inactive) or **Mount Datastore on Additional Hosts** (if the datastore is active). 2. Select the host(s) and click **OK**.	A VMFS datastore that is unmounted from all hosts is marked as inactive. You can mount the unmounted VMFS datastore. If you unmount an NFS or a vVols datastore from all hosts, the datastore disappears from the inventory. To mount the NFS or vVols datastore that has been removed from the inventory, use the New Datastore wizard.

Operation	Steps	Notes
Remove datastore	1. Move or migrate virtual machines from the datastore. Unmount the datastore. 2. Right-click the datastore and select **Delete Datastore**. 3. Click **OK** to confirm the deletion.	Deleting a datastore permanently destroys it and all its data, including virtual machine files. You are not required to unmount the datastore prior to deletion, but you should.

In the vSphere Client, you can use the datastore file browser to examine and manage the datastore contents. To get started, right-click the datastore in the inventory pane and select Browse Files. In the datastore file browser, you can select any of the options listed in Table 11-4.

Table 11-4 Datastore File Browser Options

Option	Description
Upload Files	Upload a local file to the datastore.
Upload Folder	Upload a local folder to the datastore.
Download	Download a file from the datastore to the local machine.
New Folder	Create a folder on the datastore.
Copy To	Copy selected folders or files to a new location on the datastore or on another datastore.
Move To	Move selected folders or files to a new location on the datastore or on another datastore.
Rename To	Rename selected files.
Delete	Delete selected folders or files.
Inflate	Convert a selected thin virtual disk to thick.

When you use the vSphere Client to perform VMFS datastore operations, vCenter Server uses default storage protection filters. The filters help you avoid data corruption by displaying only the storage devices that are suitable for an operation. In the rare scenario in which you want to turn off the storage filters, you can do so using the following procedure:

Step 1.   In the vSphere Client, select the vCenter Server instance in the inventory pane and navigate to **Configure > Settings > Advanced Settings > Edit Settings**.

Step 2.   Specify one of the filter names described in Table 11-5 and set its value to **False**.

Table 11-5 Storage Filters

Filter	Description
config.vpxd.filter.vmfsFilter (VMFS filter)	Hides storage devices (LUNs) that are used by a VMFS datastore on any host managed by vCenter Server.
config.vpxd.filter.rdmFilter (RDM filter)	Hides storage devices (LUNs) that are used by an RDM on any host managed by vCenter Server.
config.vpxd.filter. sameHostsAndTransportsFilter (Same Hosts and Transports filter)	Hides storage devices (LUNs) that are ineligible for use as VMFS datastore extents because of incompatibility with the selected datastore. Hides LUNs that are not exposed to all hosts that share the original datastore. Hides LUNs that use a storage type (such as Fibre Channel, iSCSI, or local) that is different from the original datastore.
config.vpxd.filter. hostRescanFilter (Host Rescan filter)	Automatically rescans and updates VMFS datastores following datastore management operations. If you present a new LUN to a host or a cluster, the hosts automatically perform a rescan, regardless of this setting.

NOTE You should consult the VMware support team prior to changing device filters.

Managing Raw Device Mappings (RDMs)

You can use the following procedure to add an RDM to a virtual machine:

Step 1. In the vSphere Client, open the settings for a virtual machine.

Step 2. Click **Add New Device** and select **RDM Disk**.

Step 3. Select a LUN and click **OK**.

Step 4. Click the **New Hard Disk** triangle to expand the RDM properties.

Step 5. Select a datastore to hold the RDM. It can be the same as or different from where the virtual machine configuration file resides.

Step 6. Select either **Virtual Compatibility Mode** or **Physical Compatibility Mode**.

Step 7. If you selected Virtual Compatibility Mode, select a disk mode: **Dependent, Independent–Persistent**, or **Independent–Nonpersistent**.

Step 8. Click **OK**.

You can use the following procedure to manage paths for the storage devices used by RDMs:

Step 1.   In the vSphere Client, right-click the virtual machine in the inventory pane and select **Edit Settings**.

Step 2.   Select **Virtual Hardware > Hard Disk**.

Step 3.   Click the device ID that appears next to Physical LUN to open the Edit Multipathing Policies dialog box.

Step 4.   Use the Edit Multipathing Policies dialog box to enable or disable paths, set multipathing policy, and specify the preferred path.

If the guest OS in your virtual machine is known to have issues using the SCSI INQUIRY data cached by ESXi, you can either modify the virtual machine or the host to ignore the cached data. To modify the virtual machine, you can edit its VMX file and add the following parameter, where scsi$X$:Y represents the SCSI device:

```
scsiX:Y.ignoreDeviceInquiryCache = "true"
```

To modify the host, you can use the following command, where *deviceID* is the device ID of the SCSI device:

```
esxcli storage core device inquirycache set --device
deviceID --ignore true
```

Managing NFS Datastores

The Network File System (NFS) protocol is the NAS solution that ESXi supports. Version 3 and Version 4.1 are the only supported versions of the NFS client in vSphere. NFS was originally created by Sun Microsystems, but it has been an open source solution for a number of years. When mounting NFS datastores on an ESXi host, be sure to observe the following best practices:

- On ESXi, the NFS Version 3 and NFS Version 4.1 clients use different locking mechanisms. You cannot use different NFS versions to mount the same datastore on multiple hosts. In NFS Version 3, the file locking daemon runs on the ESXi host as a client, while in NFS Version 4.1, the file locking daemon runs on the server side or storage.

- ESXi hosts can make use of both NFS Version 3 and Version 4.1 if the previous rule is observed.

- ESXi hosts cannot directly upgrade NFS Version 3 to NFS Version 4.1.

- NFS datastores must have folders with identical names mounted on all ESXi hosts, or functions such as vMotion may not work.

- If an NFS device does not support internationalization, you should use ASCII characters only.

How you configure an NFS storage device for use with VMware varies by vendor, so you should always refer to the vendor documentation for specifics.

The following is the procedure to configure an NFS server (but refer to vendor documentation for specifics on how to carry out this procedure):

Step 1.   Use the VMware Hardware Compatibility List to ensure that the NFS server is compatible. Pay attention to the ESXi version, the NFS server version, and the server firmware version.

Step 2.   Configure the NFS volume and export it (by adding it to /etc/exports), using the following details:

- NFS Version 3 or Version NFS 4.1 (only one protocol per share)
- NFS over TCP

Step 3.   For NFS Version 3 or non-Kerberos NFS Version 4.1, ensure that each host has root access to the volume. The typical method for this is to use the **no_root_squash** option.

Step 4.   If you are using Kerberos, ensure that the NFS exports provide full access to the Kerberos user. In addition, if you are going to use Kerberos with NFS Version 4.1, you need to enable either AES256-CTS-HMAC-SHA1-96 or AES128-CTS-HMAC-SHA1-96 on the NFS storage device.

To prepare an ESXi host to use NFS, you must configure a VMkernel virtual adapter to carry NFS storage traffic. If you are using Kerberos and NFS Version 4.1, you should take the following additional steps:

Step 1.   Ensure that the DNS settings on the ESXi hosts are pointing to the DNS server that is used for DNS records for Kerberos Key Distribution Center (KDC). This will most likely be the Active Directory server if that is being used for name resolution.

Step 2.   Configure NTP because Kerberos is sensitive to time drift.

Step 3.   Configure Active Directory for Kerberos.

To create (mount) an NFS datastore in vSphere, you need the IP address or DNS name of the NFS server as well as the path to the share (folder name). When using Kerberos, you need to configure the ESXi hosts for Kerberos authentication prior to creating the NFS datastore.

NOTE   Multiple IP addresses or DNS names can be used with NFS Version 4.1 multipathing.

You can use the following procedure to create an NFS datastore:

Step 1.   In the vSphere Client, right-click a data center, cluster, or ESXi host object in the inventory pane and select **Storage > New Datastore**.

Step 2.   Select **NFS** as the new datastore type.

Step 3.   Select the correct NFS version (Version 3 or Version 4.1). Be sure to use the same version on all ESXi hosts that are going to mount this datastore.

Step 4.   Define the datastore name (with a maximum of 42 characters).

Step 5.   Provide the appropriate path for the folder to mount, which should start with a forward slash (/).

Step 6.   Set **Server** to the appropriate IPv4 address, IPv6 address, or server name.

Step 7.   Optionally, select the **Mount NFS Read Only** checkbox. (This can only be set when mounting an NFS device. To change it later, you must unmount and remount the datastore from the hosts.)

Step 8.   If using Kerberos, select **Kerberos** and define the Kerberos model as one of the following:

- **Use Kerberos for Authentication Only (krb5)**: This method supports identity verification only.
- **Use Kerberos for Authentication and Data Integrity (krb5i)**: This method supports identity verification and also ensures that data packets have not been modified or tampered with.

Step 9.   If you selected a cluster or a data center object in step 1, then select the ESXi hosts to mount this datastore.

Step 10.   Verify the configuration and click **Finish**.

To rename or unmount an NFS datastore, you can use the same procedure as described for VMFS datastores in Table 11-3. To remove an NFS datastore from the vSphere inventory, you should unmount it from every host.

Storage DRS and SIOC

This section provides details on configuring and managing Storage DRS and Storage I/O Control (SIOC).

Configuring and Managing Storage DRS

To create a datastore cluster using the vSphere Client, you can right-click on a data center in the inventory pane, select New Datastore Cluster, and complete the wizard. You can use the following procedure to enable Storage DRS (SDRS) in a datastore cluster:

Step 1.   In the vSphere Client, select the datastore cluster in the inventory pane and navigate to **Configure** > **Services** > **Storage DRS**.

Step 2.   Click **Edit**.

Step 3.   Select **Turn ON vSphere DRS** and click **OK**.

You can use similar steps to set the SDRS Automation Mode to No Automation (Manual) or Fully Automated. You can set Space Utilization I/O (SDRS Thresholds) Latency. You can select or deselect Enable I/O Metric for SDRS Recommendations. You can also configure the advanced options, which are Space Utilization Difference, I/O Load Balancing Invocation Interval, and I/O Imbalance Threshold.

You can add datastores to a datastore cluster by using drag and drop in the vSphere Client. Each datastore can only be attached to hosts with ESXi 5.0 or later. The datastores must not be associated with multiple data centers.

If you want to perform a maintenance activity on an SDRS cluster member datastore or its underlying storage devices, you can place it in Maintenance Mode. (Standalone datastores can be placed in Maintenance Mode.) SDRS has recommendations for migrating the impacted virtual machine files, including virtual disk files. You can let SDRS automatically apply the recommendations, or you can manually make recommendations. To place a datastore in Maintenance Mode using the vSphere Client, right-click the datastore in the inventory pane, select Enter SDRS Maintenance Mode, and optionally apply any recommendations.

The Faults tab displays a list of the disks that cannot be migrated and the reasons.

If SDRS affinity or anti-affinity rules prevent a datastore from entering Maintenance Mode, you can select an option to ignore the rules. To do so, edit the settings of the datastore cluster by selecting SDRS Automation > Advanced Options and setting IgnoreAffinityRulesForMaintenance to 1.

When reviewing each SDRS recommendation on the Storage SDRS tab in the vSphere Client, you can examine the information described in Table 11-6 and use it when deciding which recommendations to apply.

Table 11-6 SDRS Recommendations

Recommendations	Details
Priority	Priority level (1–5) of the recommendation. (This is hidden by default.)
Recommendation	Recommended action.
Reason	Why the action is needed.
Space Utilization % Before (source) and (destination)	Percentage of space used on the source and destination datastores before migration.
Space Utilization % After (source) and (destination)	Percentage of space used on the source and destination datastores after migration.
I/O Latency Before (source)	Value of I/O latency on the source datastore before migration.
I/O Latency Before (destination)	Value of I/O latency on the destination datastore before migration.

You can use the following procedure to override the SDRS datastore cluster automation level per virtual machine:

Step 1. In the vSphere Client, right-click a datastore cluster in the inventory pane and select **Edit Settings**.

Step 2. Select **Virtual Machine Settings**.

Step 3. Select one of the following automation levels:

- **Default (Manual)**
- **Fully Automated**
- **Disabled**

Step 4. Optionally select or deselect the **Keep VMDKs Together** option.

Step 5. Click **OK**.

You can use the following procedure to create an inter-VM anti-affinity rule (that is, a rule specifying that two or more virtual machines are placed on separate datastores):

Step 1. In the vSphere Client, right-click a datastore cluster in the inventory pane and select **Edit Settings**.

Step 2. Select **Rules > Add**.

Step 3. Provide a name and set Type to **VM Anti-affinity**.

Step 4. Click **Add**.

Step 5. Click **Select Virtual Machine**.

Step 6.   Select at least two virtual machines and click **OK**.

Step 7.   Click **OK** to save the rule.

To create an intra-VM anti-affinity rule (that is, a rule which says that virtual disks for a specific virtual machine are placed on separate datastores), you use a similar procedure but set Type to VMDK-Affinity and select the appropriate virtual machine and virtual disks.

Configuring and Managing SIOC

Storage I/O Control (SIOC) allows you to prioritize storage access during periods of contention, such that critical virtual machines obtain a larger amount of storage I/O than less critical virtual machines. Once SIOC has been enabled on a datastore, ESXi hosts monitor the storage device latency. If the latency exceeds a predetermined threshold, the datastore is determined to be under contention, and the virtual machines that reside on that datastore are assigned I/O resources based on their individual share values. You can enable SIOC as follows:

Step 1.   In the vSphere Client, select a datastore in the Storage inventory view and select **Configuration > Properties**.

Step 2.   Click the **Enabled** checkbox under Storage I/O Control and click **Close**.

In addition to share values, which are similar to shares defined for CPU and memory, storage I/O limits can be defined on individual virtual machines to limit the number of I/O operations per second (IOPS). By default, just as with CPU and memory resources, there are no limits set for virtual machines. In a virtual machine with more than one virtual disk, limits must be set on all of the virtual disks for that VM. If you do not set a limit on all the virtual disks, the limit won't be enforced. To view the shares and limits assigned to virtual machines, you can use the vSphere Client. To select a datastore, select the Virtual Machines tab and examine the associated virtual machines. The details for each virtual machine include its respective shares, the IOPS limit, and the percentage of shares for that datastore.

Setting SIOC Shares and Limits

As with CPU and memory shares, SIOC shares establish a relative priority in the event of contention. In the event of storage contention, virtual machines with more shares will observe more disk I/O than will a virtual machine with fewer shares. The following procedure outlines how you configure SIOC shares and limits for virtual machines:

Step 1.   In the vSphere Client, right-click a virtual machine in the inventory pane and select **Edit Settings**.

Step 2.   Expand one of the hard disks (for example, **Hard disk 1**).

Step 3.   From the Shares drop-down menu, select **High**, **Normal**, **Low**, or **Custom** to define the share value.

Step 4.   Set the Limit–IOPS drop-down to **Low** (500), **Normal** (1000), **High** (2000), or **Custom** (and enter a custom value for the IOPS limit).

Step 5.   Click **OK** to save your changes.

Monitoring SIOC Shares

To view the impact of shares on individual datastores, in the vSphere Client, select a datastore in the inventory pane, select the Performance tab, and select View > Performance. Here, you can observe the following data:

■ Average latency and aggregated IOPS

■ Host latency

■ Host queue depth

■ Host read/write IOPS

■ Virtual machine disk read/write latency

■ Virtual machine disk read/write IOPS

SIOC Threshold

The default threshold for SIOC to begin prioritizing I/O based on shares is 30 ms and typically does not need to be modified. However, you can modify this threshold if you need to. Be aware that SIOC will not function properly unless all the datastores that share drive spindles have the same threshold defined. If you set the value too low, shares will enforce priority of resources sooner but could decrease aggregated throughput, and if you set it too high, the result might be higher aggregated throughput but less prioritization of disk I/O.

The following procedure allows you to modify the threshold:

Step 1.   In the vSphere Client Storage Inventory view, select a datastore and select the **Configuration** tab.

Step 2.   Select **Properties** and under Storage I/O Control, select **Enabled** if it is not already selected.

Step 3.   Click **Advanced** to modify the threshold for contention; this value must be between 5 ms and 100 ms.

Step 4.   Click **OK** and then click **Close**.

The procedure to reset the threshold to the default is similar:

Step 1.   In the vSphere Client Storage Inventory view, select a datastore and select the **Configuration** tab.

Step 2.   Select **Properties** and under Storage I/O Control, select **Advanced**.

Step 3.   Click **Reset**.

Step 4.   Click **OK** and then click **Close**.

iSCSI, iSER, NVMe, and PMem

This section provides details on configuring and managing iSCSI and iSER adapters. It also provides details on configuring and managing Non-Volatile Memory Express (NVMe) and PMem devices.

Managing iSCSI

To utilize iSCSI storage, you must configure an iSCSI adapter on your ESXi host. You can choose from the following list of adapters.

- **Independent hardware iSCSI adapter**: This is a third-party adapter that offloads the iSCSI and network processing and management from your host. It does not require a VMkernel virtual adapter (that is, VMkernel port).

- **Software iSCSI adapter**: This adapter uses standard NICs to connect a host to a remote iSCSI target on the IP network. It requires a VMkernel virtual adapter.

- **Dependent hardware iSCSI adapter**: This third-party adapter depends on VMware networking and iSCSI configuration and management interfaces. It requires a VMkernel virtual adapter.

- **VMware iSER adapter**: This adapter uses an RDMA-capable network adapter to connect a host to a remote iSCSI target. It requires a VMkernel virtual adapter.

Each adapter type involves a unique set of requirements and configuration steps. The high-level steps for configuring iSER with ESXi are as follows:

Step 1.   Install and view an RDMA-capable network adapter.

Step 2.   Enable the VMware iSER adapter.

Step 3.   Modify the general properties for iSER adapters.

Step 4.   Configure port binding for iSER.

Step 5.   Configure dynamic or static discovery for iSER on an ESXi host.

Step 6.   Set up CHAP for an iSER storage adapter.

Step 7.   Set up CHAP for the target.

Step 8.   Enable jumbo frames for networking.

To enable the VMware iSER adapter, you can use the **esxcli rdma iser add** command. The adapter then appears on the host's Storage Adapter page in the vSphere Client, in the category VMware iSCSI over RDMA (iSER).

To configure the iSER port binding, create a VMkernel virtual adapter, connect it to a virtual switch to which the appropriate RDMA-enabled physical adapter is connected as an uplink, and use the Network Port Binding tab of the iSER storage adapter to bind the virtual adapter to the physical adapter. iSER does not support NIC teaming. You should configure the port binding to use only one RDMA-enabled physical adapter and one VMkernel adapter per virtual switch.

This section provides details on configuring and managing Non-Volatile Memory Express (NVMe) and PMem devices.

Managing VMware NVMe

As described in Chapter 2, *Non-Volatile Memory Express (NVMe)* devices are a high-performance alternative to SCSI storage. There are three mechanisms for NVMe:

- **NVMe over PCIe**: NVMe over PCIe is for local storage, and NVMe over Fabrics (NVMe-oF) is for connected storage.

- **NVMe over Remote Direct Memory Access (RDMA)**: NVMe over RDMA is shared NVMe-oF storage using RDMA over Converged Ethernet (RoCE) Version 2 transport.

- **NVMe over Fibre Channel (FC-NVMe)**: FC-NVMe is shared NVMe-oF storage using Fibre Channel transport.

Chapter 2 describes the requirements for each of these mechanisms.

After you install the hardware for NVMe over PCIe, ESXi detects it as a storage adapter that uses PCIe. You can use the vSphere Client to view the storage adapter and storage device details. No other configuration is needed.

NVMe over Fabrics Shared Storage

When using NVMe storage for shared storage, you must not mix transport types on the same namespace. You should ensure that the active paths are presented because a path cannot be registered until it has been discovered.

Table 11-7 identifies additional information about NVMe-oF vs. SCSI over Fabrics storage.

Table 11-7 SCSI over Fabrics and NVMe over Fabrics Comparison

Shared Storage Capability	SCSI over Fabrics	NVMe over Fabrics
RDM	Supported	Not supported
Coredump	Supported	Not supported
SCSI-2 reservations	Supported	Not supported
Clustered VMDK	Supported	Not supported
Shared VMDK with multi-writer flag	Supported	Supported in vSphere 7.0 Update 1 and later
vVols	Supported	Supported in vSphere 8.0 and later
Hardware acceleration with VAAI plug-ins	Supported	Not supported
Default MPP	NMP	HPP (NVMe-oF targets cannot be claimed by NMP.)
Limits	LUNs=1024, paths=4096	Namespaces=32, paths=128 (maximum 4 paths per namespace in a host)

To use FC-NVMe, you must add an appropriate supported adapter and use the following procedure to add the controller to the host:

Step 1.   In the vSphere Client, select the host in the inventory pane and navigate to **Configure > Storage > Storage Adapters**.

Step 2.   Click **Controllers > Add Controller**.

Step 3.   Select one of the following options:

   a. Automatically Discover Controllers: Click **Discover Controllers** and select a controller.

   b. Enter Controller Details Manually: Provide the subsystem NQN, the worldwide node name, and the worldwide port name. Optionally, provide an admin queue size and keepalive timeout.

Configuring ESXi to Support RDMA

You can configure ESXi 7.0 and later hosts to access shared NVMe devices using RDMA over Converged Ethernet (RoCE) Version 2. The host must have a network adapter that supports RoCE Version 2, and you must configure a software NVMe over RDMA adapter.

For hosts with a NIC that supports RoCE Version 2, the vSphere Client shows both the network adapter component and the RDMA component. You can select the host in the inventory pane and navigate to Configure > Networking > RDMA Adapters. Here you can see the unique names assigned to the RDMA devices, such as vmrdma0. For each device, you can see its paired uplink (that is, its integrated NIC, such as vmnic9). To complete the host configuration, you can use the following procedure:

Step 1. Create a new VMkernel virtual network adapter on a vSphere Standard or Distributed Switch and configure its uplink to use the RDMA paired uplink (for example, vmnic9).

Step 2. Select the host and navigate to **Configure > Networking > RDMA Adapters**.

Step 3. Select the appropriate RDMA device (for example, vmrdma0) and select **VMkernel Adapters Bindings** in the details pane.

Step 4. Verify that the new VMkernel adapter (for example, vmk2) appears.

Step 5. Select the host and navigate to **Configure > Storage > Storage Adapters**.

Step 6. Click the **Add Software Adapter** button.

Step 7. Select **Add Software NVMe over RDMA Adapter**.

Step 8. Select the appropriate RDMA adapter (for example, vmrdma0) and click **OK**.

Step 9. In the list of storage adapters, identify the new adapter in the category VMware NVME over RDMA Storage Adapter and make note of its assigned device number (for example, vmhba71).

Step 10. To identify the available storage devices, select the storage adapter (for example, vmhba71) and select **Devices** in the details pane. You can use these devices to create VMFS datastores.

Configuring HPP

As described in Chapter 2, *High-Performance Plug-in (HPP)* is the default plug-in that claims NVMe-oF targets. NVMe over PCIe targets default to the VMware

Native Multipathing Plug-in (NMP). You can use the **esxcli storage core claimrule add** command to change the claiming plug-in in your environment. For example, to set a local device to be claimed by HPP, use the **--pci-vendor-id** parameter and set the **--plugin** parameter to **HPP**. To change the claim rule based on an NVMe controller model, use the **--nvme-controller-model** parameter.

To assign a specific HPP Path Selection Scheme (PSS) to a specific device, you can use the **esxcli storage hpp device set** command with the **-pss** parameter to specify the scheme and the **--device** parameter to specify the device. The available HPP PSS options are explained in Table 2-6 in Chapter 2. To create a claim rule that assigns the HPP PSS by vendor and model, you can use **esxcli storage core claimrule add** with the **-V** (vendor), **-M** (model), **-P** (plug-in), and **--config-string** parameters. In the value for **--config-string**, specify the PSS name and other settings, such as "**pss=LB-Latency,latency-eval-time=40000**".

NOTE   Enabling HPP on PXE-booted ESXi hosts is not supported.

After using these commands, you should reboot the hosts to apply the changes.

Managing PMem

PMem devices are non-volatile dual in-line memory modules (NVDIMMs) on the ESXi host that reside in normal memory slots. They are non-volatile and combine the performance of volatile memory with the persistence of storage. PMem devices are supported on ESXi 6.7 and later.

ESXi hosts detect local PMem devices and expose the devices as host-local PMem datastores to virtual machines. Virtual machines can directly access and utilize them as either memory (virtual NVDIMM) or storage (PMem hard disks). An ESXi host can have only one PMem datastore, but it can be made up of multiple PMem modules.

Virtual PMem (vPMem)

In vPMem Mode, a virtual machine can directly access PMem resources and use the resources as regular memory. The virtual machine uses NVDIMMs that represent physical PMem regions. Each virtual machine can have up to 64 virtual NVDIMM devices, and each NVDIMM device is stored in the host-local PMem datastore. Virtual machines must be at a minimum hardware Version 14, and the guest OS must be PMem aware.

Virtual PMem Disks (vPMemDisk)

In virtual PMem Disk (*vPMemDisk*) Mode, a virtual machine cannot directly access the PMem resources. You must add a virtual PMem disk to the virtual machine. A virtual PMem disk is a regular virtual disk that is assigned a PMem storage policy, forcing it to be placed on a host-local PMem datastore. This mode has no virtual machine hardware or operating system requirements.

PMem Datastore Structure

The PMem structure on an ESXi host has the following components:

- **Modules**: These are the physical NVDIMMs that reside on the motherboard.

- **Interleave sets**: These are logical groupings of modules. ESXi hosts read from an interleave set in turns, so if there are two modules on an ESXi host, they will be read in parallel. You can identify the way the NVDIMMs are grouped into interleave sets via the vSphere Client.

- **Namespaces**: PMem datastores are built on top of namespaces, which are regions of contiguously addressed memory ranges.

To view information about the PMem modules, interleave sets, and namespaces, you can follow this procedure:

Step 1.　In the vSphere Host Client, select **Storage** from the inventory pane.

Step 2.　Click on the **Persistent Memory** tab.

Step 3.　Click **Modules** to see the NVDIMMs that contribute to the PMem datastore.

Step 4.　Click **Namespaces** to see namespace information.

Step 5.　Click **Interleave Sets** to see how the modules are grouped into interleave sets.

To delete namespaces that were created by an operating system that was previously installed on the host machine, you can navigate to Namespaces, select the namespace, and click Delete. This frees up the PMem space, but you must reboot the host to access it.

Multipathing, Storage Policies, and vVols

This section provides information on managing storage multipathing, storage policies, and Virtual Volumes (vVols) in vSphere.

Managing Multipathing

As explained in Chapter 2, ESXi uses the Pluggable Storage Architecture (PSA), which allows plug-ins to claim storage devices. The plug-ins include the Native Multipathing Plug-in (NMP), the High-Performance Plug-in (HPP), and third-party multipathing modules (MPPs).

esxcli Commands for Multipathing

You can use **esxcli** commands to manage the PSA plug-ins. For example, you can use the following command from an ESXi shell to view the multipathing modules (plug-ins):

```
esxcli storage core plugin list -plugin-class=MP
```

You can use the following command to list all devices controlled by the NMP module. For each device, you will find details, such as assigned storage array type (SATP) and the path selection policy (PSP):

```
esxcli storage nmp device list
```

To see details for a specific device, you can provide the **--device** option with the previous command. For example, if you have a device that is identified by **mpx.vmbha0:C0:T0:L0**, you can use the following command to retrieve details for just that device:

```
esxcli storage nmp device list --device=mpx.vmbha0:C0:T0:L0
```

Table 11-8 provides information on some other **esxcli** commands that you can use with NMP.

Table 11-8 ESXLI Commands for NMP

Command	Description
esxcli storage nmp satp list	Provides information for each available SATP, including the default PSP
esxcli storage nmp psp list	Provides a description for each available PSP
esxcli storage nmp satp set --default-psp=policy --satp=satpname	Changes the default PSP policy for an SATP named satpname, where the policy is VMW_PSP_MRU, VMW_PSP_FIXED, or VMW_PSP_RR, as explained in Table 2-11 in Chapter 2

NOTE   In many cases, the storage system provides ESXi with the storage device names and identifiers, which are unique and based on storage standards. Each identifier uses the format naa.*xxx*, eui.*xxx*, or t10.*xxx*. Otherwise, the host generates an identifier in the form mpx.*path*, where *path* is the first path to the device, such as mpx. vmhba1:C0:T1:L3.

Table 11-9 provides information on some **esxcli** commands that you can use with HPP.

Table 11-9   ESXCLI Commands for HPP

Command	Description	Options
esxcli storage hpp path list	Lists which paths are claimed by HPP	**-d	--device** **-p	--path=<*path*>**
esxcli storage hpp device list	Lists devices controlled by HPP	**-d	--device=<*device*>**
esxcli storage hpp device set	Configures HPP settings	**-B	--bytes=<*max_bytes_on_path*>** **-g	--cfgfile** **-d	--device=<*device*>** **-I	--iops=<*max_iops_on_path*>** **-T	--latency-eval-time=<*interval_in_ms*>** **-M	--mark-device-ssd=<*value*>** **-p	--path=<*path*>** **-S	--sampling-ios-per-path=<*value*>** **-P	--pss=<FIXED|LB-Bytes| LB-IOPs|LB-Latency|LB-RR>**
esxcli storage hpp device usermarkedssd list	Lists devices that someone marked as SSD	**-d	--device=<*device*>**

Managing Paths with the vSphere Client

This section provides information on using the vSphere Client to manipulate the path selection policy and available paths for NMP. For information on selecting PSS for HPP, see the "Configuring HPP" section, earlier in this chapter.

A path to a storage device is represented as the storage adapter, storage channel number, target number, and LUN number (the LUN position within the target) that is used to connect to the device. For example, vmhba1:C0:T1:L3 indicates that the path uses storage adapter vmhba1, channel 0, target 1, and LUN 3. To view the storage paths for a specific device, you can use the following procedure:

Step 1.   In the vSphere Client, select a host in the inventory pane and navigate to **Configure > Storage > Storage Devices**.

Step 2.   Select the storage device.

Step 3.   Click the **Properties** tab and review the details. For NMP devices, the details include the assigned SATP and PSP.

Step 4.   Click **Paths** and review the available paths to the device. The status for each path can be Active (I/O), Standby, Disabled, or Dead. For devices using the Fixed path policy, an asterisk (*) represents the preferred path.

To disable a path to a storage device, you can follow this procedure, select a path, and choose Disable.

In the vSphere Client, you can select a VMFS datastore and navigate to Configure > Connectivity and Multipathing to review information on the paths to the storage devices backing the datastore.

To change the PSP that is assigned to a storage device, you can navigate to the device's properties page (see the previous set of steps) and click Edit Multipathing. On the multipathing page, you can choose a policy, such as VMW_PSP_FIXED, VMW_PSP_RR, or VMW_PSP_MRU, as described in Table 2-11 in Chapter 2.

Managing Claim Rules

ESXi uses claim rules to determine which multipathing module owns the paths to a specific storage device and the type of multipathing support that is applied. Core claim rules determine which multipathing module (NMP, HPP, or a third-party module) claims a device. For NMP, SATP claim rules determine which SATP submodule claims the device. Table 11-10 describes a few commands for claim rules.

Table 11-10   Sample Claim Rules Commands

Command	Description
esxcli storage core claimrule list --claimrule-class=MP	Lists the claim rules on the host.
esxcli storage core claimrule add	Defines a new claim rule. The rule may contain multiple options, such as plug-in (**-P**), model (**-M**), and vendor (**-V**). The value for the plug-in can be NMP, HPP, MASK_PATH, or a third-party plug-in name.
esxcli storage core claimrule load	Loads new claim rules into the system.
esxcli storage core claimrule run	Applies the loaded claim rules.

Managing Storage Policies

In vSphere, you can use Storage Policy Based Management (SPBM) to align storage with the application demands of your virtual machines. With SPBM, you can assign a storage policy to a virtual machine to control the type of storage that can be used by the virtual machine and how the virtual machine is placed on the storage. You can apply a storage policy as you create, clone, or migrate a virtual machine.

Prior to creating virtual machine storage policies, you must populate the VM Storage Policy interface with information about storage entities and data services in your storage environment. When available, you can use a vSphere APIs for Storage Awareness (VASA) provider to provide the information. Alternatively, you can use datastore tags.

Multiple steps are required to use storage policies, and the particular steps depend on the type of storage or services you need. This section describes the major steps.

In many cases, VM storage policies populate automatically. However, you can manually assign tags to datastores as follows:

Step 1. Create a category for the storage tags:

  a. In the vSphere Client, select **Home > Tags & Custom Attributes**.

  b. Click **Tags > Categories**.

  c. Click **Add Category**.

  d. Provide values for the following options: Category Name, Description, Tags per Object, and Associable Object Types.

  e. Click **OK**.

Step 2. Create a storage tag:

  a. Click **Tags** on the Tags tab.

  b. Click **Add Tag**.

  c. Provide values for the following options: Name, Description, and Category.

  d. Click **OK**.

Step 3. Apply the tag to the datastore:

  a. In the storage inventory view, right-click the datastore and select **Tags & Custom Attributes > Assign Tag**.

  b. Select a tag from the list and click **Assign**.

To create a VM storage policy, follow this procedure:

Step 1.   For host-based services:

a. In the vSphere Client, select **Home** > **Policies and Profiles**.

b. Click **VM Storage Policies**.

c. Select **Create VM Storage Policy**.

d. Provide values for the following options: vCenter Server, Name, and Description.

e. On the Policy Structure page, define the custom rules for the data service category.

f. Review the datastores that match the policy.

g. Review the settings and click **Finish**.

Step 2.   For vVols:

a. In the vSphere Client, select **Home** > **Policies and Profiles**.

b. Click **VM Storage Policies**.

c. Select **Create VM Storage Policy**.

d. Provide values for the following options: vCenter Server, Name, and Description.

e. On the Policy Structure page, enable rules.

f. On the Virtual Volumes Rules page, add storage placement rules.

g. Optionally, set rules for datastore-specific services.

h. On the Storage Compatibility page, review the datastores matching the policy.

i. On the Review and Finish page, verify the settings and click **Finish**.

Step 3.   For tag-based placement:

a. In the vSphere Client, select **Home** > **Policies and Profiles**.

b. Click **VM Storage Policies**.

c. Select **Create VM Storage Policy**.

d. Provide values for the following options: vCenter Server, Name, and Description.

e. On the Policy Structure page, select **Add Tag Rule** and define the tag category, usage option, and tags. Repeat as needed.

f. Review the datastores that match the policy.

g. Verify the policy settings on the Review and Finish page and click **Finish**.

VASA: Registering a Storage Provider

To collect storage entities and data services information from a VASA storage provider, you can use the following procedure:

Step 1.   In the vSphere Client, select **vCenter** in the inventory pane and navigate to **Configure > Storage Providers**.

Step 2.   Click the **Add** icon.

Step 3.   Provide the connection information for the provider, including the name, URL, and credentials.

Step 4.   Select one of the following security methods:

   a. Select the **Use Storage Provider Certificate** option and define the location of the certificate.

   b. Review and accept the displayed certificate thumbprint that is displayed.

   The storage provider adds the vCenter certificate to the truststore when the vCenter server initially connects to the storage device.

Step 5.   Click **OK**.

VASA: Managing Storage Providers

To perform management operations involving a storage provider, such as rescanning, you can use the following procedure:

Step 1.   In the vSphere Client, select **vCenter** in the inventory pane and navigate to **Configure > Storage Providers**.

Step 2.   Select a storage provider and choose one of the following options:

   ■ **Synchronize Storage Providers**: Synchronizes vCenter Server with information for all storage providers.

   ■ **Rescan**: Synchronizes vCenter Server with information from a specific storage provider.

   ■ **Remove**: Unregisters a specific storage provider, which is useful when upgrading a storage provider to a later VASA version requires you to unregister and reregister.

   ■ **Refresh Certificate**: Refreshes a certificate before it retires.

Applying Storage Policies to VMs

When performing a provisioning, cloning, or migration operation for a virtual machine, you can assign a storage policy. For example, when using the New Virtual Machine wizard, on the Select Storage page, you can select a policy in the VM Storage Policy drop-down menu to assign a storage policy to the entire virtual machine. After selecting the policy, you should choose a datastore from the list of compatible datastores. If you use the replication service provided with vVols, you should either specify a preconfigured replication group or choose to have vVols create an automatic replication group.

Optionally, you can set different storage policies for each virtual disk. For example, on the Customize Hardware page, you can select New Hard Disk and set a VM storage policy for that disk.

To change the storage policy assigned to a virtual machine, you can use the following procedure:

Step 1.   In the vSphere Client, navigate to **Menu > Policies and Profiles > VM Storage Policies**.

Step 2.   Select a storage policy and click **VM Compliance**.

Step 3.   Select a virtual machine that is currently assigned the selected policy.

Step 4.   Click **Configure > Policies**.

Step 5.   Click **Edit VM Storage Policies**.

Step 6.   Assign the appropriate policy to the virtual machine or assign separate policies to different virtual disks.

Step 7.   If you use the replication service provided with vVols, configure the replication group.

Step 8.   Click **OK**.

Configuring and Managing vVols

To use vVols, you must ensure that your storage and vSphere environment are properly configured.

To work with vVols, the storage system must support vVols and must integrate with vSphere using VASA. You should consider the following guidelines:

- The storage system must support thin provisioning and snapshotting.

- You need to deploy the VASA storage provider.

- You need to configure the following components on the storage side:

  - Protocol endpoints

  - Storage containers

  - Storage profiles

  - Replication configurations if you plan to use vVols with replication

- You need to follow appropriate setup guidelines for the type of storage you use (Fibre Channel, FCoE, iSCSI, or NFS). If necessary, you should install and configure storage adapters on your ESXi hosts.

- You need to use NTP to ensure time synchronization among the storage system components and vSphere.

To configure vVols, you can use the following procedure:

Step 1.   Register the storage providers for vVols, as described previously.

Step 2.   Create a vVols datastore by using the following steps:

  a. In the vSphere Client, right-click a host, cluster, or data center in the inventory pane and select **Storage > New Datastore**.

  b. Select **vVol** as the datastore type.

  c. Select the hosts that will access the datastore.

  d. Click **Finish**.

Step 3.   Navigate to **Storage > Protocol Endpoints** to examine and manage the protocol endpoints. Optionally, you can take the following steps:

  a. Use the **Properties** tab to modify the multipathing policy.

  b. Use the **Paths** tab to change the path selection policy, disable paths, and enable paths.

Exam Preparation Tasks

As mentioned in the section "Book Features and Exam Preparation Methods" in the Introduction, you have some choices for exam preparation: the exercises here, Chapter 15, "Final Preparation," and the exam simulation questions on the companion website.

Review All the Key Topics

Review the most important topics in this chapter, noted with the Key Topic icon in the outer margin of the page. Table 11-11 lists these key topics and the page number on which each is found.

Table 11-11   Key Topics for Chapter 11

Key Topic Element	Description	Page Number
List	vSAN characteristics	418
Section	Shutting down a vSAN cluster	424
Procedure	Creating a stretched vSAN cluster	429
Procedure	Increasing the size of a datastore	437
Procedure	Creating an NFS datastore	442
Section	Setting SIOC shares and limits	449
Table 11-10	Sample claim rules commands	452
Section	Implementing storage policies	462

Complete Tables and Lists from Memory

Print a copy of Appendix B, "Memory Table" (found on the companion website), or at least the section for this chapter, and complete the tables and lists from memory. Appendix C, "Memory Table Answers" (also on the companion website), includes completed tables and lists to check your work.

Define Key Terms

Define the following key terms from this chapter and check your answers in the glossary:

vSAN fault domain, vSAN file service, Storage I/O Control (SIOC), Non-Volatile Memory Express (NVMe), High-Performance Plug-in (HPP), PMem device, virtual PMem disk (vPMemDisk)

Review Questions

1. You are implementing encryption for a vSAN cluster in vSphere 8.0. Which of the following options is a requirement?

    a. Deploy KMIP 1.0.

    b. Deploy the KMS as a virtual machine in the vSAN datastore.

    c. Ensure that the KMS is in the vSphere compatibility matrices.

    d. Ensure that the witness host participates in encryption.

2. You want to save space in your vSAN OSA cluster by removing redundant data blocks. Which of the following steps should you take?

    a. Configure deduplication in a storage policy.

    b. Enable Deduplication only.

    c. Enable Deduplication and Compression.

    d. Enable Allow Reduced Redundancy.

3. In your vSphere 8.0 environment, you are using the datastore file browser to perform administrative tasks. Which of the following are valid options in the datastore file browser? (Choose three.)

    a. Upload files

    b. Download

    c. Mount

    d. Inflate

    e. Convert

4. For your vSphere 8.0 environment, you are comparing NVMe-oF with SCSI over Fibre Channel. Which of the following statements is true?

    a. Virtual volumes are supported with NVMe-oF in vSphere 7.0.

    b. SCSI-2 reservations are supported with NVMe-oF.

    c. RDMs are supported with NVMe-oF.

    d. HPP is supported with NVMe-oF.

5. You are using the vSphere Client to manage the storage providers. Which one of the following is not an option?

    a. Replace

    b. Synchronize Storage Providers

    c. Rescan

    d. Refresh Certificate

This chapter covers the following topics:

- Configuring and Managing Authentication and Authorization
- Configuring and Managing vSphere Certificates
- General ESXi Security Recommendations
- Configuring and Managing ESXi Security
- Additional Security Management

This chapter contains information related to VMware vSphere 8.x Professional (2V0-21.23) exam objectives 1.8.1, 1.8.1.1, 1.9.2, 4.1, 4.1.1, 4.1.2, 4.4, 4.4.1, 4.4.2, 4.3.3 and 4.10, 4.12, 4.13, 4.17.2, 4.19, 4.19.1, 4.19.2, 4.19.2.1, 4.19.2.2, 4.19.4, 4.19.5, 7.7, 7.12, and 7.12.1.

CHAPTER 12

Managing vSphere Security

This chapter covers the procedures for managing security in a vSphere environment.

"Do I Know This Already?" Quiz

The "Do I Know This Already?" quiz allows you to assess whether you should study this entire chapter or move quickly to the "Exam Preparation Tasks" section. In any case, the authors recommend that you read the entire chapter at least once. Table 12-1 outlines the major headings in this chapter and the corresponding "Do I Know This Already?" quiz questions. You can find the answers in Appendix A, "Answers to the 'Do I Know This Already?' Quizzes and Review Questions."

Table 12-1 "Do I Know This Already?" Foundation Topics Section-to-Question Mapping

Foundations Topics Section	Questions Covered in This Section
Configuring and Managing Authentication and Authorization	1, 2
Configuring and Managing vSphere Certificates	3, 4
General ESXi Security Recommendations	5, 6
Configuring and Managing ESXi Security	7, 8
Additional Security Management	9, 10

1. You are responsible for multiple vSphere environments. What must you do to enable the use of Enhanced Linked Mode in vSphere 8.0?

   a. Associate two vCenter Servers with the same external PSC.

   b. Map the external PSC of one vCenter Server to the embedded PSC of another vCenter Server.

   c. Configure vCenter Server HA.

   d. Connect two vCenter Servers to the same SSO domain.

2. You are configuring permissions in a vSphere environment. When editing an existing permission, which of the following properties can you change?

    a. Role

    b. Privilege

    c. User

    d. Object

3. You are managing certificates in your vSphere environment. By default, what types of certificates are in VECS? (Choose two.)

    a. ESXi certificates

    b. Machine SSL certificates

    c. Trusted root certificates

    d. vCenter Server certificates

4. You are responsible for performing certificate management for your ESXi hosts. Which of the following privileges do you need?

    a. Certificates.Manage Certificates

    b. Host.Manage Certificates

    c. Manage.Certificates

    d. Certificates.Manage.Host

5. You are enabling direct ESXi access using local accounts. To change the password requirements, such as minimum length, which of the following steps should you take?

    a. Select **Single Sign On** > **Configuration**.

    b. Configure Lockdown Mode.

    c. Use the **Set-PasswordControl** cmdlet.

    d. Configure Security.PasswordQualityControl.

6. You want to enable passthrough for a network device on your ESXi host. You see that an orange icon is associated with a device. Which of the following actions should you take?

    a. Reboot the host.

    b. Ignore the icon, select the device, and click **OK**.

    c. Navigate to **Configure** > **Services** and restart a specific service.

    d. Give up. The device is not compatible with passthrough.

7. You want to configure your ESXi host's acceptance level such that you cannot install VIBs signed at or below the PartnerSupported level but you can install VIBs signed at higher levels. Which option should you choose?

   a. VMwareCertified

   b. VMwareAccepted

   c. PartnerSupported

   d. CommunitySupported

8. You want to enable UEFI Secure Boot. To determine whether your ESXi host supports Secure Boot, which of the following steps should you take?

   a. Use the command **/usr/lib/vmware/secureboot/bin/secureBoot.py -c**.

   b. Check for compliance by using a host profile.

   c. Check for compliance by using Lifecycle Manager.

   d. Use the Security Profile section in the vSphere Client.

9. You need to use encryption in your vSphere environment. Which of the following should you use to configure a trust relationship between a KMS and vCenter?

   a. In the vCenter Server Appliance Management Interface (VAMI), choose **Configuration > Security > Key Providers**.

   b. In the vSphere Client, select the vCenter Server and choose **Configuration > Security > Key Providers**.

   c. In the vCenter Server Appliance Management Interface (VAMI), choose **Configuration > Encryption**.

   d. In the vSphere Client, select the vCenter Server and choose **Configuration > Encryption**.

10. You want to configure vSphere Trust Authority. Which of the following is a necessary step?

    a. Create the trusted key provider on the trusted cluster.

    b. Import the trusted key provider to the trusted authority cluster.

    c. Configure the trusted key provider for the trusted hosts on the trusted cluster.

    d. Configure the trusted key provider for the hosts on the trusted authority cluster.

Foundation Topics

Configuring and Managing Authentication and Authorization

This section describes configuration and management tasks related to vSphere authentication and authorization. Authentication tasks involve vCenter Single Sign-On (SSO), and authorization involves permissions.

Managing SSO

As explained in previous chapters, you can use the built-in identity provider vCenter SSO and external identity providers for vSphere authentication. SSO includes the Security Token Service (STS), an administration server, the vCenter Lookup Service, and the VMware Directory Service (**vmdir**). The VMware Directory Service is also used for certificate management.

Chapter 8, "vSphere Installation," discusses the following procedures:

- Adding and editing identity sources

- Adding the vCenter Appliance to an Active Directory domain

- Configuring SSO password, lockout, and token policies

This section describes the procedures for enabling Windows session authentication (SSPI) and managing STS. This section also describes how to implement and use Enhanced Linked Mode.

NOTE   The lockout policy applies only to user accounts and not to system accounts such as administrator@vsphere.local.

Enabling SSO with Windows Session Authentication

To enable Windows session authentication (SSPI), you can use the following procedure:

Step 1.   Prepare an Active Directory domain and its trusts in an SSO-trusted manner, as described at https://kb.vmware.com/s/article/2064250.

Step 2.   Join the vCenter Server to the Active Directory domain, as described in Chapter 8.

Step 3.   Install the Enhanced Authentication Plug-in.

Step 4.   Instruct vSphere Client users to select the **Use Windows Session Authentication** checkbox during login.

> **NOTE**   If you use federated authentication with Active Directory Federation Services, the Enhanced Authentication Plug-in applies only if vCenter Server is the identity provider.

Managing Service Token Service (STS)

The *vCenter Single Sign-On Security Token Service (STS)* is a web service that issues, validates, and renews security tokens. It uses a private key to sign tokens and publishes the public certificates. SSO manages the certificates that are used by STS for signing and stores the certificates (the signing certificates) in VMware Directory Service (**vmdir**). In the vSphere Client, you can use Administration > Certificates > Certificate Management > STS Signing Certificate to import and replace the STS signing certificate. Alternatively, you can use the following command-line procedure to generate a new STS signing certificate:

Step 1.   Create a top-level directory.

Step 2.   Copy the certool.cfg file into the new directory.

Step 3.   Modify the certool.cfg file to use the local vCenter Server IP address and host name.

Step 4.   Generate the key by running **/usr/lib/vmware-vmca/bin/certool --genkey**.

Step 5.   Generate the certificate by running **/usr/lib/vmware-vmca/bin/certool --gencert**.

Step 6.   Create a PEM file with the certificate chain and private key.

> **NOTE**   The certificate is not external facing, and it is valid for 10 years. You should replace this certificate only if required by your company's security policy.

To use a company-required certificate or to refresh a certificate that is near expiration, you can use the PEM file from the previous procedure and the **sso-config** utility command to refresh the STS certificate, as in the following example:

```
/opt/vmware/bin/sso-config.sh -set_signing_cert -t vsphere.local ~/
newsts/newsts.pem
```

Enhanced Linked Mode

To join vCenter Server systems in Enhanced Linked Mode, you need to connect them to the same SSO domain. For example, during the deployment of a vCenter Server, you can choose to join the SSO domain of a previously deployed vCenter Server.

When implementing Enhanced Linked Mode, you should ensure that you properly synchronize the time settings of the new appliance to match those of the previously deployed appliance. For example, if you are using the vCenter Server GUI installer to deploy two new vCenter Server systems joined in Enhanced Linked Mode to the same ESXi host, you can configure them to synchronize the time settings with the host.

You can use a single vSphere Client window to manage multiple vCenter Server systems that are joined with Enhanced Linked Mode. Enhanced Linked Mode provides the following features for vCenter Server:

- You can log in to all linked vCenter Server systems simultaneously.

- You can view and search the inventories of all linked vCenter Server systems.

- Roles, permission, licenses, tags, and policies are replicated across linked vCenter Server systems.

NOTE   Enhanced Linked Mode requires the vCenter Server Standard licensing level.

Users and Groups

By default, immediately following installation, only the localos and SSO domain (which is sphere.local by default) identity sources are available. Chapter 8 describes how to add identity sources, such as a native Active Directory (integrated Windows authentication) domain, an OpenLDAP directory service, or Active Directory as an LDAP server. It also describes how to create users and groups in the SSO domain.

NOTE   After creating a user or group, you cannot change its name.

When using the procedure in Chapter 8 to add members to a group in the SSO domain, you can add users from identity sources.

In some cases, you might want to manage multiple independent vSphere environments that have similar but separate SSO domains and users. In such scenarios, you can export SSO users by using this procedure:

Step 1.   Log on to the vSphere Web Client.

Step 2.   Select **Home** > **Administration**.

Step 3.   Select **Single Sign On > Users and Groups**.

Step 4.   Click the **Users** tab.

Step 5.   Click the **Export List** icon in the lower-right corner.

You can use a similar procedure to export SSO groups except that in step 4 you choose the Groups tab instead of the Users tab.

Privileges and Roles

To create a role in vCenter Server using the vSphere Client, you can use this procedure:

Step 1.   Click **Menu > Administration > Roles**.

Step 2.   Click the **Create Role Action (+)** button.

Step 3.   Provide a name for the role.

Step 4.   Select the desired privileges.

Step 5.   Click **OK**.

After you create custom roles, you can use those roles when assigning permissions in the same manner as you use the vCenter Server system roles and sample roles.

To clone a sample role or custom role in the vSphere Client, navigate to Administration > Roles and select the role, click the Clone Role Action icon, and provide a name for the new role. To edit a sample role or custom role in the vSphere Client, navigate to Administration > Roles and select the role, click the Edit Role Action icon, and modify the set of privileges in the role.

Permissions

To set a permission using the vSphere Client, you can use the following steps:

Step 1.   Select the object in the inventory.

Step 2.   Click the **Permissions** tab.

Step 3.   Click the **Add Permission** icon.

Step 4.   Select a user or group from the **User** drop-down menu.

Step 5.   Select a role from the **Role** drop-down menu.

Step 6.   Optionally, select **Propagate to Children**.

Step 7.   Click **OK**.

By assigning a different role to a group of users on different objects, you control the tasks that those users can perform in your vSphere environment. For example, to allow a group to configure memory for the host, select that host and add a permission that grants a role to that group that includes the Host.Configuration.Memory Configuration privilege.

Global Permissions

In some cases, you might assign a global permission and choose not to propagate to child objects. This may be useful for providing a global functionality, such as creating roles. To assign a global permission, you should use the vSphere Client with a user account that has the Permissions.Modify privilege on the root object of all inventory hierarchies. Select Administration > Global Permissions and use the Add Permission icon (plus sign). Then use the dialog that appears to select the desired user group (or user) and role.

NOTE   By default, the administrator account in the SSO domain, such as administrator@vsphere.local, can modify global permissions, but the vCenter Server Appliance root account cannot.

NOTE   Be careful when applying global permission. Decide whether you genuinely want a permission to apply to all solutions and to all objects in all inventory hierarchies.

Editing Permissions

To modify an existing permission, you can edit the permission and change role assignment. You cannot change the object, user, or user group in the permission, but you can change the role and the Propagate to Children setting. If this is not adequate, you need to remove the permission and create a new permission with the correct settings. You must do this work as a user with sufficient privileges to change permissions on the associated object.

The biggest challenge in editing permissions may be locating the permission in order to modify it. If you know the object on which a permission was created, you can select the object in the vSphere Client inventory, select Configure > Permissions, right-click the permission, and choose Change Role. Then you select the appropriate role and click OK.

If you do not already know which permission to modify or on which object the permission is assigned, you may need to investigate. Begin by selecting an object in the inventory on which you know the applied user permissions are incorrect. Select Manage > Permissions to discover all the permissions that apply to the object. Use the Defined In column to identify where each applied permission is defined. Some of the permissions may be assigned directly on the object, and some may be assigned to ancestor objects. Determine which permissions are related to the issue and where they are assigned.

Configuring and Managing vSphere Certificates

You can use the vSphere Client and vSphere *Certificate Manager* to view and manage certificates. With the vSphere Client, you can perform the following tasks:

- View trusted root certificates and machine SSL certificates.

- Renew or replace existing certificates.

- Generate a custom certificate signing request (CSR) for a machine SSL certificate.

For each certificate management task, you should use the administrator account in the SSO domain (which is vsphere.local by default).

Managing vSphere Client Certificates

You can use the following procedure to explore and take actions on the certificate stored in a VMware Endpoint Certificate Service (VECS) instance:

Step 1.   In the vSphere Client, navigate to **Home > Administration > Certificates > Certificate Management**.

Step 2.   If the system prompts you to do so, enter the credentials for your vCenter Server. The Certificate Management page shows the certificate types in the VECS. By default, the types are machine SSL certificates and trusted root certificates.

Step 3.   For more details, click **View Details** for the certificate type.

Step 4.   For the machine SSL certificates, optionally choose from the following actions:

- **Renew**
- **Import and Replace Certificate**
- **Generate CSR**

Step 5.   For trusted root certificates, optionally choose **Add**.

> **NOTE** To replace all VMCA-signed certificates with new VMCA-signed certificates, choose the Renew action for the machine SSL certificates.

If you replace an existing certificate, you can remove the old root certificate (as long as you are sure it is no longer in use).

By default, vCenter Server monitors all certificates in VECS and raises an alarm for any certificate that will expire in 30 days or less. You can change the 30-day threshold by modifying vCenter Server's advanced setting vpxd.cert.threshold.

Using Custom Certificates

To set up your environment to use custom certificates, you need to generate a CSR for each machine and each solution user and replace certificates when you receive them. You can generate the CSRs by using the vSphere Client or Certificate Manager. You can use the vSphere Client to upload both the root certificate and the signed certificates that are returned from the CA.

You can use the following procedure to generate a CSR for custom certificates:

Step 1. Verify that you meet the certificate requirements described in Chapter 7, "vSphere Security."

Step 2. In the vSphere Client, navigate to **Home > Administration > Certificates > Certificate Management**.

Step 3. If prompted to do so, enter the credentials for your vCenter Server.

Step 4. In the Machine SSL Certificate section, for the certificate you want to replace, click **Actions > Generate Certificate Signing Request (CSR)**.

Step 5. Enter your certificate information and click **Next**.

Step 6. Copy or download the CSR.

Step 7. Click **Finish**.

Step 8. Provide the CSR to your certificate authority.

Alternatively, you can use the vSphere Certificate Manager utility from the vCenter Server shell to generate the CSR, by using the command **/usr/lib/vmware-vmca/bin/certificate-manager**, selecting option 1, and providing the certificate information.

After your CA processes the CSR, you can use the following procedure to add the custom certificates:

Step 1. In the vSphere Client, navigate to **Home** > **Administration** > **Certificates** > **Certificate Management**.

Step 2. If the system prompts you to do so, enter the credentials for your vCenter Server.

Step 3. In the Machine SSL Certificate section, for the certificate you want to replace, click **Actions** > **Import and Replace Certificate**.

Step 4. Select the **Replace with External CA Certificate (requires private key)** option and click **Next**.

Step 5. Upload the certificates and click **Replace**.

Step 6. Wait for the vCenter Server services to restart.

Managing ESXi Certificates

In vSphere 6.0 and later, ESXi hosts initially boot with an autogenerated certificate. When a host is added to a vCenter Server system, it is provisioned with a certificate signed by the VMware Certificate Authority (VMCA). You can view and manage ESXi certificates by using the vSphere Client or the vim.CertificateManager API in the vSphere Web Services SDK. You cannot use the vCenter Server certificate management CLIs to view or manage ESXi certificates.

Changing the Certificate Mode

You can change the ESXi certificate mode from VMCA Mode to Custom Certificate Authority Mode or to Thumbprint Mode. In most cases, mode switches are disruptive and not necessary. If you require a mode switch, be sure to review the potential impact before you start. You should use Thumbprint Mode only for debugging.

> **NOTE** Thumbprint Mode was used in vSphere 5.5 and should not be used in later versions unless it is necessary because some services may not work. Also, in Thumbprint Mode, vCenter Server checks only the certificate format and not its validity. Even expired certificates are accepted.

To perform certificate management for ESXi, you must have the Certificates.Manage Certificates privilege.

For example, if you want to use custom certificates instead of using VMCA to provision ESXi hosts, you need to edit the vCenter Server vpxd.certmgmt.mode advanced option. In the vSphere client, you can use this procedure to change the certificate mode:

Step 1. Select the vCenter Server and click **Configure**.

Step 2. Click **Advanced Settings** and then click **Edit**.

Step 3. In the Filter box, enter **certmgmt** to display only certificate management keys.

Step 4. Change the value of vpxd.certmgmt.mode to **custom** and click **OK**.

Step 5. Restart the vCenter Server service.

Using Custom ESXi Certificates

You can switch the certificate mode from VMCA to a different root CA by using these steps:

Step 1. Obtain the certificates from the trusted CA.

Step 2. Place the host or hosts into Maintenance Mode and disconnect them from vCenter Server.

Step 3. Add the custom CA's root certificate to VECS.

Step 4. Deploy the custom CA certificates to each host and restart services on that host.

Step 5. Change Certificate Mode to **Custom CA Mode** (as described in the previous section).

Step 6. Connect the host or hosts to the vCenter Server system.

Switching Back to VMCA Mode

If you are using the Custom CA Mode, you can switch back to VMCA Mode by using this procedure:

Step 1. Remove all hosts from the vCenter Server system.

Step 2. On the vCenter Server system, remove the third-party CA's root certificate from VECS.

Step 3. Change Certificate Mode to **VMCA Mode**. (See the section "Changing the Certificate Mode," earlier in this chapter.)

Step 4. Add the hosts to the vCenter Server system.

Certificate Expiration

For ESXi 6.0 and later, you can use the vSphere Client to view information, including expiration, for all certificates that are signed by VMCA or a third-party CA. In the vSphere Client, select the host and navigate to Configure > System > Certificate. Here you can examine the Issuer, Subject, Valid From, Valid To, and Status fields. The value of the Status field may be Good, Expiring, Expiring Shortly, Expiration Imminent, or Expired.

A yellow alarm is raised if a certificate's status is Expiring Shortly (that is, if it expires in less than eight months). A red alarm is raised if the certificate's status is Expiration Imminent (that is, if it expires in less than two months).

By default, each time a host reconnects to vCenter Server, it renews any host certificates whose status is Expired, Expiring Immediately, or Expiring. If a certificate is already expired, you must disconnect the host and reconnect it. To renew or refresh the certificates, you can use the following procedure:

Step 1.   In the vSphere Client, select the host in the navigation pane.

Step 2.   Navigate to **Configure > System > Certificate**.

Step 3.   Click one of the following options:

- **Renew**: Retrieves a fresh signed certificate for the host from VMCA.
- **Refresh CA Certificates**: Pushes all certificates in the VECS TRUSTED_ROOTS store to the host.

Step 4.   Click **Yes**.

General ESXi Security Recommendations

In Chapter 7, you learned that vSphere has built-in security features and that you can take additional steps to harden ESXi. The following items are additional security measures that VMware recommends:

- Limit access to the Direct Console User Interface (DCUI), the ESXi shell, and Secure Shell (SSH). If you allow access to these items, which have privileged access to certain ESXi components, you need to ensure that only trusted users have access and that timeouts are set.

- Do not directly access ESXi hosts that are managed by vCenter Server. Although it may be possible to access a host via the DCUI, SSH, ESXi shell, API, or vSphere Host Client, you should not normally do so. Instead, you should use the vSphere Client (or vSphere Web Client) or API connected to vCenter Server to manage the ESXi host.

- Use the DCUI only for troubleshooting. Likewise, use root access to the ESXi shell only for troubleshooting.

- When upgrading ESXi components, use only VMware sources. Although a host runs several third-party packages, VMware supports upgrades to those packages only from VMware sources. Check third-party vendor sites and the VMware knowledge base for security alerts.

- You should follow the VMware security advisories at http://www.vmware.com/security/.

- Configure ESXi hosts with host profiles, scripts, or some other automation.

Hardening Guidelines

In the U.S. Department of Defense (DoD), Security Technical Implementation Guides (STIGs) provide technical, standards-based hardening guidance. Officially published STIGs are mandatory in the DoD and fill a crucial role in systems accreditation as part of the Risk Management Framework (RMF). VMware has worked with the Defense Information Systems Agency (DISA) to publish many STIGs over the years and will continue to do so. The official reference for DISA STIGs is https://public.cyber.mil/stigs/. The content that VMware has submitted to DISA is available in the VMware vSphere 8 STIG Readiness Guide at https://via.vmw.com/stig, which includes STIGs for the vCenter Server appliance, VAMI, and Lookup Service, among many others.

DISA uses the following category codes:

- **CAT I**: The exploitation of the vulnerability will directly and immediately result in loss of confidentiality, availability, or integrity.

- **CAT II**: The exploitation of the vulnerability has a potential to result in loss of confidentiality, availability, or integrity.

- **CAT III**: The existence of the vulnerability degrades measures to protect against loss of confidentiality, availability, or integrity.

STIGs are used as the baseline for hardening DoD environments. The vSphere 8 Security Configuration & Hardening Guide (SCG) is the baseline for hardening other vSphere environments. In addition to providing guidance for system design and hardware configuration, the SCG provides guidance on security controls.

In the VMware vSphere Security Baseline version 801-20230613-01 (at https://via.vmw.com/scg), you will find 126 security control items. For example, an item named esxi-8.account-password-policies explains that you can change the settings on the ESXi CIM service from its default "Start and stop with host" to "Start and stop manually" because it is a best practice to deactivate unused services. Code examples are provided for assessing and remediating each item. For each item, an applicable DISA STIG ID is provided. For the previous example, the item named esxi-8. account-password-policies is associated with DISA STIG ID ESXI-80-000228.

Configuring ESXi Using Host Profiles

You can use host profiles to set up standard secured configurations for your ESXi hosts and automate compliance.

You can consider any setting that is applied by a host profile to be important to ensuring that your hosts are secured. Some settings, such as direct ESXi permissions, may be obvious. Other settings, such as NTP settings, may not be obvious, but time synchronization issues impact integration with Active Directory, which impacts user authentication. Network settings, such as physical NIC speed, could impact the ability of a host to connect to the proper management network.

As discussed in Chapter 8, host profiles can be used to apply many host configuration settings, including security measures, such as ESXi-level permissions. You can use the vSphere Client to configure a host profile for a reference host and apply the host profile to a set of hosts. You can also use host profiles to monitor hosts for host configuration changes. You can attach a host profile to a cluster to apply it to all hosts in the cluster. These are the high-level steps:

Step 1.   Set up the reference host to specification and create a host profile.

Step 2.   Attach the profile to a host or cluster.

Step 3.   Apply the host profile from the reference host to other hosts or clusters.

To ensure that an ESXi host is properly configured according to your standards, you can ensure that it complies with its attached host profile. You can use the results to identify noncompliant settings on the host and remediate with the host profiles settings. You can use these steps to check compliance:

Step 1.   Navigate to the **Host Profiles** main view.

Step 2.   Right-click a host profile.

Step 3.   Click **Check Host Profile Compliance**.

The compliance status for each ESXi host is Compliant, Unknown, or Noncompliant. Noncompliant status indicates a specific inconsistency between the profile and the host, which you should remediate. Unknown status indicates that the compliance of the host is not known because it could not be verified. A common root cause is that the host is disconnected. You should resolve the issue and recheck compliance.

Using Scripts to Manage Host Configuration Settings

Another means to establish a standard secured configuration for ESXi hosts in a vSphere environment is to use vSphere PowerCLI, ESXCLI, or custom code leveraging the vSphere API.

> **NOTE** Starting with vSphere 7.0, the vSphere CLI package is end of life. Its capabilities are supported with more API-centric tools such as ESXCLI and Perl SDK.

From the ESXi shell, you can use the ESXCLI command set to configure the host and to perform administrative tasks. ESXCLI provides a collection of namespaces that allows an administrator to quickly discover the precise command necessary for a specific task. For example, all the commands to configure networking exist in the **esxcli network** namespace, and all the commands to configure storage exist in the **esxcli storage** namespace. Each namespace is further divided into child namespaces that comprise various functions performed under the parent namespace. For example, the **esxcli storage** parent namespace contains a **core** namespace that deals with storage adapters and devices and an **nmp** namespace that deals with path selection and storage array types. Therefore, a typical ESXCLI command is composed of multiple namespaces, and each additional namespace is used to narrow the scope of the command, ending with the actual operation to be performed.

To identify the proper ESXCLI command to perform a specific task, you can begin by entering **esxcli** at the command prompt in the ESXi shell. Because it is not a command by itself, just the entry point to the namespace hierarchy, the results will show the first level of the namespace hierarchy. The first level of available namespaces includes **device, esxcli, fcoe, graphics, hardware, iscsi, network, nvme, rdma, sched, software, storage, system, vm,** and **vsan.** You can use the brief description of each namespace shown in the results to identify which namespace is most likely to serve your need. You can press the up-arrow key on the keyboard to retrieve the last entered namespace and add the name for the next namespace. You can continue reviewing namespaces until you discover the command you need.

For example, if you are seeking a command to list all standard virtual switches, you can enter **esxcli network** to learn that it contains several namespaces, including one named **vswitch.** You can then enter **esxcli network vswitch** and learn that its namespaces are **standard** and **dvs.** Going further, you can learn that the **esxcli** network vswitch **standard** namespace contains **list.** You can conclude that the command you need is **esxcli network vswitch standard list.** Table 12-2 lists a few other examples of ESXCLI commands.

Table 12-2 Sample ESXCLI Commands

Command	Description
esxcli system account add	Creates an ESXi host local user account
esxcli system account set	Configures an ESXi host local user account
esxcli system account list	Lists ESXi host local user accounts
esxcli system account remove	Deletes ESXi host local user accounts
esxcli network ip dns server list	Lists the host's DNS servers
esxcli network nic list	Lists the ESXi host's physical network adapters
esxcli system settings advanced get /UserVars/ESXiShellTimeOut	Displays the shell interactive timeout for the host

Likewise, you can use PowerCLI to manage and configure a vSphere environment. When connecting to a vCenter Server environment, the functionality scope of PowerCLI is similar to the functionality scope of using the vSphere Client with the vCenter Server. Table 12-3 describes a few popular PowerCLI commands.

Table 12-3 Sample PowerCLI Commands

Command	Description	Example
Connect-VIServer	Connects to a vCenter Server	**Connect-VIServer vc01 -User administrator@ vsphere.local** connects to a vCenter Server named vc01 as user administrator@vsphere.local.
Get-VMHost	Retrieves information about one or more ESXi hosts	**Get-VMHost -Location MyDC** retrieves details about all ESXi hosts in a data center named MyDC.
Set-VMHost	Changes a setting or state of an ESXi host	**Set-VMHost -VMHost Host -State "Disconnected"** disconnects the host from vCenter Server.

If you want to develop code using other tools, you may want to get familiar with vSphere REST APIs. To do so, you can browse to the FQDN of your vCenter Server and select Browse vSphere REST APIs. In vCenter Server 8.0, this link takes you to the API Explorer section of the Developer Center in the vSphere Client. Here you can learn how to make GET and POST calls to query and modify the state and configuration of your ESXi hosts and other vSphere objects.

ESXi Passwords and Account Lockout

For direct ESXi host access, you can use the local root account and additional user accounts that you create directly on the host. When setting a password on these accounts, you must comply with or modify the predefined requirements. ESXi uses the Linux PAM module pam_passwdqc for password management and control. You can change the required length, change character class requirement, and allow pass-phrases by using the Security.PasswordQualityControl advanced option.

> **NOTE** The default requirements for ESXi passwords can change from one release to the next. You can check and change the default password restrictions by using the Security.PasswordQualityControl advanced option.

One step in hardening an ESXi host is to harden the password required to use its predefined local administrator account, which is called root. By default, the ESXi host enforces passwords for its local user accounts, which may be used to access the host via the DCUI, the ESXi shell, SSH, or the vSphere Client. Starting with ESXi 6.0, the default password policy must contain characters from at least three character classes (of the four character classes, which are lowercase letters, uppercase letters, numbers, and special characters) and must be at least seven characters long.

An uppercase character that begins a password and a number that ends a password do not count toward the number of character classes used. A password cannot contain a dictionary word or part of a dictionary word. For example, xQaT3!A is an acceptable password because it contains four character classes and seven characters. However, Xqate!3 is not an acceptable password because it contains only two character classes; the leading X and ending 3 do not count toward the number of used character classes. You can modify the ESXi password requirements by using the ESXi host Security.PasswordQualityControl advanced option. You can set Security.PasswordQualityControl to configure the ESXi host to accept passphrases, which it does not accept by default. The key to changing the password and passphrase requirements is understanding the syntax and functionality of the Security.PasswordQualityControl parameter, which has the following default value:

```
retry=3 min=disabled,disabled,disabled,7,7
```

The first part of the value used for this parameter identifies the number of retries allowed for the user following a failed logon attempt. In the default value, **retry=3** indicates that three additional attempts are permitted following a failed logon. The remainder of the value can be abstracted as follows:

```
min=N0,N1,N2,N3,N4
```

The values in this parameter are as follows:

- **N0**: This is the minimum number of accepted characters for passwords that contain characters from only one class; it can be disabled to disallow passwords that contain characters from only one class.

- **N1**: This is the minimum number of accepted characters for passwords that contain characters from only two classes; it can be disabled to disallow passwords that contain characters from only two classes.

- **N2**: This is the minimum number of accepted characters for passphrases, and it can be disabled to disallow passphrases. In addition, to require a passphrase, you can append passphrase=N to the end of the value, where N specifies the minimum number of words, separated by spaces, in the passphrase.

- **N3**: This is the minimum number of accepted characters for passwords that contain characters from only three classes; it can be disabled to disallow passwords that contain characters from only three classes.

- **N4**: This is the minimum number of accepted characters for passwords that contain characters from all four classes.

For example, to require a passphrase with a minimum of 16 characters and 3 words, you can set Security.PasswordQualityControl as follows:

```
retry=3 min=disabled,disabled,16,7,7,passphrase=3
```

The password requirements in ESXi 6.0 are implemented by pam_passwdqc. For more details, see the man pages for pam_passwdqc.

Account locking is supported for access through SSH and through the vSphere Web Services SDK. The DCUI and the ESXi shell do not support account lockout. By default, a user gets a maximum of 10 failed attempts before their account is locked. The account is unlocked after two minutes by default. You can modify the lockout behavior by using the host's advanced options:

- **Security.AccountLockFailures**: The maximum number of failed login attempts before a user's account is locked. Zero disables account locking.

- **Security.AccountUnlockTime**: The number of seconds that a user is locked out.

SSH and ESXi Shell Security

You can use SSH to remotely log in to the ESXi shell and perform troubleshooting tasks for the host. SSH configuration in ESXi is enhanced to provide a high security level. VMware does not support SSH Version 1 and uses Version 2 exclusively. SSH supports only 256-bit and 128-bit AES ciphers for connections.

The ESXi shell is disabled by default on ESXi hosts. If necessary, you can enable local and remote access to the shell. However, to reduce the risk of unauthorized access, you should enable the ESXi shell only when troubleshooting. If the ESXi shell or SSH is enabled and the host is placed in Lockdown Mode, accounts on the ception users list who have administrator privileges can use these services. For all

 thers, ESXi shell or SSH access is disabled. Starting with vSphere 6.0, ESXi or SSH sessions for users who do not have administrator privileges are closed.

If the ESXi shell is enabled, you can still log in to it locally, even if the host is running in Lockdown Mode. To enable local ESXi shell access, enable the ESXi shell service. To enable remote ESXi shell access, enable the SSH service.

NOTE The root user and users with the administrator role can access the ESXi shell. Users who are in the Active Directory group ESX Admins are automatically assigned the administrator role. By default, only the root user can run system commands (such as **vmware -v**) by using the ESXi shell.

You can use the following procedure to enable the ESXi shell:

Step 1. In the vSphere Client, select the host in the navigation pane.

Step 2. Navigate to **Configure > Services**.

Step 3. Select **ESXi Shell** and click **Start**.

Step 4. Optionally, click **Edit Startup Policy** and then select one of the following options:

- **Start and Stop Manually**
- **Start and Stop with Host**
- **Start and Stop with Port Usage**

Step 5. Click **OK**.

You can use a similar procedure to control local and remote access to the ESXi shell by configuring the startup policy for DCUI and SSH services.

In vSphere 8, timeout values are set by default for the ESXi shell and SSH. You can modify the Availability Timeout setting based on your needs. The Availability Timeout setting specifies the amount of time that can elapse before a user must log in after the ESXi shell is enabled. After the timeout period, the service is disabled, and users are not allowed to log in. In the vSphere Client, you can select the vCenter Server, navigate to Configure > Settings, go to the Timeout Settings, and set the Availability Timeout setting. Alternatively, you can modify the UserVars.ESXiShell-TimeOut advanced system setting.

Similarly, you can set a timeout for idle ESXi shell sessions. The Idle Timeout setting specifies the amount of time that can elapse before a user is logged out of an idle interactive session. In the vSphere Client, you can select the vCenter Server, navigate to Configure > Settings, go to the Timeout Settings, and set the Idle

Timeout setting. Alternatively, you can modify the UserVars.ESXiShellInteractive-TimeOut advanced system setting.

An SSH key can allow a trusted user or script to log in to a host without specifying a password. You can upload the authorized keys file for the root user (ssh_root_authorized_keys), an RSA key (ssh_host_rsa_key), an RSA public key (ssh_host_rsa_key_pub), a DSA key (ssh_host_dsa_key), or a DSA public key (ssh_host_dsa_key_pub) to the host directory on an ESXi host by using HTTPS PUT.

PCI and PCIe Devices and ESXi

You can use the VMware DirectPath I/O feature to pass through a PCI or a PCIe device to a virtual machine, but doing so results in a potential security vulnerability that could be triggered when buggy or malicious code, such as a device driver, is running in Privileged Mode in the guest OS. Therefore, you should use PCI or PCIe passthrough to a virtual machine *only* if a trusted entity owns and administers the virtual machine. Otherwise, you risk the host being compromised in several ways:

- The guest OS might generate an unrecoverable PCI or PCIe error.

- The guest OS might generate a Direct Memory Access (DMA) operation that causes an IOMMU page fault on the ESXi host.

- If the operating system on the ESXi host is not using interrupt remapping, the guest OS might inject a spurious interrupt into the ESXi host on any vector.

To enable passthrough for a network device on a host, you can use the following procedure:

Step 1.   In the vSphere Client, select the host in the navigation pane.

Step 2.   Navigate to **Configure > Hardware > PCI Devices** and click **Edit**.

Step 3.   Select a device with a green icon and click **OK**.

NOTE An orange icon indicates that the status of the device has changed, and you must reboot the host before you can use the device.

Disabling the Managed Object Browser

The *managed object browser (MOB)* provides a means to explore the VMkernel object model. Starting with vSphere 6.0, the MOB is disabled by default to avoid malicious configuration changes or actions. You can enable and disable the MOB manually. VMware recommends that you not enable the MOB in production systems.

To enable the MOB by using the vSphere Client, you can use the following procedure:

Step 1.   In the vSphere Client, select the host in the inventory.

Step 2.   In the right pane, click the **Configuration** tab.

Step 3.   Select **System > Advanced Settings** and click **Edit**.

Step 4.   Select **Config.HostAgent.plugins.solo.enableMob** and set its value to **true**.

ESXi Networking Security Recommendations

Chapter 7 provides VMware general network security recommendations for vSphere. For each ESXi host, you can summarize the network isolation into the following categories.

- **vSphere infrastructure networks**: Isolate these networks for their specific functions, such as vMotion vSphere Fault Tolerance, storage, and vSAN. In many cases, you may not need to route these networks outside a single rack.

- **Management network**: This network carries client API and third-party software traffic. Isolate this network such that it is accessible only by the appropriate administrators and systems. Consider using a jump box or a virtual private network (VPN).

- **Virtual machine networks**: This network may involve many networks, each with unique isolation requirements. Consider using virtual firewall solutions, such as NSX.

ESXi Web Proxy Settings

If you configure a web proxy, consider the following suggestions:

- Do not use certificates that use passwords or passphrases. ESXi does not support web proxies with passwords or passphrases, also known as encrypted keys.

- If you want to disable SSL for vSphere Web Services SDK connections, you can change the connection from HTTPS to HTTP. You should consider doing this only if you have a fully trusted environment, where firewalls are in place and transmissions to and from the host are fully isolated.

- Most internal ESXi services are accessible only through port 443. Port 443 acts as a reverse proxy for ESXi. You can change the configuration to allow direct HTTP connections but should consider doing this only for a fully trusted environment.

- During upgrades, the certificate remains in place.

vSphere Auto Deploy Security Considerations

If you use vSphere Auto Deploy, it is important to consider networking security, boot image security, and potential password exposure through host profiles.

You should secure an Auto Deploy network as you would secure the network for any PXE-based deployment method. Auto Deploy transfers data over SSL, but it does not check the authenticity of the client or of the Auto Deploy server during a PXE boot.

The boot image includes the host's public and private SSL key and certificate. If Auto Deploy rules are set up to provision the host with a host profile or host customization, the boot image includes the host profile and host customization. The root password and user passwords in the host profile and host customization are hashed with SHA-512. Other passwords, such as those to set up Active Directory using the host profile, are not protected. You can use vSphere Authentication Proxy to avoid exposing Active Directory passwords.

Ideally, you should completely isolate an Auto Deploy network.

Starting with vSphere 8.0, you can use custom certificates (that is, certificates signed by certificate authorities) with Auto Deploy. When the host starts, Auto Deploy associates a custom certificate with either a MAC address or the BIOS UUID of the ESXi host.

Controlling CIM Access

Common Information Model (CIM) is an open standard that defines a framework for agentless, standards-based monitoring of ESXi host hardware resources. The framework consists of a CIM broker and a set of CIM providers. Hardware vendors, including server manufacturers and hardware device vendors, can write providers that monitor and manage their devices. VMware has CIM providers that monitor server hardware, ESXi storage infrastructure, and virtualization-specific resources. These lightweight providers run inside the ESXi host and perform specific management tasks.

Instead of using root credentials, you can create a less-privileged vSphere user account to provide to remote applications that access the CIM interface. The required privilege for the user account is Host.CIM.Interaction.

You can use the VIM API ticket function to issue a session ID (ticket) to a user account to authenticate to CIM. You need to ensure that the account is granted permission to obtain CIM tickets.

When you install a third-party CIM VIB, the CIM service starts. To manually enable the CIM service, you can use the following command:

```
esxcli system wbem set -e true
```

You can use the API SDK of your choice to call AcquireCimServicesTicket to return a ticket that you can use to authenticate the user with vCenter Server using CIM-XML port 5989 or WS-Man port 433 APIs.

Configuring and Managing ESXi Security

This section describes procedures for securing ESXi.

Configuring the ESXi Firewall

By default, the ESXi firewall is configured to block incoming and outgoing traffic, except traffic for services that are enabled in the hosts' security profile. The firewall also allows Internet Control Message Protocol (ICMP) pings. Prior to opening any ports on the firewall, you should consider the impact it may have for potential attacks and unauthorized user access. You can reduce this risk by configuring the firewall to only allow communication on the port with authorized networks. To modify the firewall's rule set, you can use the vSphere Client to modify the host's security profile, using the following procedure.

Step 1.   In the vSphere Client, select the host in the inventory pane and navigate to **Configure > System > Firewall**.

Step 2.   Select the appropriate service name, such as the incoming SSH server (TCP 22) or the outgoing DNS client (TCP/UDP 53), and click **Edit**.

Step 3.   Examine the rule set. Change the state of any rule by selecting the rule (placing a check in the rule's box) to enable the rule or deselecting the rule to disable it.

Step 4.   Optionally, for some services, you can deselect the **Allow Connections from Any IP Address** box and enter specific IP addresses in the accompanying text box to restrict use to only those IP addresses.

Step 5.   Click **OK**.

When specifying particular IP addresses in the firewall settings, you can use the formats shown in the following examples:

- 192.168.10.0/24

- 192.168.11.2, 2001::1/64

- fd3e:29a6:0a79:e462::/64

The NFS Client firewall rule set behaves differently than other rule sets. ESXi configures NFS Client settings when you mount or unmount an NFS datastore. When you mount an NFS Version 3 datastore, the following events occur:

- If the nfsClient rule set is disabled, ESXi enables the rule set, sets allowedAll to FALSE, and adds the NFS server IP address to the list of allowed IP addresses.

- If the nfsClient rule set is enabled, ESXi adds the NFS server IP address to the list of allowed IP addresses but does not change the state of the rule set or allowedAll.

- When you mount an NFS Version 4.1 datastore, ESXi enables the nfs41client rule set and sets allowedAll to TRUE.

When you remove or unmount an NFS Version 3 datastore from a host, ESXi removes the IP address from the list of allowed IP addresses. When you remove or unmount the last NFS Version 3 datastore, ESXi stops the nfsClient rule set. Unmounting an NFS Version 4.1 datastore does not impact the firewall.

The ESXi software firewall is enabled by default. It should never be disabled while running production virtual machines. In rare cases, such as temporarily during troubleshooting, you can disable the ESXi firewall by using the **esxcli network firewall set --enabled false** command.

Customizing ESXi Services

Several optional services that are provided in an ESXi host are disabled by default. VMware disables these services to provide strong security out of the box. In a default installation, you can modify the status of the following services from the vSphere Client:

- **Running services**: DCUI, Load-Based Teaming Daemon, CIM Server, and VMware vCenter Agent

- **Stopped services**: ESXi shell, SSH, attestd, kmxd, Active Directory service, NTP daemon, PC/SC smart card daemon, SNMP server, syslog server, and X.Org server

In some circumstances, you might want to configure and enable these services. A good example of an optional service that you might decide to configure and enable in most environments is NTP because solid time synchronization is vital for many services. As another example, you might want to temporarily enable SSH while troubleshooting. To enable, disable, and configure services, you can use the following procedure:

Step 1. In the vSphere Client, select the host in the navigation pane and navigate to **Configure > Services**.

Step 2. Select a service that you want to modify and click **Start**, **Stop**, or **Restart** to immediately change the state of the service.

Step 3. To change the behavior permanently, click **Edit Startup Policy** and then choose one of the following options:

- **Start and Stop with Port Usage**
- **Start and Stop with Host**
- **Start and Stop Manually**

Step 4. Click **OK**.

Using Lockdown Mode

In vSphere 5.0 and earlier, only the root account can log in to the DCUI on an ESXi host that is in Lockdown Mode. In vSphere 5.1 and later, you can add a user to the DCUI.Access advanced system setting to grant the user access to the DCUI on a host that is in Lockdown Mode, even if the user is not granted the administrator role on the host. The main purpose of this feature is to prepare for catastrophic vCenter Server failures.

vSphere 6.0 and later include an Exception Users list. The main purpose of this list is to support the use of Lockdown Mode but still support service accounts, which must log on directly to the ESXi host. User accounts in the Exception Users list that have administrator privileges can log on to the DCUI and the ESXi shell.

As described in Chapter 7, you can place a host in Normal Lockdown Mode, Strict Lockdown Mode, or Normal Mode.

To change the Lockdown Mode setting, you can use the followings procedure:

Step 1. In the vSphere Client, select an ESXi host in the navigation pane and navigate to **Configure > Security Profile**.

Step 2. In the Lockdown Mode panel, click the **Edit** button.

Step 3. Click **Lockdown Mode** and choose either **Normal** or **Strict**.

Step 4. Click **OK**.

By default, the root account is included in DCUI.Access. You could consider removing the root account from DCUI.Access and replacing it with another account for better auditability.

Table 12-4 provides details on the behavior of an ESXi host in Lockdown Mode.

Table 12-4   ESXi Lockdown Mode Behavior

Service	Normal Mode	Normal Lockdown Mode	Strict Lockdown Mode
vSphere Web Services API	All users, based on permissions	vCenter (vpxuser) Exception users, based on permissions vCloud Director (vslauser, if available)	vCenter (vpxuser) Exception users, based on permissions vCloud Director (vslauser, if available)
CIM providers	Users with administrator privileges on the host	vCenter (vpxuser) Exception users, based on permissions vCloud Director (vslauser, if available)	vCenter (vpxuser) Exception users, based on permissions vCloud Director (vslauser, if available)
DCUI	Users with administrator privileges on the host and users defined in the DCUI.Access advanced option	Users defined in the DCUI. Access advanced option Exception users with administrator privileges on the host	DCUI service is stopped
ESXi shell (if enabled)	Users with administrator privileges on the host	Users defined in the DCUI. Access advanced option Exception users with administrator privileges on the host	Users defined in the DCUI. Access advanced option Exception users with administrator privileges on the host
SSH (if enabled)	Users with administrator privileges on the host	Users defined in the DCUI. Access advanced option Exception users with administrator privileges on the host	Users defined in the DCUI. Access advanced option Exception users with administrator privileges on the host

Managing the Acceptance Levels of Hosts and VIBs

A *vSphere Installation Bundle (VIB)* is a software package that includes a signature from VMware or a VMware partner. To protect the integrity of the ESXi host, do not allow users to install unsigned (community-supported) VIBs. An unsigned VIB contains code that is not certified by, accepted by, or supported by VMware or its partners. Community-supported VIBs do not have digital signatures. The host's acceptance level must be the same or less restrictive than the acceptance level of any

VIB you want to add to the host. For example, if the host acceptance level is VMwareAccepted, you cannot install VIBs at the PartnerSupported level. You should use extreme caution when allowing community-supported VIBs. The following list provides details on defined VIB acceptance levels:

- **VMwareCertified**: These VIBs go through thorough testing equivalent to VMware in-house quality assurance testing for the same technology. Only I/O Vendor Partner (IOVP) program drivers are published at this level. VMware takes support calls for VIBs with this acceptance level.

- **VMwareAccepted**: These VIBs go through testing that is run by a partner and verified by VMware. CIM providers and PSA plug-ins are among the VIBs published at this level. VMware directs support calls for VIBs with this acceptance level to the partner's support organization.

- **PartnerSupported**: These VIBs are published by a partner that VMware trusts. The partner performs all testing, but VMware does not verify it. VMware directs support calls for VIBs with this acceptance level to the partner's support organization.

- **CommunitySupported**: These VIBs have not gone through any VMware-approved testing program and are not supported by VMware Technical Support or by a VMware partner.

To change the host acceptance level, you can use the following command:

```
esxcli --server=<server_name> software acceptance set
```

Assigning Privileges for ESXi Hosts

Typically, users should access vSphere via vCenter Server, where privileges are managed centrally. For use cases where some users access ESXi hosts directly, you can manage privileges directly on the host. The following roles are predefined in ESXi:

- **Read Only**: Ability to view but not change assigned objects

- **Administrator**: Ability to change assigned objects

- **No Access**: No access to assigned objects (This role is the default role, and you can override it.)

In vSphere 6.0 and later, you can use ESXCLI to manage local user accounts and to configure permissions on local accounts and on Active Directory accounts. You can connect directly to an ESXi host by using the vSphere Host Client and navigate to Manage > Security & Users > Users to create, edit, and remove local user accounts.

The following user accounts exist on an ESXi host that is not added to a vCenter System:

- **root**: A user account that is created and assigned the administrator role by default on each ESXi host.

- **vpxuser**: A local ESXi user account that is created, managed, and used for management activities by vCenter Server.

- **dcui**: A user account that acts as an agent for the DCUI and cannot be modified or used by interactive users.

NOTE   You can remove the access privileges for the root user. But you should first create another user account at the root level and assign it the administrator role.

Much as with vCenter Server, each ESXi host uses role-based permissions for users who log on directly to the ESXi host rather than accessing the host through vCenter Server. ESXi allows the creation of custom roles, but these roles are applied only when a user directly logs on to the host, such as when the user uses the vSphere Host Client to connect to the host directly. In most cases, managing roles and permissions at the host level should be avoided or minimized. To create, edit, and remove roles, you can connect directly to an ESXi host by using the vSphere Host Client and navigate to Manage > Security & Users > Roles.

Using Active Directory to Manage ESXi Users

In scenarios where multiple users need to access multiple ESXi hosts directly (rather than accessing vCenter Server), you can consider enabling direct ESXi access using Active Directory. This requires joining the hosts to Active Directory and assigning roles to specific Active Directory users and groups. You can use the following steps to add an ESXi host to an Active Directory domain:

Step 1.   Verify that an Active Directory domain is available.

Step 2.   Ensure that the host name of the ESXi host is fully qualified with the domain name that matches the domain name of the Active Directory forest. For example, if the Active Directory domain name is mydomain.com and the ESXi host name is host-01, then the host's fully qualified name is host-01.mydomain.com.

Step 3.   Synchronize time between the ESXi host and domain controllers by using NTP.

Step 4.   Ensure that DNS is configured and that the ESXi host can resolve the host names of the Active Directory domain controllers.

Step 5.   In the vSphere Client, select the ESXi host in the inventory pane and navigate to **Configure > Authentication Services**.

Step 6.   Click **Join Domain**.

Step 7.   In the dialog box, specify the domain and user credentials. Optionally, specify a proxy server.

Step 8.   Enter a domain, either in the form *name*.tld or in the form *name*.tld/ *container/path*, where *name*.tld is the domain name, and */container/path* is an optional path to an organization unit where the host computer object should be created. For example, you can use domain.com/ou01/ou02 to add the host to an organization unit named ou02 that resides in an organization unit named ou01 in a domain named domain.com.

Step 9.   Click **OK**.

Configuring vSphere Authentication Proxy

You can use vSphere Authentication Proxy to add hosts to an Active Directory domain instead of adding hosts to the domain explicitly. When vSphere Authentication Proxy is enabled, it automatically adds hosts that are being provisioned by Auto Deploy to the Active Directory domain. You can also use vSphere Authentication Proxy to add hosts that are not provisioned by Auto Deploy.

To start the vSphere Authentication Proxy service and add a domain, you can use the following procedure:

Step 1.   Log on to the vCenter Server Appliance Management Interface (VAMI) as root.

Step 2.   Select **Services > VMware vSphere Authentication Proxy**.

Step 3.   Click **Start**.

Step 4.   In the vSphere Client, select the vCenter Server in the inventory pane and navigate to **Configure > Authentication Proxy > Edit**.

Step 5.   Enter the domain name and credentials of a user who can add hosts to the domain.

Step 6.   Click **Save**.

Now you can add a host to an Active Directory domain by using the procedure outlined in the section "Using Active Directory to Manage ESXi Users," but when you do so, you select the **Using Proxy Server** option in step 8.

Configuring Smart Card Authentication for ESXi

As an alternative to specifying a username and password, you can use smart card authentication to log in to the ESXi DCUI by using a Personal Identity Verification (PIV) credential, a Common Access Card (CAC), or an SC650 smart card. In this case, the DCUI prompts for a smart card and PIN combination. To configure smart card authentication, you should set up the smart card infrastructure (Active Directory domain accounts, smart card readers, smart card, and so on), configure ESXi to join an Active Directory domain that supports smart card authentication, use the vSphere Client to add root certificates, and follow these steps:

Step 1. In the vSphere Client, select the host in the inventory pane and navigate to **Configure > Authentication Services**.

Step 2. In the Smart Card Authentication panel, click **Edit**.

Step 3. In the dialog box, select the **Certificates** page.

Step 4. Add trusted certificate authority (CA) certificates, such as root and intermediary CA certificates, in the PEM format.

Step 5. Open the Smart Card Authentication page, select the **Enable Smart Card Authentication** checkbox, and click **OK**.

Configuring UEFI Secure Boot for ESXi Hosts

In versions since vSphere 6.5, ESXi supports UEFI Secure Boot, which you can enable in the UEFI firmware. With Secure Boot enabled, a machine refuses to load any UEFI driver or app unless the operating system bootloader is cryptographically signed. In vSphere 6.5 and later, the ESXi bootloader contains and uses a VMware public key to verify the signature of the kernel and a small subset of the system that includes a Secure Boot VIB verifier that verifies each VIB package installed on the host.

NOTE You cannot use Secure Boot on ESXi servers that were upgraded by using ESXCLI commands because the upgrade does not update the bootloader.

You can use the following command to run the Secure Boot validation script on an upgraded ESXi host to determine if it supports Secure Boot:

```
/usr/lib/vmware/secureboot/bin/secureBoot.py -c
```

The output is either "Secure boot can be enabled" or "Secure boot CANNOT be enabled."

To resolve issues with Secure Boot, you can follow these steps:

Step 1.   Reboot the host with Secure Boot disabled.

Step 2.   Run the Secure Boot verification script.

Step 3.   Examine the information in the /var/log/esxupdate.log file.

Securing ESXi Hosts with Trusted Platform Module

In ESXi 6.7 and later, you can use Trusted Platform Module (TPM) Version 2.0 chips, which are secure cryptoprocessors that enhance host security by providing trust assurance rooted in hardware. A TPM 2.0 chip attests to an ESXi host's identity. Host attestation is the process of authenticating and attesting to the state of the host's software at a given point in time. UEFI Secure Boot, which ensures that only signed software is loaded at boot time, is a requirement for successful attestation. The TPM 2.0 chip securely stores measurements of the software modules loaded in the ESXi host, and vCenter Server remotely verifies the measurements. The automated high-level steps of the attestation process are as follows:

Step 1.   Establish the trustworthiness of the remote TPM chip and create an attestation key (AK) on it.

Step 2.   Retrieve the attestation report from the host.

Step 3.   Verify the host's authenticity.

To use TPM 2.0 chips, you should ensure that your vSphere environment meets these requirements:

- vCenter Server 6.7 or later

- ESXi 6.7 or later host with TPM 2.0 chip installed and enabled in UEFI

- UEFI Secure Boot enabled

In addition, you should ensure that the TPM chip is configured in the ESXi host's BIOS to use the SHA-256 hashing algorithm and the TIS/FIFO (first-in, first-out) interface and not CRB (Command Response Buffer).

During the boot of an ESXi host with an installed TPM 2.0 chip, vCenter Server monitors the host's attestation status. The vSphere Client displays the hardware trust status in the vCenter Server's Monitor tab under Security with the following alarms:

- **Green**: Normal status, indicating full trust

- **Red**: Attestation failed

If the "Host secure boot was disabled" message appears in the vSphere Client, you must re-enable Secure Boot to resolve the problem. If the "No cached identity key loading from DB" message appears, you must disconnect and reconnect the host.

Securing ESXi Log Files

To increase the security of a host, you can implement the following measures:

- Configure persistent logging to a datastore. By default, ESXi logs are stored in an in-memory file system that keeps only 24 hours' worth of data and loses data during host reboot.

- Configure syslog to use remote logging from ESXi hosts to a central host, where you can monitor, search, and analyze logs from all hosts with a single tool.

- Query the syslog configuration to ensure that the syslog server and port are valid.

For details see Chapter 10, "Managing and Monitoring Clusters and Resources."

Additional Security Management

Managing vSphere security can involve other tasks, such as those described in this section.

Key Management Server

In order to use encryption in vSphere, you must be running a key management server (KMS) that has a trust relationship with vCenter Server. To add a KMS to vCenter Server, you can use the following procedure:

Step 1.   In the vSphere Client, select the vCenter Server in the inventory pane and navigate to **Configuration > Security > Key Providers**.

Step 2.   Click **Add > Add Standard Key Provider**.

Step 3.   Provide a logical name for the key provider.

Step 4.   Provide the server name, server address (FQDN), and server port for each KMS server associated with the key provider.

Step 5.   Optionally, provide other appropriate details, such as proxy details and user credentials.

Step 6.   Click the radio button next to the KMS name.

Step 7. In the Make vCenter Trust KMS window, click **TRUST**.

Step 8. Click **Make KMS Trust vCenter**.

Step 9. Select **KMS Certificate and Private Key** and click **Next**.

Step 10. In the next window, next to KMS Certificate, click **Upload File** and open an available certificate PEM file.

Step 11. In the same window, next to KMS Private Key, click **Upload File** and open an available certificate PEM file.

Step 12. Click the **Establish Trust** button.

Changing Permission Validation Settings

Periodically, vCenter Server validates its user and group lists against the users and groups in the Windows Active Directory domain. It removes users and groups that no longer exist in the domain. You can change the behavior of this validation by using the vSphere Client to edit the general settings of the vCenter Server and change the Validation and Validation Period options. If you want to disable the validation, deselect the Enable checkbox under Validation. If you want to adjust the frequency at which this validation is performed, enter a value in the Validation Period text box to specify a time, in minutes, between validations.

Configuring and Managing vSphere Trust Authority (vTA)

With vSphere Trust Authority (vTA), you can do the following.

- Provide a hardware root of trust and remote attestation to ESXi hosts.

- Restrict the release of encryption keys to only attested ESXi hosts.

- Centralize and secure the management of multiple key servers.

- Enhance the level of encryption key management that is used to perform cryptographic operations on virtual machines.

With vTA, you can run workloads in a secure environment where you detect tampering, disallow unauthorized changes, prevent malware, and verify the hardware and software stacks.

When you configure vTA, you enable the Attestation service and the Key Provider service on the ESXi host in the Trust Authority cluster. The Attestation service attests to the state of the trusted ESXi hosts, using a TPM 2.0 chip as the basis for software measurement and reporting. The Attestation service verifies that the software measurement signature can be attributed to a previously configured trusted

TPM endorsement key (EK). The Key Provider service removes the need for the vCenter Server and the ESXi hosts to require direct key server credentials. The Key Provider service acts as a gatekeeper for the key servers, releasing keys only to trusted ESXi hosts.

A trusted ESXi host must contain a TPM chip. A TPM chip is manufactured with an EK, which is a public/private key pair that is built into the hardware. You can configure the Attestation service to trust all CA certificates where the manufacturer signed the TPM chip (the EK public key) or to trust the host's TOM CA certificate and EK public key.

NOTE   If you want to trust individual ESXi hosts, the TPM chip must include an EK certificate. Some TPM chips do not.

You can use VMware PowerCLI to configure and manage vSphere Trust Authority. Alternatively, you can use vSphere APIs or the vSphere Client for at least some of the activities. To configure vTA, you can perform the following high-level tasks:

Step 1.   On a Windows system with access to the vTA environment, install PowerCLI 12.0.0 and Microsoft .NET Framework 4.8 or greater and create a local folder.

Step 2.   Add your user account to the TrustedAdmins groups on the vCenter Server managing the Trust Authority cluster and on the vCenter Server of the trusted cluster.

Step 3.   Enable **Trust Authority State**.

Step 4.   Collect information about the trusted hosts in the trusted cluster (using **Export-Tpm2CACertificate**).

Step 5.   Import the trusted host data to the Trust Authority cluster (**New-TrustAuthorityPrincipal**).

Step 6.   Create the trusted key provider on the Trust Authority cluster (using **New-TrustAuthorityKeyProvider**).

Step 7.   Export the Trust Authority cluster information from the Trust Authority cluster (using **Export-TrustAuthorityServicesInfo**).

Step 8.   Import the Trust Authority cluster data to the trusted cluster (using **Import-TrustAuthorityServicesInfo**).

Step 9.   Configure the trusted key provider for the trusted hosts on the trusted cluster (using **Register-KeyProvider** and **Set-KeyProvider**).

After configuring vTA, you can perform management operations, including those summarized in Table 12-5.

Table 12-5   vTA Operations

Operation	Key Steps
Start, stop, and restart vTA services	In the vSphere Client, select the host, navigate to Configure > Services > System and select Restart, Start, or Stop.
View Trust Authority hosts	In the vSphere Client, select the trusted cluster's vCenter Server and select Configure > Security > Trust Authority.
View vTA cluster state	In the vSphere Client, select the Trust Authority cluster's vCenter Server and select Configure > Trust Authority > Trust Authority Cluster.
Restart the Trusted Host service	In an SSH session, enter **/etc/init.d/kmxa restart**.
Add a Trust Authority host	Use PowerCLI to run **Add-TrustAuthorityVMHost**.
Add a trusted host	Use PowerCLI to run **Add-TrustedVMHost**.
Change the master key of a key provider	Use PowerCLI to run **Set-TrustAuthorityKeyProvider**.

Most of the vTA configuration and state information is stored on the ESXi hosts in the ConfigStore database. Backups of vCenter Server do not include vTA configuration. You can leverage the files that you exported during the configuration of vTA vSphere as your backup. If you need to restore vTA, use the exported files to reconfigure vTA.

TLS 1.2

By default, during fresh installation, upgrade, or migration, vSphere 8 enables TLS 1.2 and disables TLS 1.0 and TLS 1.1. Although the TLS Configurator utility can be used on ESXi 7.x environments to activate older TLS versions, ESXi 8.0 and later do not support TLS 1.0 and 1.1. Running the TLS Configurator utility on ESXi 8.0 and later silently fails, with no error reported. To use the TLS Configurator utility, you can open an SSH session to the vCenter Server and use a command to run the utility. For example, to deactivate TLS 1.0 and TLS 1.1 and activate only TLS 1.2 in an applicable environment, you can use the following commands:

```
cd /usr/lib/vmware-TlsReconfigurator/VcTlsReconfigurator./
reconfigureVc update -p TLSv1.2
```

FIPS

Federal Information Processing Standards (FIPS) are publicly announced U.S. standards that establish requirements for ensuring computer security and interoperability. FIPS 140-2 is a U.S. and Canadian government standard that specifies security requirements for cryptographic modules. vSphere uses FIPS-validated cryptographic modules to match those specified by the FIPS 140-2 standard. The goal of vSphere FIPS support is to ease the compliance and security activities in various regulated environments.

In vSphere 7.0 Update 2 and later, you can use the following steps to enable FIPS-validated cryptography on the vCenter Server Appliance, which is deactivated by default:

Step 1. In the vSphere Client, navigate to **Menu > Developer Center > API Explorer**.

Step 2. In the Select API drop-down menu, select **appliance**.

Step 3. Scroll through the categories and expand **system/security/global_fips**.

Step 4. Expand **GET** and click **Try It Out > Expand**.

Step 5. Go to the **Response** area and view the current setting.

Step 6. Expand **PUT** and enter the following into the request body.

```
{
"enabled":true
}
```

Step 7. Click **Execute**.

When enabling FIPS, it is important to consider that vCenter Server supports only cryptographic modules for federated authentication, which means RSA SecureID and some CACs do not function. In addition, non-VMware vSphere Client plug-ins may not work with FIPS, and certificates with key sizes larger than 3072 bits have not been tested.

Securing Virtual Machines with Intel Software Guard Extensions (SGX)

If Intel SGX technology is available on your hardware, your virtual machines can use Virtual Intel SGX (vSGX). You can enable vSGX on a virtual machine on an ESXi host that has compatible CPUs and SGX enabled in the BIOS. The virtual machine must use hardware Version 17 or later (with Compatibility set to ESXi 7.0 and Later) and a supported guest OS (Linux, 64-bit Windows 10 or later, or 64-bit

Windows Server 2016 or later). To enable vSGX, configure the following hardware settings:

- Go to Security Devices > SGX and select the Enable checkbox.

- Go to VM Options > Boot Options and set Firmware to EFI.

- Set the Enter Enclave Page Cache (EPC) size and select Flexible Launch Control (FLC) mode.

To enable vSGX, the virtual machine must be powered off. You can enable vSGX as you provision a new virtual machine. To remove vSGX from a virtual machine, go to Security Devices > SGX and uncheck the Enable checkbox.

Encrypting a Virtual Machine

You can use the following procedure to create a new encrypted virtual machine:

Step 1. Establish a trusted connection with the KMS and select a default KMS.

Step 2. Create an encryption storage policy or plan to use the bundled sample, VM Encryption Policy.

Step 3. Ensure that you have the Cryptographic Operations.Encrypt New privilege.

Step 4. If the host encryption mode is not enabled, ensure that you have the Cryptographic Operations.Register Host privilege.

Step 5. In the vSphere Client, launch the New Virtual Machine wizard.

Step 6. In the wizard, provide the following settings to encrypt the virtual machine:

- **Compute Resource Settings**: Select a compatible cluster or host. ESXi 6.5 or later is required.

- **Select Storage**: Select **Encrypt This Virtual Machine**, select the storage policy (from step 2), and select an appropriate datastore.

- **Virtual Machine Hardware Compatibility**: Select **ESXi 6.5 and Later**.

- **Customize Hardware Settings**: Optionally, select **VM Options > Encryption** and select virtual disks to exclude from encryption.

Step 7. Complete the wizard and click **Finish**.

To encrypt an existing virtual machine, you can use the following procedure:

Step 1. Establish a trusted connection with the KMS and select a default KMS.

Step 2. Create an encryption storage policy or plan to use the bundled sample, VM Encryption Policy.

Step 3. Ensure that you have the Cryptographic Operations.Encrypt New privilege.

Step 4. If the host encryption mode is not enabled, ensure that you have the Cryptographic Operations.Register Host privilege.

Step 5. Ensure the virtual machine is powered off.

Step 6. In the vSphere Client, right-click the virtual machine and select **VM Policies > Edit VM Storage Policies**.

Step 7. Select the storage policy (from step 2).

Step 8. Optionally, select **Configure per Disk** and set encryption as needed for each virtual disk.

Step 9. Click **OK**.

Exam Preparation Tasks

As mentioned in the section "Book Features and Exam Preparation Methods" in the Introduction, you have some choices for exam preparation: the exercises here, Chapter 15, "Final Preparation," and the exam simulation questions on the companion website.

Review All the Key Topics

Review the most important topics in this chapter, noted with the Key Topic icon in the outer margin of the page. Table 12-6 lists these key topics and the page number on which each is found.

Table 12-6   Key Topics for Chapter 12

Key Topic Element	Description	Page Number
Procedure	Change the certificate mode	481
Paragraph	Harden the ESXi password	488
Section	Configuring the ESXi firewall	494
List	VIB acceptance levels	498
Section	Configure smart card authentication	501
List	Adding a KMS to vCenter Server	503

Complete Tables and Lists from Memory

Print a copy of Appendix B, "Memory Tables" (found on the companion website), or at least the section for this chapter, and complete the tables and lists from memory. Appendix C, "Memory Table Answers" (also on the companion website), includes completed tables and lists to check your work.

Define Key Terms

Define the following key terms from this chapter and check your answers in the glossary:

vCenter Single Sign-On Security Token Service (STS), Certificate Manager, managed object browser (MOB), Common Information Model (CIM), vSphere Installation Bundle (VIB)

Review Questions

1. You want to add a global permission. Which of the following privileges do you need?

   a. Permissions.Modify Permission privilege on the vCenter root object

   b. Permissions.Modify Permission privilege on the global root object

   c. Permissions.Add Permission privilege on the vCenter root object

   d. Permissions.Add Permission privilege on the global root object

2. A yellow alarm is raised due to a host's certificate expiration date. Which of the following is a true statement concerning the state of the certificate?

   a. The certificate is expired.

   b. The certificate will expire in less than two months.

   c. The certificate will expire in more than two months and less than six months.

   d. The certificate will expire in more than two months and less than eight months.

3. You set the Security.PasswordQualityControl parameter to **retry=3 min=dis abled,disabled,disabled,7,7**. With this setting, which of the following statements is true?

   a. You cannot use passphrases.

   b. Your password can use just a single character class.

   c. Your password must include at least two character classes and seven letters.

   d. Vmware1 is an acceptable password.

4. You configured an ESXi host with a TPM 2.0 chip and enabled UEFI Secure Boot. During the boot, you get the message "No cached identity key, loading from DB." What should you do?

   a. Reinstall ESXi.

   b. Reboot ESXi.

   c. Re-enable Secure Boot.

   d. Disconnect the host from the vCenter Server and reconnect.

512 VCP-DCV for vSphere 8.x Cert Guide

5. You want to have a backup in case you ever need to restore vSphere Trusted Authority. What should you do?

    a. Keep a copy of the files that you exported while configuring vTA.

    b. In the vSphere Client, choose Backup vTA Configuration.

    c. Clone the vCenter Server.

    d. Use the vCenter Server File Backup feature.

This chapter covers the following topics:

- vCenter Server Backup
- Upgrading to vSphere 8.0
- Using vSphere Lifecycle Manager
- Managing ESXi Hosts
- Monitoring and Managing vCenter Server

This chapter contains information related to VMware vSphere 8.x Professional (2V0-21.23) exam objectives 1.6, 4.5, 4.7, 4.11, 4.13, 4.14, 4.17.1, 5.8, 5.9, 5.9.2, 5.12, 5.13, 5.13.1, 5.13.2, 6.3, 7.9, 7.9.1, 7.9.2, 7.9.3, 7.9.4, 7.9.5, and 7.9.6.

## CHAPTER 13

Managing vSphere and vCenter Server

This chapter covers topics related to managing vCenter Server and vSphere components.

"Do I Know This Already?" Quiz

The "Do I Know This Already?" quiz allows you to assess whether you should study this entire chapter or move quickly to the "Exam Preparation Tasks" section. In any case, the authors recommend that you read the entire chapter at least once. Table 13-1 outlines the major headings in this chapter and the corresponding "Do I Know This Already?" quiz questions. You can find the answers in Appendix A, "Answers to the 'Do I Know This Already?' Quizzes and Review Questions."

Table 13-1 "Do I Know This Already?" Foundation Topics Section-to-Question Mapping

Foundation Topics Section	Questions
vCenter Server Backup	1, 2
Upgrading to vSphere 8.0	3, 4
Using vSphere Lifecycle Manager	5–7
Managing ESXi Hosts	8
Monitoring and Managing vCenter Server	9, 10

1. You want to back up your vCenter Server. Which of the following approaches is valid?

   a. Use the vSphere Client to perform a file-based backup.

   b. Use the vSphere Client to perform an image-based backup.

   c. Use the vCenter Server Appliance Management Interface to perform a file-based backup.

   d. Use the vCenter Server Appliance Management Interface to perform an image-based backup.

2. You want to restore your vCenter Server. Which of the following options are valid? (Choose three.)

   a. SCP

   b. FTP

   c. TFTP

   d. HTTPS

   e. SMB

3. You want to upgrade a vSphere 7.x environment to vSphere 8.0. Which of the following is the appropriate order?

   a. Virtual machines, ESXi hosts, vCenter Server

   b. ESXi hosts, vCenter Server, virtual machines

   c. vCenter Server, ESXi hosts, virtual machine hardware, VMware Tools

   d. vCenter Server, ESXi hosts, VMware Tools, virtual machine hardware

4. You plan to upgrade a Windows-based vCenter Server to vCenter Server Appliance 8.0 and want to transfer data in the background. Which of the following types of data can be transferred in the background following the upgrade?

   a. Configuration data only

   b. Configuration data and performance data

   c. Historical and performance data

   d. Data from the embedded database

5. You are preparing to use Lifecyle Manager. Which of the following is the smallest installable component (metadata and binary payload) for ESXi?

   a. An update

   b. An upgrade

   c. A patch

   d. A VIB

6. You want to enable Quick Boot for all the hosts in your vSphere cluster. In the vSphere Client, where should you go to enable it?

   a. Menu > Lifecycle Manager

   b. Menu > Host and Clusters > DRS Cluster Settings

   c. Menu > Host and Clusters > HA Cluster Settings

   d. Menu > Host and Clusters > ESXi Host Settings

7. You want to use Lifecycle Manager to update ESXi firmware. Which of the following is a requirement?

   a. Firmware baselines

   b. VMware-provided add-on

   c. Vendor-provided plug-in

   d. Vendor-provided baselines

8. You want to manage the services running in an ESXi host. Which of the following actions is not available using the vSphere Host Client?

   a. Starting a service

   b. Stopping a service

   c. Removing a service

   d. Changing a service's policy

9. You are examining the health state in the vCenter Server Appliance Management Interface (VAMI). What color indicates an alert, where one or more components may be degraded?

   a. Red

   b. Orange

   c. Yellow

   d. Gray

10. You are repointing a vCenter Server to an existing domain. Which of the following is not a valid resolution setting involving conflicts among the settings between the old and new domains?

    a. Delete

    b. Copy

    c. Skip

    d. Merge

Foundation Topics

vCenter Server Backup

To provide backup and recovery protection for your vCenter Server, you can use the integrated file-based backup feature. Alternatively, you can perform image-based backups by using the vSphere API.

The vCenter Server Appliance Management Interface (VAMI) provides a file-based backup feature for the vCenter Server. If you need to restore the vCenter Server, you can use the vCenter Server installer to deploy a new vCenter Server Appliance and to restore the database and configuration from the file-based backup. You can configure the backup to stream the data to a target by using FTP, FTPS, HTTP, HTTPS, SFTP, NFS, or SMB.

When planning a vCenter Server backup, you should consider the following details:

- When a vCenter Server High Availability (HA) cluster is involved in a backup, only the primary vCenter Server is backed up.
- Protocol choices have impacts:
    - FTP and HTTP are not secure protocols.
    - A backup server must support at least 10 simultaneous connections for each vCenter Server.
    - You must have read and write permissions on the backup target.
    - FTPS supports only Explicit Mode.
    - HTTP or HTTPS requires WebDAV on the backup web server.
    - To support an HTTP proxy server, you can use only FTP, FTPS, HTTP, or HTTPS.
    - You can use IPv4 or IPv6 URLs for the vCenter Server and file backup, but mixing IP versions between the backup server and the vCenter Server is unsupported.
- After a restore completes, the following configurations are restored:
    - Virtual machine resource settings
    - Resource pool hierarchy and setting
    - Cluster-host membership
    - DRS configuration and rules

- The state of various vSphere components may change following a restore, depending on the changes made since the backup. For example, the following items may be impacted:

    - Storage DRS datastore cluster configuration and membership

    - Standby Mode for some ESXi hosts where DPM is used

    - Distributed switch configuration (Consider exporting the switch configuration prior to restoring vCenter Server.)

    - Content libraries and library items

    - The registration of virtual machines on ESXi hosts (Some virtual machines may be orphaned or missing from the vCenter Server inventory.)

    - The host membership of a vSphere HA cluster (The vCenter Server may be out of sync with the actual current membership.)

    - Security patches, which may be missing following a restore (You should re-apply the missing patches.)

If you have prepared a supported target server, you can use the following procedure to schedule a file-based backup of the vCenter Server:

Step 1. Log on to the VAMI (https://*vCenterFQDN*:5480) as root.

Step 2. Click **Backup > Configure**.

Step 3. Enter the backup location details:

- **Backup Location**: Provide the protocol, port, server address, and folder.

- **Backup Server Credentials**: Provide the username and password with write privileges.

Step 4. Configure the schedule and time.

Step 5. Optionally, provide an encryption password.

Step 6. Provide a number of backups to retain or select **Retain All Backups**.

Step 7. Optionally, select **Stats, Events, and Tasks** to back up historical data.

Step 8. Click **Create**.

You can manually back up a vCenter Server in the VAMI by selecting Backup > Backup Now.

To restore a vCenter Server, launch the vCenter Server installer (described in Chapter 8, "vSphere Installation") on your desktop (Windows, Linux, or Mac) and use the following procedure:

Step 1.   On the Home page, click **Restore**.

Step 2.   On the next page, click **Next**.

Step 3.   Accept the license agreement and click **Next**.

Step 4.   Provide the backup location and credentials for the backup file to be restored. For the backup location, specify the protocol, which can be FTP, FTPS, HTTP, HTTPS, SFTP, NFS, or SMB, and the FQDN or IP address of the backup server. For example, to restore from an FTP server with IP address 192.168.100.101, you can specify ftp://192.168.100.101.

Step 5.   Click **Next** to connect to the backup server and then use the wizard to select the folder that contains the backup metadata. Click **Select**.

Step 6.   Review the backup information and click **Next**.

Step 7.   Continue using the wizard to provide connection details (FQDN, credentials, and certificate information) for the ESXi host or vCenter Server to which the appliance will be restored.

Step 8.   When prompted in the wizard, provide a name and a root password for the vCenter Server Appliance.

Step 9.   Select a deployment size (from Tiny to X-Large).

Step 10.   Select the storage size (from Default to X-Large).

Step 11.   Select a datastore and provide virtual disk and network settings for the appliance.

Step 12.   On the Ready to Complete Stage 1 page, click **Finish**.

Step 13.   When the OVA deployment finishes, click **Continue** to proceed to Stage 2.

Step 14. Continue navigating the wizard, and when it prompts you for Single Sign-On credentials, provide the credentials and click **Validate and Recover**.

Step 15. On the Ready to Complete page, review the details, click **Finish**, and click **OK**.

NOTE If a restore fails, power off and delete the partially restored VM. Then try to restore the VM again.

NOTE You must power off the active, passive, and witness nodes in a vCenter Server HA cluster prior to restoring. You must reconstruct the cluster after a restore operation completes successfully.

If you prefer to use an image-based backup, you can leverage the vSphere API. For image-based backups, you should consider the following:

- You must ensure that the vCenter Server uses a fully qualified domain name (FQDN) with correct DNS resolution or configure its host name to be an IP address.

- If DHCP is used, you must configure the restored vCenter Server's IP address back to the original value.

- Ensure that all vSphere component clocks are synchronized.

- The set of restored configurations for image-based restoration is identical to the set for file-based restoration.

- The impact on the state of vSphere components of an image-based restoration is nearly identical to the impact of a file-based restoration.

To perform an image-based backup or recovery of vCenter Server, you must use a third-party product or custom code.

Backing Up and Restoring vSphere with Tanzu

This section provides an overview of the backup and restore process for vSphere with Tanzu.

vSphere with Tanzu backup and restore process involves multiple layers and tools, as described in Table 13-2.

Table 13-2 Backup Scenarios for VMware with Tanzu

Scenario	Tools	Comments
Back up and restore vSphere pods	Velero Plugin for vSphere	Install and configure the plug-in on the Supervisor cluster.
Back up Tanzu Kubernetes cluster workloads Restore to a cluster provisioned by the Tanzu Kubernetes Grid Service	Velero Plugin for vSphere	Both Kubernetes metadata and persistent volumes can be backed up and restored. Velero snapshotting (not Restic) is used for persistent volumes.
Back up Tanzu Kubernetes cluster workloads Restore to a conformant Kubernetes cluster not provisioned by the Tanzu Kubernetes Grid Service	Standalone Velero and Restic	If you require portability, use standalone Velero. You must include Restic for stateful applications.
Restore vCenter Server Configuration	vCenter Server	Restore from vCenter Server file-based backup.
Restore Supervisor cluster	vCenter Server, Velero Plugin for vSphere, and Standalone Velero and Restic	Restore vCenter Server and let it re-create the Supervisor cluster control plan VMs. Restore cluster workloads from backup using the plug-in or standalone Velero and Restic.

The Velero Plugin for vSphere can be used to back up and restore vSphere with Tanzu workloads. It does not back up the Supervisor state. To install and configure the plug-in, you can take the following steps.

Step 1. Create an S3-compatible object store.

Step 2. Install and configure the Data Manager.

Step 3. Install the Velero vSphere Operator Services on the Supervisor cluster.

Step 4. Use the vSphere Client to enable the Velero vSphere Operator cluster service and create a namespace for the Velero instance.

Step 5. Provide the proper permissions to the namespace.

Step 6. Create a config map to specify that the plug-in will be installed on the supervisor cluster.

Step 7. Use the Velero vSphere Operator CLI to run the **velero-vsphere** command.

To back up a stateless vSphere pod, you can use the following command, where *mybackup* is the name you assign to the backup and *mynamespace* is the name of namespace you want to back up.

```
velero backup create mybackup -include-namespaces mynamespace
```

To restore a vSphere pod from a backup, you can use the following command, where *mybackup* is the name of the backup from which you want to restore:

```
velero restore create --from-backup mybackup
```

Upgrading to vSphere 8.0

This section provides details on upgrading a vSphere environment to vSphere 8.0. For information on installing a new vSphere 8.0 environment, see Chapter 8.

To upgrade a vSphere 6.7 or 7.x environment to vSphere 8.0, you should upgrade the major components in the following order:

1. vCenter Server

2. ESXi hosts

3. VMware Tools on the virtual machines

4. Virtual machine hardware

NOTE   For vCenter Server 6.0 and earlier, you should upgrade to vSphere 6.7 and then upgrade to vSphere 8.0. For vSphere 6.5, you can first upgrade to 6.7 or 7.x and then upgrade to 8.0.

You should back up vCenter Server prior to upgrading it. For details, see the section "vCenter Server Backup," earlier in this chapter.

To upgrade your environment to use vCenter Server 8.0, you need to either upgrade an existing vCenter Server Appliance or migrate from an existing Windows-based vCenter Server. When you upgrade or migrate a vCenter Server that uses an external Platform Services Controller (PSC), you converge the PSC into a vCenter Server Appliance.

Prior to upgrading to vCenter Server 8.0, you should consider its compatibility with other vSphere components, as summarized in Table 13-3.

Table 13-3   vCenter Server 7.0 Compatibility

Component	Compatibility
vCenter Server Appliance	You can upgrade vCenter Server Appliance 6.7 and higher to 8.0. You should check for back-in-time exceptions. No back-in-time exceptions exist for vCenter Server 8.0 upgrades at the time this book was written, but some exist for vCenter Server 7.0 upgrades, as identified at https://kb.vmware.com/s/article/67077.
vCenter Server for Windows	You can migrate vCenter Server for Windows 6.7 (with or without an embedded PSC) to a vCenter Server Appliance 8.0.
vCenter Server database	vCenter Server 7.0 and later use PostgreSQL for the embedded database. vCenter Server does not support external databases.
ESXi hosts	vCenter Server 8.0 can be deployed to ESXi 6.5 or later, and it can manage ESXi 6.7 or later.
Host profiles	vCenter Server 8.0 requires Version 6.7 or later ESXi and host profiles. (For Version 6.5 ESXi and host profiles, you need to first upgrade to 7.0 and then to 8.0.)
VMFS	vCenter Server 8.0 supports VMFS 3 and later but can only create VMFS 5 and VMFS 6 datastores.
Virtual machines and VMware Tools	Review the ESXi upgrade documentation for specific upgrade options, which are dependent on the current versions.
Auto Deploy	If you currently use Auto Deploy, when you upgrade to vCenter Server 8.0, VMware recommends that you use Auto Deploy to upgrade hosts to ESXi 8.0.
vSphere Distributed Switch (vDS)	Upgrade to vDS 6.7 before upgrading vCenter Server.
Network I/O Control (NIOC)	Upgrade to NIOC Version 3 before upgrading vCenter Server.
vSAN	VMware recommends that you synchronize versions of vCenter Server and ESXi to avoid potential faults.
vSAN disk version	Supported versions and paths may be impacted by the current version and upgrade history. See https://kb.vmware.com/s/article/2148493.
Legacy Fault Tolerance (FT)	If you use Legacy FT on any virtual machines, you must turn off or upgrade the Legacy FT feature prior to a vCenter Server upgrade or migration.

vCenter Server Data Transfer

If you migrate a Windows-based vCenter Server or upgrade a vCenter Server with an external PSC, you need to transfer data to the embedded PostgreSQL database in the target vCenter Server Appliance. At a minimum, you must transfer configuration data. You can choose whether you want to transfer historical data and performance metrics data. Specifically, you can choose one of the following options:

- **Configuration data**: Transferring just configuration data minimizes downtime during the upgrade.

- **Configuration and historical data**. You can choose to transfer historical data (usage statistics, tasks, and events) during an upgrade (impacting the downtime) or in the background following the upgrade.

- **Configuration, historical, and performance data**: You can transfer the configuration data during the upgrade and transfer the remaining data in the background following the upgrade.

NOTE The option to transfer data in the background following an upgrade is applicable only in scenarios where the source vCenter Server uses an external database.

You can monitor the background data transfer by using the VAMI. You can pause and cancel the data transfer.

Upgrading vCenter Server Appliance

You should address the following prerequisites prior to upgrading a vCenter Server Appliance to Version 8.0:

- Ensure that the clocks of all the vSphere components are synchronized.

- Ensure that the system has the minimum hardware and software components.

- Ensure that the target ESXi host is not in Lockdown Mode, Maintenance Mode, or Standby Mode.

- Ensure that the target ESXi host is not part of a fully automated DRS cluster.

- Verify that port 22 is open on the source vCenter Server Appliance and that port 443 is open on the ESXi host on which the source vCenter Server Appliance is running.

- Verify that the source appliance has sufficient free space to accommodate data that is used for the upgrade.

- If the source vCenter Server uses an external database, determine its size and ensure that you account for it in the size of the new appliance.

- Ensure that network connectivity exists between the vCenter Server or ESXi that hosts the source vCenter Server Appliance and the new vCenter Server Appliance.

- If you plan to set the system name to a FQDN, ensure that forward and reverse DNS records are created.

Upgrading a vCenter Server Appliance is a two-stage process: (1) Deploy the OVA and (2) transfer the data and configure the vCenter Server Appliance. For a vCenter Server with an external PSC, you can use the following procedure for Stage 1:

Step 1.   Launch the vCenter Server (GUI) installer and select **Upgrade**.

Step 2.   Review the upgrade process on the first wizard page and click **Next**.

Step 3.   Accept the license agreement and click **Next**.

Step 4.   Provide the following information for the source vCenter Server:

- Provide the address, HTTPS port, SSO credentials, and root password for the source vCenter Server.
- Provide the address, HTTPS port, and credentials for a user with administrative privileges for the ESXi host (or vCenter Server) that is hosting the source vCenter Server.

Click **Connect**.

Step 5.   Follow the wizard prompts to accept the certificate and accept the plan to converge the source vCenter Server and external PSC into a single vCenter Server Appliance.

Step 6.   Follow the wizard prompts to provide the following information for the target environment that will host the new vCenter Server Appliance:

- If you are connecting to a vCenter Server, provide the address, HTTPS port, SSO credentials, and root password for the vCenter Server. Select a data center and an ESXi host (or cluster).
- If you are connecting to an ESXi host, provide the address, HTTPS port, and credentials for a user with administrative privileges for the ESXi host.

Step 7.   Follow the wizard to configure the new vCenter Server Appliance with the following information:

- Virtual machine name
- Root user password

- Deployment size (which can be Tiny to X-Large, as described in Table 1-10 in Chapter 1, "vSphere Overview, Components, and Requirements")
- Storage size (which defaults to X-Large, as described in Table 1-11)
- Datastore
- Temporary network used to transfer data from the source vCenter Server to the new vCenter Server

Step 8. Click **Finish**.

Step 9. Click **Continue** to proceed to Stage 2.

NOTE The identical Stage 1 procedure can be used when upgrading a vCenter Server Appliance with an embedded PSC, except the wizard does not prompt you to accept the plan to converge an external PSC.

For a vCenter Server with an external PSC, you can use the following procedure for Stage 2:

Step 1. Review the Stage 2 details and click **Next**.

Step 2. Wait for the pre-upgrade check to finish and respond to any of the following messages:

- **Errors**: Read each message, click **Logs** to obtain a support bundle, and troubleshoot. You cannot proceed with the upgrade until errors are corrected.
- **Warnings**: Read each message and click **Close**.

Step 3. Specify the replication technology by choosing one of the following options:

- **This Is the First vCenter Server in the Topology That I Want to Converge**
- **This Is a Subsequent vCenter Server** (and also provide the IP address and HTTPS port of the partner vCenter Server)

Step 4. On the Select Upgrade Data page, choose the type of data transfer, as described in the section "vCenter Server Data Transfer," earlier in this chapter.

Step 5. Complete the wizard and wait for the transfer and setup operations to complete.

Step 6. Decommission the source external PSC.

NOTE The Stage 2 procedure to upgrade a vCenter Server Appliance with an embedded PSC is similar, but instead of being prompted for the replication technology, you are prompted (again) for information for connecting to the source vCenter Server and host environment (that is, the vCenter Server or ESXi host where the source vCenter Server resides).

Migrating vCenter Server for Windows to vCenter Server Appliance

Before migrating a vCenter Server for Windows to vCenter Server Appliance, you need to do the following:

- If the vCenter Server service is running as a user other than the Local System account, ensure that the account is a member of the Administrators group and has the Log On as a Service, Act as Part of the Operating System, and Replace a Process Level Token permissions.

- Verify that the vCenter Server and PSC certificates are valid and reachable.

- Verify that the network connection to the domain controller is functioning.

- Verify that neither the source vCenter Server nor the PSC instance is using a DHCP IP address as the system name.

When you migrate vCenter Server for Windows to vCenter Server Appliance, the installer performs an environment precheck that includes the following items:

- Sufficient storage space in the source server

- Validity and compatibility of SSL certificates and system names

- Network connectivity, ports, and DNS resolution

- Database connectivity

- Proper credentials and privileges for the Single Sign-On and Windows administrator accounts

- NTP server validation

The following limitations apply when you migrate vCenter Server for Windows to vCenter Server Appliance 8.0:

- Local Windows OS users and groups are not migrated to the guest OS (Photon OS) of the new appliance. You should remove any vCenter Server permissions to local Windows users prior to the migration.

- At the end of the migration, the source vCenter Server is turned off, and any solutions that are not migrated become unavailable. You should leave the source vCenter Server powered off to avoid network ID conflicts with the target vCenter Server Appliance.

- Migration of Windows-based vCenter Server instances that use custom ports for services other than Auto Deploy, Update Manager, vSphere ESXi Dump Collector, or HTTP reverse proxy is not supported.

- Only one network adapter setting is migrated to the target vCenter Server Appliance. If the source uses multiple IP addresses, you can select which IP address and network adapter settings to migrate.

To migrate a Windows-based vCenter Server with an embedded PSC to vCenter 8.0, you can use the following procedure:

Step 1.   Run the VMware Migration Assistant on the Windows server that runs vCenter Server and follow these steps:

    a. Download and mount the vCenter Server installer.

    b. Log on to Windows as an administrator.

    c. Double-click on **VMware-Migration-Assistant.exe**.

    d. Leave the Migration Assistant running until the migration is complete.

Step 2.   Migrate the vCenter Server instance to an appliance by following these steps:

    a. Using the Stage 1 procedure for upgrading a vCenter Server Appliance as a guide, launch the vCenter Server GUI installer but choose **Migrate** rather than Upgrade.

    b. Provide connection information for the source Windows-based vCenter Server.

    c. Provide information on the target server (vCenter Server or ESXi host) to deploy the vCenter Server Appliance.

    d. Provide appliance information, such as root password, compute deployment size, storage deployment size, and datastore.

    e. Configure the temporary network used to transfer data from the source vCenter Server to the new vCenter Server and select **Continue to Stage 2**.

    f. In Stage 2, provide credentials for the Single Sign-On administrator and for the Windows system. If the Windows system is connected to an Active Directory domain, provide credentials for an appropriate domain user.

    g. Complete the wizard and click **Finish** on the Ready to Complete page.

    h. Click **OK** to confirm the shutdown of the source Center Server.

    i. Monitor the data transfer and configuration process.

> **NOTE** If the Windows-based vCenter Server uses an external Update Manager, run the Migration Assistant on the Update Manager machine before running it on the vCenter Server.

To migrate a Windows-based vCenter Server with an external PSC to vCenter 7.0 or later, you can use the previous procedure as a guide, but you should run the VMware Migration Assistant in the Windows-based PSC prior to running it in the vCenter Server. You should also decommission the source external PSC following the migration.

Upgrading ESXi and Virtual Machines

After upgrading to vCenter Server 8.0, you can use Lifecycle Manager to upgrade ESXi hosts and virtual machines, as described in the section "Using vSphere Lifecycle Manager," later in this chapter.

Using Update Planner

You can use the Update Planner to examine available vCenter Server updates and upgrades. You can produce interoperability reports for associated VMware products with your source (current) and target vCenter Server versions. You can generate pre-update reports to help ensure that your system meets the minimum software and hardware requirements. The report identifies potential upgrade issues and provides potential remedy actions. To use Update Planner, you must join the VMware Customer Experience Improvement Program (CEIP).

You can use the following procedure to perform an interoperability check of VMware products in your environment against the current vCenter Server version:

Step 1. In the vSphere Client, select a vCenter Server in the inventory pane and navigate to **Monitor > Interoperability**.

Step 2. Review the Product Interoperability report, which should contain all the available products in your environment.

Step 3. If a VMware product in your environment is not automatically detected, you can use the following steps to manually add the product to the list and regenerate the Product Interoperability report:

   a. For each missing product, click **Add Product** and select the VMware product and version.

   b. Click **Done**.

   c. Regenerate the Product Interoperability report and review the product list.

Step 4. Click **Export** to save the report as a comma-separated values (CSV) file.

You can use the following steps to create an interoperability report on the compatibility of your environment's VMware products against a target version of vCenter Server:

Step 1. In the vSphere Client, select a vCenter Server in the inventory pane and navigate to **Updates > Update > Target Version**.

Step 2. Select a target vCenter Server version (major upgrade or minor update) and click **OK**.

Step 3. Click **Product Interoperability**.

Step 4. Review the Product Interoperability report, which should contain all the available products in your environment.

Step 5. If a VMware product in your environment is not automatically listed or is undetected, you can use the following steps to manually add the product and regenerate the Product Interoperability report:

   a. For each missing product, click **Modify Product List** and select the VMware product and version.

   b. Click **Done**.

   c. Regenerate the Product Interoperability report and review the product list.

Step 6. Click **Export** to save the report as a comma-separated values (CSV) file.

A report that provides pre-update information identifies potential problems that might prevent the completion of a software upgrade or update. It includes a list with actions that you must address to ensure a successful upgrade of vCenter Server. You can use the following steps to run prechecks and generate reports providing pre-update information:

Step 1. In the vSphere Client, select a vCenter Server in the inventory pane and navigate to **Updates > Update > Target Version**.

Step 2. Select a target vCenter Server version (major upgrade or minor update) and click **OK**.

Step 3. Click **Source Pre-checks** and view the report.

Step 4. Click **Export** to save the report as a comma-separated values (CSV) file.

After you address issues identified in the report, you can use the VAMI to perform administrative tasks to apply patches and updates.

Using vSphere Lifecycle Manager

In vSphere 8.0, you have choices for methods and tools to facilitate the deployment and lifecycle management of ESXi host. You can use an ESXi installer image or VMware vSphere Auto Deploy to deploy hosts. Using vSphere Auto Deploy can result in hosts deployed in Stateless Mode. Using an ESXi installer image results in hosts being deployed in Stateful Mode. Depending on the deployment method, you can use a variety of tools and methods for host updates and upgrade. For example, you can use Update Manager baselines, the ESXi Image Builder CLI, ESXCLI, or vSphere Auto Deploy. In any case, the ESXi image may change at runtime due to some solution installing software automatically or a service changing a setting.

VMware *vSphere Lifecycle Manager (vLCM)* provides simple, centralized lifecycle management for ESXi hosts and clusters by using images and baselines. Specifically, lifecycle management of a vSphere cluster refers to tasks such as installing and updating host firmware and ESXi. Beginning in vSphere 7.0, vLCM encompasses and enhances the functionality that Update Manager provided for earlier vSphere releases. It is a service that runs in vCenter Server and is automatically enabled in the vSphere Client. It can work in an environment with direct access to the Internet or access via the proxy setting of the vCenter Server. It can also work with Update Manager Download Service (UMDS) in a secured network with no access to the Internet. In such cases, you use the UMDS to download updates to the vLCM depot, or you import them manually.

Chapter 8 provides information on the implementation of vLCM.

Beginning with vSphere 7.0, vLCM enables you to use images or baselines. An *image* represents a desired software specification to be applied to all hosts in a cluster. An image is a description of which software, drivers, and firmware to run on a host. You can apply a single image to all hosts in a cluster to ensure consistency. Updates to software and firmware occur in a single workflow. The use of images with vLCM enables new functionalities, including image recommendations, automated firmware updates, and hardware compatibility checks.

You can use baselines in vSphere 8.0, much as you could in previous vSphere versions, to perform the following tasks:

- Upgrade ESXi 6.7 and 7.0 hosts to ESXi 8.0
- Patch ESXi 6.7, 7.0, and 8.0 hosts
- Install and update third-party software on ESXi hosts

Starting with vSphere 7.0, you can use vLCM images to perform the following tasks on a set of hosts at the cluster level:

- Install a desired ESXi version on each host

- Install and update third-party software on each ESXi host

- Update the firmware of each ESXi host

- Update and upgrade each ESXi host in a cluster

- Check the hardware compatibility of each host against hardware compatibility lists, such as the *VMware Compatibility Guide* and the *vSAN Hardware Compatibility List*

NOTE   The ability for vLCM to manage clusters leveraging baselines and baseline groups has been deprecated. It is still supported in vSphere 8.0, but the support will be dropped in a future vSphere release. In vSphere 8.0, leveraging images is preferred over leveraging baselines.

You can start using vLCM images as you create a cluster. Otherwise, you can switch from using baselines to images later. After switching a cluster to use images, you cannot revert the cluster back to using baselines. However, you can move the hosts to another cluster that uses baselines. If you set up an image for a cluster and remediate all the hosts in the cluster, then all standalone VIB and non-integrated agents are deleted from the hosts.

vLCM has several components, including a service named vSphere Lifecycle Manager that runs in vCenter Server and uses the embedded vCenter Server PostgreSQL database. It communicates with agents running in each ESXi host.

vSphere Lifecycle Manager uses a desired-state model based on images that represent both the target software and target configuration of the host. To use images, all hosts must be ESXi 7.0 or later, they must be stateful, and they must be from the same hardware vendor.

NOTE   Starting with vCenter Server 7.0 Update 1, ESXi 7.0 Update 1, and NSX-T 3.1.0, a vCLM-enabled cluster can manage installation of ESXi and NSX-T VIBs. Starting with vSphere 7.0 Update 1, you can leverage vLCM to upgrade a Supervisor cluster to the latest version of vSphere with Tanzu and upgrade the ESXi version of the hosts in the Supervisor cluster.

You can leverage vLCM for VMware Tools and virtual machine hardware upgrade operations on virtual machines running on ESXi 6.7, ESXi 7.0, and ESXi 8.0 hosts.

To get started using vLCM, in the vSphere Client, you can navigate to **Menu > Lifecycle Manager** (which is called the Lifecycle Manager home view) and select a vCenter Server. Here you can configure vLCM by using the **Settings** tab. Table 13-4 describes the available settings for vLCM remediation.

Key Topic

Table 13-4   Lifecyle Manager Remediation Settings

Setting	Description
Quick Boot	You can enable Quick Boot to skip the hardware reboot during remediation.
Cluster Settings	You can disable vSphere Distributed Power Management (DPM), HA admission control, and FT for an entire cluster during remediation.
VM Power State	You can power off, suspend, or leave alone the power state of running VMs during remediation.
VM Migration	You can migrate or leave alone powered-off and suspended VMs during remediation.
Maintenance Mode Failures	You can control the number of retries and the delay between retries in the case that a host fails to enter Maintenance Mode.
PXE Booted Hosts	You can allow the installation of software for solutions on the PXE-booted ESXi hosts.
Removable Media Devices	You can automatically disconnect all virtual machine removable media devices prior to remediation and automatically reconnect afterward.

When working with images, the following settings are applicable: Quick Boot, VM Power State, VM Migration, Maintenance Mode Failures, HA Admission Control, and DPM.

NOTE   Starting with vSphere 7.0 Update 2, a new option called Suspend-to-Memory (STM) is available for vLCM clusters that use images, and it is dependent on Quick Boot.

When working with baselines, the following settings are applicable: Quick Boot, VM Power State, VM Migration, Maintenance Mode Failures, PXE Booted Hosts, and Removable Media Devices.

You can perform the following tasks from the Lifecyle Manager home view:

- Browse the vSphere Lifecycle Manager depot.

- Trigger the synchronization of updates with the configured online depots.

- Trigger the synchronization of hardware compatibility data.

- Import offline depots manually.

- Import ISO images to use for the creation of upgrade baselines.

- Create and manage baselines and baseline groups.

- Configure the default vSphere Lifecycle Manager download source.

- Add a URL to an online depot to the list of download sources.

- Enable or disable downloading from a download source.

- Configure host remediation settings.

- Configure virtual machine rollback settings.

In vSphere with Tanzu with vSphere networking, you can use vLCM for a cluster with a single image. To get started, you can use the vSphere Client to select the cluster and enable it for Workload Management. The requirements are as follows:

- ESXi 7.0 Update 1

- VMware vSphere 7 Enterprise Plus with Add-on for Kubernetes license

- vCenter Server 7.0 Update 1

In the vSphere Client, you can use the Workload Management interface to upgrade the Supervisor cluster. You can use vLCM to upgrade the host's ESXi version.

To use vLCM with vSphere with Tanzu with vSphere networking, you need vCenter Sever 7.0 Update 2 and ESXi 7.0 Update 2 or later.

About VMware Update Manager

With vSphere 7.0, VMware Update Manager (VUM) was rebranded as vSphere Lifecycle Manager, which includes new features, such as the ability to provide ESXi lifecycle management at a cluster level.

VMware Update Manager Download Service (UMDS)

VMware *Update Manager Download Service (UMDS)* is an optional module of vLCM whose primary function is to download data when vCLM does not have Internet connectivity. You can configure a web server on UMDS to automatically export the downloads to make them available to Lifecycle Manager. Alternatively, you can export the data from UMDS to a portable media drive. UMDS and vLCM must be of the same version and update release.

UMDS is a 64-bit Linux application that is bundled with the vCenter Server Appliance 8.0. You can use that bundle to install UMDS on a separate Linux system. You cannot upgrade UMDS on a Linux system. Instead, you can uninstall UMDS, perform a fresh installation, and continue using an existing patch store. To install UMDS, you can use the following procedure:

Step 1. Log on to a supported Linux system, such as Ubuntu (14.04, 18.04, 18.04 LTS, or 20.04 LTS) or Red Hat Enterprise Linux (7.4, 7.5, 7.7, or 8.1). If you select Red Hat Enterprise 8.1, install the libnsl package Version 2.28 or later.

Step 2. Verify that you have administrative privileges.

Step 3. Open a command shell.

Step 4. Copy VMware-UMDS-8.0.1-build_number.tar.gz to the Linux server.

Step 5. Run the **vmware-install.pl** script.

Step 6. When prompted, accept the EULA, select an installation directory, provide proxy settings, and specify the directory for storing patches.

To connect UMDS to third-party vendor websites, you can use the following command:

```
vmware-umds -S --add-url https://web1.vendor1.com/index.html
/index.xml --url-type HOST
```

To export data from UMDS to a specific location that serves as a shared repository for vSphere Lifecycle Manager, you can use the following command, where *repositoryPath* represents a valid path to the shared repository:

```
vmware-umds -E -export-store repositoryPath
```

Baselines and Images

vSphere Lifecycle Manager supports the use of baselines and baseline groups that are available in previous vSphere releases for host patching and upgrade operations. It supports multiple types of baselines, including predefined baselines, recommendation baselines, extension baselines, and custom baselines.

Predefined baselines cannot be edited or deleted. To examine the predefined baselines in the vSphere Client, select Lifecycle Manager > Baselines. The predefined baselines are categorized as host security patches, critical host patches, and non-critical host patches.

Recommendation baselines, which are predefined baselines generated by vSAN, appear by default when for vSAN cluster members. You can use recommendation baselines to update a cluster with recommended critical patches, drivers, updates, and supported ESXi version for vSAN. You can create a baseline group containing multiple recommendation baselines, but only if you do not include other baseline types in the group. The vSAN recommendation baselines are typically refreshed every 24 hours for Lifecycle Manager instances with Internet access.

Custom baselines are baselines that you create. Patch baselines can be dynamic or fixed. With dynamic baselines, you specify the criteria for patches to be automatically included in the baseline. You can manually include or exclude patches from dynamic baselines. With fixed baselines, you manually select the patches to include.

If you have the VMware vSphere Lifecycle Manager.Manage Baselines privilege, you can use the following procedure to create a dynamic baseline:

Step 1.   In the vSphere Client, select **Menu > Lifecycle Manager**.

Step 2.   If necessary, select the vCenter Server system in the **Lifecycle Manager** menu.

Step 3.   Select **Baselines > New > Baseline**.

Step 4.   In the wizard, provide the following baseline information:

- Name and (optionally) description
- Type: **Upgrade**, **Patch**, or **Extension**

Click **Next**.

Step 5.   On the Select Patches Automatically page, set the criteria for adding patches to the baseline:

a. Select the **Automatic Update** checkbox.

b. On the Criteria tab, specify the values for the following options to restrict which patches are included in the baseline:

- Patch Vendor
- Product (You can use an asterisk at the end to allow any version number.)
- Severity
- Category
- Release Date (You can specify a date range.)

Click **Next**.

c. On the Matched tab, optionally deselect patches that matched the criteria but that you want to permanently exclude.

d. On the Excluded and Select tabs, view which patches are excluded and which patches are included.

Step 6.   On the Select Patches Manually page, optionally select specific patches from the set of patches that do not meet the criteria for automatic inclusion to include in the baseline.

Step 7.   On the Summary page, click **Finish**.

Extension baselines contain additional (VMware or third-party) software modules for hosts, such as device drivers. You can install additional modules by using extension baselines and update the modules by using patch baselines.

NOTE   Starting with vSphere 7.0, the vendor name of VMware for inbox components has changed from VMware, Inc to VMware. If you filter the components by VMware, the results contain both VMware, Inc for 6.x patches and VMware for 7.0 patches.

If a user has the View Compliance Status privilege, you can use the Updates tab for a selected object to view the object's compliance with baselines or images. You can select a host or cluster that is managed with baselines and click on Updates > Baselines. From there, you can do the following tasks:

- Check the compliance of hosts or clusters against baselines and baseline groups.

- Attach and detach baselines and baseline groups to hosts or clusters.

- Perform a remediation precheck.

- Stage patches or extensions to prepare for remediation.

- Check the compliance of ESXi hosts against an image.

- Remediate hosts against baselines and baseline groups.

- Remediate hosts that are part of a vSAN cluster against system-managed baselines.

You can select a cluster that is managed with an image and click on Updates > Images. From there, you can do the following tasks:

- Export, import, and edit the image used by the cluster.

- Upgrade the firmware of the ESXi hosts in the cluster.

- Check for and examine recommended images for the cluster.

- Check for hardware compatibility for a selected ESXi version against the vSAN HCL.

- Check the compliance of the ESXi hosts against the image.

- Run a remediation precheck.

- Remediate the ESXi hosts against the cluster's image.

You can select a host and then select Updates > Hosts > Hardware Compatibility to check the host hardware against the *VMware Compatibility Guide*. You can select a host and then select Updates > Hosts and then select VMware Tools or VM Hardware to check and upgrade the VMware Tools version and virtual hardware version of the virtual machines.

Table 13-5 provides definitions of vSphere Lifecycle Manager terms.

Table 13-5 Lifecycle Manager Definitions

Term	Definition
Update	A software release that makes small changes to the current version, such as vSphere 7.0 Update 1, 7.0 Update 2, and so on.
Upgrade	A software release that introduces major changes to the software. For example, you can upgrade from vSphere 6.7 to 7.0 and 8.0.
Patch	A small software update that provides bug fixes or enhancements to the current version of the software, such as 7.0a, 7.0 Update 1a, and so on.
VIB (vSphere Installation Bundle)	The smallest installable software package (metadata and binary payload) for ESXi.
VIB metadata	An XML file that describes the contents of the VIB, including dependency information, textual descriptions, system requirements, and information about bulletins.
Standalone VIB	A VIB that is not included in a component.
Depot	The hosted version of updates provided by VMware, OEMs, and third-party software vendors, containing the metadata and the actual VIBs.
Offline bundle/ offline depot	An archive (ZIP file) that contains VIBs and metadata that you use for offline patching and updates. A single offline bundle might contain multiple base images, vendor add-ons, or components.
OEM (original equipment manufacturer)	A VMware partner, such as Dell, HPE, or VMware Cloud on AWS.
Third-party software provider	A provider of I/O filters, device drivers, CIM modules, and so on.

NOTE   During the synchronization of a depot, vLCM downloads only the VIB metadata.

In vSphere releases prior to 7.0, VIBs are packaged into bulletins. Starting with vSphere 7.0, VIBs are packaged into components, which are created by VMware, original equipment manufacturers, and third-party software providers. A component is much like a bulletin with extra metadata containing the component name and version. VMware bundles components together into fully functional ESXi images. Original equipment manufacturers bundle components into add-ons that are delivered via the VMware online depot as offline bundles. Third-party vendors create and ship drivers packaged as components.

vLCM can consume bulletins and components. It lists the available components as bulletins when baselines are used to manage a host or cluster. When images are used, vSphere Lifecycle Manager works only with components.

The *ESXi base image*, which is the ESXi image that VMware provides with each release of ESXi, is a complete set of components that can boot up a server. A base image has a friendly name, has a unique version that corresponds to the ESXi release, and is hosted in the VMware online depot. Alternatively, you can download an ESXi installer ISO file and an offline bundle (ZIP file) that contains the ESXi version from my.vmware.com.

A vendor *add-on* is a collection of components that you can use to customize an ESXi image with OEM content and drivers. You cannot use vendor add-ons on their own. You can use a vendor add-on to add, update, or remove components that are part of the ESXi base image. You can use the vSphere Client to view the list of components that a vendor add-on adds to or removes from an ESXi base image.

Prior to vSphere 7.0, OEMs created custom images by merging their content with the stock VMware-provided image. OEMs release custom images in accordance with the major and update releases of vSphere. Starting with vSphere 7.0, in addition to releasing custom ISO images and offline bundles, OEMs can release ZIP files that contain only the vendor add-on. This approach decouples the release cycle of OEMs from the release cycle of VMware.

vLCM can consume software updates delivered as an online depot, as an offline depot, or as an installable ISO image. An online depot is a hosted version of the software updates. Starting with vSphere 7.0, the default, the VMware online depot provides vendor add-ons to hosts. The default depot also contains VMware-certified, ESXi-compatible I/O device drivers. You can use the vSphere Client to access third-party online depots containing additional components.

Offline bundles are ZIP files that contain the software metadata and the respective VIBs. Starting with vSphere 7.0, an OEM can distribute an add-on ZIP file that contains the delta between the OEM custom image and the base image that VMware provides.

A *baseline* is a set of bulletins. Patch baselines, extension baselines, and upgrade baselines contain patch bulletins, extension bulletins, and ESXi images, respectively. You can attach baselines to hosts, check compliance of a host with its associated baseline, and remediate (update) hosts by using the baseline.

You can classify baselines based on the following:

- Update type (such as patch baselines, extension baselines, and upgrade baselines)

- Content (such as fixed or dynamic)

- Predefined, recommendation, or custom baselines

- Predefined host patches (such as host security patches, critical host patches, and non-critical host patches)

You cannot modify or delete the predefined baselines. You can use the predefined baselines to create custom patch, extension, and upgrade baselines. Recommendation baselines are baselines generated automatically by vSAN. You can use recommendation baselines only with vSAN clusters.

A baseline group is a set of non-conflicting baselines that you can apply as a single entity. A host baseline group can contain a single upgrade baseline plus patch and extension baselines. For efficiency, you can attach and apply baselines and baseline groups to container objects (such as folders, vApps, and clusters) rather than to the individual underlying objects (virtual machines and hosts).

To check a cluster's compliance against an image, you can select the cluster, select Updates > Hosts > Image, and click the Check Compliance button. When you check a cluster's compliance with a Lifecycle Manager image, one of the following four compliance states is identified for each member host:

- **Compliant**: The host's image matches the image applied to the cluster.

- **Non-Compliant**: The host's image does not match the image applied to the cluster. Some potential causes are differences in the ESXi version, the firmware version, or the set of components. Another potential cause is that the host contains a standalone VIB.

- **Incompatible**: The cluster's image cannot be applied to the host. Some potential reasons are that the host's ESXi version is later than the version in the image, the host has insufficient RAM, or the host's hardware is incompatible with the cluster's image.

- **Unknown**: No compliance state information is available, perhaps because the host was recently added or the cluster's image was edited.

ESXi Quick Boot

You can use Quick Boot with vLCM to optimize the host patching and upgrade operations. When Quick Boot is enabled, vLCM skips the hardware reboot (the BIOS or UEFI firmware reboot), which reduces the time a host spends in Maintenance Mode and reduces the risk of failures.

Starting with vSphere 6.7, Quick Boot is supported on a limited set of hardware platforms and drivers. Quick Boot is not supported on ESXi 7.0 hosts that use TPM or on ESXi 6.7 hosts that use passthrough devices. To determine whether your system is compatible with Quick Book, you can run the following command in the ESXi shell:

```
/usr/lib/vmware/loadesx/bin/loadESXCheckCompat.py
```

To enable Quick Boot, you can use the following procedure:

Step 1.   In the vSphere Client, navigate to **Menu > Lifecyle Manager**.

Step 2.   From the Lifecycle Manager drop-down menu, select a vCenter Server.

Step 3.   Select **Settings > Host Remediation > Images**.

Step 4.   Click **Edit**.

Step 5.   In the Edit Cluster Settings window, select the **Quick Boot** checkbox.

Step 6.   Click **Save**.

ESXi Firmware Updates

You can use vSphere Lifecycle Manager images to perform firmware updates on cluster member hosts. Firmware updates are not available for clusters that are managed with baselines. To apply firmware updates, you must use a vendor-provided firmware and driver add-on in the image. Firmware updates are available in a special vendor depot that you access through a vendor-specific hardware support manager plug-in that registers itself as a vCenter Server extension.

The hardware support manager enables you to select a firmware add-on to include in an image and the firmware versions to be installed on the hosts. During remediation, vSphere Lifecycle Manager requests the selected hardware support manager to update the firmware on the hosts in accordance with the firmware add-on specified in the image.

In vSphere 8.0, you can deploy hardware support manager plug-ins from Dell and HPE. Dell's plug-in, which you deploy as an appliance, is part of the Dell Open-Manage Integration for VMware vCenter Server (OMIVV). HPE's plug-in, which you deploy as an appliance, is part of the HPE iLO Amplifier management tool. You should follow the vendor's specific deployment and configuration documentation. These are the main steps:

Step 1. Deploy and power on the virtual appliance.

Step 2. Register the virtual appliance as a vCenter Server extension.

Step 3. Use the plug-in's UI in the vSphere Client.

You can use the following procedure to manage the firmware on cluster member hosts that are managed with a single image:

Step 1. In the vSphere Client, select the cluster in the inventory pane.

Step 2. Examine the cluster member hosts and verify that they are from the same vendor.

Step 3. Select the cluster and click **Updates > Hosts > Image**.

Step 4. In the Image card, click **Edit**.

Step 5. In the Edit Image card, click **Firmware and Drivers Addon > Select**.

Step 6. In the dialog box, select a hardware support manager.

Step 7. Select a firmware add-on from the provided list and review the right panel, which contains information such as whether the selected add-on contains the necessary drivers for the ESXi versions in the cluster.

Step 8. Click **Select**.

Step 9. In the Image card, validate and save the image, which triggers a compliance check against the new image.

Step 10. In the Image Compliance card, review the results.

Step 11. If any host in the cluster has firmware that is non-compliant with the new image firmware, remediate that host or the cluster, using the following steps:

   a. Optionally, in the Image Compliance card, click **Run Pre-check** for the cluster or for a selected host.

   b. In the Image Compliance card, initiate remediation.

   c. To remediate all hosts in the cluster, click the **Remediate All** button. If the remediation of a single host fails, the remediation for the cluster is aborted.

   d. Alternatively, to remediate a single host, click the vertical ellipsis icon for the host and select **Remediate**.

NOTE The host vendor must match the selected hardware support manager vendor. Otherwise, a compliance check will report that the hosts are from a different vendor or will report an incompatibility. Firmware remediation will fail.

Hardware Compatibility Checks

You can use vLCM to automate the process of validating hardware compliance against the *VMware Compatibility Guide* (VCG) and *vSAN Hardware Compatibility List* (vSAN HCL), based on ESXi version. Hardware compatibility checks for vSAN cluster member hosts use the vSAN HCL for the I/O devices used by vSAN and the VCG for all other devices.

To check the hardware compatibility for a cluster, select the cluster, select Updates > Hosts > Hardware Compatibility and click Run Checks.

Exporting and Importing Cluster Images

When creating a cluster that uses a single image, in the New Cluster Wizard, you can choose Import Image from an Existing Host in vCenter Inventory and then select a reference host from the vCenter Server inventory. If you want to import an image from a host outside the vCenter Server, you can choose Import Image from a New Host. Alternatively, in the New Cluster wizard, you can choose to compose a new image and configure it. You can also export a cluster image from one vCenter Server instance and import it to another vCenter Server instance. You can use the following procedure to export the image:

Step 1. In the vSphere Client, select the cluster in the inventory pane and navigate to **Updates > Hosts > Image**.

Step 2. Click the horizontal ellipsis icon and select **Export**.

Step 3. In the Export Image dialog box, select a file format and click **Export**.

NOTE   If you intend to use the image in another vCenter Server, export it as a JSON file and as a ZIP file. You can import both the JSON file and the ZIP file to the target vCenter Server system.

You can use the following procedure to import a cluster image:

Step 1.   In the vSphere Client, select the cluster in the navigation pane and navigate to **Updates > Hosts > Image**.

Step 2.   Click the horizontal ellipsis icon and select **Import**.

Step 3.   In the Import Image dialog box, select a JSON file and click **Next**.

Step 4.   Optionally, use the Edit Image card to modify the following image elements:

- ESXi version
- Vendor add-on
- Firmware and drivers add-on
- Components

Step 5.   Resolve any issues with conflicting components or unresolved dependencies.

Step 6.   Optionally, click **Validate**.

Step 7.   Click **Save**.

Backup and Restore Scenarios

After switching a cluster from using baselines to using images, if you restore the vCenter Server from a backup made prior to the switch, the restored cluster reverts to being managed by baselines.

If you restore a vCenter Server back to a point in time prior to when you used vSphere Lifecycle Manager to remediate a cluster with a new image containing new components, a compliance check on the cluster reveals that the hosts are incompatible. In such a case, vSphere Lifecycle Manager expected the hosts to be using a different image. To fix this, you should upgrade the cluster to the new image and remediate.

Upgrading Virtual Machines

You can use vLCM to upgrade VMware Tools and the virtual machine hardware version of multiple virtual machines in a folder, vApp, host, or cluster. You can upgrade a virtual machine regardless of its power state and let vLCM change the power state of the virtual machine as needed and return it to its original state when ready. To upgrade VMware Tools, vLCM powers on the virtual machine. To upgrade the virtual machine hardware, Lifecycle Manager powers off the virtual machine.

You can use the following procedure to upgrade the hardware for a set of virtual machines by using vLCM:

Step 1. In the vSphere client, select a virtual machine container object, such as a folder or cluster, and navigate to **Updates > Hosts > VM Hardware**.

Step 2. Select the specific virtual machines to upgrade.

Step 3. Click **Upgrade to Match Host**.

Step 4. Optionally, use **Scheduling Options** to configure the upgrade as a scheduled task.

Step 5. Optionally, use **Rollback Options** and configure the following:

    a. Select or deselect the **Take Snapshot of VMs** checkbox. (It is enabled by default.)

    b. Select to keep the snapshots either indefinitely or for a fixed period.

    c. Provide a snapshot name.

    d. Optionally, provide a description.

    e. Optionally, select the checkbox to include the virtual machine memory in the snapshot.

Step 6. Click **Upgrade to Match Host**.

You can use the same procedure to upgrade VMware Tools, except you should choose Upgrade VMware Tools to Match Host in step 3. On the VMware Tools page, you can choose Set Auto Update. Optionally, you can use a virtual machine's Updates tab to turn on the Automatically Upgrade on Reboot feature.

For more information concerning VMware Tools and virtual machine hardware, such as procedures for interactive installation, host compatibility, and log levels, see Chapter 14, "Managing Virtual Machines."

Managing ESXi Hosts

In some cases, such as when you are performing host maintenance and troubleshooting activities, you may want to restart the management agents on an ESXi host. To do so using the Direct Console User Interface (DCUI), select Troubleshooting > Restart Management Agents. This operation restarts all installed management agents and services that are running in /etc/init.d on the ESXi host. Typically, these agents include **hostd**, **ntpd**, **sfcbd**, **slpd**, **wsman**, and **vobd**. When you restart the management agents, current users of the vSphere Client and vSphere Host Client lose connectivity to the host.

When troubleshooting network connectivity with a host, you can choose Test Management Network in the host's DCUI, which automatically pings the host's configured default gateway, pings the DNS server, and attempts to resolve its hostname. You can specify additional addresses for the ping tests. To restore network connectivity for a host or to renew a DHCP lease, you can choose Restart the Management Networking in the host's DCUI.

In rare situations such as the following, you may want to restore a standard switch to an ESXi host, which you can do with the Restore Standard Switch option in the DCUI:

- The distributed switch used for management is not functioning.
- You need to restore the host connection to vCenter, which uses a distributed switch.
- You do not want vCenter Server to manage the host and want to ensure that the management connection does not use a distributed switch.

You can use the vSphere Host Client interface to manage the host's services. To get started, log on to the vSphere Host Client as the root user or as another user with local administrator privileges and navigate to Manage > Services. Here you can examine the state of each ESXi service. To change the state of a service, right-click on the service and select Start, Stop, or Reset. You can also change a service's startup policy such that it automatically starts with the host or associated firewall ports or is only started manually, as illustrated in Figure 13-1. You can perform similar operations using the vSphere Client by selecting the host and navigating to Configure > System > Services.

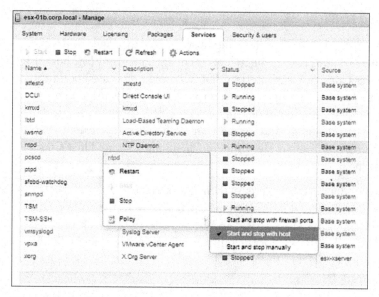

Figure 13-1   Managing Host Services in the vSphere Host Client

To manage firewall rules on an ESXi host, you can select the host in the vSphere Client and navigate to Configure > System > Firewall, as illustrated in Figure 13-2. Here you can view the currently allowed incoming and outgoing firewall services. The details for each service include the service name, the associated TCP ports, the associated UDP ports, and the allowed IP addresses. To make changes, you can use the Edit button to view all the currently defined services, select the services you want to allow, and optionally restrict the available IP addresses for the service. To perform similar operations in the vSphere Host Client, navigate to Networking > Firewall Rules.

In the vSphere Client, you can right-click on a specific host and choose from a set of available actions. For example, to address a vCenter Server connection to a host, you can choose Connection > Disconnect, wait for the task to complete, and choose Connection > Connect. To remove a host from the vCenter Server inventory, you can first choose Enter Maintenance mode and then choose Remove from Inventory.

If you want to perform maintenance activities on a host, such as upgrading its hardware, you can choose Maintenance Mode > Enter Maintenance Mode. Following the completion of a maintenance activity, you can select Maintenance Mode > Exit Maintenance Mode. To test a host's ability to be used with Distributed Power Management (DPM), you can choose Power > Enter Standby Mode.

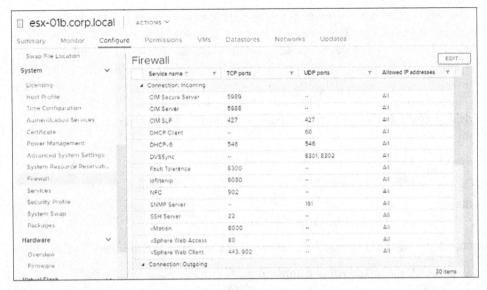

Figure 13-2 Firewall Rules in the vSphere Client

The following are some of the other options you can select for a host in the vSphere client:

- Certificates (for example, renewing certificates or refreshing CA certificates)

- Host Profiles (including Attach, Detach, Extract, Change Host Profile, or Remediate)

- Export System Logs

- Assign License

- Settings

- Move To

- Add Permission

Details on these tasks are provided elsewhere in this book.

Monitoring and Managing vCenter Server

You can use the vSphere Client and the vCenter Server Appliance Management Interface (VAMI) to configure, monitor, and manage components and resource usage of the vCenter Server Appliance.

The "VIMTOP" and "vCenter Server Management" sections in Chapter 10, "Managing and Monitoring Clusters and Resources," provide information about monitoring the resource usage of the services and database running in the vCenter Server Appliance. If database resources are low, you can consider adjusting the statistics interval, statistics level, task retention, and event retention settings. If you determine that the appliance is low on disk space, you can add more space. To increase the disk space for a vCenter Server Appliance 7.0 and later, you can use the following procedure:

Step 1.   Use the vSphere Client (or Host Client) to navigate the vSphere environment that is hosting the vCenter Server Appliance.

Step 2.   Select the vCenter Server Appliance (virtual machine), edit its settings, and increase the virtual disk size.

Step 3.   Use SSH to connect to the vCenter Server as the root user.

Step 4.   Run the following command:

```
com.vmware.appliance.system.storage.resize
```

Optionally, to see the impact of the command, you can use the following command to examine the total and used storage (in kilobytes) before and after step 4:

```
com.vmware.appliance.version1.resources.storage.stats.list
```

NOTE   If you want to keep a complete history of tasks and events for your vCenter Server, do not use the database retention options.

Monitoring and Managing vCenter Server with the VAMI

You can use the VAMI to monitor and manage specific components of your vCenter Server.

To access the VAMI, use a web browser to connect to https://*vCenter-FQDN*:5480. By default, you can log on using the root account and the password that was set during the vCenter Server deployment.

NOTE   If you are using Internet Explorer, verify that TLS 1.0, TLS 1.1, and TLS 1.2 are enabled in the security settings.

After logging in to the VAMI as root, you can perform any of the tasks described in Table 13-6.

Table 13-6 Tasks in vCenter Server Appliance Management Interface

Task	Steps/Details
View vCenter Server health status	1. Click **Summary.** 2. Examine the color of the Overall Health badge.
Reboot vCenter Server	1. Click **Summary.** 2. Click **Actions > Reboot** and click **Yes.**
Shut down vCenter Server	1. Click **Summary.** 2. Click **Actions > Shutdown** and click **Yes.**
Create a support bundle	1. Click **Summary.** 2. Click **Actions > Create Support Bundle** and save the bundle to your desktop.
Monitor CPU and memory use of vCenter Server	1. Click **Monitor.** 2. Click the **CPU & Memory** tab and use the date range drop-down menu to specify a time frame.
Monitor disk use of vCenter Server	1. Click **Monitor.** 2. Click the **Disks** tab.
Monitor network use of vCenter Server	1. Click **Monitor.** 2. Click the **Network** tab and use the date range drop-down menu to specify a time frame. 3. Examine the graph grid and use the provided table to select a packet or transmit byte rate to monitor.
Monitor database use of vCenter Server	1. Click **Monitor.** 2. Click the **Database** tab and use the date range drop-down menu to specify a time frame. 3. At the base of the graph, select specific database components to include in the graph.
Enable or disable each type of vCenter Server access	1. Click **Access.** 2. Configure each of the following options: ■ Enable SSH Login ■ Enable DCUI ■ Enable Console CLI ■ Enable Bash Shell

Task	Steps/Details

Configure network settings for vCenter Server	1. Click **Networking**.
	
	2. Click **Edit** and fill in the following networking details:
	
	  ■ DNS settings
	
	  ■ IPv4 settings
	
	  ■ IPv6 settings
	
	  ■ Proxy server settings
	
	When configuring a proxy server, you can enable HTTPS, FTP, and HTTP options. You should provide the proxy server's IP address or host name, user credentials, and a port number.

Configure the firewall rules for the vCenter Server	1. Click **Firewall**.
	
	2. Examine the existing set of rules and choose from the following commands to change the rule set.
	
	  ■ **Add**
	
	  ■ **Edit**
	
	  ■ **Delete**
	
	  ■ **Reorder**
	
	3. For each rule, include the appropriate NIC, IP address, subnet, and action (Accept, Ignore, Reject, or Return).

Configure the time settings for the vCenter Server	1. Click **Time**. 2. Click **Time Zone > Edit** and select the appropriate time zone. 3. Click **Time Synchronization > Edit** and select **Mode to Disable, Host,** or **NTP**.
Start, stop, and restart a service in the vCenter Server	1. Click **Services** 2. Select a service and click **Start, Stop,** or **Restart**.
Configure settings for updating vCenter Server	1. Click **Update**. 2. Click **Settings**, set the options for automatic update checking, and set the repository to the default or to a custom (HTTPS or FTPS) URL. Optionally provide credentials if a custom repository is used. 3. Click **Check Updates** to manually check for updates.
Change the root user password in vCenter Server	1. Click **Administration**. 2. Click **Password > Change**. Set the password and the password expiration details. If you set the password to expire, provide the number of days and an address for the email warning.

Task	Steps/Details
Configure log forwarding on the vCenter Server	1. Click **Syslog**. 2. Click **Configure** (or Edit, if you previously configured syslog hosts), enter up to three destination hosts in the **Create Forward Configuration** pane, and set the protocol and port. 3. Select one of the following protocol options: ■ **TLS**: Transport Layer Security ■ **TCP**: Transmission Control Protocol ■ **RELP**: Reliable Event Logging Protocol ■ **UDP**: User Datagram Protocol
Configure and schedule backups of the vCenter Server	1. Click **Backup**. 2. Click **Backup > Backup Now** to initiate a backup or click **Backup > Configure** to schedule backups. 3. Use the Activity table to monitor backups.

Table 13-7 describes the possible colors (icons) for the Health Status badge.

Table 13-7 Health States

Color	Meaning	Description
Green	Good	All components are healthy.
Yellow	Warning	One or more components may become overloaded soon.
Orange	Alert	One or more components may be degraded. Non-security patches may be available.
Red	Critical	One or more components may be in an unusable state, and vCenter Server may become unresponsive soon. Security patches may be available.
Gray	Unknown	No data is available.

NOTE When responding to an alert, you should begin by examining the details in the Health Messages pane.

You can use the following procedure to reconfigure the FQDN, IP address, or primary network identifier (PID) of the vCenter Server:

Step 1.   Log in to the VAMI using your administrator SSO credentials.

Step 2.   Select **Networking > Network Settings > Edit**.

Step 3.   Select the appropriate NIC and click **Next**.

Step 4.   In the Edit Settings pane, change the host name and IP address. Click **Next**.

Step 5.   In the SSO Credentials pane, provide the administrator SSO credentials. (You must provide the credentials for the administrator account in the SSO domain, such as administrator@vsphere.local.)

Step 6.   In the Ready to Complete pane, click **Finish**.

Step 7.   Monitor the progress in the taskbar, and when you are redirected to the new IP address, log in using your administrator SSO credentials.

Step 8.   On the Networking page, verify the new host name and IP address.

Step 9.   Re-register all deployed plug-ins.

Step 10.   Regenerate all custom certificates.

Step 11.   If vCenter Server HA was enabled, reconfigure vCenter HA.

Step 12.   If Active Directory was enabled, reconfigure Active Directory.

Step 13.   If Hybrid Link Mode was enabled, reconfigure Hybrid Link with Cloud vCenter Server.

NOTE   If you set an IP address as a system name during the deployment of the appliance, you can later change the primary network identifier to a fully qualified domain name. If vCenter High Availability (HA) is enabled, you must disable the vCenter HA setup before reconfiguring the primary network identifier.

Monitoring and Managing vCenter Server with the vSphere Client

You can use the vSphere Client to monitor and manage specific components of your vCenter Server, as described in this section.

Common vCenter Server Management Tasks

Using the vSphere Client, you can log on, select your vCenter Server in the inventory, and then perform any of the tasks listed in Table 13-8.

Table 13-8 Management Tasks in the vSphere Client

Task	Steps	Notes
Assign a license to your vCenter Server	1. Select the **Configure** tab. 2. Select **Settings > Licensing > Assign License**. 3. Select an existing license or enter a new license key.	This task requires the Global.Licenses privilege.
Configure statistics settings for vCenter Server	See the "Configuring Statistics Collection Settings" section, later in this chapter.	
Configure runtime settings for vCenter Server	1. Select the **Configure** tab. 2. Navigate to **Settings > General > Edit > Runtime Settings** and configure the following settings: ■ **vCenter Server Unique ID**: Specify a valid number from 0 through 63. (The default value is randomly generated.) ■ **vCenter Server Managed Address**: Can be IPv4, IPv6, a fully qualified domain name, an IP address, or another address format. ■ **vCenter Server Name**: Specify the name of the vCenter Server system (which should match the vCenter Server DNS name).	This task requires the Global.Settings privilege.
Configure user directory settings for vCenter Server	1. Select the **Configure** tab. 2. Navigate to **Settings > General > Edit > User Directory** and configure the following, which will be applied to vCenter Server Single Sign-On identity sources: ■ **User Directory Timeout**: The timeout, in seconds, for directory server connection ■ **Query Limit**: Must be enabled to set a query limit size ■ **Query Limit Size**: The maximum number of queries ■ **Validation**: When enabled, has vCenter Server validate (synchronize) known users against the directory server ■ **Validation Period**: The number of minutes between validation executions	This task requires the Global.Settings privilege.

Task	Steps	Notes
Configure mail sender settings for vCenter Server	1. Select the **Configure** tab. 2. Navigate to **Settings > General > Edit > Mail** and configure the following: ■ **Mail Server**: SMTP server information ■ **Mail Sender**: Full email address (including domain name) of the sender	This task requires the Global.Settings privilege.
Configure SNMP settings for vCenter Server	1. Select the **Configure** tab. 2. Navigate to **Settings > General > Edit > SNMP Receivers** and configure the following for one or more receivers: ■ **Enable Receiver**: Whether a receiver is enabled or disabled ■ **Primary Receiver URL**: Host name or IP address of the SNMP receiver ■ **Receiver Port**: Port number (between 1 and 65535) of the receiver ■ **Community String**: The community identifier	This task requires the Global.Settings privilege.
View port settings for vCenter Server	1. Select the **Configure** tab. 2. Navigate to **Settings > General > Edit > Ports** and examine the ports used by the web service.	
Configure timeout settings for vCenter Server	1. Select the **Configure** tab. 2. Navigate to **Settings > General > Edit > Timeout Settings** and configure the following: **Normal**: Timeout for normal operations **Long**: Timeout for long operations 3. Restart the vCenter Server system.	This task requires the Global.Settings privilege.
Configure logging settings for vCenter Server	1. Select the **Configure** tab. 2. Navigate to **Settings > General > Edit > Logging Settings** and select one of the following logging options: ■ None: Disable logging ■ Error: Show errors only ■ Warning: Show errors and warnings ■ Info: Normal logging ■ Verbose: Verbose logging ■ Trivia: Extended verbose logging	This task requires the Global.Settings privilege.

Task	Steps	Notes

Configure database settings for vCenter Server	1. Select the **Configure** tab.
	
	2. Navigate to **Settings > General > Edit > Database** and configure the following settings:
	
	  ■ Maximum Connection
	
	  ■ Task Retention (in days)
	
	  ■ Event Retention (in days)
		To limit the database growth and save storage space, you can configure the database to periodically discard task and event information.

Verify SSL certificates for legacy hosts	See the section "Verifying SSL Certificates for Legacy Hosts," later in this chapter.	
Configure advanced settings for vCenter Server (which are kept in the vpxd.cfg file)	1. Select the **Configure** tab. 2. Navigate to **Advanced Settings > Edit Settings**. Add or modify advanced settings entries, providing a name and value for each entry. (Note that you cannot delete entries.) 3. If necessary, restart the vCenter Server system.	Use Advanced Settings only when instructed to do so by VMware. This task requires the Global.Settings privilege.
Send a message to users who are logged in to vCenter Server	1. Select the **Configure** tab. 2. Navigate to **Settings > Message of the Day**, click **Edit**, and enter a message, such as a maintenance announcement or request for users to log out.	
Start, stop, and restart the services (nodes) in the vCenter Server	1. Navigate to **Administration > System Configuration**. 2. Select a node and click **Reboot Node**.	This task requires that your user account be a member of the SystemConfiguration.Administrators group.
View the health status of vCenter Server services and nodes	1. Navigate to **Administration > Deployment > System Configuration**. 2. Examine the Health Status badge for each service and node (refer to Table 13-7).	This task requires that your user account be a member of the SystemConfiguration.Administrators group.
Export a support bundle	1. Navigate to **Administration > Deployment > System Configuration**. 2. Select a node, click **Export Support Bundle**, select the services that you want to include from the two available categories (cloud infrastructure and virtual appliance), and click **Export Support Bundle**.	This task requires that your user account be a member of the SystemConfiguration.Administrators group.

Configuring Statistics Collection Settings

vCenter Server and ESXi use data counters, organized in metric groups, to collect data statistics. A data counter is a unit of information that is relevant to a specific inventory object or device. For example, the disk metric group includes separate data counters for collecting disk read rate, disk write rate, and disk usage data. Statistics for each counter are rolled up at specific collection intervals. Each data counter consists of several attributes that are used to determine the statistical value collected.

Collection levels determine the number of counters for which data is gathered during each collection interval. Collection intervals determine the time period during which statistics are aggregated, calculated, rolled up, and archived in the vCenter Server database. Together, the collection interval and collection level determine how much statistical data is collected and stored in a vCenter Server database.

You can configure statistical data collection intervals to set the frequency at which statistical queries occur, the length of time statistical data is stored in the database, and the type of statistical data that is collected. To configure a statistical interval, you can log on to the vSphere Client as a user with Performance.ModifyIntervals privilege and use the following procedure:

Step 1.   In the vSphere Client, select the vCenter Server instance in the inventory pane and navigate to **Configure > Settings**.

Step 2.   Select **General > Edit**.

Step 3.   To enable a statistics interval, select its checkbox.

Step 4.   Set the following interval attributes using the provided drop-down menus.

- **Interval Duration**: The time interval during which statistical data is collected
- **Save For**: The amount of time to keep statistics in the database
- **Statistics Level**: The level of statistical data to be collected (1 to 4)

Step 5.   Optionally, for Database Size, set the following options and examine the estimated database size and number of rows:

- Number of Physical Hosts
- Number of Virtual Machines

Step 6.   Click **Save**.

Table 13-9 provides details on the default data collection intervals.

Table 13-9 Collection Intervals

Collection Interval (Archive Length)	Collection Frequency	Default Behavior
1 day	5 minutes	Real-time (20-second) statistics are rolled up to create one data point every 5 minutes. The result is 288 data points every day. You can change the interval duration and archive length of the 1-day collection interval by configuring the statistics settings.
1 week	30 minutes	1-day statistics are rolled up to create one data point every 30 minutes. The result is 336 data points every week. You cannot change the default settings of the 1-week collection interval.
1 month	2 hours	1-week statistics are rolled up to create one data point every 2 hours. The result is 360 data points every month. You cannot change the default settings of the 1-month collection interval.
1 year	1 day	1-month statistics are rolled up to create one data point every day. The result is 365 data points each year. You can change the archive length of the 1-year collection interval by configuring the statistics settings.

The default statistics level for all statistical intervals is 1. You can set the statistics level to a value between 1 and 4, inclusive. The lower the level, the smaller the number of statistics counters used. Level 4 uses all statistics counters, but it is typically used only for debugging purposes. When setting a statistics level for a specific statistics interval, you must use a value less than or equal to the statistics level for the preceding statistics interval. Table 13-10 provides a summary of the metrics that are included for each statistics level.

Table 13-10   Statistics Levels

Level	Metrics	Best Practice
1	Cluster Services: All metrics CPU: cpuentitlement, totalmhz, usage (average), usagemhz Disk: capacity, maxTotalLatency, provisioned, unshared, usage (average), used Memory: consumed, mementitlement, overhead, swapinRate, swapoutRate, swapused, totalmb, usage (average), vmmemctl (balloon) Network: usage (average), IPv6 System: heartbeat, uptime Virtual Machine Operations: numChangeDS, numChangeHost, numChangeHostDS	Use this level for long-term performance monitoring when device statistics are not required.
2	Level 1 metrics plus the following: CPU: idle, reservedCapacity Disk: All metrics, excluding numberRead and numberWrite Memory: All metrics, excluding memUsed and maximum and minimum rollup values Virtual Machine Operations: All metrics	Use this level for long-term performance monitoring when device statistics are not required but you want to monitor more than the basic statistics.
3	Level 1 and Level 2 metrics plus the following: Metrics for all counters, excluding minimum and maximum rollup values Device metrics	Use this level for short-term troubleshooting or when device statistics are required. Due to the large quantity of data, use this level for the shortest (day or week) collection interval that suits your use case.
4	All metrics supported by the vCenter Server, including minimum and maximum rollup values	Same best practice as Level 3, except that Level 4 should be used only when you require metric rollup values that are not available in Level 3.

NOTE   If you increase the collection level, you may need to allocate more storage and system resources to avoid a decrease in performance.

Verifying SSL Certificates for Legacy Hosts

You can configure vCenter Server and the vSphere Client to check for valid SSL certificates before connecting to a host for operations such as adding a host or making a remote console connection to a virtual machine. vCenter Server 5.1 and vCenter Server 5.5 always connect to ESXi hosts using SSL thumbprint certificates. Starting with vCenter Server 6.0, VMware Certificate Authority signs the SSL certificates by default. You can instead replace certificates with certificates from a third-party CA. Thumbprint Mode is supported only for legacy hosts. To configure SSL certificate validation, you can use the following procedure:

Step 1. In the vSphere Client, select the vCenter Server object in the inventory and navigate to **Configure > Settings > General**.

Step 2. Click **Edit** and select **SSL Settings**.

Step 3. Determine the host thumbprint for each legacy host that requires validation:

a. Log in to the DCUI.

b. Select **System Customization > View Support Information** and examine the thumbprint displayed in the right column.

Step 4. Compare each host thumbprint with the thumbprint listed in the vCenter Server SSL Settings dialog box.

Step 5. If the thumbprints match, select the checkbox for the host.

Step 6. Click **Save**. Hosts that were not selected in step 5 are disconnected.

Updating the vCenter Server

You can use the VAMI or the vCenter Server Appliance shell to install minor patches.

Patching with VAMI

To update a vCenter Server Appliance, you may want to first stage the patches to the appliance, using the following procedure:

Step 1. Log on to the VAMI as root.

Step 2. Click **Update**.

Step 3. Click **Check Updates** and select one of the following:

- Check URL
- Check CDROM

Step 4.   Optionally, choose **Run Pre-check**.

Step 5.   In the Staging Options section, click **Stage**.

> **NOTE**   Other staging options include Stage and Install, Unstage, and Resume.

If you choose to use the Check URL option, the vCenter Server uses the configured VMware repository URL. The default VMware repository URL requires Internet access. If your vCenter Server is not connected to the Internet or if required by your security policy, you can configure a custom repository URL for your vCenter Server patches by using the following procedure:

Step 1.   Download the vCenter Server Appliance patch ZIP file from VMware's website (https://my.vmware.com/web/vmware/downloads).

Step 2.   On a local web server, create a repository directory under the root.

Step 3.   Extract the ZIP file into the repository directory.

Step 4.   Log on to the VAMI as root.

Step 5.   Select **Update > Settings**.

Step 6.   Set the **Repository settings**: Choose **use specified repository**, provide the URL and (optionally) the user credentials.

Step 7.   Click **OK**.

After staging the patches to the vCenter Server, you can install the patches by using the following procedure:

Step 1.   Log on to the VAMI as root.

Step 2.   Ensure that the patches are staged or use the staging procedure, but for the staging options, select **Stage and Install**.

Step 3.   Click **Update**.

Step 4.   Select the range of patches to apply and click **Install**.

Step 5.   Read and accept the end-user license agreement (EULA).

Step 6.   Wait for the installation to complete and then click **OK**.

Step 7.   If a reboot is required, click **Summary > Reboot**.

> **NOTE**   You should perform the previous procedure only during a maintenance period because the services provided by the vCenter Server become unavailable during the patch installation. As a precaution, you should also back up the vCenter Server prior to patching.

To configure vCenter Server to schedule automatic checks for available patches in the configured repository URL, you can use the following procedure:

Step 1.   Log on to the VAMI as root.

Step 2.   Verify that the correct repository URL is set and available.

Step 3.   Click **Update > Settings**.

Step 4.   Select **Check for Updates Automatically** and set the day and time (in UTC) to check for available patches.

Patching with the vCenter Server Appliance Shell

An alternate method for patching vCenter Server is to use its shell. For patching purposes, you should log on to the shell as a user with the super administrator role and use the commands in Table 13-11, as needed.

Table 13-11   Commands for Patching

Purpose	Command/Utility
View the full list of patches and software packages installed in the vCenter Server Appliance, in chronological order	**software-packages list --history**
View details about a specific patch	**software-packages list --patch** *patch_name*
Configure the vCenter Server to use a custom repository URL	**update.set --currentURL** *http://webserver / repo* **[--username** *username***] [--password** *password***]**
Configure the vCenter Server to use the default VMware repository URL	**update.set --currentURL default**
Enable automatic checks for vCenter Server Appliance patches in the current repository	**update.set --CheckUpdates enabled [--day** *day***] [--time** *HH:MM:SS***]**
Stage the patches from an attached ISO image	**software-packages stage --iso**
Stage the patches from the current repository URL	**software-packages stage --url**
Stage the patches from the repository URL that is not currently configured in the vCenter Server	**software-packages stage --url** *URL_of_the_repository*
Install the staged patches	**software-packages install --staged**
Install patches directly from an attached ISO image	**software-packages install --iso**

Purpose	Command/Utility
Install patches directly from the configured repository URL	**software-packages install --url**
Install patches directly from a repository URL that is not currently configured in the vCenter Server	**software-packages install --url** *URL_of_the_repository*
Reboot the vCenter Server following a patch installation	**shutdown reboot -r "patch reboot"**

NOTE To stage only third-party patches, include the **--thirdParty** option with the **software-packages stage** command. To directly accept the EULA, include the **--acceptEulas** option.

Managing a vCenter HA Cluster

During normal operation, the vCenter HA cluster mode is Enabled, and it is protecting the vCenter Server from hardware and software failures. When the cluster detects the failure of the Active node, the Passive node attempts an automatic failover, and the Passive node becomes the Active node. You can choose to perform a manual failover by choosing the Initiate Failover option in the vCenter HA settings in the vSphere Client. When performing a manual failover, you can choose to synchronize first or to force the failover without synchronization.

You can change the vCenter HA cluster mode to Maintenance when preparing to perform some maintenance activities. If the Passive or Witness nodes are unavailable (or recovering from a failure), a vCenter HA cluster mode may be disabled, in which case the Active node continues as a standalone vCenter Server. When the cluster is operating in either Maintenance Mode or Disabled Mode, an Active node can continue serving client requests even if the Passive and Witness nodes are lost or unreachable.

To change the vCenter HA cluster mode, you can select the Active node in the vSphere Client, select Configure > Settings > vCenter HA > Edit, and choose Enable vCenter HA, Maintenance Mode, Disable vCenter HA, or Remove vCenter HA Cluster.

You can use the following procedure to perform backup and restore operations on a vCenter HA cluster:

Step 1. Use the Active node's VAMI to obtain a file-based backup of the Active vCenter Server node. (Do not back up the Passive node or Witness node.)

Step 2. Before you begin the restore operation, power off and delete all vCenter HA nodes and remove the cluster configuration.

Step 3. Restore the Active node from the backup. The Active node is restored as a standalone vCenter Server.

Step 4. Reconfigure vCenter HA.

Repointing a vCenter Server to Another Domain

You can repoint a vCenter Server from one SSO domain to another existing domain. The steps in the procedure depend on whether the vCenter Server is the only node in the source domain and whether it is being repointed to a new domain or to an existing domain. Figure 13-3 illustrates a vCenter Server (Node A) being repointed from a single-node domain to an existing domain.

Before Repointing

After Repointing

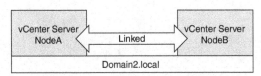

Figure 13-3 Repointing vCenter Server to an Existing Domain

Figure 13-4 illustrates a vCenter Server (Node A) being repointed from a multi-node domain to an existing domain.

Before Repointing

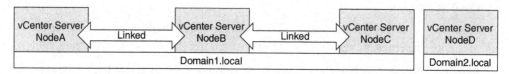

After Repointing

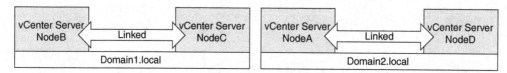

Figure 13-4 Repointing vCenter Server from a Multi-Node Domain

Figure 13-5 illustrates a vCenter Server (Node A) being repointed from a multi-node domain to a new domain that is created with the **repoint** command.

Before Repointing

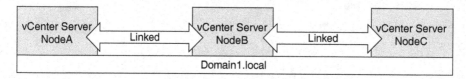

After Repointing

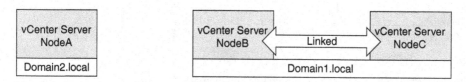

Figure 13-5 Repointing vCenter Server to a New Domain

If the source domain contains multiple (linked) vCenter Servers, then the repointing process involves additional steps to shut down the vCenter Server and unregister it from the source domain. If the vCenter Server is repointed to a new domain, you do not need to run a precheck or supply the replication partner parameters. Repointing is only supported with vCenter Server 6.7 Update 1 and later. You should back up each node prior to repointing.

To repoint a vCenter Server to another domain, you can use the following procedure:

Step 1.   If multiple vCenter Servers exist in the source domain:

   a. Shut down the chosen vCenter Server.

   b. To unregister the chosen vCenter Server from the source domain, log in to one of the other nodes in the source domain and run the following command, where *username* and *password* are credentials for the source SSO domain administrator account:

```
cmsso-util unregister --node-pnid Target_vCenter_FQDN
--username --passwd password
```

   c. Power on the chosen vCenter Server.

Step 2.   Ensure that the chosen vCenter Server is powered on.

Step 3.   If joining an existing domain:

   a. Ensure that a target replication partner (a vCenter Server in the existing domain) is powered on.

   b. Optionally, run the following precheck mode command from the chosen vCenter Server, which fetches tagging and authorization (roles and privileges) data and checks for conflicts between the source and destination:

```
cmsso-util domain-repoint -m pre-check --src-emb-admin
Administrator --replication-partner-fqdn Replication_
Partner_FQDN --replication-partner-admin Existing_Domain_
Admin --dest-domain-name Existing_Domain
```

   The precheck writes the conflicts to the /storage/domain-data directory.

   c. Optionally, check conflicts and apply one of the following resolutions to all conflicts or separately to each conflict:

   ■ **Copy:** Creates a duplicate copy of the data in the target domain

   ■ **Skip:** Skips copying the data in the target domain

   ■ **Merge:** Merges the conflict without creating duplicates

   The default resolution mode for tags and authorization conflicts is **Copy.**

Step 4.   Run the following **execute** command, which applies any precheck data and either repoints the chosen vCenter Server to the existing domain or creates a new domain for repointing:

```
cmsso-util domain-repoint -m execute --src-emb-admin
Administrator --replication-partner-fqdn Replication_
Partner_FQDN --replication-partner-admin Existing_Domain_
Admin --dest-domain-name Existing_Domain
```

If the chosen vCenter Server is being pointed to a new domain, you do not need to supply the replication partner parameters.

Exam Preparation Tasks

As mentioned in the section "Book Features and Exam Preparation Methods" in the Introduction, you have some choices for exam preparation: the exercises here, Chapter 15, "Final Preparation," and the exam simulation questions on the companion website.

Review All the Key Topics

Review the most important topics in this chapter, noted with the Key Topic icon in the outer margin of the page. Table 13-12 lists these key topics and the page number on which each is found.

Table 13-12   Key Topics for Chapter 13

Key Topic Element	Description	Page Number
Procedure	Restoring vCenter Server	520
Table 13-3	vCenter Server 7.0 compatibility	524
List	Prerequisites for upgrading vCenter Server Appliance	525
Section	Migrating vCenter Server for Windows to vCenter Server	528
Table 13-4	Lifecycle Manager remediation settings	534
Procedure	Creating a dynamic baseline	537
Procedure	Enabling Quick Boot	542
Table 13-6	Management tasks using the VAMI	550
Table 13-8	Management tasks using the vSphere Client	554

Complete Tables and Lists from Memory

Print a copy of Appendix B, "Memory Tables" (found on the companion website), or at least the section for this chapter, and complete the tables and lists from memory. Appendix C, "Memory Table Answers" (also on the companion website), includes completed tables and lists to check your work.

Define Key Terms

Define the following key terms from this chapter and check your answers in the glossary:

vSphere Lifecycle Manager (vLCM), image, Update Manager Download Service (UMDS), ESXi base image, add-on, baseline

Review Questions

1. You need to restore the vCenter Server from a file-based backup. Which of the following will not be restored?

    a. Resource pool hierarchy and setting

    b. vSphere DRS cluster state

    c. Cluster-host membership

    d. vSphere DRS configuration and rules

2. You plan to upgrade a Windows-based vCenter Server to vCenter Server Appliance 8.0 and want to transfer data in the background. Which of the following can be included in the background transfer?

    a. Configuration data only

    b. Configuration data and performance data

    c. Performance data

    d. Data from the external database

3. You are configuring remediation setting for Lifecycle Manager. Which of the following settings is available only when working with baselines?

    a. PXE Booted Hosts and Removable Media Devices

    b. Quick Boot and VM Power State

    c. VM Migration and Admission Control

    d. VM Migration and Maintenance Mode Failures

4. Your vCenter Server is offline, and the distributed switch for an ESXi host management network is not functioning. Which of the following steps might fix the ESXi management connectivity?

   a. Use the vSphere Host Client to restart ESXi networking.

   b. Use the vSphere Client to restart ESXi networking.

   c. Use SSH to restart ESXi networking.

   d. In the DCUI, select Restore Standard Switch.

5. You are repointing a vCenter Server to an existing domain. In which of the following scenarios would you need to run a precheck?

   a. Multiple vCenter Servers exist in the target domain.

   b. Multiple vCenter Servers exist in the source domain.

   c. A single vCenter Server exists in the target domain.

   d. A single vCenter Server exists in the source domain.

This chapter covers the following topics:

- Creating and Configuring Virtual Machines
- Managing Virtual Machines
- Advanced Virtual Machine Management
- Content Libraries

This chapter contains information related to VMware vSphere 8.x Professional (2V0-21.23) exam objectives 1.9.3, 4.8, 4.8.1, 4.8.2, 4.8.3, 4.9, 4.9.1, 4.9.2, 4.9.3, 4.10, 4.10.1, 5.7, 7.1, 7.2, 7.3, 7.6, 7.6.1, 7.9, and 7.9.4.

## CHAPTER 14

Managing Virtual Machines

This chapter provides details on managing virtual machines.

"Do I Know This Already?" Quiz

The "Do I Know This Already?" quiz allows you to assess whether you should study this entire chapter or move quickly to the "Exam Preparation Tasks" section. In any case, the authors recommend that you read the entire chapter at least once. Table 14-1 outlines the major headings in this chapter and the corresponding "Do I Know This Already?" quiz questions. You can find the answers in Appendix A, "Answers to the 'Do I Know This Already?' Quizzes and Review Questions."

Table 14-1 "Do I Know This Already?" Foundation Topics Section-to-Question Mapping

Foundation Topics Section	Questions
Creating and Configuring Virtual Machines	1–3
Managing Virtual Machines	4–6
Advanced Virtual Machine Management	7, 8
Content Libraries	9, 10

1. You are creating a virtual machine in your vSphere 8.0 environment, and you want the virtual disk and NVDIMM devices to share the same PMem resources. Which of the following options should you choose?

    a. In the Memory settings, select PMem.

    b. In the Memory settings, select Standard.

    c. In the Storage Type settings, select PMem.

    d. In the Storage Type settings, select Standard.

2. You want to change the logging for the VMware Tools installation, such that vminst.log is sent to the host but vmmsi.log remains in the virtual machine. Which option should you choose?

   a. vmx.log.guest.level = "warning"

   b. vmx.log.guest.level = "info"

   c. vmx.log.guest.level = "verbose"

   d. vmx.log.guest.level = "trivia"

3. You want to deploy new virtual machines using linked clones. Which of the following should you use?

   a. vSphere API

   b. vSphere Client

   c. vSphere Host Client

   d. vCenter Management Interface

4. You are updating a virtual machine and want to use hardware Version 14. Which of the following compatibility settings should you choose?

   a. ESXi 7.0 and later

   b. ESXi 6.7 Update 2 and later

   c. ESXi 6.7 and later

   d. ESXi 6.5 and later

5. You want to control the host compatibility for your virtual machines at various levels of the inventory. On which of the following objects can you set the Default VM Compatibility option?

   a. Cluster

   b. VM folder

   c. Virtual machine

   d. Template

6. Which option should you choose to minimize the time required to create a virtual machine snapshot?

   a. Snapshot the memory and quiesce the file system

   b. Snapshot the memory but do not quiesce the file system

   c. Quiesce the file system but do not snapshot the memory

   d. Do not quiesce the file system or snapshot the memory

7. You want to enable Microsoft virtualization-based security (VBS) for a Windows virtual machine in a vSphere environment. Which of the following is a requirement?

    a. vSphere 7.0 or later

    b. Virtual machine hardware Version 17 or later

    c. IOMMU

    d. Windows 8 or later

8. You are considering whether to use vGPUs for some of the virtual machines in your vSphere environment. Which of the following is not a common use case for vGPUs?

    a. Fast provisioning

    b. High-end graphics in VDI

    c. Machine learning

    d. Artificial intelligence

9. You are setting permissions for a vCenter Server. You want to ensure that a specific user can manage the vCenter Server's content libraries and content but can only view content libraries belonging to other vCenter Servers. Which settings should you make?

    a. Grant the read-only role as a global permission and the administrator role on the vCenter Server.

    b. Grant the content library administrator role as a global permission and the administrator role on the vCenter Server.

    c. Grant just the administrator role on the vCenter Server.

    d. Grant just the content library administrator role on the vCenter Server.

10. You want to add items to the content library. Which of the following is not a valid choice?

    a. You can import a vApp.

    b. You can select a virtual machine and choose Clone to Template in Library.

    c. You can import an ISO.

    d. You can migrate a virtual machine to the library.

Foundation Topics

Creating and Configuring Virtual Machines

You can use the vSphere Client to create and manage virtual machines. The associated procedures are intuitive. The following sections summarize the procedures and provide some related details, such as the required privileges.

Creating a New Virtual Machine

The following permissions are required when creating a virtual machine:

- Virtual Machine.Inventory.Create New on the destination folder or data center

- Virtual Machine.Configuration.Add New Disk on the destination folder or data center (when adding a new disk)

- Virtual Machine.Configuration.Add Existing Disk on the destination folder or data center (when adding an existing disk)

- Virtual Machine.Configuration.Configure Raw Device on the destination folder or data center (when using a Raw Device Mapping [RDM] or SCSI passthrough device)

- Virtual Machine.Configuration.Configure Host USB Device on the destination folder or data center (when attaching a virtual USB device backed by a host USB device)

- Virtual Machine.Configuration.Advanced Configuration on the destination folder or data center (when configuring advanced virtual machine settings)

- Virtual Machine.Configuration.Change Swapfile Placement on the destination folder or data center (when configuring swap file placement)

- Virtual Machine.Configuration.Toggle Disk Change Tracking on the destination folder or data center (when enabling change tracking on the virtual machine's disks)

- Resource.Assign Virtual Machine to Resource Pool on the destination host, cluster, or resource pool

- Datastore.Allocate Space on the destination datastore or datastore folder

- Network.Assign Network on the network where the virtual machine will be connected

To create a virtual machine, you can use the New Virtual Machine wizard and select Create a New Virtual Machine. In the wizard, you should provide all required information, including compute resource (host, cluster, resource pool, or vApp), storage type and location, virtual machine compatibility, guest OS, Windows virtualization-based security (for a Windows virtual machine), and hardware customization.

When selecting the storage type on a host that has PMem memory, you can select either the Standard or PMem radio button. If you chose PMem storage for a virtual machine, its default virtual disk, new virtual disk, and NVDIMM devices share the same PMem resources. You should adjust the size of newly added devices. The wizard alerts you if issues exist.

Powering On a VM

To power on a virtual machine from the vSphere client, you can right-click the virtual machine and choose Power On. The following are some likely causes of power-on failures:

- The evaluation period (or license) has expired.

- Permissions are insufficient.

- There is insufficient storage space to create files, such as the swap file.

- The assigned MAC address conflicts with VMware reserved MAC addresses.

- The operation would violate admission control.

Opening a Console to a VM

To open a console to a virtual machine, you can use an integrated web-based console or the independent VMware Remote Console (VMRC). To use the integrated web-based console, you should ensure that the virtual machine is powered on, select it in the inventory pane, and either choose Launch Web Console in the vSphere Client or Open Browser Console in the vSphere Host Client.

To use the VMRC to access a virtual machine, you should first ensure that it is installed on your local system and, if necessary, prepare a proxy server. Then you can launch it from the vSphere Client or the vSphere Host Client. In the vSphere Client, select the virtual machine in the inventory pane and select Summary > Launch Remote Console. In the vSphere Host Client, select the virtual machine in the inventory pane and select Console > Launch Remote Console.

To configure a proxy server for VMware Remote Console, you can browse to vmrc://settings or use the menu if VMware Remote Console is already open. Then choose Preferences in the appropriate menu:

- **Windows**: Select VMRC > Preferences.
- **macOS**: Select VMware Remote Console > Preferences.
- **Linux**: Select File > Remote Console Preferences.

The main steps are to select the Enable Proxy for Remote Virtual Machine option and to set the appropriate settings, such as the proxy server's host name or IP (IPv4 or IPv6) address and port, and optionally provide user credentials. The specific steps depend on the OS type (Windows, Linux, or macOS).

NOTE   In VMRC Version 11.0, the VMWARE_HTTPSPROXY environment variable, which is used to set a proxy server in previous versions of VMRC, is ignored after the previous procedure is applied. To use authentication with the proxy server, you must use the previous procedure instead of the environment variable.

Installing and Upgrading VMware Tools

You can install VMware Tools in the guest OS of a virtual machine to enable several features that improve manageability and smooth user interaction. To interactively install VMware Tools, in the vSphere Client, you can right-click on a virtual machine, select Guest OS > Install VMware Tools, and select Mount, which connects the virtual machine's first virtual CD-ROM disk drive to the appropriate VMware Tools ISO file, based on the guest operating system. If Autorun is configured in the guest OS, the VMware Tools installation may begin automatically. Otherwise, you might need to interactively launch the installer in the guest OS. For example, you might need to launch **d:\setup.exe** in a Windows 64-bit guest OS. In many cases, the default installation is adequate. If you need non-default components, such as the Guest Introspection Thin Agent driver, select Custom Setup.

NOTE   The open source implementation of VMware Tools for Linux is Open VM Tools.

Whenever a new VMware Tools version is available, such as following an ESXi upgrade, you should consider upgrading your virtual machines. You should always upgrade VMware Tools prior to upgrading the virtual machine hardware. You can use the same procedure as you used to install VMware Tools, except you choose Upgrade VMware Tools.

Previous versions of vSphere allow you to use Update Manager to upgrade virtual machine hardware and VMware Tools. In vSphere 7.0 and later, you can use the vSphere Client directly to upgrade the hardware and VMware Tools for a set of virtual machines in a container, such as a folder or cluster, as described in the "Upgrading Virtual Machines" section in Chapter 13, "Managing vSphere and vCenter Server."

VMware Tools Lifecycle Management provides a simplified and scalable approach for installing and upgrading VMware Tools. You can configure your virtual machine to automatically check for and apply VMware Tools upgrades each time you power on your virtual machine. Automatic Tools upgrades are not supported for Solaris or Netware guests. The prerequisites for automatic VMware Tools upgrades are that the virtual machines must be hosted by ESX/ESXi 3.5 or later, must be managed by vCenter Server 3.5 or later, must be using VMware Tools shipped with ESX/ESXi 3.5 or later, and must be running a guest OS that is supported for ESX/ESXi 3.5 and vCenter Server 3.5 or later.

You can set the vmx.log.guest.level option as described in Table 14-2 to control the use of log files for VMware Tools installation.

Table 14-2   Installer Log Options

Value	Description
vmx.log.guest.level = "off"	Logging to the host is disabled. (This is the default value.)
vmx.log.guest.level = "error"	vminst.log and vmmsi.log remain in the virtual machine and are not sent to the host.
vmx.log.guest.level = "warning"	vminst.log and vmmsi.log remain in the virtual machine and are not sent to the host.
vmx.log.guest.level = "notice"	vminst.log and vmmsi.log remain in the virtual machine and are not sent to the host.
vmx.log.guest.level = "info"	vminst.log is sent to the host, but vmmsi.log remains in the virtual machine.
vmx.log.guest.level = "verbose"	vminst.log and vmmsi.log are sent to the host.
vmx.log.guest.level = "trivia"	vminst.log and vmmsi.log are sent to the host.

When using the **setup.exe** command to install VMware Tools, you can use the **/mg** or **"LOGMODE=G"** options to control and suppress logging to the host. To suppress logging during automatic upgrades, you can set the **install-vmxGuestLog Disabled** parameter to **true** in the tools.conf file. To use the tools.conf file in some versions of Windows, you might need to create the file and deal with a hidden application data or program data file. To do so, you could open a text editor (such as Notepad) using Run as Administrator. If you change the tools.conf file, you do not need to restart VMware Tools. By default, the Tools service checks the configuration file for changes every 5 seconds.

Shutting Down a Guest

To stop a virtual machine gracefully from the vSphere client, you can right-click the virtual machine and choose Power > Shutdown Guest. To perform this operation, which safely stops the guest OS and powers down the virtual machine, VMware Tools must be running in the guest OS. If Shutdown Guest is not available for a virtual machine, a likely cause is that VMware Tools is not installed or not running.

Cloning a Virtual Machine

You can clone a virtual machine to a template. The following privileges are required for cloning a virtual machine to a template:

- Virtual Machine.Provisioning.Create Template from Virtual Machine on the source virtual machine

- Virtual Machine.Inventory.Create from Existing on the virtual machine folder where the template is created

- Resource.Assign Virtual Machine to Resource Pool on the destination host, cluster, or resource pool

- Datastore.Allocate Space on all datastores where the template is created

To clone a virtual machine to a template, in the vSphere client, right-click the virtual machine, select Clone > Clone as Template, and complete the wizard. In the wizard, provide a template name, folder, compute resource, and datastore.

> **NOTE** You cannot change the storage policy if you clone an encrypted virtual machine.

You can clone a virtual machine to a create a new virtual machine. The following privileges are required to clone a virtual machine to create a new virtual machine:

- Virtual Machine.Provisioning.Clone Virtual Machine on the virtual machine you are cloning

- Virtual Machine.Inventory.Create from Existing on the data center or virtual machine folder

- Virtual Machine.Configuration.Add New Disk on the data center or virtual machine folder

- Resource.Assign Virtual Machine to Resource Pool on the destination host, cluster, or resource pool

- Datastore.Allocate Space on the destination datastore or datastore folder

- Network.Assign Network on the network to which you assign the virtual machine

- Virtual Machine.Provisioning.Customize on the virtual machine or virtual machine folder (when customizing the guest operating system)

- Virtual Machine.Provisioning.Read Customization Specifications on the root vCenter Server (when customizing the guest operating system).

You can clone a virtual machine to create a new virtual machine by right-clicking the virtual machine and selecting Clone > Clone to Virtual Machine. In the wizard, you should provide all the required information, such as name, compute resource, compatibility, and storage. The procedure is much like the procedure in the "Deploying a Virtual Machine from a Template" section, later in this chapter, including the option to customize the guest OS.

NOTE   You cannot use the vSphere Client to clone a virtual machine using linked clones or instant clones. You can do so with API calls.

If the source virtual machine has an NVDIMM device and virtual PMem hard disks, the destination host or cluster must have an available PMem resource. If the virtual machine has virtual PMem hard disks but does not have an NVDIMM device, the destination host or cluster must have an available PMem resource. Otherwise, all hard disks of the destination virtual machine use the storage policy and datastore selected for the configuration files of the source virtual machine.

Converting Between a VM and a Template

You can easily convert a virtual machine to a template. To do so in the vSphere client, right-click a powered-down virtual machine and choose Template > Convert to Template.

You can convert a template to a virtual machine. This is useful when you want to install new software and guest OS updates in the template. To do so, in the vSphere client, right-click the template and select Convert Template to Virtual Machine. You need to have the following privileges:

- Virtual Machine.Provisioning.Mark as Virtual Machine on the source template

- Resource.Assign Virtual Machine to Resource Pool on the target resource pool

Deploying a Virtual Machine from a Template

The following privileges are required for deploying a virtual machine from a template:

- Virtual Machine.Inventory.Create from Existing on the data center or virtual machine folder
- Virtual Machine.Configuration.Add New Disk on the data center or virtual machine folder (when adding a new virtual disk)
- Virtual Machine.Provisioning.Deploy Template on the source template
- Resource.Assign Virtual Machine to Resource Pool on the target host, cluster, or resource pool
- Datastore.Allocate Space on the target datastore
- Network.Assign Network on the target network (when adding a new network card)
- Virtual Machine.Provisioning.Customize Guest on the template or template folder (when customizing the guest operating system)
- Virtual Machine.Provisioning.Read Customization Specifications on the root vCenter Server (when customizing the guest operating system)
- Virtual Machine.Edit inventory.Create New on the destination folder or data center
- vApp.Import

To deploy a virtual machine from a template, in the vSphere client, right-click the template and select Clone Deploy from Template. In the wizard, you should provide all required information, such as name, compute resource, compatibility, storage, and guest customization options. The guest customization choices are Select an Existing Specification, Create a Specification, and Create a Specification from an Existing Application.

Customizing the Guest OS

When you clone a virtual machine to a template or to a new virtual machine, you have the option to customize the guest OS. In addition, other scenarios may allow you to customize a guest OS. This section describes guest OS customization.

You can customize the guest OS to change the computer name, network settings, and guest OS licensing to prevent conflicts in the environment. During a cloning operation, you can provide the customization settings or select a prebuilt customization specification.

Guest OS customization requires a supported guest OS installed on SCSI node 0:0 and VMware Tools. Windows guest customization requires ESXi Version 3.5 or later. Linux guest customization requires Perl in the guest OS. To customize a Linux guest OS, you need to install VMware Tools 10.10.10 or later and enable the enable-custom-scripts option (which is disabled by default).

Optionally, you can create a custom application for vCenter Server to use to generate computer names and IP addresses during guest customization. To do so, create a custom script based on the sample reference script (sample-generate-name-ip.pl) found at https://kb.vmware.com/s/article/2007557 and configure the associated vCenter Server advanced settings. For example, set config.guestcust.name-ip-generator.program to c:\perl\bin\perl.exe and set config.guestcust.name-ip-generator.arg1 to c:\sample-generate-name-ip.pl.

You can use the following procedure to create a guest customization specification for Linux:

Step 1. In the vSphere Client, navigate to **Menu > Policies and Profiles > VM Customization Specifications**.

Step 2. Click the **Create a New Specification** icon.

Step 3. On the Name and Target OS page, enter a name and a description for the customization specification, select **Linux** as the target guest OS, and click **Next**.

Step 4. On the Computer Name page, configure one of the following options in order to assign the computer name:

- **Use the Virtual Machine Name**
- **Enter a Name in the Clone/Deploy Wizard**
- **Enter a Name** (For this option, enter a name in the provided box and optionally select the **Append a Numeric Value** checkbox.)
- **Generate a Name Using the Custom Application Configured with vCenter Server** (For this option, optionally enter a parameter to pass to the application.)

Step 5. Enter the domain name and click **Next**.

Step 6. Select the time zone and click **Next**.

Step 7.   On the Customization Script page, optionally provide a script to run in the guest OS and click **Next**.

Step 8.   On the Network page, choose one of the following options:

- **Use Standard Network Settings**: Select this option to use DHCP to assign IP configuration.
- **Manually Select Custom Settings**: Select this option to have vCenter Server prompt the user to provide the IP configuration for each virtual NIC when using the guest customization specification.

Click **Next**.

Step 9.   On the DNS Settings page, enter the DNS server and domain settings.

Step 10.   Complete the wizard and click **Finish**.

To create a guest customization specification for Windows, you can use the previous procedure with the following modifications:

- On the Name and Target OS page, select Windows as a target guest OS and optionally select Generate a New Security Identity (SID).

- On the Set Registration Information page, enter the virtual machine owner's name and organization and click Next.

- On the Windows License page, provide a Windows product key. For a Windows Server specification, either select the Per Seat option or configure the maximum concurrent connections for the Per Server option. Click Next.

- On the Set Administrator Password page, configure the password, optionally select Automatically Logon as Administrator, and click Next.

- On the Networking page, if you choose Manually Select Custom Settings, use the DNS tab to provide DNS server details and click WINS to provide WINS details.

- On the Set Workgroup or Domain page, either provide a workgroup name or provide user credentials and a domain name and click Next.

Whenever you create a new virtual machine by deploying from a template or by cloning, you can use the wizard to select the Customize the Operating System checkbox and select the appropriate specification. To customize an existing virtual machine, in the vSphere client, right-click the virtual machine in the inventory pane, select Guest OS > Customize Guest OS, and select the appropriate specification.

As needed, you can manage guest customization specifications by navigating to Menu > Policies and Profiles > VM Customization Specifications. Here, you can import guest customization specifications. You can also select a particular specification and select one of the following actions:

- Edit Customization Spec

- Duplicate Customization Spec

- Export Customization Spec

- Delete Customization Spec

Deploying OVF/OVA Templates

Another method for deploying virtual machines is to leverage *Open Virtual Format (OVF) templates* or *Open Virtual Appliance (OVA) templates*. You can use the vSphere Client to deploy an OVF or OVA template. You can export a virtual machine, virtual appliance, or vApp as an OVF or OVA template to create virtual appliances that can be imported by other users. Compared to other methods, using an OVF template to export and import virtual machines provides the following benefits:

- Compressed data (which means faster downloads and uploads)

- Validation of the OVF by vCenter Server prior to importing

- Encapsulation of multiple virtual machines

OVA is essentially a single-file distribution of an OVF package. Prior to vSphere 6.5, the Client Integration Plug-in is required to export and import OVF and OVA templates. Starting in vSphere 6.5, you can only export to OVF. Deploying a virtual machine from an OVF template is commonly referred to as *deploying an OVF*.

To deploy an OVF, you can use the following procedure:

Step 1. In the vSphere Client, right-click on a cluster in the inventory pane and select **Deploy OVF Template**.

Step 2. On the Select OVF Template page, specify the path to the OVF file as a URL or local file and click **Next**.

Step 3. Use the wizard to provide information for the new virtual machine, such as name, folder, and compute resource.

Step 4. On the Review Details page, verify the OVF template details, such as publisher, download size, and size on disk. Click **Next**.

Step 5. Complete the wizard by providing typical details for a new virtual machine, such as storage policy, storage location, and network configuration.

Step 6. Optionally, customize the deployment properties on the Customize Template page.

Step 7. Optionally, select a binding service provider on the vService Bindings page.

Step 8. On the Ready to Complete page, click **Finish**.

Managing Virtual Machines

This section covers reoccurring activities that you might perform regarding virtual machines.

Configuring Virtual Machine Hardware

When creating or upgrading a virtual machine, you can configure the virtual machine compatibility setting, which controls the ESXi versions on which the virtual machine can run. The compatibility setting controls which virtual machine hardware version is used. The main use cases for configuring the compatibility setting to a version earlier than the default for the host are to maintain compatibility with older hosts and to standardize virtual machine deployment in the environment. The main downside of configuring the compatibility setting to a version earlier than the default for the host is that the virtual machine may not be able to use virtual hardware features supported by the host and may not achieve the best performance. Table 14-3 describes virtual machine compatibility options.

Table 14-3 Virtual Machine Compatibility Options

Compatibility Setting	Hardware Version
ESXi 8.0 and later	Hardware Version 20
ESXi 7.0 Update 2 and later	Hardware Version 19
ESXi 7.0 Update 1 and later	Hardware Version 18
ESXi 7.0 and later	Hardware Version 17
ESXi 6.7 Update 2 and later	Hardware Version 15
ESXi 6.7 and later	Hardware Version 14
ESXi 6.5 and later	Hardware Version 13
ESXi 6.0 and later	Hardware Version 11

Compatibility Setting	Hardware Version
ESXi 5.5 and later	Hardware Version 10
ESXi 5.1 and later	Hardware Version 9
ESXi 5.0 and later	Hardware Version 8
ESX/ESXi 4.0 and later	Hardware Version 7
ESX/ESXi 3.5 and later	Hardware Version 4

The compatibility setting impacts the supported features for the virtual machine. Table 14-4 lists some of the feature sets available in recent hardware versions.

Table 14-4 Features by Recent Virtual Machine Hardware Versions

Feature	Version 20	Version 19	Version 18	Version 17	Version 15	Version 14	Version 13
Maximum memory (GB)	24,560	24,560	24,560	6128	6128	6128	6128
Maximum number of logical processors	768	768	768	256	256	128	128
Maximum number of cores (virtual CPUs) per socket	256	64	64	64	64	64	64
NVMe controllers	4	4	4	4	4	4	4
Maximum NICs	10	10	10	10	10	10	10
USB 3.1 SuperSpeedPlus	Yes	Yes	Yes	Yes	No	No	No
Maximum video memory (GB)	8	8	8	4	2	2	2
Dynamic DirectPath	Yes	Yes	Yes	Yes	No	No	No
PCI hot adding support	Yes	Yes	Yes	Yes	Yes	Yes	Yes
Virtual precision clock device	Yes	Yes	Yes	Yes	No	No	No
Virtual watchdog timer device	Yes	Yes	Yes	Yes	No	No	No
Virtual SGX device	Yes	Yes	Yes	Yes	No	No	No
Virtual RDMA	Yes	Yes	Yes	Yes	Yes	Yes	Yes
NVDIMM controller	1	1	1	1	1	1	No

Feature	Version 20	Version 19	Version 18	Version 17	Version 15	Version 14	Version 13
NVDIMM devices	64	64	64	64	64	64	No
Virtual I/O MMU	Yes	Yes	Yes	Yes	Yes	Yes	No
Virtual TPM 2.0	Yes	Yes	Yes	Yes	Yes	Yes	No
Microsoft VBS	Yes	Yes	Yes	Yes	Yes	Yes	No

To control the default hardware compatibility for new virtual machines, you can set the Default VM Compatibility setting at the host, cluster, or data center level. The settings on a host override the settings on a cluster, which override the settings on the data center. To make the settings on a host or cluster, you must have the Host. Inventory.Modify Cluster privilege. To make the settings on a data center, you must have the Datacenter.Reconfigure Datacenter privilege.

You can upgrade the compatibility level of an existing virtual machine but should first upgrade VMware Tools. For example, you can select a virtual machine and use the Compatibility > Schedule VM Compatibility Upgrade option to upgrade the compatibility the next time you restart the virtual machine. Optionally, you can select Only Upgrade After Normal Guest OS Shutdown to upgrade compatibility during regularly scheduled guest maintenance.

You can change the number of virtual CPUs used by a virtual machine. Specifically, you can set the number of cores and the number of cores per socket. In ESXi 8.0, the maximum number of virtual CPU sockets is 128. To configure a virtual machine with more than 128 virtual CPUs, you must use multicore virtual CPUs.

By default, you cannot add CPU resources to a virtual machine when it is turned on. To change this behavior, you can enable the virtual machine's CPU hot adding option, but the following conditions apply:

- For best results, set virtual machine compatibility to ESXi 5.0 or later.

- Hot adding multicore virtual CPUs requires compatibility set to ESXi 5.0 or later.

- You can use hot adding to increase the number of virtual CPUs for a virtual machine that already has more than 128 virtual CPUs.

- You can disable hot adding for virtual machines with guest operating systems that do not support CPU hot adding.

- For virtual machines with compatibility set to ESXi 4.x and later, to support CPU hot adding, set Number of Cores per Socket to 1.

- Hot adding CPU resources to a virtual machine disconnects and reconnects all USB passthrough devices.

To enable CPU hot adding, the following prerequisites apply:

- The latest VMware Tools version must be installed.

- The guest operating system must support CPU hot adding.

- Virtual machine compatibility must be set to a minimum of ESX/ESXi 4.x or later.

- The virtual machine must be turned off.

- The Virtual Machine.Configuration.Settings privilege is required.

CPU identification (CPU ID) masks control the visibility of CPU features to the guest OS. Masking CPU features can impact a virtual machine's availability for migration using vMotion. For example, if you mask the AMD No eXecute (NX) or the Intel eXecute Disable (XD) bits, you prevent the virtual machine from using those features, but you allow the virtual machine to hot migrate to hosts that do not include this capability.

NOTE   Changing the CPU compatibility masks can result in an unsupported configuration. Do not manually change the CPU compatibility masks unless instructed to do so by VMware Support or a VMware Knowledge Base article.

During specific management operations, such as creating a virtual disk, cloning a virtual machine to a template, or migrating a virtual machine, you can set the provisioning policy for the virtual disk file. You can use Storage vMotion or other cross-datastore migrations to transform virtual disks from one format to another. The available virtual disk provisioning policies are described in Table 14-5.

Table 14-5   Virtual Disk Provisioning Policies

Provisioning Policy	Description	Sample Use Case
Thick provisioned lazy zeroed	All the provisioned space is allocated during creation. Data is zeroed on the first demand from the virtual machine.	Minimizes the risk of exhausting free datastore space.
Thick provisioned eager zeroed	All the provisioned space is allocated and zeroed (erased) during creation.	Required for some clustering features, such as Fault Tolerance. Provides the best performance.
Thin provisioned	Space is allocated and zeroed on demand, as needed, up to the provisioned space.	Fastest method to provision and migrate virtual disks.

You can change a virtual disk from the thin format to thick format by navigating to Datastore > Files in the vSphere Client and choosing the Inflate action for the virtual disk file. The vSphere Client does not provide a deflate option. To change a virtual disk provisioning type from thick to thin, you can migrate the virtual machine storage and select the appropriate policy.

Creating and growing a virtual disk provisioned for thick provisioned eager zeroed may take significantly longer than with a virtual disk provisioned for thick provisioned lazy zeroed.

You can configure virtual machines with virtual disks greater than 2 TB (large-capacity virtual disks), but you must meet resource and configuration requirements. The maximum size for large-capacity virtual disks is 62 TB. You should avoid using the maximum size because some operations, such as those involving snapshots and linked clones, may not finish when the maximum amount of disk space is allocated to a virtual disk. Operations such as snapshot quiescence, cloning, Storage vMotion, and vMotion in environments without shared storage can take significantly longer to finish. The following conditions and limitations apply to virtual machines with large-capacity disks:

- You must use a guest OS that supports large-capacity virtual hard disks.

- Target hosts for migration and cloning operations must use ESXi 6.0 or later.

- NFS, vSAN, and VMFS Version 5 or later datastores are supported.

- Fault Tolerance is not supported.

- BusLogic Parallel controllers are not supported.

To increase the size of a virtual disk, you need the following privileges:

- Virtual Machine.Configuration.Modify Device Settings on the virtual machine

- Virtual Machine.Configuration.Extend Virtual Disk on the virtual machine

- Datastore.Allocate Space on the datastore

To control how a virtual disk is impacted by snapshots, you can set the disk mode for a virtual disk to the settings described in Table 14-6.

Table 14-6 Virtual Disk Mode Settings

Disk Mode	Description
Dependent	Included in snapshots.
Independent–Persistent	Not included in snapshots.
	All data written is written permanently to disk.

Disk Mode	Description
Independent–Nonpersistent	Not included in snapshots.
	Changes are discarded when you turn off or reset the virtual machine.

You can set shares for a virtual disk, and they work much like CPU or memory shares for a virtual machine. The disk shares provide a relative priority for accessing the disk during periods of disk I/O contention for the underlying storage. The values Low, Normal, High, and Custom are compared to the sum of all shares of all virtual machines on the host. To control the maximum amount of disk I/O for a virtual disk, you can set the virtual disk's Limit–IOPS value. By default, the virtual disk is set for normal shares and unlimited IOPS.

You can add virtual disks to virtual machines, including new virtual disks, existing virtual disks, and raw device mappings (RDMs). To add an RDM to a virtual machine, you need to use an account with the Virtual Machine.Configuration.Configure Raw Device privilege, select a target LUN, choose where to store the mapping file, choose a compatibility mode (physical or virtual), and select a disk mode. Disk modes are not available for RDMs using physical compatibility mode.

A storage controller is included by default when you create a virtual machine. You can add additional SCSI controllers (BusLogic Parallel, LSI Logic Parallel, LSI Logic SAS, and VMware Paravirtual SCSI), AHCI, SATA, and NVM Express (NVMe) controllers. The following limitations apply to storage controllers:

- ESXi 4.x and later compatibility is required for LSI Logic SAS and VMware Paravirtual SCSI.

- ESXi 5.5 and later compatibility is required for AHCI SATA.

- ESXi 6.5 and later compatibility is required for NVMe.

- BusLogic Parallel controllers do not support large-capacity disks.

- Disks on VMware Paravirtual SCSI controllers may not provide the expected performance if they have snapshots or if the host's memory is overcommitted.

Before changing the storage controller type, you should ensure that the guest OS has the drivers for the target controller type, or the disks will become inaccessible. Likewise, in the following cases, adding storage controller types to a virtual machine that uses BIOS firmware may cause boot problems and require you to fix the issue by entering the BIOS setup:

- If the virtual machine boots from LSI Logic SAS or VMware Paravirtual SCSI, and you add a disk that uses BusLogic, LSI Logic, or AHCI SATA controllers

- If the virtual machine boots from AHCI SATA, and you add BusLogic Parallel or LSI Logic controllers

NOTE   Adding additional disks to virtual machines that use EFI firmware does not cause boot problems.

Editing Virtual Machine Options

You can edit a virtual machine and use the VM Options tab for multiple purposes, such as setting VMware Tools scripts, controlling user access to the remote console, configuring startup behavior, and changing the virtual machine name, as summarized in Table 14-7.

Table 14-7   Settings on the Virtual Machine Options Tab

Options	Description
General Options	You can set the virtual machine name. In addition, you can view the configuration file location, working location, and guest OS type and version.
VMware Remote Console Options	You can set the locking behavior and simultaneous connections.
Encryption	You can adjust the encryption settings.
Power Management	You can configure the suspend virtual machine behavior.
VMware Tools	You can set the VMware Tools scripts behavior, VMware Tools upgrade settings, and guest OS time synchronization settings.
Boot Options	You can set the boot delay and force entry into the BIOS or EUFI setup screen.
Advanced	You can adjust the acceleration and logging settings, debugging and statistics, swap file location, and latency sensitivity.
Fibre Channel NPIV	You can set the virtual node and port worldwide names (WWNs).

A virtual machine name must be unique within the folder where the virtual machine is located. If you move a virtual machine to a different datastore folder or host that already has a virtual machine of the same name, you must change the virtual machine's name to keep it unique. Changing a virtual machine name impacts how the virtual machine is identified by vCenter Server and does not impact file (or folder) names or the guest OS. After changing a virtual machine name, you can leverage Storage vMotion to migrate the virtual machine, which renames the associated files to match the new virtual machine name.

You can encrypt a virtual machine by editing its storage policies or by editing VM Options. Before encrypting a virtual machine, you must meet the following prerequisites:

- Establish a trusted connection with the KMS and select a default KMS.
- Create an encryption storage policy (or plan to use the sample VM encryption policy).
- Ensure that the virtual machine is powered off.
- Verify that you have the required privileges:
    - Verify that you have the Cryptographic Operations.Encrypt New Privilege.
    - If the host encryption mode is not enabled, verify that you have the Cryptographic Operations.Register Host privilege.

You can use the following procedure to encrypt a virtual machine:

Step 1. In the vSphere Client, right-click the virtual machine in the inventory pane and navigate to **VM Policies > Edit VM Storage Policies**.

Step 2. Use one of the following methods:

- Select an encryption storage policy to apply to the virtual machine and its virtual disks and click **OK**.
- Click **Configure per Disk**, select the encryption storage policy for VM, select an encryption or other storage policies for each virtual disk, and click **OK**.

Step 3. Optionally, encrypt the virtual machine or both the virtual machine and disks from the Edit Settings menu in the vSphere Client:

a. Right-click the virtual machine and select **Edit Settings**.

b. Select the **VM Options** tab and open **Encryption**. Choose an encryption policy. If you deselect all disks, only the VM home is encrypted.

Step 4. Click **OK**.

Configuring Guest User Mappings

You can enable guest OS access for some of your SSO user account to facilitate some administrative tasks, such as upgrading VMware Tools. You can use the following procedure to enroll SSO users to user accounts in guest operating systems by using SSO certificates. Subsequent guest management requests use an SSO SAML token to log in to the guest OS:

Step 1. In the vSphere Client, select a powered-on virtual machine in the inventory pane and navigate to **Configure > Guest User Mappings**.

Step 2. Enter your username and password and click **Log In**.

Step 3. In the Guest User Mappings pane, click the **Add** button.

Step 4. In the dialog box, select the SSO user.

Step 5. Specify a guest OS username and click **OK**.

Editing OVF Details

You can use the following procedure to edit a virtual machine's OVF settings to customize the OVF environment, OVF transport, and boot behavior after OVF deployment. This information is preserved when you export the virtual machine as an OVF template:

Step 1. In the vSphere Client, select a virtual machine in the inventory pane and navigate to **Configure > Settings > vApp Options**.

Step 2. Click the **Edit** button.

Step 3. If vApp options are not enabled, select the **Enable vApp Options** checkbox.

Step 4. Click the **OVF Details** tab.

Step 5. Set the OVF Environment Transport option to one of the following:

- **ISO Image**: Mounts an ISO image with the OVF template to the CD-ROM drive.
- **VMware Tools**: Initializes the guestInfo.ovfEnv variable with the OVF environment document.

Step 6. Optionally, enable the **Installation Boot** option and set the delay time, in seconds, to automatically reboot the virtual machine after OVF deployment.

Step 7. Click **OK**.

Creating and Managing Virtual Machine Snapshots

You can use a virtual machine snapshot to capture the state and data of a virtual machine at a specific point in time. A snapshot preserves the following information:

- Virtual machine settings
- Power state
- Disk state
- Memory state (optional)

To take a snapshot, in the vSphere client, you can right-click a virtual machine, select Snapshots > Take Snapshot, and provide a snapshot name. Optionally, you can provide a snapshot description and select Snapshot the Virtual Machine's Memory. Also, you can optionally choose Quiesce Guest File System. Quiescing the file system requires the virtual machine to be powered on, VMware Tools to be running, and Snapshot the Virtual Machine's Memory to be deselected.

NOTE   To minimize the impact to a running virtual machine and to reduce the time required to take a snapshot, do not snapshot the memory state or quiesce the guest file system.

After creating a snapshot, you can use the Snapshot Manager to view the snapshot hierarchy of the virtual machine, which appears as a tree with branches, as illustrated in Figure 5-2 in Chapter 5, "vCenter Server Features and Virtual Machines." To open the Snapshot Manager from the vSphere client, right-click the virtual machine and choose Snapshots > Manage Snapshots. In the Snapshot Manager, the snapshot that appears above the You Are Here icon is the parent snapshot. If you revert to a snapshot, that snapshot becomes the parent snapshot. If you take a snapshot of a virtual machine that already has at least one snapshot, the new snapshot is a child of the parent snapshot.

To revert a virtual machine to a specific snapshot, select the snapshot in the Snapshot Manager for the virtual machine and select Revert To. To do this, you must have the Virtual Machine.Snapshot Management.Revert to Snapshot privilege on the virtual machine.

When you revert the virtual machine to a snapshot, you return its virtual disks and settings to the state captured in the snapshot. If the snapshot includes the memory state, reverting to the snapshot returns the virtual machine's memory to that state. You can revert the virtual machine to any available snapshot in the Snapshot Manager. Subsequent snapshots from this point create a new branch of the snapshot tree.

When you revert to a snapshot, no snapshots are removed, but you lose the virtual machine's current disk state. In other words, all changes to disk data made since the last snapshot are permanently lost. If you revert to a snapshot without memory state, the virtual machine is in the powered-off state.

You can delete a snapshot for a running virtual machine without disrupting its end users. Deleting a snapshot removes your ability to revert to that snapshot's state in the future. To delete a specific snapshot, select the snapshot in the Snapshot Manager for the virtual machine and select Delete. Optionally, to delete all snapshots, select Delete All.

If the virtual machine is in a state where it has no snapshots but has one or more delta disks contributing to the active state of the virtual machine, then the vSphere Client may provide a "Consolidation Needed" warning. In this state, you can right-click the virtual machine in the vSphere client and select Snapshots > Consolidate. The system merges the data from delta disks into the base disks and deletes the delta disks. In normal conditions, your virtual machine is in a state where the Consolidate option is not available.

Migrating Virtual Machines

To migrate a virtual machine by using the vSphere Client, you can right-click the virtual machine in the inventory pane, choose Migrate, and complete the wizard. The details for completing the wizard depend on the migration type. The required privileges for each migration type are covered in Chapter 5. You can use the Recent Tasks pane to monitor the progress of your migration.

To cold migrate a virtual machine, you can use the following procedure:

Step 1. In the vSphere Client, right-click a powered-off virtual machine and select **Migrate**.

Step 2. Select one of the following migration types:

- **Change Compute Resource Only**
- **Change Storage Only**
- **Change Both Compute Resource and Storage**
- **Migrate Virtual Machine(s) to a Specific Datacenter**

Click **Next**.

Step 3. If you select a migration type that includes a cross-host migration, select the destination compute resource (**Host**, **Cluster**, **Resource Pool**, or **vApp**), verify that no issues exist in the Compatibility panel, and click **Next**.

Step 4.   If you select a migration type that includes a cross-datastore migration, select the virtual disk format (**Same as Source**, **Thin Provisioned**, **Thick Provisioned Lazy Zeroed**, or **Thick Provisioned Eager Zeroed**), select the appropriate policy in the VM Storage Policy menu, and select the destination, as described here:

- To store all the virtual machines in a datastore, select the datastore and click **Next**.

- To store all the virtual machines in a Storage DRS cluster, select the cluster and click **Next**.

- To store the virtual machine configuration files and virtual disks in separate locations, click **Advanced** and configure the destination for the configuration files and each virtual disk. Click **Next**.

Step 5.   For cross-host migrations, select the destination network for the virtual machines and click **Next**. Alternatively, you can click **Advanced** to assign separate networks to individual virtual machine network adapters.

Step 6.   Click **Finish**.

To perform a hot cross-host (vMotion) migration, you can apply the previous cold migration procedure with the following changes:

- Start with a powered-on virtual machine.

- Select to change the compute resource only.

- You are not prompted to select a destination datastore.

- Select either Schedule vMotion with High Priority or Schedule Regular vMotion.

To perform a hot cross-data store (Storage vMotion) migration, you can apply the previous cold migration procedure with the following changes:

- Start with a powered-on virtual machine.

- Select to change storage only.

- You are not prompted to select a destination host.

To perform a hot cross-host and cross-data store (vMotion without shared storage) migration, you can apply the previous cold migration procedure with the following changes:

- Start with a powered-on virtual machine.

- Select to change both the compute resource and storage.

- Select either Schedule vMotion with High Priority or Schedule Regular vMotion.

- As described in Chapter 5, you can use the vSphere Client to hot-migrate virtual machines across vCenter Servers that do not use Enhanced Linked Mode. The source must use vCenter Server 7.0 Update 1c or later, and the target vCenter Server must be 6.5 or later. If you want to clone the virtual machine across the vCenter Servers, the source must be Version 7.0 Update 3 or later. To perform this migration, you can use the following steps:

Step 1.   Right-click the virtual machine and choose **Migrate**.

Step 2.   Select **Cross vCenter Server Export**.

Step 3.   Use the **New vCenter Server** option to provide the target vCenter Server's fully qualified name (or IP address) and user credentials.

Step 4.   Use the wizard to select the target cluster, datastore, network, and other options, much as you would do with other migrations types.

Advanced Virtual Machine Management

This section covers topics related to the configuration and management of virtual machines that are not covered elsewhere in the book.

Managing OVF Templates

To export a virtual machine into a self-contained OVF template, you can select the virtual machine and then select Actions > Template > Export OVF Template. You must have the vApp.Export privilege. In the export wizard, you must provide a name and can optionally provide a description and configure advanced options. In the advanced options, you can include details concerning BIOS, UUID, MAC address, boot order, PCI slots, and other settings.

You can browse the VMware Virtual Appliance Marketplace to discover and download virtual appliances provided by VMware and VMware partners. The cost and licensing for each appliance are controlled by the provider.

Virtualization-Based Security

Starting with vSphere 6.7, you can enable *Microsoft virtualization-based security (VBS)* on supported Windows guest operating systems. VBS is a Microsoft feature for Windows 10 and Windows Server 2016 operating systems that uses hardware and software virtualization to enhance system security by creating an isolated, hypervisor-restricted, specialized subsystem. Windows typically uses hashed credentials stored in memory, including Active Directory credentials, that may be subject to the pass-the-hash exploit. In VBS, to mitigate the pass-the-hash exploit, you can enable a feature called Credential Guard that keeps account of hash information outside the memory of the Windows instance. If the hardware TPM chip is not available or is not enabled in the BIOS, Windows still uses VBS, and you can still enable Credential Guard, but the credentials are not as secure.

On a traditional (non-virtual) Windows server, to prepare for VBS, you should ensure that its BIOS, firmware, and operating system are set to use UEFI firmware, Secure Boot, hardware virtualization (Intel VT/ADM-V), and IOMMU. You can enable VBS in the Windows operating system. When you reboot Windows, the Microsoft hypervisor loads and leverages virtualization to bring up additional Windows components, including the credential management subsystem, in a separate memory space. All subsequent communications between Windows and Windows components are via RPC calls run through a Microsoft hypervisor-based communications channel.

In vSphere, to use VBS, you must use virtual hardware Version 14 or later. The virtual machine must be set to use UEFI firmware, Secure Boot, hardware virtualization (Intel VT/ADM-V), and IOMMU. In the virtual machine settings, enable the Virtualization Based Security checkbox on the VM Options tab. Finally, you must enable VBS by editing the group policy.

Enabling VBS for a virtual machine does not automatically enable virtual TPM, but you can add a virtual TPM device. A virtual TPM doesn't have a hardware-based vault. Instead, the data that it secures is written to the NVRAM file, which is encrypted using VM encryption, providing strong encryption and virtual machine portability.

Managing VMs by Using PowerCLI

VMware PowerCLI is a command-line scripting tool built on Windows PowerShell that provides cmdlets for managing and automating VMware products, including vSphere. You can install PowerCLI on a workstation or server in your vSphere environment and use PowerCLI to automate some aspects of your virtual machine management.

The main prerequisites for installing PowerCLI 12.0 on a Windows system are the presence of .NET Framework 4.7.2 or later and Windows PowerShell 5.1. For Linux and macOS systems, the requirements are .NET CORE 3.1 and PowerShell 7. The main steps to install PowerCLI are to download the product to the system and run the following command in the PowerShell console:

```
Install-Module VMware.PowerCLI -Scope CurrentUser
```

In many cases, you need to change the execution policy, which by default is set to the most secure policy (Restricted). For example, to change the policy to RemoteSigned, you can use the following command:

```
Set-ExecutionPolicy RemoteSigned
```

The Connect-VIServer cmdlet allows you to connect to a vCenter Server. The Get-VM cmdlet allows you to collect information about virtual machines. You can use the following commands to connect to a vCenter Server named server1.vsphere. local (using the administrator@vsphere.local account and the password VMware1!) and display information for all of its managed virtual machines:

```
Connect-VIServer -Server server1.vsphere.local -Protocol http -User
'administrator@vsphere.local' -Password 'VMware1!'
Get-VM
```

To start a virtual machine named win-01, you can use the following commands:

```
Get-VM win-01 | Start-VM
```

You can use PowerCLI to create virtual machines from specifications provided in an XML file. The XML content could provide detailed specifications for multiple virtual machines. For example, you can use the following sample XML content, which represents the minimum specifications for two virtual machines named MyVM1 and MyVM2, each having a 100 GB virtual disk:

```
<CreateVM>
   <VM>
      <Name>MyVM1</Name>
      <HDDCapacity>100</HDDCapacity>
   </VM>
   <VM>
      <Name>MyVM2</Name>
      <HDDCapacity>100</HDDCapacity>
   </VM>
</CreateVM>
```

If you save the sample content to a file named MyVMs.xml, you can use the following commands to read the file, parse the XML content into a variable, and create a virtual machine based on each specification:

```
[xml]$s = Get-Content myVM.xml
$s.CreateVM.VM | foreach {New-VM -VMHost $vmHost1 -Name $_.Name
-DiskGB $_.HDDCapacity}
```

You can use PowerCLI to migrate virtual machines. Consider a scenario where you need to automate frequent, massive migrations of virtual machines between datastores to prepare for storage array upgrades. At the lowest level, you need a command that migrates a virtual machine to a specified datastore. For example, you can use the following command to migrate a virtual machine named MyVM1 to a datastore named DS2:

```
Get-VM MyVM1 | Move-VM -Datastore DS2
```

Configuring VMs to Support vGPUs

In vSphere 8.0, you can enable virtual machines to use the processing power of available *graphics processing units (GPUs)*. GPUs are specialized processors developed for parallel processing, primarily for rendering graphical images. In vSphere, the main use case for a GPU is to support high-end graphics in virtual desktop infrastructure (VDI). Recently, the need to support artificial intelligence (AI) and machine learning (ML) has also emerged as a major use case.

You can use GPUs in different manners in a vSphere environment. For AI/ML use cases, the GPU configuration choice is mostly impacted by the size and complexity of the problem being solved. For VDI, the GPU configuration choice is impacted by the end user's graphics needs. The configuration involves either sharing GPUs with multiple virtual machines or dedicating some GPUs to specific virtual machines. Table 14-8 summarizes the potential GPU configuration for specific AI/ML use cases.

Table 14-8 Use Cases and GPU Configurations

GPU Configuration	Sample Use Cases	Details
GPU sharing	ML development and testing	Good fit for small problems and for the ML inference phase
Dedicated GPU	Data science	Commonly used for development and training in ML models
Dedicated multiple GPUs per VM	Advanced power ML users tackling large problems	Highest-performing GPU model

For the VMware Horizon VDI use case, depending on your hardware, you may have multiple options for sharing GPUs. For example, with NVIDIA hardware, you can choose to share GPUs using the NVIDIA vGPU (GRID) technology or the Virtual Shared Graphics Acceleration (vSGA) technology. In the vSGA model, the vSphere hypervisor presents a virtual VMware SVGA 3D GPU to each virtual machine. In the GRID model, each hardware GPU presents multiple virtual GPUs that the hypervisor passes through to the virtual machines. In the GRID model, you can use a vGPU profile to assign a portion of the GPU hardware to a virtual machine.

The vSGA model tends to be flexible and cost-effective for supporting virtual desktops running office, video, and 2D CAD applications. But the performance of the GRID model may be preferred for virtual desktops running 3D modeling software. For a side-by-side comparison of the vSGA and GRID models, see Figure 14-1.

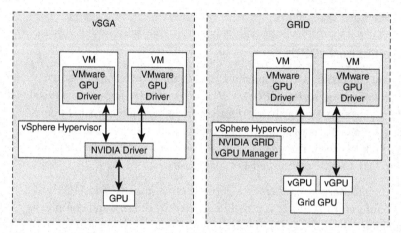

Figure 14-1 Comparison of the vSGA and GRID Models

The procedure to configure the GPU hardware, ESXi host, and virtual machine depends on your choice for GPU configuration. For example, you can use the following procedure to implement the GRID model using a vGPU profile (named grid_p100-8a) to allow a virtual machine to use up to 8 GB of the GPU's memory:

Step 1.   Obtain the NVIDIA vGPU software and license.

Step 2.   In the vSphere Client, select the ESXi host in the inventory pane and navigate to **Configure > Hardware > Graphics > Host Graphics**.

Step 3.   Click **Edit**.

Step 4.   Select the **Shared Direct (Vendor Shared Passthrough Graphics)** option.

Step 5.   Reboot the host and enter Maintenance Mode.

Step 6.   In the ESXi Shell, enter the following command but replace the path with the actual path to the downloaded VIB file:

```
esxcli software vib install -v /vmfs/volumes/ARL-ESX14-
DS1/ NVIDIA/NVIDIA-VMware_ESXi_6.7_Host_Driver_390.42-1OEM.
670.0.0.7535516.vib
```

Step 7.   Exit Maintenance Mode.

Step 8.   Edit the virtual machine settings and select the option to add a new device.

Step 9.   From the New PCI device drop-down, select **NVIDIA GRID vGPU**.

Step 10.   From the GPU Profile drop-down, select an appropriate profile, such as **grid_p100-8a**.

Step 11.   For the virtual machine guest OS, install the appropriate NVIDIA vGPU driver.

Managing EVC Mode and CPU Affinity

As described in Chapter 5, you can configure per-VM EVC. The requirements are ESXi 7.0 or later, vCenter Server 7.0 or later, and virtual hardware 14 or later. You can change EVC mode for a virtual machine only while it is powered off. To change EVC mode using the vSphere Client, select the virtual machine, select Configure > VMware EVC > Edit, and choose an option in the Change EVC Mode dialog box. The options include Disable EVC, Enable EVC for AMD Hosts, Enable EVC for Intel Hosts, and Custom. If you select an option to enable EVC, you can then select a baseline CPU set, much as you would when configuring EVC for a cluster, as described in Chapter 4, "Clusters and High Availability." Optionally, you can use the Graphics Mode (vSGA) drop-down to select either Baseline Graphics or D3D 11.0 class features.

To determine the EVC mode for a virtual machine, select the virtual machine and examine VMware EVC in the Configure tab. When per-VM EVC is enabled, the tab reflects the per-VM EVC setting. When per-VM EVC is deactivated, the tab reflects the EVC setting of the cluster or host.

Typically, you should allow running virtual machines to use any of the hosts' processors, but if you want to restrict which of a host's CPUs can be used to service a virtual machine, you can configure CPU affinity. To configure CPU affinity using the vSphere Client, select the virtual machine, choose Edit Settings, and navigate to Virtual Hardware > CPU > Scheduling Affinity. For Processor Affinity, you specify particular processors and processor ranges, separated by commas. For example, 0,2,4-6 indicates that the virtual machine can use processors 0, 2, 4, 5, and 6.

Content Libraries

This section provides details for implementing and using content libraries to provide templates, ISOs, and other content across multiple vCenter Servers in a vSphere environment.

Introduction to Content Libraries

A *content library* is a container object for virtual machine templates, vApp templates, ISO images, and other files that you may want to share among multiple vCenter Servers in a vSphere environment. Content libraries allow you to share templates and other files in a manner that provides consistency, compliance, efficiency, and automation when deploying workloads at scale.

A content library contains and manages content in the form of library items. A single library item consists of one file or multiple files. For example, an OVF template is a set of files with the OVF, VMDK, and MF file extensions. When you upload an OVF template to the library, you upload the entire set of files, which the library represents as a single item.

When creating a content library, you can choose to create a local content library or a subscribed content library. With a local library, you store and manage content in a single vCenter Server instance. After creating a local library, you can publish it to make it available for subscription. From another vCenter Server instance, you can create a subscribed content library with a subscription to the published library. With a subscribed library, you can control when to download the subscribed content— either immediately or as needed.

Historically, content libraries supported OVF templates but not standard virtual machine templates. Starting with vSphere 6.7 Update 1, content libraries support virtual machine templates in addition to OVF templates.

Creating a Content Library

To create a content library, you must have one of the following privileges on the vCenter Server instance:

- Content Library.Create Local Library
- Content Library.Create Subscribed Library

In addition, you must have the Datastore.Allocate Space privilege on the target datastore.

You can use the following procedure to create a content library:

Step 1.   In the vSphere Client, select **Menu > Content Libraries** and click the **Create a New Content Library** icon.

Step 2.   On the Name and Location page, enter a name and select a vCenter Server instance for the content library. Click **Next**.

Step 3.   On the Configure Content Library page, select the type of content library that you want to create:

- **Local Content Library**: By default, a local content library is accessible only in the vCenter Server instance where you create it. Optionally, you can select **Enable Publishing** to make the content of the library available to other vCenter Server instances.

- **Subscribed Content Library**: This option creates a content library that subscribes to a published content library.

Click **Next**.

Step 4.   On the Add Storage page, select a storage location for the content library contents and click **Next**.

Step 5.   On the Ready to Complete page, review the details and click **Finish**.

Publishing a Content Library

You can publish an existing content library. For example, to publish an existing local, non-subscribed library, you can use the following procedure:

Step 1.   Use the vSphere Client to navigate to **Content Libraries**.

Step 2.   Right-click on an existing content library and select **Edit Settings**.

Step 3.   Select the **Enable Publishing** checkbox.

Step 4.   Click the **Copy Link** button to copy the URL of your library that you can paste into the settings of a subscribed library.

Step 5.   Select **Enable User Authentication** for access to this content library and set a password for the library.

Step 6.   Click **OK**.

NOTE   When you enable authentication for the content library, you effectively set a password on the static username vcsp, which you cannot change. This is a user account that is not associated with vCenter Single Sign-On or Active Directory.

Subscribing to a Content Library

When using the previous procedure to create a subscribed content library, you must provide the following information:

Step 1. In the **Subscription URL** text box, enter the URL address of the published library.

Step 2. If authentication is enabled on the published library, select **Enable Authentication** and enter the publisher password.

Step 3. Select a download method for the contents of the subscribed library: **Immediately** or **When Needed**.

Step 4. If prompted, accept the SSL certificate thumbprint. The SSL certificate thumbprint is stored on your system until you delete the subscribed content library from the inventory.

> **NOTE** The transfer service on the vCenter Server is responsible for importing and exporting content between the subscriber and the publisher, using HTTP NFC.

Content Library Permissions

Content libraries are not direct children of the vCenter Server object in the vSphere inventory. Instead, content libraries are direct children of the global root. This means that permissions set on a vCenter Server do not apply to content libraries, even if they are set to propagate to child objects. To assign a permission on a content library, an administrator must grant the permission to the user as a global permission. Global permissions support assignment of privileges across solutions from a global root object.

Consider the following scenarios:

- If a user is granted the read-only role as a global permission and the administrator role at a vCenter Server level, the user can manage the vCenter Server's content libraries and content but can only view content libraries belonging to other vCenter Servers.

- If a user is granted the content library administrator role as a global permission, the user can manage all content libraries and content in all vCenter Server instances.

- If a user is not granted any global permission but is granted the administrator role at a vCenter Server level, the user cannot view or manage any libraries or content, including the vCenter Server's local content libraries.

vCenter Server provides a predefined sample role, content library administrator, that allows you to give users or groups the privileges required to manage selected content libraries. You can modify the role or use it as an example to create custom roles. A user who is assigned the content library administrator role on a library can perform the following tasks on that library:

- Create, edit, and delete local or subscribed libraries.

- Synchronize a subscribed library and synchronize items in a subscribed library.

- View the item types supported by the library.

- Configure the global settings for the library.

- Import items to a library.

- Export library items.

NOTE You cannot set permissions on a content library directly.

Content Library Synchronization Options

When configuring the subscribing library, you can choose either to download all libraries' content immediately or download library content only when needed. The first option starts the full synchronization process immediately. It includes the full content, including the metadata and actual data. The latter option starts the synchronization process for just the metadata immediately. The metadata contains information about the actual content data, allowing users to view and select the associated templates and ISOs. In this case, the actual data is synchronized only as needed when subscribed library objects are demanded. The impact of the on-demand synchronization is that storage space may be saved for the subscribing library, but a delay may exist each time a library item is selected.

To enable automatic synchronization, select the option Enable Automatic Synchronization with the External Library in the subscribed library settings. Consider the fact that the automatic synchronization requires a lot of storage space because you download full copies of all the items in the published library.

The content library synchronization method has an impact on VM provisioning time and datastore space usage. If an object is not already downloaded when you go to use it, you may have to wait while the subscribed content library downloads it from the published library. To optimize VM provisioning time, consider setting the download method to Immediately. To optimize datastore space usage, consider setting the download method to When Needed.

Adding Items to a Content Library

You can import items such as OVA/OVF templates and vApps to a content library from your local machine or from a web server. You can also import ISO images, certificates, and other files. You can add to a content library an item that resides on a web server, or you can add items to a content library by importing files from your local file system.

You can import an OVF package to use as a template for deploying virtual machines and vApps. You can also import other types of files, such as scripts or ISO files. To import a file, in the vSphere client, right-click a content library, choose Import Item, select a file, and assign the item name.

You can also add content to a library by cloning VMs or templates to the library, as described in the following steps:

Step 1.   In the vSphere Client, navigate to the virtual machine or template that you want to clone and select one of the following cloning tasks:

- Right-click a virtual machine and select **Clone > Clone to Template in Library**.
- Right-click a VM template and select **Clone to Library**.

Step 2.   Depending on the selection in the previous step, complete the cloning wizard. For example, if you selected a VM template and chose **Clone to Library**, then you can use the following steps to create a new template in the content library:

a. Select the **Clone As** option and choose to create a new template.

b. From the Content Libraries list, select the library in which you want to add the template.

c. Enter a name and description for the template.

d. Optionally, select the configuration data that you want to include in the template. You can select to preserve the MAC addresses on the network adapters and include extra configuration.

e. Click **OK**.

Deploying VMs by Using a Content Library

You can deploy virtual machines from the VM templates in your content library by using this procedure:

Step 1.   In the vSphere client, select **Home > Content Libraries**.

Step 2.   Select a content library and click the **Templates** tab.

Step 3.   Right-click a VM template and select **New VM from This Template**.

Step 4.   On the Select Name and Location page, enter a name and select a location for the virtual machine.

Step 5.   Optionally, to apply a customization specification to your virtual machine, select the **Customize the Operating System** checkbox and click **Next**.

Step 6.   On the Customize Guest OS page, select a customization specification or create a new one and click **Next**.

Step 7.   On the Select a Resource page, select a host, a cluster, a resource pool, or a vApp to run the deployed VM template and click **Next**.

Step 8.   On the Review Details page, verify the template details and click **Next**.

Managing VM Templates in a Content Library

Beginning with vSphere 7.0, you can efficiently manage VM templates by checking them out of the content library, making the necessary changes, and checking them back into the content library. To check out a VM template, open the content library, select the template, and choose Check out VM from This Template. In the wizard, provide details such as name and location for the virtual machine. You can still deploy new virtual machines from the template while it is checked out.

To check a virtual machine back to the VM template, shut down the virtual machine, open the content library, select the template, and choose Check VM to Template. In the wizard, add a short description of your changes in Check in Notes. The system creates a new version of the template.

To revert a VM template to a previous version, you can select the template in the content library, use the vertical timeline to locate a previous state, click the ellipsis button, and select Revert to This Version.

Exam Preparation Tasks

As mentioned in the section "Book Features and Exam Preparation Methods" in the Introduction, you have some choices for exam preparation: the exercises here, Chapter 15, "Final Preparation," and the exam simulation questions on the companion website.

Review All the Key Topics

Review the most important topics in this chapter, noted with the Key Topic icon in the outer margin of the page. Table 14-9 lists these key topics and the page number on which each is found.

Table 14-9   Key Topics for Chapter 14

Key Topic Element	Description	Page Number
List	Permissions to create a virtual machine	576
List	Permissions to clone a virtual machine	580
Procedure	Creating a Linux guest customization specification	583
Procedure	Creating a Windows guest customization specification	584
List	Conditions for CPU hot adding	588
List	Requirements for virtual machine encryption	593
Section	Migrating virtual machines	596
Section	Configuring VMs to support vGPUs	601
Procedure	Subscribing to a content library	606

Complete Tables and Lists from Memory

Print a copy of Appendix B, "Memory Tables" (found on the companion website), or at least the section for this chapter, and complete the tables and lists from memory. Appendix C, "Memory Table Answers" (also on the companion website), includes completed tables and lists to check your work.

Define Key Terms

Define the following key terms from this chapter and check your answers in the glossary:

Open Virtual Format (OVF) template, Open Virtual Appliance (OVA) template, Microsoft virtualization-based security (VBS), VMware PowerCLI, graphics processing unit (GPU), content library

Review Questions

1. Which of the following is a requirement for guest OS customization?

    a. ESXi 5.0 or later

    b. VMware Tools 11.0 or later

    o. A supported guest OS installed on SCSI node 0:0

    d. A supported guest OS installed on any SCSI node

2. You want to create a virtual machine that can use up to 4096 MB of video memory. Which compatibility option should you choose?

    a. ESXi 7.0 and later

    b. ESXi 6.7 Update 2 and later

    c. ESXi 6.7 and later

    d. ESXi 6.5 and later

3. You are snapshotting production virtual machines and want to minimize the impact to users and the performance of the guest OS and its applications. Which option should you choose?

    a. Snapshot the memory and quiesce the file system

    b. Snapshot the memory but do not quiesce the file system

    c. Quiesce the file system but do not snapshot the memory

    d. Do not quiesce the file system or snapshot the memory

4. In your vSphere 8.0 environment, you want to export a virtual machine for portability to other systems. Which approach should you use?

    a. Export to OVF

    b. Export to OVA

    c. Export as a VM template

    d. Export as a VMDK

5. You want to add items to the content library. Which of the following is not a valid choice for importing?

    a. ISO file

    b. OVA

    c. A running virtual machine

    d. OVF

## CHAPTER 15

Final Preparation

Congratulations on making it through all the technical chapters in this book. Now you are ready for your final preparation for taking the VMware vSphere 8.x Professional (2V0-21.23) exam. This chapter contains two sections: "Getting Ready" and "Taking the Exam."

Getting Ready

Here is a list of actions and considerations that you should address prior to taking the exam:

- Review the VCP-DCV 2023 or current certification requirements, as described in the Introduction in this book.

- If you are taking an updated version of the VMware Professional vSphere 8.x exam rather than 2V0-21.23, download the corresponding online appendix from the Pearson companion website. Use the appendix, written by the authors of this book for each exam update, as your guide for preparing for the exam. The appendix covers product and exam changes. It provides an updated table that maps exam objectives to chapters and sections in this book.

- Gain hands-on experience with vSphere 8. If you have not done so already, you should access a vSphere 8 environment and use it to practice performing the procedures described in this book. If you do not have a suitable vSphere 8 environment, consider using VMware Hands-on Labs (http://labs.hol.vmware.com) to search for vSphere and vSAN offerings. You can follow the lab exercises as designed or use them as a playground to gain hands-on familiarity with specific vSphere features that may be difficult for you to implement in your own lab, such as vSAN or vVols. The following are examples of labs that might be helpful:

  - VMware vSphere 8: What's New (HOL-2311-01-SDC)

  - VMware vSphere: Advanced Topics (HOL-2211-02-SDC)

  - VMware vSphere: Security Getting Started (HOL-2211-03-SDC)

  - VMware vSAN 8: Quick Start—Lightning Lab (HOL-2308-91-HCI)

- Practice performing most of the procedures that are described in this book.

- Review the following items in each chapter in this book until you have them committed to memory:

  - The "Do I Know This Already?" questions at the beginning of each chapter

  - The key topics table at the end of each chapter

  - The key terms at the end of each chapter

  - The "Review Questions" at the end of each chapter

- Take the practice exams included with the book. The standard edition includes two exams, and the premium edition includes two more exams. If you miss any questions, read the provided explanation and the related section in this book. Continue taking the practice exams until you feel you know and can explain each answer. If you are preparing for an updated version of the exam, be sure to look for updated practice exam questions.

- Prior to registering for the exam, create an account with VMware Certification, at https://mylearn.vmware.com/MgrReg/login.cfm?ui=www_cert.

- Create an account at Pearson Vue (www.vue.com), which delivers all VMware career certification exams. To register for the 2V0-21.23 exam, use the information in the Introduction of this book to navigate to 2V0-21.23 exam details and click the Schedule Exam link. Follow the link to log in with your VMware Certification account. After successfully logging in, you will be redirected to the Pearson Vue website to complete the registration. In the wizard, you select the exam location, date, and time and provide payment.

NOTE Currently, you can choose to take the exam at home or in a Pearson Vue testing center. To take the exam at home, you must meet strict requirements, such as compatibility for audio, camera, and bandwidth. Pay careful attention to all the requirements and precheck information before choosing this option.

Taking the Exam

Here is a list of recommendations for the day of the exam:

- Bring two forms of identification that include your photo and signature. You cannot bring personal items such as laptops, tablets, phones, watches, pagers, wallets, or notes into the examination room. You may be able to place some of these items into a locker, but you should avoid bringing larger items into the testing facility.

- Arrive at the exam center 30 minutes prior to the scheduled exam start time so you have ample time to complete the sign-in procedure and address personal needs. During the sign-in procedure, you should expect to place personal belongings in a locker, provide credentials, review the test regulations, and sign the agreement.

- Be sure to pay attention to the rules and regulations concerning the exam. For example, follow the venue's protocol for requesting help during the exam and for signaling your completion of the exam. Each venue's rules may be unique.

- Pay close attention to the wording of each question and each choice. (The exam format is multiple choice, provided via a web-based user interface.) The following are some examples of what to expect:

  - Some questions may ask you to select "which statement is correct," and some questions may ask you to select "which statement is incorrect."

  - Most questions call for you to select a single choice from a list of multiple choices. Whenever a question calls for you to select more than one choice, it does so explicitly by including a phrase such as "Select two."

  - Read each question carefully enough to ensure that you successfully interpret feature names and terminology. For example, when a question contains the word *heartbeat*, you need to carefully determine if it is referring to an HA network heartbeat, an HA datastore heartbeat, a VMFS heartbeat, a VMware Tools heartbeat, or some other heartbeat.

  - Questions tend to be written in a concise manner, and at first glance, you might think that insufficient details are provided. For example, a question could provide a symptom and ask you to select three actions that you should take to troubleshoot the issue. Your first thought might be that you would take analytical steps or remediation steps that are not provided as choices for the question. You might even consider the provided choices to be unpractical or insufficient. Do not get frustrated. Just select the best choices that fit the question.

  - Questions that ask you to select multiple choices to accomplish a specific task may not clearly state whether all the selected choices must be performed or whether performing just one of the selected choices is sufficient. Although you may wish the question was worded more clearly, you should see that only one set of choices fits the question.

- Strive for good time management during the exam. For the 2V0-21.23 exam, you need to answer 70 questions in 135 minutes. You could, for example, allow yourself 1.5 minutes per question, leaving 30 minutes at the end of the exam to review your marked questions. A timer is provided in the top-right corner of the exam user interface, along with the number of remaining questions. You might want to watch for the following milestones and pick up your pace when necessary:

- With 50 questions remaining, at least 105 minutes left

- With 30 questions remaining, at least 75 minutes left

- With 10 questions remaining, at least 45 minutes left

- Don't allow yourself to spend too much time on a question. For example, if a question is tricky or if more than one choice seems to fit for a question that calls for a single choice, determine which choice is most likely the choice that VMware wants. In some cases, you might find it easier to answer the question by focusing on which choices to eliminate.

- Be sure to answer all questions. You will not be penalized for incorrect answers. Guessing provides an opportunity for a higher score.

- Whenever you are unsure of an answer or feel rushed to make a decision, answer it the best you can, select the box to mark the question for review, and continue forward.

- After answering all the questions, use the Review Page, which identifies all questions that you marked for review and all questions that are incomplete. If sufficient time remains, use the links provided on the review page to return to any questions that you marked or any questions that are identified as incomplete.

Answers to the "Do I Know This Already?" Quizzes and Review Questions

"Do I Know This Already?" Answers

Chapter 1

1. b. Explanation: vCenter Server Essentials Plus, which is included in vSphere Essentials Plus, supports vMotion.

2. b. Explanation: Proactive HA minimizes VM downtime by proactively detecting hardware failures and placing the host in Quarantine Mode or Maintenance Mode.

3. d. Explanation: Security Token Service (STS) provides Security Assertion Markup Language (SAML) tokens, which are used to authenticate users to other vCenter components instead of requiring users to authenticate to each component.

4. a. Explanation: During vCenter Server Appliance deployment, you must create an SSO domain or join an existing SSO domain.

5. c. Explanation: You should deploy the vCenter Server appliance in the Large Environment configuration because the Medium Environment configuration supports only 4000 virtual machines.

6. d. Explanation: Changing the host boot type between legacy BIOS and UEFI is not supported after you install ESXi 7.0.

7. a, b, and c. Explanation: If you plan to schedule file-based backups using the vCenter Server Appliance Management Interface (VAMI), you must prepare an FTP, FTPS, HTTP, HTTPS, or SCP server with sufficient disk space to store the backups.

8. a, b, and d. Explanation: For Windows and Mac users of vSphere 8.0, VMware supports Microsoft Edge 79 and later, Mozilla Firefox 60 and later, and Google Chrome 75 and later.

9. d. Explanation: Aria Automation is cloud automation software that speeds up the delivery of infrastructure and application resources on-premises and in the public cloud.

10. b. Explanation: VMware Cloud Foundation (VCF) delivers a simple path to the hybrid cloud by leveraging a common infrastructure and consistent operational model for on-premises and off-premises data centers.

Chapter 2

1. c. Explanation: NPIV requires the use of virtual machines with RDMs. An RDM is a mapping file containing metadata that resides in a VMFS datastore.

2. a. Explanation: A vSphere pod requires ephemeral storage to store Kubernetes objects, such as logs, emptyDir volumes, and ConfigMaps.

3. b. Explanation: Symmetric Multiprocessing Fault Tolerance (SMP-FT) is supported when PFFT is set to 0 and Data Locality is set to Preferred or Secondary DRS should be automated. You should disable vSphere HA datastore heatbeats.

4. b. Explanation: If you choose RAID 5/6 and PFTT=2 for a 100 GB virtual disk, the required capacity is 150 GB, and the usable capacity is 67%.

5. a. Explanation: The following are the VAAI primitives for NAS: Full File Clone, Fast File Clone/Native Snapshot Support, Extended Statistics, and Reserve Space.

6. d. Explanation: Protocol endpoints (PEs) are logical I/O proxies, used for communication with virtual volumes and the virtual disk files.

7. a. Explanation: When the VMware NMP receives an I/O request, it calls the appropriate PSP, the PSP selects an appropriate physical path, and the NMP issues the I/O request.

8. c. Explanation: A VM storage policy for tag-based placement is helpful for storage arrays that do not support VASA and their storage characteristics are not visible to the vSphere client.

9. a. Explanation: The available vSAN storage policies include PFTT, SFTT, Data Locality, Failure Tolerance Method, Number of Disk Stripes per Object, Flash Read Cached Reservation, Force Provisioning, Object Space Reservation, Disable, Object Checksum, and IOPS Limit for Object.

10. b. Explanation: If the space used on datastore A is 82% and on datastore B is 79%, the difference is 3. If the threshold is 5, Storage DRS will not make migration recommendations from datastore A to datastore B.

Chapter 3

1. d. Explanation: On a vSS, you can set the following network policies: Teaming and Failover, Security, Traffic Shaping, and VLAN.

2. b. Explanation: The following NIC teaming options are available on vSS and vDS: Route Based on Originating Virtual Port, Route Based on IP Hash, Route Based on Source MAC Hash, and Use Explicit Failover Order.

3. a. Explanation: Distributed virtual switches can do both inbound and outbound traffic shaping, whereas standard virtual switches handle just outbound traffic shaping.

4. c. Explanation: If you reserved 1.0 Gbps for virtual machine system traffic on a distributed switch with 8 uplinks, then the total aggregated bandwidth available for virtual machine reservation on the switch is 8.0 Gbps (8 uplinks times 1.0 Gbps per uplink). Each network resource pool can reserve a portion of the 8 Gbps capacity. Because you already reserved 512 Mbps for one network resource pool, you have 7.5 Gbps (8.0 Gbps - 512 Mbs) remaining for other network resource pools. See Figure 3-3 for a similar example.

5. c. Explanation: When marking traffic, you can create a rule to configure qualifiers to identify the data to be tagged and set Action to Tag.

6. c. Explanation: A vDS supports up to 64 LAGs. LACP support is not compatible with software iSCSI port binding or nested ESXi.

7. a. Explanation: The required vDS configuration for the virtual switch teaming policy health check is at least two active physical NICs and two hosts.

8. c. Explanation: Cisco Discovery Protocol (CDP) support was introduced with ESX 3.x. CDP is available for standard switches and distributed switches that are connected to Cisco physical switches. Link Layer Discovery Protocol (LLDP) is supported in vSphere 5.0 and later for vDS (5.0.0 and later), but not for vSS.

9. a. Explanation: With DirectPath I/O in a vSphere 7.0 environment, a virtual machine can be part of a cluster, but it cannot migrate across hosts.

10. a. Explanation: The available services for a custom stack are Management, vMotion, IP-based storage, Provisioning, Fault Tolerance logging, vSphere Replication, vSphere Replication NFC, and vSAN.

Chapter 4

1. b and d. Explanation: An EVC requirement is that the hosts must be attached to a vCenter Server. The options for VMware EVC are Disable EVC, Enable EVC for AMD Hosts, and Enable EVC for Intel Hosts. You can apply a custom CPU compatibility mask to hide host CPU features from a virtual machine, but VMware does not recommend doing so.

2. c. Explanation: When the DRS migration threshold is set to Level 3, the default level, DRS expands on Level 2 by making recommendations to improve VM happiness and cluster load distribution.

3. b. Explanation: Resource pools are container objects in the vSphere inventory that are used to compartmentalize the CPU and memory resources of a host, a cluster, or a parent resource pool. You can delegate control over each resource pool to specific individuals and groups.

4. c. Explanation: The main use case for scalable shares is a scenario in which you want to use shares to give high-priority resource access to a set of virtual machines in a resource pool, without concern for the relative number of objects in the pool compared to other pools.

5. d. Explanation: Set Define Host Failover Capacity By to Dedicated Failover Hosts to designate hosts to use for failover actions.

6. b. Explanation: The medium virtual machine monitoring level sets Failure Interval to 60 seconds and Reset Period to 24 hours.

7. c. Explanation: For PDL and APD failures, you can set VMCP to either issue event alerts or to power off and restart virtual machines. For APD failures only, you can additionally control the restart policy for virtual machines by setting it to Conservative or Aggressive.

8. a. Explanation: Predictive DRS is a feature in vSphere 6.5 and later that leverages the predictive analytics of VMware Aria Operations, formerly known as vRealize Operations (vROps), and vSphere DRS. Predictive DRS must be configured and enabled in both vCenter Server and Aria Operations.

9. d. Explanation: vSphere Fault Tolerance can accommodate symmetric multiprocessor (SMP) virtual machines with up to eight vCPUs.

10. a. Explanation: If a vCenter service fails, VMware Service Lifecycle Manager restarts it. VMware Service Lifecycle Manager is a service running in vCenter server.

Chapter 5

1. d. The first object that you must create in a vSphere inventory is a data center (with the exception of a folder to contain data centers).

2. d. Explanation: A subscribed library is a library whose content you cannot change or publish. It receives its content from a published library.

3. b. Explanation: The file named *<vmName>*-flat.vmdk is the virtual machine data disk file. It is commonly called the flat file. *<vmName>*. vmdk is the virtual machine data disk file.

4. a. Explanation: The parent (current) snapshot is always the snapshot that appears immediately above the You Are Here icon in the Snapshot Manager. The parent snapshot is not always the snapshot that you took most recently.

5. a. Explanation: The SIO controller provides serial and parallel ports and floppy devices, and it performs system management activities. One SIO controller is available to the virtual machine, but it cannot be configured or removed.

6. c. Explanation: The VM Options table includes General Options, Encryption Options, Power Management, VMware Tools, VBS, Boot Options, Advanced Options, Fibre Channel NPIV, and vApp Options.

7. c and d. Explanation: To perform a standard, cross-vCenter Server migration with Enhanced Linked Mode, you must meet the following requirements: The associated vCenter Servers and ESXi hosts must be Version 6.0 or later. The cross-vCenter Server and long-distance vMotion features require an Enterprise Plus license. The vCenter Server instances must be time-synchronized with each other for correct vCenter Single Sign-On token verification. Both vCenter Server instances must be in the same vCenter Single Sign-On domain.

8. c. Explanation: You can simultaneously perform one Storage vMotion and four vMotion operations involving a specific host.

9. b. Explanation: To avoid network saturation, you can use traffic shaping to limit the average bandwidth and peak bandwidth available to vMotion traffic.

10. c. Explanation: One of the most popular use cases for instant clones is a just-in-time virtual desktop infrastructure (VDI) deployment. Instant clones enable you to perform large-scale deployments by allowing you to create virtual machines from a controlled point in time. For example, VMware Horizon uses instant clones to improve the provisioning process for virtual desktops.

Chapter 6

1. d. Explanation: Use cases for vSphere with Tanzu include providing a familiar single stack for containers and virtual machines and streamlining the development of modern applications.

2. b. Explanation: Aria Operations is commonly used for continuous performance optimization and intelligent remediation.

3. a. Explanation: Aria for Logs is commonly used to decrease time and effort spent on root cause analysis and centralized log management and analysis.

4. a and e. Explanation: Horizon includes instant clones, which together with VMware Dynamic Environment Manager, and VMware App Volumes dynamically provides just-in-time (JIT) delivery of user profile data and applications to stateless desktops.

5. c and d. Explanation: VMware App Volumes is a set of application and user management solutions for VMware Horizon, Citrix Virtual Apps and Desktops, and Remote Desktop Services Host (RDSH) virtual environments.

6. d. Explanation: vSphere Replication does not require separate licensing. Instead, it is included as a feature of specific vSphere license editions, including vSphere Standard.

7. b and c. Explanation: Site Recovery Manager (SRM) use cases include disaster recovery and data center migrations. For data replication, SRM integrates with vSphere Replication and supported storage-based replication products.

8. c. Explanation: VMware Cloud Foundation (VCF) is a hybrid cloud platform built on full-stack hyperconverged infrastructure (HCI) technology. Its main components include Cloud Builder and SDDC Manager.

9. a. Explanation: VMware HCX is a workload mobility platform that simplifies application migration, workload rebalancing, and business continuity across on-premises data centers, private clouds, and hybrid clouds.

10. a. Explanation: NSX is commonly used with zero-trust security and multi-cloud networking.

Chapter 7

1. d. Explanation: The key size requirement is 2048 to 16,384 bits, not 1024 to 16,384 bits.

2. a. Explanation: vCenter Server supports these certificate modes for ESXi: VMware Certificate Authority, Custom Certificate Authority, and Thumbprint Mode.

3. a. Explanation: In vCenter Server 8.0, the system roles include read-only, administrator, no access, no cryptography administrator, trusted infrastructure administrator, and no trusted infrastructure administrator.

4. a. Explanation: To migrate a virtual machine with Storage vMotion, the user must have the Resource.Migrate Powered On Virtual Machine on the virtual machine or folder and Datastore.Allocate Space on the destination datastore.

5. d. Explanation: In normal lockdown mode, user accounts that are in the Exception Users list and that have administrator privileges on the host can access the DCUI. Also, users identified in the host's DCUI.Access advanced option can access the DCUI.

6. a. Explanation: By default, this password must have at least eight characters, one lowercase character, one numeric character, and one special character.

7. b. Explanation: To list the available security associations, you can use the command **esxcli network ip ipsec sa list** in ESXi.

8. b. Explanation: Concerning encrypted vMotion across vCenter Server instances, you must use the vSphere APIs, encrypted vMotion migration of unencrypted virtual machines is supported, and vMotion migration of encrypted virtual machines is not supported.

9. d. Explanation: Some settings can be disabled in a vSphere environment. To reduce potential risk, consider setting isolation.tools.ghi.launchmenu.change to TRUE.

10. b. Explanation: You can implement VMware NSX to add a distributed logical firewall, microsegmentation, and additional security measures to your vSphere environment.

Chapter 8

1. a. Explanation: The ESXi installation prerequisites include downloading the ESXi installer ISO and preparing the hardware system to boot from it.

2. b. Explanation: There is a default installation script included with the ESXi installer. The default ks.cfg installation script is in the initial RAM disk at /etc/vmware/weasel/ks.cfg.

3. c. Explanation: Prior to running the deployment command, you can run a pre-deployment check by using the command **vcsa-deploy install --verify-only** *path-to-JSON-file*.

4. a. Explanation: VECS does not store ESXi certificates. ESXi certificates are stored locally on the ESXi hosts in the /etc/vmware/ssl directory.

5. d. Explanation: All users have must have the object of class inetOrgPerson. All groups must have the object of class groupOfUniqueNames. All groups must have the group membership attribute uniqueMember.

6. c. Explanation: A user must be a member of the CAAdmins group to perform most certificate management operations, such as using the **certool** command.

7. a. Explanation: You should not select the Use Machine Account option if you plan to rename the machine. Instead, you need to select Use Service Principle Name (SPN) and provide the SPN, UPN, and password.

8. a. Explanation: In scenarios where vCenter Server is installed in a secured network with no Internet access, you can install the Update Manager Download Service (UMDS) and use it to download updates.

9. d. Explanation: For the Passive node, connect NIC 0 to the Management network and NIC 1 to the vCenter HA network. For the Witness node, connect NIC 1 to the vCenter HA network.

10. b. Explanation: The following kernel boot options have been deprecated and are no longer supported in ESXi 7.0: **--no-auto-partition**, **autoPartition CreateUSBCoreDumpPartition**, and **autoPartitionDiskDumpPartitionSize**.

Chapter 9

1. a. Explanation: To add physical adapters to a vSS, you can select the host, navigate to Configure > Networking > Virtual Switches, select the switch, and select Manage Physical Adapters. In the wizard, click the Add Adapters (green plus sign) button.

2. b. Explanation: You can set the VLAN ID to 0 (external switch tagging), 1 to 4094 (virtual switch tagging), or 4095 (virtual guest tagging).

3. d. Explanation: You can change the general setting of a vDS, including Name, Number of Uplinks, Network I/O Control (enable or disable), and Description.

4. a. Explanation: You can change the Advanced settings for a vDS, including MTU (in bytes), Multicast Filtering Mode (Basic or IGMP/MLD Snooping), Discovery Protocol, and Administrator Contact.

5. a. Explanation: When creating a VMkernel adapter, you should configure the VMkernel Adapter IP, MTU, Stack, and Available Services settings.

6. c. Explanation: NIOC applies shares to each of the following network traffic types: management traffic, Fault Tolerance (FT) traffic, NFS traffic, vSAN traffic, vMotion traffic, vSphere Replication (VR) traffic, vSphere Data Protection backup traffic, and virtual machine traffic.

7. b. Explanation: For port mirroring, you can select one of the following session types: distributed port monitoring, remote mirroring source, remote mirroring destination, or encapsulated remote mirroring (L3) source.

8. a. Explanation: The number of ports in each port channel must match the number of physical NICs that will be aggregated on the host (the minimum is two). The same hashing algorithm must be used for the port channel and the associated LAG on the vDS. All the NICs in a LAG must be configured with the same speed and duplexing.

9. b. Explanation: You can enable the VLAN and MTU and the Teaming and Failover health checks.

10. d. Explanation: You can use the following to qualify data: IP address (to identify packets by source and destination addresses and ports), MAC address (to identify packets by source and destination addresses and by VLAN), and system traffic (to identify data by system traffic type).

Chapter 10

1. c. Explanation: If you initially selected the Skip Quickstart option, you should add hosts manually. If you previously used Quickstart but selected Configure Networking Settings Later, you can add hosts by using Quickstart but must manually configure the host networking.

2. a, b, and c. Explanation: The default value for CPU and Memory Limit is unlimited. The default value for Reservation Type is Expandable.

3. a. Explanation: Define Host Failover Capacity can be set to Cluster Resource Percentage, Slot Policy (powered-on VMs), Dedicated Host Failures, or Disabled.

4. b. Explanation: To configure Virtual Machine Component Protection (VMCP) in a vSphere HA cluster, you can select Failures and Responses > Datastore with PDL and choose Issue Events or Power Off and Restart VMs.

5. c. Explanation: You need to install a supported vendor-supplied vSphere Client plug-in and register the proactive HA provider. Ensure that vSphere HA and DRS are enabled. To allow remediation actions, you need the Host.Config. Quarantine and Host.Config.Maintenance privileges.

6. b. Explanation: If the guest OS reports that memory paging is occurring, you should increase the memory size of the virtual machine.

7. a. Explanation: If a virtual disk is thin provisioned, you may be maximizing the use of your storage space while decreasing the virtual machine's performance and increasing its risk of denial of service.

8. b. Explanation: %DRPTX is the percentage of transmit packets dropped. It indicates that the physical network adapter cannot meet the demand, perhaps due to load from other virtual machines.

9. a. Explanation: Warning, Information, and Audit are valid event types. Another valid type is Alert, which indicates that a fatal problem has occurred in the system.

10. c. Explanation: The ESXi host agent log contains data related to the agent that manages and configures the ESXi host and its virtual machines.

Chapter 11

1. c. Explanation: In hybrid clusters, magnetic disks are used for capacity, and flash devices serve as a read cache and a write buffer. In a hybrid cluster, 70% of the flash space is used for the read cache, and 30% is used for the write buffer.

2. d. Explanation: To use Quickstart to configure a vSAN cluster, the hosts must use ESXi 6.0 Update 2 or later. The hosts must have a similar network configuration to allow Quickstart to configure network settings based on cluster requirements. You can use Quickstart to enable vSAN in the cluster. vSAN uses local storage.

3. d. Explanation: A datastore is expandable when the backing storage device has free space immediately after the datastore extent.

4. b. Explanation: Multiple IP addresses or DNS names can be used with NFS Version 4.1 multipathing.

5. b. Explanation: Select the datastore, enable Configuration > Properties > Storage I/O Control, click Advanced, and modify the threshold for contention (which must have a value between 5 ms and 100 ms).

6. d. Explanation: If you want to perform a maintenance activity on an SDRS cluster member datastore or its underlying storage devices, you can place it in Maintenance Mode. To place a datastore in Maintenance Mode using the vSphere Client, right-click the datastore in the inventory pane, select Enter SDRS Maintenance Mode, and optionally apply any recommendations.

7. a, d, and e. Create a new VMkernel virtual network adapter on a virtual switch and configure its uplink to use the RDMA paired uplink (for example, vmnic9). Navigate to Configure > Networking > RDMA Adapters to review the bindings. Select Add software NVMe over RDMA adapter.

8. b. Explanation: In vPMem mode, a virtual machine can directly access PMem resources and use the resources as regular memory.

9. c. Explanation: FIXED and LB_RR are path selection schemes (PSS) used by the HPP module. VMW_PSP_FIXED is the NMP path selection module that uses a preferred path.

10. a and b. Explanation: To configure vVols in a vSphere 7.0 environment, you need to configure the following components on the storage side: protocol endpoints, storage containers, storage profiles, and replication configurations (if you plan to use vVols with replication).

Chapter 12

1. d. Explanation: To join vCenter Server systems in Enhanced Linked Mode, you need to connect them to the same SSO domain. External PSCs are not used in vSphere 8. ELM does not require vCenter HA.

2. a. Explanation: In a vSphere environment, you cannot change the object, user, or user group in a permission, but you can change the role.

3. b and c. Explanation: The Certificate Management page shows the certificate types in the VMware Endpoint Certificate Service (VECS). By default, the types are machine SSL certificates and trusted root certificates.

4. a. Explanation: To perform certificate management for ESXi, you must have the Certificates.Manage Certificates privilege.

5. d. Explanation: You can change the required length, change the character class requirement, and allow passphrases by using the Security.PasswordQuality-Control advanced option.

6. a. Explanation: An orange icon indicates that the status of the device has changed, and you must reboot the host before you can use the device.

7. b. Explanation: If the host acceptance level is VMwareAccepted, you cannot install VIBs at the PartnerSupported level.

8. a. Explanation: You can use the following command to run the Secure Boot validation script on an upgraded ESXi host: **/usr/lib/vmware/secureboot/bin/secureBoot.py -c**

9. b. Explanation: To configure a trust relationship between a KMS and vCenter, in the vSphere Client, select the vCenter Server, navigate to Configuration > Key Management Servers, and click Add.

10. c. Explanation: Multiple steps are needed. For example, on the Trust Authority cluster, you should import trusted host data and create the trusted key provider. A final step is to configure the trusted key provider for the trusted hosts on the trusted cluster (using Register-KeyProvider and Set-KeyProvider).

Chapter 13

1. c. Explanation: The vCenter Server Appliance Management Interface (VAMI) provides a file-based backup feature for the vCenter Server. Alternatively, you can perform image-based backups by using the vSphere API.

2. b, d, and e. Explanation: When restoring from backup, you can choose the location and the protocol. Valid protocol choices are FTP, FTPS, HTTP, HTTPS, SFTP, NFS, or SMB.

3. d, Explanation: To upgrade a vSphere 7.x environment to vSphere 8.0, you should upgrade the major components in the following order: vCenter Server, ESXi hosts, Virtual machines - VMware Tools, Virtual machines - virtual machine hardware

4. c. Explanation: If you choose to transfer configuration, historical, and performance data, you can transfer the configuration data during the upgrade and transfer the remaining data in the background following the upgrade. The option to transfer data in the background following an upgrade is applicable only to scenarios where the source vCenter Server uses an external database.

5. d. Explanation: A vSphere Installation Bundle (VIB) is the smallest installable software package (metadata and binary payload) for ESXi.

6. a. Explanation: To enable Quick Boot, navigate to Menu > Lifecycle Manager, select a vCenter Server, and enable the Quick Boot checkbox in the cluster settings at Settings > Host Remediation > Images.

7. c. Explanation: Firmware updates are available in a special vendor depot that you access through a vendor-specific hardware support manager plug-in that registers itself as a vCenter Server extension. Firmware updates are not available for clusters that are managed with baselines.

8. c. Explanation: To change the state of a service, you can right-click on the service and select Start, Stop, or Reset. You can also change a service's startup policy such that it automatically starts with the host or associated firewall ports or is started only manually.

9. b. Explanation: When the Health Status badge color is orange, it indicates an alert, and one or more components may be degraded. Non-security patches may be available.

10. a. Explanation: Optionally, you can check conflicts and apply one of the following resolutions to all conflicts or separately to each conflict: Copy, Skip, or Merge.

Chapter 14

1. c. Explanation: When selecting the storage type on a host that has PMem memory, you can select either the Standard or PMem radio button. If you chose PMem storage for a virtual machine, its default virtual disk, new virtual disk, and NVDIMM devices share the same PMem resources.

2. b. Explanation: With the vmx.log.guest.level = "info" setting, vminst.log is sent to the host, but vmmsi.log remains in the virtual machine.

3. a. Explanation: You cannot use the vSphere Client to clone a virtual machine using linked clones or instant clones. You can do so with API calls.

4. c. Explanation: The compatibility setting controls which virtual machine hardware version is used. Setting the compatibility to ESXi 6.7 and later uses hardware Version 14.

5. a. Explanation: To control the default hardware compatibility for new virtual machines, you can set the Default VM Compatibility setting at the host, cluster, or data center level.

6. d. Explanation: To minimize the impact to a running virtual machine and to reduce the time required to take a snapshot, do not snapshot the memory state or quiesce the guest file system.

7. c. Explanation: In vSphere, to use VBS, you must use virtual hardware Version 14 or later. The virtual machine must be set to use UEFI firmware, Secure Boot, hardware virtualization (Intel VT/ADM-V), and IOMMU.

8. a. Explanation: The main use case for vGPUs is to support high-end graphics in virtual desktop infrastructure (VDI). Recently, the need to support artificial intelligence (AI) and machine learning (ML) has also emerged as a major use case.

9. a. Explanation: If a user is granted the read-only role as a global permission and the administrator role at a vCenter Server level, then the user can manage the vCenter Server's content libraries and content but can only view content libraries belonging to other vCenter Servers.

10. d. Explanation: You can import items such as OVA/OVF templates and vApps to a content library. You can also import ISO images. You can also add content to the library by cloning VMs or templates to the library.

Review Question Answers

Chapter 1

1. c. Explanation: Fault Tolerance is supported for up to two vCPUs in vSphere 8.0 Standard.

2. d. Explanation: VMware Directory Service for the vCenter Single Sign-On (SSO) domain (vsphere.local) is a service in vCenter Server Appliance.

3. b. Explanation: To install ESXi 8.0, ensure that the hardware system has 4 GB or more of physical RAM. VMware recommends 8 GB or more for production environments.

4. c and d. Explanation: You must run the GUI deployment from a Windows, Linux, or Mac machine that is in the network on which you want to deploy the appliance.

5. b. Explanation: VMware Cloud Foundation (VCF) is the industry's most advanced hybrid cloud platform. It provides a complete set of software-defined services for compute, storage, networking, security, and cloud management to run enterprise apps in private or public environments.

Chapter 2

1. d. Explanation: ESXi 6.5 and later supports VMFS versions 5 and 6, but not version 3.

2. c. Explanation: Ruby vSphere Console (RVC) is a command-line interface used for managing and troubleshooting vSAN. RVC provides a cluster-wide view and is included with the vCenter Server deployment.

3. a. Explanation: VASA storage providers are software components that integrate with vSphere to provide information about the physical storage capabilities.

4. a. Explanation: MRU is the default path selection policy for most active/passive storage devices.

5. b. Explanation: Thick eager zeroed is the slowest method for virtual disk creation, but it is the best for guest performance.

Chapter 3

1. b. Explanation: When you enable traffic shaping for a standard switch or port group, you can configure the options Average Bandwidth, Peak Bandwidth, and Burst Size.

2. c. Explanation: At the distributed port level, you can override policies applied to the distributed port group and apply unique policies to a distributed port.

3. b. Explanation: In vSphere 8.0, the default settings for a distributed port group are static binding, elastic port allocation, and eight ports.

4. d. Explanation: Single Root I/O Virtualization (SR-IOV) is a feature that allows a single Peripheral Component Interconnect Express (PCIe) device to appear as multiple devices. It is useful for supporting an application in a guest OS that is sensitive to network latency. SR-IOV-enabled devices provide virtual functions (VFs) to the hypervisor or guest operating system.

5. b. Explanation: After configuring NetFlow on a vDS, you can configure monitoring policies on vDS port groups and ports.

Chapter 4

1. b. Explanation: Enhanced vMotion Compatibility (EVC) is a cluster feature. The source and target processors must come from the same vendor class (AMD or Intel) to be vMotion compatible. Clock speed, cache size, and number of cores can differ between source and target processors.

2. b. Explanation: When the DRS Migration Threshold is set to Level 2, DRS expands on Level 1 by making recommendations in situations that are at or close to resource contention. It does not make recommendations just to improve virtual machine happiness or cluster load distribution.

3. b. Explanation: If the primary host detects datastore heartbeats for a secondary host but no network heartbeats or ping responses, it assumes that the secondary host is isolated or in a network partition.

4. d. Explanation: Hosts must use static IP addresses or guarantee that IP addresses assigned by DHCP persist across host reboots.

5. a. Explanation: To use Wake-on-LAN (WoL) with DPM, you must ensure that vMotion is configured, the vMotion NIC must support WoL, and the physical switch port must be set to automatically negotiate the link speed.

Chapter 5

1. b. Explanation: Although making snapshots may be a useful step for a backup utility, a snapshot is not by itself a backup. A snapshot does not provide a redundant copy of data. If the base flat file is lost or corrupt, you cannot restore the virtual machine by reverting to a snapshot.

2. a. Explanation: You can enable or disable hardware acceleration. You can set debugging and statistics to run normally, record debugging information, record statistics, or record statistics and debugging.

3. a. Explanation: The vMotion process involves the following phases: Compatibility check, Pre-copy, Iterations of Pre-copy, and Switchover.

4. c. Explanation: During a vMotion migration without shared storage the virtual disk data is transferred over the vMotion network.

5. a. Explanation: During an instant clone (vmFork) operation, the system quiesces and stuns the source virtual machine, creates and transfers a checkpoint, customizes the destination MAC address and UUID, and forks the memory and disk.

Chapter 6

1. b. Explanation: Aria Orchestrator is a key component of vRA that provides custom workflows to support anything as a service (XaaS).

2. d. Explanation: VMware Horizon is commonly used for remote users, kiosk and task users, and call centers.

3. b. Explanation: To configure replication, in the vSphere Client, navigate to Home > Site Recovery > Open Site Recovery.

4. d. Explanation: VMware HCX is a workload mobility platform that simplifies application migration, workload rebalancing, and business continuity across on-premises data centers, private clouds, and hybrid clouds.

5. d. Explanation: The following are the common uses cases for NSX: Adoption of zero-trust security; Multi-cloud networking; Automated network deployment; and Networking and security for cloud-native applications (containers).

Chapter 7

1. c. Explanation: Do not use CRL distribution points, authority information access, or certificate template information in any custom certificates.

2. b. Explanation: You cannot modify permissions on the following entities that derive permissions from the root vCenter Server system: custom fields, licenses, roles, statistics intervals, or sessions.

3. d. Explanation: By default, the services that are running in ESXi include DCUI, Load-Based Teaming, CIM Server, and VMware vCenter Agent.

4. b. Explanation: You should remove any expired or revoked certificates from the vCenter Server to avoid MITM attacks.

5. d. Explanation: Prerequisites for enabling UEFI boot for your virtual machines are UEFI firmware, virtual hardware Version 13 or later, VMware Tools Version 10.1 or later, and an operating system that supports UEFI Secure Boot.

Chapter 8

1. d. Explanation: In the first stage when using the GUI installer, you navigate through the installation wizard, choose the deployment type, provide the appliance settings, and deploy the OVA. In the second stage you use a wizard to configure the appliance time synchronization, configure vCenter Single Sign-On (SSO), and start the services in the newly deployed appliance.

2. d. Explanation: When adding an Active Directory over LDAP identity source, you need to provide required information such as the name, the base DN for users, and the base DN for groups.

3. d. Explanation: The vSphere Lifecyle Manager service is available via the vSphere Client immediately after vCenter Server deployment. No special steps are required to install vSphere Lifecyle Manager.

4. c. Explanation: A rule can identify target hosts by boot MAC address, SMBIOS information, BIOS UUID, vendor, model, or fixed DHCP IP address.

5. b. Explanation: After selecting Remediate and selecting the hosts, you need to click Pre-check Remediation to determine whether the selected hosts are ready for remediation.

Chapter 9

1. b. Explanation: You can set VLAN ID to 0 (external switch tagging), 1 to 4094 (virtual switch tagging), or 4095 (virtual guest tagging).

2. c. Explanation: As a rollback plan, you should export the distributed switch configuration prior to upgrading. In the export wizard, choose the option to include the distributed port groups.

3. c. Explanation: Edit the distributed port group setting. In the settings, click General and then, from the Network Resource Pool drop-down menu, select the network resource pool and click OK.

4. d. Explanation: The provisioning stack supports traffic for virtual machine cold migration, cloning, and snapshot migration. It also supports the Network File Copy (NFC) traffic used for cloning virtual disks during long-distance vMotion. You can use this stack to isolate provisioning traffic by placing it on a separate gateway. The default stack provides networking support for management traffic and for all VMkernel traffic types.

5. a. Explanation: To enable NetFlow in a distributed port group, select the distributed port group, select Configure > Policies, click Edit, and then, on the Monitoring page, select Enable NetFlow or Disable NetFlow.

Chapter 10

1. c. Explanation: Optionally, you can set Memory Reservation to a numeric value (the default is 0) and a unit of measure (MB, GB, MHz, or GHz).

2. c. Explanation: In the Aria Operations GUI, locate the appropriate vCenter Server adapter instance. Select the adapter, choose Advanced Settings, and set Provide Data to vSphere Predictive DRS to True.

3. d. Explanation: To disable admission control, set Define Host Failover Capacity to Disabled.

4. a. Explanation: VIMTOP is a tool you can run in vCenter Server Appliance to see resource usage for services that are running.

5. d. Explanation: vmware.log is in the same folder as the virtual machine configuration file.

Chapter 11

1. c. Explanation: To provide the encryption keys for a vSAN datastore, you must implement a key management server (KMS) cluster server that is KMIP 1.1 compliant and is in the vSphere compatibility matrices.

2. c. Explanation: To enable deduplication and compression for an existing vSAN OSA cluster, edit the vSAN services in the cluster and enable Deduplication and Compression. (In vSAN OSA, a separate option to enable just deduplication is not provided.)

3. a, b, and d. Explanation: The options in the datastore browser include Upload Files, Upload Folder, Download, New Folder, Copy To, Move To, Rename To, Delete, and Inflate.

4. d. Explanation: The default storage module that claims NVMe-oF is HPP. NVMe-oF targets cannot be claimed by NMP. vSphere 8 enables NVMe-oF support for vVols.

5. a. Explanation: When using the vSphere Client to manage the storage providers, you can select a storage provider and choose Synchronize Storage Providers, Rescan, Remove, or Refresh Certificate.

Chapter 12

1. b. Explanation: To assign a global permission, you should use the vSphere Client with a user account that has the Permissions.Modify Permission privilege on the root object of all inventory hierarchies.

2. d. Explanation: A yellow alarm is raised if a certificate's status is Expiring Shortly (that is, if it expires in less than eight months).

3. a. Explanation: With this setting, passwords of one and two character classes are disabled, and so are passphrases. An uppercase character that begins a password and a number that ends a password do not count toward the number of character classes used.

4. d. Explanation: If the "Host secure boot was disabled" message appears in the vSphere Client, you must re-enable Secure Boot to resolve the problem. If the "No cached identity key, loading from DB" message appears, you must disconnect and reconnect the host.

5. a. Explanation: You can leverage the files that you exported during the configuration of vTA vSphere as your backup. If you need to restore vTA, you can use the exported files to reconfigure vTA.

Chapter 13

1. b. Explanation: After a restore completes, the following configurations are restored: virtual machine resource settings, resource pool hierarchy and setting, cluster-host membership, DRS configuration, and rules.

2. c. Explanation: If you choose to transfer configuration, historical, and performance data, you can transfer the configuration data during the upgrade and transfer the remaining data in the background following the upgrade.

3. a. Explanation: When working with baselines, the following settings are applicable: Quick Boot, VM Power State, VM Migration, Maintenance Mode Failures, PXE Booted Hosts, and Removable Media Devices. When working with images, the following settings are applicable: Quick Boot, VM Power State, VM Migration, Maintenance Mode Failures, HA Admission Control, and DPM.

4. d. Explanation: In rare situations, such as when the distributed switch used for management is not functioning, you may want to restore a standard switch to an ESX host, which you can do with the Restore Standard Switch option in the DCUI.

5. b. Explanation: If the source domain contains multiple (linked) vCenter Servers, the repointing process involves additional steps to shut down the vCenter Server and unregister it from the source domain.

Chapter 14

1. c. Explanation: Guest OS customization requires a supported guest OS installed on SCSI node 0:0 and VMware Tools. Windows guest customization requires ESXi Version 3.5 or later. Linux guest customization requires Perl in the guest OS.

2. a. Explanation: The compatibility setting controls which virtual machine hardware version is used. Setting the compatibility to ESXi 7.0 and later uses hardware Version 17, which is the minimum version that support 4 GB video memory.

3. d. Explanation: To minimize the impact to a running virtual machine and to reduce the time required to take a snapshot, do not snapshot the memory state or quiesce the guest file system.

4. a. Explanation: You can export a virtual machine, virtual appliance, or vApp as an OVF or OVA template to create virtual appliances that can be imported by other users. Starting in vSphere 6.5, you can only export to OVF.

5. c. Explanation: You can import items such as OVA / OVF templates and vApps to a content library. You can also import ISO images. You can also add content to the library by cloning VMs or templates to the library.

Glossary

A

add-on: In vSphere Lifecycle Manager, a collection of components that you can use to customize an ESXi image with OEM content and drivers.

App Volumes: A set of application and user management solutions for VMware Horizon, Citrix Virtual Apps and Desktops, and Remote Desktop Services Host (RDSH) virtual environments.

AppDefense: A data center endpoint security product that protects applications running in vSphere.

B

baseline: In vSphere Lifecyle Manager, a set of bulletins.

C

Certificate Manager: A command-line utility that you can use to generate certificate signing requests (CSRs) and replace certificates for machine and solution users.

client performance charts: vSphere charts that enable you to view performance metrics in different ways, depending on the selected object and metric type.

cluster: A set of ESXi hosts that are intended to work together as a unit.

Common Information Model (CIM): An open standard that defines a framework for agentless, standards-based monitoring of ESXi host hardware resources. The framework consists of a CIM broker and a set of CIM providers.

content library: A repository (container) for objects such as virtual machine templates, vApp templates, ISO images, and files that you might want to share among multiple vCenter Servers in a vSphere environment.

CPU Ready Time: A metric that indicates the amount of time a VCPU is ready to work (that is, has a workload and is ready to be scheduled) but is waiting to be scheduled on hardware. High CPU Ready Time is a sign of CPU contention.

D

data center: A container object in the vSphere inventory that is an aggregation of all the different types of objects used to work in virtual infrastructure.

disk group: A group of local disks on an ESXi host that contributes to the vSAN datastore.

Distributed Resource Scheduler (DRS):   A vSphere feature that balances VM workload in a cluster based on compute usage. It includes live (vMotion) migrations of VMs, when necessary.

E-F

ESXi base image: The ESXi image that VMware provides with each release of ESXi, which is a complete set of components that can boot up a server.

ESXTOP: A utility that provides a detailed real-time look at resource usage from the ESXi Shell.

EtherChannel: A logical channel formed by bundling together two or more links to aggregate bandwidth and provide redundancy. Other acceptable names for Ether-Channel (an IOS term) are port channel (an NX-OS term) and link aggregation group (LAG).

G

graphics processing unit (GPU):   A specialized processor developed for parallel processing, primarily for rendering graphical images.

H

High-Performance Plug-in (HPP):   The default plug-in that claims NVMe-oF targets.

host profile: A feature that enables you to encapsulate the configuration of one host and apply it to other hosts.

hybrid cloud: A cloud that is a combination of a private cloud, a public cloud, and on-premises infrastructure.

I-L

I/O filter: A software component that can be installed on ESXi hosts and can offer additional data services to virtual machines.

image: In vSphere Lifecyle Manager, a description of which software, drivers, and firmware to run on a host.

Intel Software Guard Extension (SGX):   A processor-specific technology that enables application developers to protect code and data from disclosure or modification.

M

managed object browser (MOB):   A web-based interface that provides you with a means to explore the VMkernel object model.

microsegmentation: A type of network segmentation that decreases the level of risk and increases the security posture of a data center by providing granular control and distributed stateful firewalling. It effectively allows you to place a firewall on each VM network connection.

Microsoft virtualization-based security (VBS):   A Microsoft feature for Windows 10 and Windows Server 2016 operating systems that uses hardware and software virtualization to enhance system security by creating an isolated, hypervisor-restricted, specialized subsystem.

N

NetFlow: A switch feature that collects IP network traffic as it enters or exits an interface. NetFlow data provides an overview of traffic flows, based on the network source and destination.

network resource pool: A mechanism that enables you to apply a part of the bandwidth that is reserved for virtual machine system traffic to a set of distributed port groups.

Non-Volatile Memory Express (NVMe) device: A high-performance alternative to SCSI storage.

O

Open Virtual Appliance (OVA) template: A single-file distribution of an OVF package.

Open Virtual Format (OVF) template: A set of files with the OVF, VMDK, and MF file extensions.

P-Q

PMem device: A non-volatile dual in-line memory module (NVDIMM) on the ESXi host that resides in a normal memory slot.

port mirroring: A process that allows administrators to duplicate everything that is happening on one distributed port to then be visible on another distributed port.

Predictive DRS: A feature that leverages the predictive analytics of vRealize Operations (vROps) Manager and vSphere DRS to provide workload balancing prior to the occurrence of resource utilization spikes and resource contention.

private VLAN (PVLAN):   An extension of the VLAN standard that is not double encapsulated but that allows a VLAN to effectively be subdivided into other VLANs.

Proactive HA: A vSphere feature that minimizes VM downtime by proactively detecting hardware failures and placing the host in Quarantine Mode or Maintenance Mode.

Proactive High Availability (Proactive HA):   A feature that integrates with select hardware partners to detect degraded components and evacuate VMs from affected vSphere hosts before an incident causes a service interruption.

R

raw device mapping (RDM):   A mapping file that contains metadata that resides in a VMFS datastore and acts as a proxy for a physical storage device (LUN), allowing a virtual machine to access the storage device directly.

resource pool: A container object in the vSphere inventory that is used to compartmentalize the CPU and memory resources of a host or cluster.

S

Single Root I/O Virtualization (SR-IOV):   A feature that allows a single Peripheral Component Interconnect Express (PCIe) device to appear as multiple devices to the hypervisor (ESXi) or to a virtual machine's guest operating system.

Site Recovery Manager (SRM):   A VMware business continuity solution that you can use to orchestrate planned migrations, test recoveries, and disaster recoveries.

Skyline: A proactive support technology developed by VMware Global Services that is available to customers with an active Production Support or Premier Services agreement.

stateless caching: A type of caching in which Auto Deploy does not store ESXi configuration or state data within the host. Instead, during subsequent boots, the host must connect to the Auto Deploy server to retrieve its configuration.

Storage I/O Control (SIOC):   A vSphere feature that allows you to prioritize storage access during periods of contention, ensuring that the more critical virtual machines obtain more I/O than less critical VMs.

Storage vMotion: The hot cross-datastore migration of a virtual machine.

T-U

template: An object in the vSphere inventory that is effectively a non-executable virtual machine.

Trusted Platform Module (TPM):   A chip that is a secure cryptoprocessor that enhances host security by providing a trust assurance rooted in hardware as opposed to software.

V

vApp: A container object in vSphere that provides a format for packaging and managing applications.

vCenter Converter: A free solution that automates the process of converting existing Windows and Linux machines into virtual machines running in a vSphere environment.

vCenter HA: A native high availability solution for vCenter Server Appliance.

vCenter Single Sign-On (SSO):   An authentication broker and security token exchange infrastructure.

vCenter Single Sign-On Security Token Service (STS):   A web service that issues, validates, and renews security tokens.

VIMTOP: A tool you can run in vCenter Server Appliance to see resource usage for services that are running.

virtual LAN (VLAN):   A logical partition of a physical network at the data link layer (Layer 2).

Virtual Machine Component Protection (VMCP):   A vSphere HA feature that can detect datastore accessibility issues and provide remediation for impacted virtual machines.

virtual machine snapshot: A copy that captures the state of a virtual machine and the data in the virtual machine at a specific point in time.

virtual PMem disk (vPMemDisk):   A regular virtual disk that is assigned a PMem storage policy, which forces it to be placed on a host-local PMem datastore.

Virtual Trusted Platform Module (vTPM):   A software-based representation of a physical TPM 2.0 chip.

virtual volume: An encapsulation of virtual machine files, virtual disks, and their derivatives that are stored natively inside a storage system.

Virtual Volumes (vVOLs):   An integration and management framework that virtualizes SAN/NAS arrays, enabling a more efficient operational model.

vMotion: The hot cross-host migration of a virtual machine.

VMware Certificate Authority (VMCA):   A certificate authority (CA) that is responsible for issuing certificates for VMware solution users, certificates for machines running required services, and certificates for ESXi hosts. It provisions each ESXi host, each machine in the environment, and each solution user with a certificate signed by VMCA.

VMware Cloud (VMC):   An integrated cloud offering jointly developed by AWS and VMware that provides a highly scalable, secure service that allows organizations to seamlessly migrate and extend their on-premises vSphere-based environments to the AWS cloud.

VMware Directory Service (vmdir):   An identity source that handles SAML certificate management for authentication with vCenter Single Sign-On.

VMware Endpoint Certificate Service (VECS):   A local (client-side) repository for certificates, private keys, and other certificate information that can be stored in a keystore. VECS is a mandatory component that is used when VMCA is not signing certificates.

VMware Enhanced Authentication Plug-in: A plug-in that provides integrated Windows authentication and Windows-based smart card functionality. In the vSphere 6.5 release, the VMware Enhanced Authentication Plug-in replaced the Client Integration Plug-in.

VMware Horizon: A platform for securely delivering virtual desktops and applications in private and hybrid clouds.

VMware Lifecyle Manager: A service that replaces VMware Update Manager and adds features and capabilities for ESXi lifecycle management at the cluster level.

VMware PowerCLI: A command-line and scripting tool built on Windows PowerShell that provides cmdlets for managing and automating VMware products, including vSphere.

VMware Service Lifecycle Manager: A vCenter Server service that monitors the health of services and takes preconfigured remediation action when it detects a failure.

VMware Tools: A set of software modules and services, including services that can communicate with the VMkernel.

VMware Update Manager Download Service (UMDS):   An optional module of vSphere Lifecycle Manager, whose primary function is to download data when Lifecyle Manager does not have Internet connectivity.

VMware vSphere Lifecycle Manager: A service that runs in vCenter Server and provides simple, centralized lifecycle management for ESXi hosts and clusters by using images and baselines.

Aria Automation: An automation platform for private and multi-cloud environments.

Aria for Logs: A software product that provides intelligent log management for infrastructure and applications for any environment.

vSAN fault domain: A set of hosts that are members of a vSAN cluster. Fault domains provide additional protection against outage in the event of a rack or blade chassis failure.

vSAN Express Storage Architecture (ESA):   An alternative architecture for vSAN that uses single-tiered storage pools.

vSAN file service: A file service on a vSAN cluster, which enables you to create file shares. It provides vSAN-backed file shares that virtual machines can access as NFS Version 3 and NFS Version 4.1 file shares.

vSphere Client: An HTML5-based GUI used for administration in vSphere.

vSphere Distributed Switch (vDS):   A single virtual switch for all associated hosts in a data center. It provides centralized provisioning, monitoring, and management of virtual networks for associated hosts and virtual machines.

vSphere Fault Tolerance (FT):   A feature that provides continuous availability for a virtual machine (the primary VM) by ensuring that the state of a secondary VM is identical at any point in the instruction execution of the virtual machine.

vSphere HA: A vSphere feature that provides automated failover protection for VMs against host, hardware, network, and guest OS issues. In the event of host system failure, it performs cold migrations and restarts failed VMs on surviving hosts.

vSphere Installation Bundle (VIB):   An ESXi software package, created and signed by VMware and its partners, that contains solutions, drivers, CIM providers, and applications.

vSphere inventory: A collection of managed virtual and physical objects.

vSphere Replication: An extension to VMware vCenter Server that provides hypervisor-based virtual machine replication and recovery.

W-Z

witness host: A stretched vSAN component that consists only of metadata and acts as a tiebreaker.

Index